STUDIES IN JOSEPHUS' REWRITTEN BIBLE

SUPPLEMENTS TO THE
JOURNAL FOR THE STUDY
OF JUDAISM
FORMERLY STUDIA POST-BIBLICA

EDITOR
JOHN J. COLLINS
THE DIVINITY SCHOOL, UNIVERSITY OF CHICAGO

ASSOCIATE EDITOR
FLORENTINO GARCÍA MARTÍNEZ
QUMRAN INSTITUTE, UNIVERSITY OF GRONINGEN

ADVISORY BOARD
J. DUHAIME
A. HILHORST
M. A. KNIBB
M. MACH
J. T. A. G. M. VAN RUITEN
J. SIEVERS
G. STEMBERGER
J. TROMP
A. S. VAN DER WOUDE

VOLUME 58

STUDIES IN JOSEPHUS'
REWRITTEN BIBLE

STUDIES IN JOSEPHUS' REWRITTEN BIBLE

Louis H. Feldman

SBL
Society of Biblical Literature
Atlanta

STUDIES IN JOSEPHUS' REWRITTEN BIBLE

Copyright © 1998 by Koninklijke Brill NV, Leiden,
The Netherlands

This edition published under license from Koninklijke Brill NV,
Leiden, The Netherlands by the Society of Biblical Literature.

All rights reserved. No part of this work may be reproduced or transmitted in any form or by any means, electronic or mechanical, including photocopying and recording, or by any means of any information storage or retrieval system, except as may be expressly permitted by the 1976 Copyright Act or in writing from the Publisher. Requests for permission should be addressed in writing to the Rights and Permissions Department, Koninklijke Brill NV, Leiden, The Netherlands.

Authorization to photocopy items for internal or personal use is granted by Brill provided that the appropriate fees are paid directly to The Copyright Clearance Center, 222 Rosewood Drive, Suite 910, Danvers, MA 01923, USA. Fees are subject to change.

Library of Congress Cataloging-in-Publication Data

Feldman, Louis H.
  Studies in Josephus' rewritten Bible / by Louis H. Feldman.
    p. cm. – (Supplements to the Journal for the study of Judaism ; v. 58)
  Originally published: Leiden ; New York : Brill, 1998.
  Includes bibliographical references and index..
  ISBN-13: 978-1-58983-195-7 (paper binding : alk. paper)
  ISBN-10: 1-58983-195-0 (paper binding : alk. paper)
  1. Josephus, Flavius. Antiquitates Judaicae. 2. Bible. O.T. –Criticism, interpretation, etc., Jewish. 3. Judaism–Apologetic works–History and criticism. I. Title. II. Series.

DS116.J743F45 2005
933–dc22   2005029539

Printed in the United States of America
on acid-free paper

To my sisters and brother:
Betty (of blessed memory), Rose, Dorothy, Gertrude,
and Morris,

whose love and devotion to each other and
to me know no bounds.

Hineh mah tov umah na'im shevet 'ahim gam yahad.

TABLE OF CONTENTS

Preface XIX

I Man's Decline after Creation 1
   1. Biblical Geography 1
   2. The Earliest Language 2
   3. The Original Bliss of Mankind 3
   4. The Story of Cain and Abel 8
   5. The Decline from the Golden Age 10
   6. Summary 15

II Noah 17
   1. Introduction 17
   2. Apologetic Concerns 19
   3. Noah's Virtues 26
   4. The Relationship of the Biblical and Greek Floods 27
   5. Noah's Emergence from the Ark 30
   6. Summary 35

III Jethro 38
   1. Introduction 38
   2. The Treatment of Jethro in Other Ancient Sources 39
   3. Jethro's Qualities of Character, according to Josephus 46
   4. The Attitude of Jethro the Non-Jew toward Jews .. 49
   5. The Role of G-d in the Jethro Narrative 49
   6. Jethro the Non-Proselyte 50
   7. "Improvements" in the Story: Clarifications, Increased Plausibility 52
   8. Summary 52

IV Aaron 55
   1. Introduction: The Problem Confronting Josephus .. 55
   2. Aaron's Virtues 57
   3. Aaron as Spokesman 64
   4. Summary 72

TABLE OF CONTENTS

V The Pharaohs	74
1. Introduction	74
2. Josephus' Portrayal of Nebuchadnezzar, Belshazzar, and Darius	74
3. Philo's Portrait of the Pharaohs	75
4. The Rabbinic Portrait of the Pharaohs	78
5. Josephus' Portrait of the Pharaohs	82
6. Summary	89
VI Korah	91
1. Introduction	91
2. The Treatment of Korah by Philo and Pseudo-Philo	92
3. Korah in the Rabbinic Tradition	94
4. The Qualities of Josephus' Korah	97
5. Josephus on Korah's Rebellion as an Attack on the Priesthood	100
6. The Rebellion as Motivated by Jealousy	101
7. The Political Aspects of the Rebellion	101
8. "Improvements" in the Story: Clarifications, Increased Drama	104
9. Summary	109
VII Balaam	110
1. Introduction	110
2. Balaam the Soothsayer	113
3. Other Positive Qualities of Balaam	116
4. Apologetics	117
a. Refutation of the Charge that Jews Hate Non-Jews	117
b. Jews Do Not Hate the Romans	118
c. Jews Do Not Rebel	120
d. Jews Are Not Busybodies	121
e. Reduction of Gentile Anti-Judaism	121
f. Appeal to Stoicism	126
5. Emphasis on Military Details	127
6. Miracles	128
7. Preaching against Assimilation	130
8. "Improvements" in the Story: Clarifications, Increased Drama	131
9. Summary	134

VIII Ehud 137
1. Introduction 137
2. The Portrayal of Ehud in Pseudo-Philo's *Biblical Antiquities* and in Rabbinic Literature 137
3. The Virtues of Ehud 139
4. The Rehabilitation of Eglon 144
5. "Improvements" in the Story: Clarifications, Increased Suspense and Drama 146
6. Summary 151

IX Deborah 153
1. Introduction: The Insignificance of Deborah for Josephus 153
2. The Role of G-d in the Deborah Pericope 156
3. The Role of Jael 159
4. The Song of Deborah 160
5. Summary 162

X Gideon 163
1. Introduction 163
2. The Qualities of Gideon 165
3. The Role of G-d and Miracles 170
4. Political Lessons 171
5. "Improvements" in the Story: Clarifications, Increased Suspense and Drama 172
6. Summary 175

XI Jephthah 177
1. Introduction 177
2. Jephthah's Qualities of Leadership 177
3. Jephthah's Virtues 179
4. Jephthah's Vow 182
5. Summary 191

XII Ruth 193
1. Introduction: The Problem 193
2. Why Josephus Includes the Ruth Pericope 194
3. The Character of Ruth 194
4. The Role of G-d in the Ruth Pericope 196
5. Intermarriage and Conversion 196

TABLE OF CONTENTS

	6. Dramatic Embellishment	199
	7. Summary	201

XIII Joab 203
    1. Introduction: Joab in the Rabbinic Tradition 203
    2. Joab's Virtues 204
    3. Joab's Negative Qualities 206
    4. Josephus' Treatment of Joab as a Lesson in the Disastrous Consequences of Civil Strife 208
    5. The Disastrous Effects of Envy 209
    6. Summary 213

XIV Absalom 215
    1. Introduction 215
    2. Absalom as an Archexample of Impiety in Blood Relations 215
    3. Absalom's Positive Qualities of Body and of Spirit 220
    4. Political Lessons 223
    5. "Improvements" in the Story: Clarifications, Increased Suspense and Drama 225
    6. Summary 228

XV Jeroboam 230
    1. Introduction: Characterization of Jeroboam in Rabbinic Thought 230
    2. The Importance of Jeroboam for Josephus 233
    3. The Negative Qualities of Jeroboam: His Lack of Wisdom 233
    4. Jeroboam's Intemperate Nature 234
    5. Jeroboam's Impiety 234
    6. Jeroboam and Democracy 237
    7. Jeroboam as Ancestor of the Revolutionaries of Josephus' Day: *De nobis fabula narratur* 237
    8. Assimilation 240
    9. Dramatic Build-up 240
    10. Summary 242

XVI Rehoboam 244
    1. Introduction 244
    2. The Qualities of a Leader 246

	3. The Portrait of Rehoboam as a Commentary on the Civil Strife of Josephus' Day	253
	4. The Rehabilitation of Rehoboam	255
	5. Summary	261
XVII	Asa	263
	1. Introduction	263
	2. The Rabbinic Account of Asa	263
	3. Asa's Virtues	264
	4. Apologetics	269
	5. Summary	271
XVIII	Ahab	273
	1. Introduction	273
	2. The Rabbinic Portrait of Ahab	274
	3. Ahab's Wickedness according to Josephus	276
	4. Ahab's Positive Qualities	278
	5. Apologetics	284
	6. Hellenizations	285
	7. Summary	289
XIX	Elijah	291
	1. Introduction	291
	2. Elijah's Qualities of Leadership	295
	3. Elijah's Qualities of Character	297
	4. The Miracles Performed by Elijah	298
	5. Elijah the Zealot	302
	6. Rationalizations in the Narrative	303
	7. Dramatic Enhancement	304
	8. Summary	305
XX	Jehoshaphat	307
	1. Introduction	307
	2. The Rabbinic Portrait of Jehoshaphat	309
	3. The Power of Jehoshaphat	310
	4. The Virtues of Jehoshaphat	311
	5. Political Theory	316
	6. Apologetics	318
	7. Summary	320

XXI	Jehoram, King of Israel	322
	1. Introduction	322
	2. Jehoram's Qualities of Character	322
	3. "Improvements" in the Story: Avoidance of Discrepancies	331
	4. Summary	332
XXII	Elisha	334
	1. Introduction	334
	2. Elisha's Power as a Prophet	336
	3. Elisha's Loyalty to Elijah	337
	4. Elisha's Virtues	338
	5. A Gentler Elisha	344
	6. Miracles	344
	7. "Improvements" in the Story: Increased Drama, Elimination of Anthropomorphisms	348
	8. Summary	350
XXIII	Jehu	352
	1. Introduction	352
	2. The Portrait of Jehu in Rabbinic Literature	352
	3. The Cardinal Virtues of Jehu	353
	4. Jehu and Civil Strife	358
	5. "Improvements" in the Story: Clarifications, Better Motivation and Drama	360
	6. Summary	361
XXIV	Hezekiah	363
	1. Introduction: The Problem	363
	2. Hezekiah's Qualities of Character	367
	3. Apologetics	371
	4. Josephus' Theology	373
	5. Summary	374
XXV	Isaiah	376
	1. Issues	376
	2. Josephus' Concern with Priestly Matters	379
	3. Submissiveness to the Superpower	381
	4. References to David and to the Messiah	382
	5. Isaiah as Prophet	389

	6. Summary	391
XXVI	Jonah	393
	1. Introduction: Issues	393
	2. The Importance of Jonah to Josephus, the Historian	394
	3. The Role of G-d in Josephus' Treatment of Jonah	397
	4. The Problem of G-d's Repentance and the Truth of Jonah's Prophecy	400
	5. Josephus' Handling of the Miracles in the Book	402
	6. The Issue of Jew and Non-Jew: the Universalism of the Book of Jonah vs. the Particularism of Jonah and the Israelites	404
	7. Proselytes and "G-d-Fearers" in the Book of Jonah	409
	8. Hellenizations in Josephus' Account	412
	9. Summary	415
XXVII	Manasseh	416
	1. Introduction	416
	2. The Portrait of Manasseh in Rabbinic Literature	416
	3. The Impiety of Manasseh	418
	4. Manasseh's Attack on the Prophets	420
	5. Manasseh's Repentance	420
	6. Summary	423
XXVIII	Josiah	424
	1. Introduction	424
	2. The Rabbinic Account of Josiah	424
	3. Josiah as the Embodiment of the Cardinal Virtues	426
	4. Summary	435
XXIX	Jehoiachin	437
	1. Introduction: The Problem	437
	2. The Qualities of Jehoiachin	440
	3. The Political Implications of Josephus' Treatment of Jehoiachin	442

	TABLE OF CONTENTS	

    4. The Rehabilitation of Jehoiachin in Rabbinic Literature and in Josephus 444
    5. Summary 448

XXX Zedekiah 450
    1. Introduction: The Problem in Josephus' Portrait of Zedekiah 450
    2. Josephus' Portrait of Nebuchadnezzar 452
    3. Josephus' Defense of Zedekiah 455
    4. Summary 461

XXXI Gedaliah 463
    1. Introduction 463
    2. Gedaliah's Virtues 464
    3. Contemporary Associations 465
    4. Why the Whitewash of Gedaliah? 468
    5. "Improvements" in the Story: Elimination of Improbabilities 470
    6. Summary 471

XXXII Ezra 473
    1. Introduction: The Problem 473
    2. Ezra as Priest and Scribe in the Rabbinic Tradition 475
    3. Ezra's Genealogy in Josephus 476
    4. The Virtues of Ezra: Wisdom 477
    5. Ezra as Political Leader 480
    6. Josephus' Aims: Moralizing about Intermarriage 483
    7. Apologetics for the Jews in Josephus' Account of Ezra 485
    8. Summary 487

XXXIII Nehemiah 489
    1. Introduction: The Problem 489
    2. Nehemiah as a Political Figure 490
    3. Apologetics for the Jews 495
    4. The Problem of Intermarriage 497
    5. Summary 498

XXXIV	Ahasuerus	500
	1. The Rabbinic Portrayal of Ahasuerus	500
	2. Josephus' Portrait of Ahasuerus	503
	3. Novelistic, Romantic, and Dramatic Elements	508
	4. Summary	511
XXXV	Esther	513
	1. Introduction	513
	2. The Qualities of Esther and of Mordecai	513
	3. Novelistic, Romantic, and Dramatic Elements	516
	4. Apologetic Elements	529
	5. Resolution of Difficulties in the Biblical Narrative	532
	6. The Role of G-d	534
	7. Summary	537

Conclusion 539
1. Introduction 539
2. Josephus' Violation of His Promise Not to Add
   to or Subtract from the Biblical Narrative 539
3. Factors That Influenced Josephus in His Rewriting of the Bible 543
   1. Josephus' Non-Jewish Audience 543
   2. Josephus' Jewish Audience 543
   3. Concern with Assimilation and Intermarriage 544
   4. Respect for the Prophets 544
   5. Regard for the Priesthood and Especially for
      the Temple in Jerusalem 545
   6. Concern to Show That His Biblical Heroes Are
      Fully Comparable to Pagan Heroes 546
      a. Good Birth 546
      b. Precociousness 546
      c. Handsome Stature 547
      d. Wealth 547
      e. Wisdom 547
      f. Courage 548
      g. Temperance 548
      h. Justice (including especially respect for truth,
         humanity (φιλανθρωπία), mercy, hospitality,
         gratefulness, and generosity) 549
      i. Piety 550

TABLE OF CONTENTS

7. Qualities of Leadership 551
8. Importance of Repentance 551
9. Respect for Law and Order 552
10. Respect for the Concept of a Just War 552
11. Contempt for the Masses 553
12. Disdain for Demagogues 553
13. Realistic Attitude and Even High Regard for the Superpower of the Day 553
14. Opposition to Messianic and Messianic-like Movements 554
15. Contempt for the Revolutionaries of His Own Day 555
16. Abhorrence of Civil Strife 556
17. Loyalty to Rulers 556
18. Loyalty to Mentors and Friends 556
19. Tolerance and Respect toward Non-Jews and Especially Non-Jewish Leaders 557
20. Tolerance toward Non-Jewish Religions 558
21. Insistence that Gentiles Do Not Hate Jews . 558
22. Compliments by Non-Jews 558
23. Concern to Refute the View That Jews Are Aggressive in Seeking Converts 559
24. Insistence that Jews Are Not Busybodies 560
25. Establishment of the Historicity of Biblical Events 560
26. Improvements in the Narrative through Removal of Difficulties and Contradictions 560
27. Stylistic Improvements 562
28. Hellenization of the Narrative for His Greek Readers 563
29. Increased Suspense, Drama, and Irony 563
30. Derogatory View of Women 564
31. Increased Romantic Element 565
32. Introduction of Wise Sayings 565
33. Appeal to Philosophic Interests 566
34. Interest in Military Details 567
35. Analysis of the True Motives of People 567
36. G-d's Reward for Those Who Obey His Laws and Punishment for Those Who Do Not 567

	37. De-emphasis on G-d's Role in History	568
	38. De-emphasis on Miracles	568
	39. Resolution of Theological Problems	570

Abbreviations 571

Bibliography 573

Indices 585
    1. Ancient Texts 585
        Jewish Scriptures 585
        Apocrypha 600
        Pseudepigrapha 600
        Dead Sea Scrolls 601
        Philo 601
        Pseudo-Philo 603
        Josephus 604
        Other (Alleged) Graeco-Jewish Writers 619
        Rabbinic and Allied Literature 620
        New Testament 628
        Christian Church Fathers 628
        Koran 629
        Passages from Classical Greek Authors 629
        Passages from Classical Latin Authors 633
    2. Names and Subjects 636
    3. Greek, Latin, Hebrew, and Aramaic Words ... 646
    4. Modern Scholars 660

PREFACE

The present volume, consisting of 35 studies of various portions of Josephus' *Jewish Antiquities*, is an attempt to examine the oldest systematic commentary on the historical books of the Bible that has come down to us. In particular, it focuses on the following questions: 1) how do Josephus' modifications reflect his views on issues that were confronting Jews of his day? 2) how does Josephus, in his rewritten Bible, answer anti-Jewish canards, especially that Jews hate non-Jews? 3) how does his commentary reflect his attitude toward intermarriage, assimilation, and defection from Judaism? 4) how does it reflect his attitude toward non-Jewish philosophy, religion, and historiography, especially Thucydides, Plato, and Stoicism? 5) how does it comment on the movement of conversion to Judaism? 6) to what degree is it a commentary on revolutionary and messianic movements of his day? 7) how does it reflect his attitude toward non-Jewish rulers? 8) how does it indicate his attitude toward the place of the Diaspora in Judaism? It considers how Josephus resolves apparent contradictions, obscurities, and theological and other questions, as well as the historicity of biblical events, which have puzzled classical commentators on the Bible. It attempts to explain cases, notably Ahab, Hezekiah, Jehoiachin, and Zedekiah, where Josephus seems to change the biblical text radically. It considers how Josephus' changes may be explained in view of his own life, notably his status as a priest and his role in the war against the Romans. Included are Josephus' interpretations of several prophets (Elijah, Elisha, Isaiah, and Jonah), several women (Deborah, Ruth, and Esther); and several non-Jewish leaders (Noah, Jethro, the Pharaohs, Balaam, and Ahasuerus). Because of the large number of studies, because of their variety, and because they are, for the most part, relatively minor figures, we can perhaps more readily see Josephus' approach.

All of these studies have previously appeared in print over a period of almost three decades in 33 different publications. However, they have been edited, corrected, and updated in many ways. In one case, that of Absalom, the original publication was in Italian; and what is presented here is a modified English version of that article. I am indebted to the following for permission to reprint versions of my articles: "Hellenizations in Josephus' Account of Man's Decline," in *Religions in Antiquity: Essays in Memory of Erwin Ramsdell Goodenough*, ed. Jacob Neusner (Leiden: Brill, 1968) 336-53; "The Portrait of Noah in Josephus, Philo, Pseudo-Philo's *Biblical Antiquities*, and Rabbinic Midrashim," *Proceedings of the American Academy for Jewish Research* 55 (1988) 31-57; "Josephus' Portrait of Jethro," in *The Quest for Context and Meaning: Studies in Biblical Intertextuality in Honor of James A. Sanders*, ed. Craig A. Evans and Shemaryahu Talmon (Leiden; Brill, 1997) 481-502; "Josephus' Portrait of Aaron," in *Classical Studies in Honor of David Sohlberg*, ed. Ranon Katzoff, Jacob Petroff, and David Schaps (Ramat Gan: Bar-Ilan University Press, 1996) 167-92; "Josephus' Portraits of the Pharaohs," *Syllecta Classica* 4 (1993) 49-63; :Josephus' Portrait of Korah," *Old Testament Essays* 6 (1993) 399-426; "Josephus' Portrait of Balaam," *Studia Philonica Annual* 5 (1993) 48-83; "Josephus' Portrait of Ehud," in *Pursuing the Text: Studies in Honor of Ben Zion Wacholder on the Occasion of His Seventieth Birthday*, ed. John C. Reeves and John Kampen (Sheffield: Sheffield Academic Press, 1994) 177-201; "Josephus' Portrait of Deborah," in *Hellenica et Judaica: Hommages à Valentin Nikiprowetzky*, ed. André Caquot, Mireille Hadas-Lebel, and Jean Riaud (Leuven-Paris: Éditions Peeters, 1986) 115-28; "Josephus' Portrait of Gideon," *Revue des Études juives* 152 (1993) 5-28; "Josephus' Portrait of Jephthah," in *The Jews in the Hellenistic-Roman World: Studies in Memory of Menahem Stern*, ed. Isaiah M. Gafni, Aharon Oppenheimer, and Daniel R. Schwartz (Jerusalem: Zalman Shazar Center for Jewish History, 1996) 67*-84*; "Reflections on John R. Levison's 'Josephus's Version of Ruth," *Journal for the Study of the Pseudepigrapha* 8 (1991) 45-52; "Josephus' Portrait of Joab," *Estudios Biblicos* 51 (1993) 323-51; "Il Ritratto di Assalonne in Giuseppe Flavio," *Rivista Biblica* 41 (1993) 3-30; "Josephus' Portrait of Jeroboam," *Andrews University Seminary Studies* 31 (1993) 29-51; "Josephus' Portrait of Rehoboam," *Studia Philonica Annual* 9 (1997) 1-23; "Josephus' Portrait of Asa," *Bulletin for Biblical Research* 4 (1994) 41-60; "Josephus' Portrait of Ahab," *Ephemerides Theologicae Lovanienses* 68 (1992) 368-84; "Josephus' Portrait of Elijah," *Scandinavian Journal of the Old Testament* 8 (1994) 61-86; Josephus' Portrait of Jehoshaphat," *Scripta Classical Israelica* 12 (1993) 159-75; "Josephus' Portrait of Elijah," *Scandinavian Journal* *of The Old Testament* 8 (1994) 61-86; "Josephus's Portrait of Jehoram, King of Israel," *Bulletin of the John Rylands Library* 76 (1994) 3-20; "Josephus' Portrait of Elisha," *Novum Testamentum* 36 (1994) 1-28; "Josephus' Portrait of Jehu," *Jewish Studies Quarterly* 3 (1996) 12-32; "Josephus' Portrait of Hezekiah," *Journal of Biblical Literature* 111 (1992) 597-610; "Josephus' Portrait of Isaiah," in *Writing and Reading the Scroll of Isaiah: Studies of an Interpretative Tradition*, vol. 2, ed. Craig C. Broyles and Craig A. Evans (Leiden: Brill, 1997) 583-608; "Josephus' Interpretation of Jonah," *Association for Jewish Studies Review* 17 (1992) 1-29; "Josephus' Portrait of Manasseh," *Journal for the Study of the Pseudepigrapha* 9 (1991) 3-20; "Josephus' Portrait of Josiah," *Louvain Studies* 18 (1993) 110-30; "Josephus' Portrait of Jehoiachin," *Proceedings of the American Philosophical Society* 139.1 (1995) 11-31; "Josephus' Portrait of Zedekiah," in *Ḥazon Naḥum: Studies in Jewish Law, Thought, and History Presented to Dr. Norman Lamm on the Occasion of His Seventieth Birthday*, ed. Yaakov Elman and Jeffrey S. Gurock (Hoboken: Ktav, 1997) 69-92; "Josephus' Portrait of Gedaliah," *Shofar* 12 (1993) 1-10; "Josephus' Portrait of Ezra," *Vetus Testamentum* 43 (1993) 190-214; "Josephus' Portrait of Nehemiah," *Journal of Jewish Studies* 43 (1992) 187-202; "Josephus' Portrait of Ahasuerus," *Australian Biblical Review* 42 (1994) 17-39; "Hellenizations in Josephus' Version of Esther," *Transactions of the American Philological Association* 101 (1970) 143-70.

CHAPTER ONE

MAN'S DECLINE AFTER CREATION

1. *Biblical Geography*

At the very beginning of his paraphrase of the Bible, Josephus presents his narrative within a Greek framework.[1] The notion of a stream, the Okeanos, flowing around the earth, is found among the Greeks from an early period; and while Herodotus (2.23) disclaims any knowledge of a river called Okeanos, he does confirm the antiquity of the notion by conjecturing that Homer or some earlier poet invented the name and introduced it into his poetry. Even when the Greeks accepted the idea of the spherical shape of the earth, they continued to apply the name Okeanos to the great outer nature of the earth as against the inner seas. This conception of a stream encircling the entire earth is introduced by Josephus in his description of the river that went out of Eden to water the garden (Genesis 2:10; *Ant.* 1.38); he thus presents biblical geography in terms intelligible to his Greek audience. This feature of Josephus' geography is unknown to the Aggadah, and is plainly an attempt to present biblical geography in Greek terms (Rappaport 1930, 2, n. 8).[2] The same tendency to identify biblical places with those familiar to the Greeks is found in Josephus' identification of the river Pishon with the Ganges River and of the land of Havilah "where there is gold" and which it encompasses as India (Genesis 2:11; *Ant.* 1.38).[3] Josephus here follows the many classical writers – Herodotus, Diodorus, Strabo, and Pliny – who identify India as the land of gold. Similarly, Havilah in Genesis 10:29 is

---

[1] The only other attempts to survey Josephus' treatment of this period are the brief studies by Droge (1989, 35-47), which acknowledges its debt to my article (1968a) in a number of points; and Basser (1987) which is, for the most part, not concerned with the Hellenizations in the account.

[2] Rappaport (1930, 76, n. 10) refuses to equate this stream with the Okeanos, and notes that Josephus distinguished between the waters surrounding the planet earth and the river flowing around the earth. But it is precisely the latter, not the former, that the Greeks identified with the Okeanos.

[3] Most of the rabbis identify the Pishon with the Nile River; see Rappaport (1930, 76-78, notes 11-12).

identified by Josephus with India. Just as Herodotus in his travels sought to identify strange and exotic foreign place-names with those familiar to the Greeks so that they would not appear so remote, so Josephus likewise adopts the old identification of the River Gihon with the Nile (Genesis 2:13; *Ant.* 1.39).[4] Similarly, in his listing of the lands settled by Japheth's sons, Josephus identifies them with various Greek countries (*Ant.* 1.122-29).

2. *The Earliest Language*

Josephus adds to the biblical narrative that in the earliest period all the animals spoke a common language (ὁμοφωνούντων) (Genesis 3:1 vs. *Ant.* 1.41). Such a detail is, to be sure, found in the Book of Jubilees (3:28) and in a few places in rabbinic literature.[5] The more common rabbinic view, however, is that only the serpent among the animals produced speech.[6] Ginzberg has noted that the older rabbinic literature does not know of an original common language spoken by man and the animals, and that, in any case, the serpent is said to have spoken Hebrew, while the other animals spoke their own language (Ginzberg 1925, 5:94, n. 58). It is interesting that Philo (*De Confusione Linguarum* 3.6) ascribes the view of a common language of animals to mythologists (μυθυπλαστοί), perhaps, we may conjecture, the same mythologists who are the source for Plato's picture of primitive man, who had the power of holding intercourse not only with men but with brute creatures as well (*Statesman* 272C) (see Lewinsky 1887, 54, n. 3). Josephus may well have been influenced by the fact that in the earliest period animals, in the Greek as in the Jewish tradition, are said to have

---

[4] See Rappaport (1930, 3, no. 12, and 79, n. 16), who cites the Septuagint on Jeremiah 2:18, Ecclesiasticus 24:27, and a number of other texts that make this identification.

[5] See Rappaport (1930, 79-80, n. 18); and Schalit (1944, 2:8, n. 15).

[6] Josephus apparently knew this view, for he says that speech was taken from the serpent (*Ant.* 1.50), the assumption being that only the serpent had previously possessed this faculty. Basser (1987, 27), suggests that Josephus understood Genesis 3:1 to mean not that the serpent was more subtle than any of the living creatures of the field (*ḥayat ha-sadeh*) but rather that the serpent was more subtle than any of the speaking ones of the field. He bases this on the fact that the Targumim on Genesis 2:7 render "living" (*ḥayah*) to mean "speaking" (*memalela'*) and notes that Josephus renders Genesis 3:14 to mean not that the serpent was cursed from among all the living creatures of the field (*ḥayat ha-sadeh*) but that the serpent was deprived of speech (*Ant.* 1.50).

had the possibility of speech, as we see in the case of Achilles' horse in the *Iliad* (19.404-17) and in Aesop's fables (see Headlam 1934, 65).

3. The Original Bliss of Mankind

The typical picture of the early generations of man in Greek literature is of man in close contact and friendship with the gods. Thus Hesiod speaks of men during the Golden Age as friendly with the immortal gods (φίλοι μακάρεσσι θεοῖσιν) (*Works and Days* 120).[7] Even in the later heroic age, Homer speaks of the god Poseidon as associating with the Ethiopians, enjoying himself by sitting at their banquets (*Odyssey* 1.22-26). Again, Nausicaa tells Odysseus that the Phaeacians are very dear to the gods (*Odyssey* 6.203). And Alcinous, the king of the Phaeacians, notes that the gods appear in manifest form among them, feast among them, and sit together with them, since they are related to them (ἐπεί σφισιν ἐγγύθεν εἰμέν) (*Odyssey* 7.201-6). Dicaearchus of Messene (ca. 310 B.C.E.) (fragment 49)[8] likewise asserts that what set the men of the earliest age apart was their "nearness to the gods" (see Dröge 1989, 37); likewise Josephus, in an addition to the Bible, presents a similar picture of Adam as being wont to resort to G-d's company (εἰς ὁμιλίαν αὐτῷ) and as taking delight in associating with him (ἡδόμενος τῇ πρὸς αὐτὸν ὁμιλίᾳ) (*Ant.* 1.45). The approaching end of this Golden Age is signalled by the fact that Adam, who had previously been associating so freely with G-d, withdraws when G-d enters the garden after his sin.

In his developed picture of the original bliss of mankind, which has no parallel in the Bible, Josephus follows a tradition found in many authors from Hesiod on (*Ant.* 1.46). Smith finds almost a hundred references to the Golden Age in classical writers, and he quotes the author of the *Aetna* (16), who says that descriptions of the Golden Age are so common that "non cessuit cuiquam melius sua tempora nosse" (K. F. Smith 1908, 194). Josephus describes this life of bliss (βίον εὐδαίμονα) as one in which men are unmolested by any evil (κακοῦ παντὸς ἀπαθῆ), with no care (φροντίδι) to fret

---

[7] On Hesiod's account of the Five Ages and its sources see Rosenmeyer (1957, 257-85).
[8] *Ap.* Porphyry, *De Abstinentia* 4.2, in Wehrli (1944, 1:24).

(ξαινόμενοι, "mangle") their souls, where all things that contribute (συντελεῖ) to enjoyment (ἀπόλαυσιν) and pleasure (ἡδονήν) spring up, through G-d's providence (πρόνοιαν), spontaneously (αὐτομάτων), without toil (πόνου) or distress (ταλαιπωρίας) on the part of man, where men live long lives and where old age (γῆρας) does not soon overtake them (*Ant.* 1.46). And in imposing his punishment upon Adam (Genesis 3:17), G-d says, in Josephus' version, that the earth will no longer produce anything of herself (αὐτομάτως) but only in return for toil (πονοῦσι) and grinding labor (τοῖς ἔργοις τριβομένοις) (*Ant.* 1.49).

The notion that early man lived free from evils and toil and that old age did not soon overtake him is found in Hesiod's description, which employs several of the words found later in Josephus: "For ere this the tribes of men lived on earth remote and free from ills (κακῶν) and hard toil (πόνοιο) and heavy sicknesses which bring the Fates upon men; for in misery men grow old (καταγηράσκουσιν) quickly" (*Works and Days* 90-93).[9] In his description of the Golden Age, Hesiod says that men lived like gods without sorrow of heart, remote and free from toil (πόνων) and grief, that they avoided old age (γῆρας),[10] that the earth of its own accord (αὐτομάτη) gave them fruit abundantly (*Works and Days* 112-20). "They dwelt in ease and peace upon their lands with many good things," he concludes, "rich in flocks and loved by the blessed gods" (118-20).[11] In contrast, in his description of the Iron Age, Hesiod stresses that men never rest from labor and sorrow by day, nor from perishing by night, "and the gods shall lay troublesome cares upon them" (*Works and Days* 176-78).

The notion of food springing up spontaneously, mentioned several times in Josephus' description of the Golden Age (*Ant.* 1.46, 49, 54), is also found in Homer's description of the Cyclopes, for whom grain sprang up without sowing or plowing (*Odyssey* 9.109). Likewise, in Plato, the Golden Age is described as a period when

---

[9] Translated by White (1914). All other translations in this chapter are from the Loeb Classical Library.

[10] Cf. Horace, who remarks that after Prometheus' theft of fire, "death, that hitherto had kept withdrawn and came but slowly, quickened its pace" (*Odes* 1.3.27-33). Headlam (1934, 66) notes that in Genesis this part of man's punishment does not appear until Noah (Genesis 6:3).

[11] Hesiod's description of the ages of the world may well come from the doctrine of Zarathustra that there will be four ages of the world, symbolized by a tree with four branches – gold, silver, steel, and iron. Cf. Reitzenstein (1926, 38 ff.).

the fruits of the earth grew of themselves (αὐτομάτης) (*Statesman* 272A). Plato, in his description of primitive man, notes that men in those days were neither rich nor poor, and hence that they were free from insolence (ὕβρις), injustice (ἀδικία), jealousies (ζῆλοι), and envies (φθόνοι) (*Laws* 3.679B 3-C 2). These men were simple-minded (εὐήθεις), believed to be true what they heard about gods and men and lived according to truth. They did not know how to suspect their fellow men of falsehood. Again, the fourth-century B.C.E. comic poet Philemon (frag. inc. 4) contrasts the miserable lot of man who must always toil with the lot of the other animals for whom the earth gives bread of its own accord. The Peripatetic Dicaearchus of Messene (fragment 49)[12] explains that primitive man's ignorance of agriculture caused him to be dependent upon food that grew spontaneously (αὐτόματα). He states that in the Golden Age men lived long lives of leisure, without toil (πόνων) or care (μερίμνης) and without disease. Iambulus (of uncertain but Hellenistic date) (*ap*. Diodorus Siculus 2.57.1), in his utopia, remarks that foodstuffs were then produced of themselves (αὐτομάτους), and that the inhabitants lived extremely long lives, reaching the age of one hundred and fifty (2.57.4). Similarly, Aratus, who lived in the fourth and third centuries B.C.E., describes the Golden Age as a time when justice ruled and men had not knowledge of "hateful strife, or carping contention, or din of battle" (*Phaenomena* 108-9), while he depicts the Silver Age as one marked by wars and cruel bloodshed (*Phaenomena* 125). The Stoic Posidonius (*ap*. Seneca, *Epistulae* 90.5-6), who lived in the second and first centuries B.C.E., contrasts the Golden Age, when the wise rulers protected the weak from the strong, with the period of decline, when vice and tyrannies came into being. In his reference to this Golden Age Ovid describes it as a period in which the trustfulness (*credulitas*) of the fish and the innocuousness and simplicity of the beasts did not result in their being caught, since all things were free from snares (*insidiis*), fear and deceit (*fraude*), and were full of peace (*Metamorphoses* 15.99-103). The Stoics[13] similarly had a glowing picture of a Golden Age, during which men lived in

---

[12] *Ap*. Porphyry, *De Abstinentia* 4.2, in Wehrli (1944, 1:24).
[13] See the passages collected by Lovejoy and Boas (1935, 260-86). To be sure, however, many of the Stoics, as Ryberg (1958, 121) and Taylor (1955, 264-66), remark, for example, Panaetius (*ap*. Cicero, *De Officiis* 2.15-16), did acknowledge that there was some progress in the history of civilization.

harmony with nature and had no blind love of gold (Seneca, *Phaedra* 486 and 527-28), and of a decline from that ideal, so that "luxury arose, deadliest of ills, a luring pest" (Pseudo-Seneca, *Octavia* 427-28).

Likewise, Josephus' picture of the Golden Age is reminiscent of that in the Epicurean poet Lucretius, with whose Latin, to be sure, Josephus probably was not acquainted[14] but who reflects traditions available to Josephus, and who remarks that at first the earth of her own accord (*sponte sua*) created crops for men, who now must toil for a lesser result (2.1158). Similarly, Lucretius describes the primitive age of man as one when man did not use the plough, but depended merely upon the sun and rains to bring forth what the earth had earlier created of its own accord (*sponte sua*) (5.933-38). Cicero recalls the Golden Age, when, "as the poets say," no force was ever applied by man to produce crops from the soil" (*De Natura Deorum* 2.63). In his picture of the return of the Saturnian Age, Virgil[15] declares that the earth, untilled, will pour forth ivy and foxglove (*Eclogue* 4.18-20); and in another picture of this Golden Age he notes that no ploughman then tilled the soil (*Georgics* 1.125).[16] Ovid, too, in his description of the Golden Age, says that the earth gave forth food of itself (*per se*) without compulsion (*nullo cogente*) (*Metamorphoses* 1.101-4). "The earth, untilled," he continues, "brought forth her stores of grain; and the fields, though unfallowed, grew white with the heavy, bearded wheat" (*Metamorphoses* 1.109-10). Elsewhere he repeats the theme that in that age the earth produced fruits without the use of the ploughshare (*Amores* 3.8.39-40).

Josephus' picture of primitive man as being unmolested (ἀπαθῆ) by any evil is reminiscent of the Stoic goal of ἀπάθεια. The Stoic Seneca quotes the passage from Virgil's *Georgics* cited

---

[14] So Thackeray (1929, 118): "Josephus, we may be sure, had but slight acquaintance with Latin literature, and these reminiscences doubtless came from an assistant." Nevertheless, it is possible that Josephus might have been acquainted with Latin, since he wrote his *Antiquities* after spending twenty years in Rome.

[15] On Virgil's picture of the Golden Age see Taylor (1955, 261-78) and Ryberg (1958, 112-31).

[16] For an excellent analysis of Virgil, *Georgics* 1.121-46, and its relation to Lucretius' theory of progress see Ryberg (1958, 119-23), who notes man's progress in the arts as evidence of G-d's wisdom and providence. Josephus, in contrast, has the more conventional view, found in Hesiod and others, that toil is G-d's punishment inflicted on man for his sins.

above (*Epistulae* 90.37), and then remarks that in those days "the very soil was more productive when untilled, and yielded more than enough for peoples who refrained from despoiling one another" (*Epistulae* 90.40). Similarly, pseudo-Seneca remarks that in that age the glad earth of her own accord (*ultro*) laid bare her fruitful breast (*Octavia* 404-5). The unknown author of the *Aetna* speaks of the carefree Saturn, in whose age "no man subdued fields to his will or sowed grain in them" (9-16). Indeed, the central ideal in the Stoic philosophy was to live according to nature (κατὰ φύσιν), as we see already, for example, in Polemo, the teacher of Stoicism's founder Zeno (*ap*. Diogenes Laertius 7.87). It is precisely this which leads G-d, according to Josephus, to prefer Abel's sacrifice, inasmuch as it was "in accordance with nature" (κατὰ φύσιν) (*Ant*. 1.54). It is true that in the rabbinic Aggada we find the notion that it was unnecessary to till the soil in the Garden of Eden to produce fruit (see Rappaport 1930, 5, no. 18, and 82, n. 24), and this is, in fact, implied in the biblical text itself; but the correspondences both in ideas and in words between Josephus and the Greek authors, especially those whom Josephus cites elsewhere, are closer.[17] And, in the last analysis, even if Josephus' version is sometimes paralleled by rabbinic midrashim, the fact that he chooses to select a given tradition, while omitting so many others, is an important indicator of his aim and method.

According to the Bible, one of the punishments meted out by G-d to Eve is that man shall rule thereafter over woman (Genesis 3:16). During the Hellenistic period the status of women was greatly ameliorated (see Tarn and Griffith (1952, 98-100); and presumably to avoid the accusation that Judaism places the woman in an utterly inferior position, Josephus completely omits this statement (*Ant*. 1.49). He does, however, repeat the common classical theme of the evil wrought by womanish counsel when he says that G-d imposed punishment on Adam for yielding (ἥττονα – being inferior to) to a woman's counsel (γυναικείας συμβουλίας) (*ibid*.). Though this is ostensibly similar to the biblical account, which says that G-d punished Adam because he hearkened to the voice of his

---

[17] On the original state of mankind in the Golden Age see Klingender (1856); Graf (1884); Bury (1920); R. H. Murray (1920, 401-46); Séchan (1929, 3-36); Türck (1931); Headlam (1934, 63-71); Lovejoy and Boas (1935); and Teggart (1947, 45-77). Of these the fullest collection of sources is that by Lovejoy and Boas, but they are little concerned with the terminology used or with comparing the sources with one another.

wife (Genesis 3:17), Josephus generalizes about womanish counsel; and in this he is reminiscent of Homer's *Odyssey*, where, after Agamemnon has described how he met his death through the contrivance of his wife Clytemnestra, Odysseus replies: "Ah, verily has Zeus, whose voice is borne afar, visited wondrous hatred on the race of Atreus from the first because of the counsels of women (γυναικείας βουλάς). For Helen's sake many of us perished, and against thee Clytemnestra spread a snare while thou wast afar" (11.436-39).

4. *The Story of Cain and Abel*

One of the difficulties in the biblical text, pointed out by such non-believers as the Emperor Julian (*Contra Galilaeos* 346E-347C) and Ḥiwi al-Balkhi (see J. Rosenthal 1947-48, 323) is that G-d is apparently capricious in accepting the sacrifice of Abel while rejecting that of Cain (Genesis 4:4-5). The Septuagint explains G-d's rejection of Cain by stating that he failed to cut his sacrifice into pieces properly (Genesis 4:7).[18] Philo (*De Sacrificiis Abelis et Caini* 27.88-89), followed by Julian (*Contra Galilaeos* 346E-347C), goes to great pains to explain the difference between Cain's offering, which, he says, was lifeless, second in age and value, and weak, and that of Abel, which was living, first in age and value, and possessed of strength and superior fatness. Similarly, the rabbis stress that Cain's gift was of the poorest quality.[19] But, as Cassuto well points out, the Bible does not contrast the gifts of Cain and Abel but merely conveys the impression that Abel brought the finest of his flock (Genesis 4:4) while Cain was indifferent (Genesis 4:3) (Cassuto 1961, 205). To show that G-d was not capricious in preferring Abel, Josephus condemns Cain because his gift had been forced from the soil "by the ingenuity of grasping man" (τοῖς κατ' ἐπίνοιαν ἀνθρώπου πλεονέκτου [καὶ] βίᾳ πεφυκόσιν) (*Ant.* 1.54). In contrast, says Josephus, Abel's offering was favored by G-d, who is

---

[18] Genesis 4:7 is so difficult to understand that the rabbis (*Yoma* 52a-b) numbered this among the five verses in the Torah the grammatical construction of which is undecided. Josephus resolves the problem by completely omitting the verse.

[19] *Genesis Rabbah* 22.5 and other passages cited by Aptowitzer (1922, 37-41, 142-44). Stein (1931, 10-11) states that since the Septuagint was not held in favor in Palestine, the source of the rabbis' comment that Cain incurred G-d's displeasure through an improper division of the sacrifice is "Hellenistic midrash."

honored by things that grow spontaneously (τοῖς αὐτομάτοις)" and (in the phrase so familiar to the Stoics) in accordance with nature (κατὰ φύσιν) (*Ant.* 1.54).[20] In addition, Josephus stresses Abel's respect for justice, his piety, and his virtue generally, in contrast to Cain's depravity and eagerness for gain (*Ant.* 1.53).[21] Josephus thus, like Philo (*De Sacrificiis Abelis et Caini* 1.2), connects Cain's name, which means "acquisition" (κτῆσις), with this quality in his character.

It was characteristic of the Stoics in antiquity to seek etymologies of proper names;[22] and Josephus elsewhere (e.g., *Ant.* 1.180, Melchisedek) adds etymologies that are not found in the Bible. The Bible, to be sure, often does give etymologies, but it omits the etymology of the name of Abel (Genesis 4:2), a fact that bothered some of the great medieval Jewish commentators, one of whom, Nachmanides, noted that the reason for this omission was that the Bible did not wish to make explicit the pessimism inherent in the meaning of the name "vanity" (*hebel*). The Hebrew reader, as Cassuto remarks, can immediately see how apt the name of Abel is in view of the fate in store for him (Cassuto 1961, 202); but this is, of course, not true for the Greek reader. Hence, Josephus gives the meaning of Abel's name as "nothing" (οὐθέν) (*Ant.* 1.52).

Similarly, Josephus' added detail about Cain's fear that in his wanderings he would fall prey (ἀλώμενος περιπέσῃ) to wild beasts (*Ant.* 1.59) is a familiar theme from Greek and Roman literature. Thus Lucretius, in his vivid description of the life of primitive man, notes that tribes of wild beasts often made rest dangerous for primitive man, who would flee in terror at night at the approach of a foaming boar or a lion (5.982-87).[23] Likewise, Josephus' exag-

---

[20] Droge (1989, 38) notes that a number of religious and philosophical thinkers, such as Theophrastus, had expressed a preference for the offering of inanimate objects, notably fruits of the earth, rather than animals; but, as he remarks, Josephus defends the biblical practice on the basis of the Hesiodic tradition, which, we may note, was highly respected in antiquity.

[21] Similarly, the Aggada praises the righteousness of Abel (see Rappaport 1930, 5, no. 22, and citations on 83, n. 28) and condemns Cain's acquisitiveness (see Rappaport, 5, no. 23, and citations on 83, n. 30). But the rabbinic parallels speak of Abel in terms that would appeal to a traditional Jewish audience; thus in *Tanhuma Balak* 11 he is referred to as righteous (*zaddik*), whereas Josephus describes his virtues in terms comparable to the cardinal virtues spoken of by Plato and Aristotle.

[22] See, e.g., Cicero, *De Natura Deorum* 2.7.64-69. For further examples and bibliography see Pease (1958, 2:709).

[23] The Aggada (*Genesis Rabbah* 22.12) and other citations in Rappaport (1930, 85-86, n. 37) are not as close to Josephus in remarking that the animals assem-

geration of Cain's travels (πολλὴν δ' ἐπελθὼν γῆν) (*Ant.* 1.60), in contrast to the Bible's statement that Cain "went out from the presence of the L-rd" (Genesis 4:16), is reminiscent of Greek parallels, notably the wanderings of Oedipus.[24]

Josephus elaborates considerably on Cain's wickedness after the murder of Abel (*Ant.* 1.60-62), and his language is highly reminiscent of Greek and Roman descriptions of the decline of man from the age of primitive simplicity.[25] The ancients generally, starting with Hesiod, agreed that the chief cause of man's decline was his greed and selfishness.[26] Hesiod describes the Iron Age, the age in which he himself lived, as one in which man used the right of might (χειροδίκαι: *Works and Days* 189, and δίκη δ' ἐν χερσί, 192) and in which man praised the evil-doer and his insolence (κακῶν ῥεκτῆρα καὶ ὕβριν, 191).[27]

5. *The Decline from the Golden Age*

Lucretius, who differs from Hesiod and Aratus in not seeing a continuous decline in man's history, condemns the building of

---

bled to demand Cain's blood. Philo (*Quaestiones in Genesin* 1.74), which Rappaport cites as a parallel, similarly says that Cain "feared the attacks of beasts and reptiles, for nature produced these for the punishment of unjust men."

[24] Cf., e.g., Sophocles, *Oedipus at Colonus* 20: "For an old man thou hast traveled far."

[25] There was also in antiquity a theory that man had risen from his former estate (e.g., Aeschylus, *Prometheus Bound* 447-506), as well as one (cf., e.g., Lucretius, 5.925-1457; see Lovejoy and Boas 1935, 192-221) that man had in some respects improved while in other respects he had declined; but the prevailing theory, as K. F. Smith (1908, 192), states, was that man had progressively degenerated. The typical presentation is that of Horace, *Odes* 3.6.46-48: "Aetas parentum, peior avis, tulit / nos nequiores, mox daturos / progeniem vitiosiorem."

[26] Of course, as Attridge (1976, 170, n. 1) points out, the theme of progressive decline is to be found in historians such as Polybius and Poseidonius, both of whose works were known to Josephus. We may also add a reference to the historian Livy (mentioned at a much later point by Josephus, *Ant.* 14.68), who likewise notes "how, with the gradual relaxation of discipline, morals first gave way, as it were, then sank lower and lower, and finally began the downward plunge which has brought us to the present time, when we can endure neither our vices nor their cure" (1.9). But the fact that Josephus does mention Hesiod (*Ant.* 1.108) in close juxtaposition to this passage and the fact that he does not mention the names of any of these historians and the fact that there are similarities of language with Hesiod would argue that his immediate source for this motif is Hesiod.

[27] Cf. Macurdy (1940, 51-55) for a parallel between Hesiod's description of the evils attending the wicked and of the happiness attending the righteous and the Bible's descriptions as found in Amos and Micah, the Hebrew prophets.

cities and the establishment of citadels by kings to be a stronghold and refuge, and, in particular, attacks the introduction of the institution of property and gold, "which easily robbed the strong and beautiful of honor, since, for the most part, however strong men are born, however beautiful their body, they follow the lead of the richer man" (5.1105-16). During the Iron Age, according to Ovid, modesty, truth, and faith fled the earth, to be replaced by tricks and plots and snares (*fraudesque dolusque insidiaeque*), violence (*vis*), and a cursed love of gain (*amor sceleratus habendi*) (*Metamorphoses* 1.127-31). Whereas, he adds, the ground, like the sunlight and the air, had previously been the common possession of all men, it was now carefully marked out by boundary-lines (*Metamorphoses* 1.135-36). During this age wealth was discovered, which led men on to crime and war and plunder and which vanquished piety (*Metamorphoses* 1.139-50).

Josephus' picture of the decline from a Golden Age (*Ant.* 1.60-62) stands within this classical tradition. Cain, he says, in his supplement to the biblical account, indulged in every bodily pleasure, increased his substance with wealth (πλήθει χρημάτων) amassed by rapine (ἁρπαγῆς) and violence (βίας), and incited to luxury (ἡδονήν) and pillage (λῃστείαν) all whom he met.[28]

In particular, Josephus' non-biblical additions of Cain's introduction of boundaries of land, his building and fortifying a city, and his ending of the life of simplicity have close classical parallels which Josephus may well have had in mind. In his description of the Germans, Caesar, in apparent praise, notes that they do not have definite quantities of land or estates of their own (*Bellum Gallicum* 6.22). Virgil remarks that in the Saturnian (Golden) Age it was unlawful to mark out fields and to divide them with boundaries (*Georgics* 1.126-27). Tibullus notes that in that age there were no boundary-stones in the fields (1.3.43-44). Ovid similarly re-

---

[28] Cf. Ovid, *Amores* 3.8.35-36, who refers to the Age of Saturn, when "the deep earth kept all lucre in darkness." Josephus similarly notes as marks of the degeneracy of the Israelites before their deliverance by the judges their drifting into living in accordance with their own pleasure (ἡδονήν) and caprice (βούλησιν) and luxury (τρυφήν) (*Ant.* 5.179-80). It is the increase in wealth (πλοῦτον) which leads to luxury (τρυφῆς) and voluptuousness (ἡδονῆς); and these lead to disregard of the laws (*Ant.* 5.132). Cf. Moses' extra-biblical attack on the tribes of Gad, Reuben, and Manasseh for seeking to live in luxury and ease (τρυφᾶν ἀπόνως) and Josephus' attack on Samuel's sons for abandoning themselves to luxury (τρυφή) and rich food (*Ant.* 4.167, 6.34).

marks that in that period surveyors did not mark off the soil with boundaries (*Amores* 3.8.41). Seneca uses similar language in noting that no sacred boundary-stones separated fields (*Phaedra* 528-29); in contrast, in the present age, the characteristics of decline are that men have marked out boundaries, established kingdoms, built cities, guarded their own dwellings, or, bent on booty, attacked other dwellings with weapons (Pseudo-Seneca, *Octavia* 420-22).

To Virgil the fact that man, even with the return of the Golden Age, will gird towns with walls is an indication that traces of his old sin remain (*Eclogues* 4.32-33). Similarly, Seneca, in his picture of the primitive age of man, notes that cities were not then surrounded by massive walls, set with many towers (*Phaedra* 531-32). And Pseudo-Seneca similarly notes that they were not then accustomed to surround their cities with walls (*Octavia* 401).

Josephus condemns Cain for putting an end to the guileless (ἀκέραιον) and generous (μεγαλόψυχον) simplicity (ἀπραγμοσύνην – a word which occurs in the works of Josephus only here) and ignorance (ἀμαθίας) in which men had lived previously and converted them to a life of knavery (πανουργίαν) (*Ant.* 1.61). This, too, is in line with the classical portrayals of the primitive age of simplicity in Homer, Plato, Virgil, and Ovid, as noted above.

In a further addition to the biblical narrative, Josephus notes in vivid detail the continued deterioration in Cain's descendants, each generation becoming worse than the previous one through inheriting and imitating its vices (*Ant.* 1.66). "They rushed incontinently (ἀκρατῶς) into battle," he adds, "and plunged (ὡρμήκεσαν) into brigandage (λῃστείαν); or if anyone was too timid (ὀκνηρός) for slaughter, he would display other forms of mad recklessness (ἀπόνοιαν θράσους) by insolence (ὑβρίζων) and greed (πλεονεκτῶν)."[29] Later, in describing the deterioration of Seth's descendants, Josephus remarks that they no longer rendered to G-d his due honors nor showed justice in dealings with their fel-

---

[29] On the depravity of Cain's posterity see also Philo (*De Posteritate Caini* 12.42-43). Philo here speaks of "a life beset with passions and vices, with its treachery and unscrupulousness, its villainy and dissoluteness." While the picture is similar, Josephus uses none of Philo's terms in describing the depravity of Cain's descendants. Cf. also *Pirqe de-Rabbi Eliezer* 22, which speaks of the descendants of Cain as those who rebel and sin and defile themselves with all kinds of immorality; but the picture and the language are more biblical than Josephus' Hellenized version. Cf. Rappaport (1930, 7, no. 33, and 86-87, n. 41).

low men but exhibited a zeal (ζήλωσιν) for vice (κακίας) twice as great as they had shown previously for virtue (*Ant.* 1.72). All this is Josephus' embellishment of a single biblical phrase): "And he [Cain] built a city" (Genesis 4:17).

Schalit has well remarked that the fact that Josephus speaks in immediate juxtaposition of the wickedness of Cain and of his building of a city indicates that he regarded the act of Cain as sinful (Schalit 1944, 2:11, 28.).[30] In this Josephus may well have had in mind the story of Romulus, who slew his brother Remus because of an argument over the city wall of Rome.[31] The account may have been familiar to him from Dionysius of Halicarnassus, with whose work Josephus was probably acquainted (see Thackeray 1930, 4:ix-x; and Shutt 1961, 92-101).

Josephus adds to the biblical account of Tubal-Cain (Genesis 4:22), whom he calls Jubel (*Ant.* 1.64), by connecting the latter's invention of the forging of metal with the art of war, a link similarly made by Hesiod (*Works and Days* 150-54), who notes the connection between the discovery of the art of metallurgy with bronze and the warlike behavior that followed. A similar point is made in Ovid's account of the Iron Age (*Metamorphoses* 1.142-43). Josephus' account is likewise reminiscent of that of the Greek Telchines, semi-divine beings in Rhodes who were skilled in metal-work, found in Strabo (14.2.7.653-54) and Eustathius (*ad Iliad*, p. 771, 55 ff.). The added statement that Jubel distinguished himself in the art of war, procuring thereby the means of satisfying the pleasures of the body, is reminiscent of Lucretius' attack on war (5.1000-1).[32]

Josephus' exalted picture of Seth's descendants (*Ant.* 1.69), completely missing from the Bible (Genesis 5:6), as inhabiting the same

---

[30] The Midrash likewise regards this as sinful but does not give details (*Genesis Rabbah* 23.1), as does Josephus. Pseudo-Philo (*Bib. Ant.* 2.3) adds that Cain continued to build cities until he had founded seven of them.

[31] Cf. Livy 1.7.2 and 1.16; Dionysius of Halicarnassus 1.87.4; and Plutarch, *Romulus* 10. On the comparison of Cain and Romulus, see Kretschmer (1909, 301), who cites Propertius 3.9.50 ("caeso moenia firma Remo") and Tibullus, 2.5.23-24, as indicating that the death of Remus was understood as a building-sacrifice. See also Ehrenzweig (1915, 1-9, and 1919-20, 65-86) and Gruppe (1920-21, 67-76).

[32] Cf. Philo (*De Posteritate Caini* 34.117): "All these people are war-makers, and that is why they are said to be workers in iron and bronze." Similarly, as Rappaport (1930, 6, no. 31, and 86, n. 39) remarks, the Aggada (see *Genesis Rabbah* 23.3 and Rashi on Genesis 4:22) condemns Tubal-Cain for inventing the weapons by means of which men can kill each other.

country without dissension (ἀστασίαστοι) is reminiscent of Thucydides, who especially bewails civil strife (3.80-83), and of Plato (*Laws* 3.678E9-679A2), who, in his description of the development of society after the great deluge, remarks that primitive men felt affection and good will towards one another and had no occasion for internecine quarrels about their subsistence. And the fact that they lived "in prosperity, meeting with no untoward incident to the day of their death" is reminiscent of Aristotle, who remarks that true happiness requires external goods (τῶν ἐκτὸς ἀγαθῶν), "for which reason some identify happiness with good fortune (εὐδαιμονίᾳ), though others identify it with virtue" (*Nicomachean Ethics* 1.8.1099A31-1099B8). Aristotle further stresses that not only is complete virtue required, but also a complete life, since many vicissitudes occur, as witness the case of Priam, who fell into misfortune in his old age; "and one who has experienced such chances and has ended wretchedly no one calls happy" (*Nicomachean Ethics* 1.9.1100A4-9). Finally, Aristotle quotes Solon as saying that no one should be called happy until he has seen the end of his life (*Nicomachean Ethics* 1.10.1100A10-11).

An interesting addition made by Josephus to the biblical text is Adam's prediction[33] of "a destruction (ἀφανισμόν) of the universe, in one case by violent fire (κατ' ἰσχὺν πυρός) and in another by a mighty deluge of water (κατὰ βίαν καὶ πλῆθος ὕδατος)" (*Ant.* 1.70).[34] While it is true that the rabbis (*Zevahim* 116a and other passages cited by Rappaport 1930, 90, n. 52), in describing the tumult that occurred when G-d gave the Torah at Sinai, speak of the possibility that the noise was that of the destruc-

---

[33] Rappaport (1930, 7, no. 37, and 88, n. 45) remarks that the picture of Adam as predicting the future is very widespread in the Aggada; but he also calls attention to the fact that the rabbis do not picture him, as does Josephus, as predicting catastrophes to his contemporaries.

[34] Rappaport (1930, 88, n. 94a) concludes that from Josephus' language it is not possible to be sure whether Josephus is referring to "the one time...the other time," i.e. two catastrophes, or to "partly...partly," i.e., one catastrophe, though he tends toward the view that Josephus is speaking of one catastrophe. But Schalit (1944, 2:13, n. 45) contends that Josephus refers to two catastrophes, noting the close parallel with the *Vita Adae*, 49-50, which speaks of two catastrophes and two tablets. We may add that Pseudo-Philo (*Bib. Ant*, 3.9) likewise speaks of two catastrophes, inasmuch as it indicates that after the flood brought upon the earth in the days of Noah G-d promises that when mankind will sin again He will judge them, not again by flood, but by famine or sword or fire or pestilence or earthquakes.

tion of the world by flood of water or by flood of fire, they do not present this as a prediction and, in fact, deny (the words are put into the mouth of Balaam) that this will take place, since G-d has sworn that He will not destroy mankind. It is just as likely, however, as Hölscher avers (though without citing evidence), that Josephus' notion is Greek (Hölscher 1916, 1959). In point of fact, Plato declares that there have been and will be hereafter many diverse destructions of mankind, the greatest by fire and water (*Timaeus* 22C-D). Heraclitus (*ap.* Diogenes Laertius 9.8 = Heraclitus, fragment 66D, 26B) likewise speculates about the conflagration (ἐκπύρωσις) which will consume the universe; and this doctrine of the ultimate absorption of the universe at the end of the *annus magnus* in a primal fire played a prominent role in the writings of the Stoics, so that Clearchus speaks of successive reintegrations of the universe from fire (*ap.* Stobaeus, *Eclogae* 1, p. 171), and Marcus Aurelius states that in the conflagration all things that exist will either pass into vapor or else be dispersed into their constituent atoms (*Meditations* 6.4). Ovid similarly notes that it was fated that the universe, including the sea, land, and sky, would be destroyed by fire, and so Zeus, to punish man's wickedness, decided to send a flood (*Metamorphoses* 1.253-61).

There is obvious Hellenization in Josephus' treatment of the sons of the angels of G-d (Genesis 6:4), for he actually compares their bold exploits with those ascribed by the Greeks to the giants (*Ant.* 1.73).[35] Josephus then, in language reminiscent of Greek tragedy, discusses the punishment by G-d of these sons of angels, for, whereas the Bible remarks merely on their wickedness and on their evil thoughts (Genesis 6:5), Josephus notes that they were overbearing (ὑβριστάς) and disdainful (ὑπερόπτας) of every virtue, being over-confident of their strength (*Ant.* 1.73).

6. Summary

Josephus presents his account of creation within a Greek framework, noting that the river Okeanos surrounded the earth; and, in general, his geography in identifying the rivers and countries al-

---

[35] Rappaport (1930, xxv, n. 2) rightly cites this as an example to refute the contention of M. Gaster (1927, 63) that Josephus adhered strictly to the biblical narrative and avoided syncretism with Greek mythology.

luded to in the first chapters of Genesis is Greek. He is likewise indebted to Greek tradition for the notion that all the animals at the beginning spoke a common language and for his picture of primal man's close contact with the Divine.

Josephus' portrayal of the original bliss of mankind, particularly the spontaneous growth of all things, has no parallel in the Bible but is clearly indebted to the Greek tradition such as is found in a number of authors starting with Hesiod. His notion that man was then affected by evil is reminiscent of the Stoic ideal of ἀπάθεια. In mentioning Eve Josephus repeats Homer's comment about the evil wrought by listening to womanish counsel.

In explaining, as the Bible does not, why G-d preferred Abel's offering to that of Cain, Josephus adopts classical terminology in remarking that Abel's gift was superior in that it grew spontaneously and was in accordance with nature, whereas Cain's had been forced from the soil and was the result of his grasping ambition. Likewise, Josephus' description of Cain's wickedness is reminiscent of Greek and Roman descriptions of the decline of primitive man from the age of simplicity due to man's greed and desire for luxury. Josephus' description of Cain's introduction of boundaries of land and his building and fortifying of cities likewise has classical parallels, as does his description of the continued degeneration of Cain's descendants. The contrasting description of Seth's descendants as living in harmony and without civil strife is reminiscent of the language of Thucydides and Plato. Finally, Adam's prediction that the world would ultimately be destroyed by fire is paralleled in Heraclitus, Plato, and the Stoic tradition. Thus, as Levison perceptively remarks, Josephus has transformed Adam into a figure of universal importance, and the history of the Jews becomes not merely a national but a world epic (Levison 1988, 110).

CHAPTER TWO

NOAH

1. *Introduction*

The pericope in which Josephus describes Noah and the Flood is an excellent example of Josephus' goals and methods, especially since this is an episode that has its counterpart in the pagan Babylonian, Greek, and Roman traditions. Thus far there have been only two studies of any note concerning this passage. The first, by Lewis,[1] is a simple summary of Josephus, which concludes, quite erroneously, as we shall see, that Josephus' treatment is a mere paraphrase of the Septuagint (Lewis 1978, 77-81). Lewis alludes only once to a pagan parallel and only twice to rabbinic parallels, and attempts no specific comparison with Philo or with Pseudo-Philo's *Biblical Antiquities*. Franxman has a more detailed paraphrase of Josephus (Franxman 1979, 86-92) and concludes that in this segment Josephus has struck a more or less even balance between version and original (Franxman 1979, 287); but he has missed several points where Josephus significantly diverges from the Bible (whether in the Hebrew or Greek version), and he alludes to no pagan parallels, to only three rabbinic parallels, to one parallel in Philo, and to none at all in Pseudo-Philo.

The first thing to strike us about the Noah pericope is its relative importance to Josephus in terms of the amount of space that he devotes to it. In the Bible (Genesis 5:28-9:29) it occupies 155 lines in the Hebrew and 217 lines in the Septuagint; in Josephus (*Ant.* 1.74-108) it occupies 215 lines. This gives a ratio of 1.30 of Josephus to the Hebrew and of .99 of Josephus to the Septuagint.[2] This compares with the ratios of Josephus to the Hebrew text for

---

[1] Lewis had been preceded by Rappaport (1930), who notes many rabbinic parallels for Josephus' additions and modifications; but Rappaport is far from complete and sometimes forces parallels where there are none. He, moreover, fails to consider that many of the modifications of Josephus, as well as Josephus' decision whether or not to include rabbinic Midrashim at any given point, may be due to a conscious appeal to his audience of Greek-speaking Jews and non-Jews.

[2] For the Hebrew text I have used the standard edition with the commentary

the following personalities: Abraham, 1.20; Isaac, 1.04; Jacob, 1.08; Joseph, 1.63 (Joseph's dreams and subsequent enslavement, 3.26; Joseph and Potiphar's wife, 5.45; the final test of Joseph's brothers ending with Judah's speech before Joseph, 4.09; the deaths of Jacob and Joseph, .27); Moses, 1.17; Jethro, 2.16; Aaron, .62; Korah, 3.41; Balaam, 2.09; Joshua, .79; Ehud, 2.45; Deborah, .63; Gideon, .90; Jephthah, .94; Samson, 1.52; Ruth, .74; Samuel, 1.87; Saul, 2.19; David, 2.31; Joab, 2.46; Absalom, 1.83; Solomon, 2.56; Jeroboam, 2.16; Rehoboam, 2.35; Josiah, 1.71; Asa, 1.39; Ahab, 1.98; Elijah, 1.52; Jehoshaphat, 2.01; Jehoram of Israel, 1.93; Elisha, 1.11, Jehu, 2.01; Jonah, .67; Hezekiah, 2.18; Manasseh, .91; Jehoiachin, 1.58; Zedekiah, 7.45; Gedaliah, .91; Daniel, 1.32; Ezra, 1.22; Nehemiah, .24, and Esther, 1.36. Hence, in comparison with his treatment of other biblical personalities, Noah is of considerable interest to Josephus.

The second thing, though unnoticed by previous commentators, to strike us about Josephus' Noah narrative is that it is much less concentrated than is the Bible's. In Genesis, after Noah is first mentioned as the son of Lamech (5:29), the narrative continues with the account of man's wickedness and G-d's decision to wipe out the human race and his directions to Noah to build an ark (chapter 6), the description of the Flood (chapter 7), the subsiding of the waters and Noah's sacrifice to G-d (chapter 8), G-d's commandments to Noah, the covenant of the rainbow, and Noah's drunkenness and nakedness (chapter 9), and the genealogy of Noah's sons (chapter 10). The net effect of this presentation is to highlight the character of Noah. In Josephus the centrality of Noah is very much diminished, inasmuch as after he is first mentioned (*Ant.* 1.74) and we are told of the wickedness of mankind (*Ant.* 1.75) and of G-d's instructions to Noah to build an ark (*Ant.* 1.76-78), there is a long digression concerning the date of the Flood (*Ant.* 1.80-88), followed by an account of the Flood itself and of the abating of the waters (*Ant.* 1.89-92), which, in turn, is followed by another digression, noting non-Jewish witnesses to the historicity of the Flood (*Ant.* 1.93-95), after which comes mention of G-d's covenant with Noah sealed with the rainbow (*Ant.* 1.99-

---

of Meir Loeb Malbim (New York: Friedman, s.a.); for the Septuagint I have used the edition of Alfred Rahlfs, *Septuaginta* (Stuttgart: Privilegierte Württembergische Bibelanstalt, 1935); for Josephus I have used the Loeb Classical Library edition of Henry St. John Thackeray, *Josephus*, vol. 4 (London: Heinemann, 1930).

NOAH   19

103), followed by another digression, explaining the longevity of the patriarchs (1.104-8), followed by the account of the refusal of Noah's grandsons and later descendants to colonize the plains (*Ant.* 1.109-12), the building of the Tower of Babel (*Ant.* 1.113-21), the table of nations descended from Noah's sons Japheth and Ham (*Ant.* 1.122-39), and, finally, the story of Noah's drunkenness and nakedness (*Ant.* 1.140-42). Hence, whereas Noah's drunkenness is mentioned in the Bible four chapters (and ninety verses) after its first reference to Noah, in Josephus this incident is mentioned only sixty-five paragraphs later, even though the account of the Flood itself is considerably condensed.

2. *Apologetic Concerns*

In each case of digression in Josephus, it will be noted, the chief factor is apologetic, namely to explain the apparent discrepancy in the chronology of this period (*Ant.* 1.80-88), the apparent objection to the historicity of the whole narrative (*Ant.* 1.93-95), the apparent objection to the Bible's statement about the long lives of the patriarchs (1.104-8), and the fact that the Greeks and the other nations, which claim such antiquity, are actually descended from the biblical Noah (*Ant.* 1.122-39).[3] Connected with this factor of apologetics may be the desire not to build up Noah too much, inasmuch as he is the direct ancestor of what the Talmud refers to as the "Sons of Noah," that is, all Gentiles (*Sanhedrin* 56a-60a). We may note that in Pseudo-Philo also, while there are not as many digressions as in Josephus, from the first mention of Noah until the statement of his death there are three chapters (3.4-5.8, that is, 33 subsections), much of which is taken up with an extra-biblical list of the names of the descendants of Noah and an extra-biblical census of their numbers (4.2-5.8), Pseudo-Philo's motive also, presumably, is apologetic, namely, to diminish, on the one hand, the relative importance of Noah himself, while, on the other hand,

---

[3] Cohen (1979, 32) notes that Josephus (*Ant.* 1.17) promises to narrate everything in proper order (κατὰ τὴν οἰκείαν τάξιν) and that he felt free to set in order (τάξαι) the biblical material thematically, since Moses left what he wrote in a scattered condition (σποράδην), "just as he received each several instruction from G-d." This is true, but what must be added is that the rearrangement is motivated not merely by stylistic but also, more particularly, by apologetic considerations.

endeavoring to show that the nations of the world are actually derived from Noah.

That Josephus' account is motivated, above all, by apologetic concerns may be deduced especially from the fact that his Gentile readers would, in this episode, be expected to equate Noah with Deucalion of the Greek flood, as, indeed, we find in Philo (*De Praemiis* 4.23).[4] It is true that Josephus makes no such equation, presumably because he wished to keep the Pentateuch's words concerning G-d "pure of that unseemly mythology (ἀσχήμονος μυθολογίας) current among others" (*Ant.* 1.15); but the parallel would certainly be recognized by his readers, especially in view of Josephus' terminology, as we shall see. Indeed, there is good reason to believe that Josephus was thinking of such a parallel from the fact that he goes out of his way to note a resemblance between the angels (ἄγγελοι) of G-d who consorted with women and begot sons who were overbearing and disdainful of every virtue (Genesis 6:2), and the giants, who, according to the Greeks, did audacious exploits (*Ant.* 1.73). That others had made the equation of Noah with Deucalion seems clear from the statement of the Church Father Theophilus in the second century, noting that both called mankind to repentance (*Ad Autolycum* 2.19). Theophilus also, we may note, inveighs against those who had said that Noah's Flood was as locally limited as Deucalion's (*Ad Autolycum* 3.29).[5] Indeed, Celsus bitterly attacks Jewish writers who alter the Deucalion story (*ap.* Origen, *Contra Celsum* 1.19, 4.11, 4.42). Finally, we may also suggest that Josephus was acquainted with the story of the Ogygian Flood (mentioned by Varro, *ap.* Augustine, *De Civitate D-i* 21.8 and Nonnos 3.204 ff.), since he, in a curious departure from both the Hebrew text and the Septuagint (Genesis 13:18, which mentions the

---

[4] Colson, ed. and trans. (1939, 8:451-52) says that this is the only instance where Philo makes an explicit equation between a biblical personage and a character in Greek mythology. That others, however, had made such equations is clear from such a passage as *De Confusione Linguarum* (2.2-5), where Philo notes the identification made by impious (δυσσεβεῖς) scoffers in their godlessness (ἀθεότητος) of the story of the Tower of Babel with the account of the attempt of the giants to pile Mount Pelion on Ossa on top of Olympus in order to reach heaven.

[5] Similarly, Lactantius reproaches the heathen for claiming that Noah was merely another name for Liber (i.e. Dionysus, the god of wine) *(De Origine Erroris* [*PL* 6.326-27]), presumably because of the incident of his planting a vineyard and becoming drunk (Genesis 9:20-21).

"oaks of Mamre"), speaks of Abraham as living near an oak called Ogyges (*Ant.* 1.186).⁶

The very first problem that confronts the reader of the biblical narrative of the Flood is to explain why G-d, Who is perfect and presumably unchanging, should have changed His mind and repented (*vayinaḥem*, Genesis 6:6) that He had created man. We may remark that the oldest manuscripts of the Septuagint (Genesis 6:7) have "was angry" (ἐνεθυμήθη, "took to heart"); other manuscripts read "pondered," presumably to avoid this problem. Philo is clearly troubled by the theological problem and attacks those who regard the passage as meaning that G-d changes His mind (*Quod D-us Immutabilis Sit* 5.21-22). Indeed, he says explicitly that those who interpret the words to mean that G-d repented are wrong, since G-d is without change. Rather, the meaning is that G-d was concerned or reflected on the reason why He had made man. Similarly, the rabbis render, "And the L-rd was *comforted* that He had made man in the earth" (*Sanhedrin* 108a), although some leave the anthropomorphism intact and translate "repented," citing, in typically Midrashic fashion, an analogy with a father who rejoices when a son is born to him although he knows that he will eventually die (*Genesis Rabbah* 27.4). One of the rabbis, Rabbi Nehemiah, however, is troubled by this and understands the verb "repented" as "consoled," and explains that G-d was consoled that He had not created man as an angel, since then He would have brought about a revolt of the angels against Him, while Rabbi Levi explains it to mean that G-d was comforted that He had made man from the earth and that he would, presumably, therefore, be subject to death (*ibid.*). Pseudo-Philo piously quotes the passage as it appears in the Hebrew text and translates "repented" (*penitet me*) (3.3). Such a notion is an obvious anthropomorphism, as admitted by such medieval commentators as Ibn Ezra and Nachmanides. It is not surprising that Celsus, Marcion, and Ḥiwi al-Balkhi cite the passage in support of their claim that G-d is not omniscient (see Rosenthal 1947-48, 327). Josephus, in a fashion often paral-

---

⁶ Astour (1965, 212) notes that Ogygos (or Ogyges), who was the ancient king of the region where Cadmus the Phoenician later built Thebes and after whom one of the seven gates of Thebes was named, had a wife named Thebe. Her name and that of the city of Thebes (Astour, 158) may be derived from the Hebrew word *tevah* ("ark," "chest"), which is employed in the Noah story in the Bible (Genesis 6:14 ff.).

leled elsewhere, seeking to avoid such theological hornets' nests, solves the problem by omitting the passage altogether (*Ant.* 1.73).

Another theological problem arises when we ask why G-d should have created man only to destroy him in the Flood. In the Bible G-d justifies this action with the single statement to Noah that He is doing so because man has filled the earth with violence (Genesis 6:13). Josephus anticipates the objection that it would have been reasonable (σῶφρον, "discreet," "prudent," "temperate") for G-d not to have created man rather than to create him and later destroy him.[7] "No," says G-d in a strong apology, "it was the outrages (οἷς ἐξύβριζον) with which they met my reverent regard (εὐσέβειαν, 'piety') and goodness (ἀρετήν) that constrained me to impose this penalty upon them" (*Ant.* 1.100). Philo, without raising the problem considered by Josephus, also stresses that the biblical statement that the earth was filled with injustice (Genesis 6:13) is as much as to say that no part of it remained empty and so able to receive and support righteousness (*Quaestiones in Genesin* 1.100 on Genesis 6:13). We may note that Philo and Pseudo-Philo do not expand on this verse. The rabbis, on the other hand, in predictable fashion, identify the chief sins of the generation of the Flood as immorality (*Genesis Rabbah* 26.5 and parallel sources cited by Ginzberg [1925, 5:173, n. 17), idolatry, violence (*Genesis Rabbah* 31.6 and parallel sources cited by Ginzberg [*ibid.*]), and rapacity (*Genesis Rabbah* 31.3-5). Josephus likewise mentions the immorality of the age, when he notes that many angels now consorted with women and begot sons who were overbearing (ὑβριστάς) and disdainful of every virtue (παντὸς ὑπερόπτας καλοῦ) because of their confidence in their strength (διὰ τὴν ἐπὶ τῇ δυνάμει πεποίθησιν) (*Ant.* 1.73). Josephus' notice here, particularly its reference to the overweening pride (ὑβριστάς, a key word in Greek tragedy) of this generation, is clearly redolent of Greek tragedy, where νέμεσις follows ὕβρις.[8] The fact that Josephus repeats the

---

[7] One is reminded of the famous debate which lasted for two and a half years, between the schools of Hillel and Shammai as to whether it would have been better if man had never been created (*'Eruvin* 13b).

[8] Josephus similarly presents his depiction of the generation of the Tower of Babel in terms of ὕβρις and νέμεσις (*Ant.* 1.113-19). Following the typical Greek sequence of prosperity, insolence, and punishment, Josephus first notes their prosperity (εὐδαιμονεῖν, *Ant.* 1.113), then their insolence (ὕβρις, *Ant.* 1.113), and finally their punishment through the discord (στάσις, *Ant.* 1.117) which G-d created among them.

idea that the generation obliterated by the Flood had been guilty of ὕβρις (οἷς ἐξύβριζον) (*Ant.* 1.100) shows that he views the punishment meted out by G-d as the νέμεσις which follows the ὕβρις of a Greek tragedy. Ovid, likewise, as we have noted, in his description of the Iron Age, which was the generation of the Flood, is explicit in enumerating the evils of the age: immodesty, falsehood, trickery, slyness, plotting, swindling, violence, greed, injustice, and contempt for the gods (*Metamorphoses* 1.128-62). Similarly, Lucian mentions that the Flood was brought on men because they were very insolent (ὑβρισταὶ κάρτα) and did unlawful deeds (ἀθέμιστα ἔργα) (*De Syria Dea* 12).

A reader of the Bible might well be disturbed by the fact that G-d decided to destroy the world by a flood without apparent warning. Hence, Josephus goes so far as to have Adam already preaching to his contemporaries the destruction of the universe (ἀφανισμὸν...τῶν ὅλων), at one time by a violent fire (καθ' ἰσχὺν πυρός) and at another by a mighty deluge of water (κατὰ βίαν καὶ πλῆθος ὕδατος),[9] with the result that two pillars were erected, one of brick and one of stone, not merely, as Josephus says, to inform mankind of the astronomical discoveries of Adam's day but also by implication to warn mankind of the impending destruction of the earth (*Ant.* 1.70-71). Philo also speaks of such an alternation of fire and flood, noting that "because of the constant and repeated destructions by water and fire the later generations did not receive from the former the memory of the order and sequence of events in the series of years" (*De Vita Mosis* 2.48.263). Pseudo-Philo, on the other hand, speaks of these alternatives only *after* the Flood, when he has G-d declare that if men sin He will judge them by famine, sword, fire, or pestilence, but not again by a flood (3.9). The rabbis, to be sure, speak of the tumult accompanying the giving of the Torah at Sinai and the question put by the heathen kings to the pagan prophet Balaam as to whether a flood of water or a flood of fire might be coming to engulf the

---

[9] There is some question, as we have noted, as to whether Josephus is referring to two catastrophes that may destroy the earth or whether he means a single catastrophe, whereas the world will be destroyed partly by water and partly by fire. It is more likely that two catastrophes are referred to; in the one case, Josephus is saying, a brick pillar will survive, whereas in the other case (water) a stone pillar remains. Josephus' passage recurs almost verbatim in the Pseudepigrapha in *Vita Adae et Evae* (49.3). Cf. the eschatological apocalypse in *Sibylline Oracles* (3.689-90): "And G-d shall judge all with war and sword, and with fire and cataclysms of rain."

earth (*Zevaḥim* 116a); but they do not speak of G-d pondering whether to destroy the earth by water or by fire in the days of Noah, nor do they present it as a prediction that a cataclysm will not occur, inasmuch as G-d has already sworn that He will not destroy mankind. In other places, where the alternatives of a flood of fire and a flood of water are mentioned as ways by which G-d will destroy the earth, it is in connection with the ridicule which Noah's fellow men pour upon him when they see him building an ark and when he warns them that G-d will bring a flood upon them (*Sanhedrin* 108a-b). We may here suggest that Josephus' source may well be Plato's *Timaeus*, to which we have called attention and which declares that "there have been, and will be hereafter, many diverse destructions of mankind, the greatest by fire and water, though other lesser ones are due to countless other causes" (22C). Plato here explains that conflagrations and floods alternate in destroying the inhabitants of the earth, the former allowing the dwellers by the sea to survive, the latter allowing those who live in mountainous regions to do so. But the closest parallel to Josephus is Ovid, who alone, like Josephus, speaks of a divine pondering in connection with the Deluge as to whether to destroy the earth by fire or by water. Because thunderbolts are the usual weapons of Jupiter (Zeus), one might have expected, as Ovid indicates, that Jupiter would have preferred to use them, but he decided not to do so when he remembered that it had been fated that there would come a time when earth, sea, and heaven itself would burn (*Metamorphoses* 1.253-61).

The reader of the account in Genesis may well wonder why both G-d and Noah did not do more to warn mankind of the impending destruction. The Bible states merely that G-d saw that the wickedness of man was great (Genesis 6:5) and that Noah was a righteous and wholehearted man (Genesis 6:9), but it does not indicate that either G-d or Noah did anything to get mankind to repent so as to avert doom. Likewise, neither Philo nor Pseudo-Philo says anything about any attempt by G-d or Noah to induce the inhabitants of the earth to repent. The rabbis, by contrast, as we have noted, expatiate on Noah's attempts to induce his fellow men to mend their wicked ways, only to have them deride him (*Sanhedrin* 108a-b). The very fact that Noah waited for many years, until the cedars which he had planted had grown, was due to his desire to warn his fellow men to repent in the meantime (*Tanhuma Noah* 5); indeed, Noah took fifty-two years (*Pirqe de-Rabbi Eliezer* 23) or 120 years (*Sifre Numbers*, end) (cited by Ginzberg 1925, 5:174, n. 19, with parallels), in order to induce the evil-doers to repent. In fact, the rabbis interpret the phrase "a righteous man" which is applied to Noah in Genesis 6:9, to mean that he was one who forewarned others, since only such a person deserves this designation (*Genesis Rabbah* 30.7). Josephus, similarly, stresses that Noah, in indignation (δυσχεραίνων) at the conduct of his fellow men, and viewing their counsels with displeasure (ἀηδῶς ἔχων), urged them to come to a better frame of mind (διάνοιαν), and to change their deeds (τὰς πράξεις μεταφέρειν) (*Ant.* 1.74).[10] Moreover, Josephus, in his downplaying of theological concerns, does not agree with that rabbinic tradition which ascribes to G-d the credit for Noah's concern with preaching to his fellow men (*Book of Jashar* 5.6-8, 11). In a unique apology for Noah, Josephus adds that Noah feared that his fellow inhabitants, far from listening to his pleas, would even murder him;[11] and so he, with his wives (γυναικῶν), sons, and sons' wives, left the country (*Ant.* 1.74). This statement is cal-

---

[10] Thackeray (1930, 4:35, n. c) remarks that Book 1 of the *Sibylline Oracles* (which contains Jewish, Christian, and even some pagan material) devotes fifty lines to two of Noah's addresses. The parallels, however, which he cites with 1 Peter 3:20 and with 2 Peter 2:5 in the New Testament are not apt, since in the latter instance we read of Noah as a herald (κήρυκα) of righteousness, an honorific term that does not necessarily indicate that he preached to his fellow men. This portrait of Noah the preacher is reminiscent of a Cynic proclaiming "diatribes" on street corners – a scene that was frequent during this period of antiquity, as we can see from the works of Horace (see especially *Satires* 2.3), Menippus, Meleager, Petronius, Epictetus, Dio Chrysostom, and Seneca the Younger. It was such diatribes that profoundly influenced the style of Paul in his sermon to the Athenians on the Areopagus (Acts 17:22-31). See Hadas 1959, 142-46; Bultmann 1910; and Wendland 1912, 75-81.

[11] Rabbinic tradition, as we have noted, remarks on the derision which his contemporaries cast upon Noah (*Sanhedrin* 108b) and indicates that if his fellow men had really known why he had entered the ark they would not have allowed him to do so (*Genesis Rabbah* 32.8); but the rabbis do not speak of threats against Noah's life. Ginzberg (1925, 5:177-78, n. 25), remarking that Josephus' detail that Noah emigrated to another country is unique with him, comments that Josephus probably wished thus to explain how the ark came to rest on Mount Ararat in Armenia, whereas Noah had lived in Palestine. But, we may counter, it is not remarkable for the ark to have floated in the flood-water that had lasted so long. It seems more likely that Josephus introduced this detail to defend Noah against a possible charge of having deserted his fellow men in order to save his own life and those of his family. We may, as a parallel, note Virgil's defense of Aeneas' departure from Troy in Book 2 of the *Aeneid* against similar possible charges.

culated to answer the implied charge that Noah should not have separated himself from his fellows but should have sought to influence them to repent.

Again, one might well be critical of G-d for his negativism in simply seeking to destroy the human race without presenting any plan to start anew. The Greek reader might well have contrasted this apparent divine callousness with the statement in Aeschylus' *Prometheus Bound* that Zeus intended to blot out (ἀιστώσας) the entire race of mankind and to create (φιτῦσαι) another new race (232-33). Similarly, Ovid notes Zeus' promise to the other gods on Olympus that he will replace the wicked race of men with another race of wondrous origin not like the earlier one (*Metamorphoses* 1.250-52). The Bible declares simply G-d's decision to destroy the inhabitants, with no indication that He had any positive goal of starting anew to complement this negative decision (Genesis 6:13). Neither Philo nor Pseudo-Philo nor the rabbis have any parallel to Josephus' unique comment, offered to defend G-d against the accusation of mere negativism, that G-d had decided not merely to blot out the existing race of mankind but to replace it with another race free of vice (*Ant.* 1.75).

3. *Noah's Virtues*

One of the most enigmatic phrases in the biblical account of Noah is the statement that Noah was a man "righteous and wholehearted in his generations" (*zaddik tamim hayah bedōrōtav*) (Genesis 6:9), which the Septuagint renders δίκαιος, τέλειος ὢν ἐν τῇ γενεᾷ αὐτοῦ ("just, perfect in his generation"). Professor David Daube has called my attention to the parallel in Luke 16:8 in the parable of the steward. Philo quotes the Septuagint and consequently praises Noah to the highest degree (*Quod D-us Immutabilis Sit* 25.117), since he says that justice is the chief of the virtues (*De Abrahamo* 5.27). Inasmuch as Noah is perfect, Philo declares that he possessed all the virtues (*De Abrahamo* 6.34); and yet, he, too, qualifies this view by remarking that the statement that Noah was perfect in his generation indicates that he was not absolutely good but only in comparison with the men of his time (*De Abrahamo* 7.36). Pseudo-Philo describes Noah as *iustus et inmaculatus in progenie tua* ("a just man and unblemished in his generation"); but he, too, qualifies this praise of Noah by saying that Noah found grace and mercy (*gratiam et misericordiam*) (3.4), implying that

Noah did not really deserve all the kindness and concern shown to him by G-d, whereas the Bible speaks more positively about Noah in declaring that he found favor (*ḥen*) in the eyes of the L-rd (Genesis 6:8).

The rabbis similarly found themselves in a dilemma. To declare Noah, the ancestor of all non-Jews ("sons of Noah") perfect would, indeed, raise a question as to how Moses and the Torah marked any advance. Indeed, there is a debate in the Talmud as to how righteous Noah really was. One view, that of the second-century Rabbi Nehemiah (*Genesis Rabbah* 30.9) and of the third-century Resh Laqish (*Sanhedrin* 108a) is that Noah deserves even greater praise, since he was righteous in a wicked generation. On the other hand, the third-century Rabbi Judah (*Genesis Rabbah* 30.9) and Rabbi Johanan ben Nappaḥa (*Sanhedrin* 108a) remark that Noah was righteous only in comparison with those of his time. Rabbi Johanan even goes so far as to declare that Noah was so lacking in faith that if the water of the Flood had not reached his ankles he would not have entered the ark (*Genesis Rabbah* 32.6). We may suggest here that one factor in this debate was perhaps the fact that the Church Fathers looked upon Noah as a type of the Christ and stressed that he was pleasing to G-d despite the fact that he was not circumcised (see Lewis 1978, 158-61). Josephus, likewise seeking to steer an even course between excessive praise for the father of the Gentiles and a disdainful sneer, twice remarks that G-d loved Noah for his righteousness (τῆς δικαιοσύνης ἠγάπησε, ἐπὶ δικαιοσύνῃ...ἀγαπῶν) (*Ant.* 1.75 and 1.99) but omits completely the statement that he was perfect.

4. *The Relationship of the Biblical and Greek Floods*

There is a striking similarity between Josephus' language in stating that G-d had put into Noah's mind (ὑποθεμένου) "the device and means of salvation on this wise" (μηχανὴν...καὶ πόρον πρὸς σωτηρίαν) (*Ant.* 1.76), and the account of the flood in Apollodorus (whose date is uncertain, though he was probably a contemporary of Josephus), where we read that Deucalion constructed his ark through the advice (ὑποθεμένου) of Prometheus (1.7.2). Again, the second-century Lucian, using language similar to that of Josephus, declares that Deucalion's salvation was on this wise (ἡ δὲ σωτερίη ἥδε ἐγένετο), namely, that he (Deucalion) built a large chest (λάρνακα) into which he put his children and their wives (παῖδάς τε καὶ γυναῖκας ἑαυτοῦ) (*De Syria Dea* 12; cf. Josephus, *Ant.* 1.73: σὺν τῇ μητρὶ τῶν παίδων καὶ τοῖς τούτων γυναιξίν). That Josephus was, indeed, thinking of Deucalion is, moreover, indicated by the fact that the word which Josephus uses for Noah's ark (λάρνακα, *Ant.* 1.77) is the same word which is used by Apollodorus (1.7.2), by Lucian (*De Dea Syria* 12), and by Josephus' contemporary Plutarch (13.968F), in connection with the ark of Deucalion, rather than the word employed by the Septuagint (κιβωτός, Genesis 6:14) and by Philo (*De Plantatione* 11.43).[12]

That Josephus' choice of the word λάρναξ for Noah's ark is significant is to be seen from the fact that when the same word "ark" (*tevah*) occurs in the Bible of the container where Moses' mother placed him when he was an infant (Exodus 2:3), whereas the Septuagint renders it by the word θίβις (a word presumably derived from the Hebrew), Josephus, perhaps because he wished to avoid a word which is not found in classical writers, does not use the word λάρναξ, which he had used for Noah's ark. Instead Josephus adopts the word πλέγμα ("plaited basket") (*Ant.* 2.224), even though λάρναξ would appear to be the appropriate word for a basket in which a baby is exposed, to judge from Simonides (37.1), Apollonius of Rhodes (1.622), and Diodorus Siculus (5.62).

It would seem, moreover, that Josephus adopted the word λάρναξ directly from Nicolaus of Damascus, whom he quotes (even to the point of giving the number of the book – 96 – where the passage appears) as saying that many refugees found safety on a certain mountain in Armenia at the time of the flood, including a man, transported in an ark (λάρνακος)[13] "who might well be (γένοιτο δ' ἄν) the same man of whom Moses, the Jewish legislator, wrote" (*Ant.* 1.94-95). That Josephus, indeed, identified Noah with the survivor of the Babylonian flood is clear from his remark that the Flood and the ark are mentioned by all who have written histories of the barbarians, whereupon he cites, in particular, Berossus, Hieronymus the Egyptian (the author of an ancient his-

---

[12] It is this same word, λάρναξ, that Josephus employs when he refers to the remains of the ark in Armenia "in which report has it that Noah was saved from the flood" (*Ant.* 20.25). We may here suggest that one factor that led Josephus to select the word λάρναξ for Noah's ark was his desire to reserve the word κιβωτός for the Ark of Covenant.

[13] In Berossus (*ap.* Syncellus 53-56) the ship of the Deluge is called σκάφος, πλοῖον, and ναῦς, but not λάρναξ; and hence it would seem that Josephus has adopted the word rather from the account of Deucalion.

tory of Phoenicia), and Mnaseas of Patara (*Ant.* 1.93-94). Especially significant is Josephus' statement that the dove which Noah sent to explore the condition of the earth returned smeared with mud (πεπηλωμένης) (*Ant.* 1.92), a detail which is not found in the Bible (Genesis 8:11) but does appear in Berossus (*ap.* Syncellus, 53-56) (see Thackeray 1930, 4:44-45, n. b). Finally, that Josephus identified Noah with the survivor of the Babylonian flood is further clear from a passage in his work *Against Apion* (1.130), in which he states that Berossus mentions an ark (λάρναξος, though this is not actually the term used by Berossus) in which Noah was saved when it landed on a mountain in Armenia. In the passage in question, Berossus refers to Xisuthrus, rather than Noah, as we see from Syncellus, who here quotes Berossus; but the fact that Josephus relates the passage as pertaining to Noah shows that he (and presumably his readers) had identifed the two.

We may remark that such an identification of Jewish religious concepts with pagan ideas is seen already in the *Letter of Aristeas* (16), where the presumably Jewish author identifies G-d with Zeus: "G-d...is He Whom all men worship, and we, too, Your Majesty, though we address Him differently, as Zeus and Dis." In making this equation, the author is following in the time-honored footsteps of Herodotus, who constantly makes such equations: for example, the Egyptian deities Pasht and Isis are equated with Artemis and Demeter (2.59), and Horus with Apollo (2.144). Philo also notes that atheist intellectuals denounce the Jewish inconsistency in, on the one hand, proclaiming that the Bible is unique, while, on the other hand, including in the Bible stories that are very similar to the Greek myths. They cite, in particular, the parallel between the story of the attempt of the Giants to reach heaven by piling Mount Pelion on Ossa on Olympus, which is said to be similar to the story of the Tower of Babel (*De Confusione Linguarum* 2.2-5). Josephus' contemporary Plutarch likewise cites what he considers to be conclusive evidence identifying Tabernacles and even the Sabbath as festivals in honor of Dionysus (*Quaestiones Conviviales* 4.6.2).

In response to the charge that the Flood is only a myth, Josephus, in addition to citing the evidence of Berossus and others (*Ant.* 1.94), as noted above, also remarks that relics of the ark have long been preserved in Armenia (*Ant.* 1.95), though elsewhere he states that the remains of the ark are still to be seen in a district called Carron (*Ant.* 20.24-25), presumably identical with Korduene in Mesopotamia near the Armenian border, where rabbinic sources (Onkelos on Genesis 8:4; see Ginzberg (1925, 5:186, n. 48, and parallels noted there) and Berossus agree that the ark came to rest. Neither Philo nor Pseudo-Philo nor the rabbis – none of them being historians – cite external evidence for the historicity of the Flood, nor do they claim that remains of the ark are still to be seen.

5. *Noah's Emergence from the Ark*

When Noah emerges from the ark, the Bible declares simply that he built an altar unto the L-rd (Genesis 8:20), but it gives no reason for the sacrifices which Noah then proceeds to offer. Neither does Pseudo-Philo (3.8), who simply quotes the biblical text. Philo asks why Noah did so when he had not been ordered to do so, and he replies that it was an act of gratitude (*Quaestiones in Genesin* 2.50 on Genesis 8:20). The rabbis also ask how Noah was able to arrive at the idea of sacrificing, and they typically, with their emphasis on the process of reasoning, conclude that he was able to deduce it logically from the fact that G-d had commanded him to take into the ark more clean than unclean animals, the surplus being presumably for the sacrifices later to be offered (*Genesis Rabbah* 34.9). Another explanation, to be sure found only in late sources,[14] is that Noah brought the sacrifice because he sought forgiveness for his sins. Josephus, attempting to give a reasonable explanation, states that Noah, fearful that G-d might send another flood, offered a sacrifice to beseech Him not to do so (*Ant.* 1.96).

There is an obvious anthropomorphism in the biblical statement, retained in the Septuagint, that G-d smelled the sweet savor of Noah's sacrifice (Gen. 8.21). Philo removes the anthropomorphism by explaining that the word "smelled" means "accepted," "for G-d is not of human form (ἀνθρωπόμορφος), nor has he need of nostrils or any other parts as organs" (*De Congressu Quaerendae Eruditionis Gratia* 21.115). Likewise, Pseudo-Philo removes the anthropomorphism by paraphrasing "and it was accepted" (*acceptum est*) by the L-rd as "an odor of rest" (*odor*

---

[14] See Ginzberg (1925, 5:186, n. 49), who cites *Zohar Ḥadash*, Noah 29a, and parallels.

requietionis) (3.8). Josephus once again avoids the problem by omitting this detail (*Ant.* 1.92) and by stating simply that Noah sacrificed to G-d and that G-d, Who loved him for his righteousness, signified to him that He would grant his prayers (*Ant.* 1.99).

The figure of Noah gains in stature through the fact that he does not sacrifice to G-d silently, as in the Bible (Genesis 8:20), but expresses concern for the future of mankind and, like Abraham (Genesis 18:23-30), reasons with G-d that He might maintain the primitive good order (εὐταξίας) of nature and not send another calamity upon mankind,[15] but spare those who, because of their goodness (χρηστότητα), had survived the Flood (*Ant.* 1.96). In the biblical account, the attention is focused on G-d, Who promises not to make any wholesale destruction of man in the future (Genesis 8:21-22). Josephus shifts the attention to Noah, who, through his pleading that if there were another flood the just people would suffer still more than the miscreants who had perished in the first deluge, persuades G-d to promise that there would be no such deluge again in the future (*Ant.* 1.97). In Genesis G-d makes His promise without reference to Noah (9:11); but Josephus exalts Noah by having G-d say that it is at Noah's petition that He has decided to refrain in the future from exacting such a penalty for the crimes of men (*Ant.* 1.99). Noah thus becomes a champion of mankind, similar to Abraham, asking G-d not to send another flood, so that men may devote themselves to recultivating the earth and building cities – the hallmark of civilization.

In Genesis 8:21 there would seem to be a theological problem in the apparent allusion to a doctrine of original sin, since G-d declares that He "will not again curse the ground any more for man's sake, for the imagination of man's heart is evil from his youth." Philo seems to subscribe to a doctrine of original sin when he declares that man's inclination toward evil exists from his youth, "which is all but from his very swaddling bands, as if he were to a certain extent united, and, at the same time, nourished and grown, with sins" (*Quaestiones in Genesin* 2.54 on Genesis 8:21). Pseudo-Philo quotes the biblical passage without elaboration (3.9).[16] The rabbis have ambiguous feelings on the matter. On the one hand,

---

[15] The Aggada also knows of Noah's motive in sacrificing; see *Tanḥuma Noah* 1 (ed. Buber, 17).

[16] The manuscripts of Pseudo-Philo (3.9), however, read *desiit*, and the meaning would then be that the guise (*figura*) of man's heart has ceased (*desiit*) from

in answer to the question of the Emperor Antoninus, Rabbi Judah the Prince was at first ready to subscribe to the view that the evil impulse bears sway over a man even from the formation of the embryo, and only later promulgated the view that the evil impulse prevails only from the moment of birth (*Sanhedrin* 91b). On the other hand, they insist that the impulses natural to man are not in themselves evil (*Genesis Rabbah* 9.7). Josephus, seeking to avoid theological controversy, omits this passage completely from his paraphrase (*Ant.* 1.92).

One of the anomalies of Jewish law is that in the case of the prohibitions of blasphemy, murder, and theft, the Noachides ("Sons of Noah," that is, Gentiles) are subject to greater legal restrictions than are Jews. Thus, for example, the killing of a fetus by a non-Jew is regarded as murder but is not so regarded if done by a Jew (*Sanhedrin* 57b). To be sure, the Septuagint renders Genesis 9:6: "He that sheds a man's blood, instead of his blood shall his own be shed," but the rabbinic interpretation, as applicable to Gentiles, punctuates the verse differently: "He who sheds the blood of man within a man [i.e., an embryo], shall his blood be shed" (*Sanhedrin* 57b). Elsewhere, as we have noted, Josephus was amply aware of rabbinic tradition; but here he avoids such an interpretation and renders simply: "I [G-d] exhort you to refrain from shedding human blood, to keep yourselves pure from murder and to punish those guilty of such crime" (*Ant.* 1.102). It would have been embarrassing, presumably, to have G-d expect more of Gentiles than of Jews, and hence Josephus omits any such interpretation. On the contrary, Josephus goes so far as to declare that

---

his youth, which clearly contradicts the biblical verse and makes no sense. Cohn (1898, 310), plausibly emends *desiit* to *desipit*, "is foolish," and the emendation is adopted by Harrington (1976, 1:70). Jacobson (1996) 1:321, with some diffidence, declares that Cohn's reading, while weak and unexpected, just might be right and that, in any case, nothing better has been suggested. He then, however, calls attention to a reading, *desciit*, from this passage of Pseudo-Philo recorded in Helinand's thirteenth-century *Chronicon*, as cited by Smits (1992, 204), and remarks, without coming to a final conclusion, that this may be the correct reading. We may here state that from a transcriptional point of view there is little to choose between *desipit* and *desciit*, both of which involve the insertion of a single letter; but from the point of view of sense and usage *desciit* seems clearly superior, since *desipit* means "is foolish" and only occasionally is used with a moral color, whereas the biblical text reads "is evil." Hence, the verb *descisco*, of which *desciit* is in the perfect tense and which means " has revolted," "has deviated," "has degenerated," is closer to the original sense.

abortion is prohibited for Jews (*Ag. Ap.* 2.202), going beyond the rabbis themselves, who, while opposing abortion by Jews, did not regard it as a variety of murder.

Josephus, in his eagerness to point out parallels between Jewish and non-Jewish stories and symbolism, notes that the rainbow, which G-d established as a token of a covenant between Him and man (Genesis 9:13), is "among the people there" (παρὰ τοῖς ἐκεῖ) believed to be G-d's bow (τόξον) (*Ant.* 1.103). Inasmuch as the context of the Noah story is Babylonia, the reference would seem to be to the Babylonians rather than to the Greeks; but since, as we have noted, the Greeks commonly equated their gods and their tales with those of other peoples, the reader would more probably identify the bow with the implement of the deities Apollo and Artemis, both of whom are called τοξοφόρος, "bow-bearing" (Homer, *Iliad* 21.483; *Homeric Hymn to Apollo* 13.126). A favorite epithet of both Artemis (Sophocles, Fragment 401) and especially of Apollo (*Iliad* 1.14, etc.) is ἑκήβολος ("attaining his aim," understood by later writers as "far-shooting"). The rainbow to the Greeks, however, was Zeus' sign of war or of a storm that forces people to stop their work and afflicts their flocks (Homer, *Iliad* 17.547-50). It is interesting that Philo, perhaps because of this association of the rainbow with war, argues that the bow that is spoken of in this biblical passage cannot be the rainbow, inasmuch as the bow in Genesis has its own special nature and substance, whereas the rainbow does not (*Quaestiones in Genesin* 2.64 on Genesis 9:13-17). Pseudo-Philo says nothing about the rainbow in that part of his narrative dealing with Noah, but mentions it only when he quotes G-d's assurance to Moses that his (Moses') rod will be a sign comparable to Noah's rainbow in His sight (19.11). The rabbis apparently are troubled that G-d should have set the rainbow in the cloud as a kind of afterthought of the Flood and that He seemingly did not have the forethought to do so earlier. Hence, they declare (*'Avot* 5:6) that the rainbow is one of the ten things created on the eve of the Sabbath of creation at twilight. Josephus carefully avoids stating that G-d created the rainbow, but rather declares that He displayed (ἀποσημαίνων) it; presumably, it had been created long before (*Ant.* 1.103). Moreover, in the Bible there is a clearly anthropomorphic picture in G-d's statement that He will look upon the rainbow that He may remember His covenant with mankind (Genesis 9:16). Philo, Pseudo-Philo, and the rabbis omit reference to this last anthropomorphism, while Josephus reduces the anthropomorphism by having G-d state that by His bow He will indicate the truce from destruction by flood that men are to have (*Ant.* 1.103).

Neither the Bible (Genesis 9:18) nor Philo nor Pseudo-Philo nor the rabbis say anything about the descent of Noah's sons from the mountains to the plains after the Flood; and only later does the Bible note that the generation of the Tower of Babel found a plain in the land of Shinar and dwelt there (Genesis 11:2). Josephus, however, declares that Noah's three sons were the first to descend from the mountains to the plains (εἰς τὰ πεδία) and persuaded the rest of mankind, who, fearing another flood, were afraid of settling in the plains and hence reluctant to make a descent (κατάβασιν) from the heights (ἀπὸ τῶν ὑψηλῶν), to take courage and to follow their example (*Ant.* 1.109). The rabbis similarly remark on mankind's fear of a second flood (*Pirqe de-Rabbi Eliezer*, 11); but a much closer parallel to Josephus' account will be found in Josephus' favorite, Plato, who notes that only the hill shepherds – "small sparks of the human race preserved on the tops of mountains" – managed to escape the Flood, and that since the cities in the plain and on the seacoast were utterly destroyed they feared to descend (καταβαίνειν) from the heights (ἐκ ... τῶν ὑψηλῶν) into the plains (ἐπὶ τὰ πεδία) (*Laws* 3.677B1-3).

The discussion that follows in Josephus, which has no parallel in the Bible, in Philo, in Pseudo-Philo, or in rabbinic literature, of the failure of Noah's descendants to send out colonies (στέλλειν ἀποικίας), notwithstanding their increase in population (πολυανθρωπίαν) (*Ant.* 1.110-12), is, indeed, reminiscent of Herodotus' description of the founding of Etruria by Lydians due to lack of food, presumably owing to overpopulation (1.94). To be sure, the Midrash also notes a rapid increase in the post-Flood population, remarking that women gave birth to sextuplets (*Pirqe de-Rabbi Eliezer*, 24); but it says nothing about the founding of colonies. Josephus also cites another motive that should have persuaded Noah's descendants to send out colonies, namely so that the inhabitants might not quarrel with one another (μὴ στασιάζοιεν) (*Ant.* 1.110), a motive which is reminiscent of that which leads Abraham to divide his land with Lot (*Ant.* 1.169). It is, as we have noted, such quarreling (στάσις, in Corcyra) which Thucydides so bewails (3.82-84) and which David asks his sons to cease (*Ant.* 7.372) and which Solomon requests G-d to be free from (*Ant.* 7.337).

The episode of the drunkenness of Noah raises the question why, if it was Ham who had seen his naked father, Noah pronounced a curse not upon the culprit but upon Ham's son Canaan. Philo raises this question and replies, though with no biblical basis, that both father and son practiced the same wickedness and, secondly, that actually the father, Ham, in any case, felt greatly saddened by the fact that his son Canaan had been cursed (*Quaestiones in Genesin* 2.77 on Genesis 9:27). Elsewhere Philo goes to great lengths to explain that Canaan actively participated in the insult to Noah and that wheras Ham is a name for vice in the quiescent state, Canaan is its name when it passes into active movement (*De Sobrietate* 10.44-48). Pseudo-Philo omits the incident altogether, presumably because he felt it unbecoming. The rabbis explain that Noah could not curse Ham himself because the latter had already been blessed by G-d (Genesis 9:1) (*Genesis Rabbah* 36.7). Others say that Canaan deserved to be cursed because it had been he who had drawn the attention of Ham to Noah's nakedness and drunkenness (*Genesis Rabbah* 36.7). Still others actually declare that Canaan had castrated Noah (*Pirqe de-Rabbi Eliezer*, 23). Josephus, however, realizing that such rabbinic interpretations are not really derived from the plain meaning of the text, prefers to abide by its literal meaning and explains very simply and reasonably that Noah did not curse Ham himself because of his nearness of kin (συγγένειαν) (*Ant.* 1.142). To justify the severity of the punishment, Josephus adds that Ham showed the sight of his naked father to his brothers with mockery (ἐπιγελῶν) (*Ant.* 1.141), a detail paralleled in Philo (*De Sobrietate* 7.32).

6. *Summary*

On the one hand, Josephus desired to highlight the character of Noah, the ancestor of the "Sons of Noah," the nations of the world, and he thus defends him against the charge that he had not done enough to induce his fellow men to repent of their wickedness; consequently, Josephus notes that Noah had actually urged them to do so but feared that they would murder him. Moreover, Josephus points out that after the Flood, in foreshadowing Abraham's reasoning with G-d, Noah appealed to G-d asking Him to maintain good order and not to repeat the calamity of the Flood in the future. He thus emerges as a true champion of mankind. Again, he portrays Noah as presenting a rational reason for instituting sacrifices. With such a portrayal Josephus sought to compliment the Gentiles, the descendants of Noah. He likewise presents a plausible reason why Noah cursed not Ham, who had revealed Noah's nakedness, but his son Canaan.

On the other hand, Josephus set for himself the goal of defending and glorifying the Jewish people by reducing the role of Noah, who was, after all, not a Jew, and by not demanding more of the Sons of Noah than of the Jews, as did the rabbis, in those commandments incumbent upon both. In particular, the fact that Josephus' account is much less concentrated than it is in the Bible would appear to diminish the centrality of Noah. Furthermore, whereas the Bible speaks of Noah as perfect, a statement that might well have raised the question as to wherein Abraham and Moses were superior to him, Josephus very carefully omits this remark.

Inasmuch as during the period that Josephus was writing his *Antiquities*, the Jews were experiencing some success in winnng converts (see Feldman 1993, 288-341), pagan intellectuals had counterattacked with ridicule of Jewish theology and past leadership. Hence, Josephus felt obliged to defend his people and, in particular, the historicity of the Bible upon which Jewish history rested. In the case of the Noah story, he does so not merely by appealing to the evidence of such non-Jewish writers as Berossus, who had mentioned a flood, but also by employing language which would clearly identify the biblical Flood with the one associated with the Greek mythical figure Deucalion. What is particularly striking is that Josephus uses the same word for Noah's ark as that found in Apollodorus, Lucian, and Plutarch with reference to the ark of Deucalion while avoiding the Septuagint's term.

Moreover, Josephus has removed troublesome anthropomorphisms and has defended G-d against the charge of capriciousness and, in particular, against the accusation of being merely negative in seeking to destroy the human race. Since the rainbow was regarded by the Greeks as a symbol of war, Josephus defends G-d against the accusation that he had created such an unfortunate symbol by saying nothing to the effect that he had actually created the rainbow but rather that he merely displayed it.

The fact that Josephus casts the generation of the Flood in the classical mold of those who have shown insolence and who now receive their deserved punishment presents the narrative in the outline of a Greek tragedy, which his intellectual readers would surely have understood and appreciated. Parallels with Plato and Herodotus, as well as with Apollodorus and with motifs later found in Lucian, would likewise serve to make the narrative more readily intelligible to a Greek audience. In particular, Josephus' point that sending out colonies avoids quarrels within a population and his consequent criticism of Noah's descendants for not sending out such colonies would have found a responsive chord among his readers who recall the motives of colonization by the Greeks as described by Herodotus.

The distinctive flavor of Josephus' version may be especially appreciated when it is compared with that of Philo, Pseudo-Philo's *Biblical Antiquities*, and the rabbis, particularly in the midrashic tradition. In general, Philo is more philosophical and more attuned to allegory, and Pseudo-Philo is intent on remaining closer to the biblical text, while the rabbis take greater liberties, but with no primary interest in apologetics, whereas Josephus' chief goal is precisely to defend his people against the canards that were circulating so widely in his day.[17]

---

[17] I am grateful to Professors Daube Daube and Daniel Schwartz for helpful suggestions in connection with this essay. We may here comment on an article by Paul (1985, 473-80), in which the author argues that Josephus' substitution of the word παῦλαν ("truce") for the word *berit* (Genesis 9:9, Septuagint διαθήκην, *Ant.* 1.103) is due to his desire to dissociate himself from the New Testament's emphasis on the doctrine of the "new covenant." We may, however, reply that if, indeed, Josephus is thus writing an anti-Christian manifesto, we would have expected him to be more open about it, since he had nothing to fear from the Christians at the time that he wrote the *Antiquities*, inasmuch as they were few in numbers and were hardly held in favor by the Emperor Domitian, during whose reign Josephus issued his work. A polemic which takes about 1,900 years to be recognized as such is hardly an effective polemic. Moreover, the fact that Josephus, in passages whose authenticity has seldom been questioned, is so laudatory of John the Baptist and James, who is termed "the brother of the one called the Christ" (*Ant.* 18.116-19 and 20.198-200), seems hardly consistent with this view that he was carrying on a polemic against Christianity. The absence of the term διαθήκην, we may suggest, is due to Josephus' desire to avoid the *national* complications of the covenant and to his eagerness (especially important in view of his relations with and his indebtedness to the Roman government) to view Judaism as a religion rather than as a state, as Amaru (1980-81, 201-29) has suggested.

CHAPTER THREE

JETHRO

1. Introduction

In view of the fact that he is writing for a primarily non-Jewish audience, it should not be surprising that Josephus is particularly careful, in his portrayal of non-Jewish personalities in the Bible, not to offend his pagan readers. We may see this in Josephus' more favorable portrayal of Pharaoh in connection with Sarai (*Ant.* 1.165), of Pharaoh in connection with Joseph and his brothers (*Ant.* 2.185), of the Pharaoh of the Exodus (*Ant.* 2.238-53), of Balaam (*Ant.* 4.107), of Nebuchadnezzar (*Ant.* 10.217), of Belshazzar (*Ant.* 10.246), of Darius (*Ant.* 10.254), and of Ahasuerus (*Ant.* 11.216).

One criterion of the importance of a given biblical figure for Josephus is the sheer amount of space that he devotes to him as compared with the attention which he gives to other personalities. In the case of Jethro, the Bible devotes fifty-six lines (Exodus 2:16-21 [8 lines] and 18:1-27 [forty-eight lines]) to him; Josephus devotes 121 lines (*Ant.* 2.257-64 and 3.63-74). This gives a ratio of 2.16 for Josephus in relation to the Hebrew, and 1.68 in relation to the Septuagint. Hence, we can see that for Josephus Jethro, like another non-Jew, Balaam, is definitely one of the more important biblical personalities.[1]

---

[1] For comparative purposes we may note the following ratios of lines in Josephus (Loeb text) to lines in the Hebrew (Malbim's edition): Noah, 1.30; Abraham, 1.20; Isaac, 1.04; Jacob, 1.08; Joseph, 1.63; Moses, 1.17; Aaron, .62; Korah, 3.41; Balaam, 2.09; Joshua, .79; Ehud, 2.45; Deborah, .63; Gideon, .90; Jephthah, .94; Samson, 1.52; Ruth, .74; Samuel, 1.87; Saul, 2.19; David, 2.31; Joab, 2.46; Absalom, 1.83; Solomon, 2.56; Jeroboam, 2.16; Rehoboam, 2.35; Josiah, 1.71; Asa, 1.39; Ahab, 1.98; Elijah, 1.52; Jehoshaphat, 2.01; Jehoram of Israel, 1.93; Elisha, 1.11; Jehu, 2.01; Jonah, .67; Hezekiah, 2.18; Manasseh, .91; Jehoiachin, 1.58; Zedekiah, 7.45; Gedaliah, .91; Daniel, 1.32; Ezra, 1.22; Nehemiah, .24; Esther, 1.36.

2. The Treatment of Jethro in Other Ancient Sources[2]

It would appear that in antiquity there was a sharp difference of opinion in the evaluation of the personality of Jethro. There were those, notably Demetrius, Artapanus, Ezekiel the tragedian, and Josephus, who elevated him; there were those, notably Philo the philosopher, who basically denigrated him; there were those who were divided, notably in the rabbinic tradition; and there were those, notably the writers in the Apocrypha and Pseudepigrapha, who ignored him.

Demetrius, a chronographer, who apparently lived in Egypt during the latter half of the third century B.C.E. (so Holladay, *Fragments*, 1.51-52) notes, in his summary of Exodus 2:15-21, that Moses fled to Midian, where he was married to Zipporah, the daughter of Jethro ('Ιοθώρ), whom he identifies as the son of Raguel (*ap.* Eusebius, *Pr. Ev.* 9.29.1). The fact that he then traces the ancestry of Jethro back to Abraham, through the latter's marriage to Keturah, would clearly elevate the status of Jethro. It would also resolve the embarrassing problem of Moses' apparent intermarriage with Zipporah, a Midianite, since it turns out that both Moses and Zipporah are directly descended from Abraham. It will be recalled that it is likewise through Abraham's marriage with Keturah that the historian Cleodemus-Malchus, who apparently lived at some time between 200 B.C.E. and 50 B.C.E. (so Holladay 1983, 1:246), proudly reports that a son was born, whose daughter was married to the greatest Greek hero, Heracles (*ap.* Josephus, *Ant.* 1.240-41). Moreover, the fact that Jethro is mentioned by Demetrius as the son of Raguel solves the problem of his name in the Book of Exodus, where it is first given in the Septuagint (the Hebrew text does not give his name at this point), which was clearly Demetrius' source, as Jethro ('Ιοθόρ) (Exodus 2:16) and then as Raguel ('Ραγουήλ, Hebrew Reuel) (Exodus 2:18); it also solves the problem of the apparent identity with Jethro of Hobab (Septuagint 'Ιωβάβ), who in Judges 4:11 is re-

---

[2] There has been no comprehensive treatment of role of Jethro in ancient sources. Baskin (1983, 45-74) discusses at some length his portrayal in rabbinic and patristic literature, while dealing only briefly with Philo (62-65) and Josephus (65-66). She does not mention at all the treatment of Jethro by Demetrius, Artapanus, and Ezekiel.

ferred to as the father-in-law of Moses, since Demetrius here says that Hobab was the son of Raguel.

Perhaps a century after Demetrius, the historian Artapanus (*ap.* Eusebius, *Pr. Ev.* 9.27.19)[3] likewise aggrandizes Jethro by referring to him as the chief (ἄρχοντι) of the region even though the Bible identifies him merely as "the priest of Midian" (Exodus 2:16). In view of the apologetic nature of much of Artapanus' work, it should not be surprising that he adds the extra-biblical detail that Jethro, whom he refers to as Raguel, wanted to wage war against the Egyptians in order to establish the throne for his daughter and son-in-law. Such a remark would clearly raise Jethro's stature in the eyes of Jewish readers, who would feel grateful to him for his concern. When, according to Artapanus, Moses declined to join in this plan because of his regard for his own people, who presumably would have been accused of lacking patriotism since one of their number was waging war against the country where they were living, Raguel ordered the Arabs to plunder Egypt.[4]

Ezekiel, the author of the tragedy *The Exodus*, dating from perhaps the second century B.C.E.,[5] considerably enhances the status of Jethro. In one of the fragments (*ap.* Eusebius, *Pr. Ev.* 9.28.4b) his daughter Zipporah refers to him, as had Artapanus, as chief (ἄρχων) of the state. Far from being merely a priest he is called both ruler (τύραννος) and general (στρατηλάτης). He not only rules (ἄρχει) but also judges (κρίνει) the people (presumably the latter attribute arises from the fact that it is Jethro who gives Moses advice as to how to construct a judicial system). Moreover, Ezekiel (*ap.* Eusebius, *Pr. Ev.* 9.29.4) truly glorifies Jethro by presenting him in the role of interpreter of Moses' dream. This is most remarkable, inasmuch as nowhere in the Bible do we find a non-Jew interpreting a dream for a Jew, but rather the reverse, as in the case of the dreams of Pharaoh and of Nebuchadnezzar (so

---

[3] Artapanus' date is apparently somewhere between the middle of the third and the middle of the second century B.C.E. See Holladay 1983, 1:189-90. There is considerable debate among scholars, as Holladay (1983, 1.189) remarks, as to whether he was Jewish or pagan, with the consensus being that he was Jewish, despite the religious syncretism in much of his work.

[4] There is some question as to the meaning of Artapanus' Greek here. For alternate translations see Holladay (1983, 1:238, n. 77).

[5] This is the conclusion of the most exhaustive treatment of this playwright, Jacobson (1983, 5-13), as well as of the most recent extensive discussion, that by Holladay (1989, 2:308-12).

Jacobson 1983, 92). The fact, furthermore, that Jethro is able to interpret the dream without any mention of divine help offers a considerable contrast to the methods employed by Joseph and Daniel in the Bible.[6]

Jethro's interpretation in Ezekiel's tragedy that the dream signifies that Moses will judge and lead mankind and will see present, past, and future, is, of course, a tremendous compliment to Moses, but it also glorifies the interpreter as one who is able to perceive this. This portrayal of Jethro as ruler and as interpreter of dreams, in effect, converts him into a kind of biblical Joseph, especially as elaborated by Josephus. The fact that Jethro is portrayed as a military leader converts him into a kind of doublet of Moses, as described in the Bible and especially as elaborated by Josephus. The notion of a priest-ruler is surely reminiscent of the role of the Hasmonean priest-rulers, notably Simon and John Hyrcanus.

What is striking in Philo's portrait of Jethro is that it is almost completely negative.[7] Presumably the basis for this is his Midianite origin. The most severe criticism that Philo, the Platonist, can make of anyone is that he prefers seeming to being, conceit to truth; and that is precisely the charge that he makes against Jethro, deriving these traits from the very name of Jethro, which he says means "uneven" (περισσός) (*De Agricultura* 10.43).[8] Jethro, consequently, stands for variability and inconsistency. Jethro, he says, "values the human above the divine, custom above laws, profane above sacred, mortal above immortal, and in general seeming above being" (*De Mutatione Nominum* 17.104). It is hard to imagine a more devastating attack, coming as it does from a Platonist. Again, he declares that Jethro corresponds to the "commonwealth peopled by a pro-

---

[6] Jacobson (1983, 37-38) notes several narrative details in which Josephus is reminiscent of Ezekiel and concludes that he was familiar with the latter's play. Though the *argumentum ex silentio* is never conclusive, it seems surprising, if Josephus did know the work of Ezekiel, that he does not mention Moses' dream and the interpretation by Jethro, especially in view of Josephus' great interest in dreams.

[7] Baskin (1983, 62) notes only the unfavorable comments about Jethro in Philo; she neglects to cite *De Specialibus Legibus* 4.33.173-174, which speaks of the excellent (ἄριστα) and useful (συμφέροντα) advice given to Moses by Jethro.

[8] This is the most common epithet applied to Jethro. Its meaning is "superfluous," "over-wise." Colson (1929, vol. 2) translates it as "worldling" in *De Sacrificiis Abelis et Caini* 12.50 and as "worldly-wise" in *De Gigantibus* 11.50; Whitaker (1930, vol. 3) translates it as "uneven" in *De Agricultura* 10.43; Colson (1934, vol. 5) renders it as "superfluous" in *De Mutatione Nominum* 17.103.

miscuous horde, who swing to and fro as their idle opinions carry them" (*De Ebrietate* 10.36). Indeed, he declares that the mythical Proteus, constantly changing form as he did, is most clearly typified by Jethro (*ibid.*). He bows down to the opinions of the multitude and will undergo any manner of transformation in order to conform with the ever-varying aspirations of human life. To a Platonist such as Philo this is well nigh the ultimate sin.

Indeed, Philo completely perverts the biblical account of Jethro's visit to Moses. It is almost as if Philo's text of the Bible ended with the statement, "What you are doing is not good" (Exodus 18:17). According to Philo's version, Jethro suggests to Moses that "he should not teach the only thing worth learning, the ordinances of G-d and the law, but the contracts which men make with each other, which as a rule produce dealings where the partners have no real partnership." He is accused of trying to convince Moses "to give great justice to the great and little justice to the little" (*De Mutatione Nominum* 17.104). Rather than praise Jethro for giving such excellent advice to Moses, Philo here (*De Mutatione Nominum* 17.105) and elsewhere (*De Ebrietate* 10.37) describes him as "seeming wise" (δοκησίσοφος) and as being concerned with little else than things human and corruptible. In enumerating four classes of children – one who obeys both parents, one who obeys neither, one who obeys only the father (that is, right reason), and one who obeys only the mother (that is, mere variable and unstable convention) – Philo says that the last, which, he explains, symbolizes the one who bows down to the opinions of the masses, is most clearly typified by Jethro (*De Ebrietate* 9.35-10.36). Indeed, Jethro, who in the Bible is depicted as dispensing excellent advice to Moses on how to administer his judicial system (Exodus 18:17-23), is described by Philo as having seven daughters who represent the unreasoning element (*De Mutatione Nominum* 19.110). Philo undoubtedly has in mind Plato's allegory of the ship (*Republic* 6.488) when he condemns Jethro as playing the demagogue (*De Ebrietate* 10.37). Instead of welcoming Jethro's statement, "Now I know that the L-rd is greater than all gods" (Exodus 18:11) Philo vehemently condemns Jethro as a blasphemer, first because the word "now" implies that he had never previously understood the greatness of G-d and secondly because he dares to compare G-d with other gods (*De Ebrietate* 11.41-45).

And yet, Philo is not completely negative in his portrayal of

Jethro. We do see a favorable side of Jethro in the gratitude that he exhibits toward Moses for having aided his daughters when they were driven away by some shepherds when they were drawing water at a well. Indeed, Philo elaborates considerably on the scene. Jethro shows real exasperation that his daughters did not bring the stranger along so that he might be thanked for his kindness. "Run back," he tells them, "with all speed, and invite him to receive from me first the entertainment due to him as a stranger, secondly some requital of the favor which we owe to him" (*De Vita Mosis* 1.11.58-59). This overwhelming concern with showing hospitality to the stranger would surely have endeared Jethro to a Greek audience that worshipped Ζεὺς Ξένιος. Again, in the treatise *De Specialibus Legibus* (4.33.173-74), Philo compliments Jethro for having given Moses excellent advice (ἄριστα συνεβούλευσεν) which was useful (συμφέροντα), namely to choose others to adjudicate less important matters while keeping the greater matters for himself and thus giving himself time to rest. But such favorable comments are few. In particular, we may note that Philo nowhere refers to Jethro, as do the rabbis, as a proselyte to Judaism. In any case, the two sides of Jethro may reflect his two names, Jethro having negative associations and Reuel (Raguel), meaning "the shepherding of G-d," having positive associations (*De Mutatione Nominum* 17.105).

We may well wonder why Pseudo-Philo in his *Biblical Antiquities* does not mention Jethro at all, especially since he does ascribe an extra-biblical prophetic dream to Miriam (9.10). Perhaps this omission may be explained as arising from Pseudo-Philo's polemic against intermarriage (as seen in Moses' marriage with the Midianite Zipporah in Exodus 2:21 and with the nameless Ethiopian woman in Numbers 12:1), which we see, for example, in his extra-biblical statement that Tamar's intent in having relations with Judah was to prevent her being joined with Gentiles (9.5), in his stress on the incident of the Midianite women (and we must not forget that Jethro was a priest of Midian) who led the Israelite youths astray (18.13-14), and in the unique detail that the Levite's concubine of Judges 19:25 had transgressed against her husband by having relations with foreigners (45.3).

Unlike Philo, the rabbis were, on the whole, positively inclined toward Jethro, presumably because they found it hard to believe that Moses, the greatest prophet in Israel who had ever lived (Deuteronomy 34:10), would associate with anyone of less than high repute and, in fact, would marry the daughter of an idol-worshipper.[9] Indeed, the sheer volume of comments about him in rabbinic literature is a sure indication of his importance for their tradition.

The rabbis were apparently troubled by the fact that Jethro was a pagan priest; and, actually, we find a debate (*Mekilta, Yitro* 1) as to whether the term *kohen* as applied to him (Exodus 2:16) indicates that he was a priest or, more neutrally, that he was a chief – an appellation that we have already noted in Artapanus and Ezekiel. According to one view, he counselled Pharoah to throw Israelite baby boys into the Nile River but later repented (*Exodus Rabbah* 27.6). Another tradition relates that Pharaoh had three advisers – Balaam, Job, and Jethro; Balaam advised Pharaoh to cast the Israelite babies into the river, Job was silent, and Jethro fled. Because he refused to join in the scheme, the tradition holds, his descendants were privileged to sit in the Sanhedrin (*Sanhedrin* 106a). It is true that Jethro was viewed by some as an idolater of the worst sort, so much so that we hear that there was not an idol on earth that he had not worshipped (*Mekilta, Beshallah* 1) and that he permitted his daughter Zipporah to marry Moses only on condition that their first son would be raised to worship idols (*Mekilta, Yitro* 1). On the other hand, we hear that even before Moses came to Midian Jethro was excommunicated by his neighbors for giving up his idolatry (*Exodus Rabbah* 1.32).

The tradition is similarly divided in commenting on the reaction of Jethro to the miracles performed by G-d. One view, transmitted by the third-century Rav, is that he actually became a proselyte to Judaism (*Tanḥuma* B, *Exodus* 71); in fact, according to one view, he became a proselyte even before Moses came to his home (*Exodus Rabbah* 1.32). Indeed, he becomes, for the rabbis, the prototype of proselytes (*Mishnat Rabbi Eliezer*, p. 304 [ed. H. G. Enelow]); and the very change of his name from Jether to Jethro ("enlarges") is cited to illustrate G-d's love for proselytes. In striking contrast to Esau, who though born of Israelite parents chose to abandon his ancestral beliefs, Jethro, though born a non-Jew, chose a life of piety (*Exodus Rabbah* 27.2). The fact that Jethro left his very comfortable home in order to meet Moses in the desert shows his sincerity, in the eyes of the rabbis, in the lengths that he was willing

---

[9] On the rabbinic attitude toward Jethro see Bamberger (1939, 182-91; and Baskin (1983, 47-61).

to go in order to become a convert (*Mekilta, Yitro* 1).[10] The other view, expressed by Rav's contemporary Samuel, is that he felt sympathetic for the sufferings of the Egyptians (*Sanhedrin* 94a) and that he converted to Judaism only after he had heard what had happened to Amalek (*Exodus Rabbah* 27.6).

So highly is Jethro regarded that, according to one tradition, the very Presence (*Shekinah*) of G-d greeted him when he came to visit Moses (*Mekilta, Yitro* 1) – another indication that Jethro became a convert, inasmuch as the traditional term for conversion is "to be taken under the wings of the *Shekinah*." One factor in this tradition recognizing Jethro as a proselyte apparently was the concern that a non-Jew should have been responsible for the reorganization of the Jewish judicial system; and, indeed, the rabbis explain that Moses gave credit to Jethro for this even though, in fact, the changes had been commanded by G-d, in order to give merit to Jethro as a convert (*Sifre Numbers* 80) and to his descendants and in order to give greatness to Jethro in the eyes of Moses and all Israel (*Sifre Numbers* 78; *Mishnat Rabbi Eliezer*, p. 304). Indeed, the fact that Jethro blessed G-d (Exodus 18:10) shows his superiority to Moses and the rest of the Israelites in that they had failed to bless Him before Jethro arrived (*ibid.*). There is even a view that it was Jethro who was responsible for the revelation of the Torah in its complete form, inasmuch as G-d was afraid, after Jethro had been responsible for the reorganization of the judicial system, that the Israelites might think that it was he who was the source of their whole system of law (*Pesiqta de-Rav Kahana* 12.11).

There is likewise a difference of opinion as to the reason for Jethro's departure from Moses. On the one hand, the view is expressed that Moses dismissed Jethro because he did not want him, a non-Jew, to be present at the moment of revelation at Sinai (*Tanḥuma* B, *Exodus* 75); on the other hand, we have the view justifying Jethro's departure so that he might spread the knowledge of monotheism among his fellow Midianites (*Tanḥuma* B, *Exodus* 73, *Mekilta, Yitro* 2). In effect, the contradictory views about Jethro

---

[10] Baskin (1983, 74), after surveying the evidence with regard to the treatment of Jethro in the writings of the Church Fathers, concludes that, aside from Aphraates and Cyril of Alexandria, Jethro remains a virtual nonentity in Christian exegesis. We may suggest that one reason for this neglect was that the Fathers may have been aware of the rabbinic tradition that Jethro became a proselyte to Mosaic Judaism, a type of Judaism which Christianity claimed to supersede.

parallel the divergent views of the rabbis with regard to the reception of proselytes; side by side with the prevalent view welcoming them[11] was the view of those such as Rabbi Ḥelbo (*Qiddushin* 70b, *Yevamot* 47b, *Niddah* 13b), who regarded them as being as injurious to Israel as a scab.

3. *Jethro's Qualities of Character, according to Josephus*

Josephus, in his portrait of the non-Jew Jethro, is particularly concerned to answer the charge that Jews hate non-Jews. Unlike Philo and the rabbis, who are, as we have seen, divided in their views of Jethro, Josephus presents a uniformly favorable picture of him. In the first place, when the reader is introduced to him, he is described as a priest held in high veneration (πολλῆς ἠξιωμένου τιμῆς) by the people of the country (*Ant.* 2.258). Presumably this is intended to counteract the implication of the biblical text that the shepherds drove away Jethro's daughters (Exodus 2:17), which, we may assume, they would not have done if they had had respect for Jethro himself. This would also counter the impression found in the rabbinic tradition, if, as seems likely, Josephus was acquainted with at least some of it, that Jethro was *persona non grata* among his neighbors and was even excommunicated for giving up his idolatry. Again, when Jethro comes to Moses to congratulate him upon his victory over Amalek, the Bible states that he came accompanied by his wife and her sons (Exodus 18:5); Josephus, seeking to build up the stature of Jethro, has him come alone so as to focus the spotlight upon him (*Ant.* 3.63).

Connected with the quality of φιλανθρωπία is the virtue of showing gratitude, in accordance with the definition of justice as rendering every man his due (Plato, *Republic* 1.332A). In the case of Jethro, Josephus elaborates considerably on the scene in which Jethro is represented as saying to his daughters after they tell him how Moses had delivered them from the shepherds and had drawn water for them, "Where is he? Why have you left the man? Call him, that he may eat bread" (Exodus 2:20). In Josephus' version the shepherds' insolence (ὕβριν) is spelled out as such, as is Moses' beneficence (εὐεργετηθεῖσαι); and Jethro specifically bids his daughters not to allow such benevolence (εὐποιίαν) to be in vain

---

[11] See especially Bamberger (1939) and Braude (1940).

or unrewarded and to bring Moses to him so as to receive the gratitude (χάριτος) that was his due. He commends his daughters for their zeal (σπουδῆς) for their benefactor (εὐεργετηκότα) (*Ant.* 2.261). In the Bible there is no statement that Jethro actually thanked Moses; we are merely told that Moses was content to dwell with Jethro (Exodus 2:21). In contrast, Josephus' Jethro, upon Moses' arrival, tells him of his (Jethro's) daughters' testimony to the help which he had rendered and expresses admiration for his gallantry (ἀρετῆς). He adds that it is not upon those who had no sense of gratitude for these meritorious services (ἀναισθήτους εὐεργεσιῶν) that he had bestowed this help but on persons well able to requite a favor, "indeed to outdo by the amplitude of the reward the measure of the benefit" (*Ant.* 2.262). In fact, in a startling addition to the biblical text Josephus even adopts Moses as his son (*Ant.* 2.263).[12] The key point is that Jethro is actually identified here as a barbarian; clearly, Josephus' point is to stress that, far from being prejudiced against barbarians, actually, the greatest leader of the Jews married a barbarian and that he was even adopted by a barbarian. In terms of the striking impact upon a reader, only Alexander the Great's marriage with a Persian princess would be comparable. We may also add that not only does Jethro show gratitude but he appreciates it when others show it. Thus we are told that when he meets Moses he is profuse in eulogies of the Israelites for their gratitude (εὐχαριστίᾳ) to Moses (*Ant.* 3.65).

We may well ask what was the motive and what was the setting for Jethro's visit to Moses (Exodus 18:1). In the Bible this comes immediately after the description of the Israelites' victory over the Amalekites (Exodus 17:8-16); and we are told that Jethro heard of all that G-d had done for Moses and for Israel and, in particular, how G-d had brought the Israelites out of Egypt (Exodus 18:1). In the rabbinic tradition there is a debate as to exactly when Jethro came to congratulate Moses. The view of Rabbi Joshua ben Hananiah, adhering to the order in the biblical text, is that Jethro heard of the battle with the Amalekites, which is mentioned immediately before this passage, as we have noted; the view of Rabbi

---

[12] Rappaport (1930, 100-1) notes that elsewhere Josephus states that Abraham adopted Lot (*Ant.* 1.154) and that neither this adoption nor that by Jethro is mentioned in the Bible. He suggests that perhaps Josephus took over into the Bible an institution known from Rome.

Eleazar ben Pedat is that he heard of the miraculous dividing of the Red Sea, since the passage refers to G-d's leading the Israelites out of Egypt; and the view of Rabbi Eleazar of Modin is that Jethro heard of the giving of the Torah at Mount Sinai (*Zevaḥim* 116a). The last is clearly the most difficult to sustain, inasmuch as the account of the revelation at Sinai is not to be found until after Jethro's visit (Exodus 19-20), though it is perhaps alluded to in the statement that Jethro came to Moses in the wilderness, where Moses was encamped at the mountain of G-d (Exodus 18:5). Significantly, Josephus, in his effort to build up the stature of Jethro, goes out of his way and out of the biblical order in prefacing the visit of Jethro with the remark that the Israelites had reached Mount Sinai (*Ant.* 3.62). This gives a more important setting for the visit, since it puts Jethro in immediate juxtaposition with the central event in Israelite history and makes of his visit more than a mere congratulation for military victory. Likewise, whereas the Bible says nothing about the feast which Moses arranged in honor of his father-in-law, Josephus not only does so but adds further honor to Jethro by remarking that the feast took place near the very site where Moses had seen the burning bush (*Ant.* 3.63).

One of the most delicate problems for Josephus must have been how to deal with the scene in which Jethro criticizes the way in which Moses had been administering justice (Exodus 18:14). In the Bible Jethro comes right out with his criticism: "What is this that you are doing for the people? Why do you sit alone?" Such a criticism must have been disconcerting for Moses, especially since there is no indication in the biblical text that Jethro took Moses aside so as to avoid embarrassing him in the presence of the Israelites. On the other hand, in Josephus' version Jethro shows real sensitivity so as to avoid embarrassing his son-in-law. We are told that when he sees the way Moses administers affairs he holds his peace (ἡσυχίαν ἦγε, "kept quiet") at the moment (τότε), inasmuch as he is reluctant to hinder any who would avail themselves of the talents of their chief. It is only after the tumult of the crowd has subsided that he then discreetly takes Moses aside and in utter privacy (συμμονωθείς, "be alone in private with someone") he instructs him what it is necessary to do (*Ant.* 3.67).

4. The Attitude of Jethro the Non-Jew toward Jews

In view of the frequent negative statements on the part of non-Jews toward Jews, particularly with regard to Jewish theology, circumcision, the Sabbath, dietary laws, credulity, begging, and alleged Jewish influence (see Feldman 1993, 149-76), Josephus was particularly eager, notably in the essay *Against Apion*, to demonstrate that there were famous non-Jews who appreciated the virtues of the Jews in the realms of wisdom, courage, temperance, and justice (see Feldman 1958-59, 27-39).

Hence, we see a significant change in Josephus' account of Jethro's meeting with Moses (Exodus 18:5). Whereas in the biblical version we read only that Jethro came with Moses' sons and his wife to Moses and are told nothing of his feelings in meeting his son-in-law, Josephus remarks that Raguel (i.e. Jethro) went with gladness (ἀσμένως, "with pleasure") and that he welcomed (δεχόμενος) Moses (*Ant.* 3.63). One would have expected that since it was Jethro who was visiting Moses it would be Moses who would go out to greet Jethro; and, indeed, this is what we find in the biblical text (Exodus 18:7), where we are told that Moses went out to meet his father-in-law and did obeisance to him and kissed him. In Josephus' version, however, while we are told that Moses rejoiced at the visit of his father-in-law there is no description of Moses actually greeting Jethro, and the stress is placed on Jethro's acknowledgment of the greatness of Moses.

5. The Role of G-d in the Jethro Narrative

In the case of Jethro, the biblical narrative six times mentions G-d in noting what G-d had done for Moses and for the Israelites and in indicating Jethro's sacrifice of thanksgiving to G-d for these successes (Exodus 18:1 [*bis*], 18:9, 18:10, 18:11, 18:12). Josephus (*Ant.* 3.63), on the other hand, omits totally Jethro's rejoicing for all the good which G-d had done to Israel (Exodus 18:9) and his blessing G-d for delivering the Israelites from the Egyptians (Exodus 18:10). Indeed, Jethro speaks not of G-d but of Moses' success, and he expresses admiration for Moses for the gallantry (ἀνδραγαθίας) which he had devoted to the salvation of his friends (*Ant.* 3.65). Again, when Aaron and his company get Jethro to join them, they sing the praises of their general, Moses (*Ant.* 3.64), whereas in the

Bible Jethro blesses G-d (Exodus 18:10).

Likewise, in the biblical version, when Jethro gives his counsel to Moses as to how to administer justice, he mentions G-d no fewer than three times within a single verse: "G-d be with you! You shall represent the people before G-d, and bring their cases to G-d" (Exodus 18:19). He then tells Moses to choose men such as fear G-d as his subordinate judges (Exodus 18:21). Indeed, lest the reader think that it is Jethro, the non-Jew, who is advising Moses what to do, the biblical Jethro is very careful to state that Moses is do what Jethro advises only if G-d commands him to do so; in other words, Jethro's suggestions required divine sanction (Exodus 18:23). In place of all this spiritual advice, which may well raise the question whether Jethro is not, at least with respect to the administration of justice, superior to Moses, Josephus' Jethro counsels Moses to select capable (ἀγαθούς, "good") Hebrews (*Ant.* 3.68); later he recommends the appointment of upright and just persons (ἀγαθοὶ καὶ δίκαιοι) (*Ant.* 3.72), and he specifically limits his advice to mundane (ἀνθρωπίνων, "human," "worldly") matters (*Ant.* 3.70).

Indeed, in what follows, it now appears that Jethro, the ruler experienced presumably in military affairs, who had begun by giving judicial advice, gives military advice to Moses, since he tells him how to draw up (ἐξετάσεις) his army and how to divide it into groups of ten thousands, thousands, five hundreds, hundreds, and fifties (*Ant.* 3.70). This is a case of one general talking to another, and the result would surely add greater appeal to Josephus' military-minded Roman readers. In place of the biblical statement in which Jethro, as we have seen, after giving his advice to Moses, expressly declares that Moses should do so only if G-d commands him thus (Exodus 18:23), Jethro omits the giving of veto-power for the reorganization to G-d. Instead, by organizing his judicial and military systems thus, says Jethro, Moses will have more time to spend in gaining the favor of G-d for the army (*Ant.* 3.72).

6. *Jethro the Non-Proselyte*

Josephus was clearly aware that the Romans were sensitive to the great expansion of the Jewish population, especially through proselytism. In the Bible, as we have noted, when Moses tells Jethro all that the L-rd has done to Pharaoh and the Egyptians, Jethro rejoices for all the good which G-d has done to Israel, he blesses G-d for having delivered them from the Egyptians, he declares that he now knows that the L-rd is greater than all gods because of His saving the Israelites, he offers a sacrifice to G-d, and Aaron comes with all the elders to eat bread with him (Exodus 18:8-12). What is striking in this brief passage is that Jethro is brought into immediate juxtaposition with the mention of G-d no fewer than six times, as we have noted. It is not surprising, consequently, as we have remarked, that, according to rabbinic tradition, especially in view of Jethro's outright statement that the L-rd is greater than all gods, Jethro is represented as having become a proselyte to Judaism. Consequently, Josephus, in his sensitivity to the proselyting movement, quite carefully omits Jethro's statement about G-d's greatness.

Moreover, the biblical narrative actually states that Jethro offered a burnt offering and sacrifices to G-d (Exodus 18:12), an act that would seem to indicate, as some of the rabbis noted above deduced, that he had come to accept the belief in the Israelite G-d. Josephus, sensitive to the Roman opposition to proselytism by Jews, has quite obviously made a deliberate change in having Moses offer the sacrifice (*Ant.* 3.63).[13]

Furthermore, in distinct contrast to Jethro's outright taking the lead in his blessing of G-d in the Bible (Exodus 18:10) and his offering of sacrifices to G-d (Exodus 18:12) and in contrast to the clearly subordinate role of Aaron in merely coming with the Israelite elders to eat bread with Jethro (Exodus 18:12), Josephus, in the apparent realization that such a role would, in effect, make Jethro a convert to Judaism, makes Aaron the prime mover in chanting hymns to G-d as the author and dispenser of salvation and liberty to the Israelites (*Ant.* 3.64). Jethro's role is clearly subordinate; Aaron merely gets him to join him (προσλαβόμενος).

---

[13] Augustine (*Locutionum in Heptateuchum* 82) suggests that perhaps Jethro handed over the sacrifice to Moses so that the latter might offer it to G-d; but there is no hint of this in the text.

7. *"Improvements" in the Story: Clarifications, Increased Plausibility*

One basic reason for Josephus' writing of a paraphrase of the Scripture was that he sought to clear up obscurities in the text and apparent contradictions in the biblical text. In the case of Jethro, the reader is befuddled by the fact that Jethro seems to be called by no fewer than seven names – Jethro (Exodus 3:1), Jether (Exodus 4:18), Putiel (Exodus 6:25), Reuel (Numbers 2:18), Hobab (Numbers 10:29), Keni (Judges 1:16), and Heber (Judges 4:11).[14] Aware of this, Josephus regularly calls him Raguel, but remarks that his surname was Ietheglaeus, that is, Jethro (*Ant.* 2.264).

One means by which Josephus seeks to "improve" upon the biblical narrative is through providing better motivation and through increasing the plausibility of events. In connection with Moses and Jethro, there is an improbability in the biblical text in that Moses asks Jethro for permission to return to Egypt even though he does not yet know (until the following verse) whether those who are seeking him are still alive (Exodus 4:18). In Josephus' version the setting is more reasonable: it is only after learning that the Pharaoh from whom he had fled is dead that Moses asks Jethro for permission to return to Egypt (*Ant.* 2.277).

8. *Summary*

To judge from the amount of space that he devotes to him, Jethro, like another non-Jewish biblical figure, Balaam, was clearly of great interest to Josephus. Prior to Josephus his personality had occasioned a great deal of controversy. On the one hand, such Hellenistic-Jewish writers as Demetrius, Artapanus, and Ezekiel the tragedian had elevated his stature; others, notably Philo, had, on the whole, denigrated him; others, notably the rabbinic tradition, were divided in their opinions; and still others, notably the writers of the books of the Apocrypha and the Pseudepigrapha, had chosen to ignore him.

---

[14] Albright (1963, 1-11) resolves the problem by asserting that Reuel (Numbers 10:29) is the clan name of Hobab. He notes that in the Septuagint text of Genesis 25:3 it actually appears as the name of a clan affiliated with Midian.

Josephus, in his portrait, presents a uniformly favorable picture of Jethro. He is particularly concerned to answer the frequently heard charge that Jews hate non-Jews. In an addition to the biblical text, Jethro is presented as a priest who is held in high veneration by the people of his country. Josephus heightens the gratitude which Jethro expresses to Moses for helping his daughters when they were driven away by the shepherds. Not only does he give his daughter Zipporah in marriage to Moses, but he, who is termed a barbarian by Josephus, actually adopts Moses as his son. He shows remarkable sensitivity in not criticizing Moses openly for his failure to delegate authority, but rather takes him aside and advises him in private in order to avoid embarrassing him in the presence of the Israelites. Again, in reply to the frequent criticisms of Jews by non-Jews in pagan literature, Josephus depicts Jethro as welcoming Moses with gladness. Whereas in the Bible Jethro blesses G-d for the Israelites' successes, in Josephus he expresses admiration for Moses for his gallantry. In contrast to the Bible, where, in counselling Moses, Jethro mentions G-d several times – a factor that might well raise a question as to whether Jethro may not have G-d's ear, so to speak, to a greater degree than Moses himself – , in Josephus he presents his advice in human terms. Again, whereas in the Bible Jethro tells Moses that he is to listen to his advice only if G-d sanctions it, in Josephus he limits his advice to mundane matters. Indeed, a good deal of the advice is presented in terms of a recommendation to Moses to reorganize his people militarily; and instead of seeking G-d's sanction for this reorganization we are told that by doing so Moses will have more time to spend in seeking to gain greater favor from G-d for his army.

A major problem that confronted Josephus was what to do with the biblical passage in which Jethro mentions G-d over and over again and even acknowledges that he now knows that G-d is greater than any other god. That this passage could be and was, indeed, interpreted to indicate that Jethro actually became a proselyte to Judaism would have been a source of great embarrassment to Josephus in view of the sharp antagonism that had been caused by the success of the Jews in his day in converting so many non-Jews to Judaism. To have Jethro offer sacrifices to G-d, as he does in the Bible, would, in effect, have indicated his conversion to Judaism; and so Josephus, quite delicately, has Moses offer the sacrifice. For the same reason Jethro is likewise subordinated to Aaron in chanting hymns to G-d.

Josephus avoids apparent contradictions, notably in the many names of Jethro. He likewise avoids improbabilities, particularly in Moses' asking Jethro for permission to return to Egypt when he actually does not yet know whether those who were seeking to kill him are still alive; Josephus' version explains that he makes his request because he has learned that the Pharaoh who was seeking to kill him has died.

CHAPTER FOUR

AARON

1. *Introduction: The Problem Confronting Josephus*

For Josephus, as for Philo and the Rabbis, the biblical figure of Aaron presented several major problems. In the first place, though older than his brother Moses he is clearly subordinate to him; and so one cannot help but wonder whether Aaron may not have felt jealous and resentful at not being chosen by G-d to lead the Israelites. In the second place, though the biblical tradition is clear regarding Moses' overall supremacy, Aaron is certainly portrayed as superior to him as a speaker in an era in which oratorical ability was regarded as a *sine qua non* for an effective leader. In the third place, Aaron's appointment as the first high priest to head the all-important religious cult of the Jews is due to his brother, Moses, and might therefore appear to be a case of nepotism. Finally, Aaron's role in the making of the golden calf when Moses was delayed in returning from his rendezvous with G-d raises serious questions as to why he, unlike the masses of the Israelites, was not punished and, in fact, was permitted to remain as high priest.

Philo resolves these problems by resorting to allegory and by underscoring that Aaron, admirable though he was, was subordinate to Moses. While it is true that the logical nature was the mother of both Moses and Aaron (*De Migratione Abrahami* 14.78), Moses, Philo says, is mind at its purest, while Aaron is its word; each has been trained for holy things, the mind to grasp them and the word to express them (*De Mutatione Nominum* 37.208). The fact, however, that Aaron is here equated with the word, λόγος, does indicate his importance for him, inasmuch as he uses the same term, λόγος, to refer to the "idea of ideas," "the first-begotten Son of the uncreated Father," "a second G-d," and "the man of G-d."[1]

---

[1] Philo, *De Migratione Abrahami* 18.103; *De Posteritate Caini* 18.63; *De Confusione Linguarum* 11.41. The symbolism is particularly effective in Philo's version of the scene in which Aaron and Hur hold up Moses' hands during the battle of the Israelites against Amalek (Exodus 17:12). Philo explains that Aaron is the Word (λόγος) and that Hur is Light (φῶς), that life has no clearer light than truth, and that Moses' aim is to show by means of these symbols that the doings of the wise

Moreover, the ancients, in general, appreciated the importance and power of speech, as we see, for example, in the fact that, according to Thucydides, one of the four crucial attributes of Pericles, the role model par excellence of the statesman, was his ability to persuade, since, as he says, "he who determines upon a policy and fails to lay it clearly before others is in the same case as if he never had a conception of it" (2.60.6).

And yet, for Philo Aaron is clearly "second" (δεύτερος, *Legum Allegoria* 3.44.128), hence inferior to Moses, who represents consummation, the perfect man who stands on the borderline between the uncreated and the perishing form of being (*De Somniis* 2.35.234). Aaron represents the one who acquires virtue by toil and hence falls short of its full achievement (*Legum Allegoria* 3.46.135), in contrast to Moses, who receives it easily without toil directly from the hands of G-d. Aaron represents high spirit which must be curbed by reason; he is the man who makes gradual progress (*Legum Allegoria* 3.45.132). His revelation is, therefore, clearly less direct than that of Moses (*Legum Allegoria* 3.33.103). As to the charge that Moses was guilty of nepotism in appointing his own brother as high priest, Philo emphasizes that the choice was made on Aaron's merits; he also adds – an argument not found in Josephus – that further proof that Moses was not guilty of such nepotism is the fact that he did not appoint his own sons to such positions of power (*De Vita Mosis* 2.28.142).[2]

The rabbinic tradition is even more positively disposed toward Aaron. Indeed, in a number of passages he is viewed as completely equal to his brother (see Ginzberg 1925, 5:424, n. 152). Every attempt is made to exonerate him of blame in connection with the Golden Calf incident. Though, according to tradition, Aaron had preceded Moses as prophet and spokesman for the Israelites in Egypt, he was not at all envious of his brother for assuming the leadership subsequently and, in fact, rejoiced at his success (*Tanḥuma Exodus* 27). He represents the height of piety, particularly in his keeping silent (Leviticus 10:3) upon seeing two of his sons bathed in blood (*Leviticus Rabbah* 20.4). In fact, his acceptance

---

man are upheld by the most essential of all things, namely the Word and Truth (*Legum Allegoria* 3.15.45).

[2] For Josephus to have made this point might have been viewed by his Roman audience as a criticism of the Emperor Vespasian for having appointed his son Titus as his successor.

without complaint of the divine decree with respect to his sons' death is compared to the faith exhibited by Abraham when ordered to sacrifice his son Isaac (*Sifra* 46a). Aaron is especially praised as well for his love of peace (*'Avot* 1.12), in contrast to Moses, who insists on applying the law strictly. Most remarkably, there is even a tradition that Aaron is one of those few who never sinned and that he died only because death was decreed for all humans after the machinations of the serpent (*Sifre Deuteronomy* 338-39).

2. Aaron's Virtues

That Josephus seeks to honor Aaron is clear from his variation on the biblical scene in which Aaron welcomes Moses when he returns to Egypt from Midian. In the biblical version G-d tells Aaron to meet Moses, and then the two brothers go and gather together all the elders of the people of Israel (Exodus 4:27-29). In Josephus' pericope, after Aaron, at G-d's bidding, goes to meet Moses, the two of them do not go to gather the elders but rather are met, presumably on the latter's own initiative, by the most distinguished (ἀξιολογώτατοι) of the Hebrews, who had learnt of Moses' coming (*Ant.* 2.279).

One of the issues raised by Korah in his revolt is Moses' appointment of Aaron as high priest, which would seem to be a case of nepotism. In the biblical narrative G-d simply tells Moses to appoint Aaron and his sons to serve as priests with no indication of their qualifications for the office (Exodus 28:1). Josephus, himself a priest and undoubtedly sensitive to the charge that those who are priests have no other qualifications than the mere fact of their birth, is careful to remark that Aaron's virtue (ἀρετήν) rendered him more deserving than all others to obtain this dignity (τιμῆς) (*Ant.* 3.188).[3] Over against this remark stands the amazingly frank

---

[3] In the sentence that follows, Josephus states that Moses, convening the people in assembly, recounted "his merits, his benevolence, and the perils which he had sustained in their behalf" (*Ant.* 3.188). Thackeray (1930, 4:407) in his translation in the Loeb Library edition, understands this to refer to Moses' merits, benevolence, and perils. But if we read αὐτοῦ, as the manuscripts have it and as the Latin version of Cassiodorus suggests with its rendering *eius*, rather than *suam*, the reference would appear to be to Aaron's virtue rather than to Moses', which would further qualify him for the high priesthood.

extra-biblical statement, in which the Josephan Moses admits that if the decision had been entrusted to him he would have adjudged himself worthy of the honor both because of self-love that is innate in everyone and because of his being conscious of having labored abundantly for the salvation of the people (*Ant.* 3.190). The fact, however, that G-d chose otherwise (*Ant.* 3.189-90) is a clear indication that Aaron was actually superior to himself as far as the position of priest and minister (ὑπηρετήσοντος, "rendering service") goes. Moses then adds that because G-d Himself had chosen Aaron to be high priest He could not but accept the prayers offered by him on behalf of the Israelites (*Ant.* 3.191).

The ancients looked upon music as so integral a part of education that they regarded it as the very pinnacle of wisdom. Hence, we should not be surprised that Josephus makes a point of mentioning, in reference to Moses' song upon crossing the Red Sea (Exodus 15:1-18), that Moses himself composed a hymn to G-d "to enshrine His praises and the thankfulness [of the Israelites] for His gracious favor" (*Ant.* 2.346). Similarly, Aaron, in an addition to the Bible, is presented as chanting hymns of thanksgiving to G-d for their salvation and liberty, as well as singing the praises of Moses as general in the battle against Amalek (*Ant.* 3.64).

Furthermore, in enumerating the unique qualifications of Aaron for the high priesthood (*Ant.* 3.192), Josephus calls attention to his prophetical gift (προφητείαν) as one of the qualities in which he excelled all others.

A major component of courage, the second of the cardinal virtues, is sheer endurance in the face of adversity. It is this quality of steadfastness which Aaron displays, according to an extra-biblical remark by Josephus, when his sons, Nadab and Abihu, die. The Bible says very simply that Aaron held his peace (Leviticus 10:3); but Josephus elaborates: the death of his sons, he says, was a misfortune for Aaron, regarded as a man and as a father, but the blow was valiantly (γενναίως) borne (καρτερηθεῖσα) by him because he had a soul steeled (στερρός, "strong," "sturdy," "powerful," "solid," "firm," "hard") against accidents (συμπίπτοντα), since he believed that it was by G-d's will that the tragedy had occurred (*Ant.* 3.208).

Temperance, the third of the cardinal virtues, is shown particularly in self-control. It is this quality – a combination of courage and self-control – which Josephus praises most highly in Aaron in describing his valiant self-control when his sons, Nadab and Abihu, die (*Ant.* 3.208).

As to justice, the fourth of the cardinal virtues, it is significant that when Moses, in an extra-biblical comment, explains the choice of Aaron to be high priest, he states that G-d has judged him worthy of this honor, knowing him to be "the more just (δικαιότερον) of us," that is, more just than Moses himself (*Ant.* 3.190).[4]

Regarding the fifth virtue, namely piety, one notable exception to Josephus' general downgrading of the role of Aaron is to be seen in the fact that whereas in the Bible it is Moses alone who is mentioned as taking the bones of Joseph with him (Exodus 13:19), in accordance with the latter's request (Genesis 50:25), Josephus declares that both Moses and Aaron brought the bones with them (*Ant.* 2.319). Inasmuch as attending to the dead and to their wishes is regarded as particularly meritorious (see Rabinowitz 1971, 8:442-46), this deed brings great credit to Aaron. One problem is that priests are not permitted to have contact with the dead, except for their nearest relatives (Leviticus 21:1-4; *Ant.* 3.277); and the high priest is not even permitted this. One may, therefore, ask how Aaron, the first high priest, can be presented here as having contact with the dead. The explanation may be that Aaron at this point had not yet been consecrated as high priest.

Another indication of Aaron's piety may be seen in the fact, not mentioned in the Bible (Exodus 18:12), that after the victory over Amalek, Aaron with his company, joined by Moses' father-in-law Raguel (Jethro), chanted hymns of thanksgiving to G-d as the author and dispenser of their salvation and their liberty (*Ant.* 3.64).

Of course, the biggest blot on Aaron's record for piety is his participation in the creation of the golden calf. According to the biblical account, when the Israelites saw that Moses was delayed in descending from Mount Sinai they told Aaron to make gods for them, whereupon Aaron advised them to bring their golden earrings to him. He is then said to have fashioned the gold with a graving tool and made a molten calf. He then built an altar before it and proclaimed that on the following day there would be a

---

[4] This is the rendering of the Latin version by Cassiodorus: *hunc sacerdotem nobis credidit iustiorem*. Thackeray (1930, 4:408-9), in the Loeb version, translates: "knowing him to be the most deserving among us," while suggesting, as alternative renderings, "the more deserving of us (twain)" or "knowing better than ourselves who is the more worthy."

festival for G-d (Exodus 32). When Moses descended and found the golden calf, he berated Aaron, asking him what the people had done to him that he should have brought such a great sin upon them (Exodus 32:21). Aaron then blamed the people for pressuring him and claimed that when he threw their gold into the fire a calf emerged (Exodus 32:24). That the Bible does, however, hold Aaron accountable, together with the Israelites, for making the golden calf is clear from the statement that it was Aaron who had allowed the people to break loose (Exodus 32:25), as well as from the closing verse of this chapter: "And the L-rd sent a plague upon the people, because they made the calf, which Aaron made" (Exodus 32:35). The Bible itself emphasizes the contrast between Aaron and the sons of Levi, who rallied to Moses' side and killed three thousand of the sinners (Exodus 32:26-29). Aaron's culpability is clear also in Moses' later summary of these events, for he remarks that G-d was so angry with Aaron that he was ready to destroy him, but that Aaron was saved by Moses' prayer on his behalf (Deuteronomy 9:20).

Philo, who, as we have noted, generally aggrandizes the portrayal of Aaron, does not omit mention of the golden calf incident, but blames it upon the Israelites, "men of unstable nature" (*De Vita Mosis* 2.31.161-62, *De Ebrietate* 24.95-96, 32.124-26), and says nothing about Aaron's role. Pseudo-Philo, while mentioning the incident and Aaron's involvement, strives mightily to exonerate him (12.2). He quotes Aaron as telling the people, when they insist that he make gods for them to serve, to have patience, since Moses, whom they assumed to have died because of his delay in descending from the mountain, will return and bring the Law to them. The people, however, are reported to have refused to listen to him, whereupon Aaron, in fear of them, tells them to bring their earrings to him. Moreover, whereas in the Bible Aaron admits to Moses that it was he who threw the earrings into the fire (Exodus 32:24), in Pseudo-Philo it is the people who are said to have thrown them into the fire (12.3).

The rabbis, clearly troubled that one who had participated, and indeed played a leading role, in such a grave sin should have been appointed high priest, might have adopted the solution, as they did, for example, in the case of the similarly embarrassing accounts of Reuben's intercourse with his father's concubine Bilhah (Genesis 35:22), of David's sins with Uriah and Bathsheba (2 Samuel

11:2-17), and of Amnon's incestuous intercourse with his sister Tamar (2 Samuel 13:1-14), of declaring that these episodes are to be read in the synagogue but not translated (Mishnah, *Megillah* 4:10); and, indeed, the rabbis do declare that what they term the second account of the golden calf, that is, Moses' accusation of Aaron and Aaron's defense (Exodus 32:21-25), is to be read but not translated (Mishnah, *Megillah* 4:10).[5] Refusing, however, to resort to censorship of the first account, the rabbis attempt to exonerate Aaron by insisting that his very life was threatened by the people, that he feared that he would suffer the same fate as Hur, who, indeed, is said to have been put to death by the people when he opposed them, and that Aaron agreed to make the golden calf only after procrastinating as long as possible (*Exodus Rabbah* 41.7, *Sanhedrin* 7a). It is Aaron's love of peace that deterred him from putting to death those who worshipped the golden calf (see *Eliyahu Rabbah* 13.63 and 31.157); indeed, unlike Moses, who insisted on applying the law strictly, he is depicted as using every device in order to reconcile litigants (*'Avot de-Rabbi Nathan* A 12). In fact, it was because of his love of peace that he was chosen to be high priest (*Exodus Rabbah* 37.2); and consequently he becomes the role model for those who prefer peaceful persuasion as the best means of instilling love of the Torah, whence Hillel's dictum: "Be of the disciples of Aaron, loving peace and pursuing peace, loving people and bringing them near to the Torah" (*'Avot* 1:12).

Generally speaking, Josephus' way of handling problem passages in the Bible is not to omit them, inasmuch as, presumably, some of his readers, notably those who had access to the Septuagint, would regard doing so as an act of blatant censorship. His preferred method is rather to reinterpret such passages. How, then, can we explain Josephus' total omission of the incident of the golden calf? If we examine other passages which Josephus totally omits, we see that the overwhelming majority of them fall into two categories: either the omission is to protect the reputation of a character, such as Moses, whose status as *the* prime leader and lawgiver it is crucial for Josephus the apologist to defend, or the passages in question are such as would impugn the Jews' reputation

---

[5] The Gemara on this passage (*Megillah* 25a) further states that there are some biblical texts that are neither read nor translated, but the Vilna Gaon, in his commentary, declares that these words should be omitted.

for tolerance and loyalty to the nation where they lived and offered ammunition to Jew-baiters in his non-Jewish audience. In the case of Aaron, the incident of the golden calf certainly raises the fundamental question of his qualifications for the high priesthood, about which Josephus, who is so proud of his priestly ancestry that this is the very first matter that he mentions in his autobiography (*Life* 1), must have been especially sensitive. While it is true that including this incident, by lowering the reputation of Aaron, would have raised still further the standing of Moses, Josephus apparently felt that the price to pay was too great.

We may see a similar instance of an incident in which Josephus faced a dilemma as to whether he should include a biblical criticism of Aaron. In Leviticus 10:16-20 we read that after the sudden death of Aaron's sons Nadab and Abihu, Moses was angry with the remaining sons, Eleazar and Ithamar, for burning the goat offering instead of eating it. Actually, it is clear that Moses was really angry with Aaron himself, since it was he who had offered the sacrifice (Leviticus 9:15). Josephus chooses not to include this incident both because it is a further indictment of Aaron's worthiness to be high priest and because it also includes Aaron's rejoinder (Leviticus 10:19) to Moses, which leaves the latter speechless and serves, in effect, as a counter-rebuke to Moses.

We may cite another incident involving Aaron which Josephus has passed over in complete silence, namely where he and Miriam criticize Moses for marrying a Cushite woman. To have included such a passage would have exposed the Jews – and Aaron and Miriam in particular – to the charge of prejudice, especially since, as we have noted, the Jews had been accused of misanthropy by even so sympathetic a writer as Hecataeus of Abdera (*ap.* Diodorus 40.3.4).[6] In particular, Aaron and Miriam would seem in this in-

---

[6] Schäfer (1996, 12*) points out that it is Hecataeus who, for the first time in history, combines the *misoxenia* motif with the Exodus tradition and thus created or transmitted a powerful argument against the Jews. He is consequently not convinced of the overall pro-Jewish attitude in Hecataeus' version of the Exodus tradition. The fact, however, that Hecataeus goes out of his way to speak of the Jewish way of life as "somewhat" (τινα) unsocial and hostile to foreigners (ἀπάνθρωπόν τινα καὶ μισόξενον βίον) would seem to indicate a real effort to tone down the accusation of misanthropy. Hecataeus is here simply trying, clearly sympathetically, to explain the origin of the Jewish attitude toward anthropomorphism and other religious ideas and practices which were otherwise well nigh universal. No doubt others built on Hecataeus' views concerning Jewish opposition

stance to be betraying their prejudice against the much respected Ethiopians, who were renowned for their wisdom, piety, and bravery,[7] who are termed blameless by Homer (*Iliad* 1.423), and from whom, according to one theory (Tacitus, *Histories* 5.2.2), the Jews themselves were said to be descended. Moreover, as presented in the Bible, the episode raises the question as to why only Miriam was punished for her criticism, whereas Aaron, who joined in it, was not. Philo resolves the problem by avoiding direct mention of the Ethiopian woman and by allegorizing Aaron as Speech and Miriam as Perception (*Legum Allegoria* 3.33.103). Josephus, again seeking to protect the reputation of his priestly ancestor, omits the episode altogether.

Connected with the quality of φιλανθρωπία is that of compassion. On this point, whereas the Bible declares that all the congregation was ready to stone Moses and Aaron after the unfavorable report of the spies (Numbers 14:10), in Josephus Moses and Aaron, instead of panicking, show their compassion for the people, thus exhibiting true leadership in their ability to analyze the cause of the people's depression (*Ant.* 3.307). Rather than condemning the people for their lack of faith they exonerate them on the ground of their ignorance and pray to G-d that He rid them of this ignorance and calm their spirits. In the Bible it is Moses alone who prays, and he says nothing in defense of the people but rather prays that G-d pardon them for complaining against him (Numbers 14:19).

One biblical incident in which both Moses and Aaron are criticized for lack of faith is that at Meribah, where, during a water shortage, Moses and Aaron gather the Israelites, and where Moses, instead of following G-d's instructions to speak to the rock (Numbers 20:8) actually smites it with his rod (Numbers 20:10). Thereupon G-d, blaming Aaron (whose role in the incident seems unclear) as well as Moses, declares that as punishment neither of them will enter the Promised Land. Such an incident casts aspersions upon the reputation for faith of both Moses and Aaron, and so it is not surprising that Josephus omits it completely. Likewise,

---

to Greek religious ideas and practices, but selectively and without his sympathy for Moses' achievements.

[7] See Diodorus 3.2; Pomponius Mela 3.85; Seneca, *Hercules Furens* 38-41; Lactantius Placidus on Statius, *Thebaid* 5.427. Cf. Snowden (1970, 144-47; and 1983, 46 and *passim*).

the Bible, when recounting the death of Aaron, has G-d tell Aaron that he is to die because he rebelled against His command at the waters of Meribah (Numbers 20:24), but Josephus' version makes no mention of this sin (*Ant.* 4.83).

3. *Aaron as Spokesman*

One measure of the importance which Josephus assigns to a given biblical figure is the sheer amount of space that he gives to him as compared with the Bible. In the case of Aaron his activities are covered in 461 lines of the Hebrew Bible[8] (613 lines in the Septuagint), whereas in Josephus (*Ant.* 2.279, 319; 3.54, 64, 188-92, 205-11, 307, 310; 4:15, 18, 21, 23-24, 26-34, 46, 54-58, 64-66, 83-85) he appears in 287 lines. This gives a ratio of .62 for Josephus as compared with the Hebrew and .47 as compared with the Septuagint. This means that in terms of the ratio of Josephus to the biblical coverage, Aaron is approximately half as important as Moses, for whom the figures are 1.17 in comparison with the Hebrew and .83 in comparison with the Septuagint. Moreover, in the case of Aaron, the Book of Exodus mentions him 101 times, whereas in the portion of the *Antiquities* parallel to this book Josephus refers to him by name only eight times.[9] Indeed, whereas in the biblical account of the consecration by Moses of Aaron as high priest Aaron is mentioned by name sixteen times (Exodus 29:1-46), in Josephus' version Aaron is mentioned by name only once (Ant. 3.205-7); clearly, for Josephus, what is crucial is not the personal consecration of Aaron but rather the institution of the high priesthood.

According to the biblical version, when G-d first directs Moses to lead the Israelites out of Egyptian bondage his reply is to ask G-d to appoint another person on the ground that he is not eloquent and indeed suffers from a speech impediment (Exodus 4:10;

---

[8] Exodus 4:14-16, 27-31; 5:1-21; 7:1-13, 19-21; 8:1-21; 9:8-10, 27-28; 10:3-8, 16-18; 11:10; 12:1, 28-31, 43, 50; 16:2-3, 6-7, 9-10, 33-34; 17:10; 19:24; 24:1, 9-10, 14; 28:1-3, 35-39; 29:44; 30:30; 32:1-25, 35; Leviticus 8:1-36; 10:3; Numbers 6:22-27; 12:1-12; 14:5, 26-35; 16:3, 10-11, 16-22; 17:6-25; 18:1-7; 20:2, 6, 10, 12, 23-29.

[9] We may also note that the Bible, in citing Miriam's song at the Red Sea, speaks of "Miriam the prophetess, the sister of Aaron," rather than of Miriam as the sister of Moses (Exodus 15:20). Josephus, however, omits Miriam's song altogether.

cf. 6:12). Thereupon G-d angrily replies that He knows that Aaron can speak well (*daber yedaber*), that he will speak for Moses to the people, and that Moses will be to him as G-d (Exodus 4:14). In view of the significance which the ancients attached to speaking ability, it is not surprising that Josephus omits both passages referring to Moses' speech impediment. Indeed, whereas Moses and Aaron go together to Pharaoh, with Aaron as the spokesman (Exodus 5:1), in Josephus Moses goes alone (*Ant.* 2.281); in fact, in his final encomium of Moses, Josephus makes a special point of stating that Moses found favor in every way in speech and in public addresses (*Ant.* 4.328). Thus, when Aaron does accompany Moses it is not because Moses cannot speak effectively. As to the above divine remark that Moses was to be to Aaron as G-d, such a statement raises serious theological problems for a religion that is so insistent on not deifying human beings; hence it is not surprising that Josephus omits this remark and others like it.

Likewise, in the biblical version, it is Aaron who performs many of the miracles, though it is apparently not by virtue of any innate ability or at his own initiative but, rather, in response to a divine command mediated through Moses. Even so, one may well wonder why Moses does not perform all the miracles himself, especially since no eloquence of speech is involved. Thus, at the very beginning of Moses' mission, when he returns from Midian to Egypt and meets the elders of the people of Israel, it is Aaron who speaks all the words which G-d had spoken to Moses and who performs the signs in the sight of the people, with the result that the people believe (Exodus 4:30). In Josephus' version this role of Aaron is completely eliminated; rather, in a suspenseful passage leading to a climax, it is Moses who, after failing to convince the Israelite leaders by a mere description of the miracles, then proceeds to perform them before their eyes, whereupon they are amazed by the astonishing spectacle and take courage (*Ant.* 2.280).

Immediately thereafter we are told that Moses and Aaron went to Pharaoh and requested that he allow the Israelites to leave Egypt (Exodus 5:1). Pharaoh, in turn, berates the two of them by name for taking the Israelites away from their work (Exodus 5:4). In Josephus, however, again Aaron is removed from the spotlight, and we read only that Moses betook himself to the Egyptian king, now that he was assured of the agreement of the Israelites to follow his orders and of their love of liberty (*Ant.* 2.281). Elsewhere in the Bible, while it is true that Aaron never speaks to Pharaoh alone, Pharaoh frequently addresses himself to both brothers (Exodus 8:4, 21; 9.27; 10.16-17). Indeed, it is to Moses and Aaron jointly that G-d gives his formal charge (just before the enumeration [Exodus 6:14-25] of the heads of the families of the Israelites) to speak to the people of Israel and to Pharaoh to lead the Israelites out of Egypt (Exodus 6:13); significantly Josephus omits this passage (*Ant.* 2.291).

In fact, whereas in the Bible G-d tells Moses that Aaron is to be his prophet, and that Aaron is to be his spokesman in demanding that Pharaoh release the Israelites from bondage (Exodus 7:1-2), Josephus totally omits this passage (*Ant.* 2.284). Again, in the Bible G-d instructs Moses and Aaron that when Pharaoh tells them to prove themselves by working a miracle, Moses is to instruct Aaron to cast his rod down before Pharaoh so that it may become a serpent (Exodus 7:8-9); they then follow these instructions, and when the Egyptian magicians do a similar feat of magic, Aaron's rod swallows up their rods. In Josephus, however, it is Moses, rather than Aaron (Exodus 7:10), who now performs the miracle with his rod in the presence of Pharaoh and whose rod makes the circuit of the Egyptians' rods, which merely look like pythons, and devours them all (*Ant.* 2.284, 287). Moses' accomplishment here is all the more impressive because, according to Josephus' addition, the king had previously ridiculed him (*Ant.* 2.284).

Similarly, Aaron in the biblical narrative, no less than Moses, is the object of recrimination by the Israelites' foremen when Pharaoh increases the tasks imposed upon them (Exodus 5:19-21). In Josephus' version it is Moses alone whom the Israelites hold accountable for the increased severity of their labors (*Ant.* 2.290).

Significantly, just after G-d formally charges Aaron and Moses with the task of leading the Israelites out of captivity, the Bible states important facts concerning Aaron's personal life, namely that he married Elisheba, the daughter of Amminadab, the sister of Nahshon, and that she bore him four sons – Nadab, Abihu, Eleazar, and Ithamar (Exodus 6:23). This notice certainly elevates the stature of Aaron, inasmuch as this marriage allied him with one of the most distinguished families of the tribe of Judah. Nahshon, his brother-in-law, we may note, was chieftain of the tribe of Judah (Numbers 2:3, 10:14), which consisted of 74,600 men (Numbers 2:3-4), was the first to present his offering at the dedication of the Tabernacle (Numbers 7:12-17), and headed the line of march in the desert. Moreover, according to a well-known rabbinic tradition (*Soṭah* 37a, *Mekilta Beshalaḥ* 5), when at the Red Sea none of the tribes wished to be the first to enter the sea, it was Nahshon who, with complete faith that the miracle would occur, sprang forward and descended first into the sea. Additionally, Nahshon was an ancestor of King David (Ruth 4:20-22, 1 Chronicles 2:10-15); hence the marriage of Aaron with Elisheba joined the two main hereditary lines among the Israelites, that of the high priesthood and that of the kingship. All this is, very significantly, omitted by Josephus (presumably because it would elevate Aaron too highly), as is the genealogy of the house of Levi, from which Moses and Aaron were descended (Exodus 6:16-20).

Likewise, according to the biblical version of the plagues, it is Aaron alone who performs the first three plague miracles, namely those of blood (Exodus 7:20), frogs (Exodus 8:2), and vermin (Exodus 8:13). In the Josephan version it is G-d who Himself performs these miracles directly, with no mention of the role of Aaron or, for that matter, of Moses (*Ant.* 2.294, 296, 300). Again, after the plague of the vermin, Pharaoh calls Moses and Aaron and grants them permission to offer sacrifices to G-d (Exodus 8:25); but in Josephus' version Pharaoh makes this offer to the "Hebrews," with no mention of Aaron (or Moses) in particular (*Ant.* 2.302). In the instance of two other plagues, the sixth (boils) (Exodus 9:8) and the eighth (locusts)(Exodus 10:3), Aaron and Moses appear jointly before Pharaoh, though it is Moses himself who performs the miracle; in Josephus the roles of Moses and Aaron are totally eliminated (*Ant.* 2.304, 306). Again, after the plagues of hail (Exodus 9:27) and locusts (Exodus 10:16) Pharaoh summons both Moses and Aaron, but in Josephus there is no mention of either (*Ant.* 2.305). Finally, at the conclusion and summary of the plagues, the Bible states that Moses and Aaron performed all these wonders before Pharaoh (Exodus 11:10), but in Josephus it is Moses alone whose role is mentioned (*Ant.* 2.314).

Similarly, we read that the whole congregation of the people of Israel murmured against both Moses and Aaron in the wilderness and expressed the wish that they had died in Egypt, where they had sat by fleshpots and eaten to the full (Exodus 16:2-3); but in Josephus' version the complaint is directly solely at Moses (*Ant.* 3.11-12). Again, in the biblical account, Moses calls upon Aaron to be his spokesman to the congregation and to tell them that G-d has heard their complaint (Exodus 16:9). We are then told that while Aaron was speaking to the people the glory of G-d appeared in a cloud and promised the people that in the evening they would have flesh and that in the morning they would have bread (Exodus 16:10). Aaron, however, plays no role in Josephus' version; instead, we read that Moses stood in their midst and informed the people that he had come to announce that G-d would deliver them from their present straits (*Ant.* 3.24).

Likewise, during the battle with Amalek in the desert, Moses' hands grow weary; a stone is then put under him and he sits upon it, and Aaron and Hur hold up his hands (Exodus 17:12). The scene in Josephus is similar, except that it is Moses who takes the initiative of asking Aaron and Hur to support his hands, inasmuch as the Israelites prevail only when Moses holds up his hands (*Ant.* 3.54). Again, after the battle, Josephus, in an extra-biblical addition, focuses upon Moses as the hero; and Aaron and Raguel (Jethro), Moses' father-in-law, sing praises of Moses the general, "to whose merit it was due that all had befallen to their hearts' content" (*Ant.* 3.65).

The most important achievement of Moses is his role as the agent of G-d in the revelation of the Torah. Prior to Moses' ascension on Mount Sinai (though stated after this event in the Bible) Moses is told to come up with Aaron, his sons Nadab and Abihu, and seventy of the elders of Israel (Exodus 24:1-11). We are informed that they actually saw G-d and that there was under His feet a pavement of sapphire stone (Exodus 24:10). It would appear that this direct meeting with G-d would, in addition to presenting problems of human beings actually beholding G-d, detract from the uniqueness of Moses' later encounter with Him, and hence Josephus omits this completely (*Ant.* 3.75). Again, the Bible states that G-d told Moses to come up Mount Sinai bringing Aaron with him (Exodus 24:1) but then proceeds to declare that Moses, presumably alone, went down to the people and presented to them the Ten Commandments (Exodus 19:25). The fact that Moses was to bring Aaron with him would also detract from the unique role of Moses and so, not surprisingly, Josephus omits it (*Ant.* 3.84).

Likewise, in the description of the high priest's vestments, whereas the Bible states that they are to be put upon Aaron (Exodus 28:41), Josephus describes them in general without applying them to Aaron in particular (*Ant.* 3.159). Similarly, whereas the Bible states that the breastplate of judgment, containing the the Urim and the Thummim, is to be put upon Aaron's heart (Exodus 28:30), Josephus describes them, with no mention of Aaron in particular (*Ant.* 3.171). In like fashion, whereas the Bible mentions the plate of gold on Aaron's forehead (Exodus 28:38), Josephus describes the plate and the inscription upon it but with no mention of Aaron (*Ant.* 3.178).

One is tempted, as we have seen, for example, in the rabbinic tradition, to compare Aaron's acceptance without complaint of the sudden death of his sons with Abraham's supreme act of faith in his readiness to sacrifice his son Isaac when ordered to do so by G-d. If so, there was clearly a danger that Aaron might emerge as superior, at least in this respect, to Moses himself. Hence, whereas the Bible says that Aaron held his peace, presumably of his own volition (Leviticus 10:3), Josephus declares that it was Moses who required him to refrain from any thoughts of grief, since, as a priest, he was required to put homage due to G-d above his personal loss (*Ant.* 3.211).

The reason for this relative downgrading of Aaron is Josephus' desire to preserve the primacy of Moses, who was to the Jewish people as Lycurgus, for example, was to the Spartans (cf., e.g., Josephus, *Ag. Ap.* 2.154, 225). Indeed, as we have remarked, Moses was the one figure in Jewish tradition who was well known to the pagan world (see Gager 1972). In fact, in the one place in pagan literature where Aaron is mentioned by name (he is called Arruas), Pompeius Trogus makes the egregious error of referring to him as the son of Moses (*ap.* Justin, *Historiae Philippicae* 36, *Epitome* 2.16). Clearly, Trogus knows only that Aaron was subordinate to Moses. Indeed, so poorly informed was Trogus about Aaron that he then goes on to say that Aaron was created king soon after he was made priest.

Again, in order to protect the unique status of Moses as the leader of the Israelites, when the Bible states that Moses and Aaron took a census of the people (Numbers 1:17. 1:44), Josephus ascribes this census to Moses alone (*Ant.* 3.287), and this despite the fact that the taking of a census incurs divine wrath, as we see in the case of David's census (2 Samuel 24:1).

The greatest challenge to the leadership of Moses and Aaron, according to the biblical narrative, came from Korah (Numbers

16:3). Josephus, eager to preserve the primacy of Moses as the leader of the Israelites, presents the rebellion as a direct challenge to Moses alone (*Ant.* 4.15), though the main subject of the challenge is apparently the arbitrary awarding of the high priesthood to Aaron by Moses himself, who is accused of showing preference to Aaron merely because he was his brother, rather than submitting the matter to popular decision (*Ant.* 4.22). Korah's argument is that he has more right to the high priesthood than Aaron because he is both older and richer and on a par with Moses himself by birth, being his first cousin (*Ant.* 4.18-19). That the accusation is one of nepotism is clear from Josephus' comment that Moses knew that his brother had obtained the priesthood "through G-d's deliberate choice and not through any favoritism (χάριν) of his own" (*Ant.* 4.24)[10] In a powerful, extra-biblical defense, Moses is completely frank in stating that if the decision had been up to him, he would naturally have preferred to keep the high priesthood for himself, since he was a nearer kinsman to himself than was his brother, but that the choice had been made by G-d (*Ant.* 4.26). Then, whereas in the Bible it is G-d who tells Moses to open the high priesthood as a prize to the one whom He chooses (Numbers 17:5), Josephus depicts Moses as dramatically taking the initiative in offering the high priesthood as a prize to the best qualified in order to end the dissension (*Ant.* 4.29-30). The whole episode is more a contest between Moses and Korah, with the alleged nepotism of Moses in choosing his brother Aaron to be high priest as the pretext for the challenge. Aaron's victory in the contest with Korah is due to G-d rather than to Aaron's merits, and the credit goes to Moses for fighting G-d's battle and for vindicating G-d's decision (*Ant.* 4.56). For Aaron the key is to establish the legitimacy of the line of Aaron, especially since he himself was of that line. No one else would hereafter claim that high honor, Josephus

---

[10] Apparently, in this respect Josephus differs from the prevalent point of view in the Roman world that such nepotism was not at all improper. See Evans (1978, 102-28); and Saller (1982, 135, 176-82). I am grateful to Professor Ranon Katzoff for calling my attention to these discussions, as well as to his own (1986, 238-39), in which he comments on an anonymous midrash dealing, in fact, with the appointment of Aaron as high priest. The passage states that when the high priest was to be appointed, Moses would certainly be expected to exercise his influence to obtain the position for his own brother, as would happen in the case of an appointment in the Roman imperial administration (*Exodus Rabbah* 37.2).

editorializes, in view of the miserable end to which the first challengers had come.

This concern to protect the primacy of Moses may also be seen in the fact that whereas in the Bible G-d instructs Moses to tell the Israelites to inscribe each man's name upon his rod and to write Aaron's name upon the rod of Levi (Numbers 17:17), Josephus, apparently aware that this would give greater prominence to Aaron than to Moses, who no less than Aaron came from the tribe of Levi, states that Aaron wrote the name "Levite" upon his staff (*Ant.* 4.64). The end result of the whole episode, according to Josephus in an extra-biblical remark, is the restoration of peace in place of the dreaded στάσις, so that those who had previously borne malice against Moses and Aaron now renounced it (*Ant.* 4.66).

Normally, when one of the biblical heroes dies, Josephus, as we have noted, has an encomium of greater or lesser length. According to the rabbinic tradition, so beloved was Aaron by the Israelites that when he died all the congregation of Israel wept for him (Numbers 20:29) (*Sifra* 45d), whereas when Moses died only the men (Deuteronomy 34:8, literally, the sons of Israel) wept for him. But Josephus, in his concern not to build up Aaron as a person lest he rival Moses, has no word of encomium for him at all. Moses retains the role of leadership, inasmuch as it is he who reveals to Aaron that he is about to die (*Ant.* 4.83), whereas in the biblical account it is G-d who tells Moses and Aaron jointly that Aaron is to die (Numbers 20:23). For Josephus the key point is the legitimacy of the succession of the high priesthood; hence, he gives the precise date of the month when Aaron died, noting the equivalent name of the month according to the Athenian and Macedonian calendar (*Ant.* 4.84). And so, whereas in the Bible it is Moses who actually strips Aaron of his priestly garments and places them upon his son Eleazar (Numbers 20:28), in Josephus it is Aaron himself who presides over the succession, delivering his robes to Eleazar, upon whom, Josephus adds, in an important extra-biblical remark, the high priesthood descended by virtue of his age (*Ant.* 4.83).[11]

---

[11] According to Deuteronomy 10:6 Aaron died at Moserah, whereas in Numbers 20:22-28 he is said to have died at Mount Hor. According to the description of the stages in the journey of the Israelites through the wilderness, Moserah (Moseroth) is seven stages earlier than Mount Hor. Josephus avoids the problem of this discrepancy by saying nothing about Aaron's dying at Moserah. Philo (*Legum*

4. *Summary*

Four major problems confronted Josephus in his treatment of Aaron: how to deal with the fact that Aaron was actually older than his brother Moses (and presumably entitled to preference), that he was much superior to Moses as a speaker in an era when oratory was prized, that he was appointed as high priest by his brother (an apparent case of nepotism), and that he participated in the egregious sin of the making and worship of the golden calf.

Unlike Philo, who resorts to allegory, and unlike the rabbis, who aggrandize his qualities of character and explain away his shortcomings, Josephus, on the one hand, stresses Aaron's possession of the four cardinal virtues of wisdom, courage, temperance, and justice, plus the fifth cardinal virtue of piety, while, on the other hand, making sure that he nowhere eclipses Moses, whose primacy is important since a nation was known by its lawgiver. In particular, Josephus stresses Aaron's capacity as a prophet, a role which Josephus regarded as especially important, inasmuch as he saw a close kinship between the prophet and the historian in guaranteeing the truth of history. Josephus emphasizes his valiant steadfastness and self-control when he learns of the death of his two oldest sons. As to justice, the queen of the virtues, he is said to have been chosen by G-d as high priest because he was even more just than Moses himself. He displays his piety by joining Moses in taking Joseph's bones with him when they leave Egypt. Josephus, clearly in a quandary as to how to deal with his participation in the creation and worship of the golden calf, does not, like Philo, Pseudo-Philo, and the rabbis, try to exonerate him. Because this incident raised serious questions as to Aaron's worthiness to be high priest, Josephus, who was so proud of his priestly descent, felt the necessity to omit it altogether. Similarly, Josephus omits the episode in which Miriam and Aaron criticize Moses for marrying an Ethiopian woman; to have included it would have subjected Aaron to the charge of prejudice against the much respected Ethiopians and would have substantiated the charge of those who contended that the Jews hated non-Jews. Likewise, Josephus omits the

---

Allegoria 3.15.45), as we have noted, gives an allegorical interpretation of the significance of the fact that Aaron died at Mount Hor, namely that Aaron, whose name signifies Word, goes up into Hor, which signifies Light or Truth, so that the end of the Word is Truth, "which casts a beam more far-reaching than Light."

incident at Meribah in which Aaron shows lack of faith and for which he is punished, according to the Bible, by not being granted the privilege of entering the Land of Israel.

In general, Josephus downgrades the importance of Aaron by mentioning him by name far less frequently than does the Bible. There is no indication that Moses needs Aaron as his spokesman in his dealings with Pharaoh. Furthermore, Josephus omits mention of Aaron's marriage with Elisheba, the brother of Nahshon, the hero at the Red Sea and the ancestor of David, since this represents the union of the high priesthood with royalty and would perhaps thus raise Aaron to a point above Moses himself. Whereas in the Bible it is Aaron who performs the miracles of the first three plagues, in Josephus it is G-d who does so directly. Even Aaron's supreme act of faith in not complaining when his sons die suddenly is less impressive in Josephus, who declares that he abstained from mourning because he was told by Moses to do so. The rebellion of Korah is presented by Josephus as a challenge to Moses' authority rather than as a challenge to the high priesthood of Aaron. When Aaron dies there is no encomium for him personally; rather, Josephus is concerned to confirm the legitimacy of the transmission of the high priesthood to his son Eleazar.

CHAPTER FIVE

THE PHARAOHS

1. *Introduction*

An important part of Josephus' response to the charges of critics of the Jews can be seen in his treatment of non-Jewish figures, and, in particular, those who are demonstrably wicked. Here Josephus was clearly confronted with a dilemma: if he downgraded these figures he would play into the hands of those who charged that he, no less than Jews generally, was prejudiced against non-Jews; but if he showed too much regard for them he would be whitewashing enemies of the Jewish people and so would clearly offend Jews in his audience. It may, therefore, be instructive to see how Josephus deals with such figures as Nebuchadnezzar, Belshazzar, and Darius, and the various Pharaohs mentioned in the Bible.[1]

2. *Josephus' Portrayal of Nebuchadnezzar, Belshazzar, and Darius*

Just as Josephus seeks to portray Balaam in a more favorable light, so also, as we shall see, he attempts to depict Nebuchadnezzar, who was responsible for the capture of Jerusalem and the destruction of the First Temple, more positively.

Nebuchadnezzar's "son" Belshazzar is, to be sure, according to Josephus punished severely by G-d (*Ant.* 10.247), but this is because he not only had drunk from the vessels which Nebuchadnezzar had taken from the Temple (as the Bible [Daniel 5:23] indicates), but also had grievously blasphemed G-d (*Ant.* 10.233, 242). Both Philo (*Quaestiones et Solutiones in Exodum* 2.5, *De Specialibus Legibus* 1.9.53, *De Vita Mosis* 2.37-38.203-8) and Josephus (*Ant.* 4.207, *Ag. Ap.* 2.237) interpret the biblical injunction to mean that one is not permitted to revile the gods of others (Exodus 22:27 [28]); hence, Josephus' audience would understand the revulsion which Josephus felt toward Belshazzar in this respect.

---

[1] See also the essays on Jethro, Balaam, and Ahasuerus included in this volume.

Even so, however, Belshazzar emerges more favorably. In particular, whereas the Bible states that Belshazzar commanded that Daniel be given the various honors which he had promised him (Daniel 5:29), Josephus adds that he did so despite the fact that Daniel had prophesied doom for him (*Ant.* 10.246). He then notes Belshazzar's reasoning, namely that the prophecy was intended for himself and in no way attributable to the one who had interpreted it and that, in any case, Daniel was a good and just man.

As to Darius, the Bible asserts that he signed his name to an edict forbidding any petition directed toward any god or man other than himself for thirty days (Daniel 6:7, 9). One might well wonder why he should have gone along with such an arbitrary ruling. Josephus, clearly aware of this problem, explains that Darius had approved of the decree only because he had been misled by his advisers (*Ant.* 10.254). Josephus likewise protects Darius' reputation by having him not merely express the hope, as does the Bible (Daniel 6:16), that Daniel's G-d would save him and that he would suffer no harm from the beasts but also, more positively, by having him bid Daniel to bear his fate with good courage (*Ant.* 10.258). Moreover, the fact that he had cast into the lions' den not only his enemies but also their innocent wives and children (Daniel 6:24) would cast discredit upon Darius, and it is therefore significant that Josephus omits this detail (*Ant.* 10.262).

3. *Philo's Portrait of the Pharaohs*

It is significant that Philo, with whose works, as we have suggested, there is good reason to believe, Josephus was acquainted, presents a uniformly blackened picture of the Egyptian pharaohs. One may guess that his negative view was influenced by the fact that he himself was living in Egypt and was intimately involved in the Jewish community's attempts at refuting the anti-Jewish charges of his Egyptian contemporaries. The fact that Philo does not distinguish among the various pharaohs in his portrayal of them is a further indication of his strongly negative attitude.

The most general and most severe condemnation of the pharaohs may be seen in Philo's equation of Pharaoh with materialism and his picture of him rejoicing in buildings constructed of brick (*De Confusione Linguarum* 19.88). Pharaoh is enamored of "what is material and female" and knows not the First Cause (*Legum*

Allegoria 3.87.243). Indeed, "when this mind becomes enamored of the body, its efforts are expended on three things which it deems most worthy of its care and trouble – bread, meat, and drink" (*De Josepho* 26.151). For Philo, who calls Plato "most sacred" (*Quod Omnis Probus Liber Sit* 2.13), the strongest criticism of Pharaoh is that he is the mind that is king of the body, namely Egypt (*De Confusione Linguarum* 19.88, *De Fuga et Inventione* 23.124, *De Migratione Abrahami* 29.160, *De Ebrietate* 50.208, *De Abrahamo* 21.103, *De Josepho* 26.151), as well as the body in each of us (*De Josepho* 26.151). He is weak-willed and incontinent (*De Ebrietate* 51.210). Such people are irrational and lifeless, and should consequently be shunned (*De Fuga et Inventione* 23.126). Moreover, it is he whom the passions follow as their leader (*Legum Allegoria* 3.4.13). He is identified with the senses and with the search for pleasure and love of the self (*De Somniis* 2.32.215, 2.32.219, 2.42.277, *De Mutatione Nominum* 31.171, 32.173, *Legum Allegoria* 3.75.212, *De Posteritate Caini* 33.115); indeed Pharaoh crowns his self-love with madness (*De Cherubim* 23.74), thinking that his constitution is more than human (*De Posteritate Caini* 33.115). He opposes "what training and education establish for our dealings with the world of creation, and thus he will work universal confusion" (*De Ebrietate* 19.77).

Again, one sees the Platonist in Philo bitterly criticizing Pharaoh as one who, in body and soul alike, is the subject of movement and turning and change (*De Somniis* 2.32.219); things created and perishable seem to him bright and shining, so that he dwells in night and profound darkness (*De Ebrietate* 50.209). He "cannot receive the vision of timeless values, for the eyes of the soul, whereby alone incorporeal natures are apprehended, are blinded in him" (*De Sacrificiis Abelis et Caini* 19.69). In this respect he is identified with the land of Egypt (*Legum Allegoria* 3.75.212), just as he is contrasted with our paternal and our truly real wealth (*De Mutatione Nominum* 32.173). The love of pleasure, with which he is identified, is devoid of all the chief necessities, namely temperance, modesty, self-restraint, justice, and every virtue; "for no two things can be more hostile to each other than virtue is to pleasure" (*De Josepho* 26.153). He is the epitome of senselessness and wine-frenzy and ceaseless life-long intoxication and incontinence (*De Somniis* 2.30.200-1).

Over and over again Philo presents the etymology (a clearly wrong one, the correct derivation being from the Egyptian term for "the Great House") of Pharaoh as derived from the word meaning "scattering," in the sense, according to Philo, that he made scattering and undoing of continence his business (*De Somniis* 2.31.211) and, indeed, is the scatterer of all things noble and of pious thoughts and deeds (*Legum Allegoria* 3.4.12, 3.84.236, 3.87.243; *De Sacrificiis Abelis et Caini* 11.48, 19.69; *Quod Deterius Potiori Insidiari Solet* 25.95; *Quis Rerum Divinarum Heres* 12.60). His tyranny, rife with lawlessness and cruelty, is impossible to escape (*Quis Rerum Divinarum Heres* 12.60). Like an actor in a play, he "assumes a counterfeited fellowship, he, the licentious with chastity, the profligate with self-control, the unjust with justice, and in his desire to earn a good repute with the multitude invites virtue to join him" (*De Abrahamo* 21.103). He is at once boastful (*De Ebrietate* 29.111) and stiff-necked (*De Somniis* 2.27.184).

Indeed, Pharaoh is steeped in greed, is licentious and unjust, priding himself on his impiety, of which he is the crowning example (*De Mutatione Nominum* 3.19), since he dared to say "I know not the L-rd" (Exodus 5:2) (*De Somniis* 2.27.182). In fact, in saying "I know not the L-rd," he is asserting that even if there is a G-d He is not known to us" (*De Ebrietate* 6.19). Over and over again he is described as godless (*Legum Allegoria* 3.4.13, 3.75.212; *De Sacrificiis Abelis et Caini* 19.69); indeed, he is the very antithesis of G-d, since he is the mind which usurps His place (*De Somniis* 2.27.183). He is "disobedient to the commandments which law and custom regularly prescribe in these matters; but rebellion or strife-stirrer is the name for him who turns aside to their direct opposite, impiety, and becomes a leader in godlessness" (*De Ebrietate* 5.18).

In sum, he is the archetype of the foolish man (*Quod Deterius Potiori Insidiari Solet* 44.161-62; *De Mutatione Nominum* 22.128, 33.175; *De Confusione Linguarum* 9.29-30) and the wicked man (*De Somniis* 2.36.237; *Legum Allegoria* 3.75.212). In fact, in surveying all the numerous references to Pharaoh in Philo one finds not a single positive trait nor any mitigating circumstances. Undoubtedly, Philo has been influenced in this regard by the long and bitter history of hostility to the Jews in Egypt, starting with Manetho in the third century B.C.E. and culminating in his own day in the vicious remarks of Apion as cited in Josephus' essay *Against Apion*. Most of all, perhaps, he has been influenced by the terrible suffering of his fellow Alexandrian Jews in the pogrom of the year 38, which he himself reports in such graphic colors in his essays *In Flaccum* and *Legatio ad Gaium* (18-19. 120-31).

4. *The Rabbinic Portrait of the Pharaohs*

Whereas the hostility of Philo to Pharaoh was, as we have seen, couched in philosophic terms such as Plato would have used, that of the rabbis expresses itself in plain words of the strongest condemnation, undoubtedly reflecting the tremendous losses of Jewish life and property in the terrible pogroms in Egypt of 38, 66, and, above all, 116-7. Like Philo, they generally make no distinctions among the various pharaohs. Unlike Philo, however, some of the rabbis, like Josephus, as we shall see, do seek to exonerate them.

Thus, in the incident of Abraham's descent into Egypt with his wife Sarah (Genesis 12:10-20), though the biblical account would seem to exculpate Pharaoh, since it is his Egyptian princes who take the initiative to praise her to Pharaoh and since he is clearly unaware that she is married to Abraham inasmuch as she tells the Egyptians that she is his sister (Genesis 12:15), the rabbinic tradition flatly terms him "this wicked man" and declares that though he was informed by her that she was a married woman he was, nonetheless, not deterred from attempting to seduce her (*Genesis Rabbah* 41.2); and consequently, very appropriately, he was whipped by an angel and stricken with leprosy (*Tanḥuma* B, *Genesis* 33).

And yet, the rabbis, or at least some of them, had ambivalent feelings toward this Pharaoh. Thus we hear that Pharaoh felt such genuine love for Sarah that he actually wrote out a marriage contract, granting her all his gold and silver and slaves, as well as the whole province of Goshen (which was later destined to be occupied by the Israelites) (*Pirqe de-Rabbi Eliezer* 26, *Genesis Rabbah* 45.1, *Yashar Lek* 32a, *Targum Yerushalmi* Genesis 26.1). Indeed, he is reported even to have given his own daughter Hagar to her as a slave.[2]

---

[2] Ginzberg (1925, 5:244, n. 192) remarks that the rabbis contrast Abimelech, of whom they have a very high opinion, with Pharaoh, whom they utterly condemn, even though the biblical incidents involving them and Sarah are quite similar. Nevertheless, as we note here, there is apparently a minority view that sought to excuse Pharaoh as well.

Even the Pharaoh of Joseph's day, though clearly presented in a favorable light in the Bible, is blackened in the rabbinic version. Thus we are told that when Joseph wished to swear falsely he would invoke the Pharaoh's name (*Genesis Rabbah* 91.7). Again, Joseph shows distrust for him in that when presenting his brothers to Pharaoh he chooses the weakest of them so as to avoid their being drafted into the Egyptian army. This Pharaoh is likewise termed "wicked" and is accused by Judah of making false promises and of engaging in pederasty (*Genesis Rabbah* 89.4).

And yet, there is a divergent view with regard also to this Pharaoh, for when, after Joseph interprets Pharaoh's dreams and Pharaoh, in appreciation and admiration, decides to entrust the administration of Egypt to Joseph (Genesis 41:38-41), the rabbis cite a tradition that Pharaoh's astrologers, who were his counsellors, tried to dissuade him with the remark, "Do you prefer to us a slave, whom his present owner acquired for twenty pieces of silver?" Thereupon Pharaoh insists that Joseph was not only, beyond any doubt, a free-born person but also that he was descended from a noble family (*Soṭah* 36b, *Midrash Hagadol* 1.626).

The rabbis emphasize the ingratitude of the Pharaoh of the exodus for the service rendered by Joseph to the Egyptians, noting that this ingratitude ultimately led to idolatry (*Midrash Hagadol* 2.7, *Exodus Rabbah* 1.8, and *Tanḥuma* B *Exodus* 2.4), as we see in Pharaoh's statement that "I know not the L-rd" (Exodus 5:2). Moreover, though the biblical text clearly states that after the time of Joseph there arose a new king who did not know Joseph (Exodus 1:8), the Talmud, while noting the literal interpretation that the king was really new (*Soṭah* 11a; so also *Yashar Shemot* 112b, 125a-b), also cites the view that he was not really new but that his decrees were made new; and, indeed, he is described as one who did not know that Joseph had ever existed (*Soṭah* 11a). Moreover, it is said that it was Pharaoh who initiated the plan to persecute the Israelites.

Here, however, we do find a minority view that the initiative was not Pharaoh's but that of the Egyptians generally, that, in fact, he opposed the plan, reminding the Egyptians that it was a Hebrew, Joseph, who had saved their lives during the years of famine, that he was deposed by the Egyptians when he refused to listen to them, that he was incarcerated for three months, and that he was restored to the throne only when he promised to heed them (*Exodus Rabbah* 1.8). Moreover, we are told that the idea of drowning all male Israelites babies was not Pharaoh's but rather that of his adviser, who is identified as the wicked Balaam (*Soṭah* 11a, *Exodus Rabbah* 1.34, *Targum Yerushalmi* Exodus 3:23, *Yashar Shemot* 128b-30b, *Divre Hayamim* 1, *Midrash Hagadol* 2.12, 2.20). Furthermore, Pharaoh is, to some degree, exculpated in that, in response to Moses' argument that if a slave is not afforded rest at least one day a week he will die of overexertion, Pharaoh permits the Israelites to rest on the Sabbath (*Exodus Rabbah* 1.28, *Yashar Shemot* 133a, *Shibbole Ha-Leqet* 55-6).

The same punishment of leprosy, which we noted in connection with the Pharaoh of Abraham's time, is likewise inflicted upon the Pharaoh of the exodus (*Exodus Rabbah* 1.34).[3] Here, too, the rabbis castigate him in the strongest terms, invoking the tradition that in order to cure himself of this leprosy he bathed in the blood of Hebrew children.

On the whole, the rabbinic tradition[4] magnifies Pharaoh's brutality, asserting that he commanded that those Israelites who did not complete the number of bricks required of them were to be buried beween the layers of bricks (*Exodus Rabbah* 5.21, *Seder Eliyahu Rabbah* 7.44). So cruel was Pharaoh that, whereas the biblical statement is that he decreed that all male Israelite children should be cast into the river (Exodus 1:22), the rabbis have a tradition that he ordered that all male children, even those of the Egyptians, should be thus disposed of, inasmuch as his astrologers had foretold that a redeemer would be born to Israel but had been unable to tell him whether he would be a Hebrew or an Egyptian (*Tanḥuma B Exodus* 22.122, *Tanḥuma Vayaqhel* 4, *Exodus Rabbah* 1.18). In seeking to induce the midwives to enforce his decree Pharaoh is depicted as going to the length, on the one hand, of attempting to seduce them and, on the other hand, of threatening to burn them to death (*Soṭah* 11b, *Exodus Rabbah* 1.15, *Yashar Shemot* 127b). The rabbis also express their abhorrence at his claiming divinity for himself (*Exodus Rabbah* 8.2).

---

[3] According to Artapanus (*ap.* Eusebius, *Pr. Ev.* 9.27.20), the Pharaoh, Chenephres, who chose Moses to be commander in the war against the Ethiopians, died, the first man ever to contract elephantiasis, a disease which is similar to leprosy and used as a designation for it sometimes. See Holladay 1983, 1:238-39, n. 78.

[4] For the rabbinic tradition see Ginzberg (1938, 7:368-70, s.v. "Pharaoh"); and Aberbach (1971, 13:360-62).

The rabbis[5] further blacken Pharaoh's portrait by presenting a tradition that he resorted to various inducements in order to persuade his people to go to war against the Israelites, notably promising that he would lead the way in battle, that he would take no more of the booty than any of his subjects, and finally that he would, upon returning from battle, divide all his treasures among the people (*Mekilta Beshallaḥ* 1.26b-27a, *Mekilta de-Rabbi Shimon ben Yoḥai* 43-44).

The rabbis further emphasize their negative portrait of Pharaoh by stressing his boastfulness (*Exodus Rabbah* 5.14, *Midrash Song of Songs* 8a, *Midrash Proverbs* 26.101, *Tanḥuma Vaera* 5), as does Philo. Thus he is quoted as telling Moses and Aaron that he had no need of G-d since he had created himself and that he had the Nile River, which is the source of such huge fruit that it takes two asses to carry it. Furthermore, he is coupled with the classic sinners – the builders of the Tower of Babel, Sennacherib, and Nebuchadnezzar – as guilty of committing eight cardinal sins – neglect of justice, idolatry, incest, bloodshed, blasphemy, arrogance, slander, and obscenity (*Seder Eliyahu Rabbah* 15.74 and 31.117).

And yet, just as we shall see in Josephus' depiction, Moses is told to treat Pharaoh, despite his wickedness, with the deference and respect due to a sovereign (*Exodus Rabbah* 7.3), especially since the rabbis view him as the ruler of the whole world (*Exodus Rabbah* 5.14, *Midrash Hagadol* 2.43, *Tanḥuma* B *Exodus* 2.19, *Tanḥuma Vaera* 5, *Midrash Song of Songs* 7b).[6] Furthermore, according to one view (*Exodus Rabbah* 15.5 and 21.5), it is not Pharaoh who should be blamed for his wickedness and stubbornness but rather an evil spirit named Abezi-thibod, who fought against Moses by means of magic and who hardened Pharaoh's heart, thus causing the Egyptians to pursue the Israelites after the latter had been permitted to leave Egypt. Another view is that it was Uzza, the angel of Egypt, who was the great adversary of Moses and Israel in Egypt and at the Red Sea. Moreover, we do find a conciliatory view toward the Egyptians expressed by the third-century Rabbi Jonathan ben Eleazar (*Sanhedrin* 39b, *Megillah* 10b), who reports that G-d rebuked the angels when they attempted to sing a song of praise to

---

[5] See Ginzberg, 3.12 and 6.3, n. 15.
[6] See Ginzberg, 2.331 and 5.424, n. 154. Indeed, so powerful is Pharaoh in the rabbinic view that *2 Targum Yerushalmi* 1.1, in its list of those who have ruled the entire world, starts with G-d Himself and includes Pharaoh.

Him when the Israelites were saved at the Red Sea, saying, "My handiwork [the Egyptians] is drowning in the sea, and you would utter song before Me!" Most remarkably, there is even a tradition (*Pirqe de-Rabbi Eliezer* 43, *Mekilta Beshalah* 6) that Pharaoh himself was not actually drowned in the Red Sea but that he emerged to become king of Nineveh and actually took the initiative in leading his people to repent in response to the prophet Jonah's exhortations. Nevertheless, he is portrayed as thoroughly humiliated, searching for Moses and Aaron at night and mocked by the Hebrew children (*Mekilta Bo* 13, *Tanhuma B, Exodus* 26).

5. *Josephus' Portrait of the Pharaohs*[7]

In line with stress on the importance of showing respect for the ruler of the land, Josephus emphasizes the terrible effects of civil strife (στάσις) so familiar to readers of Thucydides' description of revolution at Corcyra (3.82-4). Hence, to the extent that he was the legitimate ruler of his land, Pharaoh in his role as king was above criticism for Josephus. Indeed, the only ground for criticism in the incident with Sarah was that he failed to show self-control; in the Bible (Genesis 12:11-2), significantly, the blame is put on the Egyptians, whose licentiousness Abram fears and who take the lead in praising her to Pharaoh, whereas in Josephus (*Ant.* 1.162) this frenzy for women is transferred to Pharaoh himself; and it is the fear that Pharaoh will slay him because of his wife's beauty that leads Abram to devise his scheme of pretending that she is his sister. Josephus, then, in an extra-biblical passage (*Ant.* 1.163-64), remarks that Pharaoh, not content with reports about Sarai's beauty, was fired with a desire to see her and was actually at the point of laying hands upon her, whereupon G-d inflicted upon Pharaoh the punishment that was most dreadful in Josephus' eyes, namely an outbreak of disease and political disturbance (στάσει). But even in this instance Josephus comes to Pharaoh's defense, carefully remarking (*Ant.* 1.165) that once he discovered the truth

---

[7] The most extensive bibliographies of Josephus are those by Heinz Schreckenberg, *Bibliographie zu Flavius Josephus* and *Bibliographie zu Flavius Josephus: Supplementband mit Gesamtregister* and by myself, *Josephus and Modern Scholarship* and *Josephus: A Supplementary Bibliography*. An examination of these bibliographies indicates that the subject of Josephus' portrait of the Pharaohs has not been dealt with at all previously.

about Sarai's identity (at that point her name had not yet been changed to Sarah) Pharaoh apologized to Abram, stressing that he had wished to contract a legitimate marriage alliance with her rather than to outrage her in a transport of passion. Significantly, whereas in the Bible (Genesis 12:16) it is before his discovery of her identity that Pharaoh gives Abram abundant gifts, in Josephus (*Ant.* 1.165) Pharaoh's character is enhanced by virtue of the fact that it is after the discovery of Sarai's identity and when he has nothing to gain thereby that Pharaoh gives abundant riches to Abram.

Furthermore, whereas in the Bible (Genesis 41:15) Pharaoh is impressed with Joseph's ability to interpret his dreams but shows no particular warmth toward him, Josephus' Pharaoh (*Ant.* 2.80) is clearly a more winning personality in that he actually takes Joseph by the hand and commends him for his excellence (ἄριστος) and extreme sagacity (σύνεσιν ἱκανώτατος) in asking him to interpret his dreams. We are likewise impressed by the fact that before Joseph actually gives his interpretation Pharaoh reassures him by telling him that he should suppress nothing through fear, nor should be feel the necessity to flatter him with lying speech, however grim the truth may be. These words would remind the reader of the assurances given by Achilles to Calchas the seer in Homer's *Iliad* (1.84-91).

Moreover, in the biblical text (Genesis 41:37) we read only that Joseph's advice to Pharaoh to gather food during the fat years for the lean years that will follow seemed good to Pharaoh and to all his servants. On the other hand, we admire Josephus' Pharaoh much more, inasmuch as he expresses his appreciation to Joseph with much greater enthusiasm, not merely stating that Joseph was discreet and wise (Genesis 41:39) but actually marvelling (θαυμάσαντος) at the latter's discernment (φρόνησιν) and wisdom (σοφίαν). This appreciation for Joseph is particularly to be seen in that Josephus spells out the fact (*Ant.* 2.89) that Pharaoh doubly (ἀμφοτέρων) admired Joseph, alike for the interpretation of the dream and for his counsel.

Again, whereas the biblical text (Genesis 41:45) is content, without further explanation, to state that Pharaoh called Joseph's name Zaphenath-paneah, Josephus (*Ant.* 2.91) explains the meaning of the name as "Discoverer of Secrets" and indicates that he gave this name to him because of his amazing (παράδοξον, "astonishing," "miraculous") intelligence (συνέσεως, "insight," "understanding," "perception," "sagacity"). We thus come to admire Pharaoh himself more because of the recognition that he thus gives to the erstwhile slave and prisoner. Likewise, whereas in the Bible (Genesis 47:1), when Pharaoh is told that Joseph's father and his family were coming to Egypt from Canaan, we learn nothing of Pharaoh's reaction other than that he was pleased (Genesis 45:16), Josephus' Pharaoh (*Ant.* 2.185) arouses positive feelings on the part of the reader by virtue of the warm reception that he describes Pharaoh as giving to Jacob and the latter's sons, since we are told that the king rejoiced at the news. Moreover, whereas in the Bible (Genesis 46:34) Joseph instructs his brothers, when Pharaoh asks them what their occupation is, to say that they are keepers of cattle rather than shepherds, inasmuch as every shepherd is an abomination to the Egyptians, Josephus' Pharaoh (*Ant.* 2.185) takes the initiative in asking Joseph what the occupation of the brothers is so that he, magnanimously, may permit them to continue in that work.

When Josephus comes to that portion of the Bible detailing the sufferings of the Israelites in Egypt, he is careful (in line with the Bible itself [Exodus 1:8]) to avoid the identification, which we have found prevalent in the rabbinic sources, of this oppressor Pharaoh with the one who had appointed Joseph to high estate, in order to emphasize that not all Pharaohs are identical. Indeed, Josephus (*Ant.* 2.202) very carefully remarks that not only was there a new king but that the kingdom had now passed to another dynasty. Moreover, the blame is placed not on Pharaoh but rather on the Egyptians (*Ant.* 2.201), who are described as a voluptuous and lazy people, "slaves to pleasure in general and to a love of lucre in particular." Josephus' audience would have had little difficulty accepting this statement of contempt for the Egyptian people, if we may judge from the remarks of a host of Greek and Roman writers, from Florus and Achilles Tatius to the author of the *Bellum Alexandrinum* and Juvenal.[8] As Josephus (*Ant.* 2.201-2) presents it, it is not Pharaoh but the Egyptians who are at fault, their bitter disposition toward the Israelites being due to their envy of the latter's prosperity, brought about by the latter's work ethic, which they thought was to their own detriment.

---

[8] See J. P. V. D. Balsdon, *Romans and Aliens*, 68-69 and 271, notes 61-74.

As to Pharaoh's decree that the male babies should be put to death, the Bible (Exodus 1:8-10) clearly puts the finger of blame upon Pharaoh, since we are told that it is he who said to his people that the Israelites were too numerous and too mighty. In Josephus' version (*Ant.* 2.205), on the other hand, the blame is placed upon one of the Pharaoh's sacred scribes who predicts to the king that there would be born to the Israelites one who would surpass all others in virtue and who would win everlasting renown and who would abase the sovereignty of the Egyptians. In view of this remark the reader is not likely to censure the king who, we are told (*Ant.* 2.206), was alarmed (δείσας, "was afraid") and who, consequently, as we are reminded, on this sage's advice (rather than on his own initiative), ordered all male children to be drowned in the river. Moreover, we are told, it was the Egyptians (rather than Pharaoh) who were stimulated by the advice of this scribe to exterminate the Israelites.

In addition, Josephus' Pharaoh is portrayed as less cruel than his biblical counterpart, inasmuch as in the Bible (Exodus 1:15) we read that he gave orders to the Hebrew midwives to put the male children to death, whereas Josephus (*Ant.* 2.206) specifically says that the orders were given to Egyptian midwives and explains that Pharaoh proceeded in this way because he realized that women who were his compatriots were not likely to transgress his will. If Pharaoh enforces his decree by declaring (*Ant.* 2.207) that those mothers who ventured stealthily to save their offspring are to be put to death along with their babes the reader might feel at least some understanding for such a measure in view of the importance of obedience to the law, just as the reader of Sophocles' *Antigone* must identify to some degree with Creon's position, inasmuch as non-obedience to the law, even if one feels the law to be unjust or immoral, is an invitation to something even worse, namely anarchy. Even if this Pharaoh, as we shall see, lacks self-control in his personal behavior and in this respect is subject to censure, he, *qua* ruler, must be obeyed.

But we see a very human side to Pharaoh, and consequently have much more sympathy for him, in Josephus' depiction (*Ant.* 2.232-33), unparalleled in the biblical text (Exodus 2:10), of Pharaoh's affectionate clasping (προσστερνισάμενος) of the infant Moses when Pharaoh's daughter presents him to him. Furthermore, when Moses playfully tears off the king's crown and flings it to the ground (*Ant.* 2.233), the sacred scribe who had predicted that a child's birth would lead to the abasement of the Egyptian empire rushes forward to kill Moses, warning the king of the danger to him if he allows this child to live. At this point we are told not only that the king's daughter, who was raising Moses, snatched him away to safety but that the king himself delayed to slay him out of a hesitation induced by G-d. The fact of such hesitation, even if induced by G-d, would clearly redound to the Pharaoh's credit in the eyes of Josephus' readers.

Josephus introduces an episode (*Ant.* 2.238-53), completely unparalleled in the Bible, in which Pharaoh chooses Moses as general to halt an invasion of Egypt by the much feared Ethiopians. That Pharaoh should have chosen an Israelite[9] for such a difficult and crucial task is clearly complimentary to Pharaoh and shows that he is clearly not prejudiced against the Israelites. Moreover, lest the reader think that Pharaoh is deliberately choosing Moses in order to bring about his death in battle, Pharaoh, we are told (*Ant.* 2.242), swore to do him no injury and reproached those knavish priests who had urged him to put Moses to death as an enemy.[10]

The scenes in which Moses and Aaron approach Pharaoh asking him to allow the Israelites to leave Egypt certainly offered Josephus opportunities to condemn Pharaoh. And yet, we find him evidencing rather a certain amount of understanding for Pharaoh's situation, since, we are told in an extra-biblical addition (*Ant.* 2.281), he had only recently been promoted to the throne. One might be reminded of the similar understanding that one might well feel for Zeus in Aeschylus' *Prometheus Bound* (312), where, we are told, he, too, is new to the throne and so presumably should be given a greater opportunity to establish his rule more firmly.

---

[9] That Pharaoh is aware that Moses is an Israelite is clear from Josephus' statement (*Ant.* 2.241) that when the Egyptians had recourse to oracles and divinations, they were told "to take the Hebrew for their ally." The fact that the Egyptians hoped to do away with Moses by guile through entrusting him with this extremely dangerous mission is a further indication that they were aware of Moses' origin.

[10] In this reassurance to Moses Josephus' Pharaoh is be contrasted with the portrait in Artapanus (*ap.* Eusebius, *Pr. Ev.* 9.27.7), who says that Pharaoh became jealous and sought to kill Moses, finding an opportunity to do so by naming Moses to the extremely dangerous position of commander in the war against the Ethiopians. When the war is over Pharaoh welcomes him back in words but plots against him in deed (*ap.* Eusebius, *Pr. Ev.* 9.27.11-13).

When Moses asks Pharaoh to allow the Israelites to leave, Josephus (*Ant.* 2.284) rather plausibly explains Pharaoh's angry reaction by having him charge that Moses "had once escaped from servitude in Egypt and had now effected his return by fraud and was trying to impose on him by juggleries and magic."

One of the most difficult problems in theodicy is how to explain that, on the one hand, G-d hardens Pharaoh's heart so as not to allow the Israelites to leave and, on the other hand, punishes him for refusing to allow them to go. In Josephus' version (e.g., *Ant.* 2.288) the problem is avoided, since there is no mention at all of the hardening of Pharaoh's heart; rather, we hear that Pharaoh is indignant that Moses should have thought that he could have influenced Pharaoh by the cunning and craft of his magical act with his staff.

Moreover, Josephus evokes a certain sympathy for Pharaoh's position, inasmuch as he depicts him (*Ant* 2.295) as perplexed (ἀμηχανήσας) and apprehensive (δείσας) for the Egyptians; it is his concern for his people that leads him to permit the Israelites to depart after the plague of the water turned to blood. Again, after the plague of lice, it is fear of the destruction of his people, according to Josephus' addition (*Ant.* 2.301), that induces Pharaoh to listen to reason (σωφρονεῖν). Even when, after the plague of the blood, Pharaoh is termed stubborn in refusing to allow the Israelites to leave Egypt, Josephus (*Ant.* 2.296) carefully remarks that Pharaoh was no longer (οὐκέτι) willing to be wise (σωφρονεῖν, "to be moderate," "temperate," "reasonable"), the implication being that he had previously exercised such wisdom and moderation. When, finally, Pharaoh does allow the Israelites to depart he is motivated by fear (*Ant.* 2.290) rather than by wisdom (φρονήσει, "intelligence," "sagacity," "understanding," "prudence").

To be sure, when Pharaoh, after the plague of the lice, decides to listen to reason and to allow the Israelites to leave, Josephus (*Ant.* 2.301) remarks that in his depravity he did so only in half measure; but, we may remark, while the word here translated as "depravity," φαυλότητος, may mean "poorness," "want of accomplishments or skill," or "lack of judgment," it may also be used in a good sense of plainness and simplicity of life. In any case, it is surely significant that Josephus does not here use any of the available words for wickedness, whether κακία or πονηρία or κακουργία or πανουργία in reference to Pharaoh's motivation. Moreover, realizing that Pharaoh's confessions of guilt after the plague of the hail (Exodus 9:27-30) and the plague of the locusts (Exodus 10:16) were insincere and thus would certainly not redound to his credit, Josephus omits them completely. If, finally, Pharaoh is punished, it is not because his heart was hardened (Exodus 8:19) but rather because, in Josephus' phraseology (*Ant.* 2.302) that would certainly have appealed to the Stoics in his audience, he exasperated G-d in thinking to impose upon His providence (πρόνοιαν), "as though it were Moses and not He who was punishing Egypt on the Hebrews' behalf."

Again, after the plague of the boils, in place of the troublesome statement (Exodus 9:12), which seems to indict G-d, that the L-rd hardened the heart of Pharaoh, Josephus' presentation clearly ascribes the fault to Pharaoh, in that he fails to become temperate (σωφρονιζομένου, "come to reason," "come to one's senses"). It is only after many plagues that Pharaoh loses reason (*Ant.* 2.307) and his sense for his own interest and becomes motivated by malice and knavery, the cause of this being ultimately his impiety, in accord with which he was matching himself against G-d as a deliberate traitor to the cause of virtue. Finally, however, in an addition to the Bible (Exodus 12:30), whereas previously Pharaoh had failed to listen to his servants (Exodus 10:7), he (*Ant.* 2.313) does listen to his people and returns to his senses and orders the Israelites to depart. And when Pharaoh decides to pursue the Israelites it is because he is mortified at the thought that it was the jugglery (γοητείαν, "magic," "wizardry," "deceit") of Moses that had brought about their departure (*Ant.* 2.320). If we may judge from Apuleius' *Metamorphoses*, such alleged wizardry would have aroused considerable sympathy for its victim, Pharaoh. In any case, whereas in the Bible (Exodus 14:5) both Pharaoh and his servants have a change of heart after the Israelites leave Egypt and whereas (Exodus 14:8) it is specifically Pharaoh whose heart is hardened and who takes the initiative to pursue the Israelites, in Josephus (*Ant.* 2.320) it is the Egyptians alone who repent of having let the Israelites leave and who resolve to set out after them.[11]

---

[11] We find a similar shift of blame from Pharaoh to the Egyptians regarding who takes the initiative in pursuing the Israelites in Pseudo-Philo's *Biblical Antiquities* (10.2, 10.6), which so often parallels Josephus. See my "Prolegomenon"(1971), lviii-lxvi.

6. Summary

Unlike Philo and, on the whole, the rabbinic tradition, Josephus, in order not to offend his non-Jewish readers, goes to great lengths in an effort to rehabilitate such non-Jewish leaders as Balaam, Cyrus, Belshazzar, and Nebuchadnezzar. As the leader of a nation, Pharaoh, for Josephus, deserves to be obeyed, except when he fails to show self-control, as in the incident with Sarai; and, indeed, once he discovers the truth about Sarai's relationship to Abram he apologizes and avers that he had intended to contract a legitimate marriage contract with Sarai, and he shows his sincerity by giving abundant gifts to Abram after this discovery when he has nothing to gain thereby.

Moreover, Josephus' Pharaoh is a much warmer personality in his appreciation of Joseph, particularly as we see in his explanation of the name Zaphenath-Paneah that he gives to Joseph. Moreover, Pharaoh is more magnanimous toward Joseph's brothers in permitting them to continue in their occupation as shepherds.

Unlike the rabbis and in accordance with the obvious meaning of the biblical text (Exodus 1:8), Josephus is careful to differentiate between the Pharaoh of Joseph's time and that of the exodus period, thereby clearly indicating that one should not generalize about all pharaohs. He puts the blame for the oppression of the Israelites not on Pharaoh personally but on the Egyptian people, who are depicted as a voluptuous and lazy people who are envious of the Israelites' prosperity.

As to the decree to put all male babies to death, the blame is transferred from Pharaoh to one of the Egyptian sacred scribes. Moreover, unlike the Bible, where Pharaoh gives orders to Hebrew midwives to carry out the grisly task of putting these babies to death, Josephus' Pharaoh is less cruel in entrusting this task to Egyptian midwives. Likewise, we see a very human side to Pharaoh in the fact that he affectionately clasps the baby Moses when he is presented to him by his daughter. Furthermore, Pharaoh shows that he is not prejudiced against Israelites in that he chooses Moses to lead a campaign against the dreaded Ethiopians.

In the extended negotiations between Moses and Pharaoh the reader is more likely to feel some understanding for the latter inasmuch as we are told that he had only recently been promoted to the throne. Josephus avoids the key problem of how G-d can harden Pharaoh's heart and yet proceed to punish him by omitting all mention of the hardening of Pharaoh's heart. Finally, Pharaoh's actions are explained as arising out of his concern for the welfare of his Egyptian subjects.

While it is true that Josephus' extra-biblical additions are often based on clues in the Bible itself and while it is likewise true that some of the changes are introduced lest his Greek and Roman readers find the account incredible, many of the additions, modifications, and omissions are motivated by apologetic concerns.[12]

---

[12] I am most grateful to Professor Jonathan A. Goldstein for a number of very helpful suggestions in connection with this essay.

CHAPTER SIX

KORAH

1. Introduction

It would seem that Josephus' motto in his recasting of the biblical narrative is, as it were, "De nobis fabula narratur." His version highlights those aspects that he believes are most applicable to his own day and, in particular, to his own career. In the first place, Josephus, as a proud priest, whose very first point in his autobiography (*Life* 1-2) is to stress his descent from the first of the twenty-four courses of the priests, emphasizes the dreadful consequences for those who rebel against the priests or who seek to diminish their power, as we may see in his portraits of Jeroboam and Ezra. Secondly, his portrait of Joseph, for example, focuses on the jealousy which his brothers felt toward him, just as in his own life Josephus felt that he had been the object of jealousy by John of Gischala and others. Finally, his portrait of Jeroboam, for example, underscores the dreadful political consequences of rebellion, with the clear implication that similar consequences occurred as a result of the revolution against Rome in his own day.

That Josephus regarded the Korah episode as an object lesson to teach all of the above lessons may be seen from an examination of his version, especially when we note the tremendous amount of space that he gives to this episode. For Korah the ratio of Josephus (*Ant.* 4.11-56: 198 lines) to the Hebrew text (Numbers 16:1-35: 58 lines) is 3.41, and the ratio of Josephus to the Septuagint version (75 lines) is 2.64. Thus Josephus devotes relatively more space to this episode than to almost any other, with the exception of Zedekiah (7.45) and the pericopes of Joseph and Potiphar's wife (5.45) and the final test of Joseph's brothers ending with Judah's speech before Joseph (4.09). We may suggest that one reason for his doing so, in addition to the inherent dramatic potential of the confrontation between two great leaders, is his desire to build up the central personality of the Bible, Moses, whose stature rises to even greater heights due to his overcoming so mighty an adversary. But, in addition, as we have suggested above, Josephus seeks to stress the themes of the importance of the priesthood, the dangers of jealousy, and the consequences of political rebellion. Attridge suggests that one of the reasons for the elaboration of the pericope is its suitability for exemplifying the theological message of the work (Attridge 1976, 96); but, as we shall see, it is not so much the theological as the political import of the revolt that Josephus stresses. And yet, despite its clear importance for Josephus no study has yet been attempted of his portrait of Korah.[1]

2. *The Treatment of Korah by Philo and Pseudo-Philo*

We may see a marked contrast between the attention which Josephus gives to Korah as compared with the relative neglect of Korah in Philo's works (he is mentioned by name only once, *De Fuga et Inventione* 26.145), presumably because Philo was not a priest and had no direct ties to the Temple; secondly, because he personally was apparently not subjected to jealousy on the part of his fellow-countrymen; and thirdly, because in Philo's day the revolutionaries against Rome were not yet on the verge of serious revolt.

Philo stresses three points in his discussion of Korah's rebellion (*De Vita Mosis* 2.50.277-78). In the first place, he attacks the pride which the Levites felt because they were superior in numbers to the priests; this reminds us of a frequent theme in Greek mythology, seen, for example, in the punishment inflicted upon Niobe for boasting, of ὕβρις ("overweening pride") leading to νέμεσις ("retribution"). Second, he stresses the dreadful consequences of the chaos which occurs when subjects attack their rulers and thus confound the order of the commonwealth. Third, while it is true that Philo's Levites, as in Josephus' account, challenge the selection of Aaron as high priest, it is not on account of nepotism that they attack Moses; rather, they challenge Moses' statement that he had acted under divine direction in choosing his brother as high priest. It is this last point that Philo emphasizes most of all, since his chief concern is theological, and the Levites' objection challenges the very concept of divine revelation. For Philo the contest is between G-d and Korah's impiety (*De Vita Mosis* 2.50.279), be-

---

[1] There have, of course, been a number of studies of Josephus' portrait of Moses, but these mention the Korah episode only in passing. See Feldman 1984, 149-63, 908-9.

tween belief and disbelief (*De Vita Mosis* 2.50.280). The issue, in other words, is theological rather than a political contest between two views of government; and more than a personal contest between Moses and Korah is at stake. The speed of the punishment is said to attest to the truth of G-d's pronouncements (*De Vita Mosis* 2.50.284); and the fundamental parts of the universe itself, namely heaven and earth, chastise Korah's impiety (*De Vita Mosis* 2.50.285), appropriately enough by the earth swallowing up his adherents and by the heaven raining down fire upon them (*De Vita Mosis* 2.50.286-87).

Again, when Philo deals with Korah's rebellion in his essay *De Praemiis et Poenis* (13.74) he uses this episode to preach a philosophic sermon on the consequences of unreasonable (ἀλόγου) pride (φρονήματος, "presumption," "arrogance," "ambition"). We find a similar moral in Philo's essay *De Fuga et Inventione* (26.145), where he stresses that the Levites, by aiming to become kings instead of gate-keepers and thus to overthrow the established order of things, not only failed to attain their goal but even lost that which they already had. Indeed, he concludes by affirming that those who are enamored of things too great for their nature will be convicted of foolishness, "since every effort beyond our strength breaks down through over-violent straining" (*De Fuga et Inventione* 26.146). Again, the revolt is viewed in theological terms as an attack on the divine choice of the priesthood (*De Praemiis et Poenis* 13.75). While it is true that in this passage the masses accuse Moses of nepotism in selecting his brother Aaron to be high priest, Moses, according to Philo, was not greatly aggrieved at this charge; rather, what disturbed him, and presumably Philo himself, most was that they should challenge the divine origin of his appointment of Aaron (*De Praemiis et Poenis* 13.78).

Likewise, Philo, in his essay *De Fuga et Inventione* (26.145), emphasizes the philosophic point that Korah had aimed to overthrow order (τάξιν), "the most beautiful thing in human life," rather than the political point that Korah had sought to overthrow Moses' commonwealth.

Pseudo-Philo (*Bib. Ant.* 16.1), like the rabbis, ascribes the rebellion to Korah's objection against the Torah; for both Pseudo-Philo and the rabbis the law, according to Korah, is unbearable (*insufferibilis*), and in both cases a specific law such as Korah cites is that concerning the fringes (Numbers 15:37-39), though Pseudo-

Philo does not have Korah assert that that law is illogical. Again, as with the rabbis, Pseudo-Philo (16.3) seeks to emphasize the gravity of Korah's sin by stating that Korah will not be resurrected at the final judgment but will be annihilated.

3. *Korah in the Rabbinic Tradition*

The rabbinic tradition, like Josephus, builds up the figure of Korah as the mightiest adversary that Moses encountered during the sojourn in the wilderness after the exodus from Egypt. One of the seven qualities which the rabbinic sages enumerated as most appropriate for the righteous person, as we have noted, is wealth (*'Avot* 6:8). Indeed, one of the four rabbinic prerequisites for prophecy is wealth (*Nedarim* 38a); and Moses, the greatest of the prophets (Deuteronomy 34:10), is specifically said there to have acquired his great wealth from the chips of the tablets (which were fetched from a diamond quarry) given to him by G-d.

Like Josephus (*Ant.* 4.14), the rabbis stress the immensity of Korah's wealth as well. Indeed, according to the tradition preserved by Rabbi Ḥama bar Ḥanina, of the three treasures hidden by Joseph in Egypt one was revealed to Korah, one was revealed to the Roman emperor Antoninus the son of Severus, and the third is stored up for the righteous for the future time, presumably the time when the dead will be resurrected (*Pesaḥim* 119a, *Sanhedrin* 110a). Indeed, so great was Korah's wealth, according to the above passage, that, recalls Rabbi Levi, the mere keys of Korah's treasurehouse required three hundred mules to transport them, though all the keys and locks were made of leather.[2]

Like Josephus (*Ant.* 4.14), the rabbinic tradition stresses Korah's ability as a speaker, as it does that of Moses (see Feldman 1992-93, 11-12). The weight of this tradition is indicated by the fact that the rabbis derive it from the biblical word *vayiqaḥ* ("took") in the phrase introducing the Korah pericope (Numbers 16:1, "And

---

[2] For the numerous other references to Korah's wealth see Rappaport (1930, 124, n. 172), who cites the following: Jerusalem *Sanhedrin* 10.1.50a, *Exodus Rabbah* 31.3, *Leviticus Rabbah* 5.3, *Ecclesiastes Rabbah* 5.12, *Esther Rabbah* 7.4, *Tanḥuma Mishpaṭim* 8, *Tanḥuma Matot* 5, *Pirqe de-Rabbi Eliezer* 50, *Midrash Panim Aḥerim* 1, *Aggadat Esther* 56 (ed. Buber, p. 25), *Midrash Proverbs* 11.27, and *Midrash Al-Jithallal* (Jellinek, 6.107). To these Ginzberg (1928, 6:99, n. 560) adds *Numbers Rabbah* 18.13 and 22.7 and *Tanḥuma B* 4.160.

Korah took"), which seems to have nothing to do with Korah's powers of speech. Nevertheless, the rabbis explain the word to indicate that Korah convinced the Israelites with flattering words so that all the great men of Israel, including even the leaders of the Sanhedrin, allowed themselves to be persuaded (*Numbers Rabbah* 16:1, *Tanḥuma Korah* 1 [ed. Buber, 2]).

That Korah possessed the power to foresee the future appears from the rabbinic tradition that his self-confidence in challenging Moses was due to his foreknowledge that one of his descendants, the prophet Samuel, would be equal in greatness to Moses and Aaron together (Psalms 99:6) and that twenty-four of his descendants would compose psalms and sing them in the Temple (*Numbers Rabbah* 18.8); hence he felt assured that G-d would not allow the forefather of such a great prophet and such great and holy singers to perish. What he failed to realize was that his descendants would repent of their father's rebellion against Moses (*Numbers Rabbah* 18.2 and 18.8; *Tanḥuma B* 4.85 and 89).

As for Korah's followers, the rabbinic tradition states that they were the most distinguished men of the community, indeed famed throughout the whole world (*Sanhedrin* 10a). In an era in which the ability to fix the calendar and to know when to intercalate months was prized as a mark of the greatest wisdom, these adherents are here described as skilled in intercalation and in fixing the new moon. In fact, the midrashic tradition, basing itself on an interpretation of the phrase 'anshei-shem ("men of renown," literally "men of name," which is taken to mean "men skilled in the use of the Name [of G-d]"), goes so far as to assert that they even knew the correct pronunciation of the Tetragrammaton and possessed enormous power, so much so that Moses himself was afraid of them, inasmuch as he realized that he was thus unable to use the Name against them (*Shu'aib*, Numbers 16:2).

Also, like Josephus, the rabbinic tradition stresses as a motive for the revolt Korah's desire for the high priesthood (*Tanḥuma Pequdei* [ed. Buber, 1]). In particular, as in Josephus' version, Korah is jealous that Aaron, rather than he, was chosen for this position (*Numbers Rabbah* 18.4, *Tanḥuma B* 4.86-8, *Tanḥuma Korah* 3). Korah is likewise described as jealous that Moses had bypassed him and had instead appointed his cousin Elizaphan ben Uzziel as chief of the Levite division of the Kohathites (*Numbers Rabbah* 18.2).

The main point stressed by the rabbinic tradition concerning Korah is his attack upon the Torah itself and his attempt to disprove its divine origin. Thus, to illustrate how unfair and unlivable the Torah is, Korah tells the masses a story of a poor widow who was forbidden by the Torah to plow with an ox and ass together (Deuteronomy 22:10), then forbidden to sow with diverse seeds (Leviticus 19:19), then required to give first fruits (Deuteronomy 26:2), then required to leave gleanings and corners of the field for the poor (Leviticus 23:22), then required to give portions of grain to the priests and Levites (Numbers 18:8, 21), then required to give firstlings of sheep to the priests (Numbers 18:15), then required to give initial shearings of sheep to the priests (Deuteronomy 18:4), and then required to give to the priests portions of the slaughter of sheep (Deuteronomy 18:3). When she then, in exasperation, consecrated the flesh to the L-rd (Numbers 18:14) she had to give all the meat to the priests (*Midrash Psalms* 1.15).

In another attempt to reduce the Torah to absurdity Korah is represented as asking Moses whether those who are dressed in garments of *tekelet* are obliged to attach fringes to them. When Moses replies in the affirmative Korah exclaims that since the requirement is to wear fringes of *tekelet*, surely it makes no sense to require such fringes when the whole garment is of *tekelet* (Jerusalem Talmud, *Sanhedrin* 10.1.27d-28a). Similarly, he asks whether it is necessary to have a *mezuzah* at the entrance of a house full of sacred scrolls. Again, when Moses replies in the affirmative, Korah argues that inasmuch as the scrolls contain the passage found in the *mezuzah* such a requirement made no sense. Finally, realizing that Korah was contending that the Torah was not of divine origin and thus that the integrity of the Torah itself was at stake, Moses perceived that he had to call upon G-d to teach the rebels a lesson (Jerusalem Talmud, *Sanhedrin* 10.1.28a). Indeed, that the main point of Korah's rebellion was his attack on the truth of the Torah and of divine revelation may be seen from the fact that as Korah and his followers are slowly and painfully being swallowed up by the earth they continue to make their confession, "Moses is truth and his Torah is truth" (Jerusalem Targum on Numbers 16:22-34, *Tanḥuma B* 4.97, *Likkutim* 1.23b, *Beit Hamidrash* [Jellinek, 6.108]). To emphasize the point even more we are told that these words were audible throughout the entire camp, so that the people might be convinced of the wickedness of Korah's undertaking. Indeed, in order to impress the people even more, one rabbinic tradition states that Korah was one of those who were both swallowed up by the earth and burnt (*Sanhedrin* 110a, *Numbers Rabbah* 18.19, *Tanḥuma B* 4.93, *Sifre Numbers* 117).

Moreover, even this terrible double form of death was not sufficient to atone for the sins of Korah and his followers, since we hear that they are tormented in Hell and that at the end of thirty days they are cast up near to the surface of the earth only to swallowed up again (*Baba Batra* 74a, *Sanhedrin* 110a-b).[3] Here, too, the rabbinic tradition emphasizes that the main point of Korah's rebellion was his attack on the validity of revelation, since we are told that whoever on the day when they are cast back up to the earth puts his ear to the ground will hear their cry, "Moses is truth and his Torah is truth, but we are liars." Finally, even though all Israel have a portion in the world to come, the congregation of Korah, according to the view of Rabbi Akiva (Mishnah *Sanhedrin* 10:3) and of the rabbis generally (*Sanhedrin* 109b), is condemned to eternal damnation (Mishnah *Sanhedrin* 10:1).

The rabbis further denigrate Korah's reputation by representing him as slandering Moses' character by suspecting him of adultery with a married woman, so that every man warned his wife (based on Psalms 106:16) on Moses' account (*Sanhedrin* 110a).

4. *The Qualities of Josephus' Korah*

By building up the personality of Korah Josephus no doubt was simultaneously aggrandizing the character of the leader, Moses, whom he dared to oppose; and to build up Moses was crucial for Josephus, inasmuch as a nation was known primarily from the character of its founder (see Feldman 1993a, 233-87). In particular, Josephus begins his account by adding two remarks about Korah which are not found in the biblical narrative, namely that he was one of the most eminent of the Hebrews by reason both of his birth and of his wealth. While it is true that the Bible itself begins its account of Korah by giving the names of his father, grandfather, and great-grandfather (Numbers 16:1), it does not

---

[3] Also Jerusalem *Sanhedrin* 10.1.29c, Mishnah *Sanhedrin* 10:3, Tosefta *Sanhedrin* 13.89, *Tanḥuma B* 4.94, *Numbers Rabbah* 18.13, Jerusalem Targum Numbers 16:34, and *Midrash Samuel* 5.61-62.

actually say that Korah's ancestry was distinguished. Josephus, on the other hand, specifically starts off by stating that Korah was one of the most eminent of the Hebrews precisely by reason of his birth (*Ant.* 4.14). Again, while the reader of the Bible might readily recognize the relationship of Korah to Moses, since Amram, the father of Moses, and Izhar, the father of Korah, were brothers, the biblical text does not actually mention the exact relationship between them, whereas Josephus makes a point of clearly stating that Korah was of the same tribe as Moses and was his kinsman (*Ant.* 4.14). Korah himself, in his harangue to his fellow Levites, asserts that by birth he is of the same rank as Moses (being his first cousin) and hence as well qualified as Aaron and his sons for the priesthood (*Ant.* 4.19).

Wealth, which, as we have noted, is regarded in the rabbinic tradition as one of the prerequesites for a prophet, is ascribed by them to Korah in huge measure; Josephus, too, stresses Korah's possession of it. In the first place, when he introduces Korah he himself remarks that Korah was one of the most eminent of the Hebrews by reason of his riches and then adds that Korah was aggrieved at the thought that he did not have superior rank, though he had a greater right to enjoy the highest honors since he was richer than Moses without being his inferior in birth. In addition to these first two references to Korah's wealth, the pericope mentions his wealth on three other occasions (*Ant.* 4.19, 25, 26). Indeed, in the last of these passages Moses readily acknowledges that Korah surpasses both himself and Aaron in the magnitude of his possessions.

One of the four qualities of the ideal statesman, as we see in the speech which Thucydides (2.60.6) ascribes to Pericles, is, as we have stressed, the ability to present one's policy clearly and convincingly before the people. It is therefore significant that when Josephus introduces the figure of Korah one of the first points that he makes about him is his ability as a capable speaker (ἱκανὸς... εἰπεῖν), one most persuasive in addressing a crowd (δήμοις ὁμιλεῖν πιθανώτατος) (*Ant.* 4.14). This makes him a formidable opponent of Moses, inasmuch as this is a quality which Josephus has ascribed to Moses himself (*Ant.* 3.13: πλήθεσιν ὁμιλεῖν πιθανώτατος, "most persuasive in addressing a crowd"; *Ant.* 4.328: πλήθεσιν ὁμιλῆσαι κεχαρισμένος, "most agreeable in addressing a crowd"). Indeed, in the pericope about Korah this trait is specifically attributed to

Moses; when he responds to Korah's harangue he is described as gifted in addressing a crowd (πλήθεσιν ὁμιλεῖν) (*Ant.* 4.25).

That, however, the power of persuasion may be used for negative ends may be seen from the fact, noted by Mason, that in the three places where Thucydides, whom Josephus admired so much, uses the term πιθανώτατος ("most persuasive"), he does so with the indirect object "the people" (τῷ δήμῳ, 3.36.6), "the masses" (τῷ πλήθει, 4.21.3), and "the multitude" (τοῖς πολλοῖς, 6.35.2) (so Mason 1991, 300).[4] It is significant that in the first two of these citations the person who is "most persuasive" is none other than the arch-demagogue Cleon, for whom Thucydides had such contempt. The fact that Josephus says of the Emperor Gaius Caligula, whom he, of course, despised, that he knew how to reply impromptu to speeches which others had composed by long preparation and to show himself instantly more persuasive (πιθανώτερος) on the subject than anyone else, even when the greatest matters were debated (*Ant.* 19.208), is another indication that for Josephus to ascribe this trait to someone is not necessarily a compliment. Indeed, just as Korah represents the use of the power of persuasion for negative ends, so also Josephus' most formidable opponent, John of Gischala, is described as more persuasive (πιθανώτερος) than anyone else in disclosing to the enemy the plans of the high priest Ananus (*War* 4.212). Likewise, the leader of the Zealots, Eleazar, is described as most persuasive (πιθανώτατος) (*War* 4.225). Indeed, Josephus, in a moralizing comment, warns the reader not to think that the things that are said to flatter us or please us are more convincing (πιθανώτερα) than the truth (*Ant.* 8.418).

The Greeks never ceased to stress the importance of the virtue of moderation. It is precisely because of Korah's lack of moderation (σωφροσύνης) that Moses asks G-d to punish Korah by a most unusual method, namely through engulfing him and his followers in an earthquake (*Ant.* 4.49).

---

[4] Mason notes that the Pharisees are likewise described by Josephus as most persuasive (πιθανώτατοι) among the masses (δήμοις) (*Ant.* 18.15) and convincingly suggests that this hardly implies Josephus' approval of their popularity.

5. *Josephus on Korah's Rebellion as an Attack on the Priesthood*

When Moore remarks that Josephus is a somewhat disappointing source for the religion of his times and had little interest in religion for its own sake, what he is referring to is the fact that Josephus tells us less about religious beliefs and theological issues than we might expect (Moore 1927, 1:210). Surely, Josephus had a tremendous interest in religion; but the point to be made is that for him the central focus of the Jewish religion was the Temple and the priesthood of which he was such a proud member that this is the very first point that he makes in his autobiography, namely his proud status as a priest of the first of the twenty-four orders of priests (*Life* 1).

Schwartz has noted in Josephus a number of pro-priestly revisions of both the legal and narrative portions of the Bible (S. Schwartz 1990, 88-90). In particular, we may note that Josephus states that the priests alone rather than the Levites were permitted to carry the ark (*Ant.* 3.136, 4.304); that the king may do nothing without consulting the high priest and the Gerousia (*Ant.* 4.224); that Moses consigned the holy books to the priests alone (*Ant.* 4.304); and that Moses gave equal portions to the priests and the Levites from the booty taken from the Midianites (*Ant.* 4.164), whereas the Bible states that Moses assigned to the Levites ten times as much as he gave to the priests (Numbers 31:27-30).

As a priest Josephus is particularly sensitive to the attempt of the Levites to usurp the status of the priests (Numbers 16:10). In his version of Korah's revolt Josephus may well be thinking of the incident, during the procuratorship of Albinus (62-64 C.E.), in which those Levites who were singers of hymns succeeded in persuading King Agrippa II to convene the Sanhedrin and to secure permission for them to wear linen robes like the priests (*Ant.* 20.216-18). This, says Josephus, was contrary to the ancestral laws, and he ominously declares that such transgression was bound to make the Jews liable to punishment, presumably by G-d himself (*Ant.* 20.218).[5]

---

[5] On the background of this dispute see Feldman 1965, 9:504-5, n. b; Vogelstein 1889; and Meyer 1938, 721-28, especially 727.

6. The Rebellion as Motivated by Jealousy

In the Bible Korah's revolt is not motivated by jealousy of Aaron's high priesthood as such; rather, Korah claims, the method by which he was chosen to be high priest was undemocratic. Josephus adds considerable drama to the episode by ascribing the revolt to Korah's jealousy in that he regarded himself as having superior claims to the position (*Ant.* 4.19) and merely made a pretense of concern for the public welfare (*Ant.* 4.20). But the truth is that, at least on the surface, it would appear that Korah did have a point in charging Moses with nepotism in choosing his own brother for the second most important position of leadership, namely that of high priest. Josephus would seem here to be following the lead of Hecataeus (*ap.* Diodorus 40.3.4), who, in answering this implied charge of nepotism, pays Moses the supreme compliment of saying that he chose men of utmost refinement and of the greatest potential ability to head the nation as priests.[6]

7. The Political Aspects of the Rebellion

For Josephus Korah's rebellion is not so much theological or philosophical as it is political and military,[7] as we can see from his use of the word στάσις ("sedition") in his first mention of it (*Ant.* 4.12), as well as from his reference to the people who were swayed by Korah as an army (*Ant.* 4.21). Indeed, the fact that Josephus, in the brief pericope of Korah (*Ant.* 4.11-56), uses the word στάσις four times (*Ant.* 4.12, 13, 32, and 36) and the verb στασιάζω ("to revolt") twice (*Ant.* 4.13, 30) underscores the political aspect of this passage. The analogy which Josephus draws is with large armies, which become ungovernable when they encounter reverses (*Ant.* 4.11). It is a truism, according to Josephus, that under the stress of

---

[6] In this crucial decision of selecting proper priests, Moses parallels the founder of Rome, Romulus, as we see in Dionysius of Halicarnassus (*Rom. Ant.* 2.21). The importance of the appointment of proper priests may likewise be seen in the fact that, according to Livy (1.20.1), the first act of Numa Pompilius, Romulus' successor, after fixing the calendar, was his appointment of priests.

[7] Similarly, in his account of the conflict between Midian and Israel, Josephus emphasizes the political and military point of view, in contrast, for example, to Pseudo-Philo, who, as a moralist, emphasizes (particularly in 18.10) the tragic elements in the narrative. See Van Unnik 1974, 244-45.

want (ἀπορίας) and calamity (συμφορᾶς) people become enraged with each other and with their leader (*ibid.*). Josephus here has in mind a similar scene in one of his favorite authors, Thucydides (2.65.2-3), where he depicts the attitude of the fickle Athenian mob toward Pericles after the plague had afflicted them. That Josephus is here thinking also of the parallel in Thucydides (3.82-84), where he describes στάσις in Corcyra, seems clear, especially since Josephus specifically states that this was a sedition for which we know no parallel, whether among Greeks or barbarians (*Ant.* 4.12). We recall that in his prooemium to the *Antiquities* Josephus declares that he intends in his work to embrace not only the entire ancient history of the Jews but also their political constitution (διάταξιν τοῦ πολιτεύματος) (1.5). It is under this rubric of politics and, in particular, of political revolution, that he discusses the rebellion of Korah.

Moses makes it clear, in his address to the assembly, that, in view of Korah's complaint about the choice of Aaron as high priest, his and Aaron's chief aim was to avoid dissension (στασιάζοντας), and this despite the fact that Aaron held his office by the decision of G-d, as ratified by the good will of the people (*Ant.* 4.30). To Josephus the worst political behavior is that of people trooping to the assembly (ἐκκλησίαν) in disorderly wise (ἀκόσμως), with tumult (θορύβου, "turmoil," "confusion," "unrest," disorder") and uproar (ταραχῆς, "confusion," "unrest," "disturbance," "tumult," "upheaval," "disorder"), the terms θόρυβος and ταραχή being clearly synonymous and intended to emphasize the tumult (*Ant.* 4.22). Moses appeals to the people to cease from their sedition (στάσεως) and turbulence (ταραχῆς) (*Ant.* 4.32). Korah, on the other hand, is portrayed as a typical demagogue who, as such, wishes to make it appear by his words that he is concerned with the public welfare (τοῦ κοινοῦ) (*Ant.* 4.20, λέγων), whereas, in reality (ἔργῳ) he is but scheming to have the dignity of leadership transferred by the people from Moses to himself. In his demagoguery he is highly reminiscent of Cleon and Alcibiades in Thucydides' narrative, as well as of the sophists in Plato's parable of the ship (*Republic* 6.488-89). Likewise, the behavior of the Israelite masses, with their innate delight in decrying those in authority and with their opinion swayed by what anyone said (*Ant.* 4.37), recalls that of the masses of the Athenians who vent their disappointment and anger upon Pericles (Thucydides 2.65).

It is this turbulence (ταραχή) which Korah arouses and which we find referred to no fewer than four times in this brief passage describing the excitement and disorderly conduct of the people (*Ant.* 4.22, 32, 35, 36). The synonymous term, θόρυβος, and its corresponding verb, θορυβέω ("to be noisy," "to be in ferment"), and adjective, θορυβώδης ("rebellious," "restless," "tumultuous"), appear three times in the passage (*Ant.* 4.22, 37, 36). Such disorderliness brings about obliteration of the ordered beauty (κόσμος) of the constitution. Indeed, so deeply ingrained is this disorderliness and this seditious tendency that even after the rebels are swallowed up by the earth the sedition continues (*Ant.* 4.59) and, in fact, to a far greater degree and more grievously than before.

Significantly, in the Bible (Numbers 16:3) Korah's appeal to the people is cast in theological terms and as an appeal to egalitarianism, that is, that all the congregation are holy and that, consequently, Moses and Aaron have no right to lift themselves up above the rest. The central point at issue between Moses and Korah is "Who is holy?" On the one hand, Korah (Numbers 16:3) insists that everyone is equally holy (*qedoshim*); on the other hand, Moses (Numbers 16:5) replies that G-d will make known who is holy (*haqadosh*).

Josephus transposes the issue from the religious to the political plane; and the word ὅσιος ("holy") does not appear in this pericope. In Josephus Korah attacks Moses on legal grounds, that is, that he had given the priesthood to Aaron in defiance of the laws (*Ant.* 4.15), and on political grounds, namely, that Moses had acted in despotic fashion (τυράννων ... τρόπῳ) on his own initiative and without getting the approval of the popular assembly (*Ant.* 4.16). The multitude, clearly influenced in their thinking by Korah, portray themselves as favoring a meritocracy and a democracy: G-d, they say, if indeed it was He who chose Aaron to be high priest, should have selected the person most deserving of this office and should have committed the choice to the people for confirmation rather than to that person's brother (*Ant.* 4.23). Moses is accused of scheming by wicked artifice to attain power and of failing to consult the people for their approval (*Ant.* 4.17). While it is true that Moses invites the rebels to await the issue of the sacred ceremony (ἱερουργίαν), for Josephus the issue is a political one, to be determined by an election (*Ant.* 4.37); hence, Moses' proposal that Korah leave the judgment to G-d, by awaiting the casting of his ballot (ψηφοφορίαν) (*Ant.* 4.33). The language of a poltical election is continued in the next paragraph, where Moses makes his proposal: "Whosoever sacrifice G-d shall judge to be most acceptable, he shall be your elected priest" (*Ant.* 4.34). The word here used for "elected," κεχειροτονήσεται, literally means to stretch out one's hand for the purpose of giving one's vote in the assembly. Indeed, the rival claimants for the priesthood agree to act as candidates for election, with the understanding that he whose sacrifice should be received with most favor by G-d shall be declared elected (*Ant.* 4.54), where again the word for "elected" is the same verb, κεχειροτονημένος. Finally, when Aaron is confirmed in his high priesthood by the budding of his rod alone, this decision is formulated in political terms, namely that G-d had elected (χειροτονήσαντος, *Ant.* 4.66) him.

To be sure, Josephus does introduce the theme that the Korah episode proves that all is directed by Divine providence (προνοίᾳ) (*Ant.* 4.47-48); but that Josephus' aim in introducing this concept is not primarily theological but philosophical and aims to please his Roman audience, composed largely of Stoics and Epicureans, is suggested by the phrase that follows immediately thereafter, namely that the incident proves that nothing happens fortuitously (αὐτομάτως).[8] This terminology clearly reflects the Stoic conception of providence (πρόνοια) and is intended as an attack on the Epicurean notion that the world runs by its own movement (αὐτομάτως). This is the same contrast that is found in his account of Daniel, where Josephus devotes no fewer than five paragraphs to showing in detail how mistaken the Epicureans are in stating that the world runs by its own movement (αὐτομάτως) (*Ant.* 10.277-81).

8. *"Improvements" in the Story: Clarifications, Increased Drama*

Josephus in his version, tries to avoid apparent contradictions in his biblical source. One such seeming contradiction concerns the manner in which Korah and his company died. On the one hand,

---

[8] A similar contrast may be found in Josephus' discussion as to whether the miracle of the crossing of the Sea of Reeds was due to Divine providence or to accident (*Ant.* 2.347-49). There Josephus leaves the decision to the discretion of the reader (*Ant.* 2.348).

the biblical text states that the earth opened its mouth and swallowed up all the men that belonged to Korah (Numbers 16:32). Three verses later, however, we are told that fire came forth from the L-rd and consumed the 250 men who had offered incense (Numbers 16:35), presumably the 250 followers of Korah (Numbers 16:2). Josephus neatly resolves the problem by asserting that the earth swallowed up Korah's associate, Dathan, and the latter's followers (*Ant.* 4.51-53), whereas Korah's company was consumed by fire (*Ant.* 4.54-56).[9]

Another "improvement" made by Josephus in his reworking of the biblical narrative is his avoidance of undue exaggeration and the grotesque such as might provoke the ridicule of a later satirist such as Lucian. One such instance is the miraculous scene in which the earth is described as opening her mouth and swallowing up Korah and his followers (Numbers 16:31-32). In Josephus' version the event is more plausibly presented as an earthquake ("a tremor moved over the surface as when a wave is tossed by the violence of the wind") (*Ant.* 4.51); and, in fact, it is Moses himself who suggests to G-d this method of punishing Korah (*Ant.* 4.48). Likewise, whereas in the Bible we are told nothing about the fire that suddenly consumed the 250 followers of Korah other than that it came forth from the L-rd (Numbers 16:35), Josephus, well aware that his readers might find this item hard to believe, disarms them by telling them that the like of this fire had never, in the record of history, been produced by the hand of man (*Ant.* 4.55). And lest the reader question whether perhaps this fire might have been caused by being emitted from the earth by a subterranean current of heat or whether it might have broken out spontaneously in the woods from the violence of wind and mutual attrition, Josephus shows, by mentioning these alternative explanations, that he was aware of them, while likewise stating specifically that these were not the factors that produced the fire, which was rather such a flame as might be kindled at the bidding of G-d.

---

[9] Rabbinic tradition, bound by adherence to the biblical text, generally asserts that Korah was swallowed up by the earth. The only rabbinic text that explicitly states that Korah and his company were consumed by fire is *Ve-Hizhir* on *Beshallaḥ* (ed. Freimann, p. 21b), as noted by Rappaport, 124-25. The Talmud (*Sanhedrin* 110a) cites the view of Rabbi Joḥanan that Korah was neither among those who were swallowed up nor those who were burnt, as well as the view of the anonymous Tanna that Korah was one of those who were both swallowed up and burnt.

Josephus also tries to increase the dramatic interest of the biblical narrative. Indeed, the scene, from beginning to end, is much more dramatic in Josephus. In the first place, whereas the 250 men in the Bible are described simply as well-known men (*'anshei-shem*) (Numbers 16:2), Josephus depicts them as being held in high esteem by the people alike for the merits of their ancestors and for their own, in which they even surpassed their own ancestors (*Ant.* 4.54). Secondly, not only is the speech of Korah expanded from fourteen words in the Hebrew (nineteen in the Septuagint, Numbers 16:3) to 194 words (*Ant.* 4.15-19), but its rhetoric becomes considerably more violent. The strongest language in the Hebrew is *rav lakem* ("you assume too much"); in the Greek of the Septuagint this is even milder: ἐχέτω ὑμῖν ("let it be [enough] for you"). In Josephus Korah paints a picture of Moses hunting (θηρώμενον) around to create glory for himself, as if hunting for prey; he further describes his doing so in very strong language as δεινόν ("terrible," "dreadful," shocking," "horrible," "monstrous"). He accuses Moses of behaving maliciously (κακουργοῦντα). To the Romans, with their great tradition of respect for the laws, the charge that Moses had acted in defiance of the laws would be especially effective, as would the accusation that he had acted in despotic fashion. Likewise, the Romans, who felt so strongly about honorable dealings and who looked with such disdain upon *fides Punica*, would certainly have understood Korah's charge, upon which Josephus dwells at such length, that Moses had committed an outrage clandestinely, so that the victims were unaware of the plot (*Ant.* 4.16). Korah then appeals to the people's sense of fairness, noting that his qualifications of age and wealth for the priesthood were superior to those of Aaron in terms of age and wealth. The tone of Korah's address is set by the frequency in it of such words as "to use force" (βιάζεσθαι), "clandestine" (λεληθότως), "to outrage" (ἐξυβρίζειν), "scheme" (τέχνῃ), "behave maliciously" (κακουργοῦσι), and "undetected" (λανθάνειν). The impression of scheming malice left by Korah's words is continued in Josephus' own editorial comments that follow: ἐπραγματεύετο ("he was scheming"), κακοήθως ("maliciously," "malevolently," "insidiously"), and διαβολαῖς ("calumnies") (*Ant.* 4.20).

Adding to the drama is Josephus' portrayal – completely absent in the biblical text – of the multitude's reaction to Korah. In Josephus' version the multitude is described as excited (ἀνηρέθιστο, "was irritated," "was provoked") and actually bent on stoning Moses (*Ant.* 4. 22). They troop to the assembly, as we have noted above, in disorderly fashion (ἀκόσμως), with tumult and uproar (θορύβου καὶ ταραχῆς). They shout, "Pursue the tyrant!" Whereas in the Bible Moses replies briefly in a mere 97 words (137 in the Septuagint) stating his proposal that Korah and his company and Aaron take censers and that G-d will choose who should be high priest (Numbers 16:5-11), in Josephus' version Moses, in a much more elaborate speech of no less than 401 words, now fearlessly takes control of the situation and dramatically addresses not a word to the multitude but, turning instead to Korah, very honestly and cogently argues that if the choice of high priest had been up to him he would have chosen himself (*Ant.* 4.25-34). He thereupon makes the magnanimous proposal, unparalleled in the biblical text, that Aaron will now lay down the high priesthood as an open prize and will make no claim on the ground of previous selection (*Ant.* 4.29). He then uses strong language in stating that it would be out of place (ἄτοπον, "absurd," "perverse") for Korah to deprive G-d of the power of deciding to whom He should accord the high priesthood (*Ant.* 4.32). The fickle masses, as in Thucydides' portrait of the Athenians vis-à-vis Pericles (2.65), at first cease from their turbulence and their suspicions of Moses (*Ant.* 4.35) but on the following day become tumultuous once again, delighting in decrying those in authority and being swayed by whatever anyone said (*Ant.* 4.37). At this point in the biblical text Moses addresses G-d in a single sentence of fourteen words (fifteen in the Septuagint) asking Him not to accept the offering of the rebels and protesting that he himself has taken nothing from the people (Numbers 16:15). Again, this is much elaborated and dramatized in Josephus' version of no fewer than 522 words, where Moses, in effect, presents a poignant *apologia pro vita sua*, recounting all the benefits that G-d had bestowed upon the Israelites, and asking that G-d remove the rebels in no common manner, namely through an earthquake (*Ant.* 4.40-50).

In particular, the scene depicting the death of Korah and his host is made more dramatic. In the Bible we are told that each of Korah's 250 followers took his censer, put fire and incense in it, and stood at the entrance of the tent of meeting together with Moses and Aaron (Numbers 16:18). Then, as Moses finishes speaking (Numbers 16:31), the earth swallows Korah and his followers

(Numbers 16:32), while fire consumes the 250 men (Numbers 16:35). Whereas the Bible speaks of the earth as swallowing up Dathan, Abiram, and Korah and their company (Numbers 16:31-34), and states that fire consumed the 250 men who had offered the incense (Numbers 16:35), Josephus, as we have noted, distinguishes the earthquake which engulfed Dathan and Abiram and their company (*Ant.* 4.51-53) from the fire which consumed Korah and his company (*Ant.* 4. 54-56). Josephus likewise gives a more graphic picture of the earthquake, comparing the tremor to a wave tossed by the violence of a wind (*Ant.* 4.51). The reader of the biblical narrative is able to visualize the earthquake; but Josephus lets us hear it as well, noting the crash and the burst of booming sound (*Ant.* 4.51). Moreover, whereas the Bible mentions only that the earth swallowed up the rebels together with their households (Numbers 16:32), Josephus adds further graphic details: they were obliterated so swiftly that some were even unaware of their fate; in addition, the ground that had opened up for them closed again so completely that the onlookers could see no indication of what had happened (*Ant.* 4.52). Moreover, most remarkably, the kinsfolk of the victims actually rejoiced over the terrible fate of those who had perished so miserably, inasmuch as they felt that the rebels had suffered deservedly (*Ant.* 4.53).

As to the fire which consumed Korah's company, the biblical narrative tells us only the bare fact that a fire came forth from G-d and consumed the 250 adherents of Korah (Numbers 16:35). Josephus builds up a truly dramatic scene (*Ant.* 4.54-56). The 250 men assemble; then Aaron and Korah advance; there follows the spectacle of the whole company burning incense in front of the tabernacle. Suddenly the fire blazes forth. Josephus then adds, as we have noted, that a fire such as this had never prevously been made by the hand of man nor was ever ejected from the earth through a subterranean current of heat, nor spontaneously broke out in the woods due to strong winds and violent attrition (*Ant.* 4.55). One guesses that mention of the latter two parallels is Josephus' way of suggesting the possibility of a "scientific" explanation for this apparent miracle. The blaze, we are told, darted (ἄξαντος, "leaped") upon the victims, and they were consumed so completely that all trace of their bodies disappeared. Indeed, as Thackeray has remarked, Josephus' description is based on and, in fact, is intended to outdo that of the Plataean bonfire as described by Thucydides

(2.77) (Thackeray 1930, 4:503, note e, on *Ant.* 4.55). His description also contains an implied allusion to the eruption of Mount Vesuvius in the year 79, which Josephus mentions elsewhere (*Ant.* 20.144) and which is described so graphically by Josephus' younger contemporary, Pliny the Younger (6.16).

9. *Summary*

That Josephus intended his portrait of Korah to serve as an object lesson for his readers is clear from the tremendous amount of space that he gives to this pericope. In contrast to Philo, Pseudo-Philo, and the rabbinic tradition, whose chief concern is theological in stressing the fact that Korah challenged the concept of divine revelation and the reasonableness of the Torah, Josephus builds up the character of Korah by stressing his genealogy and wealth (and thus, at the same time, aggrandizes the stature of Moses, his great opponent). The fact that Korah is a most effective speaker in addressing crowds again makes him Moses' counterpart; but this same quality also serves to associate him with the demagogues whom Thucydides and Plato denounce.

As a proud priest Josephus is particularly sensitive to the attempt of a Levite such a Korah to usurp the privileges of the priests, an issue which was very much alive in Josephus' own day. The revolt is further presented by Josephus as an object lesson in the terrible effects of jealousy, a theme that appears so frequently throughout Josephus' works. In particular, Korah's jealousy of Moses is paralleled in Josephus' own life by that of his archrival, John of Gischala, toward him. Above all, the rebellion highlights the terrible consequences of sedition, another theme that pervades Josephus' works, especially under the influence of his experiences in the revolt against the Romans. Whereas Korah in the Bible bases his appeal on theological and egalitarian grounds, Josephus' Korah focuses on political and legal issues.

Finally, here as elsewhere in his "rewritten Bible," Josephus has cleared up ambiguities, such as the apparent contradiction as to whether Korah was swallowed up by the earth or consumed by fire. He has heightened the dramatic element, especially by his graphic description of the earthquake and the fire that enveloped the rebels.

CHAPTER SEVEN

BALAAM

1. *Introduction*

That the story of Balaam[1] was of great interest to Josephus may be deduced from the extraordinary amount of space that he gives to this narrative (*Ant.* 4.102-58). Thus, whereas the Hebrew (Numbers 22:2-25:9) has 164 lines and the Septuagint 261 lines, Josephus' version has 363 lines.[2] This gives a ratio of 2.21 for Josephus as compared with the Hebrew and 1.39 for Josephus as compared with the Septuagint. For the episode of the Israelite men and the

---

[1] Of studies thus far concerning Josephus' version of the Balaam pericope, Baskin (1983, 96-99) very briefly summarizes Josephus' account with a view particularly to comparing it with the rabbinic tradition. She concludes that the portrait of Balaam in Josephus is relatively tame in comparison with the rabbinic depiction but gives few details. Even the otherwise exhaustive (526 pages) treatment by Rouillard (1985) of the three chapters of Numbers on the Balaam episode has only a few scattered and extremely brief references to Josephus' account. Varneda (1986, 227-29) provides little more than a brief paraphrase of Josephus' narrative. Greene (1989, 57-106) is concerned primarily with an analysis of the biblical text about Balaam; in particular, he attempts to show that Balaam was a figure utilized by various warring groups of priests and prophets against each other's ideal self-concept and type-concept, but he has very little to say specifically about Josephus' version. The only full-scale treatment of Josephus' interpretation of the Balaam episode is by Moscovitz (1979), done under my direction. This excellent study, however, hardly exhausts the topic, and, in particular, only intermittently takes into account the relationship between Josephus' treatment of Balaam and his handling of other biblical figures.

[2] As evidence that Josephus used a Hebrew text (probably in addition to a Greek text) for his account of Balaam we may note that whereas the Hebrew text states that one of the animals sacrificed by Balak and Balaam was a bullock (Numbers 23:2), the Septuagint speaks of it as a calf, and Josephus, like the Hebrew text, identifies the animals as bullocks (*Ant.* 4.113). Again, in the Hebrew, as well as in the Aramaic Targumim, Balak and Balaam offer a bullock and a ram on every altar, whereas according to the Septuagint (and Philo, *De Vita Mosis* 1.50.277), Balak alone sacrificed the bullock; and according to Josephus it was Balaam alone who offered the sacrifice (*Ant.* 4.113). (On this latter point we may perhaps suggest that Josephus considered it logical for Balaam to do the sacrificing, inasmuch as it was he who would be uttering the curse and who required divine approval.) Likewise, we see from Josephus' paraphrase of Numbers 24:4 and 16 that he used a Hebrew text, inasmuch as he speaks of Balaam "falling upon his face," rendering *nofel*, "falling down" (*Ant.* 4.125), whereas the Septuagint reads "he saw in his sleep" (εἶδεν ἐν ὕπνῳ).

Midianite women (Numbers 25:1-9) the ratio of Josephus' 176 lines (*Ant.* 4.131-58) to the Hebrew text of 15 lines is no less than 11.73 (9.26 as compared with the Septuagint).[3] The fact that Josephus mentions Balaam once again after the conclusion of the episode with the Midianite women (*Ant.* 4.158) and says that "on this narrative readers are free to think what they please" shows that he regarded the whole account as a single narrative.

There are several reasons for Josephus' interest in the figure of Balaam. In the first place, Josephus is very much concerned with the phenomenon of prophecy, since he regarded himself as having a special gift for prediction, like his biblical namesake Joseph, one which he displays in foretelling that Vespasian will become emperor (*War* 3.400-2). Moreover, Josephus in his youth spent considerable time with the Essenes (*Life* 10), who from youth were particularly well versed in the prophetic books (*War* 2.159) and who, indeed, had a special gift for prediction themselves. Similarly, the Pharisees, with whom Josephus eventually allied himself (*Life* 12) after experimenting with the three sects of Jews, were said to have a special gift of foreknowledge (πρόγνωσιν, *Ant.* 17.43), as we see evidenced in the predictions of Pollio the Pharisee (*Ant.* 17.4) and his disciple Samaias (*Ant.* 14.174-75). Furthermore, Josephus the historian saw an integral relationship between history and prophecy (see Feldman 1990, 397-400), inasmuch as, in defending the accuracy of the biblical narrative, he declares that only the prophets had the privilege of recording the history of the Jewish people, and that the accuracy and consistency of their records are guaranteed by the fact that they were divinely inspired (*Ag. Ap.* 1.37). Finally, the biblical prophets had some standing even among pagans, if we may judge from their popularity with the second century philosophers, such as Numenius of Apamea, the Pythagorean, who, according to Origen (*Against Celsus* 4.51), quoted not only Moses but also other prophets in many passages in his writings.

In general, in his portraits of biblical figures Josephus focuses upon their personalities and aggrandizes their qualities of character. Balaam, however, is different in that he was a non-Jew and, at least according to a *prima facie* reading of the biblical text, a wicked

---

[3] The ratio of Josephus' 187 lines (*Ant.* 4.102-30) to the Balaam story proper of 149 lines (Numbers 22:2-24:25) (that is, without including the narrative of the Midianite women) is 1.26; the ratio to the Septuagint's 242 lines is .77.

figure at that. Josephus was thus clearly confronted with a dilemma here: if he showed too much regard for Balaam, he would be giving credence to a pagan prophet who had sought to curse Israel; on the other hand, if he downgraded Balaam, he would betray his prejudice against non-Jewish wise men. Nevertheless, as we shall see, Josephus gives a relatively unbiased portrayal of Balaam,[4] especially when it is compared with Philo,[5] with the rabbinic tradition,[6] with the New Testament,[7] or with the Jewish Scriptures them-

---

[4] Vermes (1973, 174) remarks that Josephus plays down Balaam's wickedness slightly by imputing all of Balaam's wrongdoing to his desire to please Balak; apart from this specific slant, he shows the same general bias toward Balaam that is exhibited in the rest of the Palestinian tradition and in the New Testament. It is our argument that Josephus' positive changes are much more substantial. Interestingly, the portrayal by Pseudo-Philo (*Bib. Ant.* 18.3) is even more favorable to Balaam than is Josephus, as Baskin (1983, 99) has noted. Origen (*PG* 12.683D) is surprisingly even-handed, blaming him for inspiring idolatry and immorality but praising him when the word of G-d is placed in his mouth. See Braverman (1974, 41-50). The chief reason, however, why Balaam is viewed more positively in patristic literature is that he was regarded as prophesying the coming of Jesus.

[5] Philo (*De Cherubim* 10.32, *De Confusione Linguarum* 31.159, and *De Migratione Abrahami* 20.113) portrays Balaam as foolish and vain. *Quod Deterius Potiori Insidiari Solet* 20.71 presents him as an empty sophist, a conglomerate of incompatible and discordant notions. *Quod D-us Immutabilis Sit* 37.181, *De Confusione Linguarum* 31.159, and *De Mutatione Nominum* 37.202 depict him as a dealer in the vanity of unfounded conjecture and as the very antithesis of true prophecy. *De Vita Mosis* 1.48.263-300, offers an extremely unfavorable picture of Balaam, charging him, in particular, with avarice.

[6] To be sure, the rabbis (*Sifre Deuteronomy* 357.2, ed. Finkelstein, 430), commenting on the verse that there has not arisen a prophet in Israel equal to Moses (Deuteronomy 34:10), assert that among the nations, such a prophet did arise, namely Balaam. In fact, the rabbis were ready to grant (*ibid.*) that in some respects Balaam was actually superior to Moses; that is, Moses did not know who spoke with him, whereas Balaam did know; moreover, Moses did not know when G-d would speak with him until he was actually addressed by G-d, whereas Balaam knew in advance (*Sifre Deuteronomy* 357.2). The reason, say the rabbis, why G-d raised Balaam to such heights was so that the Gentiles would not be able to say that if they had had a prophet of the stature of Moses they would have accepted the Torah (*Seder Eliyahu Rabbah* 26, ed. Freedman, p. 142). Indeed, an anonymous rabbinic tradition regarded the Balaam episode as so important that it singles it out as a separate book distinct from the rest of the Torah, with its statement that Moses wrote his own book and the portion of Balaam (*Baba Batra* 14b). But even those rabbinic passages which acknowledge his greatness as a prophet denigrate Balaam for his greed, envy, immorality, and bestiality (cf. *Sanhedrin* 105a, where he is said to have committed bestiality with his ass) and depict him as subject to all four of the modes of capital punishment (*Sanhedrin* 106b). He is known as Balaam the Wicked (*Sanhedrin* 105b) and, indeed, is looked upon as the very epitome of wickedness because of his skill in being able to gauge the exact moment when G-d becomes angry (*Sanhedrin* 106b). He is, thus, worse than any of those who are

selves.[8] Most significantly, however, he shifts the focus from Balaam's personality to the historical, political, and military confrontation between the Israelites and their enemies in his time. Indeed, to a considerable degree, the Balaam episode, as described by Josephus, functions as a prologue to the war against the Midianites. Furthermore, Josephus employs the prophecies of Balaam to present, in a veiled form to be sure, his own vision of the future of the Jewish people.

2. *Balaam the Soothsayer*

Clearly, Josephus was confronted with a dilemma when he came to classify Balaam. On the one hand, if he knew the rabbinic tradition, as there is good reason to think that he did, he would be aware of the high regard in which that tradition held Balaam as a

---

denied a portion in the world to come (Mishnah, *Sanhedrin* 10:2). His greatest wickedness consisted of his seeking to strike at the very heart of the Israelite religion by cursing them that they should have no synagogues or schools (*Sanhedrin* 105b). Indeed, he is identified as one of Pharaoh's counsellors who advised him to cast into the Nile River the new-born male children of the Israelites (*Sanhedrin* 106a). The Mishnah berates him for his evil eye, his haughty spirit, and his proud soul (*'Avot* 5:19). Though he was at first an interpreter of dreams and then a prophet, he sank to the level of sorcerer (*Tanḥuma B* 4.134). There are even those who find a veiled reference to Jesus in the passage which states that a *min* (heretic) asked Rabbi Ḥanina how old Balaam was, whereupon he replied that since, according to the Psalm (55:24), "Bloody and deceitful men shall not live out half their days," it follows that Balaam was 33 or 34 years (since a normal lifetime is seventy years), whereupon the *min* stated that he had seen Balaam's Chronicle in which he read that Balaam the lame was 33 years old when Phinehas the Robber put him to death (*Sanhedrin* 106b). The theory, however, that Balaam is Jesus, that the Chronicle is the Gospel, and that Phinehas is Pilate has been generally rejected. See, for example, Ginzberg (1928, 6:123-24, n. 722) and Klausner (1925, 32-35).

[7] Cf., e.g. 2 Peter 2:15: "Forsaking the right way, they [the heretics] have gone astray; they have followed the way of Balaam, the son of Beor, who loved gain from wrongdoing, but was rebuked for his own transgression; a dumb ass spoke with human voice and restrained the prophet's madness." The same theme of Balaam's unholy search for gain is to be found in Jude 1:11: "Woe to them [i.e. false teachers], for they walk in the way of Cain and abandon themselves for the sake of gain to Balaam's error." Finally, in the seer's vision of Jesus in Revelation 2:14 there is a bitter reference to Balaam as the one who inspired the Israelites to perform the cardinal sins of idolatry and immorality.

[8] When Balaam appears after the scene in Numbers 22-24 in which he is the central figure, he is depicted in negative tones. Thus in Deuteronomy 23:5 we read that G-d would not listen to Balaam but, instead, turned his curse into a blessing. Almost exactly the same statement is found in Joshua 24:10 and in Nehemiah 13:2.

prophet. Moreover, the fact that Balaam is cited, with virtually no introduction, in an extra-biblical text discovered in 1967 indicates that the name of Balaam was well known to the pagan people to whom the inscription in question (apparently dating from the eighth century B.C.E.) was addressed, so that we may infer that Balaam's prophetic status was a tradition of long standing (see Hackett 1980). On the other hand, Josephus was surely also aware of portrayals of Balaam as the epitome of wickedness. Against this background, it is only to be expected that Josephus will distinguish carefully, in his terminology, between pagan and Jewish prophets and even between the classical prophets and those latter-day prognosticators such as himself. The Septuagint, we may note, reserves the term προφήτης[9] for those who reveal the Divine will, while using the word μάντις and its cognates when referring to heathen soothsayers.[10] The prophet declares nothing which comes from himself. Josephus, in general, seems to maintain the classical distinction between μάντις and προφήτης, namely that the former has foresight and knowledge of future events, as Cicero (*De Diviniatione* 1.1) puts it (hence this role can continue after the cessation of prophecy, which occurred during the reign of Artaxerxes, according to *Ag. Ap.* 1.41), whereas the task of the προφήτης is to be the voice of G-d and to declare the knowledge of G-d to those who come for advice (see Krämer 1976, 6:790). The role of the prophet is that of a mediator, serving both as G-d's spokesman to man and vice versa. It is not until the second century C.E., under Christian influence, that the term προφήτης came to denote one who foretells the future (see Krämer 1976, 795). The μάντις was not an inspired prophet but a craftsman (δημιουργός), associated with leeches and carpenters in Homer (*Odyssey*, 17.384) (see Rose 1914, 796).

To be sure, Josephus never applies the word προφήτης to Balaam or, for that matter, to himself. Instead, he uses the terms μάντις, μαντεία, μαντεῖον, and μαντεύομαι with reference to pa-

---

[9] Rendtorff (1976, 6:812) remarks that in the Septuagint *navi* is always translated by προφήτης. Προφήτης is also the translation in a few instances for *ro'eh* (1 Chronicles 26:28, 2 Chronicles 16:7, 10) and *ḥozeh* (2 Chronicles 19:2, 29:30, 35:15).

[10] One reason perhaps why Josephus avoids using the term μάντις for biblical prophets is that the word is associated with the words μαίνομαι, "to be mad," and μανία, "madness."

gan prophecies (particularly those derived from dreams), for example, of the Egyptian seers (*Ant.* 2.241; *Ag. Ap.* 1.236, 256, 257, 258 [2], 267, 306), Balaam (*Ant.* 4.104 [2], 112, 157), the Witch of Endor (*Ant.* 6.330, 331, 338), the Babylonian soothsayers (*Ant.* 10.195), a seer in Alexander the Great's army (*Ag. Ap.* 1.203, 204), the Emperor Tiberius (*Ant.* 18.217, 223), the Delphic Oracle (*Ag. Ap.* 2.162), and soothsayers in general (*Ant.* 6.327, 331, 17.345; *War* 2.112).[11] Indeed, in this respect Josephus diminishes the stature of Balaam by stating that he was the best μάντις of his day (τῶν τότε), the implication being that he was not the best diviner of all time (the Bible does not explicitly designate him as either a prophet or a seer of any kind).[12]

And yet, Josephus, like Pseudo-Philo (*Bib. Ant.* 18.10), gives Balaam added importance to Balaam by having him offer the sac-

---

[11] In this respect Josephus parallels pagan usage, which restricted the use of the term προφήτης to a religious sphere, where it designates one who speaks in the name of a god (as in the etymology from πρό + φημί) declaring the divine will and counsel in the oracle. Historical seers and prophets who are not recipients of the oracles – the biblical parallel would be those acting without G-d's direction – are called not προφῆται but χρησμολόγοι or the like. But since Josephus wishes, on the whole, to restrict his use of the word προφήτης to those who qualify as prophets according to the Bible, he also applies these terms (μάντις, etc.) to Jews, notably Judas the Essene (*War* 1.79; *Ant.* 13.312, 313) and even himself (*War* 4.625). As we can see from the fact that he uses the term μαντεῖον with reference to the Delphic Oracle (*Ag. Ap.* 2.162), Josephus here departs from classical usage (see Fontenrose 1970, 887), which reserved the term προφήτης for one attached to an established oracular shrine, and employed the term μάντις for an unattached seer; perhaps his purpose is to stress that the μάντις merely predicts the future and is not a spokesman for the divine.

[12] Philo likewise avoids calling him a prophet and instead refers to his widespread fame for soothsaying (μαντείᾳ) (*De Vita Mosis* 1.48.264). Pseudo-Philo (*Bib. Ant.* 18.2) likewise refrains from calling Balaam a prophet and instead refers to him as an interpreter of dreams (*interpretem somniorum*). For Origen there is a question whether Balaam was or was not a prophet (*Commentary on John* 28.12 [*PG* 14.707]). Finally, he concludes that Balaam was not a prophet, inasmuch as his prophecies were involuntary and shortlived and inasmuch as he is referred to in the Septuagint not as a prophet but as a soothsayer (μάντις). Yet, just as he is not consistent and precise in his terminology for slavery (see Gibbs and Feldman 1985-86, 281-310) or in his use of terms for "city" or "village," so here, though he avoids the term in reference to Balaam, Josephus does use the word "prophet" for an Egyptian prophet (*Ag. Ap.* 1.312), for Cleodemus-Malchus the historian (*Ant.* 1.240), and the prophets of Baal opposed by Elijah (*Ant.* 8.339). Josephus also uses the word μαντεία in referring to predictions by Jews who were not prophets, such as Jotham (*Ant.* 5.253), the diviners banished by King Saul (*Ant.* 6.327), Judas the Essene (*War* 1.80; *Ant.* 13.312), the anonymous critics of Herod (*Ant.* 17.121), the diviners skilled in interpreting dreams who were sent for by the ethnarch Archelaus (*Ant.* 17.345), and Josephus himself (*War* 4.625).

rifice before he prophesies (*Ant.* 4.113); in contrast, in the Hebrew text Balaam and Balak offer the sacrifice jointly (Numbers 23:2),[13] while in the Septuagint and in Philo (*De Vita Mosis* 1.50.277) it is Balak who does so. In the same line, Josephus avoids blaming Balaam by declaring, in an addition to the biblical text (Numbers 23:4), that Balaam realized that his prophecy was governed by inflexible Fate (*Ant.* 4.113).

Again, the fact that Josephus usually abbreviates biblical poetry and presents it in indirect discourse, whereas in the case of Balaam he actually gives it added emphasis by combining his three biblical discourses into a single long, powerful prophecy, and by retaining the direct discourse of the original, serves to highlight the figure of Balaam as a gentile prophet.

3. *Other Positive Qualities of Balaam*

There was almost no quality more deeply appreciated in antiquity than hospitality. Hence, the reader will form a distinctly positive picture of Balaam by virtue of the hospitality which he shows in Josephus' additions to the biblical account. Thus, whereas the latter simply asserts that Balaam told Balak's envoys to remain overnight (Numbers 22:8), Josephus elaborates that Balaam received them in friendly fashion (φιλοφρόνως, "lovingly," "cordially," affectionately," "benevolently," "kindly," "politely," "joyfully," "gladly" – the same word which is used with regard to the hospitality shown by David [*Ant.* 7.30]) and with hospitality (ξενίᾳ) (*Ant.* 4.105). Josephus then adds that Balaam, the gracious host, gave them supper.

The portrait of Balaam is likewise made more positive by Josephus' addition to Balak's rebuke of Balaam after the latter had praised the Israelites. Whereas the Bible says, very simply, that Balak told Balaam neither to denounce them nor to bless them (Numbers 23:25), Josephus expands considerably and dramatically by describing Balak's fuming (δυσχεραίνοντος, "feeling displeasure," "being indignant," "being annoyed," "being angry," " being dismayed," "being vexed," "being distressed," "being troubled") at Balaam and his accusing him of transgressing the agreement according to which he (Balak) had obtained his services (*Ant.* 4.118).

---

[13] So also Targum Onkelos and Targum Pseudo-Jonathan on Numbers 23:2.

4. Apologetics

a. Refutation of the Charge that Jews Hate Non-Jews

The biblical Balaam narrative was a real challenge for Josephus, inasmuch as Balaam was a non-Jew, and Josephus is constantly aware of the charge that Jews are guilty of hating non-Jews. Indeed, we find in Balaam's words in the Bible (Numbers 23:9) the statement that the Israelites are a people that shall dwell alone and shall not be reckoned among the nations. Significantly, in his version of this passage, Josephus, clearly aware of the above, avoids presenting the Israelites as sundered off from all other peoples and instead words the statement in terms of the *excellence* of the Israelites as compared with other peoples, and has Balaam assert that G-d has lavished upon the Israelites the means whereby they may become the *happiest* of all peoples (*Ant.* 4.114). No one could object to such a prophecy of the Israelites' happiness; the objection, which Josephus carefully avoids mentioning, would be to their cutting themselves off from other peoples.

Indeed, in the course of Josephus' version of the Balaam narrative he has the Midianite women, when they successfully persuade the Israelite youths to give up their way of life, remark that the Israelites have customs and a way of life wholly alien (ἀλλοτριώτατα, "belonging to another," "different," "not comparable," "hostile") to all mankind, "inasmuch as your food is of a peculiar sort (ἰδιοτρόπους) and your drink is distinct from that of other men" (*Ant.* 4.137) – remarks echoing those frequently found in Graeco-Roman pagan writers, as we have noted.

Another indication of Josephus' desire to avoid attacking the religious institutions of non-Jews may be seen in his complete omission of the fact that it was to the high places of the pagan god Baal that Balak took Balaam in order to inspect the Israelites (Numbers 22:41 vs. *Ant.* 4.112).

It is particularly effective, in terms of Josephus' overall apologetic goals on behalf of the Jews, to have a non-Jew praise them. Whereas Balaam in the Bible declares that G-d has not beheld any wrong or perverseness in the Israelites (Numbers 23:21), Josephus has him go one step further in positively pronouncing them, on his own authority, the most blessed of men (*Ant.* 4.118).

It is likewise extremely effective to have Balaam, in an extra-biblical remark, state that the Israelites will never be overwhelmed by utter destruction, since Divine providence is watching over them (*Ant.* 4.127-28). It surely would have been a source of great consolation to Josephus' Jewish readers to read that a non-Jewish seer had predicted that the misfortunes that the Israelites will encounter will be slight and momentary, and that thereafter they will flourish once more (*Ant.* 4.128).

b. *Jews Do Not Hate the Romans*

Again, Josephus does not hesitate to have Balaam prophesy that the Israelites will occupy the land to which G-d has sent them and that the whole earth will be filled with their fame (*Ant.* 4.115). If Balaam foretells the calamities that will befall kings and cities of the highest celebrity (some of which, he says, have not yet been established) (*Ant.* 4.125), he is careful to keep this prophecy cryptic enough so that Gentile readers will not necessarily recognize this as referring to Rome, just as he has a similarly cryptic prophecy in connection with the interpretation of Nebuchadnezzar's dream in his pericope of Daniel (*Ant.* 10.210).

Of course, inasmuch as Josephus, especially in his paraphrases of the prophets, is highly selective, he might have simply omitted this prediction by Balaam, as he does with the passage foretelling a messianic kingdom which would destroy all previous kingdoms and which itself would last forever (Daniel 2:44), as well as the later passage in Daniel, which makes it clear that the fifth, worldwide, and everlasting empire would be ruled by a people of "saints of the Most High," that is the Jews (7:18) – a passage which would, to the obvious embarrassment of Josephus as spokesman for the Romans, imply the ultimate overthrow of Rome. The fact that he does not, on the other hand, omit the interpretation of Nebuchadnezzar's dream or the above prophecy of Balaam is an indication of Josephus' deliberate ambiguity reflective of his attempt to reach both of his audiences, the non-Jews and the Jews, the latter with these allusions to an apparently messianic kingdom which will make an end of the Roman Empire. Perhaps he felt that to omit them altogether would have been taken by Jewish readers as a clear indication that he had sold out to the Romans. In fact, Klausner goes so far as to argue that Josephus' trip to Rome in 64, despite his statements in the *War* that Rome's ascendancy was part of a Divine plan, may have actually increased his support for the cause of the revolutionaries, inasmuch as he must have been impressed by the evidence of Rome's decadence and realized that it was only a matter of time before Rome would fall (Klausner 1949, 5:167-68); hence, the passages in *Antiquities* 4.125 and 10.210 may be a clue to his real feelings.[14] In the passage (Numbers 24:17-18) corresponding to *Antiquities* 4.125, however, what Balaam predicts is that a star out of Jacob and a scepter out of Israel will conquer Edom and Seir. That this is intended as an eschatological prophecy is clear from Balaam's earlier statement that he will advise Balak what the Israelites would do to the Moabites at the end of days (Numbers 24:14). That a Messianic prophecy is likewise intended seems to be hinted at in the Septuagint's version of Numbers 24:7: "There shall come a man out of his [i.e. Israel's] seed, and he shall rule over many nations; and the kingdom of Gog shall be exalted, and his kingdom shall be increased." In any case, the passage was interpreted messianically shortly after the time of Josephus in reference to Bar Kochba (Jerusalem *Ta'anit* 69d) by Rabbi Akiva. Of course, such a messianic understanding was avoided by Josephus because of his subservience to the Romans.[15]

In the same line, Josephus is eager to avoid giving the impression that the Israelites are out to destroy their enemies mercilessly (*Ant.* 4.125), as is suggested by the biblical passage in which Balaam predicts that the G-d of Israel will "eat up the nations that are His adversaries and break their bones in pieces" (Numbers 24:8). In Josephus' much milder version we are informed merely that Balaam foretold what calamities were in store for the opponents of the Israelites without spelling out precisely what those would be (Ant. 4.125).[16]

---

[14] Moscovitz (1979, 27) suggests that it is very likely that Balaam's prophecy here is that famous "ambiguous oracle" mentioned by Josephus, which Josephus thus left in total obscurity (*War* 6.314). We may counter, however, that this seems unlikely, inasmuch as Josephus says that some of the events prophesied by Balaam had already befallen men in bygone ages, whereas the "ambiguous prophecy" was one that had yet to come to pass (*Ant.* 4.125).

[15] Josephus likewise omits all reference to the Kittim (Numbers 24:24), who are identified with the Romans, at least in later rabbinic literature (*'Avodah Zarah* 2b, *Shevuot* 6b, etc.), as well as perhaps already at Qumran. See Schürer 1973, 1:241-42, n. 30.

[16] Cf. Josephus, *War* 5.367: "G-d, who went the round of the nations, bringing to each in turn the rod of empire, now rested over Italy." De Jonge (1974, 211) deduces from the use of the word "now" in the above quotation that Josephus regarded the Romans as being powerful at the time that he wrote but not forever. We may reply, however, that the use of the word "now" is perfectly natural in the

c. *Jews Do Not Rebel*

As one who had participated in the war against the Romans and who had come to the conclusion that resistance to Rome was futile and that Rome was divinely destined to rule the world, Josephus constantly seeks to prevail upon his compatriots to give up their dream of national independence. We may see an instance of this concern where Josephus avoids terminology suggestive of an independent state (Numbers 23:21) in Balaam's remark that G-d has granted untold blessings to the Israelites and has vouchsafed to them His own providence as their perpetual ally (σύμμαχον) and guide (ἡγεμών) (*Ant.* 4.114). This rendering is clearly not merely an equivalent for the biblical concept of covenant but actually a replacement for it (see Attridge 1976, 79-80). As Josephus' Balaam puts matters, the Israelites are thus to be happy (εὐδαίμων, *Ant.* 4.114) rather than to dominate the world. It is their fame – rather than, it would seem, their sheer force – that will fill the whole earth, as we see in another of Josephus' extra-biblical additions (*Ant.* 4.115). In particular, we may note that in place of the Bible's picture comparing the Israelites to lions that do not lie down until they have eaten their prey and drunk their blood (Numbers 23:24), Josephus avoids such sanguinary particulars and speaks only of the land that the Israelites will occupy (*Ant.* 4.115-16).

Indeed, Josephus clearly shifts the focus from the land of Israel to the Diaspora when he has Balaam declare that whereas now the Israelites are circumscribed by the land of Canaan, the habitable world (τὴν οἰκουμένην), that is the Diaspora, lies before them as an everlasting habitation (*Ant.* 4.116).[17]

Josephus was similarly aware that the Romans were sensitive to the great expansion of the Jewish population, especially through proselytism. Hence, we can understand Josephus' difficulty when he came to the passage in Balaam's prophecy (Numbers 23:10)

---

context, namely a speech delivered by Josephus to his fellow-countrymen. He is there making an appeal to realism: right now (but without reference to the future, which really is irrelevant) the Romans are in firm control of the world; hence revolution makes no sense.

[17] This is clearly a plea for the viability of Jewish life in the Diaspora, as noted by Schalit (1944, 1:lxxxi). We may see a parallel in Josephus' version of G-d's blessings to Jacob (Genesis 28:13-15; *Ant.* 1.280-83): Jacob, G-d says, will have good children who both will rule over both the land of Israel and will fill all other lands (*Ant.* 1.282).

with regard to the population explosion of the Israelites: "Who hath counted the dust of Jacob or numbered the fourth part of Israel?" Josephus diplomatically omits this statement altogether.

d. *Jews Are Not Busybodies*

We can see another of the charges against the Jews reflected, for example, in the order given by Marsus, the governor of Syria, to Agrippa I, to break up the conference of various kings which the latter had convened at Tiberias on the suspicion that Agrippa was trying to foment a conspiracy against the Romans (*Ant.* 19.340-42). Hence, in an extra-biblical detail, Josephus, in introducing the narrative of Balaam, remarks that Balak, the king of the Moabites, had formed an alliance with the Midianites when he saw the Israelites growing so great and became concerned that they would seek to expand at his expense (*Ant.* 4.102). In so doing, he had not learned, says Josephus, that the Hebrews were not for interfering with other countries, G-d having forbidden them to do so. The verb which is here used for "interfering," πολυπραγμονεῖν, implies being meddlesome, being an inquisitive busybody, and is almost always employed in a pejorative sense.[18]

Moreover, it is significant that whereas in the biblical statement G-d forbids the Israelites to attack the Moabites, inasmuch as He had not given the Moabites' land to them but rather to the Moabites themselves as the descendants of Lot (Deuteronomy 2:9), Josephus broadens the statement into a sweeping general principle, namely that the Israelites do not interfere in the affairs of any other country (*Ant.* 4.102).

e. *Reduction of Gentile Anti-Judaism*

Josephus is also concerned to attribute hatred of the Jewish people not to whole nations but rather merely to individuals. Thus, whereas in the Bible it is the Amalekites as a nation who beset the Israelites in the desert (Exodus 17:8-16), in Josephus it is the kings of the Amalekites who are blamed for sending messages to the kings of neighboring tribes exhorting them to make war against the Israelites (*Ant.* 3.40).

---

[18] Cf., e.g., Herodotus 3.15; Xenophon, *Anabasis* 5.1.15; Aristophanes, *Plutus* 913; Plato, *Republic* 4.433A.

Again, whereas in the rabbinic tradition, the Moabites and Midianites join forces, despite the fact that they are bitter enemies of one another, because their hatred of the Jews is even greater (*Tanḥuma* [ed. Buber] 4.134, *Numbers Rabbah* 20.4, *Sifre Numbers* 157 [ed. Horowitz, p. 209], *Sanhedrin* 105a), Josephus assiduously avoids giving the impression that Gentiles by nature hate Jews and instead depicts the two nations as long-time friends and allies (*Ant.* 4.102). Their motive in going to war with the Israelites, according to Josephus, is thus not hatred (*Ant.* 4.103); in fact, in an extrabiblical addition, Josephus specifically says that it was not Balak's intention to fight against men fresh with success and who had been found to be only the more emboldened by reverse; rather his aim was to check their aggrandizement. Such a presentation casts the Moabites and the Midianites in a much better light.

Moreover, far from imputing anti-Jewish hatred to Balaam, Josephus presents him as himself counselling the envoys who had been sent by Balak to renounce the hatred which they bore to the Israelites (*Ant.* 4.106). By contrast, the rabbinic view (*Tanḥuma Balak* 6, *Tanḥuma* [ed. Buber, 4.136-37], *Midrash Aggadah* on Numbers 22:13 [ed. Buber, 2.134]) and that of Philo (*De Vita Mosis* 1.48.266) is that Balaam was not at all sincere in his initial refusal to accompany the envoys. In the Bible as well, Balaam does not give advice, as Josephus reports him doing here, on his own but merely reports that it is G-d who has refused to allow him to accompany the envoys (Numbers 22:13).

Moreover, Josephus' favorable picture of Balaam is enhanced by the fact that, unlike the rabbinic tradition, which connects Balaam's desire to gratify the ambassadors with his hatred of the Israelites,[19] Josephus has Balaam explicitly inquire of G-d concerning His intention with regard to the invitation of the envoys (*Ant.* 4.105). When G-d informs him that he is not to curse the Israelites (Numbers 22:12), in the biblical version Balaam tells the envoys that they must return, inasmuch as G-d refuses to allow him to accompany them (Numbers 22:13). To be sure, in Josephus' version Balaam might seem to be even more anti-Israelite, inasmuch as he makes plain to the envoys his ever readiness (προθυμίαν) and zeal (σπουδήν) to comply with their request to curse the Israelites,

---

[19] *Tanḥuma Balak* 5, 8, 12; *Tanḥuma* (ed. Buber) 4.136, 137, 142; *Numbers Rabbah* 20.12, 20.19; *Eliyahu Rabbah* 29 (ed. Friedmann, p. 142), *Aggadat Bereshit* 65 (ed. Buber, p. 131).

which, however, G-d has forbidden him to do (*Ant.* 4.105). From this statement we see, nevertheless, that Balaam's motive is not actually hatred for the Israelites but rather loyalty to his sovereign, Balak. Moreover, in stating that G-d has vetoed the envoys' request Josephus has him piously add to the biblical narrative a statement of his recognition that the G-d who refused him is the G-d who had brought him to his high renown for the sake of truth and its prediction (πρόρρησιν).[20]

Josephus' favorable portrayal of Balaam may also be discerned in the scene in which he is said, in an extra-biblical addition, to have received a magnificent reception from Balak (*Ant.* 4.112). According to the Bible, Balak begins by berating Balaam, asking why he had not come to him hitherto and whether the reason was that Balak was not able to honor him sufficiently (Numbers 22:37). Josephus, on the other hand, is here clearly stressing that the relationship between Balak and Balaam is, in the first instance, one motivated by friendship rather than by their hatred of the Israelites. In contrast, we find the rabbis describing the reception which Balak gave to Balaam as very cheap and poor;[21] and Philo, who, to be sure, remarks that the interview began with friendly greetings, proceeds immediately to note that these were followed by Balak's censure of Balaam for his slowness and failure to come more readily (*De Vita Mosis* 1.50.275).

Again, the meeting is presented by Josephus not as an occasion for the parties to express their hatred for the Israelites but rather for them to plan their military defeat. Thus, it is the Israelites' camp (στρατόπεδον, *Ant.* 4.112, clearly a military term) that Balak and Balaam go to inspect, rather than, as the Bible would have it, "a portion of the people" (Numbers 22:41). Similarly, the mountain to which they, in an extra-biblical addition, go in order to inspect the Israelites' camp is located by reference to its distance from the camp (*Ant.* 4.112). Moreover, it is implied in the biblical text that it was Balak who took the initiative to escort Balaam

---

[20] The fact that Josephus here uses the word πρόρρησις does not indicate that he regards Balaam as a prophet comparable to the Hebrew prophets, inasmuch as πρόρρησις is employed by him of predictions in a dream (e.g., Joseph's dream, *Ant.* 2.15; the butler's dream, *Ant.* 2.65; the baker's dream, *Ant.* 2.72; Amram's dream, *Ant.* 2.217) or of predictions in general (e.g., of Pharaoh's seer, *Ag. Ap.* 1.258).

[21] *'Avot de-Rabbi Nathan* A 23 (ed. Schechter, p. 48); *Tanḥuma Balak* 11; *Tanḥuma* (ed. Buber) 4.140.

(Numbers 22:41), whereas in Josephus it is Balaam who apparently asks to be conducted to one of the mountains in order to inspect the disposition – which would certainly include their fighting capacity – of the Israelites' camp (*Ant.* 4.112).

Indeed, Balaam is depicted in Josephus as succumbing only to persistent pressure by Balak (*Ant.* 4.107). Thus the Bible states very simply that Balak sent yet again princes, more in number and more honorable than those whom he had sent previously to ask Balaam to come to him (Numbers 22:15). In Josephus Balak's entreaties (δέησιν, "supplication," "plea") are urgent and persistent, while Balaam agrees to consult G-d anew not out of audacity or greed, but only in order to give these new envoys some gratification (*Ant.* 4.107). Indeed, it is this desire to gratify Balak and his representatives that Josephus cites as Balaam's motive in several other additions to the biblical text (*Ant.* 4.121, 123, 127). Even when Balaam, instructed by G-d to accompany them, agrees to do so, Josephus, in an extra-biblical addition, not only does not blame Balaam but even seems to castigate G-d, since we are told that Balaam did not realize that G-d had deluded him in giving him this order (*Ant.* 4.107).[22] To be sure, Josephus proceeds to defend G-d's action by remarking that He was angry that Balaam should have tempted Him thus a second time; Philo, however, puts Balaam himself in a more unfavorable light by stating that his second consultation of G-d was once again pure pretense (*De Vita Mosis* 1.48.268). Even Balak emerges in a more favorable light, inasmuch as Josephus totally omits the attempt made by Balak, according to the Bible, to influence Balaam with the promise of power and money in order to get him to curse the Israelites (Numbers 22:17-18 vs. *Ant.* 4.107).

Josephus makes every attempt to depict Balaam's purpose in cursing the Israelites as due to his friendship with Balak rather than to hatred of the Israelites or greed, the motives that Philo (*De Vita Mosis* 1.48.267-68), the New Testament (2 Peter 2:15, Jude 1.11), and rabbinic literature (Mishnah 'Avot 5.19, 1 'Avot de-Rabbi Nathan 29 (ed. Schechter, p. 88), and 2 'Avot de-Rabbi Nathan 49 (ed. Schechter, p. 125) attribute to him. Thus, in an extra-biblical addition, Balaam declares that it was his earnest prayer to do no de-

---

[22] As Baskin (1983, 97) has noted, Josephus here appears to agree with the rabbinic tradition (*Numbers Rabbah* 20.9, 20.11) in indicating that it was G-d who had led Balaam astray by directing him to accede to the request of the envoys.

spite to Balak's desire to have him curse the Israelites but that G-d is mightier than his own wish "to do this favor" (*Ant.* 4.120-21). Again, he reiterates that it was his earnest desire to gratify Balak and the Midianites and that, indeed, it would be unseemly to reject their request (*Ant.* 4.123). Hence, when, against the biblical version, in which it is Balak who proposes to Balaam a second attempt to curse the Israelites (Numbers 23:27), Josephus has Balaam himself suggest that new altars be erected and additional sacrifices be offered (*Ant.* 4.123), the change is intended to depict that Balaam's motive is his close friendship with Balak.

Indeed, whereas in the Bible, when the angel rebukes him, Balaam responds penitently, declaring that he had sinned unknowingly and offering to return home (Numbers 22:34), Philo remarks that Balaam was dissimulating, "for why should he ask about a matter so evident?" and that his real intention continued to be to do harm to the Israelites (*De Vita Mosis* 1.49.274).[23] In Josephus' version there is no indication of any such lack of sincerity on the part of Balaam; in fact, in an extra-biblical remark, the blame is actually put upon G-d, who has to exhort him to pursue the way on which he has set out (*Ant.* 4.111).

Commentators have long wondered why the Midianites are introduced into the biblical account, when actually the story concerns only Balak the king and Balaam the prophet of Moab (Numbers 25:6-18). In reply, we may suggest that Josephus was well aware that Ruth, a Moabite, was the ancestress of King David (*Ant.* 5.336); and hence he was careful not to impute such groundless hatred to the Moabites as a whole, as the Bible does. Indeed, whereas in the biblical text of the story of Balaam the Moabites are mentioned thirteen times and the Midianites only twice, in Josephus' version the ratio is almost exactly reversed, with the Moabites mentioned only twice and the Midianites nine times. In particular, whereas in the Bible the Israelites' harlotry is with the daughters of Moab (Numbers 25:1), with the Midianites merely participating in it (Numbers 25:6-18), in Josephus, although in his parting advice, Balaam tells the Midianite princes to instruct their women to seduce the Israelite youths and thus to induce them thus to worship the gods of the Midianites and the Moabites, the actual seduction

---

[23] So also the rabbinic tradition (*Numbers Rabbah* 20.14-15, *Tanḥuma* (ed. Buber, 4.139).

is carried out by the Midianite women (*Ant.* 4.126-30); and the war that follows is waged against the Midianites (*Ant.* 4.131-64), with no mention made of the role of the Moabites in the entire narrative. Again, it is not the Midianites as a nation, as in the Bible, but rather their leaders who are responsible for the ploy whereby the Midianite women seduce the Israelite men (*Ant.* 4.126).

As to the Israelites themselves, in contrast to the Bible, which states that Balaam told the envoys sent by Balak that they should return because G-d had refused to allow him to accompany them to curse the Israelites without giving a reason for G-d's veto (Numbers 22:13), Josephus uses the opportunity to speak apologetically on behalf of the Israelites by declaring that the reason why G-d had refused Balak's request was that the Israelites were in favor with Him (*Ant.* 4.106).

If we wonder why Josephus omits mention of the death of Balaam, this may be due to the fact that he was killed in battle, together with the Midianite kings (Numbers 31:8). To be sure, Josephus does mention this battle (*Ant.* 4.161); but if he had included Balaam as a participant in and casualty of it, readers might get the impression that Balaam, like the Midianites, was anti-Jewish. Hence, by omitting this detail Josephus shows himself consistent in his portrayal of Balaam as not a conspirator against Israel but rather as simply a professional soothsayer (so Moscovitz 1979, 30).

f. *Appeal to Stoicism*

In the case of Balaam, Josephus' statement, in an addition to the biblical text (Numbers 23:4), that when Balaam offered his sacrifice before prophesying he saw the indications of inflexible Fate (ἄτροπον) (*Ant.* 4.113), casts him as something of a Stoic sage.

The concept of Providence, so central in Stoic thought, is introduced several times by Josephus in the Balaam pericope. Thus, Balaam proclaims that G-d has vouchsafed His own providence to the Israelites as their personal ally and guide (*Ant.* 4.114). He further declares that the Israelites have been invested by the providence of G-d with superabundant valor (*Ant.* 4.117). Again, in his parting advice, Balaam tells Balak that G-d's providence is watching over the Israelites to preserve them from all ill (*Ant.* 4.128). Finally, we are told that it was by divine providence (θείᾳ προνοίᾳ) that Balaam was prevented from cursing the Israelites

(*Ant.* 4.157). Likewise, in the biblical text, after Balak and Balaam offer their sacrifices, G-d plays an active role in putting His words into Balaam's mouth (Numbers 23:16), whereas Josephus, with his stress on the concept of Providence, is clearly appealing to a Stoic audience in remarking that Balaam realized that G-d had bestowed untold blessings upon the Israelites and had granted them His own providence (πρόνοιαν) as their perpetual ally and guide (*Ant.* 4.114).

5. *Emphasis on Military Details*

Josephus not only gives us an extended portrait of Moses as a general but he also presents Moses' people as soldiers. Thus Balaam tells the envoys who have come to him that the army whom he has been requested to curse is in favor with G-d (*Ant.* 4.106); thereby the confrontation between the Moabites-Midianites and the Israelites is put on a military basis, rather than on one of anti-Jewish hatred. Indeed, the Israelites are referred to several times as an army where this military aspect is missing in the biblical original (*Ant.* 4.106, 116, 122, 140). Moreover, whereas the Bible states that Balak took Balaam and brought him to the high places of Baal, whence he sees a portion of the people (Numbers 22:41), in Josephus Balaam is presented as a kind of general who desires to inspect the disposition of the Israelites' camp (στρατόπεδον) (*Ant.* 4.112). Likewise, Josephus has Balaam refer to the Israelites as a blessed army (στρατός) (*Ant.* 4.116). Such military phraseology continues with the Josephan Balaam's statement that not even one of the enemies of the Israelites will return victorious so as to gladden the hearts of child and wife (*Ant.* 4.117). That the latter phrase has military associations is clear from the fact that it is so similar to the language used by Homer with regard to the warrior Sarpedon (*Iliad* 5.688) and, negatively, by Tyrtaeus (frag. 6-7, line 6) of the opposite of the warrior, namely the beggar who wanders about with his little children and his wedded wife.

Josephus' emphasis on the military aspects of the confrontation between the Moabites-Midianites and the Israelites (*Ant.* 4.112) serves to underscore the military prowess of the Israelites, just as does his related stress on Moses as a general.

Because the Jews had been reproached with cowardice by such Jew-baiters as Apollonius Molon (*ap. Ag.Ap.* 2.148), it is particularly effective that the non-Jew Balaam remarks that the Israelites have been invested by the providence of G-d with superabundant valor (ἀνδρείας) (*Ant.* 4.117). Moreover, there is greater effect in Balaam's blessing of the Israelites because he originally intended, as Josephus indicates, to curse them (*Ant.* 4.120-22).

6. *Miracles*

Undoubtedly, one of the greatest challenges that Josephus faced with regard to his credibility as an historian was what to do with the story of Balaam's ass that spoke.[24] Josephus might have omitted the incident, as he did several other episodes in the Bible. Instead, only at the very end of the whole episode of Balaam and not rather in direct connection with the ass episode do we meet the familiar words of Josephus: "On this narrative readers are free to think what they please" (*Ant.* 4.158).[25]

We may guess that Josephus was not deterred from including the narrative of the speaking ass because his audience was probably familiar with the account of Achilles' horse, Xanthos, which likewise speaks after being unfairly accused by his master (Homer, *Iliad*, 19.408-17). And just as Balaam's ass speaks because G-d willed it, so Xanthus is said to have spoken because the goddess Hera gave him speech. Thus both narratives clearly acknowledge that human speech is not natural for animals.

Even so, Josephus has taken several steps to make the narrative of the talking ass more credible. In the first place, whereas the story of the speaking ass is the subject of fifteen verses in the Bible (Numbers 22:21-35), in Josephus this is reduced to four short paragraphs (*Ant.* 4.108-11). In the second place, in the Bible Balaam

---

[24] Pseudo-Philo (*Bib. Ant.* 18.9), though mentioning the ass, says nothing to indicate that it spoke.

[25] Moscovitz (1979, 18) suggests that perhaps Josephus postponed his customary declaration that the reader may believe as he pleases to the end of the Balaam narrative, where it is added as an afterthought, because the whole incident of the ass was so trivial and insignificant in Josephus' eyes. The incident, however, hardly seems so trivial in view of the fact that Josephus does devote four paragraphs to it. More likely, the reason for the postponement was that it is not only the incident of the ass that might strike readers as incredible, but the whole of the Balaam episode, since the very idea that an individual such as Balaam had the power to curse a whole nation and that he could be prevented from doing so by divine intervention might likewise stretch credibility.

smites his ass three times, whereas Josephus mentions his doing so only once (*Ant.* 4.108-9). Thirdly, the Bible has the ass speaking twice, whereas in Josephus she speaks only once (*Ant.* 4.109). Fourthly, whereas the Bible states that the L-rd actually opened the mouth of the ass (Numbers 22:28), Josephus is less direct in asserting merely that the ass became conscious of the divine spirit approaching her (*Ant.* 4.108). In so doing Josephus has transformed a potentially embarrassing story into a credible tale in the eyes of his non-Jewish audience by adopting a method of inspiration ultimately traceable to Plato (*Symposium* 202E-3A) that explained the working of the Delphic Oracle (so Levison 1994, 123-38). Fifthly, instead of saying that G-d actually opened the mouth of the ass, Josephus says that the ass broke out in human speech because G-d so willed it (*Ant.* 4.109). Sixthly, readers might well have wondered why an ass with the supernatural power to speak should be sensitive to pain, as she is in the biblical account (Numbers 22:28); and so Josephus represents the ass as insensible to the blows with which Balaam smote her (*Ant.* 4.108). Seventhly, in the Bible when the ass speaks, Balaam evidences no amazement that his animal should be speaking (Numbers 22:29). Josephus, aware that his readers would obviously wonder why a man hearing an animal speak shows no astonishment, specifically declares that Balaam was aghast (ταραττομένου, "confounded," "put into confusion," "embarrassed," "frightened," dismayed," "bewildered") at hearing his ass speak thus with a human voice (*Ant.* 4.110). Similarly, when the angel rebukes Balaam for striking the ass (Numbers 22:32), the Bible gives no indication that Balaam was at all surprised (Numbers 22:34), whereas Josephus, clearly aware that his readers would wonder that Balaam was not amazed by the angel's intervention, states that Balaam was terrified (καταδείσας) (*Ant.* 4.111).

In any case, the picture painted of Balaam in this incident is much harsher in the Bible than in Josephus; in the former, Balaam is angry (Numbers 22:27) and even threatens to kill the animal (Numbers 22:29), whereas Josephus omits both points; and, indeed, Balaam is, in effect, excused on the ground that he had failed to understand that it was G-d's purpose that kept the ass from serving him on his mission (*Ant.* 4.109).[26] Moreover, whereas in

---

[26] In the Targumim it is the ass herself which reproaches Balaam for failing to

the Bible the ass speaks in direct discourse reproaching Balaam (Numbers 22:30), the strength of the ass' rebuke is considerably diminished by Josephus' mere report of it (*Ant.* 4.109).

7. *Preaching against Assimilation*

A dilemma confronted Josephus in his interpretation of the episode of the Midianite women: if he portrayed this favorably, he would be condoning the assimilation and intermarrige forbidden by the Torah (Deuteronomy 7:3); and yet, he was aware that too strenuously voiced an objection against intermarriage would play into the hands of those opponents of the Jews who charged them with misanthropy and illiberalism.

On the one hand, as we have noted, Josephus is careful to avoid offending non-Jews and their religion; on the other hand, assimilation and intermarriage did pose problems for him. That this was, indeed, a serious issue is intimated by Josephus' remark that as a result of the seduction a sedition (στάσις) far worse even than that of Korah broke out among the Israelites (*Ant.* 4.140). Of course, as we have noted, Josephus might have omitted the seduction incident as he does a number of others. But apparently Josephus felt the need to use the episode to lecture to contemporary Jews (so Troiani 1986, 343-53); and so, he not only includes it, but his account of the Israelites' sin with the Midianite women (Numbers 25:1-9) expands the story from nine verses to twenty-five paragraphs (*Ant.* 4.131-55) (see van Unnik 1974, 241-61).

That Josephus, in his version of the incident, has the danger of intermarriage in mind would seem to be indicated by his added notice that the Israelites implored the Midianite women to be their brides (*Ant.* 4.132) and that the latter, in turn, declared that they would be content (ἀγαπήσομεν) to live out their lives with them as their wedded wives (*Ant.* 4.135). That Josephus has the contemporary situation of the Jews in view here would seem to be indicated by the fact that he omits the Bible's particular place names, that is, Shittim and Ba'al Pe'or, thus making the story a generic tale that presumably is intended to have a direct application to the time in which he is writing, when some Jews were likewise being

---

understand the ways of G-d, whereas Josephus states, in an editorial-like comment, that Balaam failed to understand G-d's purpose.

seduced by the temptations of Hellenism (see Feldman 1989a, 66).

In particular, the speech of Zambrias (*Ant.* 4.145-49) sounds very much like the summary of arguments that assimilated Jews of Josephus' day might have used (so van Unnik 1974, 258-59; and S. Schwartz 1990, 177), namely attacking the tyranny (*Ant.* 4.146, 149, a word twice repeated) of the commandments and advocating liberty (ἐλευθέρων, *Ant.* 4.146, a key word throughout the *Antiquities*) of action. Apparently, the danger which Josephus is highlighting here is intermarriage: significantly, it is intermarriage between Jewish men and Moabite-Midianite women that he castigates (*Ant.* 4.135, 148), whereas Philo (*De Vita Mosis* 1.54.295-304), Pseudo-Philo (*Bib. Ant.* 18.13-14), and the rabbis (*Sanhedrin* 106a) present the view that the great sin committed by the Israelites was surrender to illicit passion. Similarly, we may remark, Josephus has elaborated his account of Samson's relations with alien women (Judges 14:1-16:31, *Ant.* 5.286-313) as a lesson to Hellenized Jews of his own day who sought assimilation with the Gentiles through intermarriage (see Feldman 1988a, 194-204, 210-14).

8. *"Improvements" in the Story: Clarifications, Increased Drama*

One basic feature of Josephus' paraphrase of Scripture is his concern to resolve apparent contradictions in the biblical text. One major difficulty in the Balaam pericope is that in Numbers 22:20 G-d instructs Balaam to accompany the envoys that have been sent to him, whereas a mere two verses later G-d expresses his anger at Balaam for doing this (Numbers 22:22). The rabbis resolve this contradiction by insisting that since Balaam wanted to act wickedly he was permitted to do so, inasmuch as "a man is divinely assisted in treading the path he desires" (*Tanḥuma, Balak* 8; *Tanḥuma* [ed. Buber] 4.137; *Numbers Rabbah* 20.12). Josephus resolves the problem by having G-d express indignation that Balaam should have tempted Him and by having Balaam misunderstand G-d's sarcasm in permitting him to go with the envoys (*Ant.* 4.107).

Josephus also tries to increase the dramatic interest of the biblical narrative. We may see an example of this in Josephus' version of the incident where, having seen the Israelites, Balaam begins to prophesy (*Ant.* 4.113). According to the Bible G-d first puts a word into Balaam's mouth and tells him to return to Balak (Numbers 23:5), so that only later does Balaam take up his parable. On the other hand, in Josephus' version G-d plays no direct role, and instead Balaam proceeds directly and more dramatically to prophesy immediately after his sacrifice (*Ant.* 4.113). Moreover, in the biblical version Balaam delivers three brief prophetic discourses; Josephus' Balaam is dramatically much more effective by combining his prophecies into a single discourse (*Ant.* 4.114-17). The fact that Josephus presents Balaam's prophecy in direct discourse (so noted by Moscovitz 1979, 20), whereas Josephus generally either omits biblical poetry or refers to it in brief summary (e.g., Jacob's benediction [*Ant.* 2.194-195], the Song at the Sea of Reeds [*Ant.* 2.346], Moses' farewell songs [*Ant.* 4.303, 4.320], the song of Deborah [*Ant.* 5.205-9], David's mourning for the deaths of Saul and Jonathan [*Ant.* 7.6], David's lament for Abner [*Ant.* 7.42], David's songs [*Ant.* 7.305], and Jeremiah's lamentations [*Ant.* 10.78]), serves to highlight the importance of this prophecy.

Furthermore, Josephus' description of Balaam as one who is no longer his own master (οὐκ ὢν ἐν ἑαυτῷ) (*Ant.* 4.118) is definitely reminiscent of the Platonic concept of ecstatic possession (*Phaedrus* 245A), whereby the god enters, for example, into the Pythian priestess at Delphi and uses her vocal organs as if they were his own (Plato, *Laws* 2.672B).[27] That Josephus is using the concept of "ecstasy" in a sense different from the Septuagint, where it sometimes refers to a deep sleep, is especially clear in the Balaam pericope. In the Bible, we recall, Balaam says, "All that the L-rd will speak, that must I do" (Numbers 23:26). Josephus not only expands this statement but also uses Hellenistic terminology in explaining that it is not up to a person to be silent or to speak

---

[27] See Dodds 1951, 77 and 94-95, n. 84. The god within the diviner speaks out from the person in a strange voice or in an unintelligible way (cf. Euripides, *Bacchae*, 300, 1124). Indeed, Euripides (*Bacchae* 298 ff.) has Teiresias claim that Dionysus is the god of ecstatic prophecy. In the ecstatic state understanding no longer belongs to the individual (cf. Plato, *Ion* 534B). Cf. Philo (*Quaestiones in Genesin* 3.9), who similarly defines the ecstasy of prophets as a state when the mind is divinely possessed and becomes filled with G-d, so that it is no longer within itself, inasmuch as it receives the divine spirit to dwell within it. Moscovitz (1979, 56, n. 9) states that Josephus' references to himself as being "inspired" (ἔνθους, *War* 3.353, 4.33) make it extremely unlikely that he has in mind ecstatic possession in the Hellenistic sense; but the important question here is how his non-Jewish readers would interpret the word used by him. It seems likely that they would, in fact, understand it in line with Plato's usage in his dialogues. It further seems reasonable to assume that Josephus, who apparently knew Plato's works, as we have noted, would have been aware of the connotations of the word.

when possessed by the spirit of G-d, "for that spirit gives utterance to such language and words as it will, whereof we are all unconscious" (*Ant.* 4.119). To be sure, there is a difference between this view of ecstasy and the claim that the Pythian priestess at Delphi was actually possessed by the god Apollo, who used her vocal chords as if they were his own, so that she presented Apollo's utterances in the first person, whereas Balaam presents G-d's words in the third person. Again, Josephus draws on the prevalent theory of ecstasy in stating that one is wholly impotent who, pretending to a foreknowledge of human affairs drawn from his own breast, refrains from speaking what G-d suggests and thus violates His will (*Ant.* 4.121). In particular, his use of the phrase that "once G-d has gained prior entry, nothing within us is any more our own," is typical of Platonic and Hellenistic descriptions of ecstasy.

There is further increased drama in Josephus' version of the events surrounding Balaam's parting advice. In the Bible, after Balaam blesses the Israelites he and Balak go their respective ways (Numbers 24:25). In Josephus' version, Balak expresses his fury by summarily dismissing Balaam, granting him no reward (*Ant.* 4.126). And then, just as he is on the point of crossing the Euphrates, Balaam, in Josephus' version, sends for Balak and the Midianite princes and presents them with a scheme for overcoming the Israelites (*Ant.* 4.126-30).

The Bible itself does not itself immediately link the apparent end of the Balaam episode (Numbers 24:25) with the incident involving the Israelite youths with the Moabite women (Numbers 25:1-5), and only at a later point (Numbers 31:16) associates Balaam with the incident. Josephus, on the contrary, like the rabbis,[28] makes Balaam, as was just mentioned, the originator of the Midianites' scheme (*Ant.* 4.126-30). Van Unnik notes the significant fact that Josephus expands at great length (*Ant.* 4.126-51) the story of the seduction of the Israelite youths by the women, whereas he deals only briefly with the Phinehas episode (*Ant.* 4.152-55), even though the two accounts are of approximately equal length in the Bible (Numbers 25:1-5 and 6-13) (see van Unnik 1974, 243). In particular, Josephus, like Philo (*De Vita Mosis* 1.53.294-55.304 and

---

[28] See *Sanhedrin* 106a and parallels cited by Rappaport(1930, 126, n. 180). In Philo (*De Virtutibus* 7.34-35) the advice comes from the Midianites rather than from Balaam.

De Virtutibus 7.34-42), shows a strong interest in the erotic psychology reflected in Balaam's advice,[29] whereas the Talmudic parallels make no reference to this. Josephus' version is also considerably more romantic than that of Philo in that the women (Josephus [*Ant.* 4.131], like the Bible [Numbers 25:6] changes them from Moabites to Midianites) at first surrender to the youths without any conditions; but once they perceive that the latter have been ensnared by passion, they, following Balaam's advice, depart from them (*Ant.* 4.130). The men, now, in a most romantic touch, in the depths of their despondency, offer the women all that they possess. They implore them, in the manner typical of the later Hellenistic novels, with tears, which they confirm with oaths, ironically, despite their own immorality, invoking their G-d as arbiter of their promises, so as to render themselves an object of the women's compassion (*Ant.* 4.133); and they entreat them to stay. The women, in turn, demand that the Israelite lovers give up their laws and customs (*Ant.* 4.134-38).

9. *Summary*

The importance of the Balaam pericope for Josephus may be seen from the extraordinary amount of space that he gives to the narrative, especially to the incident of the Israelite youths and the Midianite women. Josephus was clearly in a dilemma in his portrait of Balaam in that if he gave too positive a portrayal he would not only be going against the simple meaning of the biblical text but would also be in a position of praising one who sought to curse the Jews. On the other hand, Josephus wished to avoid the charge that Jews look down upon non-Jewish men of wisdom. The result is a relatively unbiased portrait in sharp contrast with the negative picture painted by Philo, the New Testament, and the rabbis. Josephus develops such a portrayal by shifting the focus from Balaam's personality to the historical, military, and political confrontation between Israel and her enemies.

To be sure, Josephus never applies the term προφήτης to Balaam but rather refers to him as a μάντις. But Josephus adds to

---

[29] Braun (1938, 104) notes a parallel in Aristophanes' *Lysistrata*, where similarly the women break off relations with their husbands and threaten to leave them unless they fulfill certain political conditions, whereupon the men submit.

Balaam's stature by elaborating on the hospitality that he shows to Balak's envoys.

To a high degree, Josephus seeks in his paraphrase of the Bible to answer the charges of those who are hostile to the Jews. One of these charges is that Jews hate non-Jews, as shown by their sundering themselves off from them. In the Balaam pericope Josephus, by skilful changes of the biblical narrative, shifts the emphasis from the Jews' separatism for its own sake to their excellence and their future happiness. It is particularly effective to have a non-Jew, Balaam, praise the Israelites, and to do so to an extent that goes beyond the biblical text.

Josephus was confronted with a dilemma as to what to do with Balaam's prophecy which was understood by near-contemporary rabbinic tradition as announcing the coming of a messiah and the overthrow of the Roman Empire. His solution, as with a similar prophecy in the Book of Daniel, is to adopt a stance of deliberate ambiguity, so that Jews would not accuse him of omitting the prophecy, while non-Jews would not suspect him of disloyalty to the Roman Empire for including it. Again, in place of covenant theology which would be regarded by the Romans as a challenge to their rule of Judaea, Josephus has Balaam predict future fame and happiness for the Jews, rather than political domination by them. Moreover, he shifts attention from Canaan to the dispersion of the Jews in the Diaspora. Furthermore, he omits the biblical Balaam's reference to the population explosion of the Jews, since the Romans were so sensitive about the tremendous increase in the number of the Jews, particularly through proselytism. In addition, Josephus is careful to stress, as an important principle of their policy, that the Jews do not interfere in the affairs of other countries.

Inasmuch as an important goal of Josephus' revision of the Bible is to counter hatred of the Jews, it is particularly significant that Balaam urges Balak's envoys to give up just such hatred. As for Balaam himself, in Josephus' view his motive in seeking to curse the Israelites is not Jew-hatred but rather loyalty to his sovereign. The meeting of Balak and Balaam is presented not as an exercise in Jew-hatred but as a planning session to find a way of defeating the Israelites militarily. In any case, Balaam is depicted as succumbing only to persistent pressure by Balak. Balaam's initial decision to refrain from cursing the Israelites is presented as sincere; indeed, the blame for the reversal is actually put on G-d Himself.

Josephus makes a particular appeal to his non-Jewish readers by his constant reference to Providence (πρόνοια), a central concept in Stoic thought. Though he realizes that miracles, particularly that of the speaking by Balaam's ass, might make his narrative less credible, he nonetheless does mention the episode, perhaps because readers would think of the parallel of Achilles' speaking horse; however, he takes a number of steps to make it more plausible.

The fact that Josephus not only includes but very considerably expands the narrative of the Midianite women is apparently due to his desire to preach to his Jewish readers about the dangers of intermarriage. This expansion, replete with erotic motifs and with the description of Balaam's ecstatic state in prophesying, clearly increases the drama of the entire episode.

CHAPTER EIGHT

EHUD

1. *Introduction*

Josephus' treatment of the brief biblical episode of Ehud is a good illustration of his procedures in rewriting the Bible both in modification and in omission. In particular, Josephus, in his version, is careful not to offend his non-Jewish audience while, at the same time, instilling a sense of pride in his Jewish readers. Moreover, Josephus, the critical historian, is concerned to make the story more credible by omitting obscurities and other difficulties.

That this episode is of great interest to Josephus may be seen from the sheer amount of space that he devotes to it as compared with that which he gives to other episodes. For the episode of Eglon and Ehud (Judges 3:12-30), which comprises 29 lines in the Hebrew text and 71 lines in Josephus (*Ant.* 5.185-97), the ratio is 2.45 (the ratio of Josephus to the Septuagint version A is 1.54 and to version B 1.37).[1] From this comparison we can already see that this pericope was of very great interest to Josephus, presumably because the figure of Ehud supplied an excellent role model of bravery and ingenuity and a compelling answer to the charges of those hostile to Jews, just as did the episodes pertaining to Joseph, and also because the pericope itself was of great dramatic interest in a long work with many more drab than exciting episodes.

2. *The Portrayal of Ehud in Pseudo-Philo's* Biblical Antiquities *and in Rabbinic Literature*

Ehud is not mentioned by Pseudo-Philo, unless we choose to identify him, as do Ginzberg and Perrot and Bogaert, with Zebul.[2]

---

[1] For a discussion of versions A and B see Jellicoe (1968, 280-83).

[2] There is a question, in view of the considerable difference in spelling, as to whether Pseudo-Philo's Zebul (*Bib. Ant.* 29) is, indeed, to be identified with the biblical Ehud (Ioudes in Josephus). Ginzberg (1928, 6:184, n. 21) suggests that Zebul is a corruption of Iehud and points out that there is a parallel to such an interchange of Z and I in *Biblical Antiquities* 47.1, where most manuscripts read

Iambri and where the reference is clearly to Zambri. As to the interchange of D and L, there is likewise a parallel to this in *Biblical Antiquities* 44.2, where the manuscripts read Dedila and where the reference is clearly to Delila. Moreover, Pseudo-Philo's reference to Zebul comes directly after his pericope on Cenez (Kenaz), just as in the Bible the reference to Ehud (Judges 3:15) comes immediately after mention of Othniel the son of Kenaz (Judges 3:11) and just as in Josephus the story of Eglon (*Ant.* 5.186) immediately follows the reference to Kenaz (*Ant.* 5.184), who in Josephus takes the place of Othniel. Perrot and Bogaert (1976, 2:165) conclude that Pseudo-Philo's Zebul must correspond to the Bible's Ehud. Jacobson (1996, 2:822) contends that this identification is almost surely wrong, since it would require us to believe that the same error occurred five different times in chapters 29 and 30.5. To be sure, Pseudo-Philo (*Bib. Ant.* 34.1) does mention a certain Aod, the spelling of whose name is closer to that of Ehud; but this Aod is a magician who bears no resemblance to the biblical Ehud. Perrot and Bogaert suggest that it was necessary to distinguish the judge Ehud on the basis of his well-known characteristic, his lefthandedness; but the Hebrew word *semal*, "left," also designates Satan-Sammael, whence finally the Latin Zebul (Zabulus, the devil, Beelzebul).

If we accept the identification of Ehud with Pseudo-Philo's Zebul, we shall have to explain why he does not mention the most remarkable of Ehud's achievements, namely his assassination of Eglon, while, on the other hand, he cites several other details concerning him not found in the Book of Judges. In the first place, Zebul in Pseudo-Philo (*Bib. Ant.* 29.1) is the direct successor to Cenez, the foremost hero in the entire *Biblical Antiquities*. Indeed, his first act as successor to Cenez (*Bib. Ant.* 29.1) is to gather the Israelites together and to acknowledge the labor with which Cenez worked for the benefit of the people throughout his life. His second act (*ibid.*) is to grant to Cenez's daughters, inasmuch as Cenez had no sons, a greater portion of the national inheritance than the other Israelites. His third act (*Bib. Ant.* 29.3) is to set up a treasury for the L-rd, with the instruction that the Israelites not contribute material obtained from idols to this. Finally, we are told that Zebul judged the people for twenty-five years. This datum contrasts both with the Hebrew text about Ehud, which says nothing about his rulership, and the Septuagint (Judges 3:30), which asserts that he judged the Israelites until he died, implying, though not directly stating, via the statement that the land had rest for eighty years, that Ehud ruled the Isrelites during this period, as well as with Josephus (*Ant.* 5.197), who states directly that Ehud ruled the Israelites for eighty years. Thereafter, we are given Zebul's farewell address to the people in which he exhorts them to obey the law (*Bib. Ant.* 29.4). What is striking is that Pseudo-Philo's account of Zebul reproduces none of the ingredients of the biblical account of Ehud. Perhaps, it may be suggested, in view of the tremendous liberties that Pseudo-Philo takes with the narrative of Cenez, who is not even a judge in the Bible (there it is his son Othniel who is a judge [Judges 3.9]), it should not be surprising that he presents a totally new picture of Ehud. We should point out, however, that his portrait, though at variance with that in the Bible, is completely positive, as is that of Josephus.

We may add that when Zebul is mentioned in *Biblical Antiquities* 30.5 the *editio princeps* spells his name Iebul, which, to be sure, removes one of the above problems of transcriptional probability. Nevertheless, the simplest and the most likely explanation is to identify Zebul with the Zebul, the ruler of Shechem, mentioned in the Book of Judges itself (9:28-41). This would then be another instance, like that of Kenaz, where Pseudo-Philo has built up a figure who is mentioned only briefly in the Book of Judges.

As to the rabbinic tradition, there are two major points to be made. In the first place, there is one remark (*Genesis Rabbah* 99.3) about Ehud that is clearly positive. Here we are told that when Jacob blessed his son Benjamin, comparing him to a wolf that devours (Genesis 49:27), he was alluding to the judge, Ehud, descended from Benjamin (Judges 3:15), who seized King Eglon's heart, that is, deceived him. That this notice is not intended to be critical of Ehud may be seen from the high regard that this midrash has in general for Benjamin and, in particular, from the fact that it quotes the tradition cited by Rabbi Berekiah that after Ehud assassinated Eglon he went forth to the place where the ministering angels sat in order, presumably in approval of his deed.

What is especially remarkable, however, is the respect in which the rabbinic tradition holds Eglon, Ehud's antagonist, who, though he is identified as the grandson of the wicked King Balak, who had hired the soothsayer Balaam to curse the Jews (*Yalquṭ* 665), is praised for showing respect to G-d by rising from his throne when Ehud tells him that he has a message from the L-rd (Judges 3:20; *Sanhedrin* 60a); indeed, as a reward for this, Eglon is said to have had Ruth as his descendant (*Nazir* 23b); and her descendant, King David, is described as sitting on the throne of the L-rd (*Ruth Rabbah* 2.9). In fact, the Talmud, citing the precedent of Eglon, argues *a fortiori* that if that king, who was only a heathen and who knew but an attribute of G-d's name, nevertheless rose from his seat, how much more so should an Israelite rise when he hears G-d's name (*Sanhedrin* 60a). Such respect for Eglon, we may surmise, reflects the general attitude of respect which the rabbis had for rulers, simply in virtue of their office.[3]

3. *The Virtues of Ehud*

In view of the importance which the ancients, both Greeks and Jews, attached to physical attractiveness, the biblical statement, with which Ehud is introduced, namely that he had a shriveled ("obstructed") right hand (Judges 3:15),[4] would certainly not enhance

---

[3] Cf., e.g., the statement of Rabbi Ḥananiah, prefect of the priests, in '*Avot* 3:2: "Pray for the welfare of the government, for if it were not for fear of it, one man would swallow his fellow alive."

[4] The Revised Standard Version translates "a left-handed man"; but the Hebrew

the reader's regard for him but would simply confirm the impression given by anti-Jewish tales about the appearance of Moses, for example. Josephus might have solved this problem by following here, as he generally does elsewhere in this part of the *Antiquities*, the Septuagint version (in both of its major recensions), which reads ἀμφοτεροδέξιον, that is, that Ehud was ambidextrous. He is, however, quite clearly aware here, as he generally is elsewhere, of the Hebrew reading, and moreover must have been influenced by the fact that when Ehud embarks upon his mission of assassinating Eglon he girds his sword on his right thigh (Judges 3:16) presumably because he was left-handed. Accordingly, Josephus provides a very neat solution to this problem: he says that Ehud was superior (ἀμείνων, "better") with his left hand and derived all his strength from it but says nothing about his right hand being shriveled (*Ant.* 5.188).[5] Moreover, whereas the Bible states that Ehud assassinated Eglon by stretching out his left hand and removing his sword from his right thigh, whereupon he thrust it into Eglon's belly (Judges 3:21), Josephus, aware of the negative attitude of the ancients toward left-handed people,[6] omits all mention of Ehud's use of his left hand and says merely that he smote Eglon in his heart (*Ant.* 5.193). The Roman reader would, consequently, think of the parallel with the great Roman hero, Gaius Mucius Scaevola (Livy 2.12), who, in a similarly daring exploit, killed the scribe of the Etruscan king Porsinna and then, to show his disdain for suffering, thrust his right hand in the fire into which he was about to be flung.[7]

Josephus is at every point eager to underline the leadership qualities of such figures as the judges and the kings of Israel, espe-

---

reads *'ish 'iṭer yad-yemino*, which the Targum Jonathan renders as "a man with a shriveled right hand." On the key word, *'iṭer*, Rashi cites its use in Psalms 69:16, where the meaning is "closed." C. Cohen (1971, 14:178) notes that the word *'iṭer* is of "the nominal construction that is usually utilized for physical defects – e.g., 'blind,' 'dumb,' and 'deaf.'"

[5] The fact that Ehud thus derived all his strength from his left hand might imply that his right hand was useless; but the Latin version, significantly, reads *in laeva manu maximam fortitudinem habens*, that is, that he had the *greatest* strength in his left hand but without stating that he had no strength at all in his right hand.

[6] See Fordyce (1961, 205-6), commenting on Catullus 45.

[7] That Josephus was acquainted with Livy's history would seem to be indicated by the fact that he cites Livy in his account of Pompey's capture of Jerusalem (*Ant.* 14.68).

cially since the race of mankind, according to him, is by nature morose and censorious (*Ant.* 3.23). In fact, however, in the Hebrew Bible, there is no indication that Ehud was a judge at all, since we are told merely that the land had rest for eighty years (Judges 3:30). By contrast, the Septuagint (both versions, Judges 3:30) adds that he judged the Israelites until he died. Josephus combines the two readings and declares that Ehud held the office of governor (ἡγεμονίᾳ) for eighty years (*Ant.* 5.197). This would make Ehud's rule the longest in the entire period of the judges. For Josephus, who attached such great importance to the rule of law and order, Ehud's extended term of office was all the more impressive, inasmuch as the period of the Judges was marked, as he says over and over again by disregard of the order (κόσμου) of the constitution (πολιτείας) and contempt for the laws (νόμων) (*Ant.* 5.132, 179). Josephus has encomia for only a select few of his biblical heroes; yet he sees fit to praise Ehud by remarking that even apart from his extraordinary exploit in killing the king of the enemy, he was deserving to obtain praise (*Ant.* 5.197), presumably because he restored respect for law and order.

In the case of Ehud we see this quality of leadership displayed in his success in exhorting his fellow Israelites to assert (ἀντιλαμβάνεσθαι, "grasp for," "seize," "attain") their liberty (ἐλευθερίας) (*Ant.* 5.194). This notice is to be contrasted with the biblical statement, according to which Ehud merely told his fellow Israelites to follow quickly, "for the L-rd has given your enemies, the Moabites, into your hands" (Judges 3:28). Here it is G-d who gets all the credit; there is no exhortation, and there is no mention of the key Josephan theme of "liberty."

Ehud's success in persuading his fellow Israelites may be further seen in what follows, where we are told that they, welcoming his announcement, rush to arms and send heralds throughout the country to give the signal by sounding rams' horns (*Ant.* 5.194). Ehud's achievement in arousing his fellow Israelites is seen as well in the added detail that before the garrison of the Moabites could be mustered the host of the Israelites was upon them (*Ant.* 5.195). By way of parallel to all this the Bible has only the brief statement, "And they went down after him" (Judges 3:27).

A major problem that concerned Josephus, as it would any reader or interpreter of the Bible is how to justify the obvious trickery employed by Ehud in assassinating Eglon the king of

Moab. In this connection, we should recall how strongly the Romans, Josephus' primary audience, felt about deceit, as we see, for example, in Livy's disdain for the Alban leader Mettius Fufetius, who broke his treaty with Rome (1.27-28), and for the Carthaginians, who were known for their faithlessness (*fides Punica*). We can see Josephus' uneasiness on this matter elsewhere in his treatment of the deceitfulness of Jacob, Simeon, and Levi. In the case of Ehud, however, the fact that his action was necessary in order for the Israelites to reassert their liberty puts his deed on a different plane, and so Josephus does not hesitate to follow the biblical narrative.

A quality of major importance for a hero is ingenuity. To be sure, Ehud does not possess wisdom in the same sense as do other biblical personalities, but he shows himself certainly clever, in that whereas the Hebrew text states simply that the children of Israel sent a present (or presents, according to the Septuagint, in both major versions[8]) via him to Eglon, the king of Moab (Judges 3:15), Josephus, in an extra-biblical addition, has Ehud (whom he calls Judes) very cleverly plan his murder of Eglon by becoming familiar with him, courting (θεραπεύων, "paying respect," "rendering homage," "flattering," "being obsequious") and cajoling (ὑπερχόμενος, "approaching someone subserviently or flatteringly") him with presents, whereby he manages to endear himself to those attending the king (*Ant.* 5.189). Again, displaying a cleverness reminiscent of Odysseus in the episode with Polyphemus the Cyclops, Ehud, in an extra-biblical touch, arranges to fall into conversation[9] with the king and even gets him to order his henchmen to depart so that they may be alone (*Ant.* 5.191). One is reminded of the similar tactics successfully employed by Antipater, who by means of many cajoling presents (δώροις ὑπελθών) managed to induce

---

[8] From the fact that Josephus here uses the plural, "gifts," one may infer that he employed the Septuagint text in his paraphrase of this part of the Book of Judges. However, in his paraphrase of the very same verse of Judges Josephus (*Ant.* 5.188) says that Ehud was superior with his left hand and therefrom derived all his strength, which would seem to reflect the Hebrew text (Judges 3:15), which states that Ehud had a shriveled right hand, whereas the Septuagint, in both major versions, says that he used both hands alike (ἀμφοτεροδέξιον).

[9] To be sure, the Latin version reads instead of "fell into conversation" that Eglon sought his solitude ("retreat," "secrecy," "retirement") (*eius secretum*); but the Greek ὁμιλίαν, "conversation," is definitely the *lectio difficilior* and is to be preferred here.

King Aretas of Arabia to furnish an army to reinstate Hyrcanus (*War* 1.126). The most outstanding example of the successful use of such tactics is to be seen in Agrippa I, who spent money in paying court to Gaius Caligula, with whom he consequently rose to higher favor (*Ant.* 18.167).

Furthermore, the fact that Ehud is able to engage Eglon in conversation (ὁμιλία - the word implies a confidential discussion or personal talk) (*Ant.* 5.191) and thus to divert the king's attention is a clear indication of his mental acuity.

As to the virtue of courage and skill in battle, it is significant that whereas the Bible introduces Ehud in general terms as a "deliverer" (*moshia'*) (Judges 3:15), Josephus refers to him as most brave (ἀνδρειότατος) in daring (τολμῆσαι) and most able (δυνατώτατος, "most mighty") in using his body for the accomplishment of deeds (ἔργα) (*Ant.* 5.188). We may note that though, as we have remarked, Josephus speaks of many of the biblical heroes as brave in his extra-biblical additions, only four others – Joshua (*Ant.* 3.49), Abimelech the son of Gideon (*Ant.* 7.142), Sibbechai the Hushathite (*Ant.* 7.301), and Elhanan the son of Jaare-oregim (*Ant.* 7.302) – are referred to in the superlative as "most brave," used of Ehud here.

As to daring, the verb τολμάω, "to dare," which is employed in both a positive and a negative sense by Josephus, is used approvingly of Abraham (*Ant.* 1.155), Samson (*Ant.* 5.298), Jonathan the son of King Saul (*Ant.* 6.111), David (*Ant.* 6.210 and, by implication, 6.177), and Daniel (*Ant.* 10.256). It is also used of a certain Eleazar, who is described as a youth of daring enterprise who stimulated his comrades by frequently making fearful havoc of the Romans at Machaerus, one of the last fortresses to fall to the Romans after the destruction of the Temple (*War* 7.196). In reading the Josephan passage about Ehud's daring exploit Josephus' Roman audience might well have thought of a similar exploit by the youths Nisus and Euryalus, who boldly entered the enemy lines in search of their leader Aeneas (Virgil, *Aeneid* 9.176-502); their exploit, however, is solely military in nature; and, moreover, they receive advance permission from the Trojan chiefs before setting out, whereas Ehud's mission involves clever planning and, so far as we can tell, is undertaken without prior consultation.

As for the description of Ehud as δυνατώτατος, "most mighty," this epithet is found in Josephus of only one other biblical figure,

Jephthah, who is described as a mighty man by reason of the valor of his forefathers (διὰ τὴν πατρῴαν ἀρετήν) and has his own troop of mercenaries which he maintained himself (*Ant.* 5.257). Jephthah, we may add, is, like Ehud, a judge of the Israelites; and, in a number of additions to the Bible (e.g., *Ant.* 5.258, 260, 261), Josephus stresses his qualities of leadership as well.

One might perhaps fault Ehud as less than brave, given the detail, added by Josephus that at the crucial point when he is just about to plunge his dagger into Ehud he is beset by fear (*Ant.* 5.192); but a closer examination of Josephus' text reveals that it is not cowardice that is the source of Ehud's fear here. He certainly is determined to go through with the attempt to assassinate Eglon; his only fear is that he may fail to inflict a mortal blow.[10]

4. *The Rehabilitation of Eglon*

Ehud's assassination of Eglon presented Josephus with at least two problems of major importance. In the first place, Josephus is very sensitive, as we have noted, to the charge that Jews hate non-Jews. It is, therefore, significant that in mentioning King Eglon's subjugation of the Israelites Josephus not only castigates the latter for doing what was evil in the sight of the L-rd (Judges 3:12) but also blames them for their lack of a functioning government (ἀναρχίας) and for their failure to obey the laws (*Ant.* 5.185), a theme likewise mentioned in Josephus' description of the state of the Israelites just before the judgeship of Keniaz, Ehud's predecessor (*Ant.* 5.179), and repeated in his account of the behavior of the Israelites shortly after the death of Ehud (*Ant.* 5.198). Josephus then adds that it is out of his contempt (καταφρονήσαντα) for the Israelites' disorder (ἀκοσμίας) that Eglon made war upon them.[11] Significantly, in the Bible Eglon is depicted as the means by which

---

[10] In the Latin version (*Ant.* 5.192) Ehud is beset with fear lest he not be able to strike Eglon "most bravely" (*fortissime*), but this seems most likely to represent a paraphrase, rather than a translation, of the Greek.

[11] The Latin version of the *Antiquities* (5.186) speaks of Eglon as *despiciens inhonestam conversationem*, that is, having contempt for the shameful ("dishonorable," "disgraceful") intercourse of the Israelites; but it seems unlikely that Eglon would despise the Israelites for their intercourse with foreign women. Likewise, the Latin version states that Eglon *praesumeret*, that is, took the initiative, in attacking the Israelites; but it seems more likely that he was reacting to the Israelites' anarchy rather than that he made a preemptive strike against them.

G-d punishes the Israelites for their neglect of Him (Judges 3:12), whereas in Josephus Eglon acts on his own, with no mention of G-d's role, in taking advantage of the Israelites' anarchy (*Ant.* 5.186).

If, then, Eglon inflicts bodily injury (κακώσεως)[12] upon the Israelites, it is occasioned, according to Josephus, in an extra-biblical comment, by the anarchy (ἀναρχία, *Ant.* 6.84) which prevailed after Joshua's death and which represents the very opposite of the aristocratic rule that prevailed under Moses and Joshua and that was restored by Ehud after the eighteen years of anarchy (Judges 3:14). Josephus equates such anarchy with disorder (ἀκοσμίαν) and contempt (ὕβριν) of G-d and the laws, as we see in his remark that after the judgeship of Jair the Israelites degenerated into such a state before the appearance of another true leader, Jephthah (*Ant.* 5.255).

The above theme of the dreadful consequences of anarchy and civil strife pervades much of Josephus' paraphrase of the *Antiquities*. Furthermore, one might almost say that that same theme is the central motif of the *Jewish War*. Josephus is particularly concerned to emphasize the importance of showing respect for the legitimate ruler of a nation, even if that ruler may be guilty of performing reprehensible acts. One may readily understand why Josephus adopts this position, inasmuch as he was recipient of a multitude of favors from Roman autocrats.

In the case of Eglon, we may note that the Bible remarks that he formed an alliance with Ammon and Amalek (Judges 3:13); this would surely diminish, at least for Josephus' Jewish readers, their regard for Eglon, inasmuch as the Ammonites were almost constantly at war with the Israelites and inasmuch as especially the Amalekites were the people who, though unprovoked, had attacked the Israelites during the latter's sojourn in the desert after the Exodus. Josephus, realizing that mention of such an alliance would demean the status of Eglon, very carefully omits all mention of it.

Alter suggests that the Bible is actually poking fun at Eglon's stu-

---

[12] Thackeray (1934, 5:85) translates οὐδὲν τῆς εἰς τὸ πλῆθος κακώσεως παρέλιπεν as "he ruthlessly molested the people," but this rendering is at variance with Josephus' care to avoid downgrading non-Jews, especially their rulers. The more literal – and more likely – translation would thus seem to be that "he omitted nothing of bodily injury (κακώσεως, "devastation," "ruin") against the multitude."

pidity, but Josephus has too much regard for legitimate rulers, as we have noted, to give such an impression (Alter 1981, 19-20). We may note that Josephus totally omits reference to the fact, which might well be a source of ridicule, that Eglon was very fat (Judges 3:17), as well as the statement that when Ehud killed him the fat closed upon the blade (Judges 3:22).[13] Moreover, whereas the Bible mentions the gruesome detail that when Ehud thrust his sword into Eglon's belly his excrement came out (Judges 3:22), Josephus passes over this indelicate remark (*Ant.* 5.193). In particular, we may note that whereas the biblical pericope mentions that Eglon was defecating (Judges 3:24)[14] and therefore was not interrupted by his servants, Josephus, finding such a detail unseemly in reference to a monarch, explains the failure of the servants to come to his aid sooner by remarking that they thought that he had fallen asleep (*Ant.* 5.193).

5. *"Improvements" in the Story: Clarifications, Increased Suspense and Drama*

One basic motivation for Josephus' writing of a paraphrase of the Scripture was to clear up obscurities in the text. Thus, it is not clear from the biblical text whether Ehud had previously not consulted the Israelites before undertaking his plan to assassinate Eglon or whether he had acted in consultation with the Israelites, inasmuch as the text simply states that the Israelites sent tribute through him and then declares, without explaining the connection, that Ehud made a sword for himself (Judges 3:16). Josephus clarifies the matter by stating that after assassinating Eglon, Ehud reported the matter secretly to the Israelites at Jericho and exhorted them to

---

[13] To be sure, in the former passage (Judges 3:17), the Septuagint, in both major versions, reads that Eglon was ἀστεῖος (that is, "elegant," "charming," "refined," "handsome"); but in the latter passage (Judges 3:22) it is clear that Eglon is very fat, since the Greek, again in both versions, states that when Ehud plunged his weapon into him, the fat (στέαρ) closed in upon the blade.

[14] The Hebrew text reads *mesik hu' et ragelav* ("he is covering his feet"), but the Targum Jonathan, basing itself on *Yevamot* 103a, understands this as a euphemism for moving one's bowels. The Septuagint (version B) reads: ἀποκενοῖ τοὺς πόδας, that is, "he is draining [exhausting] his feet," clearly a euphemism for evacuating. Version A reads: ἀποχωρήσει τοῦ κοιτῶνος, that is, "in the retreat of the bed-chamber"; but the word ἀποχωρήσει also means "voidance" and is used especially of excretions.

assert their liberty (*Ant.* 5.194). The fact that they welcomed the news would suggest that they were previously unaware of Ehud's plan.

As the story stands in the Bible, there are a number of additional difficulties; indeed, it crowds into the space of a few verses the highest concentration of rare and unique vocabulary in the literature of ancient Israel (so Halpern (1988, 40). Moreover, there are a number of apparent implausibilities.[15] In the first place, one wonders why the biblical narrator states that after presenting Israel's tribute Ehud turned back from the sculptured stones (*pesilim*, "quarries") near Gilgal (Judges 3:19). It would seem to be a long and useless journey for him to first depart from Eglon's capital, perhaps Medeba, then cross the Jordan to Gilgal, and finally return to the capital again. So great is this problem that Wiese adopts the radical solution of postulating that the first half of the verse is an addition by a learned scribe (Wiese 1926, 4-5). Kraeling, followed by Rousel, defends the received text by asserting that since at the time that Ehud presented the tribute Eglon was likely to be attended by enough armed guards to impress the Israelite delegation with his power, Ehud could not possibly have hoped to see the king in private at that moment (Kraeling 1935, 206-7; Rösel 1977, 270-71). The trip to Gilgal was necessary in order for Ehud to receive a divine message from the *pesilim*, while Eglon, in his eagerness to hear what he had learned there, readily admitted him to a private interview. But, we may remark, the text says not that Ehud went to Gilgal but merely that he went from Gilgal, nor is there any indication that this was the site of an oracle or that the *pesilim* were oracular stones.

A second difficulty is to be found in the fact that Ehud, after returning from Gilgal tells the king that he has a secret errand, whereupon those that stood near the king retire (Judges 3:19); but immediately thereafter we read that Ehud came to him and again told the king that he had a message for him (Judges 3:20). In verse 19 Eglon is in a large audience-chamber, but in the next verse he is in a private room. One solution is to suppose that Eglon dismissed his retinue and then received Ehud alone; another is to postulate that the first report of Ehud's message was announced by an attendant (Judges 3:19); but, as Moore points out, neither solu-

---

[15] See Kraeling (1935, 205-10) and Rösel (1977, 270-72).

tion is exegetically plausible, and he resolves the problem by suggesting that we have two separate sources here (Moore 1898, 95-96). Kraeling, for his part, assumes that the storyteller is somewhat sloppy here and leaves a few things to the imagination of his readers, notably that the king retired to his private chambers and that Ehud was conducted there by the king's servants (Kraeling 1935, 207).

A third and truly major difficulty is to explain how Ehud managed to escape. Glaser postulates that there was a small chamber within Eglon's upper chamber (Judges 3:24), the former being a privy, and that Ehud made his escape by sliding down through the toilet (Glaser 1932, 81-82). But why should we suppose that Eglon locked the door upon leaving the room to go to the alleged privy? Indeed, the fact that Ehud managed to get out unsuspected would seem to indicate that he came down the stairs in normal fashion (so Rösel 1977, 271-72). So puzzling is this question of how Ehud managed to escape that in the most recent treatment of this problem Halpern devotes no fewer than eighteen pages to solving the mystery (Halpern 1988, 43-60).

Fourthly, why, as Halpern appositely remarks, did the king's courtiers fetch a key and unlock the doors that the key had locked (Judges 3:25) (Halpern 1988, 44)? Why did they not check the unlocked access that Ehud had used?

What is most remarkable about the above four difficulties is that all of them are resolved by Josephus by simply omitting these problematic details: there is no mention of Ehud's trip to Gilgal, no second address of Ehud to the king, no indication that the small chamber was a privy, and no suggestion as to how Ehud escaped other than that he locked the door as he left.

We may also wonder how Ehud was able to hide a two-edged sword (*ḥerev*, Judges 3:16) a cubit (about eighteen inches) in length under his clothing.[16] The Septuagint, in both major versions, to be sure, reduces the sword to a large knife (μάχαιρα) a span (σπιθαμή, about nine inches) long; but Josephus resolves the credibility

---

[16] This problem is cited by Rösel (1977, 270), who concludes that it was perhaps a pointed weapon (which works more rapidly and leaves fewer traces) rather than a sickle-shaped sword; but neither the Hebrew *ḥerev* nor the Greek μάχαιρα lends itself to such an interpretation, whereas Josephus' ξιφίδιον would do so much more.

problem by turning the weapon into a mere dagger (ξιφίδιον) and by not indicating its length at all (*Ant.* 5.190).

If we wonder why Eglon should have been so foolish as to grant a member of a subdued tribute-paying nation a private conference with no one else present, Josephus explains that Ehud had won his confidence with frequent gifts, had come back with an allegedly divine interpretation of a dream, and had managed to engage the king in a conversation (*Ant.* 5.191).

Still, we might suppose that Eglon must have shrieked when assailed, so that his many attendants would have heard him, especially since, according to the biblical text Ehud thrust his sword into Ehud's fat belly (Judges 3:21), in which case death would have been delayed considerably. In Josephus' version the death blow is inflicted not to the belly but to Eglon's heart (*Ant.* 5.193), which certainly would have greatly hastened his end.

Moreover, in view of the question why the guards would have supposed that Eglon was defecating for so long (Judges 3:24), Josephus offers a much more reasonable scenario, namely that they supposed that he had fallen asleep (*Ant.* 5.193).

One means by which Josephus seeks to "improve" upon the biblical narrative is through providing better motivation and through increasing the plausibility of events. Thus we may wonder how Ehud had come to be so well-known to King Eglon as to be trusted by him. Josephus adds to the biblical narrative in noting that Ehud lived in Jericho,[17] the capital of Eglon's kingdom (*Ant.* 5.188), and that he had become familiar with the king prior to the assassination attempt (*Ant.* 5.189). As to why the guards did not suspect that something was wrong when they did not hear from the king, Josephus (*Ant.* 5.190) explains that it was summer-time and that the guards were relaxed both because of the heat and because they had gone to lunch.

Josephus also tries to increase the dramatic interest of the biblical narrative. In our pericope, the Bible (Judges 3:20) very prosaically has Ehud tell Eglon that he has a message from G-d for him. Aside from the fact that it would seem implausible that a pagan king would be so gullible as to be allow himself to be deceived in this manner, there is nothing very original or exciting in such a narrative device. In Josephus' version (*Ant.* 5.193) Ehud's strata-

---

[17] In the Latin version it is Eglon, and not Ehud, who is residing in Jericho (*Ant.* 5.188).

gem is much more exciting; there, as in the Bible, he does claim to have a message from G-d, but what he tells Eglon is that he has a dream to disclose to him by commandment of G-d. At this point, overjoyed at news of this dream, Eglon actually leaps up from his throne, whereupon Ehud has the opportunity that he sought to stab him with his dagger. In this connection we may also note Josephus' interest in dreams in that he records no fewer than fifty dreams (along with their truth and fulfillment in every case).

There is also increased drama in Josephus' portrayal (*Ant.* 5.195) in Josephus' account of the reaction of Eglon's courtiers to the discovery of his corpse. In the Bible (Judges 3:25) we read only that they opened the doors of the upper room and found that the king had fallen down to the ground dead. Josephus (*Ant.* 5.195) adds to the drama by stating that when they found the corpse they stood in helpless perplexity (ἀμηχανίᾳ, "want of resources").

There is a further increase of drama in Josephus' description (*Ant.* 5.196) of the rout of the Moabites that follows Ehud's deed. Whereas the Bible (Judges 3:29) says merely that the Israelites killed ten thousand strong, able-bodied Moabites and that none escaped, Josephus (*Ant.* 5.196) adds poignant details: some were massacred on the spot; the rest took flight to seek safety in Moab, whereupon the Israelites pursued them and massacred multitudes of them at the ford of the Jordan.

One of the ways in which Josephus heightens interest in his narrative is by increasing suspense. In the narrative of the assassination of Eglon Josephus adds to the suspense, while also enhancing the reader's admiration for Ehud's ingenuity by building up more effectively to the assassination itself. In particular, we have the added detail, noted above, that Ehud (*Ant.* 5.189) won the confidence of Eglon by courting and cajoling him with presents. The suspense is heightened by the added ironic fact (*Ant.* 5.190) that it was while he was actually bringing his gifts to Eglon that he secretly girt a dagger about his right thigh. There is further added suspense in that Ehud and the king now fall into conversation. Lastly, we have a final suspenseful touch, unparalleled in the biblical version, which also gives a more human flavor to the story, namely (*Ant.* 5.192) that fear overtook Ehud lest he strike amiss and not deal a mortal blow. It is at this point that Ehud makes use of the brilliant device by which he gets the king to rise, namely telling him that he has a dream to disclose to him by commandment of G-d. There is further suspense in the fact that, according to Josephus' extra-biblical comment (*Ant.* 5.195), Eglon's courtiers remained ignorant of his fate for a long time before they discovered his body.[18]

6. *Summary*

The fact that Josephus devotes so much space to the episode of Eglon and Ehud indicates how significant this was to him. Because he realized how important physical appearance was for a hero he omits the statement that Ehud had a shriveled right hand and instead states that he was superior in the use of his left hand. He adds considerably to Ehud's stature by asserting that he held the office of governor for eighty years, longer than any other judge. We see Ehud's quality of leadership in his success in exhorting his fellow Israelites to assert their liberty – a leitmotif in the history of the Jewish people as Josephus portrays it. Josephus was definitely sensitive to the charge of trickery that might have been made against Ehud, but inasmuch as the latter acts in the name of liberty this appears in a different light. On the contrary, his cleverness in courting Eglon and in engaging him in conversation would be admired even by Gentile readers. Because the Jews had been reproached with cowardice Josephus, in an extra-biblical addition, takes care to describe Ehud as most brave in daring and most mighty in the use of his body for the accomplishment of deeds.

Josephus is eager not to cast aspersions on non-Jews, especially their leaders. Hence, instead of blaming Eglon for subjugating the Israelites he places the onus upon the Israelites themselves for their anarchy and for their failure to obey the laws – another common theme in Josephus. For the same reason he also omits such disparaging elements as Eglon's obesity and his defecation.

Josephus clarifies a number of obscurities in the biblical text. Thus he makes it clearer that the Israelites were previously unaware of Ehud's plan to assassinate Eglon. Moreover, there are a number of difficulties and improbabilities in the biblical story, notably Ehud's apparently useless trip to the sculptured stones near Gilgal, Ehud's double approach to the king, the lack of a plausible explanation as to how Ehud managed to escape, and the

---

[18] I am grateful to my student, Howard M. Sragow, for several fine insights in connection with this essay.

failure of the king's courtiers to check the unlocked access that Ehud had used. In all of these cases Josephus resolves the problem by simply omitting the details in question. On the other hand, he satisfactorily explains how Eglon came to trust Ehud, namely because the latter had won his confidence with frequent gifts and because he had come to him with an allegedly divine interpretation of a dream – a detail which also increases the dramatic interest of the narrative. He plausibly explains as well that the reason why the king's guards did not suspect foul play was that they were relaxed on account of the summer heat and their being away for lunch. Finally, Josephus has added to the suspense of the pericope by building up more effectively to the assassination itself, especially by noting that Ehud felt fear lest he strike amiss and not deal Eglon a mortal blow.

CHAPTER NINE

DEBORAH

1. *Introduction: The Insignificance of Deborah for Josephus*

With the tremendous rise in recent years of interest in the portraits of women in ancient literature it is surprising that scholarship has neglected Josephus' presentations of women in Jewish history[1]. His pericope dealing with the prophetess and judge Deborah should be of particular interest in this connection because of her prominence in the Bible itself.

In order to appreciate what Josephus has done with the figure of Deborah, it may be helpful to consider how she appears both in rabbinic tradition, with which, as we have indicated, there is ample reason to think Josephus was well acquainted, and in the *Biblical Antiquities* of Pseudo-Philo, Josephus' presumed contemporary.[2] The first thing that strikes us in such an examination is the brevity of Josephus' account, especially as compared with that of Pseudo-Philo, this despite the fact that the former very often expands greatly on the biblical narrative, as for example in the case of the early years of Moses. The story of Sisera, Deborah, Barak, and Jael, which in the Bible (Judges 4:1-5:31) comprises 104 lines (64 of which are in the Song of Deborah) (172 lines in Version A in the Septuagint; 166 lines in Version B in the Septuagint), is reduced to 66 lines in Josephus (*Ant.* 5.200-210), giving a ratio of .63

---

[1] An examination of the bibliographies of Josephus (Schreckenberg 1968 and 1979) and Feldman (1984 and 1986) indicates that until 1986 there was only one attempt to survey Josephus' attitude toward women – Stagg and Stagg (1978, 45-48). This is not only brief but omits many passages, particularly where Josephus paraphrases the Bible, and has nothing to say about Josephus' version of the Deborah episode. The authors conclude (p. 45) that "Josephus is more restrained than many of his day, but he definitely reflects a male bias, consciously or not." Since then the brief but valuable survey by Amaru (1988, 143-70) has appeared. In addition, Brown (1992) includes brief studies of Josephus' portraits of Deborah, Jephthah's daughter, Hannah, and the Witch of Endor.

[2] Cf. Feldman 1971, xxvii-xxxi. See also Delling (1971, 1-18), who, on the basis of his study of the Hymn of Deborah in Pseudo-Philo and, in particular, its account of Abraham's readiness to sacrifice his son Isaac, concludes that Pseudo-Philo was a pious Jew who lived in Palestine about 100 C.E. with similarities to the author of the *Paralipomena Jeremiae*.

of Josephus to the Hebrew text (.38 to Version A of the Septuagint, .40 to Version B of the Septuagint), whereas Pseudo-Philo, in a work of a mere sixty-five chapters covering the period from creation to the death of Saul, devotes no fewer than four chapters (30-33) and a total of 304 lines[3] (118 of which are the Song of Deborah) to the pericope.

At the very beginning of his version of the Deborah narrative Josephus sets the scene for a Greek tragedy, for we are told, in a passage that has no counterpart in the Bible (compare Judges 4:3), that for twenty years the Israelites suffered (πάσχοντες) and failed to learn from their adversity (ἤνυσαν μήτε αὐτοὶ φρονεῖν ὑπὸ τῆς δυστυχίας ὄντες ἀγαθοί); and G-d sought to tame their insolence (ὕβριν) because of their lack of good sense (ἀγνωμοσύνη, "obstinacy", "rudeness", "harshness", "ingratitude") with regard to Him, so that they might change their ways and in the future be wise (σωφρονῶσιν, "be moderate", "come to their senses") (*Ant.* 5.200). One is reminded here of the statement of the chorus in Aeschylus' *Agamemnon* (176-78) that Zeus, who has guided men to think (φρονεῖν), has laid down the rule that wisdom comes only through suffering (πάθει μάθος). Indeed, the prevailing lesson in so much of Greek tragedy is that one must learn moderation. In fact, the sin with which Josephus charges the Israelites here, ἀγνωμοσύνη, appears to be a synonym for arrogance;[4] and it is their insolence, ὕβρις, the foremost sin in Greek tragedy, which G-d now proposes to tame.

Josephus adds an interesting touch at the beginning of his pericope (*Ant.* 5.200) with the extra-biblical detail that Deborah's name means a "bee" in Hebrew. We may note that Josephus seldom adds etymologies of the names of his biblical characters and that when he does it is usually to denigrate them. For example (*Ant.* 1.205), he gives the etymologies of Moab ("of the father") and of Ammon ("son of the race"), the sons of Lot resulting by incest with his daughters. That his etymology of Deborah's name is, indeed, also intended as derogatory is to be seen from the fact that the Talmud cites this same meaning of her name as an indica-

---

[3] I use the text of Harrington 1976.
[4] Cf. Euripides, who in his *Bacchae*, 885, declares that the divine might punishes those who honor insolence (ἀγνωμοσύναν) and those who, in their madness, do not promote the interests of the gods. It is this same lack of good sense (ἀγνωμονοῦντος) which Josephus ascribes to Pharaoh (*Ant.* 2.296).

tion that she was haughty (*Megillah* 14b), since Scripture declares that she sent for and called Barak instead of going to him as would befit a woman (Judges 4:6).[5]

As to the overall stature of Deborah, this depends to a considerable degree upon the relative importance assigned to the other major figures in the story – Sisera, Barak, and Jael. The rabbinic tradition builds up the figure of Sisera by stating that he had achieved the status of a world-conqueror by the age of thirty,[6] a veritable Alexander the Great, whereas in the Bible Sisera is merely a local commander (Judges 4:2). The Bible, moreover, says nothing about his size or strength, whereas again the rabbis build him up by declaring that he was so huge that when he bathed in a river enough fish were caught in his beard to feed a multitude, that it required nine hundred horses to pull the chariot in which he rode (a detail derived, presumably, from the statement in the Bible that he had nine hundred chariots of iron [Judges 4:3]), and that when he spoke the mightiest of walls fell down and animals were paralyzed with fear. As to the number of troops arrayed against the Israelites, the rabbis declare that Sisera led thirty-one previously unconquered kings and no fewer than 40,000 armies, each consisting of 100,000 men, that is, a total of four billion soldiers.[7] Pseudo-Philo (*Bib. Ant.* 31. 2) similarly exaggerates the size

---

[5] The objection that the bee is the source of honey with which the land of Israel is said to flow (Deuteronomy 8:8) and hence that this must be a laudatory reference does not hold, inasmuch as, according to rabbinic tradition, the honey referred to in Deuteronomy derives from dates rather than from bees. Brown (1992, 91, n. 66) avers that Josephus' reference to "bee" in the *Antiquities* is not negative; but the key question is why Josephus bothers to give us the meaning of her name in the first place. And once one asks this question one would think of the associations of the bee, as noted above. Brown, 73, notes that the word which Josephus uses for "bee," μέλισσα, denotes a priestess of Delphi, and further remarks that such priestesses had no contact with men. She then concludes that this analogy with the bee would imply that Deborah was asexual, and she wonders (p. 74) whether Josephus' omission of the fact that Deborah was the wife of Lappidoth (Judges 4:4) has significance. But there is no indication in either the biblical text or in Josephus that Deborah was asexual; and the omission of the name of her husband may more readily be explained by the fact that Lappidoth plays no role in the narrative as related in the Bible.

[6] *Aguddat Aggadot* 77-78, *Abba Gorion* 27-28, *Neveh Shalom* 47-48, cited by Ginzberg (1928, 6:195, n.72).

[7] *Abba Gorion* 27, *Aguddat Aggadot* 77, *Neveh Shalom* 47, cited by Ginzberg (1928, 6:197, n. 80).

of Sisera's army by declaring that the number of its slain in one hour was ninety times 97,000 men[8], that is 8,730,000 men – all this in contrast to the simple statement of the Bible that Sisera had nine hundred chariots (Judges 4:3). To be sure, Josephus also exaggerates Sisera's numbers, stating that his army consisted of 300,000 footsoldiers, 10,000 horse, and 3,000 chariots (*Ant.* 5.199); but the exaggeration is nowhere near as great as in the rabbinic tradition or in Pseudo-Philo. Moreover, Josephus says nothing about the size or physical prowess of Sisera, presumably because he seeks to diminish the role of the miraculous in the biblical narrative.

2. *The Role of G-d in the Deborah Pericope*

In view of Josephus' de-emphasis elsewhere on theology and theodicy, it is all the more remarkable that in the Deborah pericope Josephus does stress the role of G-d, doing so, however, only, it would seem, to avoid aggrandizing the character of Deborah. Thus, whereas in the Bible (Judges 4:6), as well as in rabbinic tradition (*Megillah* 14b) and in Pseudo-Philo (*Bib. Ant.* 31.1), it is Deborah who summons Barak and informs him that G-d had commanded him to gather his troops for battle, in Josephus, while it is true that Deborah summons Barak (*Ant.* 5.202), she adds that G-d directly promised the Israelites salvation and chose Barak as their general (*Ant.* 5.201). This role of G-d in the choice of Barak is further emphasized in a dramatic scene added by Josephus (*Ant.* 5.203); for whereas in the Bible Barak says to Deborah merely "If thou wilt go with me, then I will go; but if thou wilt not go with me, I will not go," whereupon she replies that she will surely go with him (Judges 4:8-9), in Josephus she replies with indignation (ἀγανακτήσασα, "being vexed", "feeling a violent irritation"), stressing the role of G-d in his selection: "Thou resignest to a woman a rank that G-d has bestowed on thee!" (*Ant.* 5.203). Josephus here once again betrays his misogyny, since the indignation of his Deborah is caused by the fact that a man seeks to surrender to a woman a role that G-d has bestowed

---

[8] By a striking coincidence Josephus (*War* 6.420) gives the same figure, 97,000, for the number of those taken captive during the war leading to the destruction of the Temple. See my note in Feldman (1971, cxii).

upon him. Apparently, G-d does not want women in positions of military or political leadership.

Conversely, Josephus does nothing to invest the character of Deborah with an element of piety. In contrast, the rabbis, playing on the name of her husband Lappidoth (Judges 4:4: "flames"), say that she was so called because she used to make wicks for the Sanctuary (*Megillah* 14a). Again, the statement that she sat under a palm tree (Judges 4:5) is taken by the rabbis as an indication of her modesty (*Megillah* 14a), since in choosing the non-leafy palm tree as the site of her court sessions she took care to avoid the possibility of the scandal of appearing to be alone with men in a secluded place. Similarly, in Pseudo-Philo, Deborah is sent by the L-rd after the people have fasted for seven days (*Bib. Ant.* 30.5). She thereupon very piously, and speaking like a prophetess, addresses them, reminding them of G-d's previous acts of salvation, and predicts that G-d will show compassion for them now, but that they will begin to sin after her death. In particular, she alludes to the covenant which G-d had made with the patriarchs (*Bib. Ant.* 30.7), a point never mentioned in Josephus' account, since he consistently plays down the biblical stress on the covenantal land of Israel (so Amaru 1980-81, 201-29), inasmuch as this was the focal point for the revolutionaries of his own day.

As to Israel's actual battle against Sisera, the general of the Canaanites, the prose version of the biblical narrative states merely that the L-rd routed Sisera and all his chariots and that his entire army was annihilated, with Sisera alone fleeing on foot (Judges 4:12-16). The poetic song of Deborah that follows adds that the stars from their courses fought against Sisera and that the torrent of the river Kishon swept them away (Judges 5:20-21). The rabbis make much of this latter remark, affirming that Sisera's hosts were annihilated by the hosts of heaven, that is the stars and the angels (*Leviticus Rabbah* 7 [end]). The Talmud, expanding on the biblical verse (Judges 5:20), declares that as soon as the stars of heaven descended upon Sisera's soldiers and heated their iron staves, they went down to the brook of Kishon to cool them, whereupon, following G-d's command, the Kishon, which had long before pledged to participate in Sisera's defeat, swept them away into the sea (*Pesaḥim* 118b)[9]. Again, whereas in the biblical Song of Debo-

---

[9] Cf. also *Leviticus Rabbah* 7 (end), *Abba Gorion* 27, *Aguddat Aggadot* 77, *Neveh*

rah the angel of the L-rd declares that the inhabitants of Meroz should be cursed (Judges 5:23), presumably because they had failed to assist Barak and Deborah in the struggle against Sisera, the Talmud cites an alternate opinion that Meroz was the name of a constellation (*Mo'ed Qatan* 16a). Similarly, in Pseudo-Philo, when Deborah calls upon Barak to lead the fight against the Canaanites, she sees a vision of the constellations preparing to fight on behalf of the Israelites (*Bib. Ant.* 31.1). There follows a scene in which G-d disrupts the movements of the stars and orders them to hasten to confound the enemy and to break their strength, whereupon the stars "burned up" (*incenderunt*) Sisera and his forces (*Bib. Ant.* 31.2). Finally, both the rabbis (*Panim Aherim* 74, as noted in Yannai's hymn *Uvechen Vayehi Bahazi Halailah* near the end of the Passover Haggadah) and Pseudo-Philo (*Bib. Ant.* 32.16) connect Israel's victory over Sisera and Passover night, the former declaring that it occurred at midnight on Passover, and the latter comparing it to the night when G-d smote the first-born of the Egyptians.

Josephus, on the other hand, while aware of the biblical statement that the stars fought against Sisera, again avoids miraculous and grotesque elements and more plausibly declares that "amidst the clash of arms there came up a great tempest with torrents of rain and hail" (*Ant.* 5.205). He then explains that because of the strong wind that blew rain into the faces of the Canaanites, their vision was obscured, so that they were unable to make effective use of their bows and slings, while because of the cold the foot-soldiers could not use their swords. The Israelites, on the other hand, had the storm at their backs and hence were less hindered by it. One is reminded here of Josephus' rationalized version of the Israelites' crossing of the Sea of Reeds, with its added extra-biblical details, that is, that torrents of rain descended from heaven, along with crashing thunder and flashes of lightning, so that swelling, wind-swept billows enveloped the Egyptians (*Ant.* 2.343).

Neither the Bible, the rabbis, nor Pseudo-Philo gives any indication that Barak was dismayed by the host arrayed against him; but Josephus, in the interest of making the picture more dramatic,

---

Shalom 47, *Aggadat Bereshit* 1. 2, Tosefta *Sotah* 3.14, cited by Ginzberg (1928, 6:197, n. 81); and *Alphabet of Ben Sira* (*Blau Festschrift*), p. 269), cited by Rappaport (1930, 128, n. 197).

declares that the Israelites and Barak were terror-stricken at the multitude of the enemy (*Ant.* 5.204). He then adds the extra-biblical detail that Barak actually resolved to retreat, while it was Deborah who restrained him and who ordered him to stand in battle on that very day. The fact that Deborah thus saves the day might seem to contradict the view that Josephus is seeking to downgrade her role; but, we may remark, when she does so it is because, as a prophetess, she is sure, as she declares, that the Israelites will be victorious and that G-d will participate (συλλήψεσθαι) in the battle (*Ant.* 5.204). This role of Deborah as a prophetess is one which Josephus' Graeco-Roman audience could readily understand, since at the most famous oracle in Greece, that at Delphi, it was women who uttered the prophecies and since the most famous prophets in Roman tradition, the Sibyls, were likewise women. Elsewhere, moreover, it is the figure of Barak whom Josephus builds up, so that whereas, according to the rabbis, he, like most of his companions, was an ignoramus (*Exodus Rabbah* 10.48), Josephus not only has no equivalent to this detail but in paraphrasing Judges 4:23, which declares that G-d subdued Jabin, the king of Canaan, whose general was Sisera, Josephus says that it was Barak who slew Jabin and razed his city to the ground (*Ant.* 5.209).

3. *The Role of Jael*

Josephus was clearly in a quandary as to what to do with the incident in which Jael killed Sisera, since if he built this up too greatly it would detract from Deborah's achievement. In the Bible Jael's role is clearly subordinate to that of Deborah and Barak. The rabbis, on the contrary, build up her part in the narrative, noting that she was unusually beautiful and that even her voice aroused desire (*Megillah* 15a); and they increase the erotic element by noting that Sisera had sexual relations with her seven times on the day that he fled from battle (*Yevamot* 103a, *Nazir* 23b), and that she gave Sisera to drink from the milk of her breasts (*Niddah* 55b). Another rabbinic tradition has it that G-d attached His name to those of Joseph, Paltiel (the husband of Michal), and Jael to attest to the fact that they had successfully withstood sexual temptation (*Leviticus Rabbah* 23.10). Pseudo-Philo, similarly, paints an erotic scene by remarking that Jael was very fair, that she decked herself with her ornaments when she went out to meet Sisera, and that she scattered roses upon her bed (*Bib. Ant.* 31.3).

Josephus, on the other hand, who is wont to build up the erotic element in his narrative, avoids such elements as would detract from the sheer heroism of Jael. In particular, we may note that whereas in the Bible it is Jael who takes the initiative in going out to meet Sisera and in enticing him to enter her tent, while falsely assuring him that he has nothing to fear (Judges 4:18), Josephus, well aware that this description could lead to a charge of deceit and of violation of the etiquette of hospitality, makes Sisera take the initiative to ask Jael to conceal him (*Ant.* 5.207). Indeed, the veritable climax of the account is to be found in Josephus' statement that when Jael showed the dead Sisera to Barak the victory thus redounded (περιέστη, "passed to," "devolved upon," "came round to") to a woman (εἰς γυναῖκα) (*Ant.* 5.209). Hence, the victory is credited to Jael, rather than to Deborah. If this seems surprising in view of Josephus' notorious misogyny, we may remark that since the main target of his misogyny in this episode is, after all, Deborah, he was ready even to build up Jael so as to downgrade the importance of Deborah.

4. *The Song of Deborah*

The most striking difference between Josephus, on the one hand, and the Bible, the rabbinic tradition, and Pseudo-Philo, on the other hand, is the former's total omission of the Song of Deborah. In the Bible this song (Judges 5) occupies an entire chapter of thirty-one verses. In Pseudo-Philo it likewise takes up an entire chapter (32), which is itself almost three times as long as its biblical parallel. The simple explanation of its omission by Josephus is that he is writing a history and not a book of poetry. Indeed, we may note that Josephus similarly omits the Songs of Moses (Exodus 15:1-18) and of Miriam (Exodus 15:21).[10] In the Exodus context Josephus does, to be sure, add that after their great victory over Pharaoh the Israelites "passed the whole night in melody and

---

[10] As Brown (1992, 90-91, n. 60) remarks, Josephus consistently omits poetic material, such as the Song of Hannah (1 Samuel 2:1-10; *Ant.* 5.347); to this we may add his omission of the Song of Moses just before his death (Deuteronomy 33:1-29; *Ant.* 4.329) and David's lament for Saul and Jonathan (2 Samuel 1:19-27, *Ant.* 7.4).

mirth, Moses himself composing in hexameter verse a song to G-d to enshrine His praises and their thankfulness for His gracious favor" (*Ant.* 2.346). Here, however, there is no indication that Deborah even sang a song, let alone there being no citation of its contents, for example, the statement in the Song (Judges 5:14-18) that the tribes of Reuben, Dan, and Asher did not join in the fight against the Canaanites, that Ephraim, Benjamin, Zebulun, Issachar, and Naphtali fought to the death, that the battle took place at Taanach near the waters of Megiddo (Judges 5:19), that Meroz (whoever he was) did not come to the help of the Israelites (Judges 5:23), and – a human touch that would have heightened the interest of the narrative – that the mother of Sisera gazed out the window looking for the return of her son (Judges 5:28).

Above all, Josephus has omitted the embellishments so remarkable in Pseudo-Philo's version of the Song, notably Deborah's review of Israelite history, with its emphasis on the touching scene of Abraham's readiness to sacrifice his son Isaac (Pseudo-Philo, *Bib. Ant.* 32.1-4). Nor does Josephus present a farewell speech by Deborah, such as we find in Pseudo-Philo (*Bib. Ant.* 33.1-5), which is reminiscent of Moses' farewell address in its poignancy and in its piety, just as he lacks the beautiful lament for Deborah by the people: "Behold, a mother is perished out of Israel, and a holy one who bore rule in the house of Jacob, who made fast the fence about her generation, and her generation shall seek after her" (*Bib. Ant.* 33.6). The net effect of this eulogy, we may suggest, is to present a portrait of Deborah as a mother in Israel, fully comparable to the matriarchs, to the patriarchs, and to Moses. Josephus, on the other hand, says nothing about Deborah's death other than that she and Barak died simultaneously, as if to say that they were of equal importance in the struggle against the Canaanites, whereas in the Bible, in Pseudo-Philo, and in rabbinic literature it is clearly Deborah who is the more important figure. Moreover, where the Bible's account of this episode ends with the indeterminate statement that after the death of Sisera "the land had rest for forty years" (Judges 5:31), Josephus specifically affirms that it was Barak who held command of the Israelites for forty years (*Ant.* 5.209). Thus, despite Barak's initial refusal to carry out his commission and despite his cowardly behavior before the battle, Josephus' portrayal of him reflects his opposition to a woman filling such a role. It is his way of saying that even a bad male leader is better than a good female one (so Brown 1992, 81).

5. *Summary*

Josephus, especially when his account is compared with those of the rabbis and of Pseudo-Philo, has, in his misogyny, both reduced the length of the episode and the importance of Deborah, downgrading her in her role as poetess, military leader, and judge (so Brown 1992, 71). On the contrary, it is the roles of Barak and Sisera that are built up. Through rationalizing he avoids the miraculous and the grotesque so prominent in rabbinic literature and in Pseudo-Philo, though he stresses the importance of the role of Divine help in order to depreciate still further the stature of Deborah. He has diminished the element of Deborah's piety so prominent in the rabbis and in Pseudo-Philo. Rather, it is her role as a prophetess, which Josephus' Graeco-Roman audience would have allowed to women, that is stressed. Moreover, it is to Jael, rather than to Deborah, that the victory over Sisera is ascribed. The most striking difference between the accounts in the Bible, the rabbis, and Pseudo-Philo, on the one hand, and Josephus, on the other hand, is Josephus' total omission of the Song of Deborah, including even factual details mentioned in the Song. By omitting the Song he has reduced her to a prosaic figure, hardly more prominent than any of the other judges and prophets and certainly not the central figure that she is especially in Pseudo-Philo's *Biblical Antiquities*. In his summary of the period Josephus implies that Deborah and Barak, the military leader of the Israelites in the struggle against the Canaanites, were of equal importance and ignores the predominant role of Deborah.

CHAPTER TEN

GIDEON

1. *Introduction*

In portraying the judge Gideon Josephus was in something of a dilemma. On the one hand, the Bible itself seems to have reservations about him, in that it states that G-d sent Gideon to save Israel (Judges 6:14), and yet, as far as his family background goes, Gideon describes himself as being the youngest in his father's household and coming from the poorest family of the tribe of Manasseh (Judges 6:15); nor, for that matter, does the Bible explicitly state that he actually saved Israel – a claim that is to be found in the biblical accounts of the judges Othniel (Judges 3:9), Ehud (Judges 3:15), Shamgar (Judges 3:31), and Tola (Judges 10:1).

There is a similar apparent ambiguity in Josephus' presumed contemporary, Pseudo-Philo,[1] in his *Biblical Antiquities*, who describes Gideon, seemingly in praise, as the most mighty (*fortissimus*) among all his brothers (35.1), but who also states that he made and worshipped idols and would have deserved rebuke except for the fact that in that case people would say that it was Baal who was chastising him for destroying his sanctuary of that god at an earlier date (*Bib. Ant.* 36.3-4). This ambiguity is particularly striking in view of Pseudo-Philo's extended passage of high praise for another judge, Kenaz (*Bib. Ant.* 25-28), who is known in the Bible only as the father of the judge Othniel (Judges 3:9).

There would seem to be similar ambiguity in the rabbinic tradition with regard to Gideon. Thus, the Talmud quotes the passage placing him with Jephthah, Samson, and Samuel, and even with Moses and Aaron, as having been sent by G-d to save the Israelites (1 Samuel 12:11) (*Rosh Hashanah* 25a-b); Gideon is likewise praised for his filial piety in sacrificing his father's bullock after the angel appeared to him, even though he would have transgressed no fewer than seven commandments, were it not for the fact that he was obeying an explicit divine commandment (Jerusalem Talmud, *Megillah* 1.14.72c). And yet, on the other hand, the rabbinic

---

[1] For the date see Feldman (1971, xxvii-xxxi; and 1974, 305-6).

tradition also states categorically that Gideon, Jephthah, and Samson were the three least worthy (*qalei 'olam*, "light ones of the world") characters (*Rosh Hashanah* 25b). Indeed, so worthless do the rabbis regard Gideon that it is from him that they deduce the principle that Jerubaal (i.e. Gideon, so named because, according to the Bible [Judges 6:32], he had broken down the altar of Baal), who was the lowliest in rank in his generation, is like Moses (the greatest man who ever lived) in his generation and that, consequently, the most worthless, once he has been appointed a leader of the community, is to be accounted like the mightiest of the mighty (*Rosh Hashanah* 25b).

One clue, as we have seen, as to the importance which Josephus assigns to a biblical personality is the sheer amount of space that he assigns to him as compared with the amount of attention which that character receives in the Bible. As for Gideon, the ratio of Josephus (*Ant.* 5.213-33: 135 lines in the Loeb Classical Library text) to the Hebrew text (Judges 6:11-8:35: 150 lines) is .90 and to Rahlfs' text of the Septuagint (245 lines) is .55. Thus, clearly, Gideon is for Josephus one of the least important biblical figures; but this, as we shall see, is due to Josephus' omissions of whole episodes which either would reflect badly on Gideon or would not suit Josephus' overall apologetic goals. Indeed, in his concern to protect the high status of Gideon Josephus is comparable to the New Testament book of Hebrews (11:32-34), which speaks of him in the same breath as Barak, Samson, Jephthah, David, Samuel, and "the prophets." Hebrews then proceeds to state, in a note of extreme praise, the common denominator of these figures, namely that through faith they "conquered kingdoms, enforced justice, received promises, and stopped the mouths of lions, quenched raging fire, escaped the edge of the sword, won strength out of weakness, became mighty in war, put foreign armies to flight." It is hard to imagine greater compliments than these, especially the bracketing of Gideon with those who, from the point of view of the author of Hebrews, were the supreme figures in human history prior to Jesus, namely the Hebrew prophets, the alleged predicters of the coming of Jesus himself.

2. The Qualities of Gideon

The first of the thirty-six stages in praising a person was, according to the Greek rhetorician Theon, to laud his ancestry (Spengel 1854, 2:60-130; Talbert 1980, 135). As for Gideon, his genealogy was anything but prominent, if we may judge from the Bible, which quotes Gideon himself as saying that his family was the poorest in the tribe of Manasseh and that he himself was the least in his father's house (Judges 6:15). Josephus, however, rehabilitates him by remarking, in an editorial comment, that Gideon was one of the foremost (ἐν ὀλίγοις) among the tribe of Manasseh (*Ant.* 5.213). Indeed, we may remark, Josephus embellishes the genealogy not only of Gideon but also of Jephthah (*Ant.* 5.257) and Samson (*Ant.* 5.276) – precisely the three judges who are singled out by the rabbis as the least worthy leaders of the Israelites (*Rosh Hashanah* 25b).

If we ask to what degree Gideon, in Josephus' portrait, attains the standard cardinal virtues, we see that he is depicted as a model (ἄκρος, "topmost," "highest") of every virtue (ἀρετήν) (*Ant.* 5.230). His supremacy of virtue is likewise seen in Josephus' extrabiblical addition that G-d showed Gideon in a dream the hatred that human nature bears to those of surpassing merit (τοὺς ἀρετῇ διαφέροντας), the reference clearly being to himself (*Ant.* 5.215).

Gideon's wisdom is shown by his ability to use calculated reflection (λογισμός) in making decisions. As Josephus puts it, he showed this quality, in particular, in not attacking the enemy on the basis of an arbitrary decision (αὐτοκράτορι λογισμῷ) (*Ant.* 5.230).

Inasmuch as the chief virtue of the judges was their courage in the face of the enemy, we should not be surprised to find Josephus consistently highlighting this virtue. In the case of Gideon, the Bible paints a picture of Gideon beating out wheat in the winepress in order to enable his father to flee from Midian (Judges 6:11). Realizing that portraying Gideon's father as fleeing before the enemy would not enhance the son's portrait, Josephus makes no mention of such a flight; but, aware that he had to explain why Gideon was beating out wheat in a winepress, he states that he feared to do so openly on the threshing floor (*Ant.* 5.213). Moreover, Gideon's military achievement in overcoming the enemy is all the greater in Josephus' version because he so much dramatizes the oppression that the Israelites were suffering; in particular, the drama is enhanced by Gideon's bitter and sarcastic remark to the spectre that pronounces him blessed and beloved of G-d. "Indeed," he says, "this is a signal proof of his favor that I am now using a winepress instead of a threshing floor!" (*Ant.* 5.213).

Again, the achievement of Gideon in overcoming the Midianite enemy is all the greater because when a spectre in the form of a young man bids him to undertake the leadership in regaining liberty for the Israelites, he replies that this is impossible, inasmuch as the tribe to which he belonged was small in numbers and inasmuch as he was so young (*Ant.* 5.214). In the Bible the task is not as great, inasmuch as we have only Gideon's statement, "Please, O L-rd, with what shall I save Israel?" (Judges 6:15).

Moreover, Gideon's courage is magnified not only by the fact that he is able to overcome the Midianites with a meager force of three hundred men but also, as Josephus adds, by the fact that these three hundred were fearful and trembling and, therefore, in effect, cowards (*Ant.* 5.217).

The Bible, moreover, paints a picture of a Gideon who is so fearful that G-d tells him to take his lad, Purah, with him to the camp of the Midianites so that he may be strengthened by what he hears there (Judges 7:10). Josephus, realizing that the mention of Gideon's taking the lad would suggest that the terror was not so great and hence that Gideon's fear is really groundless, replaces the lad with a soldier and adds that Gideon derives his courage (φρόνημα) and confidence (θάρσος) from overhearing what the enemy was saying (*Ant.* 5.218).

Again, in attempting to dissuade the Israelites from choosing a king, Samuel reminds them that God sent the judges Jerubaal (Gideon), Bedan (i.e. Samson), Jephthah, and Samuel to save them from their enemies (1 Samuel 12:11). In Josephus' version the list of judges is reduced to two, Jephthah and Gideon, who consequently gain in importance; secondly, there is no specific mention of G-d's sending them, and so their own achievement is heightened; and thirdly, they act as generals (στρατηγούντων) and not as mere messengers of G-d (*Ant.* 6.90).

The third of the cardinal virtues, temperance (σωφροσύνη), was a quality of supreme importance to the Greeks, as we have seen. As for Gideon, the fact that Josephus juxtaposes his being moderate (μέτριος) and his being a model of every virtue would seem to indicate that he regarded Gideon's quality of moderation as particularly characteristic of him (*Ant.* 5.230). Thus Gideon, like Moses, emerges as a Stoic-like sage.

Closely connected with moderation is the quality of modesty. We see Gideon's modesty in his reply to the spectre, which has taken the form of a young man, who charges him to seek to regain liberty for the Israelites (*Ant.* 5.214). To be sure, even in the Bible Gideon states that his clan is the poorest in the tribe of Manasseh and that he is the youngest in his father's household (Judges 6:15). Josephus' Gideon is even more modest in that he compares himself not to the others in his father's household but states that he himself was but young and too feeble for great exploits (*Ant.* 5.214).

Moreover, Josephus makes Gideon's victory over the Midianites a lesson in the importance of modesty. The Bible states that G-d told Gideon that the people with him were so numerous that they would think that it was by their own efforts that they were able to overcome the Midianites, and He therefore devises a scheme whereby they are to be drastically reduced in numbers so that they will realize that the victory is due to G-d (Judges 7:2). In Josephus, while the general outline and the purpose of G-d's scheme remain the same, the truism of human nature is invoked, namely the proneness of human nature to self-love (φίλαυτον) (*Ant.* 5.215).

As for the virtue of justice, it is extremely significant that whereas the Bible says merely that the land rested for forty years in the days of Gideon (Judges 8:28) without specifically stating, as the Bible usually does for the other judges, that he judged Israel, Josephus notes explicitly that he continued for forty years to administer justice and paints a picture of him as a judge, noting that men resorted to him concerning their differences and adding that all his pronouncements had binding (κύρια) weight (*Ant.* 5.232). The net result of this change is that whereas the Bible depicts a land that passively rested for forty years, through a kind of benign neglect, Josephus portrays Gideon as actively exercising leadership in going through the land and administering justice to his people. Indeed, in his summary of the Torah's code with regard to the administration of justice, Josephus significantly uses the same word (κύριοι) to describe the binding authority that judges have, according to the Mosaic Law, to pronounce whatever sentence they see fit (*Ant.* 4.216). That this power is valid, sure, and true may be seen from the collocation of these three words (κύρια, βέβαια, ἀληθῆ) in Josephus' description of the fear of rumors, wilful hates, and irrational loves which characterize men's attitude when they have gained power (*Ant.* 6.266).

Coupled with justice is the virtue of humanity (φιλανθρωπία). In the case of Gideon Josephus was confronted with a dilemma. According to the Bible, Gideon, following instructions which he received from G-d, pulled down the altar of Baal which his father had built and the Asherah tree which was worshipped beside it and, indeed, used the wood of the Asherah to burn his offering to G-d (Judges 6:25-32). For this the men of the city would have put Gideon to death, were it not for the intervention of his father. Indeed, his father's statement becomes, as we have noted, the source of his alternate name, Jerubaal, that is, "Let Baal contend with him, because he has broken down his altar" (Judges 6:32) The reader at this point might well ask two questions: how can such zealotry be squared with the religious tolerance which Josephus claims is at the heart of Judaism, and secondly, more particularly, how could Gideon, the religious reformer, assume a name containing that of a pagan deity, namely Baal? Josephus resolves both problems very neatly by omitting the whole episode.

Closely connected with the virtue of humanity is the quality of mercy. In the case of Gideon, the Bible relates how Gideon brought the two captured kings of the Midianites, Zebah and Zalmunna, before Zether, his oldest son, with instructions to kill them. His son is too fearful, however, because of his youth, to do so, and hence Gideon kills them himself (Judges 8:18-21). The reader might well expect Gideon to show mercy toward them, especially since there was no specific divine command to kill these kings in particular, as there was in the incident involving Saul. Hence, Josephus, in his concern lest Gideon appear unmerciful, omits this incident altogether.

As for piety (εὐσέβεια), the fifth of the cardinal virtues, Gideon's piety may be seen in the fact that whereas, according to the biblical narrative, when the angel appears to him, he greets him with the words, "The L-rd is with you, mighty man of valor," thus emphasizing his courage (Judges 6:12), in Josephus' version, the angel "pronounced him blessed (εὐδαίμονα) and beloved of G-d (φίλον τῷ θεῷ) (*Ant.* 5.213). It is significant that a similar phrase is found in Josephus' encomium of the prophet Samuel, whom he describes as a man of just and kindly nature and for that reason very dear to G-d (φίλος τῷ θεῷ) (*Ant.* 6.294).

Nevertheless, Gideon would seem to lack faith, since, according to the Bible, he asks G-d for a sign to verify that it is indeed He who is speaking with him (Judges 6:17). Similarly, we may note, Moses, at the beginning of his mission, tells G-d that the Israelites will not believe that G-d actually appeared to him, thereby clearly signifying his wish for a sign to confirm that it is really G-d who spoke to him (Exodus 4:1). Significantly, in both of these instances Josephus, apparently realizing that such a desire for a sign implies a lack of faith, omits these requests. In contrast, Pseudo-Philo's Gideon, who, as we have noted, is viewed much less sympathetically than in Josephus, on two occasions does ask for signs (*Bib. Ant.* 35.6, 7).

There is one particularly embarrassing episode in connection with Gideon which would seem to cast grave doubt on his piety, namely his making an ephod of the golden earrings contributed by the Israelites from the spoil which they had taken in war (Judges 8:24-27). According to the biblical account, all Israel went astray after it, and "it became a snare unto Gideon and to his house." Pseudo-Philo makes this episode the centerpiece of his attack on Gideon, noting that Gideon made idols from the golden amulets which the Israelites contributed and that he kept on worshipping (*adorabat*) them (*Bib. Ant.* 36.3). Realizing that such a grave sin should have called forth an immediate and extreme penalty from G-d, Pseudo-Philo then explains that G-d did not punish him because people might conclude that it was not G-d who smote him but rather Baal because on a previous occasion he had destroyed the sanctuary of Baal (*Bib. Ant.* 36.4).

Josephus, we may surmise, was particularly embarrassed by this incident inasmuch as he was himself a priest – and very proud of the fact (*Life* 2) that he belonged to the first of the twenty-four courses of priests and that he was descended from the Hasmonean high priests. The ephod, we may add, was the vestment to which was bound the breastplate containing the principal vehicle for inquiring of G-d, namely the Urim and the Thummim. Inasmuch as the Torah (Deuteronomy 18:10-11) is so strict in prohibiting all other forms of divination except for this, for Gideon to have made an ephod would have been regarded as a particularly egregious breach of the Mosaic code, and so Josephus omits mention of it completely (*Ant.* 5.232).[2]

3. *The Role of G-d and Miracles*

Moreover, in the case of Gideon, the biblical text states that in the confrontation with the Midianites and Amalekites "the Spirit of the L-rd clothed (*laveshah*, Septuagint ἐνέδυσε) Gideon" (Judges 6:34). When this happens, we hear that Gideon blew the trumpet and his troops were mustered. Pseudo-Philo similarly declares that Gideon was clothed (*induit*) with the spirit of the L-rd (*Bib. Ant.* 36.2). It is, then, this spirit's power that is the direct source of Gideon's remarkable victory over the Midianites. There is no mention in Josephus of Gideon being clothed with the spirit of the L-rd (*Ant.* 5.215); rather, we are told, without any explanation as to how it happened, that instantly an army of ten thousand men appeared ready for battle under Gideon's leadership. Likewise, when the Israelites go forth to battle against the Midianites, their focus is on G-d and Gideon, as we can see from their battlecry in the Bible (Judges 7:18), whereas in Josephus the focus is on Gideon, as we can see from the battlecry, "Victory and G-d will aid Gideon!" (*Ant.* 5.225).

Again, when G-d wishes to effect a greater miracle by having Gideon encounter the enemy with a much smaller force, in the Bible He speaks to Gideon directly (Judges 7:4). Skeptical readers might well wonder at this; and so Josephus, realizing that according to the much-revered Plato (*Republic* 9.571D-572A), a person in a state of healthy, temperate self-control is most apt to touch the truth in his dreams, states that G-d appeared to him in his sleep (*Ant.* 5.215).

One of the stock charges against the Jews is credulity, as we have noted. We may discern a de-emphasis on miracles in Josephus' version of Gideon in the omission of Gideon's challenge to the

---

[2] The rabbinic tradition, though, as we have noted, it is less than fully sympathetic with Gideon, still tries (*Yalquṭ,* Judges 64) to exculpate Gideon by explaining that on the breastplate of the high priest the tribe of Joseph was represented by Ephraim alone, and that consequently, to remove the slight upon his own tribe of Manasseh, he made a new ephod substituting the name of Manasseh; moreover, this became an object of adoration only after his death, inasmuch as he consecrated it to G-d.

angel to work miracles comparable to those which the Israelites' ancestors had experienced (Judges 6:13 vs. *Ant.* 5.214), as well as his request for signs to prove that it is really G-d who has spoken to him (Judges 6:17-18). Indeed, Josephus totally omits the miracle performed by the angel of consuming with fire the flesh and the unleavened cakes offered by Gideon. Josephus likewise omits the double miracle of the fleece of wool on the threshing floor that becomes soaked with dew when all the ground around it is dry, as well as vice versa (Judges 6:36-40 vs. *Ant.* 5.215), both because, from the point of view of Gideon, the need for such miracles would indicate a lack of faith and because, from the point of view of the sophisticated reader, they would be hard to accept.

Josephus apparently realized that angels would present a problem both for his Jewish audience who, if they were purists in theology, would have difficulties with spiritual beings who were intermediaries between G-d and humans, and his non-Jewish audience, who might well ask what the difference was between these angels and the various gods and demigods of the pagan pantheon. In this connection we may note Josephus' statement that a spectre in the form of a young man (νεανίσκου) appeared to Gideon (*Ant.* 5.213), whereas the Bible declares that it was an angel (Judges 6:12).

4. *Political Lessons*

The underlying theme of Josephus' *Jewish War* is that the ill-fated revolt originated in the civil strife (στάσις οἰκεία) engendered by the Jewish "tyrants" (οἱ Ἰουδαίων τύραννοι) (*War* 1.10). The same theme of the dreadful consequences of civil strife pervades much of his paraphrase of the Bible in the *Antiquities*. In the case of Gideon, Josephus, in an editorial-like comment, notes that he pacified the wrath of the Ephraimites (Judges 8:1-3) when they were aggrieved at his success and complained that he had failed to inform them of the proposed assault on the Midianites (*Ant.* 5.231). The picture is, indeed, reminiscent of that of Neptune, who in Virgil's *Aeneid* (1.142-43) calms the storm created by Aeolus and brings back the sun, an act which brings to Virgil's mind a simile of a man who, respected for his loyalty and his merits, calms and soothes a turbulent nation with his words so that they become silent with pricked-up ears (*Aeneid* 1.148-53). In similar language, according to Josephus in an ultimate compliment, Gideon did the Hebrews a greater service than through his military success; "for he rescued them from civil strife (ἐμφυλίου...στάσεως) when they were on the brink of it" (*Ant.* 5.231).[3]

In this connection, we may note a passage which apparently contradicts a picture of Gideon as a peacemaker and as one who avoided civil strife that Josephus wishes to paint, namely the episode with the men of Succoth and Penuel (Judges 8:4-17). According to the Bible, the men of those cities, who were apparently Israelites (as we see from Joshua 13:27), had declined to help Gideon's army with bread when they were hungry; and Gideon eventually took revenge and punished them, even to the point of putting the men of Penuel to death. Such a passage reflects badly both on the hospitality of the Israelites in not feeding the hungry and on the ability of Gideon to mollify his anger and to avoid the slaughter of his countrymen. Hence, very typically, Josephus avoids these problems by simply omitting the entire incident.

5. *"Improvements" in the Story: Clarifications, Increased Suspense and Drama*

One basic reason, as we have seen, for Josephus' writing his paraphrase of the Scripture was to clear up obscurities in the text. In the case of Gideon, the biblical text, as it stands, indicates no reason why G-d chose, as His method for determining who should accompany Gideon in the attack on the Midianites, those who lapped water rather than those who knelt down to drink (Judges 7:5-7). Josephus offers a plausible explanation, namely that those who knelt down were the stalwarts, whereas those who drank hurriedly and with trepidation were the cowards and terrified of the foe (*Ant.* 5.216). Inasmuch as G-d was eager that the miracle be all the greater, he deliberately instructs Gideon to choose the latter.[4]

---

[3] Significantly, Pseudo-Philo, who, as we have noted, denigrates Gideon, omits this episode, which, in Josephus' eyes, does so much to elevate his greatness.

[4] A very different explanation is found in the rabbinic tradition (*Yelammedenu* in '*Aruk*, s.v. *Bevoah* and *Yalquṭ* 2.62, as cited by Ginzberg [1928, 6:200, n. 98]), according to which those who stopped to drink the water showed themselves to be idolaters who were worshipping their own images in the water; somewhat similarly, according to *Tanḥuma B* 1.183, they were accustomed as idolaters to bow down and consequently followed this practice when they drank water.

Another instance in the Gideon pericope where Josephus explains an obscurity is the account of the Midianite's dream as interpreted by his comrade (Judges 7:13-14). According to the biblical narrative, in the dream a cake of barley bread tumbled into the camp of Midian and turned the tent upside down. This is then interpreted to mean that the cake of barley bread was the sword of Gideon and that he would overcome the Midianites. But this interpretation does not explain the connection between Gideon and the barley cake, whereas Josephus does offer an explanation, namely that of all seeds the barley is regarded as the vilest, and that of all Asiatic races the most ignominious is that of the Israelites and hence the most similar to barley; and among the Israelites at that moment the high-spirited party must be Gideon and his comrades; hence the barley-cake overcoming the tents of the Midianites was an indication that Gideon would conquer them (*Ant.* 5.220).[5]

Again, the Bible states that Gideon put into the hands of all his men horns and empty pitchers, with torches inside the pitchers (Judges 7:16). It does not, however, explain why the torches were handled in this way. Josephus does offer such an explanation, namely to prevent the enemy from detecting the approach of the Israelites (*Ant.* 5.223). Furthermore, Josephus offers a plausible extra-biblical explanation for the rout of the Midianites and their allies, namely the diversity of their languages, a factor of which the biblical narrative makes no mention (Judges 7:22 vs. *Ant.* 5.226).

Another "improvement" made by Josephus in his reworking of the biblical narrative is avoidance of undue exaggeration and the grotesque such as might provoke the ridicule of a later satirist such as Lucian. In the case of Gideon, one such exaggeration – actually threefold – is the biblical description of the army of the Midianites and their allies as "like locusts for multitude," with camels "without number, as the sand which is upon the seashore for multitude" (Judges 7:12). Josephus is considerably more restrained: the camp is described as merely covering a large area, and there is no comparison with locusts; the camels are simply very numerous (πλείστην), and there is no comparison with sand (*Ant.* 5.224).

---

[5] A very different explanation of the dream is to be found in the rabbinic tradition (*Leviticus Rabbah* 28.6), according to which the cake of barley bread indicates that the Israelites would be granted victory as a reward for bringing the offering of an omer of barley.

Josephus also tries to increase the dramatic interest of the biblical narrative. One method which Josephus employs in the Gideon pericope is to concentrate the drama. Thus, according to the Bible Gideon's army was reduced from twenty-two thousand to ten thousand by eliminating those who were faint-hearted (Judges 7:3), and then G-d ordered Gideon to further reduce these ten thousand to three hundred so that the miracle of their victory over the Midianites would be all the greater (Judges 7:4-8). The drama is heightened in Josephus, who has the reduction of the army effected in a single step, from ten thousand to three hundred (*Ant.* 5.215).

Moreover, there is increased drama in the setting for the scene of the test as to who should remain to fight on the side of Gideon. In the Bible there is no indication as to the time of the day (Judges 7:4), whereas Josephus dramatically declares that G-d counselled Gideon to march his troops to the river towards midday, precisely when the heat was most intense (*Ant.* 5.216).

There is likewise increased drama in Josephus' description of the rout of the Midianites. According to the biblical version, the Midianite army ran, cried out, fled, and finally turned on one another (Judges 7:21-22). Josephus' description is much more dramatic: in the first place, we are told that the Midianite soldiers were still sleeping, and we are further informed that confusion and panic seized them (*Ant.* 5.226). The scene is highly reminiscent of another such rout, as embellished by Josephus, namely that in which Abraham fell upon the Assyrians, similarly at night, in an attack in which he, like Gideon in our passage, caught the enemy by surprise before they had time to arm (*Ant.* 1.177). There, too, we are given similar vivid details of the slaughter of the enemy, some of whom Abraham and his army slew while they were still asleep (see Feldman 1984a, especially 46). Whereas the Bible states that the L-rd set every man's sword against his fellow (Judges 7:22), Josephus makes the scene much more dramatic by asserting that few of the Midianites were actually slain by their enemies, that more were killed by the hand of their allies, and that what brought about such confusion was the diversity of their languages; he further adds that once confusion set in, the Midianites killed all whom they met, mistakenly taking them for enemies, and that the carnage was great (*Ant.* 5.226). The hopelessness of the Midianites' situation is greatly increased by Josephus' added detail that they were caught in a valley encompassed with impossible ravines (*Ant.*

5.227), whereas the Bible simply states that the Israelites pursued after the Midianites (Judges 7:23).[6]

6. Summary

Whereas the Bible, Pseudo-Philo's *Biblical Antiquities*, and the rabbinic tradition are ambiguous in their attitude toward Gideon, Josephus, like the New Testament, has a very high opinion of him, regarding him as a model of every virtue. In particular, he elevates his genealogy and exaggerates his possession of the cardinal virtues: wisdom, as seen by his ability to use calculated reflection in making decisions; courage, as seen particularly by his overcoming the Midianites with a meager force of three hundred cowards; temperance, exemplified by the modesty which he displays when approached to lead the mission against the Midianites; justice, as shown by the fact that all his judicial pronouncements had binding weight; and piety, highlighted by his epithet "beloved of G-d."

In order to protect the Jews from the charge of intolerance toward other religions, Josephus omits the incident in which Gideon pulled down the altar of Baal which his father had built and destroyed the Asherah tree which was worshipped beside it. Likewise, in order to defend the Jews from the charge of inhumanity, Josephus omits the incident in which Gideon kills the two captured kings of the Midianites. Furthermore, Josephus omits the episode, which would cast doubt on his piety, in which Gideon makes an ephod, which the Israelites later worshipped, out of the earrings contributed by them.

In order to elevate the personal achievements of Gideon Josephus diminishes the role of G-d. Thus, he omits the statement that the spirit of the L-rd clothed Gideon. Moreover, because skeptical readers might well wonder at the scene in which G-d addresses Gideon directly, Josephus, realizing that such scenes were accepted as true by such respected writers as Plato when presented as occurring in dreams, has G-d appear to Gideon in his sleep. Likewise, because his audience might question angelic appear-

---

[6] As Thackeray (1934, 5:103), in his note on this passage, points out, the death-trap, the "impassable valley" in which the enemy is cooped up and annihilated, is a familiar feature, as we see, for example, in Josephus' added details in his description of the rout of the Benjaminites (*Ant.* 5.162).

ances, Josephus substitutes a spectre in the form of a young man instead. Furthermore, because his audience might also have their doubts about the occurrence of miracles, Josephus omits Gideon's request to the angel to perform such miraculous signs as a verification that G-d had spoken to him, as well as the various miracles actually effected by the angel.

In addition, because he realized how dearly the Jews had paid for their civil strife during the war against the Romans, Josephus stresses the achievement of Gideon in assuaging the Ephraimites when they complained to him, noting that he thereby performed a greater service than he did through his military success. Likewise, in order not to highlight civil strife among the Israelites, he omits the incident in which Gideon takes revenge on the Israelites of Sukkoth and Penuel, who had failed to feed his hungry troops.

Finally, Josephus "tidies" up the biblical text by clarifying obscurities, such as the reason why G-d chose, as the method for determining who should accompany Gideon in the campaign against the Midianites, those who lapped water rather than those who knelt down to drink. Likewise, he explains the significance of the otherwise obscure reference to the cake of barley bread in the dream of the Midianite. He also clarifies the reason for the confusion in the rout of the Midianites, namely the diversity of their languages. Moreover, he omits undue exaggeration in the description of the size of the army of the Midianites. Finally, he greatly increases the dramatic element, particularly in his description of the rout of the Midianites.

CHAPTER ELEVEN

JEPHTHAH

1. Introduction

In his portrayal of Jephthah[1] Josephus was confronted with a dilemma. On the one hand, as he does throughout the *Antiquities*, he seeks to elevate the leadership qualities also of Jephthah, especially in view of the attempt of anti-Jewish writers to belittle or disregard such Jewish heroes as Moses (Philo, *De Vita Mosis* 1.1.1-2; Josephus, *Ag. Ap.* 2.145, 290). On the other hand, how could Josephus praise Jephthah when Jephthah had committed the heinous act of sacrificing his own daughter? Josephus might have resolved this problem by omitting the episode entirely, as he did a number of such embarrassing incidents, just as the Talmud enjoins that certain embarrassing or difficult passages are to be read but are not publicly paraphrased in the Targum (*Megillah* 25a-b). Josephus' solution, as we shall see, is to praise and exaggerate Jephthah's positive qualities of character while singling out and condemning those qualities which deserve criticism.

2. Jephthah's Qualities of Leadership

Josephus is at every point eager to underline the leadership qualities of such figures as the judges and the kings of Israel, especially since the race of mankind, according to him, is by nature morose and censorious (*Ant.* 3.23), and since the great Greek historian

---

[1] There has been no extended study of Josephus' portrait of Jephthah thus far. The most recent comprehensive study of Jephthah, by David Marcus (1986), alludes to Josephus' treatment only very briefly (notably on page 8) in passing to note that according to him Jephthah's vow was literally carried out. Amaru (1988, 143-70), the only comprehensive treatment of women in Josephus, mentions Jephthah's daughter only once (on page 169), noting that generally in Josephus daughters are not of much interest to Josephus save as their actions reflect upon their fathers; in this case Jephthah's daughter is not so much the victim of her father's vow as a martyr to her father's victory and to the liberation of her fellow citizens. The most recent study, that of Brown (1992, 118-27) focuses on Jephthah's daughter rather than on Jephthah himself and is concerned primarily with comparing Josephus' account with that of Pseudo-Philo.

Thucydides had stressed that only great and foresighted leadership can overcome the defects of the masses (2.65). Hence, when the Biblical text states that vain (*reiqim*, Septuagint κενοί, "empty, vain, devoid of wit, pretentious") men had gathered around Jephthah (Judges 11:3), this is clearly an indication of his lack of proper leadership. Indeed, the rabbis denigrate Jephthah precisely by citing this passage to illustrate the popular saying that "a bad palm will usually make its way to a grove of barren trees" (*Baba Qamma* 92b).

We may note that in the Bible there is a clear parallel between Jephthah and Abimelech, who likewise is of illegitimate origin (Judges 8:31) and who also gathers around himself idle (*reiqim*, Septuagint κενούς) mercenaries (Judges 9:4); but whereas Josephus retains the Bible's derogatory portrayal of Abimelech he removes these elements in his depiction of Jephthah and, without describing their character, states merely that Jephthah paid wages to those who resorted to him (*Ant.* 5.260). Indeed, whereas in the biblical text Abimelech is described as merely the son of Gideon's concubine and is not as such called a bastard (Judges 8:31), Josephus refers to him expressly as a bastard (*Ant.* 5.233); on the other hand, Jephthah is called the son of a harlot, no less (Judges 11:1), but Josephus uses a circumlocution in referring to his birth by a father "through an amorous desire" (*Ant.* 5.259). Moreover, whereas in the biblical text the Israelite people and their leaders ask one another who will begin to fight against the Ammonites (Judges 10:17-18), Josephus is more explicit in declaring that they lacked a leader to take command (στρατηγήσοντος) (*Ant.* 5.257).[2]

Jephthah turns out to be the true leader of his flock. Whereas the Bible declares that Jephthah, after being named commander of the Israelite forces, passed over to the children of Ammon to fight against them and that the Lord delivered them into his hand (Judges 11:32), Josephus emphasizes Jephthah's concern (ἐπιμέλειαν, "care, attention, consideration") for his people and the speed (ὀξεῖαν) with which he acted (*Ant.* 5.261). Indeed, the term ἡγεμονία ("leadership"), is twice applied to Jephthah, where

---

[2] A similarly clear statement about the lack of leadership and the consequent filling of the void by Jephthah is found in Pseudo-Philo's *Biblical Antiquities* (39.1): "Behold now, we see the strait which encompasseth us... and there is no leader to go in and out before our face."

there is no equivalent in the biblical original (*Ant.* 5.258, 260). Moreover, we gain some conception of his qualities as a leader in Josephus' eyes from the fact, not to be found in the biblical text (Judges 11:6-8), that Jephthah is twice promised the command of the Israelites not merely for the immediate campaign against the Ammonites but for all time (*Ant.* 5.258, 260). The Israelites' need for Jephthah's leadership is underlined by the word, for which there is no equivalent in the biblical text (Judges 11:8), ἐκλιπαρησάντων, indicating that they made earnest entreaty to have him lead them (*Ant.* 5.260). Indeed, Josephus paints a scene, in which the elders of Gilead succeed in persuading Jephthah to assume the leadership against the Ammonite enemy (*Ant.* 5.258), highly reminiscent of the scene in Homer's *Iliad* (9.225-655), in which a delegation sent by Agamemnon attempts (in that case, however, unsuccessfully) to persuade Achilles to resume fighting against the Trojans, or the scene, likewise in Homer's *Iliad* (9.529-605), mentioned by Phoenix in his discourse to Achilles in that book, in which Meleager refuses over and over again to resume fighting against the Kuretes until his wife finally persuades him. The fact that Jephthah, like Meleager, in the end does bow to the entreaties of his people highlights the very positive portrait of him that Josephus paints.

Josephus, moreover, emphasizes the difference between Jephthah and the Ephraimites in that whereas the Bible says simply that when Jephthah called upon the Ephraimites for help they did not deliver the Israelites from the hand of the Ammonites (Judges 12:20), Josephus stresses the contrast by remarking that they ought to have come even before being asked and to have sped into arms (*Ant.* 5.267).

3. *Jephthah's Virtues*

In view of the importance which the ancients attached to genealogy, Josephus, in the case of Jephthah, was confronted with the most embarrassing fact that Jephthah was the son of a harlot (*zonah*) (Judges 11:1), a word which the Septuagint renders literally (πόρνης). The Targum renders this word by *pundaqita* ("innkeeper," as it does in the case of Rahab [Joshua 2:1]). Josephus neatly sidesteps the issue of Jephthah's birth by omitting the word "harlot" altogether, stating that he did not have the same mother as his brothers (οὐ γὰρ ὄντα ὁμομήτριον) and that he was a stranger (ξένον) who had been brought upon (ἐπαχθεῖσαν) his brothers through the father's amorous desire (δι' ἐρωτικὴν ἐπιθυμίαν) (*Ant.* 5.159),³ thus supplying here, as elsewhere, an erotic motif which his readers, as we have suggested, would surely have welcomed. Josephus goes further in adding the extra-biblical comment extolling Jephthah's ancestry when he declares that Jephthah was a mighty man by reason of the valor of his forefathers (διὰ τὴν πατρῴαν ἀρετήν) (*Ant.* 5.257), thus transferring the valor to Jephthah's forefathers, whereas the Bible speaks of Jephthah himself as a mighty man of valor (Judges 11:1). In contrast, the rabbis clearly belittle Jephthah when they remark that Jephthah in his generation was like Samuel in his (*Rosh Hashanah* 25b), in order to teach the moral that the most worthless, once he has been appointed a leader in the community, is to be regarded as the mightiest of the mighty. Josephus, moreover, arouses the sympathy of the reader⁴ by remarking not merely, as does the biblical text (Judges 11:2), that his brothers had cast him out but also that Jephthah had been flagrantly (περιφανῶς, "evidently," "obviously") wronged (ἀδικουμένῳ) by his brothers (*Ant.* 5.258) and that they had scorned his helplessness (ἀσθενείας, "weakness," "feebleness") (*Ant.* 5.259). Josephus thus carefully omits the reason given by the brothers for their abuse of Jephthah in the biblical text, namely that he was the son of another woman.

Of the four (or actually five) cardinal virtues which Josephus ascribes over and over again to his biblical heroes in extra-biblical remarks, Jephthah is portrayed as possessing courage, temperance, and justice but is clearly deficient in wisdom and piety.

---

³ Ginzberg (1928, 6:202, n. 106) suggests the possibility that Josephus read *zarah* ("strange") instead of *zonah* ("prostitute"). This, however, seems unlikely in view of the fact that the Septuagint, which Josephus certainly knew, reads πόρνης ("prostitute"). More likely, Josephus derived support for his interpretation from the reference to Jephthah as the son of another woman (*'ishah 'aḥeret*) (Judges 11:2). The Septuagint renders this last phrase as ἑταίρας, "courtesan" (as opposed to a common prostitute, πόρνη, and hence in contradiction to the biblical statement in 11:1 that Jephthah's mother was a prostitute); and we may suggest that the original Greek in 11:2 read ἑτέρας, "other," "another" rather than ἑταίρας.

⁴ There is a striking contrast between Josephus and Pseudo-Philo's *Biblical Antiquities* in their attitude toward Jephthah's expulsion. Whereas Josephus arouses the reader's pity for Jephthah, Pseudo-Philo places the blame on Jephthah in stating that his brothers cast him out because he was jealous (*zelaret*) of them (*Bib. Ant.* 39.2).

As to his qualities as a fighter, Josephus adds to the biblical description by noting that Jephthah, after being asked to take command, promptly (ὀξεῖαν, "quick," "fast," "immediate") took charge of affairs (*Ant.* 5.261). Furthermore, to underscore the magnitude of Jephthah's military achievement, whereas the Bible states simply that the Ammonites were subdued by the Israelites (Judges 11:33), Josephus introduces the extra-biblical comment that Jephthah delivered his countrymen from a servitude which they had borne for eighteen years (*Ant.* 5.263). Moreover, it is specifically as generals (στρατηγούντων, *Ant.* 6.90) that he and Gideon are extolled by the prophet Samuel when he recalls nostalgically the leadership of the judges prior to the Israelites' demand for a king. Significantly, whereas in the biblical text, Samuel evokes the leadership of Jerubbaal, Barak, Jephthah, and Samuel (1 Samuel 12:11), in Josephus' version only Jephthah and Gideon are mentioned, and they are praised as superior to kings (*Ant.* 6.90).

That Jephthah possesses the virtue of moderation is clear from Josephus' extra-biblical remark, that Jephthah threatened to be avenged on the Ephraimites unless they showed themselves moderate (σωφρονῶσιν, "be temperate," "be reasonable," "be sensible," "have control of one's senses") (*Ant.* 5.268; compare Judges 12:3).

That Jephthah placed a premium on justice is clear from Josephus' account of his negotiations with the Ammonites (*Ant.* 5.261-62) and with the Ephraimites (*Ant.* 5.267-68). Josephus emphasizes that the Ammonites had no just grievance against the Israelites and, indeed, ought rather to have been grateful to them for having left them Ammonitis, which they might easily have seized (*Ant.* 5.262). He likewise makes a point of adding that Jephthah did not go to war with the Ephraimites before first explaining carefully how they had been delinquent and secondly issuing a warning before actually taking up arms (*Ant.* 5.267-68). Here Josephus is making clear that Jephthah conformed to the Roman code, familiar from Cicero, that war should be undertaken only after repeated provocations and only after due warning (*De Officiis* 1.11.34-36 and *De Re Publica* 3.23.34-35).

4. *Jephthah's Vow*

When it came to Jephthah's piety, Josephus might have adopted the approach of the author of the Epistle to the Hebrews (11:32-34), who cites Jephthah in the distinguished company of Gideon, Barak, Samson, David, Samuel, and the prophets as outstanding models who through faith conquered kingdoms, enforced justice, and performed miracles. In dealing with Jephthah's vow to sacrifice whatever would first come forth from his house to greet him upon returning from battle victoriously (Judges 11:31), however, Josephus was obviously confronted with more than one dilemma. On the one hand, it is not clear from the Hebrew text whether Jephthah was vowing to sacrifice whatever animal would come forth, since the relative pronoun used is of undetermined gender. The Septuagint has the masculine gender: whoever shall first come out (ὁ ἐκπορευόμενος ὃς ἂν ἐξέλθῃ). Both the Hebrew and the Greek appear to imply that Jephthah had in mind a person, since they say "whoever goes out to greet from the door(s) of my house"; and while it is true that animals were kept in the home, the word "goes out to greet" (*yaza' liqrat*) seems to imply a deliberate choice by a person endowed with reason, intellect, and will, rather than an animal.[5] Moreover, the statement that this creature will belong to the L-rd (Judges 11:31) likewise implies a person, since such a phrase is used in the Bible only with reference to people. Already in the seventeenth century Pfeiffer had cogently asked what kind of vow it would be if some prince or general should promise to offer the first calf that would meet him after a victory, since even without a vow Jephthah would have been expected to offer not one but many sacrifices after obtaining victory (Pfeiffer 1679, 356).[6] Besides, it is reasonable to assume that the Israelite custom of maidens coming out to greet a victorious general must have been

---

[5] Note the unusually strong language used by Moore (1898, 299): "That a human victim is intended is, in fact, as plain as words can make it; the language is inapplicable to an animal, and a vow to offer the first sheep or goat that he comes across – not to mention the possibility of a unclean animal – is trivial to absurdity."

[6] A further indication, as the rabbis note, that an animal could not have been intended is the possibility, or even likelihood, that the first animal that would have come out to greet him would have been a dog or donkey or horse or camel, all beasts unfit for sacrifice (*Genesis Rabbah* 60.3, *Leviticus Rabbah* 37.4). Hence, the rabbis conclude, the vow was illegitimate.

known to Jephthah.[7] Hence, Marcus concludes that the language of the vow appears to be inappropriate if the reference is to animals (David Marcus 1986, 13-14). Indeed, it cannot have been accidental that it was Jephthah's daughter who came to greet him after his victory (so Baumgartner 1915, 248-49).

Thus, for Josephus to follow closely the biblical text would definitely have cast Jephthah in a very bad light and would have raised the question about the Israelite envoys' mental acuity in begging someone to become their leader who was ready to sacrifice a human being, especially since such a practice stands in such direct contradiction to all that Judaism preaches. Moreover, Josephus' readers would probably have been aware of the close parallel with the legend[8] of Idomeneus, king of Crete, who, when caught in a storm on his return from Troy, vowed that he would sacrifice to Poseidon whoever would first meet him when he landed; and this turned out to be his own son. They might also have been aware of another close classical parallel, namely Maeander, the son of Cercaphos and Anaxibia, who vowed that if he would be victorious in the war with Pessinus in Phrygia he would sacrifice to the Great Mother the first person who would come out to greet him (Pseudo-Plutarch, *De Fluviis* 9.1). Hence, Josephus, in his eagerness to avoid the charge that the Israelite leaders were simply foolish in selecting a leader who would make such a rash vow, very carefully uses the neuter gender in reference to what Jephthah had vowed to sacrifice, namely that he would offer up the first thing (πᾶν ὅ τι καὶ πρῶτον) that would chance (συντύχοι, "meet with," "fall in with," "happen to," "befall")[9] to meet him (*Ant.* 5.263).

Josephus, given his concern to save the reputation of Jephthah, might have escaped from the above dilemma by adopting the view

---

[7] So Miriam and the Israelite women (Exodus 15:20) at the Sea of Reeds, and similarly the Israelite women in the time of Saul and David (1 Samuel 18:6).

[8] Servius on Virgil, *Aeneid* 3.121-22, 11.264; *First and Second Mythographers*, in Bode (1834, 1:195, 2:210). In both Servius and in the two citations in Bode the vow is to sacrifice the first thing (*res*) that would meet Idomeneus. As in the case of Euripides' two plays on the sacrifice of Iphigenia, there are two versions of the Idomeneus story mentioned in Bode. In one the sacrifice actually takes place; in the other we are told that he had merely wished to sacrifice his daughter but did not go through with it.

[9] The same verb with a similar meaning is found in Euripides, *Hecuba*, 1182, and *Rhesus*, 864.

of some later commentators, such as David Kimhi,[10] who remarks that the biblical text enigmatically declares not that Jephthah offered up his daughter as a burnt offering but rather that "he did to her his vow which he had vowed" (Judges 11:39); and since Jephthah had said that whatever would come forth to greet him would "be to the L-rd" (Judges 11.31) he merely dedicated her, as a kind of Vestal Virgin, to the eternal service of G-d. As support for such an identification we may note that the Bible remarks not that Jephthah's daughter bewailed her forthcoming death but rather her virginity (Judges 11:38) (so David Marcus 1986, 31), and adds, after the statement that Jephthah fulfilled his vow, the remark that his daughter had not known any man (Judges 11:39), which might be interpreted to mean that the fulfillment of the vow consisted of her being dedicated to perpetual virginity. Josephus, on the other hand, in order to avoid the possible implication that she was not actually sacrificed and in order to preclude the obvious comparison with the pagan Vestal virgins, omits completely her request to bewail her virginity, having her ask rather to bewail her youth (νεότητα) (Judges 11:37 vs. *Ant.* 5.265). Similarly, we may surmise, Josephus omits the biblical statement that Jephthah's daughter wailed over her virginity upon the mountains (Judges 11:38), since he wished to avoid comparisons with the pagan Artemis,[11] who resided on the mountains. Likewise, Josephus, in his concern to play down apparent similarities between Judaism and paganism and to stress the uniqueness of the Jewish religion, omits the annual festival bewailing the sacrifice of Jephthah's daughter (Judges 11:39-40 vs. *Ant.* 5.266), presumably because it would strike his predominantly pagan readers as very similar to the

---

[10] See David Marcus (1986, 8-9), who notes that Kimhi's interpretation was adopted by such eminent traditional commentators as Levi ben Gershon in the fourteenth century, Abravanel in the fifteenth century, Yehiel Hillel Altschuler in the eighteenth century, and Malbim in the nineteenth century, as well as by such more recent scholars as Hengstenberg, Reinke, Auberlen, Cassel, Keil, Delitzsch, Köhler, and König, among others. See Moore 1898, 304.

[11] Sypherd (1948, 14) notes that according to Epiphanius Jephthah's daughter was worshipped as the goddess Kore-Persephone by the people of Shechem and was thus elevated to the rank of a deity by the side of Artemis herself. We may also suggest that another factor in Josephus' omission of the statement that Jephthah's daughter asked to be allowed to wail upon the mountains is that the Hebrew word here (Judges 11:37, *veyaradeti*), as well as the Septuagint rendering (καταβήσομαι), literally means not to wail but to "descend" upon the mountains; and the obvious objection is that one ascends rather than descends a mountain.

laments for Persephone at Eleusis in Greece, for Osiris in Egypt, for Tammuz in Babylonia, for Attis in Asia Minor, and for Adonis in Syria.[12]

Moreover, Josephus, apparently aware that the average reader, like the Talmudic rabbis (*Ta'anit* 4a), would understand that Jephthah actually vowed to offer up as a burnt offering the first thing that would greet him, explicitly declares that Jephthah proceeded to sacrifice her as a burnt-offering (ὡλοκαύτωσεν) (*Ant.* 5.266). Furthermore, just as the Bible seeks to draw a parallel between Jephthah's daughter and Isaac, both of whom are to be sacrificed by their fathers (*Ant.* 1.225, 5.266) and both of whom are referred to as an only child (Genesis 22:2: *yeḥideka*, Septuagint ἀγαπητόν; Judges 11:34: *yeḥidah*, Septuagint μονογενής), so Josephus reinforces this parallelism by referring to Jephthah's daughter (*Ant.* 5.264) by the same term, μονογενής, which he uses of Isaac (*Ant.* 1.222),[13] thereby drawing, by implication, a stark contrast between Abraham and Jephthah.

Thus, in a rare move, Josephus, who clearly, as we have noted, had aggrandized the character of Jephthah, proceeds to criticize him openly for lacking two of the five virtues, namely wisdom and piety. Specifically, he remarks that Jephthah "had not by reflection (λογισμῷ, 'calculation,' 'reasoning')[14] probed (διαβασανίσας, 'weigh carefully', 'test thoroughly') what might befall or in what aspect the deed would appear to them that heard of it" (*Ant.* 5.266). In other words, before making his vow, Jephthah should have used his reasoning powers and been wise enough to calcu-

---

[12] See Theodor H. Gaster (1975, 2:431-32. Moore (1898, 305) notes, moreover, that the parallel with Iphigenia is instructive, inasmuch as Iphigenia was originally a name of Artemis Tauropolos, at whose festival a human sacrifice was enacted.

[13] Note that Josephus is here clearly adopting the reading of the Hebrew text rather than that of the Septuagint (Genesis 22:2), which reads ἀγαπητόν, "beloved," presumably because the translators were troubled by the fact that Isaac was not Abraham's only son. Note also that the biblical text is ambiguous in that it declares that Jephthah's daughter was an only child and then adds the seemingly superfluous statement that Jephthah had no other child by himself and his wife (Judges 11:34). Kimchi and Abravanel explain that Jephthah had other children, as well as those whom he had adopted from his wife's previous husband. Josephus, in his apparent eagerness to stress the parallel between Jephthah's daughter and Isaac and in his concern to dramatize the pathos of the scene states simply that she was an only child (*Ant.* 5.264).

[14] Attridge (1976, 113, n. 5) avers that λογισμός is a virtue close to σωφροσύνη; but it is actually much closer to reasoning and hence to σοφία.

late that the first entity to greet him after his victory would be his own daughter; or he should have realized that his vow was actually invalid, as, indeed, the rabbis, declare.[15] Incidentally, in Philo the term λογισμός refers to human reasoning (that is, the rational faculty)[16], coupled with insecure conjectures, and is contrasted with faith (πεπιστευκέναι) in G-d (*Legum Allegoria* 3.81.228).

In an incident highly reminiscent of Jephthah's vow, we find the lack of this same quality of λογισμός on the part of Saul in that, in the flush of victory, he invokes a curse upon anyone who would desist before nightfall from slaughtering the Philistine enemy and take food (*Ant.* 6.117); in that case, as in that of Jephthah, it turns out that it is his own child, Jonathan, who has breached the oath and whom he determines to slay (*Ant.* 6.126); and it is only the sympathy of all the people for Jonathan that prevents him from doing so. There, too, according to Josephus it is loss of control of reason (λογισμοῦ) which leads Saul to invoke his rash curse (*Ant.* 6.116).

In every case, as Josephus points out, that is, not only of Jephthah but also of Saul (*Ant.* 6.116) and Haman (*Ant.* 11.277), it is success or prosperity that leads to loss of control by reason. This formulation derives, of course, from Solon (fragment 1) and Greek tragedy: success or wealth begets satiety, which, in turn, begets overweening pride; and this ultimately brings forth nemesis or ruin. Indeed, a clue that Josephus views the whole Jephthah episode in terms of a Greek tragedy may be seen in the fact that whereas in the Bible we are told merely that when Jephthah returned from battle his daughter came out to meet him with timbrels and dance (Judges 11:34), in Josephus' version Jephthah experiences a reversal (περιπίπτει) (Judges 11:34), this verb being a cognate of the very word which, in Aristotle's famous analysis, denotes the περιπέτεια, the sudden reversal of circumstances on which the plot of a tragedy hinges, such as Oedipus' discovery

---

[15] Consequently, the rabbis bluntly declare that Jephthah is to be classed with the fools who do not distinguish between vows (*Ecclesiastes Rabbah* 4.7). For citations and discussion see Ginzberg (1928, 6:203, n. 109). The rabbis point out that Jephthah was unaware that he could have paid into the Temple treasury in lieu of his vow; and the high priest of his day, Phinehas, could have absolved him from it (Jerusalem Targum on Judges 11:39). The scholars of Jephthah's time, however, had forgotten the Halakhah and so they decided that he must keep his vow.

[16] See Philo, *De Mutatione Nominum* 39.223; *Quis Rerum Divinarum Heres* 53.265; *De Specialibus Legibus* 4.8.49; *De Praemiis et Poenis* 5.28. In the last passage we are told that λογισμός deals with intelligible things, the end of which is truth.

of his parentage (*Poetics* 11.1452A22-30). Indeed, Josephus here emphasizes the ironic contrast between Jephthah's fair achievements (τοῖς κατωρθωμένοις) and a calamity far different from them (κατ' οὐδὲν ὁμοίᾳ) (*Ant.* 5.264).

Furthermore, instead of commending Jephthah for being faithful to his vow, as some of the Church Fathers were later to do,[17] Josephus condemns him outright, as do the rabbis, for performing a sacrifice that was neither sanctioned by law (νόμμον) nor well-pleasing to G-d (*Ant.* 5.266). Josephus, moreover, plays down Jephthah's association with G-d (*Ant.* 5.266), thus lessening the reader's perception of his piety. For example, in the biblical text Jephthah tells the elders of Gilead that he will become their head "if you bring me back to fight with the children of Ammon and the L-rd delivers them before me" (Judges 11:9)[18] The elders likewise appeal to G-d, declaring to Jephthah that "the L-rd will be witness between us" (Judges 11:10); and Jephthah, in turn, likewise, we are told, spoke all his words before the L-rd. In Josephus' version there is no reference to G-d: "When the Hebrews made earnest entreaty and swore to confer the command upon him forever, he took the field" (*Ant.* 5.260). Again, "He installed the army in the city of Masphath." Likewise, in the Bible we hear that the spirit of the L-rd came upon Jephthah (Judges 11:29), that Jephthah made a vow to the L-rd (11:30) that whoever came forth to greet him after his successful battle would belong to the L-rd (11:31); but in Josephus' version there is no mention at all of G-d and we hear only that Jephthah prayed for victory without any indication as to whom he addressed the prayer (*Ant.* 5.263). Again, we are told in the Bible that the L-rd gave the Ammonites into Jephthah's hand (Judges 11:32), but Josephus again omits the role of G-d and says merely that Jephthah destroyed many cities and carried off spoil (*Ant.* 5.263). All this stands in contrast to Josephus' contemporary, Pseudo-Philo, who in his narrative of Jephthah mentions G-d no fewer than fourteen times.[19] Indeed, even when the

---

[17] See Penna (1961, 163), who cites Augustine in particular. Jerome (*Adversus Jovinianum* 1.23 (*PL* 23.253), on the other hand, is clearly influenced by Josephus and the rabbis when he declares that Jephthah was rebuked by several of the Hebrews (*plerisque Hebraeorum*) for his rash vow (*voti temerarii*).

[18] Cf. the comment on this Biblical text by Trible (1984, 95), that by appealing conditionally to G-d Jephthah further decreases the power of the elders while enhancing his own authority.

[19] 39.4, 39.5 (twice), 39.6 (twice), 39.7, 39.8 (twice), 39.9, 39.10, 39.11, 40.1

Josephan Jephthah does mention G-d it is not, as in the Bible, as judge between the people of Israel and the people of Ammon (Judges 11:27), but rather as the G-d of history, who in the past had conferred land for the Ammonites, which they continued to possess for the next three hundred years (*Ant.* 5.262).

On the other hand, Josephus was obviously embarrassed by Jephthah's seeming admission that the Ammonites possessed what they had as a gift from their god Chemosh (Judges 11:24), since this would seem to ascribe to Chemosh power to bestow land upon his worshippers.[20] Pseudo-Philo, apparently realizing that the Ammonites were polytheists, speaks of the gods who have given them their inheritance (*Bib. Ant.* 39.9). Josephus resolves the problem by omitting all reference to Chemosh or to the gods of the Ammonites.[21]

We may note, furthermore, that when Josephus finds flaws in such biblical heroes as Samson and Saul, he attributes them to human nature. In the case of Jephthah, Josephus might perhaps have made the excuse that a vow to offer human sacrifice was not against the law in Jephthah's time; but to do so this would have implied that the law was subject to development – a doctrine that would have opened up the floodgates to the dangerous possibility of further changes in the law in his own time. Josephus, moreover, was obviously troubled by the fact that despite what one would expect in light of the utter abhorrence of human sacrifice by the Jews, the biblical text contains no condemnation of Jephthah.[22]

(twice), 40.4. Pseudo-Philo focuses on G-d, who first punishes Israel for serving other gods but then repents of his anger.

[20] McKenzie (1966) remarks that this statement illustrates the extremely primitive belief of early Israel. We may assume that Josephus recognized and was embarrassed by it and that he resolved the dilemma by omitting the reference to Chemosh altogether. The traditional Jewish commentators, we may note, such as Radak and Ralbag, resolve this problem by asserting that in stating "Is it not that which Chemosh your god gives you to possess," Jephthah was speaking sarcastically.

[21] Another instance where Josephus avoids a problem in the biblical text is in connection with the contradiction between Judges 11:2, which declares that Jephthah was driven out by the sons of Gilead's wife, and Judges 11:7, where Jephthah turns bitterly to the elders of Gilead and asks why they had excluded him from his father's house. Here Josephus (*Ant.* 5.258) resolves the contradiction by having Josephus reproach the elders for not having aided him when he was wronged by his brethren.

[22] Indeed, as David Marcus (1986, 47) remarks, the lack of such a condemnation is one of the major reasons cited by those who deny that Jephthah actually

Hence, Josephus offers no justification or excuse but rather condemns him outright, stating baldly, in a clear addition to the Scriptural text, that the sacrifice of Jephthah's daughter was neither sanctioned by the law (νόμιμον) nor well-pleasing (κεχαρισμένην) to G-d (*Ant.* 5.266), even though in the Bible G-d says not a word of condemnation of Jephthah.

Indeed, it is significant that whereas the Bible employs direct discourse in order to dramatize the tragedy, in Josephus the narrator tells the story in order to teach a moral. As Marcus notes, it has often been alleged that the narrator of the biblical account employs an elliptical style in order to cast a veil over the final act so as to spare the reader the gruesome details (David Marcus 1986, 39); if so, we may remark that Josephus does not follow suit, clearly because he intends to criticize Jephthah and to teach a moral thereby. It is notable that whereas Josephus appears to praise Saul for respecting his oath, which would appear to us rash, to slay anyone who ate food before pursuing the enemy, more than the tender ties of fatherhood and of nature, he condemns Jephthah outright for adhering to his vow (*Ant.* 6.126). The difference, it would seem, is that Jephthah's vow was a purely personal one, to express exaltation upon his victory, whereas Saul's has a national purpose, that is, following up a military triumph.

Like Isaac (*Ant.* 1.232) and Jonathan (*Ant.* 6.127), in similar circumstances, Jephthah's daughter in Josephus learns her destiny without recrimination (*Ant.* 5.265). On the other hand, Josephus did not want to make a heroine out of Jephthah's daughter, both because it would detract from the stature of Jephthah and because he himself has a derogatory view of women (see Feldman 1986b, 115-28; and Amaru 1988, 109). We can see such downgrading of women in his extra-biblical remark (*Ant.* 5.264) that Jephthah chided his daughter for her haste in coming to meet him. Moreover, whereas Isaac reacts with positive joy when informed that he is to be sacrificed and actually rushes to the altar (*Ant.* 1.232),[23] and whereas Jonathan is said to surrender himself nobly and mag-

---

sacrificed his daughter. On the contrary, the biblical Jephthah is a true follower of G-d (Judges 11:9) and piously calls upon G-d to judge between Israel and Ammon (Judges 11:27), so that the spirit of G-d rests upon him (Judges 11:29).

[23] The consent of the one being sacrificed is an important prerequesite for the efficacy of the sacrifice. See Feldman (1984-85, 243-45) and especially the comparison and contrast with the sacrifice of Iphigenia.

nanimously (*Ant.* 6.127), and both, in extra-biblical additions in Josephus, make eloquent speeches welcoming death under these circumstances, Jephthah's daughter accepts her fate in a purely negative way, without displeasure (οὐκ ἀηδῶς). Instead of actively asserting her joy at being sacrificed for such a cause, as do Isaac and Jonathan, and in contrast to her biblical counterpart, who delivers a speech asking that her father live up to his vow, "now that the L-rd has avenged you on your enemies" (Judges 11:36), Josephus represents her as passively accepting the fact that she must die in exchange for her father's victory and the liberation of her fellow-citizens (*Ant.* 5.265).[24] Moreover, whereas Pseudo-Philo elevates Jephthah's daughter by giving her a name, Seila (*Bib. Ant.* 40.1), and by having her specifically ask her father not to annul his vow (*Bib. Ant.* 40.3), with the clear implication that she was aware that it could be so, and by having her explicitly say that she fears that her death will be unacceptable if she does not offer herself willingly, Josephus keeps her nameless, has her request her father that he act in accordance with her vow, and says nothing about her eagerness to offer herself willingly lest her death be unacceptable (*Ant.* 5.266).

We may, furthermore, contrast Pseudo-Philo's pious and theological approach with Josephus' purely political stress. His emphasis that Jephthah's daughter must die for her fellow citizens would surely remind some of Josephus' readers of the Roman concept of *devotio*, whereby a person (e.g., Decius Mus in Livy 8.9) deliberately seeks death among the enemy for the sake of the nation (see Rose 1970, 333); if he succeeded in getting killed it was deemed a sign that the gods had accepted his vow and would grant victory to the nation. Seidenberg remarks that Judith, Tamar, Jael, and Rahab are named and even honored in the Bible, but only because of their patriotic service in aiding and at times even saving the state (Seidenberg 1966, 53). This is not the case, says Seidenberg, with Jephthah's daughter, who did nothing for her country. Josephus,

---

[24] There is a unique parallel, found in no other source, between Josephus and Pseudo-Philo (*Bib. Ant.* 40.2) in the statement of Jephthah's daughter that she cannot be sorrowful at her death because she sees her people delivered. However, in Josephus the daughter learns that she must die for this cause and accepts her fate, whereas in Pseudo-Philo she positively asserts her acceptance by asking rhetorically, "Who is it that can be sorrowful in their death when they see the people delivered?"

to be sure, adds the editorial comment, as we have noted, that Jephthah's daughter is to die in return for her father's victory and the liberation of her fellow-citizens (*Ant.* 5.265), but she herself makes no such statement; indeed, she passively learns and accepts that she must die thus.

Again, whereas Samson is admired for "his valor, his strength, and his nobility at death" (*Ant.* 5.317), Josephus says not a word, in either praise or condemnation, of Jephthah's daughter for her readiness to be sacrificed, just as he avoids the pathos of her direct address to her father (Judges 11:36 vs. *Ant.* 5.265-66).

5. *Summary*

Confronted with the dilemma of how to portray Jephthah positively when he had committed the heinous act of sacrificing his own daughter, Josephus exaggerates Jephthah's good qualities of character while condemning those which deserve criticism. On the one hand, Jephthah is a true and caring leader of his flock. Josephus omits the fact that he is the son of a harlot. He stresses the magnitude of Jephthah's military achievement, adding that he delivered his countrymen from a servitude that the Israelites had borne for eighteen years. His possession of the virtue of moderation may be seen in his warning to the Ephraimites to show moderation. His devotion to justice appears from Josephus' addition that he did not go to war with the Ephraimites before carefully explaining to them how they had been delinquent.

In dealing with Jephthah's vow to sacrifice whatever would first come to greet him upon his returning victoriously from battle and his subsequent sacrifice of his own daughter, who was the first to greet him, Josephus was confronted with several dilemmas. To avoid the charge that the Israelite leaders were foolish to select a leader who would make such a rash vow, Josephus uses the neuter gender in reference to what Jephthah had vowed to sacrifice. To eliminate apparent similarities to pagan practices Josephus omits the statements that Jephthah's daughter wailed over her virginity and that a festival was held annually lamenting her sacrifice. Josephus criticizes Jephthah openly for not using his reasoning powers before making the vow and for his impiety in carrying it out. Apparently troubled by the lack of condemnation of Jephthah in the Bible, Josephus states outright that the sacrifice was not sanctioned by the law and was not pleasing to G-d. On the other hand, Josephus does not make a heroine out of Jephthah's daughter (this is especially evident when her attitude is compared with that of Isaac when about to be sacrificed or when she is compared with her counterpart in Pseudo-Philo's *Biblical Antiquities*) because it would detract from Jephthah's stature and because he had a derogatory view of women.

In contrast to Pseudo-Philo, Josephus lessens the role of G-d in Jephthah's military victories. Moreover, embarrassed by Jephthah's admission that the Ammonites had what they had as a gift from their god Chemosh, Josephus omits reference to Chemosh or to the gods of the Ammonites.

CHAPTER TWELVE

RUTH

1. *Introduction: The Problem*

The biblical personalities hitherto considered are, for the most part, of considerable significance, and Josephus generally accords them corresponding importance and length of treatment. How, though, does Josephus treat personalities of lesser importance?

We may well ask why Josephus devotes relatively little space to the Ruth pericope (114 lines in the Greek of the Loeb Library version) as against 202 lines in the Septuagint text (in the Rahlfs text). In fact, we may ask why he incorporates this pericope at all, inasmuch as the episode in itself has no reference to military victories or defeats or personal exploits of note and is historically of little importance. Indeed, we may note that in Josephus' version the role of Ruth herself is very much reduced, in line with his general misogynistic attitude. In particular, we may note Josephus' omission of her kindness (*ḥesed*, Ruth 1:8) toward others. Moreover, we may note that in two passages Ruth is reduced to the status of a mere child (παῖς) (*Ant.* 5.324, 328). Furthermore, in place of the vivid dialogue of the biblical text, we have events told in the third person; we may note, in particular, that 753 of the 1296 (58%) words in the biblical book consist of direct quotations, thereby adding to its vividness, whereas in Josephus' version there are only 72 words of direct quotations in the 776 words of text, making a percentage of only 9%. Indeed, Ruth's role, which is so central in the biblical narrative, is very much de-emphasized. We may also ask why Josephus, in contrast to his usual practice, does not highlight the erotic motif in the scene where Ruth lies down next to Boaz (Ruth 3:7; *Ant.* 5.329). If we ask why Josephus does not omit it altogether, as he does other such embarrassing episodes, we may reply that in those instances the episodes reflected badly on the Jewish people, and Josephus, as an apologist, deemed it best to omit them, whereas in the case of the Ruth episode this factor was absent.

2. *Why Josephus Includes the Ruth Pericope*

The chief answer as to why Josephus included the Ruth pericope would appear to be supplied at the very end of the passage, as it is at the very end of the biblical text, namely to provide the genealogy of King David, who is the great-grandson of Ruth. In this connection, we may suggest that Josephus was actually of two minds when it came to David. On the one hand, he could not omit the narrative because of the popularity of David in his own right among Jewish readers. On the other hand, Josephus had a personal stake in downgrading David because he himself was descended from the Hasmonean kings rather than from the line of David; moreover, inasmuch as we can see from the New Testament (Matthew 1:1-7, Luke 3:23-38, and Romans 1:3) that the tradition was well established of a Messiah descended from David, Josephus, aware that such a Messiah would be a political leader who would establish an independent Jewish state, realized how inflammatory that Messianic tack was in that this was precisely the goal of the revolutionaries of his own day in their war against the Romans. Hence, while, on the one hand, he felt that he could not omit the Ruth story altogether, on the other hand he was careful not to draw too much attention to it: hence, his diminution of dialogue and care not to highlight the erotic element.

3. *The Character of Ruth*

In our discussions of other biblical personalities we have noted Josephus' embellishing of such qualities as their genealogy, physical attractiveness, wealth, and their possession of the cardinal virtues. In the case of Ruth, if, as we have suggested, Josephus was acquainted with rabbinic traditions, he might well have known the tradition, which would certainly have enhanced her status, that she was the daughter of no less than the king of Moab himself (*Midrash Ruth Rabbah* 2.9); but he makes no mention of this tradition. Again, he might have mentioned, but does not, the tradition that Ruth was so beautiful that no man could look at her without falling passionately in love with her (*Midrash Ruth Rabbah* 2.4). He likewise does not mention the tradition of the great wealth of Mahlon, Ruth's first husband (Targum Ruth 1.1).

Likewise, as we have seen in Josephus' embellishments of the wondrous circumstances surrounding the birth of figures such as Moses and Samson, he might have mentioned, especially since he recounts the whole episode in order to highlight Ruth's descendants, the tradition that she herself had been barren and was forty years old when she bore Obed, that Boaz was eighty, and that her giving birth to a son was against all expectation (*Midrash Ruth Rabbah* 7.14). Again, Josephus is silent.

Inasmuch as the whole episode is recounted in order to call attention to Ruth's descendant, David, Josephus might also have mentioned that David's mighty opponent, Goliath, was the son of Orpah, Ruth's sister-in-law (*Soṭah* 42b, *Tanḥuma* B 1.208, *Ruth Rabbah* 1.14, *Ruth Zuta* 49, *Midrash Samuel* 20.106-8) (cited by Ginzberg 1928, 6:250, n. 27). The fact that this tradition is also to be found in Pseudo-Philo (*Bib. Ant.* 61.6), with whom, as we have noted, Josephus shares so many traditions, makes it even more likely that Josephus knew of it. Here was a tradition made to order for Josephus, since it would bring into direct juxtaposition David, the focal point of the Ruth pericope, and his great adversary, Goliath. But again, silence.

As for the cardinal virtues, we hear little of Ruth's wisdom, courage, temperance, justice, or piety. We do, to be sure, hear of her generosity in giving her mother-in-law all the barley-meal which she had received from Boaz (*Ant.* 5.326), whereas in the Bible she gives her only what she had left after she herself was satisfied (Ruth 2:18). In particular, we would, in view of the biblical text, have expected embellishment of her piety in leaving her country and its paganism and embracing the life of an Israelite; but all we are told is that she refused to be persuaded by her mother-in-law Naomi to stay in her native land and opted to join Naomi "to be her partner in all that should befall" (*Ant.* 5.322). The only aspect of her piety that Josephus does mention is her remembrance of her late husband (*Ant.* 5.325) and her regard for her mother-in-law in seeking her permission before going out to glean (*Ant.* 5.324) and in obeying her behests in all things (*Ant.* 5.329). Likewise, Boaz does show appreciation for Ruth's loyalty (εὐνοίας) to her mother-in-law (*Ant.* 5.325), though this is not expanded upon.

4. *The Role of G-d in the Ruth Pericope*

Levison affirms that the various additions and modifications of the Bible in Josephus' version of the Ruth pericope are all intended to demonstrate G-d's role in elevating ordinary people to lives of felicity in accordance with his statement in the proem to the *Antiquities* (1.20) (Levison 1991). If so, however, we may well ask why, whereas the Tetragrammaton (the word "L-rd") occurs seventeen times (1:6, 8, 9, 13, 17, 21 [*bis*]; 2:4 [*bis*], 12 [*bis*], 20; 3:13; 4:11, 12, 13, 14) in the Hebrew and in the Septuagint versions of Ruth, the word "G-d" occurs three times (1:16 [bis]; 2:12), and the word "Almighty" referring to G-d occurs twice (1:20, 21), making a total of twenty-two mentions of G-d, in Josephus, the word "G-d," in his version, which is sixty per cent as long as the Hebrew original (776 words in Josephus vs. 1296 words in the Hebrew text) and thirty-six per cent as long as the Septuagint (2147 words), appears exactly once, namely at the very end of the pericope (*Ant.* 5.337). Indeed, we may wonder why Josephus states that he was compelled to include the narrative in order to demonstrate the power of G-d (*Ant.* 5.337) when he actually does not mention the role of G-d at any stage of the story, from the famine at the beginning to the fruitful marriage of Ruth and Boaz at the end.

In general, as we have often noted, Josephus tends to assign less prominence to the role of G-d in his paraphrase of the Bible, since he is writing not as a theologian but as a historian, noting the consequences of the actions of his most important human characters. If so, we may ask why Josephus introduces G-d at all here. Our suggestion is that in writing his *Antiquities* he has two audiences in mind, one more skeptical of divine interference, the other (as seen, for example, in Livy's preface) looking upon history as a series of divine acts intended to preach morality to the reader. Apparently, he intended to deal at length with theological matters in a projected separate work (*Ant.* 1.25, 192; 3.143; 4.198; 20.168) which, it would seem, however, he never actually wrote.

5. *Intermarriage and Conversion*

As we see in his handling of the intermarriages of Esau, Joseph, Moses, Samson, and Solomon, among others, Josephus was in a quandary. On the one hand, the Bible explicitly prohibits intermarriage (Deuteronomy 7:3); but, on the other hand, too strenuous an objection to the practice on his part would play into the hands of those who accused the Jews of misanthropy and illiberalism.

Significantly, whereas in the Bible it is only after the death of their father Elimelech that his sons Mahlon and Chilion take wives of the women of Moab (Ruth 1:4), Josephus, on the contrary, indicates that it was Elimelech himself who took Moabite women as wives for his sons (*Ant.* 5.319), presumably to indicate that Jews are not prejudiced against non-Jews, even Moabites, this despite the fact that the Torah declares that no Moabite may enter the "assembly of the L-rd" (Deuteronomy 23:3) because they had shown hostility to the Israelites during their forty years of wandering in the desert after the Exodus.[1] Moreover, again to show that Jews are not hostile to non-Jews, Josephus' picture of the two Moabite daughters-in-law of Naomi arouses even more sympathy than does the biblical version. In the latter, when they are urged to return to their homeland of Moab, they reply very simply, "Nay, but we will return with thee unto thy people" (Ruth 1:10). In Josephus, by contrast, we are told that the daughters-in-law had not the heart (ἐκαρτέρουν, "endured") to be parted from Naomi (*Ant.* 5.321). And Josephus would have us give even greater credit to the daughters-in-law in light of his extra-biblical detail that Naomi actually begged (παραιτουμένη) and implored (παρεκάλει) them to return (*Ant.* 5.321-22).

We may well ask why Josephus refers to Ruth only once as a Moabitess (*Ant.* 5.319), whereas the biblical text designates her thus on six occasions (1:22; 2:2, 6, 21; 4:5, 10).[2] Moreover, we may ask why Josephus has totally omitted all references to Ruth's conversion to Judaism, so crucial in the biblical account, in Ruth's own words: "Thy people shall be my people, and thy G-d my G-d" (Ruth 1:16) or again, in the words of Boaz: "It hath fully been told me...how thou hast left thy father and thy mother, and the land of

---

[1] The rabbis have a tradition that Deuteronomy's exclusion of Moabites from entering "the congregation of the L-rd" applies only to males, not to females (*Pesiqta de-Rav Kahana* 16.124a). Hence, it was Halakhically permissible for Ruth to convert to Judaism. Josephus, however, does not mention this tradition, nor does he raise the issue of whether it was Halakhically permissible for Ruth to become a convert.

[2] We may also note that whereas the biblical text specifically enumerates Moabite women among those foreign women whom King Solomon loved (1 Kings 11:1), Josephus omits the Moabites from his version of the list (*Ant.* 8.191).

thy nativity, and art come unto a people that thou knowest not heretofore" (Ruth 2:10)

As to the almost total omission of the identification of Ruth as a Moabitess, we may note that Josephus, in his summaries of Jewish laws pertaining to marriage (*Ant.* 3.274-75, 4.244-45; *Ag. Ap.* 2.199-203) omits the prohibition of marrying Amorites and Moabites, presumably because he wished to avoid the charge that Jews are illiberal toward other peoples.

The subject of proselytism was an extremely delicate one. As the Romans saw a decline in religiosity (see, for example, the preface to Livy's history), they became more and more bitter about those who were trying to draw them away from their ancestral religion and values. The expulsion of the Jews from Rome in 139 B.C.E. (Valerius Maximus 1.3.3) and, apparently, in 19 C.E. (Josephus, *Ant.* 18.81-84; Tacitus, *Annals* 2.85; Suetonius, *Tiberius* 36; Dio Cassius 57.18.5a) had been connected with the alleged attempt of the Jews to convert non-Jews to Judaism (see Feldman (1993a, 300-4); and we must note that such drastic action had taken place despite the generally favorable attitude of the Roman government toward the Jews.

Josephus, therefore, had to be extremely careful not to offend his Roman hosts by referring to the inroads that the Jews were making through proselytism into the Roman populace; hence his remarkable silence about the conversion of Ruth to Judaism. It is surely significant that in the *Antiquities*, aside from the passage about the conversion of the royal family of Adiabene (which was, after all, under Parthian domination, and hence of no immediate concern to the Romans) (*Ant.* 20.17-96), Josephus nowhere propagandizes for proselytism. If, in the essay *Against Apion*, he declares that the Jews gladly welcome any who wish to share their customs (*Ag. Ap.* 2.261), he is careful to note that Jews do not take the initiative in seeking out proselytes and that, in fact, they take precautions to prevent foreigners from mixing with them at random (*Ag. Ap.* 2.257). Moreover, Josephus himself makes a point of stressing that when the Galilean Jews tried to compel some non-Jews to be circumcised as a condition for dwelling among them, he refused to allow any compulsion to put upon them, declaring that everyone should worship G-d in accordance with the dictates of his own conscience (*Life* 113).

Hence, whereas in the biblical text, it is Ruth who takes the iniative to indicate her desire to join her mother-in-law and the Israelite people, with her words "thy people shall be my people, and thy G-d my G-d" (Ruth 1:16), and makes the dramatic statement, indicating the degree of her sincerity, that she wishes to join her mother-in-law even in death itself, in Josephus, on the other hand, we are simply told that Ruth could not be persuaded to remain in Moab (*Ant.* 5.322). She makes no declaration of her intention to join her mother-in-law's religion. We are merely told that Naomi "took her with her, to be her partner in all that should befall" (*Ant.* 5.322).

6. *Dramatic Embellishment*

In the view of the way in which Josephus over and over again increases the dramatic component in his version of biblical pericopes, one would have expected him to make much of the emotional scene in which Naomi tries to get her daughters-in-law Ruth and Orpah not to accompany her as she returns to her homeland in Bethlehem (Ruth 1:8-18). The use of direct discourse and the mention of the lifting up of their voices and weeping again and again surely make this one of the most moving scenes in the entire Bible. All this, however, is reduced to two short paragraphs in Josephus, none of it in direct discourse, and with no mention of their raising their voices or weeping (*Ant.* 5.321-22).

As it stands, the biblical narrative has all the elements of a romantic tale. Ruth, a foreigner and a Moabitess at that, arrives in a strange land, Canaan, and by sheer chance happens to glean in a field belonging to Boaz, who, unbeknownst to her, was a kinsman of her late husband and who receives her with warm hospitality. When she returns to Naomi, it comes as a complete surprise to the latter that she had gleaned in the field of Boaz, and she blesses G-d for bringing about this happy coincidence (Ruth 2:19). *A priori*, knowing what we do of the way in which Josephus builds up the romantic and erotic elements in such episodes as that of Joseph and Potiphar's wife, the Israelite men and the Midianite women in the desert, Samson, David and Solomon and their affairs, Herod and his infatuation with Mariamne, and the affair of Anilaeus' affair with a Parthian general's wife (*Ant.* 18.340-52), we should surely expect him to exploit the erotic possibilities here as well. In fact, however, Josephus totally omits the first meeting of Ruth and

Boaz in which she poignantly asks Boaz why she should have found favor in his sight, seeing that she is a foreigner (Ruth 2:8-14 vs. *Ant.* 5.324). In Josephus' version there is no such suspense, since Boaz immediately finds out all the details about his visitor, Ruth, from his steward (*Ant.* 5.324). Hence, whereas the welcome that he gives to Ruth in the Bible is due to the code of hospitality required toward any stranger, in Josephus he welcomes her because of his kinship and his loyalty to her mother-in-law (*Ant.* 5.323). Surely, then, Josephus has here missed an opportunity to build on a more romantic scene, utilizing the biblical data. Instead he passes over as quickly as possible this and other potentially romantic scenes.

Moreover, Josephus disregards the makings of another very romantic scene, namely the incident where Naomi instructs Ruth to wash and anoint herself and to lie down in Boaz's threshing floor next to him and to uncover his feet (Ruth 3:2-4). After Boaz has eaten, drunk, become merry, and fallen asleep, he discovers the presence of an unknown woman next to him, who then proceeds to introduce herself and to remind him that he is a near kinsman. The scene is, indeed, highly reminiscent of that in the *Homeric Hymn to Aphrodite* in which we learn of Aphrodite's visit to Anchises at night in a herdsman's hut. To judge from the way Josephus treats other such incidents, especially the story of Esther, one would have expected an elaborate description of Ruth's beauty and of her cosmetic preparations here. In Josephus there is, however, nothing of Ruth's washing and anointing herself in preparation for the assignation (*Ant.* 5.328). Moreover, realizing that the reader might well wonder how an upright person could put herself in such a sexually compromising situation, Josephus specifically says that she regarded it as a pious (ὅσιον) duty to gainsay the behests of her mother-in-law in nothing (*Ant.* 5.329). And when Boaz wakes up towards midnight, Josephus adds, seeking to underscore Ruth's modesty, that she first of all asked him to pardon her (*Ant.* 5.330).[3] Moreover, realizing that most readers would assume that under such circumstances Boaz would have sexual relations with Ruth, Josephus specifically adds that Boaz roused Ruth at daybreak (in the Bible [Ruth 3:14] she herself takes the initiative to rise early) before anyone should see that she had slept there, "since it was

---

[3] Josephus cites a further indication that Boaz and Ruth did not have sexual relations before marriage, namely the detail that their child was born a year after their marriage (*Ant.* 5.335).

wise to guard against scandal of that kind, and the more so when nothing had passed" (*Ant.* 5.330). It might perhaps be thought that Josephus avoids further elaboration of the scene of Boaz and Ruth lying together on the threshing floor in order to preserve the reputation of her descendant, David; but this seems unlikely in view of the fact that Josephus not only does not omit or excuse the affair of David with Bathsheba but actually embellishes it (*Ant.* 7.130-58).

On the other hand, one might have expected, especially since the Ruth pericope comes immediately after the Samson episode, that Josephus would have emphasized the contrast between the morality of Boaz and Ruth, particularly in circumstances so tempting to immorality, and the immoral behavior of Samson, despite his Nazirite status. Likewise, the Ruth story comes just before the account of the immoral behavior of the sons of the high priest Eli, and Josephus might well have contrasted Ruth's behavior with theirs. We might, moreover, have expected Josephus to echo the rabbinic tradition that Ruth did not wash or anoint herself or dress herself beautifully on the way to her meeting with Boaz on the threshing floor until after she had arrived there in order not to attract attention from bystanders (*Shabbat* 113b). We might have expected, too, a speech about the value of chastity such as Joseph delivers to Potiphar's wife (*Ant.* 2.51-52). Again we are disappointed.

7. *Summary*

The Ruth pericope appears to be of so little importance to Josephus that one wonders why he included it at all, inasmuch as the story has little significance for the political history of Israel.

In contrast to the rabbinic tradition, Josephus says nothing about Ruth's outstanding genealogy, beauty, or wealth. Unlike his delineations of other biblical figures he is likewise silent about her wisdom, courage, temperance, and justice. His only added touches concern her piety toward her mother-in-law Naomi.

Though Josephus does say at the end of the pericope that he included the story in order to show the power of G-d, he systematically excludes mention of G-d throughout it until this very last comment.

Because the issue of Jewish proselytism was such a sensitive one for the Romans, who looked upon it as a threat to their national traditions, Josephus is careful to avoid any mentioning of Ruth's conversion.

Though we would have expected Josephus to take advantage of the opportunities to develop the dramatic, romantic, and erotic elements in the Ruth pericope, he clearly avoids doing so. Again, one might have expected him to contrast the morality of Boaz and Ruth with the immoral behavior of Samson and of Eli's sons, which stand in immediate juxtaposition with the Ruth pericope, but he does not.

There would appear to be three major reasons why Josephus has not taken advantage of the wonderful opportunities for embellishment afforded by the Ruth episode. In the first place, as we have noted in his treatment of a woman of such major importance as Deborah, he is a misogynist. If he does build up Esther it is only because she was a queen and contributed mightily toward saving the Jewish people from their enemies. Secondly, if he devotes so little attention to the central personality in this whole narrative, namely Ruth herself, it is because she is, in the Jewish tradition, depicted as the prototype of proselytes; and the Romans, Josephus' patrons, were extremely sensitive about the success of the Jews in winning proselytes during this period. If, on the other hand, he does not omit the episode altogether it may well be because he realized that some of his readers would be Jews who would expect some mention of the noteworthy story of David's ancestress, Ruth. Finally, if, at the end of the pericope (*Ant.* 5.337) Josephus states that the reason why he included the narrative of Ruth at all is to show how easy it is for G-d to promote even ordinary folk to rank so illustrious as that to which he raised her descendant, David, this may reflect his bias, as a descendant of the Hasmoneans, against the royal family of David. Josephus resolved the problems posed by the biblical story of Ruth by recounting the episode as briefly as possible and by highlighting Ruth herself as little as possible.[4]

---

[4] I should like to express my gratitude to Moshe J. Bernstein and John R. Levison for a number of suggestions in connection with my treatment of Ruth.

CHAPTER THIRTEEN

JOAB

1. *Introduction: Joab in the Rabbinic Tradition*

If we assume that Josephus had considerable acquaintance with the traditions later codified by the rabbis, his portrait of Joab is of considerable interest, inasmuch as the rabbis seem to have had ambivalent feelings toward him. On the one hand, as we would expect in the case of a general, he is praised for his bravery, as we see from his daring exploits in entering the Amalekite capital and killing so many of the men singlehandedly. He is also praised for his hospitality, a quality so much admired by the ancients (so that it is almost the leitmotif of Homer's *Odyssey*), as we see in the comment by Rabbi Judah in the name of Rab, that his home was open to all (*Sanhedrin* 49a). Furthermore, in a society which placed such a premium upon helping the poor, Rabbi Judah is quoted as saying that Joab would merely taste a meager meal of fish broth and hashed fish and then share the rest with the poor (*ibid.*). Likewise, in an age rife with robbery and licentiousness, he is praised for having a house free from such disturbances (*ibid.*). Again, though in the Bible Joab is presented as skilled merely in military matters and there would seem to be not even the slightest hint that he was a great scholar, the rabbis, who, of course, placed such emphasis upon Torah scholarship, report a tradition that he was actually the president of the Sanhedrin (Jerusalem *Makkot* 2.31d, *Tanḥuma B* 4.166, *Tanḥuma Mase'ei* 12, *Numbers Rabbah* 23.13, *Pesiqta Rabbati* 11.43b).[1] In addition, we have the view, expressed by Rabbi Abba ben Kahana, based upon his reading of the statement that David was able to execute justice for all the people because Joab was over the host (2 Samuel 8:15-16), that if not for Joab David would not have been able to devote himself to the study of the Torah. He is likewise lauded for his piety, as we may infer from the statement that he was blessed with pious descendants, among them priests

---

[1] See Ginzberg (1928, 6:258, n. 76), who remarks that in these sources the Tahchemonite is identified with Joab, who bore this name, meaning "the wise," because he was the head of the academy (2 Samuel 23:8).

and prophets (Targum 1 Chronicles 2:54). He is also depicted as having a keen insight into human nature, as we see from the tale in which he came to the realization that a father has a greater love for a child than does a mother (*Beit Hamidrash*, ed. Adolf Jellinek, 5.52-53). He is even described by Rabbi Johanan as justifying his slaying of Abner according to the law of the Sanhedrin (*Sanhedrin* 49a).[2] Indeed, that there was great sympathy for Joab in the rabbinic tradition, despite the fact that it was the ever-popular David whom he offended by killing Abner and Amasa, may be discerned from the statement that by executing Joab Solomon transferred David's curse to his own posterity.[3]

But the rabbinic tradition about Joab is far from one-sided. Thus we find a devastating attack upon him for his lack of faith in his campaign against Edom, where, in a moment of despair, he charged G-d with deserting him, whereupon David supposedly became so enraged at his lack of faith that he intended to slay him (*Midrash Psalms* 60.1). Moreover, Solomon is depicted as justifying his orders to put Joab to death on the ground that he had rebelled against King David by being about to join Absalom (*Sanhedrin* 49a). Finally, if, indeed, Joab was successful in war, it was not because of his skill as a military commander but rather because David executed justice and righteousness over all his people (*ibid.*).

2. *Joab's Virtues*

Inasmuch as Joab was commander in chief of the army of the great King David we are not surprised to find Josephus aggrandizing his military achievements. Thus, whereas the Bible is content merely to state that Joab and Abishai pursued Abner (2 Samuel 2:24), Josephus transfers the initiative solely to Joab, emphasizes that the enemy were routed (τραπέντας), and adds a number of details to illustrate Joab's persistence, namely, that he did not relax the pursuit but himself pressed after the enemy, and that he gave orders

---

[2] Indeed, the slaying is justified on the ground that Abner was indifferent to effecting a reconciliation between Saul and David (Jerusalem *Soṭah* 1).

[3] Cf. *Sanhedrin* 48b-49a, Jerusalem *Qiddushin* 1.16a, *Midrash Samuel* 25.123-24, *Tanḥuma B* 4.167, *Tanḥuma Mase'ei* 12, *Numbers Rabbah* 23.13, cited by Ginzberg (1928, 6:278, n. 10). In particular, Jerusalem *Makkot* 2.31a and *Midrash Samuel* 25.124 remark on the great loss sustained by Israel through Joab's death.

to his soldiers to follow at their heels and not to grow weary in dealing out death (*Ant.* 7.13). We see the same quality of determination in Josephus' added details concerning Joab's pursuit of Abner. Thus, whereas the Bible states very simply that Joab and Abishai pursued Abner (2 Samuel 2:24), Josephus adds that Joab and Abishai found cause for pressing with still greater zeal (σπουδῆς, "energy," "earnestness," "insistence") after Abner with incredible speed and determination (προθυμίᾳ, "zeal," "eagerness," "confidence") (*Ant.* 7.16).

Josephus similarly stresses Joab's bravery in his account of the encounter with the Ammonites. Whereas the Bible says merely that the Ammonites fled before him (2 Samuel 10:13), Josephus adds to Joab's reputation for bravery by noting that the Ammonites resisted stoutly for a while, that Joab killed many of them, and that he compelled all the rest to turn and flee (*Ant.* 7.126). Moreover, the Bible ascribes the victory not only to Joab but also to David's servants (2 Samuel 11:1), whereas Josephus mentions only Joab in giving credit for the victory (*Ant.* 7.129). Furthermore, in contrast to the Bible, which reports cryptically that Joab took "the city of waters" (2 Samuel 12:27), Josephus adds that Joab inflicted great damage and explains that he cut off the Ammonites' water and other supplies, so that they were in a very pitiable condition for lack of food and drink, since they were dependent upon a small well (*Ant.* 7.159).

Joab exhibits the quality of modesty when he writes to King David inviting him to come to the capture of the city of Rabbah so that the victory might be ascribed to David even though it was Joab who had all but completed the conquest of the city. When David receives Joab's letter, he commends, in an extra-biblical remark, Joab's loyalty (εὐνοίας) and faithfulness (πίστεως) (*Ant.* 7.160).

Moreover, it is a distinct compliment to Joab that whereas in the Bible it is the servants of David who take up the dead Asahel and bury him, with no mention made of burial of the other nineteen who had been slain, let alone of the role of Joab (2 Samuel 2:32), in Josephus it is Joab who assumes the responsibility of arranging for the burial, and not merely of Asahel but also of the other nineteen who had been slain (*Ant.* 7.18).

And yet, in his concern not to aggrandize the virtues of Joab excessively, Josephus very significantly, in citing Joab's appeal to his brother Abishai exhorting him to fight bravely against the Ammonites, omits the biblical statement in which Joab twice mentions the name of G-d, once urging Abishai to prove strong "for the cities of our G-d" and once asking the L-rd to do that which seems good to Him" (*Ant.* 7.125)

3. *Joab's Negative Qualities*

In the proem to his *Antiquities* Josephus summarizes the Bible as recounting "all sorts of surprising reverses, many fortunes (τύχαι) of war, heroic exploits of generals, and political revolutions" (*Ant.* 1.13) One might say that Joab, expecially in Josephus' version, epitomizes these topics in a negative sense.

In the last analysis, Joab turns out to be a coward. Thus, in the Bible, after he hears of the death of Adonijah, Joab, we are told, fled to the tabernacle of the L-rd and took hold of the horns of the altar (1 Kings 2:28). Josephus is more explicit in stating that Joab was greatly afraid (περιδεής) and then proceeds to give the reason for this fear, namely that he had been more friendly to Adonijah than to King Solomon (*Ant.* 8.13).

In particular, the Josephan Joab is a study of a traitor, ironically and most significantly, the very quality with which Josephus had been charged. Thus, whereas in the Bible before slaying Asahel, Joab's brother, Abner warns him not to follow him, adding that if he kills him, "How should I hold up my face to Joab your brother?" (2 Samuel 2:22). In Josephus' version Joab's later slaying of Abner is all the more condemned because we are told of Abner's friendly relations (παρρησίαν, "candor," "frankness," "friendly relationship") with his brother Joab (*Ant.* 7.15).

Josephus likewise presents Joab as more directly contradicting the orders of King David. Whereas the Bible says that Joab thrust three darts through the heart of Absalom (2 Samuel 18:14), it is clear that he did not actually kill him, inasmuch as we read that ten young men who bore Joab's armor surrounded him and killed him (2 Samuel 18:15). In Josephus' version, on the other hand, Joab orders that he be shown where Absalom is hanging, and he himself then kills him (*Ant.* 7.241).

In the biblical narrative Joab shows the quality of solicitude for King David's peace of mind when he perceives that the king really wants to be reconciled with his son Absalom, and so he devises a scheme whereby the king, with an easy conscience, might recall

Absalom (2 Samuel 14:1). Josephus, however, while noting that Joab urged David to be reconciled with Absalom, detracts from the credit due to Joab, inasmuch as, in his version, it is David, rather than Joab, who has the initial intention of sending for Absalom (*Ant.* 7.181). Moreover, in an extra-biblical addition Joab's motive is not concern for David but rather zeal for Absalom's cause (*Ant.* 7.186, 193).

Furthermore, in the scene in which Joab berates David for mourning for his son Absalom, Josephus' Joab is much less understanding of David's feelings and much harsher than he is in the Bible (2 Samuel 19:6-7 vs. *Ant.* 7.254-57). In the Bible Joab says that by his mourning David has shamed those who saved his life and the lives of members of his family, whereas in Josephus he declares that David is slandering himself. He then goes one step further than the Bible in threatening that if David persists in mourning he, Joab, will persuade the people to revolt against him.

In view of the importance which Josephus attaches to being truthful, it is particularly reprehensible for Joab to act deceitfully. Thus, in the Bible we read that when Joab approached Amasa, his sword fell out, presumably by chance (2 Samuel 20:8). Not so in Josephus, where we read that Joab artfully contrived (φιλοτεχνεῖ) to have the sword fall, as if by itself (αὐτομάτως) from its sheath (*Ant.* 7.284).

Again, if piety is one of the standard qualities associated with biblical heroes in Josephus' paraphrase of the Bible, it is the opposite quality of acting impiously (ἀνοσίως) with which Joab is characterized because he had slain Amasa and Abner (*Ant.* 8.15). In fact, in the Bible Joab attempts to justify the deed by claiming that Abner had come as a spy to deceive King David and to learn his comings and goings (2 Samuel 3:25). On the other hand, in an editorial-like comment Josephus proceeds, in an addition to the Bible, to castigate "this impious (ἀσεβές) and most unholy (παντελῶς ἀνόσιον) deed (*Ant.* 7.284).

Likewise, in the Bible, when David decides to embark on a census of the people and orders Joab to do so, Joab shows his awareness that G-d is opposed to the enumeration of the people and mentions G-d by name in his wish that G-d would add to the number of the people and questions why David would delight in such an action (2 Samuel 24:3, 1 Chronicles 21:3). Josephus' Joab, to be sure, is more explicit in telling David that there was no need for the census, but Josephus detracts from Joab's religious status by not mentioning the name of G-d at all in offering his objection (*Ant.* 7.319). Moreover, whereas in the Bible Joab is depicted as more pious in finding King David's command to conduct the census of the tribes of Levi and Benjamin downright abhorrent (1 Chronicles 21:6), in Josephus Joab omits the enumeration of these two tribes because he did not have the time to count them (*Ant.* 7.320). Josephus similarly, in encouraging his brother Abishai in the struggle against the Ammonites (*Ant.* 7.125), omits the Bible's reference to Joab's prayer that G-d should do what seems good to Him (2 Samuel 10:12, 1 Chronicles 19:13); in Josephus Joab merely exhorts his brother to fight bravely (*Ant.* 7.125).

4. *Josephus' Treatment of Joab as a Lesson in the Disastrous Consequences of Civil Strife*

In line with his constantly reiterted theme that civil strife had proven disastrous for the Jews during his own lifetime, Josephus stresses the theme of the consequences of civil strife in connection with Joab in particular. He sets the scene by referring specifically to the long war between the house of Saul and that of David as a civil (ἐμφύλιος, "of kinsmen," "internal," "domestic") war among the Hebrews (2 Samuel 3:1). Thus, whereas the biblical Abner remarks to Joab that continued fighting will lead to bitterness in the end (2 Samuel 2:26), Josephus' Abner is more specific in articulating how wrong civil strife is by stating that it is not right to stir up fellow countrymen to strife (ἔριδα) and warfare (*Ant.* 7.17)

In particular, we may note that in the Bible the anonymous old woman asks him, when he besieges the city of Abel Beth-Maacah, whether he is seeking to destroy "a city and a mother in Israel" and furthermore inquires whether he wishes to swallow up "the inheritance of the L-rd" (2 Samuel 20:19). Josephus, on the other hand, does not put it in the form of a question but rather in the form of an accusation, stressing the innocence of the people of the city: "You," she charges him, " are bent on destroying and sacking a mother-city of the Israelites which has done no wrong" (*Ant.* 7.289). In acting thus, she implies, Joab is going against the will of G-d, who had chosen kings and commanders to drive out the enemies of the Hebrews and to secure peace from them, whereas Joab was doing the work of the enemy in thus attacking fellow-Jews.

5. *The Disastrous Effects of Envy*

Josephus is clearly thinking of contemporary parallels in his constant stress on the theme of envy and its disastrous consequences. In the case of Joab it is this theme of jealousy that he especially stresses. Thus, in the Bible Joab tries to convince David that Abner's motive in coming to him was to spy (2 Samuel 3:25), whereas in the *Antiquities* (7.31) it is Josephus himself who analyzes Joab's motive and clearly indicates that it is envy, arising out of the fear that David might deprive him of his command and give Abner honors of the first rank as one who was apt (δεινόν, "clever) in understanding (συνιδεῖν) in matters of state (πράγματα) and who was quick to seize opportunities and who would help him in securing his kingdom. Josephus then specifically adds that Joab feared that he himself might be set down and deprived of his command.

This stress on Joab's envy is particularly evident in Josephus' account of David's dying charge to his son and successor King Solomon. In the Bible (1 Kings 2:5) David simply tells his son to avenge Joab's murder of Abner and Amasa. Josephus is explicit in ascribing the two murders to envy (ζηλοτυπίαν) (*Ant.* 7.386).

There can be little doubt that Josephus has recast the figure of Joab so as to parallel that of his arch-enemy John of Gischala, particularly with regard to the theme of envy. John, according to Josephus, was eager for revolution (νεωτέρων) and ambitious (ἐπιθυμίαν ἔχοντα) of obtaining command in Galilee (*Life* 70). In contrast, Josephus himself emphasizes that he himself was at this time about thirty years old, "at a time of life when, even if one restrains his lawless passions, it is hard, especially in a position of high authority, to escape the calumnies (διαβολάς) of envy (φθόνου) (*Life* 80). When John, however, observed how loyal the people of Galilee were to Josephus his envy was aroused (ἐφθόνησε) (*Life* 85). When one scheme after another to destroy Josephus failed, John, believing that there was a direct relationship between Josephus' success and his own ruin, gave way to immoderate envy (εἰς φθόνον...οὔτι μέτριον) (*Life* 122). Indeed, according to Josephus his failures to assassinate Josephus merely intensified John's envy (φθόνον) (*War* 2.614). He then tried to induce the inhabitants of the three leading cities of Galilee to abandon Josephus and to transfer their allegiance to him. Thereafter he attempted to induce the Jewish leaders in Jerusalem to deprive Josephus of his command in Galilee and to appoint John instead. Josephus writes that he was particularly distressed by the base ingratitude of his fellow-citizens, whose jealousy (φθόνον) had prompted the order to have him put to death (*Life* 204).

We may note that Josephus uses much the same language in describing John of Gischala's intention toward Josephus as πονηρός ("malign") and in depicting himself, like Abner, as being deceived by him (*Life* 86). The Galilaeans, he says, knew John to be a perjured villain (πονηρός) and consequently pressed Josephus to lead them against him (*Life* 102). He likewise speaks of John's κακουργία ("wickedness," "evil intent," "fraud") in profiting from the sale of oil (*Life* 76) and, indeed, castigates him in the most extreme terms as the most unscrupulous (πανουργότατος) and most crafty (δολιώτατος) of all who have ever gained notoriety by such infamous means (*War* 2.585).[4] John, we are told made a merit of deceit (ἀπάτην) (*War* 2.586), precisely the quality in Joab which Josephus stresses in his additions to the biblical text.

The envy (φθόνον) of even a few may bring about civil war (πολέμου ἐμφυλίου), as Josephus remarks (*War* 2.620). In particular, Josephus notes that the leaders in Jerusalem, from motives of envy (φθόνον), secretly supplied John of Gischala with money to enable him to collect mercenaries and to make war on Josephus (*War* 2.627). Envy is likewise, according to Josephus, the motive which drove the revolutionary Zealots, whom he so much despised, to massacre the nobility (εὐγένειαν, "noble ancestry," "aristocracy") (*War* 4.357). Indeed, the split in the Zealot party itself was brought about, says Josephus, by the fact that some of the revolutionaries were influenced by envy to scorn John, their former equal (*War* 4.393). Moreover, Josephus ascribes the mutiny of the Idumaeans within John's army to envy of his power, as much as to hatred of his cruelty (*War* 4.566).

After the war it is again envy (φθόνον) which was excited by Josephus' privileged position and which exposed him once again to danger (*Life* 423). He adds that numerous accusations were made against him by persons who envied him his good fortune but

---

[4] We may note that Josephus uses similar language in describing the knavish tricks (κακουργήματα) of Justus of Tiberias, Josephus' rival in historiography (*Life* 356).

that he succeeded in escaping them all through the providence of G-d (*Life* 425).

In Josephus' depiction of the relations between Joab and Abner, Joab plays the role of John of Gischala, and Abner that of Josephus. Thus, whereas in the Bible Joab seeks to turn David against Abner by telling him that Abner had come to deceive him and to spy on his comings and goings (2 Samuel 3:34), Josephus, as we have noted, goes much further in condemning Joab. In the first place, he describes Joab's course as dishonest (κακοῦργον, "malicious," "deceitful," "wrongdoing," "criminal") and evil (πονηρόν). He then proceeds to add that Joab attempted to calumniate (διαβαλεῖν, "to make someone disliked," "to put someone into a bad light," "to cast suspicion upon," "to detract from someone's reputation," "to revile," "to charge falsely") Abner to King David, "urging him to be on his guard and not to pay attention to the agreements Abner had made; for he was doing everything, he said, in order to secure sovereignty for Saul's son, and, after coming to David with deceit and guile, he had now gone away with the hope of realizing his wish and carrying out his carefully laid plans" (*Ant.* 7.31-32)

In the sequel Josephus adds further details which denigrate the role of Joab. Whereas the Bible asserts merely that Joab sent messengers after Abner (2 Samuel 3:26), Josephus declares that Joab, unable to persuade David, resorted to a course still bolder (τολμηροτέραν, "more daring," "more audacious," "more unscrupulous") in sending men in pursuit of him (*Ant.* 7.33). Josephus' Joab here practices outright deceit and misrepresentation in that he tells the men whom he sends to pursue Abner to call to him in David's name and to say that he had certain things to discuss with him concerning their affairs which he had forgotten to mention when Abner was with him. Again, whereas the biblical narrative proceeds to state very matter-of-factly that Joab took Abner aside to speak with him gently and then smote him fatally in the groin (2 Samuel 3:27), Josephus incriminates Joab much more by expanding on his deceit, noting that he greeted Joab with the greatest show of goodwill (εὔνους) and friendship (φίλος), led him apart from his attendants as if to speak with him privately, and then took him to a deserted part of the gate where he slew him (*Ant.* 7.34). Josephus quite clearly does not accept Joab's explanation that he slew Abner to avenge his brother Asahel and says outright that Abner was deceived (ἐνεδρευθείς, "plotted against," trapped," "ambushed") by him (*Ant.* 7.36). His real motive, says Josephus, was that he feared that the command of the army and that his place of honor with the king would be taken from him and given to Abner (*Ant.* 7.36). To emphasize this deceit and to teach his readers a lesson from which they may learn for the future – the very function of his history, as we may see from Thucydides (1.22) and from his own proem (*Ant.* 1.14) – Josephus comments on Joab's act by presenting an editorial reflection, that very often those who undertake disgraceful (ἀτόποις, "perverse," "wrong," "evil," "improper") acts assume (ὑποκρίνονται, "feign," "pretend") the part of truly good men in order to avert suspicion of their design (*Ant.* 7.34).

That Josephus is thinking in contemporary terms may be seen in his use of the same verb (ὑπεκρίνετο; cf. *Ant.* 7.34) in describing the hypocrisy of his great literary rival, Justus of Tiberias, in feigning hesitation on the subject of hostilities with Rome, while actually being eager for revolution (*Life* 36). Once again, Josephus takes the opportunity to preach at unusual length to the reader that from Joab's action one may perceive to what lengths of recklessness (τολμῶσιν) men will go for the sake of ambition (πλεονεξίας) and power (ἀρχῆς); and that, in their desire to obtain these, men will resort to innumerable acts of wrongdoing and that, in their fear of losing power, they perform much worse acts, "their belief being that it is not so great an evil to fail to obtain a very great degree of authority as to lose it after having become accustomed to the benefits derived therefrom" (*Ant.* 7.37-38) Hence they contrive even more ruthless deeds in their fear of losing what they have (*Ant.* 7.38). The passage clearly recalls Josephus' long editorial comment in connection with King Saul, that when men attain power they lay aside their stage masks (such as, we may suggest, Joab here shows with his deceit) and assume instead audacity (τόλμαν), recklessness, and contempt for things human and divine (*Ant.* 6.264).

We may further note Josephus' elaboration of Joab's deceit in promising Uriah that he would come to his assistance with his whole army if the enemy would throw down part of the wall and enter the city where they were stationed, while privately instructing the men who were with Joab to desert him when they saw the enemy charge (*Ant.* 7.137).

Another example of Joab's deceit, as we have noted, is to be seen in Josephus' version of Joab's act in slaying Amasa. In an extra-biblical addition, Josephus remarks that he committed this act against a brave youth because he envied him his office of commander and his being honored by the king with a rank equal to his own (*Ant.* 7.284). Josephus then adds that it was for the same reason that Joab had murdered Abner, except that for that murder he had a pretext, namely vengeance for the slaying of his brother Asahel, whereas he had no such excuse for the murder of Amasa (*Ant.* 7.285).

We may likewise note that the vice of avarice (πλεονεξία) which Josephus ascribes to Joab as a motive in his slaying of Abner (*Ant.* 7.37) is precisely the quality which, together with ambition (φιλοτιμίαν), according to Thucydides (3.82.8), was the cause of all the evils produced by the factious rivalry (φιλονικεῖν) at Corcyra.

It is, again, precisely this quality of greed which Josephus attacks in John of Gischala as his motive in obtaining a monopoly of oil (*War* 2.591-92, *Life* 74-76).[5] We may see how strongly Josephus feels about the crime of πλεονεξία in that, when he summarizes the qualities of the various revolutionary groups it is cruelty and avarice (πλεονεξία) which he ascribes to the Sicarii (*War* 7.256). Indeed, Josephus sermonizes that avarice (φιλοχρηματία) defies all punishment and concludes that a dire love of gain (κερδαίνειν) is ingrained in human nature, no other passion being so headstrong as greed (πλεονεξία) (*War* 5.558).

6. *Summary*

Like the rabbis, Josephus had ambivalent feelings toward Joab. On the one hand, he aggrandizes Joab's bravery and military achievements. Furthermore, he stresses his modesty in seeking to ascribe military victory to King David rather than to himself. In addition, Joab exhibits the quality of piety in the special regard that he has for the burial of the dead.

---

[5] It is likewise πλεονεξία which, according to Josephus, instigated the Syrians, at the outset of the war against the Romans, to murder the Judaizers in their midst, since they would then with impunity plunder the property of their victims (*War* 2.464).

On the other hand, Josephus adds details depicting Joab as a traitor and a coward. Josephus' Joab is much less understanding of David's feelings and shows less solicitude for him. Moreover, Josephus stresses his deceitfulness. The name of G-d is much less on his tongue, and, in fact, Josephus emphasizes his impiety.

In particular, in his portrait of Joab, Josephus clearly has in mind his own great rival, John of Gischala; and he uses similar language in both cases in stressing their ambition and the envy that they exhibited toward their rivals, resulting in that dreadful civil strife which, according to Josephus, was a major factor in the terrible destruction which the Jews suffered during the war against the Romans.

CHAPTER FOURTEEN

ABSALOM

1. Introduction

It is not hard to see why the story of Absalom proved of such interest in Josephus. It has all the ingredients of a fascinating novel involving the strongest emotions of kin – love and hate, rape of his sister by his brother, vengeance, and revolt against his own father. One indication, as we have indicated, of the attraction of a given biblical personality to Josephus is the sheer amount of space that he allocates to him. For Absalom Josephus (*Ant.* 7.172-257) has 580 lines, as compared with the Hebrew (2 Samuel 13:20-19:8), which has 317 lines, and as compared with the Septuagint, which has 508 lines,[1] giving a ratio of 1.83 as compared with the Hebrew and 1.14 as compared with the Septuagint. We thus see that he is of considerable interest to Josephus.

2. Absalom as an Archexample of Impiety in Blood Relations

The importance of filial piety may be seen in seen in the increased sympathy for Esau which Josephus shows (see Feldman 1988-89, 118-30). We may also discern this attribute of filial devotion in Josephus' depiction of Saul.[2] Likewise, one of the leitmotifs in both

---

[1] That Josephus was acquainted either with the Septuagint or with a Hebrew version akin to the Septuagint text for his account of Absalom may be seen from his statement that Absalom invited his brothers and his father David for a feast (*Ant.* 7.174). The Hebrew Masoretic Text says nothing about a feast (2 Samuel 13:27), but the Septuagint says that Absalom made a banquet like the banquet of a king. In the Dead Sea fragments of Samuel (4QSam$_a$), as published and commented upon by Ulrich (1989, 86), we find the exact Hebrew equivalent of the Septuagint. There appears to be some reason for thinking that Josephus' Greek text of the Bible, at least for Samuel, was a Lucianic or a proto-Lucianic text, if we may judge from the fact that whereas the Hebrew text and the Septuagint read that at the end of forty years Absalom asked his father King David for permission to go to Hebron (2 Samuel 15:7), Josephus (*Ant.* 7.196) and the Lucianic text read four in place of forty.

[2] Thus, in the Bible, after Samuel anoints Saul and sends him forth, he indicates a number of signs that will come to pass and says, in all vagueness, that when

of Josephus' major works, the *War* and the *Antiquities*, is that the tragedy of Herod was due to internal family strife. If we ask why Josephus does not discuss this quality when he deals with the story of Cain, who killed his brother Abel (*Ant.* 1.53-59) or with Abimelech, who killed all of his father's sons except one (*Ant.* 5.234), the answer would appear to be that Josephus deals with the theme of fratricide when he has characters, such as Joseph's brothers and Absalom, who are able and basically good but who succumb to irrational emotional drives. The trait, then, of *pietas*, as we have indicated, would have struck a responsive chord in the Romans, who perceived *pietas* particularly in the loving care which Aeneas showed for his father Anchises in the scene of the departure from Troy (Virgil, *Aeneid* 2.634-751).

At the beginning of the narrative Josephus arouses our sympathy for Absalom even more than does the Bible in view of the fact that his sister, Tamar, is raped by his brother, Amnon. In the Bible Tamar tells Amnon not to do "this wanton (*hanevalah*, 'impious') deed" (2 Samuel 13:12). In Josephus the deed is described as unrighteous (ἀδίκου) and unholy (μιαρᾶς, "unclean," "defiled with blood") (*Ant.* 7.168). This latter word is used in Josephus especially in connection with the slaying of blood relatives and the ritual pollution resulting therefrom,[3] and hence if, as he does, Absalom decides to avenge this indignity the reader may well understand it.[4]

---

they occur he is to do whatever his hand "finds to do" (1 Samuel 10:7). Josephus, on the other hand, uses this as an occasion to reinforce the theme of Saul's *pietas*, since Samuel specifically sends him to salute his father and his kinsfolk after the predicted signs have come (*Ant.* 6.57).

[3] Cf., e.g., *Ant.* 2.22, where Reuben tells his brother that their proposal to kill their brother Joseph would be far fouler (μιαρώτερον, "more unholy," "more abominable") than murdering someone who had not kinship with them. Again, Aristobulus I confesses to committing impious and unholy (μιαροῖς) crimes and acknowledges that swift punishment has overtaken him for the murder of his kin, namely his brother Antigonus and his mother (*Ant.* 13.316). A similar context may be seen where Herod accuses his sons of savage and unholy (μιαρόν) hatred in seeking to kill their father (*Ant.* 16.93). Likewise, when Titus addresses John of Gischala and his revolutionary allies as "most abominable" (μιαρώτατοι) (*War* 6.124 and 6.347), the implication is that they are guilty of murdering their own kinsmen. Finally, when Josephus presents his own summary of the revolutionary groups, he refers to the Idumaeans as "most abominable" (μιαρώτατοι) (*War* 7.267).

[4] In contrast, we may note, the rabbinic tradition diminishes the guilt of Amnon's crime by asserting that Tamar was not really the brother of Amnon but rather was the daughter of a captive with whom David had had relations (*Sanhedrin* 21a). According to this view, Tamar cannot be considered as one of David's chil-

To David, however, fratricide is a more serious sin; and it is significant of David's – and, presumably, Josephus' own – attitude toward fratricide that when David receives the mistaken news that Absalom has killed all of David's sons his reaction is not to bewail the loss of his numerous sons but rather to lament the fact that the murderer was the brother of the victims (*Ant.* 7.177).

The importance of maintaining family ties may be seen in Josephus' version of the speech of the wise woman of Tekoa to King David. In the biblical version she berates David for planning "such a thing [i.e., presumably, his hostility against Absalom for being responsible for the death of Amnon] against the people of G-d" (2 Samuel 14:13). In Josephus' version the focus is not on the Jewish people but on the unity of the immediate family (*Ant.* 7.185).[5]

The reverse of Absalom's attitude toward family relations is to be seen in Josephus' description of the attitude of Absalom's father, David. Whereas the Bible states that when David learned that Amnon had raped Tamar he was furious (2 Samuel 13:21), Josephus' David is described as grieved (ἤχθετο, "was vexed," "was sad"); but, he quickly adds, inasmuch as he loved Amnon greatly, he was compelled not to make him suffer (*Ant.* 7.173). Absalom, on the other hand, as we have noted, reacts to the rape with fierce, pent-up hate. Absalom's lack of sensitivity to his family may also be seen in Josephus' extra-biblical addition that he did not suffer any loss of beauty through sorrow (*Ant.* 7.189). After all, we may remark, he had not only suffered personal distress through the rape of his sister, but he saw how much sorrow he had caused to his father because of the death of his brother, for which he, Absalom, was responsible; and yet, according to his Josephan addition, he apparently cared more for his personal attractiveness than he did for his family.

A similar contrast may be seen between, on the one hand, Absalom's harboring resentment and his offenses against his fam-

---

dren, inasmuch as she was born before her mother's conversion to Judaism. See Ginzberg 1913, 4:118-19.

[5] A parallel with the wise woman's argument, that it would be utterly unreasonable if, after one son has perished, King David were to be willing to condemn another to death, may be seen in the appeal of Horatius, after he had killed his sister for bewailing the death of her betrothed, who had been slain in combat by Horatius (Livy 1.26.9).

ily and, on the other hand, David's withholding of punishment of Absalom after he learns that Amnon has been killed at Absalom's command. Indeed, we are told that David had the intention of sending for Absalom not that he might be punished but that he might be with him, inasmuch as his anger abated in the course of time (*Ant.* 7.181). Again, when David finally does send for Absalom, in place of the simple statement asking Joab to bring back Absalom (2 Samuel 14:21) we have David's extra-biblical remark that he was no longer hostile to him and that he had gotten rid of his anger and displeasure (*Ant.* 7.186).

In rebelling against his own father, Absalom exemplifies the cardinal sin of disobedience of a parent by a child.[6] Indeed, in Josephus' version, when David hears of his son's revolt, the news is completely unexpected; and he is both alarmed and surprised at the impiety (ἀσεβείας) and audacity (τόλμης) of his son (*Ant.* 7.198). Elsewhere Josephus shows how important filial obedience is by going so far as to declare that honoring parents ranks second in the Law to honoring G-d (*Ag. Ap.* 2.206). The rabbis also, in their severe condemnation of Absalom, despite the Mishnaic statement that all Israel have a share in the world to come (*Sanhedrin* 10:1), list him with such archetypes of wickedness as the kings Jeroboam, Ahab, and Manasseh, as having no portion in that world (*Sanhedrin* 103b).

David expresses particular disappointment at the ingratitude of Absalom in that he was not even mindful of having been pardoned for his sins (*Ant.* 7.198). This quality of showing gratitude is one which Josephus stresses throughout the *Antiquities*. The converse, ingratitude, may best be seen in the attitude of the Israelites to G-d despite all the benefits that they had received from Him (*Ant.* 3.312).[7] Indeed, in an addition to the Bible (Deuteronomy 21:18),

---

[6] In rabbinic literature Absalom is held forth as a prime example of the maxim, "Spare the rod and spoil the child." Noy (1971, 2:175) notes that the motif of the importance of filial obedience is found in Jewish folk sayings and in various legends centered around the Pillar of Absalom (*Yad Avshalom*) in the Kidron Valley of Jerusalem. He cites a report from Jerusalem in 1966 of a French Christian pilgrim, Bernardin Survius, that the inhabitants of Jerusalem used to bring their children to the tomb of Absalom to shout and throw stones at it, stressing the end of wicked children who defy their parents.

[7] In particular, Josephus attacks the ingratitude of Dathan, Abiram, and their followers, who, like Absalom, rebel against authority. Indeed, says Josephus, thanksgiving (εὐχαριστίας) "is a natural duty and is rendered alike in gratitude for past

Josephus presents the speech which parents give to rebellious sons, namely that it was with joy and deepest thanksgiving that they had raised them and that, in recognition of this, they should refrain from their disrespect (*Ant.* 4.261-62).

In his ingratitude Absalom is in direct contrast with his father David. Thus Josephus elaborates on the concern which David shows for the remnant of the house of Saul (2 Samuel 9:1), adding, in particular, that besides all the other qualities that he possessed was the virtue of being ever mindful of those who had benefited him at any time, precisely the quality which Absalom lacked (*Ant.* 7.111).

Furthermore, David complains that, in addition to ingratitude, Absalom has been guilty of much greater sins of lawlessness (παρανομωτέροις) in having designs upon the kingship (*Ant.* 7.198). These designs, he says, are doubly sinful in that the kingship had not been given to him by G-d, and hence he was guilty of impiety, and in that he was seeking to remove his own parent, and hence he was guilty of filial disrespect. From David's point of view the latter was sheer madness (ἀπονοίας, "despair," "desperate action," "recklessness," "folly," "insanity"). Even the common people, as we can perceive from Josephus' addition to the Bible (2 Samuel 16:21), did not expect the rift between father and son to be long-lasting (*Ant.* 7.213), presumably because they felt that it was unnatural; and hence Ahitophel urged Absalom to have relations with David's concubines as a clear indication to the public that he had no hopes of a reconciliation (*Ant.* 7.214).

If, indeed, G-d is the model of justice, He is also the model of the connected virtue of forgiveness; and this is a quality that we see particularly in Moses.[8] Here again, in this quality of forgiveness, we see a direct contrast between the father David and the son Absalom. Absalom had been unwilling to forgive his brother for the rape of his sister, but David was ready to forgive Absalom for

---

mercies and to incline the giver to others yet to come" (*Ant.* 4.212). Thus, whereas the Bible gives no reason for *mezuzot* and *tefillin* (Deuteronomy 6:8-9, 11, 18, 20), Josephus explains that they display the greatness of the benefits which Jews have received from G-d and the loving care with which G-d surrounds them (*Ant.* 4.213).

[8] Thus, in exhorting the Israelites just before his death, Moses, when he reminds them that they have more often imperilled him than has the enemy, adds immediately that he says this with no intent to reproach them, since he is loath to leave them aggrieved by recalling these things to their minds (*Ant.* 4.188-89).

the murder of his son and for leading a revolt against his rule. Indeed, whereas the Bible says that David instructed his generals to deal gently with Absalom for his sake (2 Samuel 18:5), in Josephus' version he actually implored (ἠντιβόλει, "entreated," "supplicated") them to spare Absalom and even threatened to do himself some injury if Absalom met his death (*Ant.* 7.235). Moreover, Josephus amplifies David's mourning for Absalom's death. Whereas the Bible declares that David wept and mourned for Absalom (2 Samuel 19:2), Josephus gives further details, namely that he beat his breast, tearing his hair and doing himself every kind of injury (*Ant.* 7.252).[9] Again, whereas in the biblical version David wishes that he had died for Absalom (2 Samuel 19:1), in Josephus his wish is that he had died together with Absalom (*Ant.* 7.252), thus once again stressing the close relationship that he had with his son.

We may remark that Josephus throughout his works stresses the gravity of the sins of lawlessness and rebellion. Indeed, when the Kingdom of Israel comes to an end and Josephus seeks to analyze the underlying cause of its demise, he insists that the beginning of Israel's troubles was the rebellion which it undertook against the legitimate king, Rehoboam, when it chose Jeroboam as king (*Ant.* 9.282). It is almost as if Josephus is analyzing the demise of Jewish state of his own day, which he likewise ascribes to the rebellion against the legitimate authority, in his case, Rome. To the Romans, who had such a deep and long-standing reverence for law and who were so proud of their legal tradition, such attacks on Jeroboam and Absalom for their lawlessness would be most effective.

3. *Absalom's Positive Qualities of Body and of Spirit*

Josephus, as we have seen, highlights the physical qualities of his biblical heroes. In the case of Absalom, the Bible merely speaks of his beauty, remarking that in all Israel there was no one so much to be praised for his beauty as Absalom, and that there was no blemish in him from head to foot (2 Samuel 14:25).[10] It does not,

---

[9] The rabbis (*Soṭah* 10b) have a tradition that David's lament saved Absalom from the extreme penalties of hell.

[10] The rabbinic tradition, recorded, to be sure much later, asserts that of the perfect physical qualities ascribed to Adam, Absalom inherited his hair (*Pirqe Rabbenu ha-Qadosh* [Gruenhut 1899, 3.72]).

however, mention, as does Josephus, that he had not suffered a loss of beauty, as one might have expected, through sorrow at the rape of his sister or through the lack of care proper to a king's son, or that he surpassed even those who lived in great luxury (*Ant.* 7.189). Furthermore, the Bible states as a matter of fact that he cut his hair at the end of every year and that it weighed two hundred shekels (2 Samuel 14:26). Josephus mentions the fact in a tone of wonderment and amazement and greatly exaggerates it by remarking that so great was the thickness of his hair that he could scarcely cut it within a week (*Ant.* 7.189).[11]

If we ask why Josephus ascribes, in greater measure, to Absalom the handsomeness which is the mark of his biblical heroes, we may reply that Absalom is for Josephus not so much a villain as a person of great ability, a tragic figure in the Greek sense who is essentially good but who is overcome by his passions, especially the ambition for power.[12] The fact that his father David loved him so much would seem to be a clue to the fact that he was basically virtuous. Likewise, we may note that whereas the Bible states that Absalom got himself a chariot and horses (2 Samuel 15:1), Absalom's ability is highlighted in Josephus' version by the additional fact that he was able to acquire not merely horses but a great number of them and not merely a chariot but chariots and, moreover, that he was able to do so within in a very short period of time (*Ant.* 7.194). Again, whereas the Bible says merely that Absalom used to rise up early and stand beside the way of the gate, presumably recruiting followers (2 Samuel 15:2), Josephus'

---

[11] In rabbinic literature there is a difference of opinion as to the frequency with which Absalom cut his hair (*Nazir* 4b-5a). The view of Rabbi Judah the Prince is that he cut his hair every twelve months; Rabbi Nehorai held that it was every thirty days, and Rabbi Jose said that it was every week. Rabbi Judah the Prince's view is that he was a life-Nazirite and cites as evidence the passage in which it is stated that at the end of forty years Absalom asked permission of his father to go to pay his vow – that is, presumably, of becoming a Nazirite – to the L-rd at Hebron (2 Samuel 15:7). Although he was a Nazirite and consequently prohibited from cutting his hair he was given a special dispensation to trim it from time to time because it grew so luxuriantly.

[12] See Attridge 1976, 172-73. The rabbis also raise the question of the causes of sin. They cite a catalogue of arch-sinners – Cain, Korah, Balaam, Doeg, Ahitophel, Gehazi, Absalom, Adonijah, Uzziah, and Haman – the common denominator of whose sin is that they set their eyes upon that which was not proper for them (*Soṭah* 9b).

Absalom is depicted as being even more ambitious in that he is said to do so every day (*Ant.* 7.195).

Moreover, Absalom is even more of a master psychologist in Josephus' version than he is in the Bible. In the latter we are told that when anyone had a lawsuit, Absalom would ask him from what city he had come, presumably in an attempt to give the impression of his being personally interested, and would flatter the litigant by telling him, even before hearing his case, that he was right, and then would complain about the legal system on the ground that there were not enough judges (2 Samuel 15:2-3). In Josephus Absalom likewise speaks ingratiatingly (πρὸς ἡδονήν) to the litigants, but he restricts himself to those who had lost their cases and presumably would be bitter against a system which they might well think was unjust (*Ant.* 7.195). He then wins good will by declaring that if he had had the power he would have dispensed full and equal justice to them. Thus the very fact that Josephus magnifies his virtues, such as handsomeness, and his ability to attract so many followers makes his downfall all the more tragic.

That Josephus wants us to believe that Absalom possessed not only physical qualities but also positive traits of character may be seen from the fact that whereas, according to the biblical account, Absalom summoned Joab to send him to David (2 Samuel 14:29), Josephus adds that Absalom asked Joab to appease (καταπραῦναι, "calm," "conciliate," "appease," "reconcile") his father completely (τελέως)[13] and to request that he allow him to come to see him and to speak with him (*Ant.* 7.191). Hence, Absalom is deliberately presented here as being moderate and not as being an extremist. Such an addition is particularly significant in view of Josephus' strong opposition to what he perceived as the extremism of the revolutionaries before and during the great war against Rome.[14] This same search for reconciliation on the part of Josephus' Absalom may be discerned in Absalom's words to Joab thereafter. In the first place, Absalom is cast in a better light because whereas in the Bible Absalom orders his servants to set fire to Joab's field

---

[13] The translation of the word τελέως ("completely") is omitted by Marcus (1934, 5:463).

[14] It is true that in the biblical version Absalom sends to Joab a second time, whereas Josephus omits this second attempt of Absalom to get Joab to come; but this is simply Josephus' attempt to economize in space in his narrative. In any case, he more than makes up for this omission by his insertion that Absalom sought to appease his father completely.

(2 Samuel 14:30), Josephus' Absalom gives orders to set fire to a field adjacent to that of Joab (*Ant.* 7.192). Again, when Joab reproaches Absalom for setting the fire, in the Bible, Absalom, in his defense, says nothing about his attempt to get Joab to seek a reconciliation with the king (2 Samuel 14:32), whereas Josephus' Absalom says specifically that he hit upon the scheme of setting the fire because Joab had disregarded his injunctions to reconcile (διαλλάξῃς, "bring about an agreement," "mediate," "bring about harmony," "gain someone's favor") David to him (*Ant.* 7.192). He then again requests Joab to conciliate (ἡμερῶσαι, "soften") his parent toward him. So important is this reconciliation to him that he adds that he regards his return to Jerusalem to be a greater misfortune than his exile so long as his father persisted in his anger (*Ant.* 7.192). The Bible says nothing about David's persistent anger and the implicit attempt of Absalom to assuage it (2 Samuel 14:32). It is a matter of mere guilt or innocence; as Absalom puts it, "If there is guilt in me, let him kill me." Moreover, the sense of drama and the reader's sympathy for Absalom are increased in that Joab, in an addition to the Bible (2 Samuel 14:33), out of pity for Absalom's necessity (ἀνάγκην) for reconciliation with David, intercedes on his behalf (*Ant.* 7.193).

Additionally, whereas, in the actual scene of reconciliation in the Bible, Absalom bows on his face to the ground (2 Samuel 14:33), Josephus' Absalom goes much further in his eagerness to seek a reconciliation and actually throws (ῥίψαντος, "hurl," "fling downwards," "fall down") himself upon the ground and specifically asks pardon for his sins (*Ant.* 7.193). Again, the biblical David then kisses Absalom, but in Josephus he goes much further in actually raising Absalom up and in explicitly promising to forget what had happened (*Ant.* 7.193).

4. *Political Lessons*

Josephus depicts the rise to power of Absalom as having come about through the use of techniques associated with demagogues. In the biblical version we read that Absalom would rise early and would stand outside the royal palace, and, like a modern-day politician, would greet those who had come with their lawsuits, putting out his hand, professing interest, flattering them with the view that they were right in their suit, and lamenting the injustice of the system (2 Samuel 15:2-6). By treating every man thus as his friend and equal he adopted a favorite device of demagogues. No wonder, as the biblical account concludes, Absalom stole the hearts of the men of Israel (2 Samuel 15:6).

Josephus goes further in depicting Absalom as a demagogue. He actually uses the word δημαγωγῶν ("be a demagogue," "have great influence with the people," "be a distinguished public speaker") in characterizing Absalom's currying favor with the multitude (πλῆθος) and seeking the loyalty (εὔνοιαν) of the populace (ὄχλων, the key word in Josephus' denunciation of the masses) (*Ant.* 7.196). We can see from Josephus' usage elsewhere of the same verb, δημαγωγέω, how contemptuous he was of demagogues.[15] In particular, Josephus' great rival, Justus of Tiberias, is described as a clever demagogue (ἱκανὸς δημαγωγεῖν) who, through using a charlatan's tricks of oratory, was more than a match for opponents with saner counsels (*Life* 40).

We may see a similar contempt for Absalom's demagoguery in his attraction of a great multitude (ὄχλος), which streamed (ἐπισυνέρρευσεν, "flow together," "join in mass") to him (*Ant.* 7.196), this in contrast to the biblical statement that two hundred men – clearly not a great multitude – from Jerusalem went with him as invited guests (2 Samuel 15:11).

Again, we see a political statement by Josephus against democracy in his version of the way Absalom was chosen as king by his followers. The Bible asserts that the conspiracy grew strong, that the number of his adherents kept increasing, and that a messenger came to David with the report that "the hearts of the men of Israel have gone after Absalom" (2 Samuel 15:12-13). In Josephus we have a description of a democratic political process whereby Absalom was chosen by all his followers as king, and we are told specifically that it was he who had contrived (στρατηγήσας, "be a field-commander," "use cunning," "contrive ways and means") to have this method followed (*Ant.* 7.197).

---

[15] Thus we hear that the people of Ptolemais had been persuaded to change their plans by a certain Demaenetus, who had their confidence at that time and influenced the people (δημαγωγῶν) (*Ant.* 13.330).

5. "Improvements" in the Story: Clarifications, Increased Suspense and Drama

In the Bible the wise woman's parable and its application to the case of Absalom is obscure and well nigh unintelligible (2 Samuel 14:13-17). Josephus omits the obscure biblical references to the king's guilty deeds against the people of G-d, and her statement that we are as water spilled on the ground (*Ant.* 7.184-85). In his version she comes directly to the point that it would be utterly unreasonable if, after one son has perished against the king's will, he should willingly cause the death of another.

Similarly, there is an apparent contradiction between the statement that Absalom had three sons and one daughter (2 Samuel 14:27) and the statement that he reared up for himself a pillar because he had no son to keep his name in remembrance (2 Samuel 18:18). Josephus resolves the problem by having Absalom say that if his children should perish, his name would remain in connection with the column which he erected (*Ant.* 7.243).[16]

Another "improvement" made by Josephus in his reworking of the biblical narrative is avoidance of undue exaggeration. Thus, if, as we believe, there is good reason to assume that Josephus was aware of the oral tradition as transmitted by the rabbis, there is significance in his omission of the tradition, as stated by the second-century Abba Saul (who, we are informed, was the tallest man in his generation), that on one occasion, as a grave-digger, he opened a cave and stood in the eyeball of a corpse, which, he was informed, was that of Absalom, up to his nose (*Niddah* 24b, *Numbers Rabbah* 9.24).

Another means by which Josephus seeks to "improve" upon the biblical narrative is through providing better motivation and through increasing the plausibility of events. Thus, the reader may well wonder why after David had agreed to allow Absalom to return he persisted in his refusal to see him. Josephus, the psychologist, provides anger as the motive (*Ant.* 7.192). In this way he ac-

---

[16] The rabbinic tradition, in the name of the late third-century Isaac ben Abdimi, likewise confronted with this contradiction, resolved it by asserting that though Absalom left sons they were so unfit for the kingship that Scripture spoke of them as though Absalom died childless (*Soṭah* 11a). The thirteenth-century commentator David Kimhi reconciles the apparently contradictory passages by postulating that Absalom's sons had died.

centuates his abhorrence of the sin of fratricide of which Absalom was guilty. Likewise, the reader may well ask how Absalom was able, within such a short period of time, to muster such a large following. The Bible says that whenever anyone came to him, he took hold of him and kissed him (2 Samuel 15:5-6). Josephus is more specific in stating that he made a special appeal to those who had lost their lawsuits before his father (*Ant.* 7.195). This provides a better explanation of Absalom's success, inasmuch as it is precisely the losers who are most likely to blame the system and to seek new leadership.

One of the ways in which Josephus heightens interest in his narrative is by increasing suspense. In Josephus' version Absalom is more cold-blooded and calculated in planning his revenge, and the suspense is considerably heightened (*Ant.* 7.172). In the Bible Absalom does not express surprise when he meets his sister (2 Samuel 13:20). He apparently knows that Amnon has been with her because he asks her whether Amnon has been with her. He then tells her to hold her peace; and seeking to calm her, he says, "He is your brother; do not take this to heart." In Josephus' version there is suspense when Absalom first meets Tamar after she has been raped. He gives the impression of being unaware of what had happened since he asks her why she is acting in this strange way – i.e., why she has rent her garment and poured ashes upon her head. She then informs him of the outrage (ὕβριν), whereupon he exhorts her to be quiet (ἡσυχάζειν) and to take it calmly (μετρίως, "moderately," "in due measure") and not to consider herself outraged (ὑβρίσθαι) in having been ravished by her brother (*Ant.* 7.172). Then, whereas the Bible declares that Absalom said nothing to Amnon, for he hated him (2 Samuel 13:22), the level of suspense and intrigue in Josephus is heightened because we are told that Absalom hated Amnon fiercely (χαλεπῶς) (*Ant.* 7.173). Josephus adds that he waited (παρεφύλαττεν, "be on one's guard," "be on the alert") in secret (λανθάνων, "escaping notice") for a favorable opportunity to take vengeance for Amnon's crime. The fact that Josephus uses the imperfect tense for the verb "waited" indicates that Absalom kept on waiting incessantly for his opportunity. The picture is, indeed, reminiscent of the brothers who, while smarting, as we have noted above, revealed nothing to Joseph.

The fact that Josephus twice within the same sentence refers to outrage in terms of the classical Greek ὕβρις (*Ant.* 7.172) places this scene within a familiar Greek context, that of ὕβρις and of the νέμεσις that inevitably must follow – a framework of which Josephus was fond in his reworking of the biblical narrative. The fact that Absalom urges his sister to show moderation – a quality which he notably lacks in the events which follow – increases the irony, another of the favorite themes in both Greek tragedy and in Josephus.

Another example of added suspense may be seen in Josephus' version of the biblical statement that after two years, without explicitly mentioning that it was two years after the rape of Tamar, Absalom invited his brothers and the king to a sheep-shearing celebration (2 Samuel 13:23). Josephus does not want the reader to forget the incident of the rape, since it leads up to what follows, and so he specifically mentions that it was the second year since his sister's misfortune (*Ant.* 7.174).

There is much more of a sense of drama in Josephus' account of Absalom's rebellion against his father King David. Whereas in the Bible David finally agrees to meet Absalom and kisses him (2 Samuel 14:33), there is no indication of any statements made by David in reconciliation. In Josephus' version, as we have noted, there is a much more dramatic scene as Absalom throws himself down to the ground and asks pardon for his sins, whereupon David, in turn, raises him up and specifically promises to forget what had happened (*Ant.* 7.193). It is the height of ὕβρις, then, that what immediately follows is the statement that after this experience with his father, Absalom within a very short time built an army bent on rebellion (*Ant.* 7.194). The fact that Josephus speaks of the experience "with his father" accentuates the theme of utter ingratitude on the part of Absalom and justifies the νέμεσις which follows.

One key element which renders Josephus' paraphrase more effective is increased irony. In the case of Absalom it is truly ironic that Absalom gains adherents for his illegal rebellion against the legal establishment of the state through speaking ingratiatingly to those who had come for judgment (2 Samuel 15:2-3). This irony is increased in Josephus' version in that he addresses the losers in lawsuits, hoping that they will join him against the system (*Ant.* 7.195), but, of course, ending with a complete loss on his part. We see Absalom in Josephus' version talking about law and order (εὐνομίαν, "good order," "keeping the law," "sound legal order") and justice and then find him, immediately thereafter, violating law and order and justice in fomenting a revolt against the state (*Ant.* 7.196).

Perhaps the greatest irony in the account lies in the fact, accentuated by Josephus, that it was Absalom's beauty, which was so outstanding, that brought about his downfall. In the biblical version we read only that Absalom's head got caught in a tree as he was riding on his mule during the battle against David's forces (2 Samuel 18:9). Josephus has transferred this into a case of poetic justice, since we are told that Absalom was plainly visible during the battle precisely because of his beauty and great stature; and, ironically, his hair, the source of his greatest pride and glory, became the means of his death, since his hair, we are told, became entangled in a tree, so that he remained suspended in this strange fashion (*Ant.* 7.238).[17]

6. *Summary*

In his version of the story of Absalom Josephus emphasizes the importance of family relations. The contrast is intensified between the attitude of David, who withholds punishment, and of Absalom, who harbors resentment. Josephus' emphasis on Absalom's filial impiety would find a particularly responsive chord in his Roman readers, who looked up to Aeneas as the exemplar of filial piety. Moreover, in his ingratitude Absalom is in direct contrast to his father David. In his designs upon the kingship, Absalom, in Josephus' version, is guilty of a double impiety, first against G-d, since He had not granted him the sovereignty, and secondly against his father. Here again Josephus accentuates the contrast between father and son, in that David is ready to forgive Absalom and indeed weeps for his death beyond even the picture that we find in the Bible.

Josephus clearly views the story of Absalom from his contemporary point of view, and thus he regards Absalom's greatest sin as lawlessness and rebellion against established authority. He consequently uses for him language similar to what he employs in con-

---

[17] The rabbinic tradition likewise notes the poetic justice that because Absalom was proud of his hair, therefore he was hung by his hair (Mishnah, *Soṭah* 1:8).

demning Jeroboam for his revolt against Rehoboam and in denouncing the revolutionaries of his own day for rebelling against the Roman authority.

But Absalom is not a pure villain. Rather, he is, as seen in added touches in Josephus' narrative, a highly capable and physically very attractive leader who is at first moderate and who seeks reconciliation with his father but who later is destroyed by his own excessive ambition. As an aristocrat, Josephus, in tones highly reminiscent of two of his favorite authors, Thucydides and Plato, is particularly vehement in condemning him as a demagogue who appealed to the fickle masses.

Finally, Josephus uses the opportunity, in redoing the biblical narrative, to remove obscurities and inconsistencies and to provide better motivation for events. He "hellenizes" the story by increasing the element of suspense. His account is particularly effective in highlighting ironic elements, particularly the fact that it was Absalom's most outstanding beauty, namely of his hair, which was his ultimate undoing. The story becomes, in effect, an object lesson which his pagan readers would have especially appreciated, in the inevitability with which νέμεσις follows ὕβρις.

CHAPTER FIFTEEN

JEROBOAM

1. *Introduction: Characterization of Jeroboam in Rabbinic Thought*

In the Mishnah, Jeroboam, Ahab, and Manasseh are depicted as apparently so wicked that that even though all Israelites are to have a share in the world to come, these kings have forfeited their share (Mishnah *Sanhedrin* 10:2). It is fair to assume that the reader of the Bible would conclude that of these three kings, the most reprehensible by far were Ahab and Manasseh. One thinks, for example, of the declaration in 1 Kings 16:33 that Ahab did more to provoke the Deity to anger than all the kings of Israel that were before him, as well as the statement (2 Kings 21:16) that Manasseh "shed very much innocent blood, till he had filled Jerusalem from one end to another."

Indeed, the rabbis have vivid traditions illustrating the wickedness of Ahab and Manasseh, as well as Jeroboam. Thus, for instance, according to the third-century Rabbi Joḥanan, the minor transgressions committed by Ahab were equal to the gravest ones committed by Jeroboam (*Sanhedrin* 102b). As for Manasseh, this king is said to have eliminated the name of the Deity from the Torah (*Sanhedrin* 103b).

And yet, the rabbis had ambivalent feelings about both Ahab and Manasseh. Thus, the same Rabbi Joḥanan who condemned Ahab so sharply asserts that this Israelite monarch merited to have a reign of twenty-two years because he honored the Torah, which was given in the twenty-two letters of the Hebrew alphabet (*Sanhedrin* 102b).

As for Manasseh, he is depicted as a great scholar who could interpret Leviticus in fifty-five different ways, corresponding to the years of his reign (*Sanhedrin* 103b). Indeed, the second-century Rabbi Judah bar Ilai argues that Manasseh did have a share in the world to come because he repented (Mishnah, *Sanhedrin* 10:2).

The rabbis likewise were ambivalent concerning Jeroboam. An anonymous statement ascribes to him such great scholarship that he was able to interpret Leviticus in no fewer than 103 ways, thus surpassing even Manasseh and Ahab (*Sanhedrin* 103b). He is depicted as a true disciple of the prophet Ahijah, with whom he was in the habit of discussing secret lore of the Torah – lore whose existence was wholly unknown to others (*Sanhedrin* 102a). On an occasion when the angels objected that it is unconscionable to reveal the secrets of the Torah to a man who is going to set up two calves to be worshiped, G-d asked them whether Jeroboam was at that moment righteous or wicked. When they answered that he was righteous, His retort was that He deals with persons as they are, not as they will be.

Moreover, we are told in a midrash that Jeroboam's doctrine was as pure as the new garment which Ahijah wore when he met the king (1 Kings 11:29) (*Midrash Psalms* 5.55). Inasmuch as modesty was the pre-eminent virtue of Moses (Numbers 12:3), whom the Bible calls the greatest prophet who ever lived (Deuteronomy 34:10), there is a distinct compliment of Jeroboam in the rabbinic view that at first, because of his poverty, Jeroboam refused the crown offered him, accepting it only when the people (or, according to some, the prophet Ahijah) bestowed great wealth upon him (*Aggadat Shir Ha-Shirim* 95) (cited by Ginzberg 1928, 6:307, n. 9).

Jeroboam is compared most favorably with King Solomon in that he rebuked Solomon, who, in order to exact tolls for the benefit of Pharaoh's daughter whom he had married, closed the breaches in the walls of Jerusalem (breaches which David had made to allow ready access of pilgrims to the city on festival days); consequently Jeroboam is said to have been rewarded with kingship (*Sanhedrin* 101b). That Jeroboam had a reputation for piety may also be inferred from a scenario recorded in the name of the second-century Rabbi Judah bar Ilai, wherein Jeroboam asked his righteous counsellors whether they would approve of all that he commanded; when they replied in the affirmative, he asked them whether they would execute his commands even to worship idols, whereupon they countered that a man such as Jeroboam would certainly not serve idols and that he was merely testing them (*Sanhedrin* 101b). Another scenario shifts the blame for the sin of idolatry from Jeroboam to the people (see Ginzberg 1928, 6:306, n. 9). Indeed, it is they who, intoxicated at the coronation of Jeroboam, are said to have urged him to erect idols, whereas he, unsure that they would not change their minds upon becoming sober, delayed his decision until the following day.

And yet, rabbinic tradition, citing, as its source, the biblical prediction in 1 Kings 13:34 that the house of Jeroboam would be destroyed from off the face of the earth, also condemned Jeroboam as having lost his portion in the world to come (Mishnah, *Sanhedrin* 10:2), a point that we have already noted. Indeed, he is presented as the prototype of the leader who not only sinned himself but, more importantly, caused the community to sin, so that the sin of the community was assigned to him. Thus he is the very antithesis of the true leader, Moses, who attained merit and who bestowed merit upon the community, so that the merit of the community was assigned to his credit (Mishnah, *'Avot* 5:18).

In still another respect Jeroboam was depicted by the rabbis as an anti-Moses, so to speak, namely, because of his conceit (*Sanhedrin* 101b). This is the very opposite of the quality of modesty that one rabbinic view (already noted above) assigned to him. In 1 Kings 12:26-27 Jeroboam expresses fear that the people of his kingdom, if permitted to go to Jerusalem to sacrifice, may turn to his rival, Rehoboam, the king of Judah, who was ruling there. Thus we have the irony, which the rabbis are quick to point out, that Jeroboam, who had once courageously opposed even King Solomon himself in order to encourage pilgrimages to Jerusalem, now created barriers between the people and the Temple (Jerusalem *'Avodah Zarah* 1.1.39b; *Sanhedrin* 101b).

Again, the same scenario which depicted Jeroboam as trying to delay the construction of idols demanded by the people declares as well that when he submitted to their demands he did so on condition that the members of the Sanhedrin be killed (see Ginzberg 1928, 6:306, n. 9) (or, according to others, removed from office) so that worship of the idols might be accomplished without fear. He then sent emissaries throughout the land, presenting the argument that inasmuch as the Hebrew generation of the wilderness, which was the most illustrious of all, had worshiped the golden calf without being punished severely, there should be no fear to implement a similar practice now. When these decrees were ignored by the people, Jeroboam is said to have posted guards at the borders with Judah, and these guards had orders to put to death any persons attempting to go to Jerusalem (Tosefta *Ta'anit* 4.7); however, the king's own son disobeyed the order (*Mo'ed Qatan* 28b). Moreover, the priests whom Jeroboam appointed for his shrines were from the dregs of his people, inasmuch as others declined the appointment. Indeed, not only did Jeroboam abolish the three pilgrimage festivals but he also went so far as to make an end to the observance of the Sabbath (Jerusalem '*Avodah Zarah* 1.1.39b, Jerome on Hosea 7:4-7).

Rabbi Johanan, to be sure, asks why, if the minor transgressions committed by Ahab were equal to the gravest committed by Jeroboam, Scripture makes Jeroboam rather than Ahab the exemplar of sin (*Sanhedrin* 102b). Rabbi Johanan's answer is that Jeroboam was the first to corrupt his people.

2. *The Importance of Jeroboam for Josephus*

Whereas Josephus finds some redeeming features in his portraits of Ahab and Manasseh, he paints a completely negative picture of Jeroboam. Indeed, he seems to go out of his way to stress this king's sinfulness.

One indication of the amount of interest that a given biblical personality has for Josephus may be seen in the sheer amount of space that he devotes to that personality as compared with the length of the account in the Hebrew Bible. As for Jeroboam, Josephus' account (*Ant.* 8.205-45, 265-87 [463 lines in the Loeb Classical Library text]) is 2.16 times as long as the biblical account (1 Kings 11:26-40, 12:1-14:20, 2 Chr 13:1-20, that is, 214 lines in the Hebrew text) and 1.29 times as long as the Septuagint version (360 lines in Rahlfs' text).[1] How can we explain this great attention given by Josephus to Jeroboam, in the light of the severe, unmitigated criticism which he directs toward him?

3. *The Negative Qualities of Jeroboam: His Lack of Wisdom*

Josephus, as we have observed, is vehement in his condemnation of demagogues. Thus, whereas in 1 Kings 12:30 there is mention of Jeroboam's action in setting up calves at Bethel and Dan, in Josephus it is by spoken words that Jeroboam misleads the people and causes them to transgress the laws (*Ant.* 8.229). Such demago-

---

[1] That Josephus used the Septuagint text may be seen in *Ant.* 8.236, where he follows the Septuagint in reading "his sons" rather than the Hebrew, which reads "his son" (1 Kings 13:11).

guery, according to Josephus in an editorial remark, was the beginning of the Jews' misfortunes and led to their defeat in war and their being taken captive by other peoples.

Again, like the beast in Plato's parable (*Republic* 6.492), Jeroboam was deceived by flattery, since the false prophet's goal was merely to please him (πρὸς ἡδονήν, *Ant.* 8.236).

4. *Jeroboam's Intemperate Nature*

We can see that Josephus gives clear and forceful condemnation of Jeroboam when he depicts him, in an extra-biblical comment, as the very opposite of temperate – a person who is "hot-headed" (θερμός, "hot-blooded," "passionate," "violent," "inconsiderate," "hasty") by nature (*Ant.* 8.209). Indeed, Jeroboam clearly lacks self-control, but he can and does, nevertheless, admire the self-control (ἐγκρατείας) of the prophet Iddo (*Ant.* 8.235).

5. *Jeroboam's Impiety*

The salient quality of Jeroboam, which enabled him to oppose even the great king Solomon and later to reach the heights of kingship, is his dynamism, as seen in Josephus' comment that, with his ardent nature and boundless ambition, he did not remain idle (ἠρέμει, *Ant.* 8.209). This dynamism was particularly manifest in his religious policy of prohibiting his people from going to the Temple in Jerusalem and of promoting his own religious cult.

It is significant that when Josephus paraphrases the biblical statement that Jeroboam prohibited his people from going up to offer sacrifices in Jerusalem (1 Kings 12:26-27), he makes a point of mentioning Jeroboam's fear that the people might be captivated (δελεασθέν, "ensnared," "seduced") by the Temple ceremonies and adds that Jeroboam issued this prohibition at the time when the festival of Tabernacles was to take place, that is, at the approach of the great pilgrimage festival, the most joyous in the Jewish calendar (*Ant.* 8.225). Moreover, whereas the Bible states that Jeroboam appointed a feast on the fifteenth day of the eighth month like that which was celebrated in Judah (1 Kings 12:32), Josephus, aware that there is a holiday, Tabernacles, on the fifteenth day of the seventh month and that there is no holiday mentioned in the Bible which occurs in the eighth month, indicates that Jeroboam appointed a feast in the seventh month to coincide with and, clearly, to rival and defy Tabernacles (*Ant.* 8.230)

From the point of view of Josephus, the proud priest whose ancestors were high priests (*Life* 2), a major sin on the part of Jeroboam, as we can see from an extra-biblical remark, was that he named his own priests and even made himself high priest (*Ant.* 8.238 vs. 1 Kings 12:32). This aspect of Jeroboam as false priest is emphasized by the fact that whereas the biblical text states that Jeroboam was standing by the altar ready to burn incense (1 Kings 13:1), Josephus calls greater attention to Jeroboam's impiety by describing him as ready to offer the sacrifices and the whole burnt-offerings in the sight of all the people (*Ant.* 8.231).

It is Jeroboam's decision to set up his own alternative to the Temple in Jerusalem which particularly rankles Josephus. Whereas in the Bible Jeroboam, in his address to his countrymen gives no reasons why he is preventing them from going to the Temple in Jerusalem (1 Kings 12:28), in Josephus' version, where this decision is so central, he gives no fewer than five reasons: 1) The Deity is everywhere and is not confined to merely one place; 2) Jerusalem is the city of our enemies; 3) a man built the Temple in Jerusalem, and Jeroboam likewise has made two golden heifers bearing the Divine name; 4) the two heifers are located more conveniently, so that it will no longer be necessary to make the long trip to Jerusalem; 5) Jeroboam, in egalitarian fashion, will appoint priests and Levites from among the people themselves (*Ant.* 8.227-28). Moreover, the centrality of Jerusalem for Josephus may be seen in Josephus' addition that it was from Jerusalem that the prophet Iddo had come (*Ant.* 8.231 vs. 1 Kings 13:11) and likewise in the addition that it was on his journey back to Jerusalem that a lion devoured the prophet (*Ant.* 8.241 vs. 1 Kings 13:24).

In sum, Josephus considerably enlarges upon Jeroboam's impiety (*Ant.* 8.245). Whereas the biblical text singles out his making priests from among the people as a grave sin which deserved the punishment of having the house of Jeroboam erased from the earth (1 Kings 13:34), Josephus amplifies the sin in terms which his Greek audience would understand by referring to him as committing an outrage (ἐξύβρισεν) against the Deity (θεῖον) and transgressing His laws, so that every day he sought to commit some new act more heinous (μιαρώτερον, "more unclean," "defiled [with

blood]," "horrible," "outrageous," "vile") than the reckless (τετολ-
μημένων, "bold") acts of which he was already guilty (*Ant.* 8.245).
We find similar language in Josephus' paraphrase of the biblical
remark that Jeroboam did not turn from his evil way (1 Kings
13:33). Josephus' use of the word μιαρώτερον (*Ant.* 8.245) is significant, inasmuch as it frequently has the connotation of fraternal
strife and murder, which from Josephus' point of view was also the
greatest sin of the revolutionaries in his own day.

In Josephus' amplification Jeroboam did not "cease (διέλιπεν)
nor desist (ἠρέμησεν, 'was quiet,' 'remained inactive,' 'relaxed,'
'rested') from outraging (ἐξυβρίζων) the Deity," again singling out
as his greatest sin the fact that he continued all the time to erect
altars and to appoint priests from among the common people
(*Ant.* 8.265). The same sin of ὕβρις is underlined in Josephus'
statement which has no basis in its biblical counterpart, in which
Abijah, the king of Judah, tells Jeroboam's troops that when Jeroboam "has paid the Deity the penalty for what he has done in the
past he will end his transgressions (παρανομίας) and the insults
(ὕβρεων) which he has never ceased to offer Him " (*Ant.* 8.277),
while persuading his people to do likewise (2 Chronicles 13:4-12).
This clearly calls to mind the sequence so common in Greek tragedy of ὕβρις leading to νέμεσις. Indeed, the end result of this insolence is the total defeat of Jeroboam's army and the slaughter of
500,000 of his men (2 Chronicles 13:17), a massacre which, according to Josephus' addition, surpasses any that occurred in any war,
whether of Greeks or barbarians (*Ant.* 8.284).[2] It is significant that
Josephus specifically ascribes this debacle to the Divine decision to
permit Abijah to win so wonderful a victory. Indeed, in summarizing the downfall of Jeroboam and of his descendants, Josephus, in
an extra-biblical remark, not to be found in 1 Kings 15:29, says that
they suffered fitting punishment for his impiety (ἀσεβείας) and
lawlessness (ἀνομημάτων) (*Ant.* 8.289).

Likewise, in paraphrasing the biblical statement about the evil
which Baasha, the king of Israel, did (1 Kings 15:34), Josephus
adds that he was more wicked and impious (ἀσεβής) than Jeroboam and notes specifically that he greatly outraged (ἐξύβρισεν)
the Deity (*Ant.* 8.299). Commenting on the wickedness of Baasha,

---

[2] The phrase, as Marcus (1934, 5:724) remarks, is reminiscent of Thucydides
2.47.

Josephus, in an editorial comment, remarks that he imitated Jeroboam, whom he refers to as the vilest (κάκιστον) of men (*Ant.* 8.300) He clearly looked upon Jeroboam as the paradigm of wicked impiety, inasmuch as he adds that although Jeroboam himself was dead, Baasha had revealed his wickedness as still living (*Ant.* 8.300).

6. *Jeroboam and Democracy*

It is indicative, therefore, of Josephus' negative attitude toward Jeroboam that the latter was called to power by the leaders of the rabble (τῶν ὄχλων) immediately after the death of King Solomon (*Ant.* 8.212).[3] Josephus himself shows his contempt for the masses when he remarks that the advisers of King Rehoboam of Judah were acquainted with the nature of crowds (ὄχλων), implying that such mobs are fickle and unreliable, and that they urged the king to speak to them in a friendly spirit and in a more popular style than was usual for royalty (*Ant.* 8.215).

Egalitarianism, which the aristocratically-minded Josephus despised, also comes to the fore in the extra-biblical promise, ascribed to Jeroboam, to appoint priests and Levites from among the general population (*Ant.* 8.228). To be sure, in the biblical text, we are told that Jeroboam appointed priests from among all the people (1 Kings 12:31); but it is much more effective to have this come as a promise from Jeroboam directly to his people. Josephus himself clearly opposed such egalitarianism, which smacks of the remarks made by Korah, who likewise had attacked Moses for bestowing the priesthood upon his brother Aaron (*Ant.* 4.15-19) instead of making the appointment democratically and on the basis of sheer merit (*Ant.* 4.23).

7. *Jeroboam as Ancestor of the Revolutionaries of Josephus' Day:*
De nobis fabula narratur

The theme of the dreadful consequences of civil strife, as we have pointed out, pervades Josephus' paraphrase of the Bible in the *Antiquities*.

---

[3] Weinfeld (1982, 189-94) notes that we find here the concept of the king as the servant of the people; but it is quite clear from the context that the aristocratic Josephus himself views such a relationship disparagingly.

The case of Jeroboam becomes, for Josephus, an outstanding example of the disaster brought on by secession and civil strife. Thus, when Jeroboam is first introduced by Josephus to his readers, whereas the Bible states that Jeroboam lifted up his hand against King Solomon (1 Kings 11:26), Josephus remarks that Jeroboam, "one of his own countrymen" (ὁμοφύλων, the same word which Josephus had used with reference to the revolutionaries' treatment of their fellow-countrymen, *War* 7.332), rose up against the king (*Ant.* 8.205), thus emphasizing the theme of fraternal strife. It is significant that the rabbis, as we have noted, looked with favor upon this confrontation of Jeroboam with Solomon and justified it by stressing that Jeroboam wanted to insure free access of pilgrims to the Temple, whereas in Josephus' version he is thus so severely condemned.

That Josephus viewed Jeroboam as the prototype of the revolutionaries of his own day may be seen in Josephus' extra-biblical remark that Jeroboam attempted to persuade the people to turn away (ἀφίστασθαι) and to start a revolt (κινεῖν) (*Ant.* 8.209).[4] We should also note the striking coincidence that the phrase which he uses to describe Jeroboam's sedition, that he was "ambitious of great things" (μεγάλων ἐπιθυμητὴς πραγμάτων) (*Ant.* 8.209), is so similar to that which he uses to describe the arch-revolutionary, John of Gischala, that he was always ambitious of great things (ἀεὶ ... ἐπιθυμήσας μεγάλων) (*War* 2.587). Those who responded to John's invitation are similarly depicted as always ambitious for newer things (νεωτέρων ἐπιθυμοῦντες αἰεὶ πραγμάτων), addicted to change and delighting in sedition (*Life* 87). We find similar language applied to those bold Jews in Jerusalem who were admonished by the procurator Cumanus to put an end to their ambition for newer things, that is revolution (νεωτέρων ἐπιθυμοῦντας πραγμάτων) (*Ant.* 20.109). Josephus employs similar language in describing his arch-rival Justus of Tiberias as "ambitious for newer things" (νεωτέρων ... ἐπεθύμει πραγμάτων) (*Life* 36).

It is significant that it is this aspect of fratricidal strife that is stressed when Abijah, the king of Judah, wins a great victory over the forces of Jeroboam and slays no fewer than 500,000 of them (2 Chronicles 13:17). Josephus adds, as we have noted, that the slaughter surpassed that in any war, "whether of Greeks or barbar-

---

[4] Josephus is here basing himself on the Septuagint addition (1 Kings 12:24b).

ians" (*Ant.* 8.284). This latter phrase is found also in Josephus' account of the slaying of Jesus the son of Joiada by his brother Johanan, the high priest, when Jesus was plotting to become high priest in Johanan's stead (*Ant.* 11.299).

Indeed, when the Kingdom of Israel comes to an end and Josephus seeks to analyze the underlying cause of its demise, he insists that the beginning of Israel's troubles was the rebellion which it undertook against the legitimate king, Rehoboam, when it chose Jeroboam as king (*Ant.* 9.282). It is almost as if Josephus is analyzing the demise of the Jewish state of his own day, which he likewise ascribes to the rebellion against the legitimate authority, in his case, Rome. In a word, Josephus points his finger at Jeroboam's lawlessness (παρανομίαν) (*Ant.* 9.282), the very quality which he denounces in the revolutionaries,[5] particularly in his bitter attack on the Sicarii as the first to set the example of lawlessness (παρανομίας) and cruelty (ὠμότητος) to their kinsmen (*War* 7.262). It is this lawlessness (παρανομίαν) and iniquity (ἀδικίας) which Josephus, in an editorial comment not found in his biblical source (1 Kings 15:24), stresses brought about the destruction of the kings of Israel, one after the other, in a short space of time (*Ant.* 8.314). That Jeroboam is, for Josephus, the model of lawlessness may be discerned by comparing the Bible (1 Kings 16:30), which speaks of the evil which Ahab did but which does not mention Jeroboam, and Josephus' statement that Ahab did not invent anything in his wickedness but merely imitated the misdeeds and outrageous behavior (ὕβριν) which his predecessors showed toward the Deity (*Ant.* 8.316); of these predecessors and their misdeeds, Josephus here singles out Jeroboam and his lawlessness (παρανομίαν). To the Romans, who had such a deep and long-standing reverence for law and who were so proud of their legal tradition, such an attack on Jeroboam for his lawlessness would be devastating.

---

[5] See *War* 4.134, 144, 155, 339, 351; 5.343, 393, 442; 6.122. Likewise, in the *Antiquities* Josephus make a number of changes in his paraphrase of the biblical text to emphasize the importance of observance of the laws. See, for example, 5.185 (vs. Judges 3:12); 5.198-200 (vs. Judges 4:1), 5.255 (vs. Judges 10:6); 7.130 (vs. no biblical parallel); 8.245 (vs. 1 Kings 13:33); 8.251-53 (vs. 1 Kings 14:22).

8. Assimilation

Josephus seems to have realized the danger inherent in the attraction of Stoicism. Thus, although Josephus uses Stoic terminology in connection with his proof for the existence of the Deity (*Ant.* 1.156), he is actually combatting the Stoics, as we see from the reference in the section immediately after the one containing Abraham's proof (*Ant.* 1.157).[6] Likewise, Josephus is clearly dissociating himself from the extra-biblical remarks put into the mouth of Jeroboam in the latter's address to his countrymen, which are definitely Stoic in their outlook and which are intended to refute the idea that the Deity has a special place, namely the Temple in Jerusalem: "Fellow-countrymen, I think you know that every place has Divinity in it and there is no one spot set apart for His presence, but everywhere He hears (ἀκούει) and watches over (ἐφορᾷ) His worshippers" (*Ant.* 8.227). Here Jeroboam is clearly repeating the words which are used by King Solomon when, in dedicating the Temple, he declares that the Deity is one who watches over (ἐφορᾶν) and hears (ἀκούειν) all things, and that even though the Deity dwells in the Temple He is very near to all men (*Ant.* 8.108); but it is clear that when Jeroboam repeats these words Josephus no longer identifies with them. Significantly, in the biblical passage which Josephus' Jeroboam is paraphrasing, Jeroboam says nothing about the Divine omnipresence but merely introduces the gods which he has set up as those who had brought the Israelites out of Egypt, with no philosophic justification of such an action (1 Kings 12:28).

9. Dramatic Build-up

A motif found frequently in the historical literature available to Josephus is that of the rise of the ruler from humble beginnings, as, for example, in the stories told about the upbringing of King Cyrus of Persia (Herodotus 1.95) and of Romulus and Remus. In the case of Jeroboam, whereas the Bible declares simply that his mother's name was Zeruah, a widow (1 Kings 11:26), Josephus

---

[6] So Wolfson (1947, 1:176-77, 329, and 2.78), who notes that the Chaldeans, whom Josephus describes as opposed to Abraham's views, are in Philo prototypes of the Stoics (*De Migratione Abrahami* 32.179).

adds the information, which increases the dramatic element, that he was bereaved of his father while still a child and was brought up by his mother (*Ant.* 8.205).

There is also considerable drama in the scene in which Jeroboam, upon hearing the prophet's protest against the altar which Jeroboam had built at Bethel, stretches out his hand instructing his followers to seize the prophet (1 Kings 13:4). The scene is even more dramatic, however, in Josephus' version, according to which Jeroboam was roused to fury (παροξυνθείς, "incited," "aroused emotionally," "provoked," "made angry") by the prophet's words, whereupon he stretched out his hand with orders to arrest the prophet (*Ant.* 8.233). There is further increased drama in the sequence of events following this. According to the Bible, Jeroboam's hand dried up, so that he was not able to draw it back (1 Kings 13:4). Josephus has a much more vivid scene: straightway (εὐθέως), we are told, his hand became paralyzed (παρείθη, "became exhausted," "grew weary"), and he no longer had the power to draw it back to himself but found it hanging, numb (νεναρκηκυῖαν, "grow stiff," "become paralyzed") and lifeless (νεκράν, "dead," "numb") (*Ant.* 8.233).

Likewise, the prediction of the prophet Iddo is more dramatic. In the Bible he prophesies that Jeroboam's altar will be torn down (1 Kings 13:3); in Josephus he is much more emphatic: the altar shall be broken in an instant (παραχρῆμα) (*Ant.* 8.232). Again when the prediction is fulfilled, the biblical statement is that the altar was torn down and the ashes poured out from the altar (1 Kings 13:5). Josephus is more dramatic: the altar was broken and everything on it was swept on the ground (*Ant.* 8.233). Similarly, there is greater emotion in Jeroboam's reaction when his hand is restored. The Bible declares simply that after his hand was restored the king told the prophet, whose name is given as Jadon by Josephus, to accompany him home in order to obtain a reward (1 Kings 13:7). In Josephus' version Jeroboam is overjoyed (χαίρων) (*Ant.* 8.234). The drama, moreover, is increased by the fact that the false prophet who deceives Jadon was bed-ridden through the infirmity of old age (*Ant.* 8.236).

10. *Summary*

Unlike the rabbis, who had ambivalent feelings about Jeroboam, praising him for his great learning and for standing up to King Solomon in insisting that pilgrimages to Jerusalem not be deterred, while at the same time attacking him for instituting the worship of golden calves, Josephus, the proud priest, who gives an unusual amount of attention to him as compared with his concern with other biblical figures, is unequivocally critical of him, particularly because, in words very similar to those used by Rabbi Joḥanan (*Sanhedrin* 102b), he was the first to transgress the laws (παρανομήσαντι) with regard to the sacrifices and because he had begun the process of leading the people astray, especially in refusing to allow his people to make the pilgrimage to the Temple in Jerusalem (*Ant.* 9.18). Jeroboam emerges as an earlier version of the revolutionaries of Josephus' own day in his hot-headedness.

To Josephus, whose ancestors were high priests, the major sin on the part of Jeroboam was that he set up his own alternative to the Temple in Jerusalem, that he named his own priests instead of recognizing those who were priests by birth, and that he even made himself high priest. In terms highly reminiscent of Greek tragedy, Josephus, in extra-biblical comments, denounces Jeroboam for his ὕβρις against G-d in erecting altars outside of Jerusalem and in appointing priests from among the common people. It is this ὕβρις which leads to the νέμεσις of the total defeat and slaughter of Jeroboam's army. Moreover, Josephus, who looked with contempt upon the fickle and unreliable mob, shows disdain for Jeroboam for being called to power by the leaders of the rabble.

Furthermore, it is again with a view to the contemporary scene that Josephus portrays Jeroboam as an outstanding example of the disaster wrought by secession and civil strife. It is particularly striking that the language which Josephus uses in describing Jeroboam's sedition is so similar to that which he employs to describe the archrevolutionary of his own day, his great rival John of Gischala. Likewise, in analyzing the causes of the demise of the kingdom of Israel, he insists that it all began with the rebellion against the legitimate ruler Rehoboam. Again and again he stresses Jeroboam's lawlessness, a word which must have struck a responsive chord in his Roman audience, so proud as it was of the respect of the Romans for the legal tradition. Finally, another indication that Josephus' portrait is conditioned by the contemporary scene is his clear attempt, as a priest closely connected with the Temple in Jerusalem, to dissociate himself from the extra-biblical remarks put into the mouth of Jeroboam which are highly reminiscent in their language of the Stoics, who were the most popular philosophy among intellectuals in his day, and which attempt to refute the idea that the Deity is associated with a particular place.

CHAPTER SIXTEEN

REHOBOAM

1. Introduction

To a considerable degree one might say that Josephus' rewriting of the Bible in the first half of the *Antiquities* is, to paraphrase Horace (*Satires* 1.1.69-70), a case of "De nobis fabula narratur," "The tale is told about us," that is, as the rabbis (*Soṭah* 34a) put it, in effect, *Ma'ase 'avot siman lebanim*, "What happened to the ancestors is a clue to the children." Though Josephus reassures his readers (*Ant.* 1.17) that he will neither add nor omit anything from the Scripture narrative, in point of fact he does so on almost every page, often prompted by his view that the history of his own era is repeating the past and should learn from it.[1] His portrait of Rehoboam would appear to be a good example of this tendency.[2]

One indication of the relative importance to Josephus of a given biblical personality is the sheer amount of space that he devotes to him as compared with the coverage in the Bible itself. For Rehoboam[3] the ratio of Josephus (*Ant.* 8.212-224, 246-265) to the narrative in 1 Kings (12:1-24, 14:21-31) is 3.51 and to the account in 2 Chronicles (10:1-12:16), which Josephus seems to have preferred,[4] is 2.35; the ratio of Josephus to the passage in the Septuagint version of 2 Chronicles is 1.57. The ratio to 2 Chronicles is higher than for the great majority of biblical personalities with whom Josephus deals.[5] Hence, we can see that Rehoboam was

---

[1] See my various articles as listed in my "Josephus' Portrait of Asa," *Bulletin for Biblical Research* 4 (1994) 41, n. 1.

[2] Thus far there has been only one systematic attempt to compare Josephus' account of Rehoboam with that in the Bible, namely Christopher Begg, *Josephus' Account of the Early Divided Monarchy (AJ 8,212-420)* (Leuven: University Press, 1993) 7-29, 64-85; but careful and useful as it is, this is concerned almost totally with textual comparison and only incidentally with its implications, especially as compared with Josephus' portraits of other biblical figures.

[3] For Josephus I have used the Loeb Classical Library text. For the Hebrew text I have used the standard edition with the commentary of M. L. Malbim (New York: Friedman, n.d.). For the Septuagint I have used the edition of A. Rahlfs, *Septuaginta* (Stuttgart: Privilegierte Württembergische Bibelanstalt 1935).

[4] See Begg, *op. cit.* (n. 2) 85, n. 502.

[5] See the ratios for other biblical characters in my "Josephus' Portrait of Asa," *Bulletin for Biblical Research* 4 (1994) 42,

of major interest to Josephus. This is particularly noteworthy inasmuch as the rabbinic tradition has remarkably little to say about Rehoboam,[6] especially as compared with its concern for Jeroboam.[7]

Another indication of the importance of a biblical figure for Josephus may be seen in his "editorializing" remarks, especially when he "psychologizes" about human nature on the basis of what happened to a particular biblical figure. Here we may note Josephus' generalizations (*Ant.* 8.251), in the midst of his account of Rehoboam, about the causes of degeneration into lawlessness. Likewise, we may note that it is only for those who, in his eyes, are more significant that Josephus, when reporting the death of a given figure, reflects on the character of that figure.[8] The fact that he does so for Rehoboam (*Ant.* 8.263) would indicate his importance for him and the lessons to be drawn from his life.

Still another clue to the importance of a given biblical figure is the citation by Josephus of non-Jewish authors to support the historicity of that personality. Thus, we find that Josephus (*Ant.* 1.93-95) cites the evidence of Berossus, Hieronymus the Egyptian, Mnaseas, and Nicolaus of Damascus to support the historicity of the biblical account of the Flood. Likewise, he cites (*Ant.* 2.348) the fact that the Pamphylian Sea retired before Alexander the Great as a parallel to support the historicity of the miracle of the crossing of the Red Sea. Again, on two occasions (*Ant.* 8.144-149 and *Against Apion* 1.112-125) he cites Dius, the author of a history of the Phoenicians, as well as Menander of Ephesus, to support the historicity of the relations between King Solomon and King Hiram of Tyre. Similarly, Josephus (*Ant.* 8.260-262) cites Herodotus to confirm the historicity of the Bible's account of Shishak's expedition against Rehoboam, while showing his own ability as a historian by correcting Herodotus in two details. Indeed, it is surely significant that in order to gain the confirmation of Herodotus

---

[6] The only passages of note about Rehoboam in rabbinic literature are *Horayot* 10a-b, where the rabbis emphasize that the message to be derived from Rehoboam's failure is that a king is the servant of the people rather than their ruler; and *Sanhedrin* 48b, where we are told that the curse wherewith David cursed Joab was fulfilled in David's own descendant, Rehoboam, who was afflicted with gonorrheal flux.

[7] See my "Josephus' Portrait of Jeroboam," *Andrews University Seminary Studies* 31 (1993) 30-33.

[8] See my "Josephus' Portrait of Elisha," *Novum Testamentum* 36 (1994) 4, n. 12.

(2.102 ff.), who, says Josephus, states that Sesostris reduced Palestinian Syria to slavery without a battle, Josephus (*Ant.* 8.255, 261), who identifies Sesostris with the biblical Shishak, introduces the extra-biblical statement, which certainly does not enhance the status of Rehoboam, that Shishak seized the strongest cities of Rehoboam's kingdom without a battle.

2. *The Qualities of a Leader*

To a great degree Josephus' portraits of biblical figures are lessons in leadership and its responsibility, inasmuch as he notes (*Ant.* 8.252), in accordance with the political theory expounded by Ecphantus' *Treatise on Kingship* (277.9-11; 278.10-11),[9] that the subjects of a ruler imitate his conduct, "since it is impossible to show approval of the acts of kings except by doing as they do."

It is indicative of Josephus' negative attitude toward Jeroboam that the latter was called to power by the leaders of the rabble (τῶν ὄχλων) immediately after the death of King Solomon (*Ant.* 8.212). Josephus himself shows his contempt for the masses when he remarks that the advisers of King Rehoboam were acquainted with the nature of crowds (ὄχλων), implying that such mobs were fickle and unreliable, and that they urged the king to speak to them in a friendly spirit and in a more popular style than was usual for royalty (*Ant.* 8.215).[10] That Josephus is thinking in contemporary terms in his snide remarks about the masses may be seen from a pejorative reference to them by Titus, who describes those at Tarichaeae as undisciplined, a mere rabble (ὄχλος...ἄλλως), rather than an army (*War* 3.475). Again, the word's use in connection with the mob (ὄχλον) of women and children drafted by that most despised of revolutionaries, John of Gischala (*War* 4.107), is most significant.

On the other hand, through the modifications which he makes in his narrative of Rehoboam Josephus stresses that the wise ruler will listen to responsible leaders of his people. Thus, whereas the biblical account (2 Chronicles 10:3) states that all the people of Israel came to Rehoboam to complain of their heavy yoke, in

---

[9] Cited by Begg, *op. cit.* (n. 2) 70, n. 406.

[10] On Josephus' negative attitude toward the masses see my "Josephus' Portrait of Jeroboam," *Andrews University Seminary Studies* 31 (1993) 41-43.

Josephus' version (*Ant.* 8.213) it is merely the leaders of the people and Jeroboam who come to him with their petition. Whereas in the biblical narrative (1 Kings 12:7) it is all the people who promise that they will be Rehoboam's servants forever if he agrees to lighten their burden, in Josephus (*Ant.* 8.213), with his aristocratic bent, it is the leaders alone who make this promise and who, indeed, go much further in that they declare they will actually love (ἀγαπήσειν) their servitude if treated with kindness (ἐπιείκειαν) by him; thus Josephus places much greater emphasis on Rehoboam's failure to listen to the advice of these leaders. Moreover, whereas the petition of his people in the Bible is to have him lighten their hard service without indicating the degree to which they sought alleviation of their burden, Josephus, seeking to impress upon his readers the importance of a reasonable amount of flexibility in a ruler when approached by responsible leaders, has the delegation request merely that their bondage be lightened somewhat (τι). These older advisers (*Ant.* 8.215) suggest that Rehoboam speak to the people in a friendly spirit (φιλοφρόνως, "in a friendly way," "lovingly," "cordially," "hospitably," "affectionately," "benevolently," "kindly," "politely") and in a more popular (δημοτικώτερον) manner than was usual for the royal dignity, because in this way he would secure their good will (εὔνοιαν), since subjects naturally like affability (προσηνές, "friendliness," "kindness," "pleasantness," "mildness").

There can be no doubt that Josephus agrees with these advisers, inasmuch as, in an extra-biblical addition, he explicitly states that this advice was good and beneficial, "perhaps for all occasions, or, if not all, at any rate for that particular occasion" (*Ant.* 8.216). Josephus' endorsement of this advice is also manifest from the fact that he applies the same term φιλόφρων to several biblical figures whom he much admires, notably Rebecca (*Ant.* 1.246), the Witch of Endor (*Ant.* 6.341), and David (*Ant.* 7.30), as well as others, notably Balaam (*Ant.* 4.105) and Ahab (*Ant.* 8.398) whom he seeks to rehabilitate to a considerable degree.[11] Moreover, he applies it to King Ptolemy Philometor of Egypt (*War* 7.423); the Emperor Augustus (*War* 2.37, *Ant.* 17.248), for whom he has the greatest admiration; Monobazus, the father of the pious proselyte Izates

---

[11] See my "Josephus' Portrait of Balaam," *Studia Philonica Annual* 5 (1993) 48-83; and "Josephus' Portrait of Ahab," *Ephemerides Theologicae Lovanienses* 68 (1992) 368-384.

(*Ant.* 20.24); Agrippa II (*Life* 183), who remained loyal to the Romans; Titus (*War* 6.115), and Josephus himself (*Life* 325). Of special significance is the fact that he uses this term in describing the gracious welcome which Jews give to proselytes (*Against Apion* 2.210). Josephus' identification with these advisers is also clear from his reference (*Ant.* 8.215) to them as men of kindly disposition (εὔνους), since this is an epithet which he applies to David (*Ant.* 7.41) and, indeed, to G-d himself (*Ant.* 5.98). Moreover, in an editorial-like digression he stresses (*Ant.* 16.177) that "it is most profitable for all men, Greeks and barbarians alike, to practice justice, about which our laws are most concerned; and, if we sincerely abide by them, they make us well disposed (εὔνους) and friendly to all men."

Josephus here (*Ant.* 8.213) clearly sympathizes with the delegation's request, inasmuch as in the Bible they promise merely that they will serve him if he will lighten their yoke, whereas Josephus expands on their promise, stating that they will be better disposed (εὐνούστεροι) toward him if they are treated with mildness (ἐπιείκειαν, "forbearance," "magnanaimity," "generosity," "moderation," "kindness," "considerateness," "gentleness," "mildness," "understanding," "friendliness," "geniality," "affability," "peaceableness," "reasonableness," "fairmindedness") than if they are made to fear him. With their moderate request they – and it is clear that Josephus agreed with them – hoped to gain his assent, "for they held kindness (τὸ χρηστόν, "goodness," "excellence," "uprightness," "nobility," "propitiousness," "genuineness," "kindness," "clemency," "gentleness," "benevolence," "generosity," "considerateness," "graciousness," "friendliness," "good-heartedness," "magnanimity," "worthiness," "decency," "honesty") and friendliness (φιλάνθρωπον, "kindness," "humaneness," "magnanimity," "highmindedness," "graciousness," "affability," clearly a synonym for ἐπιείκεια and τὸ χρηστόν) to be an easy matter (πρόχειρον, "ready at hand," "easily available"), especially for a young man." Again, whereas in the Bible we read merely (2 Chronicles 10:5) that Rehoboam told the delegation to come back in three days, Josephus (*Ant.* 8.214) holds out more hope that Rehoboam will show moderation by expanding on this passage through noting that the fact of his deliberating (βουλεύσασθαι) and not refusing them on the instant seemed to offer some ground for good hope.

Significantly, in his final tribute to David (*Ant.* 7.391) Josephus describes him as mild (ἐπιεικής) and kind (χρηστός) to those in trouble, just and humane (φιλάνθρωπος), thus ascribing to him all of the epithets that the leaders seek to find in Rehoboam. Again, Josephus (*Ant.* 19.334), who clearly applies this dictum as being true in his own day, reports that Agrippa I, of whom he thinks so highly, was convinced that considerate behavior (ἐπιείκειαν) is more becoming in the great than wrath. It is significant that the term is applied (*Ant.* 20.178) to the more moderate (ἐπιεικέστεροι) Jews and those of eminent rank, with whom Josephus clearly identifies, and who endeavored to reduce the tension by appealing to the procurator Felix to recall the soldiers who had attacked the Jews whose dispute with the Syrian inhabitants of Caesarea had led to bloodshed. Likewise, the term is applied (*Ant.* 20.201) is those who were the most fair-minded (ἐπιεικέστατοι) and who were most offended by the way in which James the brother of Jesus had been treated by the high priest Ananus and by the Sanhedrin.[12] Similarly, that the terms ἐπιείκεια and φιλανθρωπία represent ideals may be seen from the fact that in his edict to the world the Emperor Claudius (*Ant.* 19.290) enjoins upon the Jews to avail themselves of his kindness (φιλανθρωπία) in a more reasonable (ἐπιεικέστερον) spirit. Above all, Josephus (*Life* 176) applies the epithet ἐπιεικής to himself, asserting to the prisoners in Tiberias that they should not be intolerant of his command, inasmuch as they would not easily find another leader as considerate (ἐπιεικοῦς) as himself.

We may also note that the quality of being χρηστός, which the delegation to Rehoboam twice repeat (*Ant.* 8.213, 214) as one which they hope to find in him, is ascribed to several other personalities most admired by Josephus, namely Abraham (*Ant.* 1.200), Rebecca (*Ant.* 1.247), Isaac (*Ant.* 1.264), Jacob (*Ant.* 2.149), Joseph (*Ant.* 2,140, 157, 195), the prophet Samuel (*Ant.* 6.92, 194), Jonathan (*Ant.* 6.208), Saul (*Ant.* 6.212), King David (*Ant.* 7.43, 184, 270, 391), Jehonadab (*Ant.* 9.133), Jehoiada (*Ant.* 9.166), King Hezekiah (*Ant.* 9.260), King Jehoiachin (*Ant.* 10.100), King Zedekiah (*Ant.* 10.120), Gedaliah (*Ant.* 10.164), Ezra (*Ant.* 11.139), Nehemiah (*Ant.* 11.183), and King Ptolemy Philometor (*Ant.*

---

[12] Begg (above, note 2) 29, appositely notes that in the *Letter of Aristeas* King Ptolemy Philadelphus is praised as pre-eminent in ἐπιεικείᾳ καὶ φιλανθρωπίᾳ, two of the very qualities which the delegation to Rehoboam seek to find in him.

13.114).¹³ Significantly, this quality is assigned to those rulers and administrators, such as Jehoiachin, Zedekiah, Gedaliah, Ezra, and Nehemiah, who were, like Josephus, submissive to the superpower in authority. That this is a quality particularly to be desired in rulers is clear from Josephus' long editorial-like extra-biblical comment about Saul (Ant. 6.349) in which he emphasizes that the greatness of kings' power forbids them not merely to be bad to their subjects but even to be less than wholly good (χρηστοῖς). Furthermore, King Agrippa I, who in Josephus' eyes is the veritable ideal ruler, is described (Ant. 19.330) as not only benevolent to those of other nations but also as being even more generous (χρηστός) and more compassionate to his compatriots. Indeed, in exercising this quality the ruler is following the example of G-d Himself, as we can see from the fact that King Izates of Adiabene, the proselyte so greatly admired by Josephus, in his desperate prayer (Ant. 20.90), appeals to G-d's goodness (χρηστότητος). Significantly, in the cases of Samuel, Hezekiah, Jehoiachin, Zedekiah, Ezra, the high priest Jehoiada who saved Joash from the hands of the wicked Queen Athaliah, Jehonadab who helped King Jehu slay the priests of Baal, and Ptolemy Philometor who favored the Alexandrian Jews in their dispute with the Samaritans (Ant. 13.74, 76), he couples this quality with that of being just. Of particular significance is the fact that these two qualities are assigned to Kings Jehoiachin and Zedekiah, both of whom are rehabilitated by Josephus despite their negative portrayal in the Bible.¹⁴ Likewise, Josephus, the lackey of the Romans, makes a point of assigning the quality of χρηστότης to the Romans, as he notes, for example, when Nicanor, who is sent by the general Vespasian to persuade Josephus to surrender to the Romans, dwells (War 3.347) on the innate generosity (χρηστόν) of the Romans to those whom they have once subdued. Moreover, and very significantly, it is this quality (χρηστότητος) which Josephus (Life 423) ascribes to the Emperor Vespasian when he describes the kindness that Vespasian always displayed toward him.

---

¹³ On the term χρηστός see L. R. Stachowiak, *Chrestotes. Ihre biblisch-theologische Entwicklung und Eigenart* (Freiburg 1957) 38-39; K. Weiss, 'χρηστός', in Gerhard Kittel and Gerhard Friedrich (edd.), *Theologisches Wörterbuch zum Neuen Testament* 9 (1973) 472-488; and Ceslaus Spicq, *Notes de lexicographie néo-testamentaire* (Freiburg-Göttingen 1978) 2.971-976, cited by Begg (above, note 2) 13, n. 40.

¹⁴ See my "Josephus' Portrait of Jehoiachin," *Proceedings of the American Philosophical Society* 139 (1995) 20-21.

The virtue of humanity (φιλανθρωπία),[15] which the delegation to Rehoboam hold up as an ideal for a ruler, both when they initially come to Rehoboam (*Ant.* 8.214) and when they return on the third day to hear his response to their petition (*Ant.* 8.218), is closely connected with justice.[16] This is also a quality which Josephus assigns to his beloved Agrippa I, who, he says (*Ant.* 19.330), clearly in answer to those who had charged the Jews with being generous only to their fellow-Jews, was benevolent (φιλάνθρωπος) to those of other nations. It is also a virtue of non-Jewish rulers whom he admires, notably Cyrus (*Against Apion* 1.153), who treated Nabonnedus humanely after the latter's surrender; Xerxes (biblical Artaxerxes), who authorized the Jews' return to Jerusalem (*Ant.* 11.123); Ptolemy I, who attracted immigrants to Egypt because of his reputation for kindliness and humanity (φιλανθρωπίαν, *Against Apion* 1.186); Ptolemy Philadelphus (*Ant.* 12.32, 46), who set free the Jewish slaves in Egypt; and Julius Caesar (*Ant.* 14.195, 208) and Mark Antony (*Ant.* 14.313), who generously granted privileges to the Jews. Indeed, Josephus (*Against Apion* 2.40) assigns this quality to the Romans as a whole, who, alluding to their benevolent extension of citizenship, "in their generosity (φιλανθρωπία), imparted their name to well-nigh all mankind, not to individuals only, but to great nations as a whole." Furthermore, in his lengthy speech urging the Jews to give up the idea of rebellion, Agrippa II (*War* 2.399) tells his fellow-Jews to consider what a crime it would be to take up arms against such humane (φιλανθρώπους) opponents as the Romans; and Titus (*War* 6.333), in addressing the revolutionary leaders, asserts that they were incited against the Romans only by the reputation of the Romans for humanity (φιλανθρωπία). Above all, Josephus himself assigns this quality to his patron Titus (*War* 4.96), who refers to his humane (φιλανθρώποις) proposals and pledges of good faith in urging the inhabitants of Gischala to surrender; but the Jewish militants (*War* 5.335) mistook his humanity (φιλάνθρωπον), which was innate

---

[15] See Ceslaus Spicq, "La philanthropie hellénistique, virtu divine et royale," *Studia Theologica* 12 (1958) 169-191; idem, *Notes de lexicographie néo-testamentaire* (above, note 13) 2.922-927; Roger Le Déaut, "φιλανθρωπία dans la littérature grecque jusqu'au Nouveau Testament (Tite III,4)," in *Mélanges E. Tisserant* (Vatican City 1964) 1.255-294, cited by Begg (above, note 2) 15, n. 49.

[16] So in Philo (*Mut.* 44.255; *Mos.* 2.2.9; *Decal.* 30.164. See the discussion by Harry A. Wolfson, *Philo: Foundations of Religious Philosophy in Judaism, Christianity, and Islam* (Cambridge: Harvard University Press, 1947) 2.220, n. 146).

(*War* 6.324), for weakness, just as they had similarly mistaken the humanity of Vespasian (*War* 6.340, 341) for weakness. The fact that this, too, is a quality ascribed to G-d (*Ant.* 1.24) clearly implies that the king, as G-d's representative on earth, should embody this trait as an instance of *imitatio D-i*.

On the other hand, Josephus, commenting on the events of his own day, makes a point of noting that his arch-enemy, John of Gischala (*War* 2.587), put on a pretense of humanity (ὑποκριτὴς φιλανθρωπίας), whereas actually "the prospect of lucre made him the most sanguinary of men."

That Josephus admired the synonymous qualities of ἐπιείκεια, χρηστότης, and φιλανθρωπία may be deduced also from the fact that these are qualities that are assigned in particular by Suetonius to Josephus' patrons Vespasian and Titus. According to Suetonius (*Vespasian* 12), Vespasian was unassuming (*civilis*, "courteous," "polite," "civil," "affable," "urbane") and lenient (*clemens*, "mild," "gentle," "tranquil," "kind," "forbearing," "indulging," "compassionate," "merciful") from the very beginning of his reign until its end, "never trying to conceal his former lowly condition, but often even parading it." Again, he is said (Suetonius, *Vespasian* 22) to have been most affable (*comissimus*, "courteous," "kind," "obliging," "friendly") not only at dinner but also on all other occasions. Likewise, of Titus Suetonius (*Titus* 8) says that he was most kindly (*benevolentissimus*, "benevolent," "kind," "obliging," "generous") by nature, as shown by the fact that whereas, in accordance with a custom established by the Emperor Tiberius, all the emperors after him refused to recognize the validity of favors granted by previous emperors, unless they themselves had conferred the same favors on the same people, Titus, without even being asked, ratified them all in a single edict. Again, Titus (Suetonius, *Titus* 8) showed his generosity and affability by his remark that because he had done nothing for anybody on a certain day he had lost a day. Josephus also (*Ant.* 12.122) goes out of his way to ascribe these qualities to Vespasian and Titus, digressing, after mentioning the privileges granted by Seleucus Nicator to the Jews, to note (*Ant.* 12.122) that when the Alexandrians and Antiochians asked Vespasian and Titus to withdraw the rights of citizenship and other ancient acts of kindness (φιλανθρώπων) from the Jews they, because of their fairness and generosity (ἐπιείκειαν καὶ μεγαλοφροσύνην), refused their petition, and this, as Josephus remarks, despite their having suffered great hardships in the war with the Jews.

3. *The Portrait of Rehoboam as a Commentary on the Civil Strife of Josephus' Day*

The underlying theme of Josephus' *Jewish War* is the emphasis on the civil strife engendered by the Jewish "tyrants" whom he holds responsible for the ill-fated revolt (*War* 1.10). In particular, Josephus' *Life* is largely an account of the attempts of one of these "tyrants," John of Gischala, to interfere with Josephus' mission in Galilee. The same theme of the dreadful consequences of civil strife pervades Josephus' paraphrase of the Bible in the *Antiquities*. In particular, the case of Jeroboam becomes, for Josephus, an outstanding example of the disaster brought on by secession and civil strife.[17]

In fact, when Josephus seeks to analyze the underlying cause of the demise of the Kingdom of Israel, he insists that the beginning of the nation's troubles was the rebellion which it undertook against the legitimate king, Rehoboam, when it chose Jeroboam as king (*Ant.* 9.282). It is almost as if Josephus were analyzing the demise of the Jewish state of his own day, which he likewise ascribes to the rebellion against the legitimate authority.

It is significant that whereas the Bible (1 Kings 15:6) states that there was a continuous civil war between Rehoboam and Jeroboam, in direct contradiction to the statement (1 Kings 12:24) that after mustering his troops to fight against Jeroboam and to force an end to the rebellion, Rehoboam listened to the advice of the prophet and did not attack Jeroboam, Josephus (*Ant.* 8.223) very conspicuously omits the former statement and thus presents Rehoboam as resisting the obvious temptation to seek to put an end to the rebellion by force. Furthermore, whereas in the Bible (1 Kings 12:24, 2 Chronicles 11:4) the decision not to go to war against Jeroboam is that of all the people of Judah and Benjamin, in Josephus (*Ant.* 8.223) the decision is that of Rehoboam alone, who thus clearly obtains the credit for preventing civil war. When, to be sure, in his summary of Rehoboam's reign, Josephus (*Ant.* 8.263) asserts that all his days Rehoboam was an enemy of Jero-

---

[17] See my "Josephus' Portrait of Jeroboam" (above, note 7) 43-46.

boam, in the same sentence he declares that he reigned in great quiet (ἡσυχίᾳ). He thus clearly avoids the biblical statement that Rehoboam was constantly at war with Jeroboam. Significantly, too, whereas in the Bible (1 Kings 12:24) the prophet Shemaiah (*Ant.* 8.223) quotes G-d as asserting that Rehoboam is not to fight against his kinsmen, presumably in this particular instance Josephus uses this occasion for an editorial comment that it is not just (δίκαιον) as a general rule to make war on one's countrymen (ὁμοφύλους), thus stressing that Rehoboam was convinced by the prophet's statement. It is this failure on the part of the Jews to avoid attacks upon their own kinsmen that Josephus constantly stresses as the basic reason for their tragedies in the biblical period, as in the civil war with the Benjaminites (*Ant.* 5. 150-165), where Josephus (*Ant.* 5.151) stresses the wise advice of the Israelite elders that war ought not to be undertaken hurriedly against one's own kinsmen (ὁμοφύλους).

To be sure, Josephus (*Ant.* 8.264) acknowledges and condemns Rehoboam for being boastful (ἀλαζών) and foolish (ἀνόητος), the same epithets that he uses in condemning the Jewish revolutionaries (*War* 6.395) against the Romans, who were so haughty (ἀλαζόνας) and proud of their impious crimes and whom Josephus says (*Life* 18) that he warned not to expose their country, their families, and themselves to sure dire perils through acting so rashly (προπετῶς) and so stupidly (ἀνοήτως). It is, says Josephus (*Ant.* 8.264), because of Rehoboam's boastfulness and foolishness in not listening to his father's friends that he consequently lost his royal power.

Nevertheless, though it is true that Josephus (*Ant.* 8.251) mentions Rehoboam's unjust and impious acts, Josephus goes out of his way to explain his lawlessness and evil ways by psychologizing that such an attitude arises from the greatness of men's affairs and the improvement of their position, as if to say that it is only natural that someone under those circumstances would have been misled into unjust and impious acts and would consequently have influenced his subjects accordingly. Significantly, precisely the same phrase (μέγεθος τῶν πραγμάτων, "greatness of affairs") is used by Josephus (*Ant.* 9.223) to explain the degeneration of King Uzziah, who had started his reign so promisingly. Again, whereas we read that Rehoboam was thus misled (ἐξετράπη) into unjust acts, in the case of Jeroboam (*Ant.* 8.245) no such defense is offered for his wickedness; rather, we find not the passive but the active voice, since we are informed that he outraged (ἐξύβρισεν) G-d.

4. *The Rehabilitation of Rehoboam*

It is not unusual for Josephus to rehabilitate, to a greater or lesser degree, figures who are blackened in the Bible. Thus, of the three Israelite kings whose wickedness is most emphasized in the biblical record – namely, Jeroboam, Ahab, and Manasseh – Josephus sees positive virtues in Ahab, shifting the blame to Ahab's role-model Jeroboam (*Ant.* 8.317) and to his wife Jezebel (*Ant.* 8.318).[18]

Likewise, in his portrait of Manasseh, Josephus seems to go out of his way to rehabilitate this monarch. Thus, in details that go beyond the biblical account, we are told of Manasseh's major achievements in improving the city of Jerusalem (*Ant.* 10.44). Again, in an extra-biblical addition, we hear that the degree of Manasseh's repentance was such that he was accounted a blessed and enviable man (*Ant.* 10.45).

The degree to which Rehoboam is rehabilitated is to be seen in close conjunction with the fact that Josephus finds no redeeming features at all for his rival, Jeroboam. Indeed, in extra-biblical comments, Jeroboam is depicted as the very opposite of temperate – a person who is hot-headed by nature (*Ant.* 8.209) and who is so impious that he named his own priests and even made himself high priest (*Ant.* 8.230 vs. 1 Kings 12:32).

One method by which Josephus arouses greater sympathy for Rehoboam is through denigrating to some degree those who came to him with their demands at the very beginning of his reign. According to the Bible (1 Kings 12:5, 2 Chronicles 10:5), when the people requested that he lighten their burden, Rehoboam's reaction was simply to tell them to return in three days, and we are told merely that the people went away, with nothing added as to whether or to what degree they were disappointed. Josephus (*Ant.* 8.214), on the other hand, exhibits a somewhat negative attitude toward the people by stressing their impatience and shows greater sympathy for Rehoboam in that, in an addition to the biblical narrative, he states that Rehoboam's reply immediately (εὐθύς)

---

[18] See my "Josephus' Portrait of Ahab" (above, note 11) 373-377.

aroused their suspicions by not agreeing "on the spot" (παραχρῆμα) to their wishes. Indeed, it is clear from Josephus' addition (*Ant.* 8.214) that the people expected that he would refuse them immediately (παραυτίκα) but that apparently they were pleasantly surprised when he did not fulfill these expectations but instead chose to deliberate (βουλεύσασθαι). The fact that in this one paragraph (*Ant.* 8.214) Josephus uses three words having substantially the same meaning of "immediately" stresses the people's impatience in contrast to Rehoboam's own relative thoughtfulness and patience.

This attack on Jeroboam and rehabilitation of Rehoboam is highlighted by the rearrangement of the narrative so that instead of continuing with the story of Jeroboam (1 Kings 14:1 ff.), Josephus interrupts (*Ant.* 8.246 ff.) with the account of Rehoboam.[19] To be sure, Josephus himself (*Ant.* 8.224) explains his deviation from the order in the biblical narrative by remarking that "in this way an orderly (εὔτακτον) arrangement can be preserved throughout the history," but the real reason, or, in any case, the net effect of this rearrangement is to make the contrast between Rehoboam and Jeroboam all the greater because we see in immediate juxtaposition that whereas Jeroboam ignored the warning of the prophet Jadon Rehoboam did listen to the prophet Shemaiah and consequently repents. This highlighted contrast is likewise to be seen in the fact that whereas the Bible (2 Chronicles 11:13) states that the priests and Levites whom Jeroboam had cast out from serving the L-rd came to Rehoboam, Josephus (*Ant.* 8.248) emphasizes, by implication, the goodness of Jeroboam's counterpart, Rehoboam, in welcoming these refugees who, in an extra-biblical comment, are described as good and righteous (ἀγαθοὶ καὶ δίκαιοι). Again, whereas the Bible (2 Chronicles 12:14), in its summary of Rehoboam's reign, makes a point of stressing that "he did evil, for he did not set his heart to seek the L-rd," Josephus (*Ant.* 8.263) says nothing about his religious failings but rather focuses on his military and diplomatic deficiencies. The reason for this, we may suggest, is again to underline the contrast with Jeroboam, whose impiety and lawlessness Josephus stresses in his final summary (*Ant.* 8. 289).[20] Indeed, Josephus (*Ant.* 8.216) goes out of his

---

[19] So Begg (above, note 2) 85.
[20] Secondarily, as Begg (above, note 2) 84, n.494, suggests, Josephus may have

way to declare his belief that it was G-d who caused Rehoboam not to accept the advice of the elders and to condemn what should have been of benefit to him, whereas the Bible (1 Kings 12:15, 2 Chronicles 10:15) states that this was a turn of affairs brought about by G-d in order to fulfill the word which he had spoken through Ahijah to Jeroboam. Again, in order to lessen Rehoboam's blame for his failure to listen to the advice of the delegation which came to him at the beginning of his reign, Josephus, in his version (*Ant.* 8.216), states that when Rehoboam met with the younger advisers he first told them what the elders had said, whereas in the Bible (1 Kings 12:9, 2 Chronicles 10:9) Rehoboam asks them for their advice without telling them what the elders had said. Thereupon, in an extra-biblical addition, Josephus (*Ant.* 8.217), again shifting the blame to G-d, remarks that neither their youth nor G-d permitted the youth to discern a better course. Again, whereas in the Bible (1 Kings 12:24, 2 Chronicles 11:4) G-d, through the prophet Shemaiah, indicates that He is in some vague way directing events, in Josephus (*Ant.* 8.223) Rehoboam is actually prevented (κωλυθείς) by G-d from going to war against his countrymen. And as if it were not enough once to put the onus on G-d, Josephus, in the very same sentence (*Ant.* 8.223), reiterates that the revolt had taken place in accordance with the purpose (προαίρεσιν, "decision," "will," "intention," "plan") of G-d.

Indeed, that the people had a favorable view of Rehoboam is clear from the fact that whereas in the Bible (1 Kings 12:13, 2 Chronicles 10:13) we hear simply that the king answered the people harshly, in Josephus (*Ant.* 8.218) the people are described as excited (μετεώρου) and eager (ἐσπουδακότος) and expecting to hear something friendly (φιλάνθρωπον). Consequently, the people's disappointment is all the greater; and whereas in the Bible (1 Kings 12:16, 2 Chronicles 10:16) we are simply told of the people's response to Rehoboam, in Josephus (*Ant.* 8.219) the people's mood is graphically described: they have been struck a cruel blow (πληγέντες) and hurt (ἀλγήσαντες) as though actually experiencing what he had spoken of doing (that is, chastising them with scorpions).

Again, after presenting his decision to the people, a gentler and

---

been motivated by a desire to avoid the seeming discrepancy between 2 Chronicles 12:12, which states that Rehoboam humbled himself, and 2 Chronicles 12:14, which summarizes his reign by asserting that he did evil.

more moderate Rehoboam is presented to us. In the Bible (1 Kings 12:18, 2 Chronicles 10:18) we read merely that Rehoboam sent his taskmaster Hadoram, whom the people stone to death; but we are not told what his mission is. Josephus (*Ant.* 8.220) presents us a Rehoboam who is big enough to seek forgiveness and who explains that Hadoram's mission is "to appease and to soften the mood of the people by persuading them to forgive what he had said if there had been in it anything rash (προπετές, "passionate," "thoughtless") or ill-tempered (δύσκολον, "hostile," "stubborn," "disagreeable," "unpleasant," "difficult") owing to his youth." It is clearly to the credit of Rehoboam that he sought to distance himself from these qualities of rashness and ill temper, especially since it is the former quality that, according to an addition in Josephus (*Ant.* 6.102), Saul exhibited in offering a sacrifice wrongly in his precipitate haste, and since it is the latter quality which, again according to an addition in Josephus (*Ant.* 6.43), the Israelites displayed in their obstinate refusal to listen to the prophet Samuel's warning not to demand a king. It is the latter quality, furthermore, that the youthful advisers to Rehoboam, with whom clearly Josephus does not sympathize, mention as what he should tell the people to expect to an even greater degree than what they had experienced from his father. It is not only King Abijah, Rehoboam's son, but also Josephus himself, as we can see from his addition (*Ant.* 8.278) to Scripture, who seeks forgiveness for the unpleasant (δυσκόλων) words spoken by his father, on the grounds that he was so young and inexperienced in governing people and for the sake of his father Solomon and the benefits that the people had received from him. The fact that Josephus makes a point of stressing (*Ant.* 8.220) that Rehoboam sought to appease (καταπραύνῃ) the people certainly elevates the stature of Rehoboam, inasmuch as the same verb is used of and thus associates him with Judah (*Ant.* 2.159) in seeking to appease Joseph's wrath; it is also used of Joshua and Caleb (*Ant.* 3.310) in seeking to allay the passion of the multitude, of Absalom (*Ant.* 7.191) in sending Joab to appease David, and of the elders (*Ant.* 10.93) in mollifying the people in order to save the prophet Jeremiah from punishment.

Moreover, whereas the Bible (1 Kings 12:18, 2 Chronicles 10:18) merely reports that after Hadoram had been stoned to death Rehoboam made haste to mount his chariot to flee to Jerusalem,

Josephus (*Ant.* 8.221) shows much more sympathy for Rehoboam in implying that Rehoboam put the blame upon himself for the death of his minister, inasmuch as after learning of the death of Hadoram and thinking that he himself was actually the target of the stones, Rehoboam, in his fear that he might suffer the same fate, fled to Jerusalem. Indeed, there is, in Josephus' version (*Ant.* 8.219) at this point, more sympathy for the reasonableness of the people, and again implying greater expectations of Rehoboam's response, in that whereas in the Bible (1 Kings 12:16, 2 Chronicles 10:16) the people, seeing that Rehoboam had not listened to their petition, told him that they were cutting themselves off from his kingdom, in Josephus (*Ant.* 8.219) they merely threaten (ἠπείλησαν) to desert him.

This episode, we may add, is strikingly reminiscent of that in which Archilaus, Herod's successor, is, at the beginning of his reign, beset by the multitude with its demands for an immediate reduction of the oppression which they had suffered under Herod (*War* 2.4, *Ant.* 17.204). Like Rehoboam, Archelaus sent his general (*War* 2.8, *Ant.* 17.209) to entreat them to desist; but when this emissary was driven off by a shower of stones, whereas Rehoboam had responded by accepting personal responsibility, Archelaus responded by sending his troops, who were met with stones, whereupon he sent his entire army, who conducted a bloodbath of the Jews (*War* 2.11-13, *Ant.* 17.215-218). On the other hand, Rehoboam's readiness to accept responsibility for what had happened to his emissary is reminiscent of the description (*Life* 132-144) of Josephus' courageous assumption of responsibility for his actions when a plot had been hatched against his life at Tarichaeae in Galilee and the masses were intent upon putting him to death.

Likewise contributing to a favorable picture of Rehoboam and underlying the contrast with Jeroboam is Josephus' paraphrase (*Ant.* 8.248) of the refuge afforded by him to those who had defected from Jeroboam's kingdom. Whereas in the Bible (2 Chronicles 11:13) we hear that "the priests and Levites that were in all Israel resorted to him from all places where they lived," Josephus adds the significant words that those who took refuge with Rehoboam were good and righteous (ἀγαθοὶ καὶ δίκαιοι), clearly implying that such virtuous people would feel more comfortable with Rehoboam than with Jeroboam.

Even when Josephus mentions Rehoboam's degeneracy into evil

paths, he goes out of his way in an extraordinary digression (*Ant.* 8.251-253) in order to explain it, whereas the Bible (2 Chronicles 12:1) bluntly states that he forsook the law of the L-rd, and again, in summarizing his career (2 Chronicles 12:14), asserts, very simply and without any attempt at explanation or qualification, that "he did evil, for he did not set his heart to seek the L-rd."[21] The psychologizing explanation itself is clearly Josephus' own, since he specifically adds the word οἶμαι ("I think"). For Josephus this notion that power (τῶν πραγμάτων μέγεθος, *Ant.* 8.251) in and of itself corrupts is a matter of human nature, as we see in his similar analysis of Saul's treatment of Abimelech and his kin (Ant. 6.264-268). Another parallel may be seen in Josephus' reflection in connection with Uzziah (*Ant.* 9.223), who, he says, was led to sin "by his brilliant good fortune and the greatness of his power (μέγεθος τῶν πραγμάτων [the same phrase used of Rehoboam]) which he had not been able to direct rightly." Significantly, these similar digressions are in connection with figures whom Josephus seeks to rehabilitate.[22]

Again, the biblical text (2 Chronicles 12:5), after describing Shishak's invasion of Judaea and indicating that he had come as far as Jerusalem itself, speaks of Rehoboam humbling himself only after the prophet Shemaiah had come to him and and to the princes of Judaea and had told them that G-d had abandoned them because they had abandoned Him. Josephus, on the other hand (*Ant.* 8.255), clearly enhances the reader's regard for Rehoboam by having him and the multitude pray to G-d before the prophet addresses them. Furthermore, Josephus places greater emphasis on the contriteness of Rehoboam and the multitude, inasmuch as whereas the biblical text (2 Chronicles 12:6) declares simply that after the prophet had berated them they humbled themselves, Josephus (*Ant.* 8. 256) spells out their confession, having them assert that they had acted impiously toward G-d and had violated His ordinances and adding that they repented at once (εὐθύς) and that they hastened (ὥρμησαν) to acknowledge G-d's

---

[21] Cf. my "Josephus' Portrait of Jehoiachin" (above, note 14) 15-16, where I note that the stock phrase "did what was evil in the sight of the L-rd" occurs in the Bible in connection with twenty-five kings, but that Josephus never reproduces it as such, whereas he notes in various ways what the evil consisted of.

[22] See my "Josephus' Portrait of Saul," *HUCA* 53 (1982) 45-99; and Christopher T. Begg, "Uzziah (Azariah) of Judah according to Josephus,", *Estudios Biblicos* 53 (1995) 5-24.

justice. The fact that Josephus, in describing here the remorse of Rehoboam and of his people, states that their spirits fell (ταῖς ψυχαῖς ἀνέπεσον), using the same phrase that he (Ant. 6.329) employs in describing the repentance of Saul (τὴν ψυχὴν ἀνέπεσε), thus identifies Rehoboam, by implication, with King Saul, the master of repentance, as we see in Josephus.[23] It is, furthermore, significant that whereas the biblical text (2 Chronicles 12:7) says merely that G-d saw that the princes of Israel and King Rehoboam had humbled themselves, Josephus (Ant. 8.257) adds that G-d saw them in this state of mind confessing their sins (ἁμαρτίας ἀνθομολογουμένους). As Begg[24] has pointed out, Josephus' only other use of the verb ἀνθομολογέομαι, "to confess," is in reference to Ahab (Ant. 8.362), where Josephus describes Ahab's feeling of grief and his confession of his sins. We may add that in the case of Ahab also the biblical source (1 Kings 21:27) says nothing about Ahab's confession; and thus Josephus has, in effect, equated Rehoboam and Ahab in depicting their sincere repentance and in rehabilitating their stature.[25]

Josephus arouses further sympathy for Rehoboam by adding (Ant. 8.258) that Shishak, in sacking the Temple, did not abide by the agreement that he had made with Rehoboam, whereas the biblical account (2 Chronicles 12:9) says nothing about an agreement.

Moreover, Josephus (Ant. 8.263), in an editorial-like addition, by stating that instead of leading the life of a illustrious commander and a most brilliant statesman he reigned in great quiet and fear, seems to imply that Rehoboam had the potential to be an illustrious (ἐπιφανοῦς) general and a most brilliant (λαμπρότατος) statesman.

5. *Summary*

Rehoboam was a figure of major importance for Josephus, if we are to judge from the amount of space that he devotes to him, from his "editorializing" remarks, and from his citing of Herodotus to support his historicity.

---

[23] See my "Josephus' Portrait of Saul" (above, note 22) 91.
[24] Begg (above, note 2) 74, n. 450.
[25] See my "Josephus' Portrait of Ahab" (above, note 11) 373.

Josephus' account is intended to teach the reader how a ruler should and should not rule and, in particular, how he should deal with the masses, for whom he has considerable contempt. In particular, he stresses the importance of the qualities of mildness, kindness, and friendliness – qualities which the Romans assigned to Josephus' patrons, Vespasian and Titus, and which he himself extols in rulers, Jewish and non-Jewish, throughout his *Antiquities*. Josephus felt a need to stress these virtues because the Jews had been accused of misanthropy by a number of intellectuals.

Much of Josephus' account is intended to stress the contrast between Rehoboam and Jeroboam. His very rearrangement of the narrative highlights their juxtaposition and contrast. Whereas Jeroboam promoted civil strife, Rehoboam is depicted as avoiding attacks upon fellow-Jews. To the extent that Rehoboam is guilty of degenerating into lawlessness and impiety, Josephus "psychologizes" by explaining that this resulted naturally from the very considerable power and success that Rehoboam achieved.

Rehoboam is rehabilitated by Josephus to a great degree by depicting the people who came to him at the beginning of his reign as impatient. In summarizing his reign Josephus focuses not on his religious but on his military and diplomatic deficiencies. Most remarkably, Josephus goes out of his way to declare his belief that it was G-d who was responsible for Rehoboam's failure to accept the good advice of the older advisers at the beginning of his reign. Moreover, in an important extra-biblical addition, Rehoboam sends an emissary to seek forgiveness from the people; and when this minister is stoned to death by the people, Josephus describes Rehoboam as accepting responsibility.

In his portrait Josephus is, in effect, drawing a contrast between the way Archelaus acted murderously toward the people when they put demands upon him after the death of Herod and the relatively mild, patient, and peaceful way in which Rehoboam tried to reconcile himself with the people when they placed their demands before him following the death of Solomon. There is also an implied comparison with the calm attitude of Josephus himself in Galilee when confronted with an angry mob. Finally, Josephus places greater emphasis upon the contriteness of Rehoboam.

CHAPTER SEVENTEEN

ASA

1. Introduction

One indication of the relative importance to Josephus of a given biblical personality is the sheer amount of space that he devotes to him. As for Asa, the ratio of Josephus (*Ant.* 8.286, 290-97, 304-6, 314-15, consisting of 104 lines in the Loeb text) to the biblical text (2 Chronicles 14.1-16.14, consisting of 75 lines),[1] is 1.39, an indication that, from this point of view, he is of medium importance to Josephus.

That Asa was, however, of relative importance in Josephus' eyes may be seen from the fact that, at the conclusion of the discussion of his achievements, Josephus presents an extra-biblical encomium praising him in the highest terms by remarking that he imitated his great-great-grandfather David in courage and piety (*Ant.* 8.315). The fact that he gives such praise to a relatively minor figure as Asa is significant.

2. The Rabbinic Account of Asa

It is of particular interest to compare the rabbinic accounts of Asa, with which Josephus may well have been acquainted and which are ambivalent, with that of Josephus, which is uniformly favorable. Thus, on the one hand, the rabbis ask how it is possible that Asa did not destroy the high places, since surely he destroyed all the idolatrous cults in Palestine (*Shabbat* 56b). On the other hand, they remark that Asa showed little confidence in G-d and trusted rather in his own skill (*Sotah* 10a); indeed, in a milieu in which scholarship was so revered, they state that Asa even went to the length of forcing the scholars in his realm to enlist in his army when he went to war against Baasha the king of Israel (*ibid.*). Moreover, even the bridegroom from his chamber was not exempted on this occasion;

---

[1] The biblical account in 1 Kings (15:9-24) is much shorter and is clearly not Josephus' major source.

and it was, consequently, because of this conscription of scholars and bridegrooms, according to the tradition transmitted by the fourth-century Rava, that Asa was punished by G-d. Furthermore, the rabbis stress that the prophet Ḥanani justly rebuked Asa for trusting in princes rather than in G-d – and this despite the fact that Divine help had been visible in his conflict with the Ethiopians and the Libyans (*Lamentations Rabbah*, introduction 30, and *Midrash Psalms* 79.1). Indeed, the rabbis remark that G-d at first intended to limit the split between the kingdoms of Judah and Israel to thirty-six years and that if Asa had shown himself deserving he would have been accorded dominion over the whole of Israel (*Seder Olam* 16; Tosefta *Soṭah* 12.1-2). In fact, as the rabbis note, Asa, through his connection by marriage with the house of Omri, the king of Israel, actually contributed to the stability of his great enemy, the Kingdom of Israel (*Seder Olam* 17; Tosefta *Soṭah* 12.13); consequently, G-d resolved that the descendants of Asa should perish simultaneously with those of Omri. The rabbis note still another grievous sin committed by Asa, namely that he gave some of the treasures of Solomon which he captured from Zerah the Ethiopian king to the king of Aram, Hadrimon the son of Tabrimon (*Seder Olam* 17, *Pesaḥim* 119a). Finally, they make note of the appropriateness of the fact that Asa, who was distinguished on account of the strength residing in his feet, was afflicted at the end of his life with gout in his feet (*Soṭah* 10a). This, say the rabbis, is the disease referred to in David's curse of Joab (2 Samuel 3:29) (*Sanhedrin* 48b).

If, indeed, as we have suggested, Josephus may well have been aware of such rabbinic traditions, we may ask why his portrait of Asa systematically omits all criticisms of him.

3. *Asa's Virtues*

The chief function of a leader, as we can see for example in Thucydides' portrait of Pericles, is to put his nation in order. It is precisely this quality which Josephus emphasizes as the major achievement of Asa (*Ant.* 8.290). In this respect he is comparable to Josephus' portrayal of Saul, who likewise set the nation right (κατωρθωμένων) through his victory over Nahash, as well as through his success (κατωρθωμένοις) over the Amalekites (*Ant.* 6.81). We find the same language, significantly, in Josephus' description of David's successes wherever he went (*Ant.* 6.196, 6.335, 7.109, 8.1). Hence, by implication, Asa is compared with the two greatest kings of the Jewish people, at least as Josephus presents them.

It is, consequently, significant that whereas the Bible notes that Asa built fortified cities which he surrounded with walls, towers, gates, and bars (2 Chronicles 14:6-7), Josephus, eager to emphasize, rather, Asa's leadership in battle, totally omits these details. Again, the biblical narrative notes that Asa cried out to G-d (2 Chronicles 14:11), presumably in utter dismay. Josephus' Asa is more positive in that, in addition to crying out, he asks G-d for victory and for the destruction of many myriads of the enemy (*Ant.* 8.293). To have opposed such a huge army successfully clearly adds to Asa's reputation for bravery.

Similarly, in the Bible we are told that it is G-d who defeated the Ethiopians before Asa (2 Chronicles 14:12), whereas in Josephus' version the role of G-d is reduced to merely giving a sign that Asa would be victorious (*Ant.* 8.294), whereupon it is Asa himself who then becomes the center of attention as he encounters the Ethiopians and slays many of them. Thus, whereas, indeed, in the Bible it is G-d's victory, in Josephus the victory is Asa's, though Asa is careful to acknowledge that it was from G-d that he had received it (*Ant.* 8.295).

Likewise, whereas the Bible presents the sweeping statement that the Ethiopians fell in battle against Asa until none remained alive (2 Chronicles 14:13),[2] Josephus more plausibly has Asa slay merely *many* of the Ethiopians (Ant. 8.294). Likewise, whereas the Bible states that Asa's army plundered all the cities around Gerar (2 Chronicles 14:14), Josephus makes the statement more credible by omitting the word "all" (Ant. 8.294). On the other hand, whereas the Bible vaguely states that they carried off plunder without indicating the contents of the plunder (2 Chronicles 14:14), Josephus highlights the magnitude of the booty by specifying that it consisted of much gold and silver (Ant. 8.294).

That justice is for Josephus a key quality of Asa may be seen by comparing the biblical statement of the prophet Azariah to Asa after the latter's victory over the Ethiopians, that "the L-rd is with

---

[2] The Greek translation says that the Ethiopians fell so that they could not recover ("keep up," "preserve") themselves (ὥστε μὴ εἶναι ἐν αὐτοῖς περιποίησιν).

you while you are with him" (2 Chronicles 15:2), with Azariah's statement in Josephus, which specifically declares that Asa and his people had obtained their victory because they had shown themselves just (δικαίους) and pious (*Ant.* 8.295). We may likewise see the importance of this quality of justice in Josephus' depiction of Asa in that whereas in the Bible, when Asa hears the words of the prophet Azariah he takes courage (2 Chronicles 15:8), in Josephus the reaction of the king and the people involves rather justice, as we see from Josephus' remark that they take thought (πρόνοιαν) for what was right (δικαίου, that is, "just") (*Ant.* 8.297).

Moreover, whereas the Bible, in presenting Azariah's prophecy, says nothing about G-d's benevolence and the gratitude that one should feel for this (2 Chronicles 15:2-7), in Josephus' version Azariah advises Asa and his people not to be ungracious in refusing to accept the benevolence (εὐμενείας, "good will," "mercy," "favor," "goodness") of G-d (*Ant.* 8.297).

Josephus, as we have seen, makes a point of stressing that the main lesson to be learned from his entire history is that those who conform to the will of G-d and do not transgress His laws prosper beyond belief, whereas those who depart from the strict observance of the laws suffer irretrievable disaster (*Ant.* 1.14). It is this very point that is stressed by the prophet Azariah in an addition to the biblical text (2 Chronicles 15:2), namely, that if Asa and his people continue to be righteous (δικαίους) and pious (ὁσίους) G-d will grant them to overcome their foes and to live happily, but that if they abandon His worship, everything will turn out to the contrary and that the time would come when there would be no true prophet among them nor any priest to give righteous judgment (*Ant.* 8.296). Such a prediction would be particularly effective inasmuch as Josephus was himself a priest and regarded himself as a prophet (see Feldman 1990, 386-422, especially 397-400). The same point is made in Josephus' encomium for Asa where he remarks that Asa's prosperity demonstrates how close a watch God keeps over human affairs and how He loves good men but hates the wicked, whom He destroys root and branch (*Ant.* 8.314). The fact that Josephus here employs the neutral phrase τὸ θεῖον for the Deity is an indication that he is aiming to impress this lesson upon all his readers, including those who would not identify with the distinctively Jewish conception of G-d.

Whereas the Bible, in introducing its characterization of Asa, is content merely to state, in the most general terms, that Asa did what was right in the eyes of the L-rd and adds, "as David his father had done" (1 Kings 15:11), and whereas in the more extended account in 2 Chronicles (14:2), he is said to have done what was good and right in the eyes of the L-rd his G-d, Josephus praises him considerably more, remarking that he was of excellent (ἄριστος) character and that he actually looked to (ἀφορῶν) the Deity for guidance (*Ant.* 8.290). In particular, Josephus stresses Asa's piety, remarking that he neither did nor thought anything that did not show due regard for piety (εὐσέβειαν) and the observance (φυλακήν) of the laws (νομίμων, "customs," "traditions based on physical laws") (*ibid.*).

We likewise see greater emphasis on Asa's trust in G-d in Josephus' version of Asa's prayer when he encounters Zerah the Ethiopian with the latter's huge army. In the biblical version Asa asks for divine help, "for we rely on Thee, and in Thy name we have come against this multitude" (2 Chronicles 14:11). Josephus' Asa declares more positively that he puts his trust in G-d alone, since only G-d can make the few triumph over the many and the weak over the strong (*Ant.* 8.293). Moreover, the biblical Asa seems to suggest that it is G-d Himself who is on trial in the forthcoming battle with Zerah the Ethiopian (2 Chronicles 14:11), the implication being that if Zerah should prevail it will be a manifest blow to G-d's credibility. Josephus, seeking to avoid attributing such lack of faith to Asa, says merely that Asa cried out and prayed to G-d for victory (*Ant.* 8.293).

We see Asa's piety, moreover, in his enforcement of the biblical laws. Thus, in a passage which has no biblical parallel, Josephus states that after Asa had been warned by Azariah's prophecy he sent men throughout the country to watch over the enforcement of the (religious) laws (νομίμων) (*Ant.* 8.297).

Josephus was apparently in a quandary as to what to do with the biblical text which stated that Asa put away the prostitutes (*haqedeshim*) and removed all the idols (*hagillulim*) (1 Kings 15:12). The Greek translation goes even further and is more precise in rendering the word *haqedeshim* by τελευτάς. This would indicate that Asa had ended the Jewish mystery cults, since this word refers to the mystic rites practiced in initiations. To Josephus' pagan readers such a move would be offensive, since the mysteries were held in such high regard even by Philo, who declares that he himself had been initiated into the Greater Mysteries of Judaism (*De Cherubim* 14.49) and who had referred to Moses as one who had been instructed in all the mysteries of his priestly duties (*De Vita Mosis* 2.15.71). Moreover, in place of the reference to the Asherah (associated with Canaanite tree worship) which Asa's mother Maacah reverenced (1 Kings 15:13), the Greek version states that she made a meeting (σύνοδον) in her grove (ἄλσει); and there would surely seem to be nothing objectionable in such a meeting. Again, Josephus resolves the matter by simply omitting the reference altogether.

Quite clearly Josephus was concerned about the apparent contradiction in Asa's behavior in that, on the one hand, according to the biblical narrative, he removed his mother Maacah from being queen mother because she had an abominable image (*mifelezet*)[3] made for Asherah[4] and cut down this image and burned it (1 Kings 15:13, 2 Chronicles 15:16), but, on the other hand, he did not take away the high places where forbidden sacrifices were taking place (1 Kings 15:14, 2 Chronicles 15:17). Moreover, the Bible follows this contradiction with a further one, i.e., nevertheless, the heart of Asa was blameless all his days (1 Kings 15:14, 2 Chronicles 15:17). Josephus however resolves these contradictions by simply omitting altogether the statements about Maacah, the destruction of the image, the failure to destroy the high places, and Asa's loyalty to G-d all his days.

A problem that confronted Josephus was the apparent blot on Asa's reputation for piety posed by the biblical statement that he took silver and gold from the treasures of the house of the L-rd and sent them to Ben-hadad king of Syria (2 Chronicles 16:2). To take such sacred materials from the very Temple and to give them to a pagan king would hardly seem something which a G-d-fearing king would do. Josephus, apparently aware of this, first of all omits the specification that the gold and silver came from the Temple, and secondly attempts to justify the deed by explaining that Asa felt that he had to make an alliance with Syria in view of the fear that the army of the King of Israel was a mere forty stades (that is,

---

[3] The rabbis have a tradition that Maacah made a phallic symbol for this image and that she would copulate with it every day ('*Avodah Zarah* 44a).

[4] The Greek translation goes even further regarding the pagan practices of Maacah, since it states that she was priestess (λειτουργοῦσαν) to the goddess Astarte (2 Chronicles 15:16).

approximately five miles) from Jerusalem itself (*Ant.* 8.304).

Another major difficulty with Asa's piety is the seer Hanani's word that he had done foolishly in relying upon the king of Syria rather than upon G-d (2 Chronicles 16:7-10). The resulting angry reaction of Asa which leads him to put the seer in the stocks in prison and the further cruelties[5] which he inflicted upon some of the people at the same time is surely a severe indictment of Asa. The fact that Josephus totally omits this incident is a clear indication that he was seeking to whitewash Asa.

A further indictment of Asa may be seen in the biblical account of Asa's final illness and death (1 Kings 15:23, 2 Chronicles 16:12). The biblical narrative, clearly seeking to indict Asa, goes out of its way to remark that even when his disease became severe Asa, instead of seeking help from G-d, turned instead to physicians (2 Chronicles 16:12). Once again, Josephus, eager to protect Asa's reputation, totally omits this incident.

There is a further criticism of Asa implied in the biblical description of his funeral. There we read that the people made a great fire (*serefah*) in his honor (2 Chronicles 16:14). This sounds like a funeral pyre such as we find in Homer's *Iliad* and throughout classical pagan literature. Apparently, the translators of this passage into Greek were aware of this problem, and so they rendered it very vaguely that the people made a very great funeral (ἐκφορά, "carrying out [of a corpse to burial]"). Josephus avoids the problem altogether by simply omitting the details of the funeral.

4. *Apologetics*

In the case of Asa, Josephus has systematically removed references to his destruction of pagan cults, as we have noted. Thus, though the account of his reign in 1 Kings (15:12) is extraordinarily brief, yet we have mention of the fact that he put away the male cult prostitutes out of the land and that he removed all the idols that his father had made. In the parallel passage in 2 Chronicles (14:3, 5) we have still further details of Asa's mass destruction of pagan cult objects, namely that he took away the foreign altars and the

---

[5] The Septuagint somewhat softens this gross flaw in Asa's character by reading that he vexed (ἐλυμήνατο, "outraged," "maltreated," "harmed," "injured") some of the people (2 Chronicles 16:10).

high places, broke down the pillars and hewed down the Asherim, and took out of all the cities of Judah the high places and the incense altars. In Josephus' version we hear nothing specific about Asa's destruction of pagan cult objects; rather, the language is quite deliberately vague, with the emphasis on the positive: "He put his kingdom in order by cutting away whatever evil growths were found in it and cleansing it from every impurity" (*Ant.* 8.290). For similar reasons Josephus omits the biblical statement that when Asa heard the warning given him by the prophet Azariah he put away the idols from the land of Judah and Benjamin and from the cities which he had taken in the hill country of Ephraim (2 Chronicles 15:8).

Given Josephus' concern not to offend his pagan readers, we should also not be surprised to find that he omits the biblical statement that Asa's people entered into a covenant that they would put to death whoever, whether young or old, man or woman, would not seek the L-rd (2 Chronicles 15:12-13).

The Romans were particularly sensitive to the considerable success experienced by Jews in converting others to Judaism; and, significantly, the expulsion of the Jews from Rome on at least two occasions (139 B.C.E. and 19 C.E.) appears to have been connected with their success in winning converts (see Feldman 1993a, 300-4). According to the biblical version, when Asa was gathering his army, a number of Jews from the Kingdom of Israel who happened to be sojourning in the Kingdom of Judah deserted to him when they saw that G-d was with him (2 Chronicles 15:9). The Septuagint, in its version of the passage, declares that Asa assembled the tribes of Judah and Benjamin, together with strangers (προσηλύτους) that dwelt with them (2 Chronicles 15:9). The word here translated as "strangers" is "proselytes," and implies that they were actually converts. Again, Josephus avoids the issue by simply omitting this passage.

Josephus is also careful not to offend non-Jews politically. In particular, he is critical of messianic and messianic-like movements, since the goal of such movements was *ipso facto* a political Jewish state independent of the Romans. In view of Josephus' sensitivity to the charge that the Jews constituted a nation within a nation whose allegiance, wherever they were scattered, was to the Land of Israel and that they would be forever subversive until their return from captivity, it is instructive to note Josephus' paraphrase of the warning issued by the prophet Azariah to King Asa. According to the biblical version, if the Jews forsake G-d He will punish them by forsaking them; "they will be broken in pieces, nation against nation and city against city" (2 Chronicles 15:2-7). Josephus, in his paraphrase, introduces a new element when he declares that as a punishment G-d will scatter the Jews over the face of the earth so that they will lead a life as aliens (ἔπηλυν) and wanderers (ἀλήτην) (*Ant.* 8.296-97). From this we might conclude that the Diaspora is a curse and a punishment, whereas one would have expected Josephus, who spent the second half of his life in the Diaspora under Roman protection, to have glorified this event in Jewish history since he clearly opposed an independent Jewish state.[6] However, we must note that there is no hint here of the traditional Jewish hope that the Jews will some day be gathered together from the exile and return to the Land of Israel.

5. *Summary*

It is of interest to see how Josephus remolds a relatively obscure biblical figure, King Asa of Judah. Whereas the rabbinic tradition attacks him for trusting in himself rather than in G-d and, in particular, for drafting the sages, Josephus omits such details and, indeed, whitewashes Asa completely. He is praised particularly, in language reminiscent of Josephus' own portraits of Saul and David, as well as of Thucydides' Pericles, for putting his nation in order. So as to aggrandize Asa's bravery Josephus diminishes the role of G-d. He makes his account of Asa's courage more credible by avoiding gross exaggerations of the enemy's forces. In order to emphasize Asa's justice Josephus stresses that his very victory was due to the fact that he and his people possessed this quality. An important aspect of justice is to show gratitude, and this, too, is stressed in Josephus' portrait of Asa and his people. Josephus likewise stresses Asa's piety, an attribute which, as here, is often coupled in Josephus with justice and which was historically so prized by the Romans.

In particular, Josephus emphasizes Asa's obedience to the ancestral laws, likewise a key Roman value. And yet, because he realized

---

[6] Shochat (1953, 43-50), indeed, points to this passage as evidence that Josephus viewed the Diaspora as a punishment.

that his audience, consisting apparently primarily of non-Jews, would resent as intolerant the biblical Asa's forcible destruction of idols, tree worship, and mystery cults, Josephus omits such details. Conversely, the Bible admits that Asa did not remove the pagan high places where sacrifices to pagan gods took place, while, at the same time, declaring that his heart was blameless all his days. Again, Josephus, realizing the self-contradiction invoked, omits both statements. He likewise leaves aside the Bible's negative statement that when rebuked by the seer Ḥanani, Asa put him into prison and inflicted further cruelties upon the people at large. Furthermore, since it would have been embarrassing as showing lack of respect for other people's religious practices, as well as lack of respect for his own mother, to repeat the Bible's statement that Asa removed his mother from being queen because she had worshipped idols, he omits this detail.

Because proselytism was such a sensitive issue at the time, in view of the Jews' apparently extraordinary success during this period in attracting converts, Josephus omits the passage which implies that Asa attracted proselytes to his army. Finally, although Josephus states that the Jews have been scattered in the Diaspora because they have disobeyed G-d, he does not mention the related messianic hope that the Jews would some day be gathered together from the Diaspora and be conveyed to the Land of Israel, where they would establish a truly independent state. Such a view would, of course, be anathema to the Romans, who were always conscious of the fact that they were a minority in their own empire.

CHAPTER EIGHTEEN

AHAB

1. Introduction

We may well ask how Josephus portrays biblical rogues. Here, quite evidently, Josephus was confronted with a dilemma. On the one hand, he promises, in the proem to his *magnum opus*, the *Jewish Antiquities*, that he will faithfully reproduce the biblical narrative, neither adding to nor omitting anything (1.17); moreover, since he affirms that the main lesson to be derived from his history is that those who obey the will of G-d and do not transgress His divinely given laws will prosper beyond belief whereas those who do not will end in irretrievable disaster, he was duty bound to illustrate these principles by accentuating the disasters of those who did, indeed, violate the Torah (*Ant.* 1.14). And yet, on the other hand, it is clear that the *Antiquities* is an extended apology for the Jews, in which Josephus felt the need to defend his people against the charge that they had forfeited the protection of G-d through their heinous sins.

Of the kings of Judah and Israel, who emerge from the Bible as thoroughly wicked, none is treated at greater length by Josephus than Ahab, king of Israel.[1] He devotes 672 lines (in the *Loeb Classical Library* text) to his portrait (*Ant.* 8.316-92, 398-420) as against 340 lines in the Hebrew original (1 Kings 6:29-22:40) and 527 lines in the Septuagint version.[2] Thus Josephus has a ratio of 1.98 as

---

[1] A perusal of the bibliographies of Josephus by Schreckenberg and myself indicates that no comprehensive study has yet been attempted of Josephus' portrait of Ahab. Since the publication of these bibliographies Begg (1989, 225-45) has published an article on Josephus' treatment of Ahab; but this deals only with the narrative of Ahab's death and focuses, in particular, upon Josephus' stylistic changes vis-à-vis the Bible.

[2] That Josephus used the Greek text of the Septuagint may be seen from the fact that whereas according to the Hebrew Ahab tells Jehoshaphat to wear his own robes in battle (1 Kings 22:30), in the Septuagint and in Josephus Jehoshaphat puts on Ahab's robes before entering the line of battle (*Ant.* 8.412). There is, however, evidence that, in addition to a Greek text, Josephus also used a Hebrew text (or perhaps a Greek text which reflects the present Masoretic Text), i.e., *Antiquities* 8.322, where he has τέχνῳ, reflecting the Hebrew "son," whereas the

compared with the Hebrew text and 1.28 as compared with the Septuagint version. What is particularly striking is that Josephus devotes so much more attention relatively to Ahab than to some other kings whose reputation for virtue was outstanding.

In what we may term editorializing on the part of Josephus, he declares, commenting on the fate of King Ahab, which had been predicted by two prophets, Elijah and Micaiah, that we should realize that nothing is more beneficial than "prophecy and the foreknowledge (προγνώσεως, a term used especially by the Hippocratic school of medicine with respect to forecasts of the result of disease) which it gives, for in this way G-d enables us to know what to guard against" (*Ant.* 8.418) We may perhaps, consequently, conjecture that a major reason for this increased attention to Ahab is the latter's close association with the prophet Elijah, in whom Josephus, who himself claimed prophetic gifts (*War* 3.400-402), had a special interest. To be sure, Hezekiah was also closely associated with a prophet, Isaiah, who was certainly no less important than Elijah, but the connection of prophecy with history as a forecast of events to come is clearly more direct in the case of Ahab (see Feldman 1990, 387-94).

2. *The Rabbinic Portrait of Ahab*

In dealing with Ahab it is clear that the rabbis confronted a dilemma which was similar to that with which Josephus had to grapple; and Josephus, who apparently was well acquainted with the rabbinic tradition, resolved the problem, as they did, by presenting a balanced portrait in which he acknowledges certain defects in the king's character, while, at the same time aggrandizing other elements, notably his courage and his sincere repentance, just as he explains away various deficiencies by blaming Ahab's wife.

In his exegesis of the biblical statement that Ahab did more to provoke G-d to anger than all the kings of Israel that were before him (1 Kings 16:33), the third-century Rabbi Johanan mentions the

---

Septuagint has the plural τέκνοις (1 Kings 17:12). In addition, Josephus used an Aramaic Targum, as we see from his rendering of 1 Kings 21:27 (Septuagint 20:27), where the Hebrew text reads that Ahab went softly (*aṭ*) and the Septuagint either omits "softly" or renders it as "bent" or "bowed down," and where only the Targum reads *yaḥeif* ("barefoot"), which is clearly Josephus' reading (*Ant.* 8.362) – γυμνοῖς τοῖς ποσὶ διῆγεν.

tradition that Ahab went out of his way to write upon the gates of Samaria: "Ahab denies the G-d of Israel" (*Sanhedrin* 102b). Indeed, according to Rabbi Johanan, there was no furrow in Palestine where Ahab did not plant an idol and worship it (*Sanhedrin* 102b). The fourth-century Rabbi Aha bar Hanina, commenting on the passage that "When the wicked perish there is song" (Proverbs 11:10), cites, as an example of the wicked, the case of Ahab, as if this were the instance *par excellence*, whereupon a question is raised as to whether G-d ever rejoices over the downfall of the wicked, the implication being that even when one is as wicked as Ahab was, still G-d does not rejoice upon his downfall. Indeed, the Mishnah declares that three kings – Jeroboam, Ahab, and Manasseh – were apparently so wicked that even though all Israelites have a share in the world to come (Mishnah, *Sanhedrin* 10:1), they forfeited their share (Mishnah, *Sanhedrin* 10:2). The second-century Rabbi Judah bar Ilai then argues that Manasseh did have a share because he repented, so that only Jeroboam and Ahab are left among the arch-sinners. Of these two, Ahab was clearly the more wicked, since, according to the tradition reported by Rabbi Johanan, the minor transgressions committed by Ahab were equal to the gravest committed by Jeroboam, and the only reason why Scripture makes Jeroboam the arch-example of sinfulness is that he was the first king to engage in the sin of idol-worship (Mishnah, *Sanhedrin* 10:1).

And yet, the rabbis seemingly had ambivalent feelings about King Ahab. Thus, in a tone of pride, they state that he ruled over the whole world, that his dominion encompassed 252 (or 232) kingdoms, and that each of his seventy or one hundred and forty children had both a summer and a winter palace (*Sanhedrin* 102b). Indeed, we find in the very same tractate where the above negative comments are cited the fourth-century Rabbi Nahman ben Jacob's statement that Ahab was equally balanced between sin and merit, having performed as many good deeds as evil ones (*ibid.*). Here, too, we meet the question of the third-century Rabbi Johanan as to why Ahab merited to have a reign of twenty-two years, along with the remarkable answer that he deserved such a long reign because he honored the Torah, which was given in the twenty-two letters of the Hebrew alphabet (*ibid.*). In fact, the rabbinic tradition emphasizes the great learning of Ahab, Jeroboam, and Manasseh (*Tanhuma Exodus* 29). Furthermore, there was a tradition that Ahab was generous with his money and that because he used his great wealth to benefit scholars, half of his sins were forgiven (*Sanhedrin* 102b). Moreover, tradition ascribed to Ahab the great virtue of abstaining from slander and backbiting; in fact, in at least one important respect Ahab's generation emerges as superior even to that of the seemingly incomparable King David, namely the former did not reveal the hiding place of the prophet Elijah and the other hundred prophets, whereas David's generation often betrayed David's abode during the period when he was fleeing from Saul. Furthermore, the great victory of Ahab and his people over the Syrians is said to be due to their observance of the Sabbath.[3]

That Ahab was not viewed altogether unfavorably would further seem to be indicated by the fact that, according to the third-century Rabbi Levi, a genealogical table in Jerusalem mentioned that a certain Ben Kovesin (or Bet Koveshin) was one of the descendants of Ahab (Jerusalem Talmud, *Ta'anit* 4.2.68a, *Genesis Rabbah* 98.8). Finally, the third-century Rabbi Joseph remarks on the tremendous number of people who mourned the deaths of Ahab and Josiah (*Megillah* 3b, *Mo'ed Qatan* 28b). Indeed, the very fact that this seemingly most wicked of all kings is coupled with that exemplar of piety, Josiah, may again be an indication that Ahab was not regarded as so wicked after all. The rabbis praise his courageous leadership in battle in that he himself saddled his warhorse for the battle with Ben-hadad, whereupon his zeal was rewarded by G-d with a brilliant victory (*Yelammedenu* in *Yalquṭ* 2.219, *Tanḥuma* B 2.16, *Tanḥuma Exodus* 29).

The rabbis, of course, could not deny that Ahab had sinned grievously, but they put even greater stress than does the Bible on his wife Jezebel as the instigator of these sins (Jerusalem *Sanhedrin* 10.1.28b, *Eliyahu Rabbah* 9.49). Indeed, we hear, in a tradition cited by Rabbi Joseph that every day she weighed out gold shekels for idols (*Sanhedrin* 102b).

3. *Ahab's Wickedness according to Josephus*

Josephus could not, of course, ignore the biblical statement that Ahab was more wicked than all the kings who had preceded him

---

[3] See rabbinic citations in Ginzberg (1928, 6:311, n. 35).

(1 Kings 16:30); but even here, in a subtle way, Josephus softens the criticism by remarking that he did not make a new departure (καινίσας, "make new," "innovate") in any respect except that he hit upon (ἐπενόησεν, "consider," "find out") even more courses in his surpassing wickedness (*Ant.* 8.316); in other words, the difference beween Ahab and his predecessors was merely quantitative. Indeed, Josephus goes on to make an additional extra-biblical point, namely that Ahab closely imitated (ἐκμιμησάμενος, "imitate faithfully," "represent exactly") his predecessors in their outrageous behavior (ὕβριν) toward the Divinity (τὸ θεῖον) (*ibid*). Whereas the Bible says that it was a light thing for Ahab to walk in the ways of King Jeroboam (1 Kings 16:31), Josephus seems to shift the blame even more to Jeroboam as his role-model by stating that, in particular (μάλιστα), he emulated (ζηλώσας, "admire," "strive after") the lawlessness (παρανομίαν) of Jeroboam and that he worshipped the heifers which Jeroboam had made (*Ant.* 8.317). Indeed, when, at a later point, after the conclusion of his main narrative about Ahab, Josephus refers to Ahab's son Ahaziah, he compares him to Jeroboam, noting that he was in all respects like both his parents and like Jeroboam (*Ant.* 9.18). The fact that he then remarks that Jeroboam was the first to transgress the laws and to lead his people astray downplays Ahab's guilt, since he was simply following in the tracks of his predecessor.

Moreover, it was not merely in wickedness (πονηρίᾳ) but also, perhaps more significantly, in folly (ἀνοίᾳ) that Josephus has Ahab surpassing his predecessors (*Ant.* 8.318); such folly clearly implies lack of understanding rather than deliberate and innate depravity or viciousness.

In addition to thus highlighting Jeroboam as the precedent for Ahab's wickedness, Josephus also puts more blame on Ahab's wife, Jezebel (*Ant.* 8.318). In his extra-biblical notice she is described as being the active (δραστήριον, "forceful," "energetic") and bold (τολμηρόν, "daring," "enterprising") partner in the marriage. Even the very word for "woman" which he uses for Jezebel here is the contemptuous neuter, τὸ γύναιον, as if she did not deserve to be referred to in the feminine gender. Whereas the Bible declares that it was Ahab who erected an altar to Baal and made an Asherah grove of trees for idol-worship (1 Kings 16:32-33), Josephus ascribes to her the building of the temple to Baal and the planting of the Asherah grove, and adds that she appointed priests and false prophets to Baal (*Ant.* 8.318). Ahab's wickedness is then ascribed (*Ant.* 8.318) to the bad influences upon him of these priests and false prophets rather than to any innate wickedness on his part.

4. *Ahab's Positive Qualities*

In a number of retouches of the biblical data Josephus seeks to upgrade Ahab's stature. Thus, whereas the Bible (1 Kings 18:6) states that during the drought both Ahab and Obadiah, who was in charge of his estate, went looking for grass for fodder for the animals, Josephus, realizing that such a portrait of Ahab looking for grass was degrading for a king, mentions only Obadiah as looking for grass; Ahab joins in the search, in an extra-biblical addition, only when the prophet Elijah is being looked for (*Ant.* 8.329-30).

Moreover, even in the case which constitutes the greatest blot upon Ahab's record, his dealings with Naboth, the reader will undoubtedly feel more sympathy for Ahab because, in Josephus' addition to the biblical account (1 Kings 21:6), Ahab tells his wife Jezebel how he had been insulted (ὑβρισθείη) by Naboth, who refused his request despite his having used mild (ἐπιεικέσι, "fitting," "suitable," "reasonable") words hardly in keeping with his royal authority (*Ant.* 8.356). Moreover, whereas the Bible does not represent Ahab as expressing regret in words for his action in this case (1 Kings 21:27), in Josephus he is genuinely regretful and admits that he has acted shamefully and has been taken by the prophet Elijah in sin (*Ant.* 8.361); moreover, he actually tells the prophet that he might do with him as he wished. In the biblical version, to be sure, Ahab rents his clothes and puts on sackcloth (1 Kings 21:27), but he does not verbalize, as does Josephus' Ahab, about his feelings of grief and remorse (μετάμελος, "contrition," "repentance") for what he has done (*Ant.* 8.362).

It is this sense of remorse which is a redeeming feature of the Josephan Ahab's character as it is of Saul's and David's. Indeed, so impressed is G-d with Ahab's repentance that he promises to put off punishing his family so long as Ahab is alive (*Ant.* 8.362), whereas in the Bible He is clearly less impressed, inasmuch as He declares that he will bring evil upon Ahab's house in his son's days (1 Kings 21:29).

Moreover, Ahab, in an extra-biblical addition, is depicted as listening to the nameless prophet who tells him to hold his forces in readiness for another attack by the Syrians in the following year (*Ant.* 8.378). The biblical account simply reports the words of the prophet without indicating the reaction of Ahab (1 Kings 20:22); but Josephus says specifically that Ahab attended to what the prophet told him (*Ant.* 8.378).

Furthermore, Josephus was very sensitive about the charge of cowardice that had been made against him personally and against the Jews in general. Hence, when the Syrian king Ben-hadad besieges Samaria, whereas in the Bible Ahab meekly submits, without explanation, offering Ben-hadad everything that he has (1 Kings 20:4), Josephus does present a plausible explanation of Ahab's response, namely that Ahab did not have an army equal to Ben-hadad's, and adds that he remained in Samaria since that city was surrounded by exceedingly strong walls (*Ant.* 8.364). The reader would most likely agree that this was a sound strategy. Greater sympathy for Ahab is likewise evoked in that, in contrast to Ben-hadad's statement in the Bible demanding that his messengers should be free to take whatever they wished from Ahab's kingdom (1 Kings 20:6), Josephus' Ben-hadad is more disdainful in placing the demand in the negative, namely that whatever does not please them will be left for Ahab (*Ant.* 8.367). At this point, in Josephus' addition, Ahab expresses his righteous indignation and proceeds to exhibit his leadership in that he summons the people to an assembly and his selflessness in that he declares himself ready to give up his own wives and children to the enemy and to yield all his possessions in the interest of their safety and peace (*Ant.* 8.368).

Moreover, Josephus' Ahab is more keenly analytical in discerning the true motives of Ben-hadad. In the Bible he says, simplistically, that Ben-hadad was seeking trouble (1 Kings 20:7); Josephus' Ahab astutely asserts the hypothesis that Ben-hadad was merely seeking a pretext for making war (*Ant.* 8.369). And yet, true leader that he is and, as such, concerned first and foremost with the welfare of his people, Ahab, in an extra-biblical addition, tells his people that he will do what they think best (*Ant.* 8.369). Again, he reiterates, in a statement that has no biblical parallel (1 Kings 20:9), that his first concern was for his citizens' safety (*Ant.* 8.370).

Ahab's bravery is all the greater due to Josephus' embellishing the biblical statement describing the terror tactics of Ben-hadad's army (1 Kings 20:10). In the Hebrew Bible the Syrian king exaggerates the size of his army by saying that the dust of Samaria would not suffice for handfuls for all the people who follow him (*ibid*). In Josephus' version Ben-hadad threatens that each man in his army would take a handful of earth and erect an earthwork higher than the walls in which Ahab had such confidence (*Ant.* 8.371). Again, Josephus paints a more dire picture of the siege undertaken by Ben-hadad, inasmuch as in the Bible Ben-hadad tells his men merely to set themselves in array against the city of Samaria (1 Kings 20:12), whereas in Josephus he gives orders to build a stockade around the city, to throw up earthworks, and, indeed, to leave nothing untried that might lead to its capture (*Ant.* 8.372).

In the meantime, Josephus, in an extra-biblical addition, once again stresses Ahab's concern for his people (*Ant.* 8.373). Ben-hadad's siege leaves him in a terrible state of anxiety, together with all his people, as Josephus puts it. But he is not one to be disheartened, and so we find, in another supplement to the Bible (1 Kings 20:13), that he takes heart (θαρρεῖ, "be courageous," "be brave," "be bold," "be of good cheer") and is relieved of his fears when a certain nameless prophet assures him that the enemy will be delivered into his hand (*Ant.* 8.373). Moreover, when Ahab, wounded in battle, withdraws from the fighting, this is not, as in Scripture (1 Kings 22:34), out of concern for his own condition, but, rather, because he wishes to keep up the morale of his soldiers, who might be disheartened by the sight of their mortally wounded leader (*Ant.* 8.415). Furthermore, Josephus stresses the personal courage of Ahab, inasmuch as, whereas the Bible says merely that the wounded Ahab remained propped up in his chariot until evening (1 Kings 22:35), Josephus adds that he did so even though he was in great pain (*Ant.* 8.415).

It is Ahab's qualities of leadership which are stressed by Josephus in the statement of the nameless prophet that it would be his (Ahab's) leadership, because of the inexperience of his administrators, which would prove decisive in gaining victory over Ben-hadad (*Ant.* 8.374). In the biblical remark the prophet promises victory without indicating the role which Ahab himself will play in achieving this (1 Kings 20:14).

Josephus, moreover, develops more than does the Bible the military strategy adopted by Ahab against Ben-hadad. The Bible does not mention the following details, as Josephus does, namely that Ahab had another army waiting within the walls, and that the sons of the nobles in Ahab's army engaged the Syrian guards and killed many of them, pursuing the rest as far as the camp (1 Kings 20:19 vs. *Ant.* 8.376). Then, when Ahab saw his men winning the victory, he astutely released his second army as well. Moreover, the Bible simply states that each of Ahab's soldiers killed his man and that Ahab's men pursued the fleeing Syrians (1 Kings 20:20). In Josephus' version we are given a number of additional details that highlight the ability of Ahab as a general who is particularly adept in taking advantage of the element of surprise (*Ant.* 8.377). In particular, we are told that Ahab's men suddenly fell upon the Syrians who were unarmed and drunk since they did not expect the attack and that the Syrian king barely saved himself by making his escape on horseback. Again, Josephus stresses the role of Ahab, who, we are told, went a long way in pursuit of the Syrians (*Ant.* 8.378), whereas the Bible says merely that he went out (1 Kings 20:21). The military victory achieved by Ahab is all the greater in Josephus in that he not only, as in the Bible, captures horses and chariots but also plunders the Syrian camp, thus acquiring a large sum of gold and silver (1 Kings 20:21 vs. *Ant.* 8.378). The scene here is clearly reminiscent of the extra-biblical details in Josephus' account of how Abraham determined to help the Sodomites without delay, and how he set out in haste and fell upon the Assyrians in an attack in which he caught the enemy by surprise before they had time to arm (*Ant.* 1.177). There, too, we find the enemy incapacitated by drunkenness.[4]

Again, at the beginning of the following spring, when Ben-hadad leads his army against Ahab's forces a second time, the biblical account says merely that the battle was joined and that a hundred thousand Syrian infantry were killed by the army of Israel in one day, without a word about the leadership of Israel's army (1 Kings 20:29). By contrast, in Josephus' version we are specifically told that it was Ahab who led his forces against the Syrians (*Ant.* 8.382). Furthermore, the biblical narrative says nothing about the nature or difficulty of the battle (1 Kings 20:29), whereas Josephus adds a number of details, namely that the battle was stubbornly fought,

---

[4] In his description of David's surprise attack on the Amalekites and of his massacre of them, Josephus similarly adds that he fell upon some who, under the influence of drink, were plunged in sleep (*Ant.* 6.363).

and that it was Ahab who took the lead in putting the enemy to flight and who followed hard in pursuit (*Ant.* 8.383). Moreover, the reader would almost certainly wonder how it was possible for this small Israelite army – according to 1 Kings 20:15, when Ahab mustered all the people of Israel, he was able to gather an army of only seven thousand – to kill a hundred thousand soldiers in one day. Hence, Josephus explains that in their confusion the enemy were killed by their own chariots and by one another (*Ant.* 8.383).

We also see Ahab's wisdom in dealing with his troops in that before going into battle he is depicted, in an addition that has no counterpart in the Bible (1 Kings 22:4), as distributing pay to his army (*Ant.* 8.399). His doing so would help to ensure the loyalty of his troops, as Josephus, himself a general in Galilee in the war against the Romans, well realized (so Begg 1989a, 229-30).

Likewise, in his diplomatic initiatives Ahab is depicted more honorably by Josephus. Thus we read in the biblical Hebrew narrative that Ahab used guile in persuading (*vayesitehu*)[5] Jehoshaphat, the king of Judah, to enter into an alliance with him against the king of the Syrians (2 Chronicles 18:2); but in Josephus' version this becomes "invited" (παρεκάλεσε, "encouraged," "urged") (*Ant.* 8.398).

Similarly, Josephus has toned down the imperiousness of Ahab in his dealings with Jehoshaphat. Thus, whereas in the Hebrew Bible Ahab dictates to Jehoshaphat rather than consulting him on his battle plans (1 Kings 22:30), in Josephus the two kings agree, on an apparent plane of equality, that Ahab should remove his royal garments and that Jehoshaphat should take his place in the line of battle (*Ant.* 8.412).

Moreover, Josephus, from his own experience with the Romans in the Jewish revolt of 66-74, was well aware of the concept of a "just war," which can be waged only when there is clear evidence of a prior unjust assault and when all attempts at a peaceful solution have failed (see Cicero, *De Officiis* 1.11.34-36; *De Re Publica* 3.23.34-35). Hence, it is significant that whereas the biblical context states merely that Ahab told the servants of Jehoshaphat, the king of Judah, that Ramoth-gilead, which was in the hands of the

---

[5] The Septuagint here reads ἠγάπα, "desired"; but this is clearly a corruption of ἠπάτα, "deceived," as Marcus, on *Antiquities* 8.398 remarks.

king of Syria, really belonged to him (Ahab) (1 Kings 22:3), Josephus expatiates by giving the history of Ahab's claim, namely that the city had first belonged to his father and that it had been taken away by the father of the Syrian king (*Ant.* 8.399). Furthermore, Ahab is a respecter of peace who refuses to be party to its disruption without prior prophetic authorization (*Ant.* 8.401) (so Begg 1989a, 230-31).

Again, even though Josephus acknowledges that Ahab was guilty of idol-worship (*Ant.* 8.316-17), the picture given is far from being totally black, inasmuch as the king does show regard for the prophecy of the true prophet, Micaiah. In particular, after Micaiah foretells Ahab's death (*Ant.* 8.405), instead of fulminating against him, Ahab, we are told in an addition to the biblical narrative (1 Kings 22:24), had cause for thought (ἐννοίᾳ, "reflection," "consideration," "deliberation," "comprehension," "understanding") (*Ant.* 8.406), and that it was only because the false prophet Zedekiah convinced him, by seeming to show that he had been contradicted by a greater prophet, Elijah, and that consequently Micaiah did not speak a word of truth that he stopped listening to Micaiah. It is hard to blame Ahab in this instance, given Josephus' addition to the biblical text (1 Kings 22:24-25), i.e., Ahab took courage from the fact that when the false prophet Zedekiah struck the true prophet Micaiah he suffered no harm as a result (*Ant.* 8.408-9).

Indeed, in one of his relatively rare editorial comments, Josephus goes out of his way not to blame Ahab for heeding the false prophet. Rather, he says, "It was Fate (τὸ χρεών), I suppose (οἶμαι), that prevailed and made the false prophet more convincing than the true one, in order to hasten Achab's [Ahab's] end" (*Ant.* 8.409). The fact that in a very similar editorial comment Josephus ascribes the death of the good king Josiah not to G-d, as does the biblical text (2 Chronicles 35:21), but to destiny (πεπρωμένης, clearly a synonym for τὸ χρεών), which urged him on to do battle with Necho, the king of Egypt, "in order to have a pretext for destroying him," (*Ant.* 10.76) would clearly indicate that, in Josephus' eyes, fate is utterly capricious and makes no distinction between the good and the bad.[6] That this equation of Ahab

---

[6] See the comment by Begg (1988a, 161-62). As Begg (162, n. 13) points out, in speaking of Josiah's being wounded by one, as opposed to several, archers (2 Chronicles 35:23), Josephus actually enhances the parallel between Josiah and Ahab, since Ahab is wounded by a single bowman (1 Kings 22:34, 2 Chronicles

and Josiah is not merely a concession to his Hellenistic audience, which regarded fate as all-powerful, may be seen from the further fact that in Josephus' presentation it is not fate but G-d that urged King Amaziah of Judah in his foolish attack on King Joram of Israel (*Ant.* 9.199 = 2 Chronicles 25:20) (so Begg 1988a, 161). We may also guess that the emphasis on the fact that Ahab had been deceived by the false prophets represents Josephus' commentary on contemporary affairs and, in particular, on the misleading of the rebels against Rome by their revolutionary leaders and on the failure of true prophets – most notably, of course (at least in his own eyes), Josephus himself – to dissuade the people from following these false leaders (so Blenkinsopp 1974, 243).

5. *Apologetics*

If Josephus does criticize Ahab it is on the ground that, especially in the case of his dealings with Naboth, he violated his country's laws (πατρίους νόμους) (see *Ant.* 8.361) as against the biblical version, in which the prophet Elijah merely says, "Have you killed, and also taken possession?" (1 Kings 21:19). Realizing that the word "law" in and of itself was such an important concept to the Romans, who felt so much pride in their legal achievements, and that the possible conflict between the law of the state and the law of the Jews implied an irreconcilable conflict between the two sanctions, Josephus stressed the fairness and humanity of Jewish law. Josephus, in appraising the kings, has turned the biblical "They did what was wicked" into contempt for the constitution and failure to study and observe the laws accurately (so S. Schwartz 1990, 179).

In the biblical narrative Ben-hadad's servants tell him that they have heard that the kings of Israel are merciful and that if they put on sackcloth and ropes perhaps Ahab will spare his life (1 Kings 20:31). Josephus embellishes this by having the servants tell Ben-hadad that the Israelite kings are merciful and humane (φιλανθρώπους), the latter word denoting the direct opposite of misanthropes that the Jews were accused of being (*Ant.* 8.385).

In a similar situation, where Saul spares Agag, the king of the Amalekites (*Ant.* 6.137), Josephus, who generally does not theolo-

18:33). Similarly, we may add, he stresses that Fate involves both the innocent and the guilty in a common ruin.

gize, explains, in an unscriptural passage, that G-d refused to pardon Saul on the ground that to show mercy and kindness to the wrong-doer is to beget crime unwittingly and to encourage the increase of the oppression (*Ant.* 6.144). It is significant that there is no such Josephan criticism of Ahab, who is depicted rather, in an extra-biblical detail, as rejoicing that Ben-hadad had survived the battle and as magnanimously promising that he would show him the same honor and good will that he would accord his own brother (*Ant.* 8.386; cf. 1 Kings 20:32).

Moreover, Josephus, in an unscriptural detail, shows how much regard Ahab had for a suppliant – a crucial article of faith for the ancient Greeks and Romans, as we see, for example, in the famous scene in the *Iliad* (Book 24) in which Achilles shows regard to the aged Priam, who comes begging for the return of his son Hector, whom Achilles had slain – in that he gives his oath not to do any harm to Ben-hadad (*Ant.* 8.386). Indeed, Josephus paints a vivid scene, expanding upon the brief biblical statement (1 Kings 20:33) that Ahab caused Ben-hadad to come up into his chariot. In this Josephan expansion Ahab gives Ben-hadad his right hand, embraces him, and bids him to take heart and not be apprehensive of any outrage, whereupon Ben-hadad thanks him and promises to show himself mindful of his beneficence (εὐεργεσίας) all the days of his life (*Ant.* 8.387). Not only does Ahab then proceed to make a covenant with Ben-hadad, as mentioned in the Bible (1 Kings 20:34), but he also presents him with many gifts (*Ant.* 8.388), in accordance with the custom in establishing guest-friendships, as we see in Homer, in the instance of Glaucus and Diomedes (*Iliad* 6.212-36). When finally Josephus does criticize Ahab for being merciful toward Ben-hadad, it is not because he had allowed Ben-hadad to go free when he had been doomed to destruction in battle, but rather because he had allowed Ben-hadad, who had committed the unforgivable crime of blasphemy against G-d, to escape punishment (*Ant.* 8.391).

6. *Hellenizations*

In the Ahab pericope Josephus increases suspense with his statement, unparalleled in the biblical source (1 Kings 18:8), that Ahab sent men throughout the inhabited earth (οἰκουμένην) to look for the prophet Elijah but that they had been unable to find him (*Ant.*

8.329). This theme is repeated, and the drama increased, a few lines later, when Ahab's bailiff Obadiah, in an addition to the biblical text (1 Kings 18:10), asks Elijah whether he does not know that the king had not overlooked a single place to which he might send men to seize Elijah (*Ant.* 8.332). Likewise, whereas in the biblical account Obadiah, rather implausibly, recognizes Elijah as soon as he sees him (1 Kings 18:7), there is more drama, as well as greater plausibility, in Josephus' version, wherein when Obadiah meets the prophet he first inquires of him who he is and only then does obeisance to him (*Ant.* 8.331).

There is likewise increased drama in Josephus' version of the incident of Naboth's vineyard. Thus, in the Bible Ahab tells Naboth that he is ready to give him a better vineyard or its worth in money (1 Kings 21:2); Josephus' Ahab, more dramatically, tells Naboth that he is willing to give him any price for the vineyard (*Ant.* 8.356). Moreover, the effect of Naboth's refusal to sell him the field is more dramatic in that Ahab, in his grief, not only refuses to eat but also declines to bathe. There is likewise added excitement in that whereas in the Bible when Ahab hears that Naboth is dead he rises to go down to Naboth's vineyard in order to take possession of it (1 Kings 21:16), in Josephus' version he leaps up (ἀναπηδήσας, "jump up") from his bed in his pleasure at the turn of events (*Ant.* 8.360).

Furthermore, there is irony in Josephus' treatment of the Naboth episode, in that, according to Josephus' addition to the biblical source (1 Kings 21:9), Naboth, who is said, in an unscriptural detail, to come from an illustrious family, presides over the very assembly which condemns him to death (*Ant.* 8.358).

Finally, Josephus' version of the death of Ahab (*Ant.* 8.409, 418-420) shows his tendency to restate Jewish concepts of divine power and prophetic determination in terms of the classical Greek concepts of fate and tragic destiny, as found especially in Greek tragedy[7] and in Herodotus (see Blenkinsopp 1974, 239-62).[8] The an-

---

[7] Compare, for example, the statement of the Chorus in Euripides' *Hippolytus* when they behold the blameless Hippolytus in his stricken state. Though they feel anger at the gods (1146), yet, as they know, there is no escape from what must be (1256, τοῦ χρεών). Similarly, in Euripides' *Helen* (1301), the Dioscuri declare that they did not save their sister Clytemnestra, "for Moira's compulsion (ἀνάγκη) led where it must (τὸ χρεών)."

[8] In Herodotus (7.14-18), after a delusive dream warns Xerxes that unless he

cient reader, of course, would think of Laius and Oedipus who, as much as they tried to avoid the fate about which they had been warned by the oracle, failed to do so. Similarly, Hecabe, before giving birth to Paris, dreamed that she had given birth to a firebrand that consumed all of Troy and consequently exposed the infant, only to have him suckled by a bear, found by a shepherd, and eventually raised to fulfill the prophecy (Apollodorus 3.12.5; Hyginus, *Fabula* 91). Or again, an oracle foretold that the son of Danae, the daughter of King Acrisius of Argos, was destined to kill Acrisius, whereupon he shut her up in an underground chamber, only to have Zeus visit her and beget a child, Perseus, who, indeed, fulfilled the prophecy (Apollodorus 2.4.1; Hyginus, *Fabula* 63). Thus we see, as Chrysippus the Stoic put it, that there was no way in all of these cases to avoid the dire predictions because of the necessity that is part of Fate (so von Arnim 1905, 1:270-71).

It is significant that in the Bible it is, according to Micaiah, a lying spirit sent by G-d into the mouths of false prophets that leads Ahab to his death (1 Kings 22:19-23), whereas in Josephus Fate has taken the place of this lying spirit, and there is no mention of G-d's role at all in the deception (*Ant.* 8.409). Indeed, in a comment which has no basis in the biblical text (1 Kings 22:30), Josephus explains the motive of Ahab's disguising himself as he went into battle, namely to avoid his fated end, while also making it clear that such tricks cannot fool Fate (*Ant.* 8.412). In particular, the extra-biblical idea of τὸ χρεών ("necessity"), which he introduces here, entering into the soul of a doomed man through some psychological flaw is closely paralleled in Greek tragedy.

Indeed, we may note that of the twelve occurrences in Josephus of the term τὸ χρεών three occur in this brief section dealing with Ahab's death (*Ant.* 8.409, 412, 419).[9] Similar cases may be seen in

---

undertakes the war against Greece he would be brought low as swiftly as he became great, a similar dream occurs to Artabanus, Xerxes' uncle, warning him against opposing "what must be" (7.17, τὸ χρεόν), whereupon Xerxes is convinced that this is a divine warning.

[9] The term τὸ χρεών in Josephus seems to be equated with that which is inevitable, and, in particular, death. Thus, when David is about to die he tells his son Solomon that he is now going to his destiny (τὸ χρεών) (*Ant.* 7.383). Similarly, we are told, Baasha, the king of Israel, had no further opportunity to march against Asa, the king of Judah, because he was very soon overcome by Fate (τοῦ χρεών) (*Ant.* 8.307). Πεπρωμένος, in the sense of that which has been destined and must be, is clearly a synonym of τὸ χρεών, as we can see in Josephus' state

the doom of Saul (*Ant.* 6.335) and of Josiah (*Ant.* 10.76), as well as of Herod (*Ant.* 16.396-404).[10]

Since, as Josephus emphasizes in his proem, his history is intended to teach a moral lesson (*Ant.* 1.14), he pauses at the end of his long pericope on Ahab to preach (*Ant.* 8.419). The subject of his sermon is the power of Fate, as being so great that not even with foreknowledge is it possible to escape it, since, as he says, "it secretly enters the souls of men and flatters them with fair hope and thereby leads them on to the point where it can overcome them."

It is Josephus' general practice after discussing an important biblical personality to summarize the chief qualities of his character.[11] Significantly, there is no such summary, whether positive or

---

ment that despite the fact that Daniel had predicted an evil end for Beshazzar, the latter did not withhold from him the gifts that he had promised, on the ground that Daniel was not responsible for this doom but rather that it was part of Belshazzar's peculiar and inexorable destiny (ἀνάγκης, alternate reading πεπρωμένης) (*Ant.* 10.246). A similar usage, in the sense of one's unalterable lot, may be seen in the passage in which King Agrippa I sees an owl which he recognizes as a harbinger of woe and concludes, from this omen, that he must accept his lot (πεπρωμένην) as G-d wills it (*Ant.* 19.347). Elsewhere, in his discussion of the death of Zedekiah, Josephus stresses, as he does in the case of the prophecies made to Ahab, that what has been foretold by G-d must necessarily come to pass and at the appointed time, and that any attempt to escape from one's fate is doomed to failure (*Ant.* 10.142).

In the *War* τὸ χρεών is clearly equivalent to inexorable Fate, which even transcends death and may lead, indeed, to a premature death, as we see, for example, in Josephus' remark that Destiny (τὸ χρεών) derided Malichus' hopes of raising a national revolt against the Romans, of deposing Hyrcanus, and of mounting the throne himself (*War* 1.233). Again, we read that Fate (τὸ χρεών) outstripped Herod's zeal (*War* 1.275). A similar usage may be seen in Josephus' statement that during the siege of Jerusalem many Jews went forth to their death even before Fate (τὸ χρεών) was upon them (*War* 5.514). Furthermore, the revolutionaries, we are told, were blinded by Fate (τοῦ χρεών), which was now imminent (*War* 5.572). That τὸ χρεών is equivalent to the inevitable may be discerned from the statement of Titus to his troops that if men are doomed to an inevitable end it would be ignoble to deny to the public service what must be surrendered to Fate (τῷ χρεών) (*War* 6.49). Josephus makes it clear, when he comments on the oracle which incited the Jews to revolt against the Romans, that "it is impossible for men to escape their fate (τὸ χρεών) even though they foresee it" (*War* 6.314).

[10] This would tend to indicate that the Sophoclean elements, with their emphasis on the tragedy of Fate, are not restricted to the books ascribed to the Sophoclean assistant but are indeed found in a number of other books as well. See Feldman 1984, 827-30.

[11] Cf., e.g., Abraham (*Ant.* 1.256), Isaac (*Ant.* 1.346), Jacob (*Ant.* 2.196), Joseph (*Ant.* 2.198), Moses (*Ant.* 4.328-31), Joshua (*Ant.* 5.118), Samson (*Ant.* 5.317),

negative, for Ahab. Instead, we are, as just noted, given a sermon pointing out that Ahab's mind was deceived by the power of Fate and thus, in effect, exculpating him (*Ant.* 8.420).

7. *Summary*

In his portrait of Ahab Josephus treads a tightrope. On the one hand, he could not deny the negative traits assigned to him in the Bible and expanded upon by the rabbinic tradition. On the other hand, like the rabbis, he saw positive virtues in Ahab. In particular, Josephus shifts more of the blame to Ahab's role-model Jeroboam and to his wife Jezebel. Even in the incident with Naboth Ahab is at least partly exculpated because he had used mild words with Naboth and yet had been insulted. Moreover, as in his portraits of Saul and of David, Josephus stresses Ahab's remorse for his treatment of Naboth.

The fact that the Jews, and Josephus in particular, had been accused of being cowards adds great significance to his presentation of Ahab as a great tactician and a brave leader who is, above all, concerned for his people, as we see especially in his eagerness to keep up the morale of his soldiers even after he has been gravely wounded. Likewise, in his diplomatic activities he is depicted more honorably than in the Bible.

In a rare editorial comment Josephus goes out of his way to absolve Ahab of blame for listening to a false prophet; his doing so is due rather to inexorable and inevitable Fate, even as Fate is the culprit in effecting the end of the good king Josiah.

Moreover, Josephus uses the Ahab pericope in order to answer the recurrent charge that the Jews are guilty of hatred of mankind. Thus Ahab, in Josephus' portrait, is deliberately depicted as merciful and humane in his treatment of Ben-hadad. Indeed, Ahab establishes a guest-friendship with Ben-hadad which goes considerably beyond what we find in the Bible.

Because his work is intended for an audience that had an appreciation of Greek literature, it is not surprising that we find that in his portrait of Ahab, as in his portraits of other biblical figures,

---

Samuel (Ant. 6.292-94), Saul (*Ant.* 6.343-50), David (*Ant.* 7.390-91), Solomon (*Ant.* 8.211), and Elisha (*Ant.* 9.182).

Josephus increases suspense and dramatic excitement. In particular, the irony is accentuated, especially in his treatment of the Naboth episode. Josephus' heightening of the role of Fate and tragic destiny is highly reminiscent of their role in the Greek tragedians and Herodotus, who are his frequent models elsewhere.

CHAPTER NINETEEN

ELIJAH

1. *Introduction*

Though one might think that the prophets would be relatively unimportant in a work devoted to history, as is the *Antiquities*, for Josephus they are of supreme importance for his account of the biblical period because precision is a crucial quality in a history (*War* 1.2, 1.6; *Ant.* 1.17) and because, as he says, it is the prophets alone who, due to the inspiration which they received from G-d, guarantee the accuracy of the narratives which they committed to writing (*Ag. Ap.* 1.37). Moreover, Josephus regarded himself as having a special gift for prediction, which he used to good advantage in foretelling that Vespasian would become emperor (*War* 3.400-2).[1] Despite the fact that whole long books of the Bible are devoted to the prophecies of Isaiah, Jeremiah, and Ezekiel, by far the most popular and, from the point of view of Jewish hopes and aspirations, the most important prophet is Elijah. Indeed, his mystic presence at every circumcision and at the Passover Seder is a clue to his importance even unto today. Moreover, already the prophet Malachi prophesies that Elijah will play a key role at the end of days and will be the great reconciler of the generations. As he puts it, "Before the great and terrible day of the L-rd," G-d will send Elijah to the Jews, and "he will turn the hearts of fathers to their children and the hearts of children to their fathers" (3:23-24). Furthermore, it is said that through him the resurrection of the dead will occur (Mishnah, *Soṭah* 9:15 end). In the words of Josephus' likely contemporary Pseudo-Philo it is Elijah (whom he identifies with the biblical Phinehas) who will shut the heaven and at whose word, at the time of the resurrection, it will be reopened (*Bib. Ant.* 48.1).

And yet, as we shall see, the rabbis were in something of a quandary with regard to Elijah. On the one hand, he is depicted as a great champion of the Jewish people and as a great national hero.

---

[1] On the importance of the biblical prophets to Josephus see Feldman (1990, 387-94).

Specifically, it is he, according to tradition, who, by getting the Patriarchs and Moses to intervene with G-d, saved the Jews from being exterminated by Haman (*Esther Rabbah* 7.13, 10.9). He is said to be superior even to the angels, since an angel never assumes the form of a woman, whereas Elijah, on at least one occasion, took the form of a harlot (*'Avodah Zarah* 18b). He is even compared to Moses himself, in that both were granted revelations at Mount Sinai in similar circumstances (Exodus 3:2, 19:16-20:21, Deuteronomy 4:10-5:33, 1 Kings 19:11-12); again, just as Moses was G-d's agent in freeing the Israelites from Egyptian bondage, so Elijah will be G-d's agent in the future redemption of the Jewish people, in which Moses will also participate.[2] In a land frequently afflicted with drought he is said, in the words of the first-century B.C.E. Simeon ben Shetah, to have the keys of rain (*Ta'anit* 23a).

Most significant is Elijah's role as the forerunner of the Messiah, a role which we certainly find at least as early as the first century, when Jesus is at first believed to be Elijah. When, however, he reveals his own messianic claims, he proclaims John the Baptist as the Elijah who precedes the Messiah (Matthew 11:10-15, 17:10-13; Mark 9:11-13). If, as we have good reason to believe, Josephus was acquainted with many rabbinic traditions, he may well have been aware of the depiction of Elijah as not only a precursor but also as a close associate of the Messiah (see, for example, *Leviticus Rabbah* 34.8, *Ruth Rabbah* 5.6). It is Elijah who reveals to the third-century Rabbi Joshua ben Levi where the Messiah is to be found, i.e., among the beggars of Rome, ready to redeem the Jewish people (*Sanhedrin* 98a). Like the Messiah, Elijah plays a political role as a world conqueror (*Song of Songs Rabbah* 2.13, no. 4) who is destined to overthrow the heathen realms (*Genesis Rabbah* 71.9).

Because of his close association with the Messiah, whose principal achievement will be to create a truly independent Jewish state, we should not be surprised to find that Elijah is depicted as strongly opposed to the Roman Empire. It is he who assists Rabbi Simeon bar Yohai when the latter is fleeing from the Romans (*Shabbat* 33b) and who reproaches Rabbi Ishmael ben Yose, who had been co-operating with the Romans in delivering Jews to them for execution (*Baba Mezia* 83b-84a). Similarly, when Rabbi Joshua

---

[2] See *Pesiqta Rabbati* 4.13 for an extensive comparison of Moses and Elijah. On the juxtaposition of Moses and Elijah see also Matthew 17:3-4, Mark 9:4-5, and Luke 9:30-31.

ben Levi, who was actually acting in accordance with Mishnaic law in so doing, persuaded a Jew to surrender to the Romans and thus to save the entire Jewish community of Lydda, Elijah, who had been accustomed to visit Rabbi Joshua frequently, shunned him for a month (Jerusalem Talmud *Terumah* 8.10.46b, *Genesis Rabbah* 94.9).

The fact that Josephus' presumed contemporary Pseudo-Philo, in his *Biblical Antiquities* (48.1-2), identifies Elijah with Phinehas, the biblical zealot who took the law into his own hands (Numbers 25:7-8) and slew the Israelite Zimri who was having relations with a Midianite woman,[3] is an indication of Elijah's status as the prototype of all later zealots, including, we may presume, the revolutionaries of Josephus' own day. Similarly, in rabbinic literature Elijah is identified with Phinehas and is regarded as immortal (*Pirqe de-Rabbi Eliezer* 47; *Baba Batra* 121 b; *Genesis Rabbah* 21.5, 25.1; *Numbers Rabbah* 21.3.).

And yet, it is, apparently, precisely this identification of Elijah with Phinehas that led the rabbis to have ambivalent feelings toward Elijah. Such a leading rabbinic figure as Josephus' contemporary, Rabbi Johanan ben Zakkai, sought an accommodation with the Romans, as we can see from his arranging to have himself secreted out of the city of Jerusalem while it was being besieged by the Romans and his greeting the general Vespasian as emperor (*Giṭṭin* 56a-b; *'Avot de-Rabbi Nathan* [1] 4.22-24, [2] 6.19; and *Lamentations Rabbah* 1.5, no. 31). We see a similar readiness to reach an accommodation with the Romans on the part of Johanan's leading student, Rabbi Joshua ben Hananiah, who tried to influence the Jews not to rebel against Hadrian by telling the famous fable of the crane that extracted a thorn from the throat of a lion and that, when he demanded a reward for his deed, was told by the lion to be satisfied that he had allowed him to live (*Genesis Rabbah*

---

[3] Other passages identifying Elijah with Phinehas are in the Palestinian Targum on Exodus 6:18, Numbers 25:12, and Deuteronomy 30:4, *Numbers Rabbah* 21.3, *Tanḥuma Pinehas* 1 (cited by Ginzberg 1928, 6:316, n. 3). Ginzberg incorrectly cites *Pirqe de-Rabbi Eliezer* 44 in this connection. Add Jerome, *Quaestiones Hebraeae in Libros Regum* on 1 Samuel 2. Spiro (1953, 238) construes the identification of Phinehas and Elijah as part of a polemic against the Samaritans, inasmuch as the latter maintained that Phinehas had functioned as a priest on Mount Gerizim, emphatically denied his immortality, and insisted that his descendants continued to preside as priests among them.

64.10), the implication being that the Jews should be content not to be oppressed by the Romans.

Hence, despite his tremendous popularity, we actually find criticism of Elijah in rabbinic literature. Thus, for revealing to Rabbi Judah the Prince the divine secret that Rabbi Ḥiyya and his sons could by their prayers force G-d to fulfill their wishes, Elijah is said to have been punished by sixty flaming lashes (*Baba Meẓia* 85b). Again, G-d Himself is depicted (*Song of Songs Rabbah* 1.6, no. 1) as being so angry with Elijah for having denounced the Jews' violations of the Torah that He dismissed him and appointed Elisha in his stead. Indeed, the rabbis, far from stressing Elijah's fiery zeal, restrict his role to resolving halakhic disputes that had remained undecided and to restoring peace to the world (Mishnah, '*Eduyyot* 8:7; Tosefta, '*Eduyyot* 3.4).

Josephus, then, like the rabbis, was in a dilemma as to how much importance to give to Elijah and how to treat him. How could Josephus, who had surrendered to the Romans at Jotapata and had been given so many gifts by them – a tract of land outside Jerusalem, some sacred books, the liberation of some friends, Roman citizenship, lodging in the former palace of Vespasian, and a pension – aggrandize a figure who was apparently a forerunner of the Zealots that had fought so tenaciously against the Romans and who was so closely allied with the Messiah, whose function it was to overthrow the Roman Empire and to establish an independent Jewish state?

And yet, Josephus was clearly aware that large numbers of Jews, probably the majority certainly in the Diaspora, in his day did not speak or read Aramaic or Hebrew with any degree of fluency but rather regarded Greek as their first language and read the Scriptures in Greek. Moreover, his highlighting of certain episodes, notably the incident of Israel's sin with the Midianite women (Numbers 25:1-9, *Ant.* 4.131-55) and Samson's relations with alien women (Judges 14:1-16:31; *Ant.* 5.286-313), is directed, apparently, to those Jews who sought assimilation with Gentiles. Similarly, Josephus (*Ant.* 4.150-51) vehemently condemns Zambrias (Zimri) and bestows exalted praise upon Phinehas, "a man superior in every way to the rest of the youth" (*Ant.* 4.152), who, after all, might well have been condemned for taking the law into his own hands in putting Zambrias to death without a trial.

In view, too, of Elijah's popularity as a folk-hero of the Jewish masses, Josephus could hardly afford to downgrade him. A similar dilemma confronted him in connection with King Hezekiah, of whom there were claims that he was the Messiah.[4] Similarly, we may note, Josephus omits all reference to David as ancestor of the Messiah, despite the fact that such a tradition must have been widespread in his era, because he wished to make clear to his Hellenistic Jewish readers his own repugnance to an independent Jewish state.

One indication of the amount of interest that a given personality has for Josephus may be seen in the sheer amount of space that he devotes to him. The ratio for the Elijah episode (1 Kings 17-19, 21.17-29, 2 Kings 1.3-2.12; Josephus, *Ant.* 8.319-354, 360-362, 9.20-28) is 1.52 for Josephus as compared with the Hebrew and .96 for Josephus as compared with the Septuagint.[5] Hence, we see that Elijah is relatively important for him, but certainly less so than several other biblical personalities. It is also significant that whereas it is Josephus' practice to present an encomium for his various biblical heroes following their deaths, and whereas he has an encomium of 26 words for Elijah's successor Elisha (*Ant.* 9.182), he has none at all for Elijah.

2. *Elijah's Qualities of Leadership*

Like Thucydides and Plato, Josephus emphasizes the importance of leadership. Thus, whereas in the Bible Elijah is quoted as saying

---

[4] On the one hand, Josephus was proud of Hezekiah as a Jewish king who was noted for his virtues, especially that of piety. On the other hand, Josephus, as a descendant of the Hasmoneans, a dynasty which was not of Davidic descent, could hardly identify with the line of David. Hence, he even goes to the extreme of asserting that it was out of cowardice (δειλίας) that Hezekiah did not come out himself to meet the Assyrians when they encamped before the walls of Jerusalem and summoned him to parley with them but sent three of his friends instead (*Ant.* 10.5). Secondly, Josephus must have been wary of any claims that Hezekiah was the Messiah, inasmuch as his Roman patrons, to the extent that they were aware of the beliefs of Jewish messianism, would have objected to such a political figure who would seek to re-establish an independent Jewish state, precisely the goal of the revolutionaries against Rome in Josephus' own day whom he attacks so bitterly.

[5] There is some reason to think that Josephus used the Septuagint version for the Elijah pericope, as he did for most of the Bible, inasmuch as he agrees with the Septuagint in identifying Jehoram as the brother of Ahaziah at the point when the former succeeds to the throne (2 Kings 1:17; *Ant.* 9.27).

to the poverty-stricken widow, very simply, "Fear not" (1 Kings 17:13), Josephus has considerably expanded his words of encouragement, "Even so, be of good courage (θαρσοῦσα), and go your way in hope of (προσδοκῶσα, 'expecting,' 'anticipating') better things" (*Ant.* 8.322). Somewhat later these words of encouragement are repeated; thus, whereas in the biblical text Elijah simply tells the widow, "Give me your son" (1 Kings 17:19), Josephus' Elijah urges (παρεκελεύετο) her to take heart (θαρρεῖν) and to give her son over to him (*Ant.* 8.326). Likewise, whereas the biblical text asserts only that Elijah swore to Ahab's emissary Obadiah that he (Elijah) would show himself to Ahab on that very day (1 Kings 18:15), Josephus turns this oath into words of encouragement, Elijah bidding Obadiah to go without fear to the king (*Ant.* 8.334). In these instances Josephus' Roman audience might well have recalled the great leadership of Aeneas, who, after they have suffered so many tribulations, was able to inspire his comrades with very similar words of encouragement: "Revive your courage (*revocate animos*).... Preserve yourselves for favorable tidings (*vosmet rebus servate secundis*)" (Virgil, *Aeneid* 1.202, 207).

From the biblical statement one might conclude that Elijah was guilty of self-incrimination in that, when he flees from Jezebel to the wilderness he in his despair asks G-d to take his life, "for I am no better than my fathers" (1 Kings 19:4). Realizing that a true leader must be an example of unceasing hope to his followers, Josephus presents, in justification, an explanation of this despair, namely that Elijah felt that he was no better than his fathers that he should long for life when they were gone (*Ant.* 8.348). He thus depicts Elijah as a prototype of *pietas* in the sense, so closely identified with Virgil's Aeneas, of devotion to one's ancestors.

A great leader must be able to choose and train a successor who will carry on his work. Thus, before choosing Joshua, Moses, according to an extra-biblical detail introduced by Josephus, had already indoctrinated him with a thorough training in the laws and in divine lore (*Ant.* 4.165). Elijah's power in inspiring his successor is nowhere demonstrated more graphically than in Josephus' addition, not found in the Bible (1 Kings 19:20), that after Elijah threw his mantle upon Elisha the latter immediately began to prophesy and, leaving his oxen, followed Elijah (*Ant.* 8.354).

3. *Elijah's Qualities of Character*

One basic reason for Josephus' great interest in the prophets is that he regards them as his predecessors as historians of the past. Indeed, a crucial common denominator between prophecy and history is that the overriding goal of both is to get at the truth.[6]

Hence, when Josephus, in an addition to the Bible, states that Elijah did not flatter King Ahab in the least (οὐδὲν ὑποθωπεύσας) (1 Kings 18:18), he is establishing Elijah's credentials both as a prophet and as a historian. In addition, we may note that, according to Herodotus (1.30), who uses the very same language, the same refusal to flatter characterized the famous wise man Solon, who, when asked by King Croesus of Lydia who was the happiest man he had ever seen, refused to flatter him (οὐδὲν ὑποθωπεύσας) and answered him, "An Athenian named Tellus."

Another quality of Elijah which is stressed by Josephus is his steadfastness. Thus, the Bible reports that King Ahaziah's messengers, who had been sent by him to inquire of Baalzebub whether he would recover from his illness, informed the king that a nameless man had met them and had told them to return to the king and to inform him that he would not recover (2 Kings 1:6). In Josephus' version the man, that is Elijah, is described as actively preventing them from going any further (*Ant.* 9.21).

This steadfastness is further illustrated in Elijah's defiance of the threats of the officer of King Ahaziah, who orders him to descend from the top of a hill and to go to the king (2 Kings 1:9). This threat is magnified in Josephus, who declares that the officer threatened that if Elijah refused he would force him to go against his will (*Ant.* 9.23). In another extra-biblical addition, Josephus mentions that a second officer threatened the prophet that he would seize him by force if he did not come down willingly, but Elijah steadfastly refused (*Ant.* 9.24).

---

[6] On the crucial importance of ascertaining the truth in history, see the remarks of Josephus' idol, Thucydides (1.22.2): "As to the facts of the occurrences of the war, I have thought it my duty to give them, not as ascertained from any chance informant nor as seemed to me probable, but only after investigating with the great possible accuracy each detail, in the case both of the events in which I myself participated and of those regarding which I got my information from others."

298   CHAPTER NINETEEN

4. *The Miracles Performed by Elijah*

In connection with Elijah, Josephus, aware of his popularity with the masses, apparently had concluded that he could not utterly suppress such miracles as Elijah's raising of the widow's son from the dead (*Ant.* 8.325-27) and his spectacular victory over the priests of Baal (*Ant.* 8.336-42). That, in the popular mind, Elijah's dominant association was with miracles may be seen in the Gospels, where, immediately after mention of the miracles which Jesus and his followers perform, notably in casting out devils and in healing the sick, he is identified as Elijah (Mark 6:15). Nevertheless, Josephus tones down the miracle of the feeding of Elijah by the ravens. A skeptical pagan might well be astonished to read the biblical statement that G-d commanded the ravens to feed Elijah and might well wonder whether G-d gives commands to birds (1 Kings 17:2-4); hence in Josephus' version we are told, much more plausibly, merely that the ravens brought food to him every day, presumably of their own accord (*Ant.* 8.319). Even the extent of the miracle is toned down, in that the Bible is very specific in stating exactly what the ravens brought Elijah, namely bread and meat, and how often they came, namely in the morning and in the evening, whereas Josephus, who is generally more specific than the Bible when it comes to such details, is here apparently deliberately more vague in stating simply that the ravens brought him food every day, without indicating what they brought and exactly when they came.

When, moreover, Josephus mentions miracles he can, with a deft touch, explain the miracle in such a way as to make it more credible. Thus in the contest on Mount Carmel the biblical narrative declares that the fire of the L-rd licked up the water that was in the trench (1 Kings 18:38). Josephus, realizing that normally it is water that extinguishes fire rather than the reverse, as seems to be the case here, rationalizes the incident by stating that when the fire consumed the altar even the water went up as steam and the ground became completely dry (*Ant.* 8.342).

Likewise, Josephus makes more credible the account of the rain that miraculously descended upon the land after the contest between Elijah and the priests of Baal. In the biblical version Elijah tells Ahab to go up, since the sound of the rushing of rain is already present, even though at the moment there is no sign of rain at all (1 Kings 18:41). Josephus is more circumspect, having the prophet declare not that the rain is already present but rather that it will come in a little while (μετ' ὀλίγον) (*Ant.* 8.343). Again, when Elijah sends his servant to see whether the rain is coming, the latter is told merely to look toward the sea (1 Kings 18:43). The Josephan Elijah's instructions are more detailed and more scientific; he tells his servant precisely what to look for, namely to note whether a cloud is rising in any direction, inasmuch as until then the sky had been clear (*Ant.* 8.344).

Furthermore, Josephus has considerably diminished the miraculous aspect of the food that sustains Elijah in the wilderness whither he had fled from Jezebel. In the Bible we are told that after the angel of G-d visits him he ate and drank and went in the strength of that food for forty days and nights (1 Kings 19:8). Josephus, apparently incredulous about such a statement, is content merely to state that Elijah ate the food and gathered strength from it (*Ant.* 8.349).

Further de-theologizing may be seen in Josephus' version of the voice of G-d that came to Elijah when he had fled from Queen Jezebel to the wilderness. According to the biblical version, the word of the L-rd came to Elijah and said to him, "What are you doing here, Elijah?" (1 Kings 19:9). In Josephus' version the unidentified voice is described as coming "from someone, he knew not whom" (*Ant.* 8.350). A second time a voice tells Elijah to come out into the open on the following day. Such an unidentified voice might well remind Roman readers of Aius Locutius, the Roman deity whose very name indicates that it was merely a voice speaking and who announced to the Romans that the Gauls were coming (Varro, *ap.* Aulus Gellius 16.17.2; Cicero, *De Divinatione* 2.32.69).

Again, in the scene where Elijah flees from Jezebel to the wilderness, the Bible boldly speaks of the L-rd passing by, then declares that the L-rd was not in the wind or in the earthquake or in the fire but rather in a still small voice (1 Kings 19:11-12). Josephus rationalizes this scene by saying nothing about the presence of G-d; rather, we are told merely that the earth rumbled and Elijah saw a brilliant fiery light (*Ant.* 8.351).

Furthermore, Josephus has totally omitted the spectacular miracle whereby Elijah took his mantle and struck the Jordan River with it and thus enabled Elisha and himself to cross over on dry ground (2 Kings 2:8 vs. *Ant.* 9.28).

Apparently, angels, as intermediaries between G-d and man, presented a problem for Josephus, as they did for Philo, inasmuch as they seemed to limit G-d's uniqueness and omnipotence (see Wolfson 1947, 1:375-76). Thus, when Elijah flees from Jezebel to the wilderness, the biblical text states that an angel touched him and told him to arise and eat (1 Kings 19:5). Two verses later we read that the angel came to Elijah a second time. Josephus, however, has omitted all mention of the angel. Instead we are told that Elijah was awakened by someone, who remains nameless, and that when he arose he found food and water laid before him (*Ant.* 8.349). Moreover, the second such appearance is totally omitted.

Again, according to the biblical text, an angel instructed Elijah not to be afraid but to accompany the officers of King Ahaziah of Israel (2 Kings 1:15). In Josephus' version it is G-d Himself who instructs Elijah thus (*Ant.* 9.20). Likewise, Josephus omits the biblical statement in which an angel of the L-rd tells Elijah to accompany the third messenger sent by King Ahaziah (2 Kings 1:15 vs. *Ant.* 9.26); instead, Elijah, with no mention of a divine role in his decision, is said to go with him because he approves of the adroitness (δεξιότητα, "kindness," "tact") and courtesy (ἀστεῖον) of the manner of the king's emissary (*Ant.* 9.26). As Begg remarks, Josephus has opted not to tax the credulity of his sophisticated non-Jewish audience with a second appearance of a *deus ex machina* within a single story (Begg 1995d, 36).

Indeed, Josephus' chief interest in Elijah is not in his miracles but rather in his role as a prophet. In the proem to his *Jewish War* Josephus makes the revealing statement that he will begin his work at the point where "the historians of these events [i.e. the biblical history] and our prophets conclude" (1.18). In short, the prophet is, in effect, the patron of the historian. Hence it is not surprising that in no fewer than 169 instances Josephus introduces the word "prophet" or the verb "prophesied" where the Bible lacks it (see Feldman 1990, 389-91). In the case of Elijah there are seventeen such instances.[7]

---

[7] *Ant.* 8.319 vs. 1 Kings 17:1; *Ant.* 8.323 vs. 1 Kings 17:15; *Ant.* 8.325 vs. 1 Kings 17:15; *Ant.* 8.325 vs. 1 Kings 17:18; *Ant.* 8.327 vs. 1 Kings 17:22; *Ant.* 8.327 vs. 1 Kings 17:24; *Ant.* 8.329 vs. 1 Kings 18:7; *Ant.* 8.331 vs. 1 Kings 18:7; *Ant.* 8.337 vs. 1 Kings 18:21; *Ant.* 8.346 vs. 1 Kings 18:46; *Ant.* 8.354 vs. 1 Kings 19:21; *Ant.* 8.360 vs. 1 Kings 21:17; *Ant.* 8.362 (*bis*) vs. 1 Kings 21:27-29; *Ant.* 8.417 vs. 1 Kings 22:38; *Ant.* 9.20 vs. 2 Kings 1:3; *Ant.* 9.119 vs. 2 Kings 9:25.

Most important, perhaps in reaction to Christian claims for Jesus (see Paul 1985, 473-80; and Fornaro 1979 431-46), Josephus avoids the biblical references to Elijah as a "man of G-d" (1 Kings 17:18, 17:24).[8] Instead, the widow whose son is brought back to life by Elijah says that she now clearly realized that the Deity (τὸ θεῖον) spoke with him (*Ant.* 8.327). Again, in the Bible the officer of King Ahaziah addresses him as "O man of G-d" when he orders him to come down from the top of a hill and to go to the king (2 Kings 1:9), but Josephus omits the phrase "O man of G-d" (*Ant.* 9.23). Likewise, in the Bible, Elijah, clearly implying that he is, indeed, a man of G-d, tells the king's officer that if he is a man of G-d fire will descend from heaven (2 Kings 1:10); in Josephus' version, however, he refers to himself not as a man of G-d but as a true prophet (*Ant.* 9.23).

Perhaps the most miraculous aspect of Elijah in the biblical tradition is his going up in a whirlwind in a chariot of fire into heaven (2 Kings 1:11-12). Josephus, in accordance with his rationalizing tendency, says nothing about either a whirlwind or an ascension to heaven. Instead we are told merely that he disappeared from among men and that to this day no one knows his end (*Ant.* 9.28). The omission of the whirlwind parallels the statement in Sophocles' *Oedipus at Colonus* (1660) that no hurricane was blowing when Oedipus disappeared, while the statement that no one knows Elijah's end parallels the remark of the messenger in *Oedipus at Colonus* (1655-56) that no one of mortal men but Theseus could tell in what manner Oedipus disappeared. Moreover, as Tabor has pointed out, if Josephus had followed the biblical text and so stated that Elijah had been bodily assumed into heaven, the reader might well have concluded that Elijah had somehow escaped death, the result being that Elijah would appear superior to Moses, who definitely did die, according to both the biblical text (Deuteronomy 34:5) and Josephus himself (*Ant.* 4.326) (see Tabor

---

[8] Betz (1987, 220) concludes that this negative attitude of Josephus toward the designation "man of G-d" does not support the argument that Josephus knew of the usage of the term θεῖος ἀνήρ as a title for a worker of miracles, since if he had known this usage Josephus would have applied the title to Elijah, especially in rendering the passages in 1 Kings 17:18 and 24. Betz then concludes that the type of θεῖος ἀνήρ never existed in Hellenistic times and that it is, in fact, the imaginary product of the *Religionsgeschichtliche* school. We may remark, however, that Josephus does use the expression θεῖος ἀνήρ in connection with Moses (*Ant.* 3.180).

1989, 228-29; see also Begg 1990, 691-93). The fact that Josephus compares the disappearance of Elijah with that of Enoch, noting that in both cases they became invisible and that no one knows of their death (*Ant.* 9.28), would, moreover, seem plausible to a pagan reader, who would readily recall the similar disappearances of Aeneas (Dionysius of Halicarnassus, *Ant. Rom.* 1.64.4) and of Romulus (Dionysius of Halicarnassus, *Ant. Rom.* 2.56.2; Ovid, *Metamorphoses* 14.805-85; Ovid, *Fasti* 2.481-509; Livy 1.16) – the founders of Rome.[9]

5. *Elijah the Zealot*

The key characteristic of Josephus' remolding of the biblical portrait of Elijah is his elimination of its Zealot features. Thus, most notably, whereas in the Bible after his victory in the contest with the priests of Baal Elijah tells the Israelites to seize the prophets of Baal and himself kills them (1 Kings 18:40), in Josephus it is not Elijah but the Israelites who kill the prophets (*Ant.* 8.343).[10] Again, when Elijah, fleeing from Queen Jezebel, takes refuge in a cave and a voice asks him why he has done so, his biblical answer is that he has been very zealous (*qano' qine'ti*) for the L-rd (1 Kings 19:10); but Josephus' Elijah makes no mention of his zealotry (*Ant.* 8.350). Similarly, when, according to the biblical version, the still small voice again asks Elijah what he is doing, he replies that he has been very zealous (*qano' qine'ti*) for the L-rd (1 Kings 19:14). He then, zealot that he is, bitterly proceeds to indict the people of Israel for having forsaken the covenant, thrown down G-d's altars, and slain the prophets. All this is omitted in Josephus' version,

---

[9] Ginzberg (1928, 6:322, n. 32) cites the view of Rabbi Jose, who lived a generation after Josephus, that Elijah did not ascend to heaven (*Mekilta Baḥodesh* 4.65b, *Sukkah* 5a); but Ginzberg also cites the almost unanimous opinion of the Talmudic and midrashic literature that Elijah did not die. He sees no cogent reason for assuming that Rabbi Jose's view was prompted by a desire to combat the Christian doctrine of Jesus' ascension. That view, as he remarks, is shared by the Septuagint, which reads (2 Kings 2:11) that Elijah was taken up as it were (ὡς) into heaven, as well as by Ecclesiasticus 48:9, where the text reads that he was taken "upwards" (*ma'alah*) and "on high" (*marom*) rather than heavenward (*shamayim*).

[10] There is, to be sure, an inconsistency in Josephus on this point in that subsequently when Elijah enters the cave and is asked why he had left the city, he replies that he has done so because he has killed the prophets of Baal and is consequently being pursued by Queen Jezebel.

where the divine voice simply exhorts the prophet not to be alarmed and assures him that none of his enemies will succeed in getting him within their power (*Ant.* 8.352).

6. *Rationalizations in the Narrative*

One major goal of Josephus' re-translation, so to speak, of the Bible is to provide better motivation for and to increase the plausibility of events. Thus, we read that when Elijah came to Zarephath he saw a widow gathering sticks and called to her (1 Kings 17:10). We may well ask how Elijah knew that this was, indeed, the woman who G-d had said would feed him. Josephus clarifies matters when he says specifically that G-d revealed to him that this was the woman who was to give him food (*Ant.* 8.321). Similarly, inasmuch as the reader may well ask why the widow entrusted her son to a stranger, Elijah (1 Kings 17:19), Josephus resolves the problem by explaining that Elijah urged her to take heart and promised to restore the son to life (*Ant.* 8.326). Josephus' readers might well have been incredulous of such a miracle as restoring a dead person to life; Josephus resolves this problem by adding a single word, namely that the child "seemed" to be dead (*Ant.* 8.325). Likewise, one may wonder why G-d performed the extraordinary miracle of the revival of the son of the widow. The Bible gives no reason and states merely that the L-rd hearkened to the voice of Elijah (1 Kings 17:22). Josephus introduces such a motive, namely that G-d wished to spare the prophet from seeming to have come to her for the purpose of harming her (*Ant.* 8.327). Moreover, the scene in which Elijah stretched himself upon the child (1 Kings 17:21) must have seemed grotesque, and so Josephus omits it (*Ant.* 8.327).

The reader may also wonder as to the motive of Elijah in telling the people watching the contest between him and the priests of Baal to draw near (1 Kings 18:30). Josephus, like the rabbis,[11] cites a motive for Elijah's instructions, namely lest he be accused of trickery in secretly applying fire to the wood (*Ant.* 8.340).

---

[11] According to rabbinic tradition, to be sure recorded much later, Elijah took precautions so that the prophets of Baal would not secretly set fire to the altar (*Yalquṭ* on 1 Kings 18:25). The motif also appears in one of the paintings at Dura Europos.

Another occurrence in the biblical narrative which might well have struck readers as unrealistic is Elijah's meeting with Elisha when the latter was plowing. According to the biblical text, Elisha had twelve yoke of oxen before him (1 Kings 19:19); but since it would seem unlikely that one man would have twelve yoke of oxen, Josephus, drawing upon the biblical statement that Elisha was with the twelfth, writes, more plausibly, that there were some others with Elisha while he was ploughing (*Ant.* 8.353).

7. *Dramatic Enhancement*

Another factor in Josephus' rewriting of the Bible is his desire to enhance the sense of drama.

In the case of the Elijah pericope, when the son of the widow of Zarephath has stopped breathing, she complains to Elijah, according to the Hebrew text: "What have you against me, O man of G-d? You have come to me to bring my sin to remembrance, and to cause the the death of my son!" (1 Kings 17:18). Josephus more graphically describes her reaction to the apparent death of her son, depicting her as weeping bitterly (ἀνακλαιομένη, "weeping aloud," "bursting into tears"), injuring (αἰκιζομένη, "maltreating," "marring," "torturing") herself with her hands, and uttering such cries as her grief (πάθος, "'suffering," "calamity," "distress," "emotion") prompted (*Ant.* 8.325).

Josephus also enhances the dramatic excitement by his rendering of G-d's statement to Elijah telling him to go forth and stand before the mountain of the L-rd (1 Kings 19:11). In Josephus' version there is a nameless voice that heightens the suspense by specifying precisely when he is to come out into the open air, i.e., on the following day (*Ant.* 8.351).

Josephus also adds dramatic horror to the description of the sickness of the bowels which Elijah in his letter predicts will afflict King Jehoram. The biblical narrative states that Jehoram would be afflicted until his bowels fall out (2 Chronicles 21:15). Josephus adds poignancy to the description by remarking that Jehoram's bowels would fall out so that he would look on at his own misery without being able to help himself at all and thus would finally die (*Ant.* 9.101).

8. Summary

Though Josephus is a historian, the biblical prophets are important to him because they guarantee the accuracy of the accounts that they committed to writing. In presenting the personality of Elijah, however, Josephus, like the rabbis, was in a quandary. On the one hand, Elijah was a very popular figure in apocalyptic, sectarian, and popular circles generally who is said to have saved the Jews at crucial points in their history and who is compared to Moses himself. And yet, the fact that he was identified with Phinehas the zealot and was popularly regarded as the forerunner of the Messiah, who would by definition lead a revolt against the Roman Empire, had to make Josephus feel very uneasy about him. A similar dilemma, as we have noted, confronted Josephus regarding the good King Hezekiah, who was identified by some as the Messiah, and regarding King David, who was held to be the ancestor of the Messiah. Josephus likewise walked a tightrope in his treatment of the prophecy of Daniel which was popularly interpreted to refer to the overthrow of the Roman Empire. In short, inasmuch as Josephus was writing for both a non-Jewish and, to a lesser degree, for a Jewish audience, he had to be careful neither to denigrate nor to aggrandize the character of Elijah excessively.

On the one hand, Josephus paints a portrait of Elijah as a leader who, in words reminiscent of those of Aeneas in Virgil's *Aeneid*, encourages a poor widow, shows *pietas* in his devotion to his ancestors, and successfully trains his successor Elisha to carry on his work. Since a crucial common denominator of prophecy and history is their concern for the truth, Josephus emphasizes that Elijah steadfastly refused to flatter King Ahab and defied the threats of Ahaziah's messengers.

And yet, especially because the Jews had been subjected to ridicule because of their religious credulity, Josephus tones down the miracles associated with Elijah, such as the account of his feeding by the ravens, the display of G-d's power in the spectacular contest between Elijah and the priests of Baal at Mount Carmel, and the food that sustained Elijah in the wilderness. Again, inasmuch as angels apparently seemed to detract from G-d's uniqueness and omnipotence for him, Josephus either omits the role which angels play at several points in the biblical narrative or substitutes a nameless person or has G-d Himself assume this role. Most important, Josephus, in accordance with his rationalizing tendency, says nothing about Elijah going up to heaven in a whirlwind in a chariot of fire, but rather has him disappear in a manner highly reminiscent of Oedipus in Sophocles' *Oedipus at Colonus*.

CHAPTER TWENTY

JEHOSHAPHAT

1. Introduction

Josephus' portrait of King Jehoshaphat of Judah, a relatively minor biblical figure, will help to answer the question whether the modifications which Josephus introduces in his rewriting of the Bible are chiefly restricted to major personalities.

One indication of the relative importance to Josephus of a given biblical personality, as we have observed, is the sheer amount of space that he devotes to him. By this standard Jehoshaphat is clearly a personality of major interest for Josephus, inasmuch as the ratio of Josephus (*Ant.* 8.393-9.17, 9.19-44: 405 lines) to the Hebrew text (1 Kings 22:41-51, 2 Kings 3:7-27, 2 Chronicles 17:1-21:1: 215 lines) is 1.88, and the ratio of Josephus to the Septuagint text (311 lines)[1] is 1.30.

If, as we have noted, Josephus tends in his portraits of his other biblical heroes to gloss over their defects, it will prove of interest to see what he does with the two major failures of Jehoshaphat as noted in the Bible, namely the fact that he did not remove the

---

[1] One indication that Josephus had a Septuagintal text or a Hebrew text akin to it may be seen in the fact that our Hebrew text states that when Ahab and Jehoshaphat joined in their war against the Syrian king Ahab disguised himself but that Jehoshaphat wore his own robe (1 Kings 22:30); the Septuagint, however, states that Ahab disguised himself while Jehoshaphat wore Ahab's clothes. Josephus' version is in accordance with the Septuagint in remarking that Ahab and Jehoshaphat agreed that Ahab should remove his royal garment and that Jehoshaphat should wear Ahab's clothes (*Ant.* 8.412). Furthermore, Jehu is called a prophet as in the Septuagint (2 Chronicles 19:2, *Ant.* 9.1) rather than a seer, as in the Hebrew text. Likewise, the reference to "the prophet" in the singular reflects the Septuagint reading (2 Chronicles 20:20) in contrast to the plural which is found in the Lucianic text and in the Hebrew. Again, we read that Jehoshaphat appointed judges from among the priests and Levites (*Ant.* 9.4), adopting the order of the Septuagint (2 Chronicles 19:8) rather than the order "Levites and priests," which we find in the Hebrew text. On the other hand, there is evidence that Josephus also used either a Hebrew text or a Lucianic Greek text, rather than the Septuagint (at least as we have it), when he reads στάντας, "standing" (cf. 2 Chronicles 20:17, *'imedu*, Lucianic στῆτε) whereas the Septuagint reads σύνετε ("understand") (*Ant.* 9.11). (Several of these points are mentioned by Begg 1995b, 399).

high places of pagan worship and that he made peace with the idol-worshipping kings of Israel (1 Kings 22:43-44).

One of the questions which students of Josephus' version of the Bible have long asked is whether Josephus' changes derive from his sources or rather represent Josephus' own original interpretation. One indication that Josephus has put his personal imprint upon his version of the Bible is to be found in the emphasis upon the priesthood, which we may most readily explain as reflecting the fact that Josephus himself was a priest and, indeed, was so proud of his priestly ancestry that this is the first point that he makes about himself in his autobiography (*Life* 1).

In the case of Jehoshaphat, we may note that whereas the Bible enumerates princes, Levites, and priests whom Jehoshaphat sent to the cities of Judah to teach them the law (2 Chronicles 17:7-8), Josephus, in his version, predictably omits the Levites (*Ant.* 8.395) (nine of whom are actually mentioned by name in the biblical narrative), who were the great rivals of the priests during his lifetime. He likewise, in enumerating the officers whom Jehoshaphat appointed, omits mention of the Levites (2 Chronicles 19:11 vs. *Ant.* 9.6).

This emphasis upon the priesthood may also be seen in Josephus' version of the scene where Jehoshaphat is assured by the prophet Jahaziel that G-d Himself will take the initiative in destroying the Ammonites and Moabites. In the biblical account Jehoshaphat thereupon takes counsel with the people and appoints those who are to sing songs of praise and gratitude to G-d (2 Chronicles 20:21); we are not told who those singers are, but we may assume that they were the Levites. Josephus, on the other hand, while specifying that the singers designated by Jehoshaphat were, indeed, Levites, adds that he also appointed at the head of the people priests with their trumpets (*Ant.* 9.12).[2]

---

[2] In portraying Jehoshaphat's concern with the Temple Josephus is in accord with rabbinic tradition, which ascribed to him the ordinance forbidding anyone to ascend the Temple mount whose term of uncleanness had not expired, even though he had taken the ritual bath (*Yevamot* 7b).

2. *The Rabbinic Portrait of Jehoshaphat*[3]

An examination of the rabbinic attitude toward Jehoshaphat will indicate a more balanced picture than we find in the pages of Josephus. On the one hand, the rabbis, like Josephus, stress his piety. Thus, the rabbis raise the question whether he partook of the feast prepared for him by the wicked Ahab (2 Chronicles 18:2; *Ḥullin* 4b-5a), the clear implication being that he was so pious in his observance of the dietary laws that one could hardly imagine that he would eat under such circumstances. He is held up as such a model of piety that when Rabbi Judah the Prince cites the passage that King Hezekiah broke in pieces the brazen serpent which Moses had made because the Israelites in his time actually made offerings to it (2 Kings 18:4), the other rabbis object that surely Asa and Jehoshaphat must have destroyed it previously, since they destroyed every form of idolatry in the world (*Ḥullin* 6b). In particular, Jehoshaphat is praised for enacting an ordinance that a *ṭebul yom*, that is, one who has bathed to cleanse himself at the end of the period of his defilement but who must wait until sunset to regain his ritual purity (Leviticus 22:7), must not enter the camp of the Levites, even though the latter provision is not of Torah origin (*Yevamot* 7b). His faith in G-d is demonstrated in the fact that during the war against the Arameans, in the most desperate moments, he prayed to G-d and his entreaty was answered (Jerusalem *Berakot* 9.13b; *Midrash Psalms* 4.3).

Moreover, Jehoshaphat is frequently referred to by the rabbis as he is by Josephus as righteous (*Genesis Rabbah* 97, *Leviticus Rabbah* 30.3, *Seder Eliyahu Rabbah* 3.14). He is praised for his sense of justice, and they quote his words of instruction to judges, that they should consider that they judge not for man but for G-d (2 Chronicles 19:6; *Sanhedrin* 6b). Inasmuch as humility is the paramount virtue for which Moses himself is particularly praised (Numbers 12:3), it is significant that Jehoshaphat is singled out for praise in possessing especially this virtue, though it is not mentioned as such in either the biblical or Josephan accounts.

From a rabbinic point of view there is almost no greater virtue than respect for Torah scholars. It is therefore particularly note-

---

[3] For a useful summary of the rabbinic attitude toward Jehoshaphat see Begg (1995, 47-48).

worthy that Jehoshaphat is mentioned as one who who rose from his very throne whenever he beheld a scholar, embraced him, and kissed him, calling him "Father, Father" (*Makkot* 24a, *Ketubot* 103b), thus echoing the words spoken by Elisha when he saw his mentor Elijah go up to heaven in a whirlwind (2 Kings 2:12).

One of the seven qualities which the rabbinic sages enumerated as most appropriate for the righteous person, as we have noted, is wealth (*'Avot* 6:8). Indeed, one of the four rabbinic prerequisites for prophecy is wealth (*Nedarim* 38a); and Moses, the greatest of the prophets (Deuteronomy 34:10), is specifically said there to have acquired his great wealth from the chips of the tablets (which were fetched from a diamond quarry) given to him by G-d.

Inasmuch as one of the qualities especially appropriate for a righteous person is wealth (*'Avot* 6:8), it is significant that Jehoshaphat is spoken of as one who possessed all the gold and silver in the world, having seized it from the Ammonites (*Pesaḥim* 119a). His military power was so great that he had an army of 160,000 soldiers (*Midrash Psalms* 15.118).

On the other hand, unlike Josephus, the rabbis reproach Jehoshaphat for his alliance with the wicked Ahab (*'Avot de-Rabbi Nathan* 9.4). He is likewise criticized for arranging to have his son Jehoram marry Athaliah, who, as queen, virtually exterminated the entire royal family (*Seder Eliyahu Zuta* 3.177).

3. *The Power of Jehoshaphat*

Josephus develops the theme of Jehoshaphat's power by noting that he joined with King Ahaziah of Israel in building ships to sail as far away as Pontus and the trading-stations of Thrace (*Ant.* 9.17), whereas the Bible cites the destination of the ships as Tarshish (2 Chronicles 20:36), which Josephus elsewhere identifies as Tarsus in Asia Minor (*Ant.* 1.127), a region considerably closer to Palestine than Pontus on the Black Sea and Thrace; hence Jehoshaphat's initiative in Josephus' version appears considerably greater than it does in the biblical parallel.

Josephus goes out of his way on more than one occasion to stress Jehoshaphat's loyalty and reliability as an ally. Thus, whereas in the Bible Jehoshaphat asks his ally Jehoram the king of Israel by which way they should march against the Moabites (2 Kings 3:8), Josephus' Jehoshaphat goes much further in not only promising to assist Jehoram but also to compel the Idumaean king, who was under his authority, to join in the campaign against the Moabites (*Ant.* 9.30).

On the other hand, Josephus apparently realized that stress on Jehoshaphat's might might lead to his being compared with powerful autocratic rulers. Indeed, in the Bible we read that he built in Judah fortresses and store-cities (*'arei misekenot*, Septuagint πόλεις ὀχυράς) (2 Chronicles 17:12). The reader may very well be reminded that during the time when the Israelites were afflicted with burdensome labors in Egypt they built store-cities (*'arei misekenot*, Septuagint πόλεις ὀχυράς, the very same phrase found in both the Hebrew and the Septuagint of 2 Chronicles 17:12), namely Pithom and Raameses, for Pharaoh (Exodus 1:11). Hence, Josephus, while citing Jehoshaphat's strongholds, avoids mention of the store-cities (*Ant.* 8.396).

It is surely significant that in the very brief eulogy with which Josephus concludes his account of Jehoshaphat he singles out the fact of his having been emulous (μιμητής) of the acts of David (*Ant.* 9.44). Indeed, it is precisely Jehoshaphat's possession of the most outstanding qualities of David which Josephus proceeds to develop in his portrait of the former.

4. *The Virtues of Jehoshaphat*

In the case of Jehoshaphat, as we shall see, the virtues which Josephus stresses are his courage, justice, and piety.[4]

Josephus' Jehoshaphat, in an extra-biblical addition (1 Kings 22:4, 2 Chronicles 18:3) is a military leader with a force not smaller than Ahab's (*Ant.* 8.399). Indeed, Josephus, in a passage that has no biblical parallel (1 Kings 22:5), whether in the Hebrew or in the Septuagint version, paints a picture of Jehoshaphat, prior to his joint expedition with Ahab to recover Ramoth-Gilead, in which he and Ahab sit upon their thrones and distribute pay to their respective armies. The description is highly reminiscent of the scene described by Livy (2.12.7), in which Gaius Mucius Scaevola

---

[4] Begg (1995b, 402) notes that in Josephus Jehoshaphat becomes a much more significant ruler than in Kings but also a significantly better one than in Chronicles.

enters the Etruscan camp at the time when the soldiers are being paid, while the king is seated upon his throne.

Jehoshaphat's military stature is likewise accented by the fact that although in the Bible it is Ahab who takes the initiative before the battle against the king of Syria to say to Jehoshaphat that he, Ahab, will disguise himself, whereas Jehoshaphat is to go into battle wearing his own clothes (1 Kings 22:30), in Josephus it is a joint decision (συνέθεντο, "they put together," "came to terms," "agreed upon," "united") by Ahab and Jehoshaphat (*Ant.* 8.412). Moreover, it surely took courage for Jehoshaphat, in Josephus' version, to take his place in battle wearing Ahab's clothes, knowing full well that the enemy would concentrate their attacks on Ahab in particular as the one who had provoked the war. The subsequent battle scene itself surely does not redound to Jehoshaphat's reputation for bravery, inasmuch as Jehoshaphat is portrayed as crying out when the Syrian captains mistakenly assume that he is Ahab because he is wearing the latter's clothes (1 Kings 22:32, 2 Chronicles 18:31). The Bible then declares that G-d rescued him from this dangerous situation (2 Chronicles 18:31). In Josephus' version, however, Jehoshaphat neither cries out nor is he rescued by G-d's intervention; rather, we read only that when the Syrians saw that it was not Ahab they themselves turned back (*Ant.* 8.414).

And yet, Josephus, in order not to lose credibility, omits the exaggeration implicit in the biblical account that a great multitude was coming to attack Jehoshaphat from beyond the sea (2 Chronicles 20:1-2). Such a statement does, of course, magnify the achievement of Jehoshaphat in overcoming so vast an enemy, coming as it is from afar. But Josephus is content to say that the attackers included a large division of Arabs and says nothing of their coming from beyond the sea (*Ant.* 9.7).

Josephus is concerned not to give the impression that Jehoshaphat lost confidence in himself, as would appear from his biblical statement that he is powerless against the great multitude arrayed against him and that he does not know what to do (2 Chronicles 20:12). Josephus' Jehoshaphat prays to G-d to protect the city but gives no indication that he feels himself to be powerless (*Ant.* 9.9).

That the quality of justice is particularly prominent in Josephus' portrait of Jehoshaphat is evident from the fact that despite the relative brevity of that portrait the adjective δίκαιος is found no fewer than six times (*Ant.* 8.394, 9.4, 9.5 [*bis*], 9.33, 9.35) and the noun δικαιοσύνη once (*Ant.* 9.16) within it.

This emphasis upon Jehoshaphat's justice may be seen in the instructions which the king gives to the judges of his realm. In the biblical version Jehoshaphat places the emphasis upon the fact that it is G-d and not man for whom they judge and that therefore they should have the fear of the L-rd (2 Chronicles 19:6). He continues by stressing the guilt that they will bring on themselves and the wrath of G-d which will afflict them if they judge improperly (2 Chronicles 19:9-10). Josephus' version omits the elements of fear and guilt and stresses instead that judges should take thought of nothing so much as for justice in judging the multitude and that G-d sees everything that is done even in secret (*Ant.* 9.3). His Jehoshaphat adds an additional reason why judges should exercise the greatest care, namely that Jerusalem, which is their seat of judgment, is the site of the Temple of G-d (*Ant.* 9.5). We may remark that such an affirmation might well be expected from Josephus, as a priest of that Temple.

An integral part of justice is the showing of gratitude. In the case of Jehoshaphat, whereas after he survived the rout of his forces by the Syrians, there is no indication in the Bible that he expressed gratitude to G-d (2 Chronicles 19:4), Josephus specifically declares that Jehoshaphat thereupon betook himself to giving thanks and offering sacrifices to G-d (*Ant.* 9.2). Jehoshaphat likewise shows gratitude in Josephus' version when the Levitical prophet Jahaziel declares that G-d will fight for Judah. According to the Bible, Jehoshaphat bowed his head with his face to the ground (2 Chronicles 20:18). Josephus adds that Jehoshaphat and the multitude gave thanks to G-d, as well as doing obeisance to Him (*Ant.* 9.11).

That the virtue of piety is particularly prominent in Josephus' portrait of Jehoshaphat may be seen in the fact that the noun εὐσέβεια occurs twice (*Ant.* 9.2, 9.16) and the adjectives εὐσεβής and ὅσιος once each (*Ant.* 8.394, 9.35) in reference to him.

We may see the emphasis which Josephus places on Jehoshaphat's piety[5] in his version of the biblical statement that Jehosha-

---

[5] The rabbis similarly highlight Jehoshaphat's tremendous faith in G-d, which was the cornerstone of his piety; they note that in the war against the Aramaeans,

phat sent princes, Levites, and priests to teach in the cities of Judah (2 Chronicles 17:7-9). Josephus' Jehoshaphat shows more forceful initiative and leadership in summoning (συγκαλέσας, "calling together") the governors and priests (*Ant.* 8.395); we read, furthermore, that he kept on ordering them (ἐκέλευεν, note the force of the imperfect tense) to go not merely to Judah in general but throughout the land, indeed city by city, and not merely to teach but to teach all the people. Moreover, it is not merely, as in the Bible, that the king's emissaries have the book of the law of G-d with them: they teach the people not simply to know but to practice the laws of Moses – "both to keep them and to be diligent in worshipping G-d." The result, as stated in the Bible is that the fear of the L-rd fell upon the people (2 Chronicles 17:10), whereas in Josephus we are told that there was nothing for which the people were so ambitious and so disposed to love as the observance of the laws (*Ant.* 8.395).

Another indication of Jehoshaphat's piety may be seen in Josephus' addition to the king's question to Ahab in the Bible (1 Kings 22:7, 2 Chronicles 18:6), prior to the campaign to recover Ramoth-Gilead and after the false prophets have foretold victory, i.e., whether there is not another prophet of whom they might inquire. In Josephus' version we are told that Jehoshaphat was able to discern from the four hundred prophets' words that they were false prophets (*Ant.* 8.402). At that point, whereas in the Bible it is Ahab who then summons an officer with instructions to fetch Micaiah the prophet (1 Kings 22:8-9, 2 Chronicles 18:7-8), in Josephus it is Jehoshaphat who takes the initiative in bidding (κελεύσαντος) that Micaiah be produced (*Ant.* 8.403).

In addition, we may note that the juxtaposition of justice and piety is frequent in Josephus' additions to the biblical text.[6] Thus, almost at the very beginning of his account of Jehoshaphat, whereas the biblical narrative states that G-d was with Jehoshaphat because he followed the ways of his father (2 Chronicles 17:3), Josephus' Jehoshaphat stands on his own feet, with no mention of

---

despite the fact that an enemy held his sword at Jehoshaphat's very throat, the king entreated the help of G-d, and this was granted (*Berakot* 10a, Jerusalem *Berakot* 9.13b, *Midrash Psalms* 4.3, cited by Ginzberg 1928, 6:310, n. 30).

[6] See Attridge 1976, 115-6, n. 3. So also Dionysius of Halicarnassus remarks that the great Roman lawgiver, Numa Pompilius, introduced two virtues through which his city would become prosperous – justice and piety (2.62.5).

his father; and the reason why he wins the favorable (εὐμενές, "benevolent," "kindly," "gracious," "well-disposed") response of G-d is that he is just (δίκαιος) and pious (εὐσεβής) and daily seeks to do something pleasing (ἡδύ) and acceptable (προσηνές, "pleasant," "welcome," "friendly," "mild," "kind") to G-d (*Ant.* 8.394). Another instance of the effective juxtaposition of Jehoshaphat's justice and piety may be seen in Josephus' version of the aftermath of Judah's miraculous victory over Ammon and Moab (*Ant.* 9.16). Whereas the Bible says that thereafter the realm of Jehoshaphat was quiet (2 Chronicles 20:30), Josephus shifts the emphasis once again to Jehoshaphat himself, remarking that from that time onward he enjoyed splendid fame because of his righteousness (δικαιοσύνη) and his piety (εὐσεβείᾳ) toward G-d (*Ant.* 9.16). Likewise, in an extra-biblical addition, when the prophet Elisha is consulted by the allied kings of Israel, Judah, and Idumaea at a time of severe drought, Elisha swears that he would not answer them were it not for the sake of Jehoshaphat, who was a holy (ὅσιον) and a righteous (δίκαιον) man (*Ant.* 9.35).

Josephus does much to emphasize the role of Jehoshaphat in bringing his subjects back to the observance of the Torah. Thus, in the Bible we are told only that Jehoshaphat brought his subjects back to G-d (2 Chronicles 19:4), whereas Josephus explicitly describes how he did this, namely by teaching the people thoroughly both the laws given by G-d and the piety (εὐσέβειαν) to be shown Him (*Ant.* 9.2).

Jehoshaphat's religious sincerity may be seen in the fact that whereas, in the biblical version, when the Moabites and the Ammonites come to do battle with him, he prays to G-d stating that he is powerless against the enemy (2 Chronicles 20:5-12), Josephus' Jehoshaphat shows his true sincerity and sympathy for his people by breaking down in tears (*Ant.* 9.9).[7]

The extent of Jehoshaphat's piety may be inferred from the fact that whereas, according to the Bible, when his people are beset by the Moabites and the Ammonites, he tells them to believe in G-d and His prophets (2 Chronicles 20:20), Josephus' king spells out

---

[7] The favorable view of Jehoshaphat's weeping here does not contradict Josephus' omission of Jehoshaphat's crying out in the incident where the Syrians mistakenly assume that he is Ahab (*Ant.* 8.414). The latter, we may note, is a military situation where crying out would indicate cowardice, whereas in 2 Chronicles 20:5-12 and *Ant.* 9.9 the crying is a religious act of praying to G-d.

that they must show their faith in the prophet Jahaziel by not even drawing themselves up for battle, though, of course, that would seem to be the appropriate thing to do under the circumstances (*Ant.* 9.12). Again, whereas in the Bible Jehoshaphat tells his subjects to give thanks to G-d, since His steadfast love endures forever (2 Chronicles 20:21), in Josephus Jehoshaphat goes so far as to enjoin them to give thanks as if He had already delivered their country from the enemy, even though this is far from the case at the moment when the enemy's huge force is about to attack (*Ant.* 9.12).

Again, whereas in the Bible it is the people of Judah who bless the L-rd for their victory over Ammon and Moab (2 Chronicles 20:26), in Josephus the focus is on Jehoshaphat himself (*Ant.* 9.14). It is he who looks out over the valley where the enemy had encamped and sees it full of corpses, whereupon he rejoices at the wonderful way in which G-d had helped his nation, such that with no effort on their part He had by Himself given them the victory.

Moreover, once they had heard about the miraculous defeat of the Ammonites and Moabites, all the nations, we are told, developed a fear of G-d (2 Chronicles 20:29). In Josephus' version, however, they are struck with terror not of G-d but of Jehoshaphat, since they are convinced that G-d will henceforth fight on his side (*Ant.* 9.16).

5. *Political Theory*

It is significant that whereas the Bible, in praising Jehoshaphat, declares that he did not follow in the ways of the kingdom of Israel (2 Chronicles 17:4), Josephus, in his clear desire to promote the unity of the Jewish people, omits all reference to the ways of Israel and says, rather, that he sought to do something pleasing and acceptable to G-d (*Ant.* 8.394).

It is furthermore in the interest of stressing the importance of the unity of the Jewish people that Josephus avoids the awkward implication of the Scriptural passage that after making a marriage alliance with Ahab, the king of Israel, Jehoshaphat waited several years before visiting Ahab (2 Chronicles 18:1-2). Josephus has quietly reduced the Bible's years to "some time" (μετὰ χρόνον τινὰ) (*Ant.* 8.398). Likewise, whereas the Hebrew Bible states that it was by guile that Ahab persuaded (*vayesitehu*) Jehoshaphat (2 Chronicles 18:2), Josephus, seeking to smooth relations between the Jewish kingdoms, says that Ahab invited (παρεκάλεσε) Jehoshaphat to become his ally in a war against the king of Syria (*Ant.* 8.398). Indeed, Josephus increases considerably the warmth with which Ahab greets Jehoshaphat. According to the biblical account, Ahab killed an abundance of sheep and oxen for him and for the people who were with him (2 Chronicles 18:2); Josephus expands on this, remarking that Ahab gave him a friendly welcome (φιλοφρόνως) and splendidly (λαμπρῶς) entertained, with an abundance of grain and wine and meat, the army which accompanied him (*Ant.* 8.398).

Likewise, when Ahab approaches Jehoshaphat to induce him to join in the military action to recover Ramoth-Gilead, the Bible quotes Jehoshaphat as saying, "I am as you are, my people as your people" (1 Kings 22:4, 2 Chronicles 18:3). Josephus amplifies this, remarking that Jehoshaphat willingly offered his aid, and adds, in order that the reader may not think that Jehoshaphat was inferior in military might to Ahab, that he had a force not smaller than Ahab's (*Ant.* 8.399).

Josephus could not avoid the fact that Jehu the prophet in the biblical account does reproach Jehoshaphat, telling him that because he had helped Ahab G-d was angry with him (2 Chronicles 19:2). Josephus, however, softens the reproach by having Jehu remark that G-d was displeased (ἀηδῶς) with this act (*Ant.* 9.1).

Again, the Bible cites the castigation of Jehoshaphat by Eliezer the son of Dodavahu for joining Ahaziah, the king of Israel, in an alliance and his prophecy that as a result of this alliance G-d would destroy what they had made, namely the fleet of ships which they built in Etzion-Geber (2 Chronicles 20:37). Josephus, eager to promote the unity of the Jewish people, omits Eliezer's intervention and instead ascribes the loss of the ships to their great size (*Ant.* 9.17).[8]

This same theme of Jewish unity may be seen in another Josephan addition. The Bible states that the kings of Israel, Judah,

---

[8] In contrast, the rabbinic tradition emphasizes that Jehoshaphat was punished for his friendship with the kings of Israel by having his fleet destroyed (*'Avot de-Rabbi Nathan* 9.4, *Alphabet of Ben Sira* 14a, cited by Ginzberg 1928, 6:310, n. 27). Indeed, we hear that G-d had actually condemned Jehoshaphat to death for having joined Ahab in war and that he was saved only by his prayer (*Seder Olam* 17).

and Edom joined in an expedition against the Moabites (2 Kings 3:9). Josephus, clearly seeking to show that the alliance was more than one of convenience, adds that Jehoram, the king of Israel, came first to Jerusalem with his army and received a splended reception by Jehoshaphat there (*Ant.* 9.31). We then have Jehoram and Jehoshaphat portrayed as true partners in devising their military strategy. In the Bible it is Jehoram who makes the decision as to military strategy after Jehoshaphat asks for advice as to which way they should march (2 Kings 3:8); in Josephus the decision is a joint decision to advance through the wilderness of Idumaea, since the enemy would not expect them to attack from this direction (*Ant.* 9.31). Again, when their army lacks water, Jehoshaphat, in an extra-biblical addition, shows warm, brotherly feeling for Jehoram by comforting him; and his doing so is attributed to his righteousness (*Ant.* 9.33).

6. *Apologetics*

One of Josephus' aims in his rewriting of Scripture is to make the account more credible. Thus, while wishing to emphasize the size and power of Jehoshaphat's military forces, he apparently felt that readers would find it hard to believe the Bible's statement that the tiny state of Judah could have produced an army of 280,000 under Jehoshaphat's general Jehohanan (2 Chronicles 17:15) and another army of 200,000 under his general Amasiah (2 Chronicles 17:16). Hence, Josephus reduces the size of Jehohanan's army to 200,000 and omits Amasiah's force altogether (*Ant.* 8.397). Likewise, while it certainly underscores Jehoshaphat's power that the Arabs should have brought him as tribute 7,700 rams and 7,000 he-goats (2 Chronicles 17:11), Josephus avoids the apparent exaggeration by making their annual tribute 360 lambs and 360 kids (*Ant.* 8.396).[9]

Throughout his *Antiquities* Josephus is concerned with refuting the charge that Jews hate non-Jews. It is in line with this tolerant attitude toward the religions of others that we find Josephus omitting the biblical statement that Jehoshaphat did not seek the Baals

---

[9] The rabbis, on the contrary, exaggerate Jehoshaphat's power tremendously. Thus we hear that each division in Jehoshaphat's army consisted of no fewer than 160,000 warriors (*Midrash Psalms* 15.118).

(2 Chronicles 17:3 vs. *Ant.* 8.394). Likewise, he omits the Bible's statement that Jehoshaphat removed the pagan high places and the Asherim from the land of Judah (2 Chronicles 17:6 vs. *Ant.* 8.394).[10] Indeed, whereas, according to the Bible, the prophet Jehu, after reproaching Jehoshaphat for joining Ahab in a military alliance, remarks that there is nonetheless some good to be found in him in that he had destroyed the Asherim (2 Chronicles 19:3), Josephus very diplomatically omits mention of Jehoshaphat's destruction of the Asherim, since this would imply disrespect for the religion of others, and instead has Jehu declare in the vaguest terms that the king would be delivered from his enemies, despite having sinned, because of his good character (φύσιν) (*Ant.* 9.1).

This emphasis upon Jehoshaphat's liberal attitude toward pagans may be seen in Josephus' version of the biblical remark that the reason why the neighboring kingdoms did not make war against Jehoshaphat was that the fear of the L-rd fell upon them (2 Chronicles 17:10). In Josephus' version their fear is replaced by a positive feeling of love, since we read that the neighboring peoples continued to cherish (στέργοντες, "love," "be fond of," "like," "feel affection towards," "esteem," "think highly of") him (*Ant.* 8.396).

Moreover, Josephus, from his own experience with the Romans during the Jewish revolt of 66-74, was well aware of the concept of a "just war." Hence, it is significant that whereas the biblical account states merely that Ahab told the servants of Jehoshaphat that Ramoth-gilead, which was in the hands of the king of Syria, really belonged to him (Ahab) (1 Kings 22:3), Josephus expands this by giving the history of Ahab's claim, namely that the city had first belonged to his father and that it had been taken away by the father of the Syrian king (*Ant.* 8.399); thereby he justifies to Jehoshaphat the military action which they are jointly about to undertake. Furthermore, the Josephan Ahab is a respecter of peace who refuses to be party to its disruption without prior prophetic authorization (*Ant.* 8.401) (so Begg 1989a, 230-1).

Josephus consciously endues his paraphrase of the Bible with

---

[10] Perhaps Josephus was troubled by the fact that the Bible seems to contradict itself on this point, inasmuch as 1 Kings 22:43 says specifically that during Jehoshaphat's reign the high places were not taken away and that the people continued to sacrifice and burn incense there. Josephus resolves the problem by omitting the statements of both Kings and Chronicles on this point.

numerous contemporary implications. Thus, in the Bible, when Jehoshaphat, confronted by the invasion of the Moabites and Ammonites, prays to G-d, he says, "Didst thou not, O our G-d, drive out the inhabitants of this land before thy people Israel, and give it forever to the descendants of Abraham thy friend?" (2 Chronicles 20:7). He then reiterates the notion of an eternal divine gift of the land to the Israelites in his statement that the land has been given to the Israelites by G-d as an inheritance (2 Chronicles 20:11). In Josephus' version the central focus is not on the land but on the Temple (*Ant.* 9.9); in other words, Josephus has converted a political gift of G-d into a religious one. To be sure, he does mention the land, but it is not as an inheritance that is meant to be an independent state but rather as a dwelling place (κατοίκησιν, "dwelling," "residence").

7. *Summary*

If the sheer amount of space devoted to a biblical figure is a criterion of Josephus' interest in that figure, Jehoshaphat is of considerable importance to him. Josephus places his personal imprint upon his portrait of Jehoshaphat by downgrading the importance of the Levites and emphasizing that of the priests, to whose number he himself belonged. In particular, he develops the theme of Jehoshaphat's military and commercial power and his loyalty and reliability as an ally. He is careful, nevertheless, to avoid language that might lead the reader to compare him with autocrats such as the biblical pharaoh.

As to Jehoshaphat's virtues, Josephus stresses his courage particularly in the battle against the Syrians. He omits the embarrassing scene in the Bible in which Jehoshaphat cries out when he is surrounded by the enemy. Josephus emphasizes Jehoshaphat's justice especially in the instructions which he gives to his judges. He exhibits the quality of gratitude, which is closely connected with justice, in the thanks and sacrifices which he offers to G-d. He shows his piety in the forceful initiative and leadership which he displays in ordering his representatives to teach all the people throughout all the land, so that they will not merely know but also practice the law of Moses. Josephus' Jehoshaphat likewise shows initiative in bidding King Ahab of Israel to summon the prophet Micaiah. He shows his extreme faith in the prophet Jahaziel by instructing his people not to draw themselves up for battle, so sure is he of G-d's aid. In the interest of stressing the unity of the Jewish people, Josephus, in this diverging from several references in the biblical narrative, displays a positive attitude toward the alliance of the Jehoshaphat's Kingdom of Judah with the Kingdom of Israel.

To make his account more credible, Josephus avoids undue exaggeration regarding the size of Jehoshaphat's army. In line with his liberal attitude toward other religions, he omits the biblical references to Jehoshaphat's removal of the Baals and the Asherim and suppression of the high places. He is careful to make clear that the war against Syria in which Jehoshaphat was involved was a just war. He omits biblical expressions of a land theology which would be offensive to the Romans; his central focus, rather, is on the Temple.

CHAPTER TWENTY-ONE

JEHORAM, KING OF ISRAEL

1. *Introduction*

One criterion of the importance which Josephus assigns to his biblical personalities is the sheer amount of space that he devotes to them. From this point of view the attention given by Josephus (*Ant.* 9.27, 29-41, 51-52, 60-73, 81-86, 105-106, 112-119) to Jehoram (Joram) of Israel is rather striking as compared with the amount of space allocated to him in the Bible (2 Kings 3:1-27, 6:8-23, 7:10-20, 8:28-29, 9:15-26). This gives a ratio of 1.93 for Josephus as compared with the Hebrew text and 1.49 for Josephus as compared with the Septuagint. When one considers that Jehoram in the Bible is a relatively minor figure it is remarkable that in Josephus he gets almost as much space relatively as David and considerably more than is allotted Daniel, Ezra, Nehemiah and the good queen Esther. Indeed, the stature of Jehoram may be seen in Josephus' extra-biblical remark that when Jehoram came to Jerusalem he was splendidly (λαμπρῶς) entertained (ξενισθείς) by Jehoshaphat, the king of Judah (*Ant.* 9.31).

2. *Jehoram's Qualities of Character*

The great hero must be a true leader. We see this quality in Jehoram in that whereas the Bible states that after reconnaissance had determined that it was safe for the Israelites to leave the city of Samaria where they had been besieged, the people went out, presumably on their own, and plundered the Syrian camp (2 Kings 7:16), in Josephus it is Jehoram who takes the lead and allows the people to plunder the enemy camp (*Ant.* 9.84). They were rewarded, he adds, with no slight amount of gain but took much gold, silver, herds and flocks, as well as a quantity of wheat and barley such as they had never even dreamed of.

Wisdom (σοφία) is the prime requisite for a leader. Josephus, in an editorial comment, ascribes wisdom to Jehoram through the word of an anonymous person, who, however, clearly reflects his own thinking. That nameless speaker compliments Jehoram, when the report is brought to him that the Syrian camp is empty, by stating that the king was suspicious with the best reason (ἄριστα) and most wisely (συνετώτατα, "intelligently," "cleverly," "sagaciously," "resourcefully," "ingeniously") (*Ant.* 9.83). Another characteristic of a wise person, as we see, for example, in Moses' readiness to accept advice from his father-in-law Jethro, is willingness to listen to good counsel. We see this same quality displayed by Josephus' Jehoram in an extra-biblical comment that when one of his men suggests to Jehoram that he send horsemen to see whether the enemy are hiding or whether they really have retreated, he approves the plan (*Ant.* 9.84).

As to courage, Josephus adds to the military capability of Jehoram as one who planned carefully by noting that it was only after receiving assurances from Jehoshaphat, the King of Judah, that he went to war against the Moabites (*Ant.* 10.31; cf. 2 Kings 3:9). Moreover, whereas in the Bible Jehoram asks Jehoshaphat to join him, and it is Jehoshaphat who makes the decision to do so (2 Kings 3:8), in Josephus' version Jehoram is presented as planning carefully, as consulting with his ally Jehoshaphat, and as coming to a joint decision with him to make their advance upon the enemy, the Moabites, through the wilderness of Idumaea (*Ant.* 9.31). Josephus adds that the reason for this strategy was that the Moabites would be caught by surprise since they would not expect the allies to attack from this direction. Furthermore, on the basis of the biblical account, one might well be critical of Jehoram for leading an army to a place where there was no water for the men or for their beasts (2 Kings 3:9), whereas Josephus clearly exonerates Jehoram by explaining that the reason why they found themselves without sufficient water was that their guides had lost their way (*Ant.* 9.32).

We likewise see Jehoram's ability as a military leader in Josephus' explanation of his strategy in fighting against King Ben-hadad of Syria when the latter besieged Samaria. The Bible gives no explanation of Jehoram's strategy (2 Kings 6:24), but Josephus, himself a general in the great war against the Romans, records the extra-biblical detail that Jehoram shut himself up in Samaria, relying on the strength of its walls, inasmuch as he did not think that he was a match (ἀξιόμαχον) for the Syrians (*Ant.* 9.61). Again, whereas the Bible describes in impersonal terms the famine in Samaria when it was being besieged by King Ben-hadad of Syria (2 Kings 6:25), Josephus focuses upon Jehoram and states that it was Jehoram's own supply of necessities that was reduced, so that the cost of food escalated tremendously (*Ant.* 9.62).

Jehoram's concern for his people in times of military crisis may be seen in another extra-biblical addition in Josephus. According to the Bible, while he was being besieged in Samaria, he happened to be passing along the wall of the city when a woman appealed to him for help in a dispute with another woman with whom she had made a pact, because of the severe famine, to eat their sons (2 Kings 6:26). In Josephus' version Jehoram is depicted as totally devoted to his responsibilities. Indeed, he is described as walking around the walls every day in his fear lest, because of the famine, someone might betray the city to the enemy (*Ant.* 9.63). He spies out whether any of the enemy are within the city and, we are told, through his appearance and precautions he prevented any citizen from wishing to betray the city or from carrying out any such plan. We see his steadfastness in enforcing discipline upon the inhabitants in that we are told, in an extra-biblical remark, that when the woman approached him asking for pity, he became angry, thinking that she was about to beg for food or the like, and he consequently called down G-d's curse upon her (*Ant.* 9.64; cf. 2 Kings 6:27).

We also see Jehoram's virtue as a general in the way in which he deals with the report of the lepers about the flight of the Syrians. In the Bible the lepers tell the gatekeepers, who, in turn, inform the king that the Syrian camp is empty. The king, in turn, then tells his servants his analysis of the situation (2 Kings 7:11-12). In Josephus' version Jehoram speaks not to his servants but to his friends and commanders (ἡγεμόνας); in other words, like a good general, he holds a conference to determine strategy (*Ant.* 9.81). He then analyzes the strategy of the enemy very carefully. Whereas in the biblical narrative he states very simply that the Syrians, knowing that the Israelites are hungry, left the camp to hide in the field in order to seize them alive when they emerge from the city (2 Kings 7:12), Josephus has Jehoram bluntly declare the strategy of the Syrians to be a snare (ἐνέδραν, "ambush," "trap," "plot") and a trick (τέχνην, "ruse," "scheme") and explain their motive more fully, namely that when the Israelites go out to plunder their camp in the belief that the Syrians have fled, they may suddenly fall upon them and kill them and thus take the city without a battle (*Ant.* 9.82). Jehoram thereupon, excellent military leader and tactician that he is, urges his men to keep the city well guarded and by no means to be careless in attacking the enemy because of their withdrawal.

We see Jehoram's stature as a military leader enhanced as well in his campaign against the Syrian king, Hazael, Ben-hadad's successor. According to the biblical version, it is Ahaziah, the king of Judah, who was joined by Jehoram in the war (2 Kings 8:28), whereas in Josephus' account it is Jehoram who takes the initiative; and there is no mention of Ahaziah's accompanying him (*Ant.* 9.105). Moreover, Josephus highlights Jehoram's leadership by adding that though he was wounded in the engagement, he intended, after being healed, to continue the war against the Syrians (*Ant.* 9.105-6; cf. 2 Kings 8:29).

Another of the characteristics of a successful general is speed of decision. We see this quality in Josephus' addition that when he was told that a company of horsemen was approching, Jehoram ordered one of his own horsemen at once to go to meet them and to find out who it was who was coming (*Ant.* 9.115; cf. 2 Kings 9:17). Moreover, when he is informed that it is Jehu who is approaching,[1] whereas the Bible states that Jehoram told his retainers to prepare a chariot (2 Kings 9:21), in Josephus Jehoram himself takes the initiative and mounts his chariot (*Ant.* 9.117).

And yet, the goal of a successful military leader is not war for its own sake but rather a just peace, as we can see from Virgil's statement of the Roman mission, *pacisque imponere morem* (*Aeneid* 6.852) and from Augustus' pride (in the *Monumentum Ancyranum*) in the fact that during his rule the Temple of Janus was closed – an indication that Rome was at peace. Hence, we can appreciate Josephus' comment, in an addition to the Bible (2 Kings 8:15), that when Jehoram heard of the death of the Syrian king Ben-hadad he gladly welcomed peace (*Ant.* 9.94).

---

[1] It is apparent that here Josephus had an Aramaic text as his source, inasmuch as the Hebrew states that Jehu drove madly (*beshiga'on*), as does the Septuagint (ἐν παραλλαγῇ), while only the Targum, with its reading *keniyah*, has the meaning "in good order," whence Josephus' μετ' εὐταξίας (2 Kings 9:20). Elsewhere, however, in his account of Jehoram, as Begg (1993a, 107-8) indicates, Josephus for this pericope had several text-forms at his disposal, namely a proto-Masoretic, Septuagint, and proto-Targumic text, and not, as some have thought, primarily a proto-Lucianic text.

As to the third of the cardinal virtues, temperance, Jehoram in Josephus exhibits the quality of restraint when he repents of his anger. Thus, whereas in the Bible, he, in his anger at Elisha for not praying to G-d to alleviate the famine, sends a messenger to kill him, and it is the messenger who declares that the calamity had been sent by G-d (2 Kings 6:33), in Josephus it is Jehoram who is depicted as repenting (καταγνούς, "regretting," "reproaching himself") of his wrath against the prophet and who, fearing that the man who had been ordered to kill Elisha might already have done so, hastens to prevent the murder (*Ant.* 9.70).

We see Jehoram's possession of justice, the fourth of the cardinal virtues, in Josephus' version of the incident of the woman who made the pact with her neighbor to eat their sons. In the biblical account she does not specifically appeal to Jehoram for justice but rather asks him to save her (2 Kings 6:26-31), presumably, as he understands it in view of the famine, by providing her with food. In a crucial addition, Josephus has her beg him to judge her case against the other woman (*Ant.* 9.65), clearly because she is confident that her king is concerned for justice.

In his account of Jehoram Josephus uses extra-biblical additions to take advantage of the opportunity to answer the frequent charge that the Jews hate non-Jews and to insist, on the contrary, that Jews show compassion for non-Jews. Thus, in the biblical version, after Mesha, the king of the Moabites, sacrifices his own son as a burnt-offering to his god, we hear only that Jehoram and Jehoshaphat, the king of Judah, departed to their own lands, with no indication of their reaction to this act of desperation (2 Kings 3:27). Josephus, however, paints a picture of the humanity (ἀνθρώπινόν τι) and compassion (ἐλεεινόν)[2] shown by Jehoram and Jehoshaphat (*Ant.* 9.43). We are told that they felt pity (κατῴκτειραν) for Mesha, and that they consequently lifted the siege and returned home. Such a reaction is clearly an answer, as appears especially from the use of the word ἀνθρώπινον, to the charge that the Jews hate mankind.

We see another instance of Jehoram's compassion in Josephus'

---

[2] Ralph Marcus (1937, 6:25), in his note on *Antiquities* 9.43, indicates that Josephus' reference to the kings' compassion is based on the Septuagint, which renders the Hebrew *qezeph*, "wrath," by the Greek μετάμελος; but the latter word means "repentance" rather than "compassion"; hence, the attribution of compassion to these kings is Josephus' own creation.

depiction of the scene in which the woman who has made the pact with her neighbor to eat their sons begs him to have pity upon her (*Ant.* 9.64). In the biblical version he replies sarcastically, thinking that she is begging for food, "Whence shall I help you? From the threshing floor or from the wine press?" (2 Kings 6:27). Josephus' Jehoram is more sympathetic and omits the sarcasm, saying simply that he has neither threshing-floor nor wine press from which he might give her something at her entreaty. Furthermore, we see the empathy that Jehoram has for his people in that whereas in the Bible he merely rents his clothes upon hearing the woman's case (2 Kings 6:30), in Josephus' version he also expresses his grief in words, since we are told that he grieved sorely (σφοδρῶς) and cried out fearfully (δεινόν) (*Ant.* 9.67). Indeed, whereas in the Bible, at this point, we read that Jehoram vows to kill Elisha, though no reason is given for this outburst (2 Kings 6:31), Josephus, in an extra-biblical addition, explains that he was determined to do so out of concern for his subjects, namely because Elisha had not asked G-d to give his people an escape from their ills, notably the famine that was now besetting them (*Ant.* 9.67). In fact, when he thereafter comes to Elisha, Jehoram, in identifying himself with his people's sufferings, reproaches him, in an addition to the biblical narrative, for not having asked G-d for a deliverance from the misfortunes which had afflicted the people and for looking on indifferently while they were suffering (*Ant.* 9.70).

A particular aspect of φιλανθρωπία is the quality of hospitality. When the Syrian soldiers have been taken captive by Jehoram, while it is true that Elisha counsels him to set bread and water before them, in Josephus' version he actually uses the word for hospitality (ξενίων) in connection with Elisha's advice about what he should do for them (*Ant.* 9.59).

As to the virtue of piety, at first glance it would seem that Josephus blackens Jehoram even more than the Bible, where we are told that Jehoram did what was evil in the sight of the L-rd, though not like his father and mother Ahab and Jezebel, since he removed the pillar of Baal which his father had made. Josephus (*Ant.* 9.27), instead of thus noting that he was better than his father Ahab, states that he was very like Ahab in wickedness and adds that he displayed every form of lawlessness (παρανομίᾳ) and impiety (ἀσεβείᾳ) toward G-d, since he neglected His service (θρησκεύειν) and worshipped strange gods, precisely the opposite of what, according to the Bible, Jehoram did, i.e., removing the pillar of Baal.

As we read on, however, both in the biblical account and in Josephus, we see that the picture is far from one-sided. Thus, the biblical narrative (2 Kings 3:3) continues that Jehoram did, nevertheless, cling to the sins of Jeroboam, "who caused Israel to sin," and adds, for emphasis, that he did not turn away from it. The fact that Josephus omits the comparison with Jeroboam is significant, since Josephus, as we have noted, finds no redeeming features in Jeroboam. It is significant, then, that in his account of Jehoram Josephus omits all reference to his continuing in the ways of Jeroboam, the arch-culprit in his paraphrase of the Bible. In particular, it is striking that while Josephus points his finger at Jeroboam's lawlessness (παρανομίαν) (*Ant.* 9.282) (the very quality which he denounces in the revolutionaries and particularly in his bitter attack on the Sicarii [*War* 7.262]) and that he mentions this as characteristic also of Jehoram, nevertheless he omits the equation of Jehoram and Jeroboam that is highlighted in the Bible. Indeed, Josephus' concern to play down the Bible's attack on Jehoram may be seen in the statement that follows his description of Jehoram's wickedness, namely that he was also a man of bold action (δραστήριος) in other respects (*Ant.* 9.27). The word δραστήριος, we may note, is rarely used by Josephus in a pejorative sense (see LSJ, 448, s.v. δραστήριος, 2); hence as used here the term would seem to refer to Jehoram's active, enterprising, energetic, determined, bold, spirited and efficacious character.

Another clue that Josephus was seeking a partial rehabilitation of Jehoram is seen in the fact that whereas the Bible mentions that Jehoram conducted a census of his kingdom (2 Kings 3:6), Josephus, realizing the Bible's negative depiction of such censuses, given the plagues that followed them (cf. Numbers 26:2, 51, 62; 2 Samuel 24:9-11; 1 Chronicles 21:5-8), omits all mention of this; significantly, Josephus does mention the census conducted by the great king David, a sinfulness which David acknowledged (*Ant.* 7.319-21). We may surmise that this recasting of the relative wickedness of Jehoram reflects the appreciation by Josephus, who thought of himself as a prophet, of the fact that Jehoram permitted Elisha and other prophets to act freely.[3]

---

[3] We may note a similar rehabilitation of Jehoram in the rabbinic tradition,

Josephus' softening of his indictment of Jehoram may be seen, too, in his version of Elisha's remark to the elders sitting with him that "this murderer,"[4] that is, Jehoram, has sent a messenger to cut off his head (2 Kings 6:32). Josephus, in contrast, refers to Jehoram here as "the son of a murderer," thus shifting the blame to his father, Ahab (*Ant.* 9.68). Indeed, whereas in the Bible Elisha then predicts that the king will follow this messenger (2 Kings 6:32), Josephus specifically declares, in obvious vindication of Jehoram's character, that the king will change his mind (μεταβεβουλευμένος, "altered plans") (*Ant.* 9.69).

A clear indication that Jehoram was not impious may be seen in Josephus' version of the incident where he, Jehoshaphat the king of Judah, and the Idumaean king while advancing to war with the Moabites find themselves without water for their men or their beasts (*Ant.* 9.32). In the biblical version there is no indication that Jehoram prayed to G-d at this juncture; we are merely given his lament that G-d had delivered the three kings into the hands of the Moabites (2 Kings 3:10). In contrast, in Josephus we are told that while all were in torment, it was Jehoram most of all who felt distressed and that he called out to G-d asking what evil deed He had charged them with that He had led out the kings to deliver them without a struggle into the hands of the Moabite king (*Ant.* 9.32); the clear implication here is that Jehoram is a believer in divine justice and ready to accept G-d's verdict if, indeed, he had sinned.

Likewise, whereas, according to the Bible, Jehoram, Jehoshaphat, and the king of Idumaeans jointly consult with Elisha (2 Kings 3:12), Josephus, by noting that it was Jehoram in particular who consulted Elisha, indicates that it was he who had the greatest reverence for the prophet (*Ant.* 9.34). Moreover, whereas in the Bible, when Elisha initially refuses to prophesy, Jehoram is depicted as merely objecting to Elisha's bitter suggestion that he go to the prophets of Ahab and Jezebel (2 Kings 3:13), in Josephus' version Jehoram, clearly the suppliant, is described as begging (ἐδεῖτο) Elisha to prophesy and to save the kings (*Ant.* 9.34).

---

where we read that it was on account of the merit of their observance of the Sabbath that G-d gave victory to Jehoram and his allies over the Moabites (*Mekilta de-Rabbi Shimon ben Yoḥai* 162).

[4] The Hebrew *ben-hamerazeaḥ* is a hyphenated word meaning not "son of a murderer" but "murderer."

Elisha, in Josephus' paraphrase, is manifestly not so negative to Jehoram, for in the Bible he indignantly tells him that were it not for the respect which he had for Jehoshaphat he would neither look at him nor see him (2 Kings 3:14); in Josephus the reply is much milder: there Elisha declares merely that he would not answer him were it not for the sake of Jehoshaphat (2 Kings 3:14). Indeed, the close association of Jehoram with Elisha may be seen in Josephus' addition that when he returned from the campaign against the Moabites Jehoram brought Elisha with himself (*Ant.* 9.46). Again, it is Jehoram's obedience to Elisha that is stressed in an extra-biblical remark that it was in obedience to the prophet's word, warning him to beware of a Syrian plot to kill him, that Jehoram did not start out for the hunt (*Ant.* 9.51 vs. 2 Kings 6:10).[5]

Further indication of the close co-ordination between Elisha and Jehoram may be seen in Josephus' version of the episode of the blinding of the army of the Syrian king Ben-hadad. In the biblical account, when the army, having been blinded, enters Samaria, it is Elisha alone who asks G-d to open their eyes (2 Kings 6:20), whereas in Josephus' version we see the co-operation of Elisha and Jehoram in that the former orders the latter to shut the gates and to place his army around the Syrians (*Ant.* 9.57). Then, whereas in the Bible Jehoram asks Elisha whether he should slay them (2 Kings 6:21), in Josephus Jehoram appears more submissive to Elisha in that he asks whether it is Elisha's order (κελεύσειεν) that the enemy be shot down (*Ant.* 9.58). Again, the regard which Jehoram has for Elisha is seen in the fact that whereas in the Bible Jehoram prepares a great feast for Ben-hadad's army, in accordance with Elisha's advice (2 Kings 6:23), in Josephus Jehoram does so in obedience (πειθόμενος) to that advice (*Ant.* 9.59). Moreover, whereas the Bible states that they ate and drank, Josephus adds a further dimension by asserting that Jehoram entertained the Syrians very splendidly (λαμπρῶς) and lavishly (φιλοτίμως, "eagerly," "with an honorable escort," "honorably," "readily," "generously,"

---

[5] The fact that Jehoram, in obedience to Elisha, does not start out for the hunt may again be a compliment to Elisha in view of the traditional Jewish abhorrrence of hunting. We can see this from the question ascribed to the third-century Babylonian rabbi, Ḥanan bar Raba, "Was Moses a hunter?" in seeking to prove that the Torah was divinely revealed, inasmuch as Moses could not of his own knowledge have described the various animals mentioned in the Torah in view of the Jewish aversion to hunting (*Ḥullin* 60b).

"splendidly," "brilliantly," "with great expenditure," "sparing no expense," "magnificently") (*Ant.* 9.59).

Likewise, whereas in the Bible, when Jehoram, in his anger at Elisha for not praying to G-d to alleviate the famine, sends a messenger to kill him, it is the messenger who declares that the calamity had been sent by G-d (2 Kings 6:33), in Josephus it is Jehoram who is depicted as repenting (καταγνούς, "regretting," "reproaching himself") of his wrath against the prophet and who, fearing that the man who had been ordered to kill Elisha might already have done so, hastens to prevent the murder (*Ant.* 9.70).

Indeed, Jehoram is presented as a man of faith, in contrast to his captain who is incredulous of Elisha's prophecy that the famine will end on the following day (2 Kings 7:1-2). Specifically, we read that Elisha's words change the feelings of Jehoram and those present to one of joy, since they did not hesitate to believe the prophet, having been convinced of his truthfulness by earlier experiences, and that, in fact, the announced day of plenty made the continued famine of that day seem light to them (*Ant.* 9.72). Moreover, our sympathies are aroused for Jehoram when Jehu reviles (βλασφημήσαντος) him bitterly (πικρῶς), whereas the Bible has Jehu mention only the harlotries and sorceries of Jehoram's mother Jezebel (2 Kings 7:1-2).[6]

3. *"Improvements" in the Story: Avoidance of Discrepancies*

From time to time Josephus was confronted with discrepancies within the Books of Kings or between Kings and Chronicles. For example, we read that Ahaziah acceded to the throne of Judah in the twelfth year of Jehoram the king of Israel (2 Kings 8:25) and that he was twenty-two years old when he began his reign (2 Kings

---

[6] This partial rehabilitation of Jehoram is paralleled in rabbinic literature. Thus the rabbis clearly disapproved of Elisha's rebuke of Jehoram; and they remark that when Elisha rebuked him the spirit of prophecy forsook him, so that he had to resort to artificial means to reawaken it within himself (*Pesaḥim* 66b). On the other hand, the rabbis also condemn Jehoram for exacting usury from Obadiah, the pious protector of the prophets; and as a consequence, they say, he was pierced beween his arms, with the arrow going out at his heart, inasmuch as he had stretched out his arms to receive usury and had hardened his heart against compassion (*Exodus Rabbah* 31.9; *Tanhuma Mishpatim* 9, *Midrash Psalms* 15.6). This description contrasts with Josephus' picture, as noted above, of Jehoram as showing compassion.

8:26). Elsewhere, however, we are told that Ahaziah began his reign in the eleventh year of Jehoram (2 Kings 9:29) and that he was forty-two years old when he began his reign (2 Chronicles 22:2). Commentators, such as Radak and Malbim, puzzled by such discrepancies, suggest that Ahaziah was appointed king twice, first when his father was incapacitated, and again after his father's death. Though he usually notes a king's age at the time of death, in the case of Ahaziah Josephus avoids all problems by not bringing the start of his reign into juxtaposition with the reign of Jehoram and by not indicating his age at that time (so Begg 1993b, 464-65).

4. Summary

As in the case of two other wicked kings, Ahab and Manasseh, Josephus goes out of his way to rehabilitate Jehoram (Joram), at least partly. It is Jehoram who takes the lead in allowing his people to plunder the Syrian camp when there is some question as to whether the Syrians have planted a ruse. In addition, Jehoram possesses the cardinal virtues of wisdom, courage, temperance, justice, and piety. He shows his wisdom in the way he handles the matter of the empty Syrian camp. He displays his military ability in his careful planning in consultation with his ally Jehoshaphat the king of Judah. He holds conferences to determine strategy and analyzes the strategy of the enemy very carefully. He is capable of quick decisions. He is realistic in perceiving that he is no match for the Syrians and accordingly stays behind the strong walls of Samaria. He is depicted as totally devoted to his responsibilities and forever concerned for his people. And yet, war is not an end in itself for him; he welcomes peace. Furthermore, Jehoram shows the quality of moderation when he repents of his decision to kill the prophet Elisha.

In view of the premium which the Romans, in particular, placed upon justice, it is significant that Jehoram's subjects, as exemplified by the pitiful woman who had made a pact with her neighbor to cook their sons, have confidence that he will judge them fairly. In view of the charge of inhumanity made by detractors of the Jews, it is most effective that Josephus ascribes to Jehoram the qualities of humanity and compassion, so much stressed by the rabbis as the *sine qua non* for the Jewish people, in the incident when Mesha, king of Moab, offers his own son as a sacrifice, as well as in his reaction to the famine that afflicted his nation during the siege of Samaria. Likewise, he exhibits hospitality, so much prized by the ancients, toward the Syrian captives.

As to the fifth virtue of piety, though Josephus does say that Jehoram manifested every form of lawlessness and impiety, the picture is by no means completely negative. In particular, it is significant that he does not repeat the biblical statement that Jehoram clung to the sins of Jeroboam, the one king who, for Josephus, as for the rabbis, is the most wicked of all, primarily because he disturbed the unity of the Jewish people. On the contrary, we see Jehoram's piety in Josephus' addition that when his troops and animals are without water he prayed to G-d seeking to know what sin he had committed that had brought on this dearth; here he is clearly convinced that G-d would not have acted thus if it were not deserved. Jehoram had, as well, the greatest reverence for the prophet Elisha, to whose advice he adheres. Indeed, he is a man of faith who is convinced of the truthfulness of Elisha's prophecies.

Finally, Josephus has "improved" his narrative by avoiding discrepancies in chronology such as are found between Kings and Chronicles.

CHAPTER TWENTY-TWO

ELISHA

1. *Introduction*

In depicting the personality of Elisha, Josephus, like the rabbis, was in something of a quandary. On the one hand, Elisha was clearly inferior to Elijah, whose pupil and successor he was. Moreover, Elijah was the more popular figure in apocalyptic and popular circles and was said to have rescued the Jews at crucial points in history.

On the other hand, in view of Josephus' indebtedness to the Roman imperial family for a tract of land outside Jerusalem, the liberation of some friends, citizenship, lodging in the former palace of Vespasian, a library, and a pension, he could hardly aggrandize Elijah, a figure who was held to be the forerunner of the Messiah and who, consequently, was expected to set in motion a revolt against the Roman Empire in order to establish an independent state. Again, the fact that Josephus' presumed contemporary Pseudo-Philo, in his *Biblical Antiquities* (48.1-2), identifies Elijah with Phinehas, the biblical zealot who took the law into his own hands and slew the Israelite Zimri who was having relations with a Midianite woman (Numbers 25:7-8), would hardly endear him to Josephus, inasmuch as Elijah thereby becomes the prototype of all later zealots, including, we may presume, the revolutionaries of his own day. Since there was no such identification of Elisha with the Messiah or with Phinehas, Josephus, we may suggest, found him less controversial than Elijah and hence could present him more positively.

And yet, because Josephus was writing his *Antiquities* not only for a pagan Greek but also for a Jewish audience and because Elijah was so popular as a folk-hero of the Jewish masses, Josephus could hardly afford to downgrade him. Hence, his approach to the two figures had to be more subtle.

In the first place, one criterion of the importance which Josephus assigns to his biblical personalities is the sheer amount of space that he devotes to them. The ratio for the Elijah episode (1

Kings 17-19, 21:17-29, 2 Kings 1:3-2:12; Josephus' *Ant.* 8.319-54, 360-62, 9.20-28) is 1.52 for Josephus as compared with the Hebrew and .96 for Josephus as compared with the Septuagint.[1] For Elisha (2 Kings 2:1-25, 3:11-20, 4:1-44, 5:8-7:2, 7:16-8:15, 9:1-3, 13:14-21) the ratio of Josephus' version *(Ant.* 9.28, 34-37, 46-60, 67-74, 85-92, 106-7, 175, 178-83) as compared with the Hebrew is 1.11 and as compared with the Septuagint is .72. From this point of view Elisha would thus appear to be less important to Josephus than is Elijah; nonetheless, a key indication of Elisha's importance to Josephus as a prophet is the fact that on twenty-seven occasions[2] Josephus refers to Elisha as a prophet or uses the word "prophesied" where this is missing in the Bible, whereas he does so only seventeen times in the case of Elijah.[3] The only figure, we may add, whom Josephus designates more often as a prophet where the Bible does not is Samuel (see Feldman 1990, 389, n. 16). Another criterion of the importance of a biblical figure for Josephus is whether or not he sees fit to add an encomium when he reports the figure's death. It is thus significant that Josephus has no encomium at all for Elijah but one of twenty-six words for Elisha. Finally, Elisha is the only prophet whose deeds are described as glorious (λαμπραί) and as having been held in glorious (λαμπρᾶς) memory by the Hebrews *(Ant.* 9.46, 182). Significantly, this word, λαμπρός, is used elsewhere in Josephus only with regard to the achievements of the

---

[1] There is some reason for thinking that Josephus used the Septuagint version for his Elijah pericope, just as he does for most of the Bible, inasmuch as he agrees with the Septuagint against the Hebrew text in identifying Jehoram as the brother of Ahaziah at the point when he succeeds to the throne (2 Kings 1:17; *Ant.* 9.27).

[2] *Ant.* 8.354 vs. 1 Kings 19:19; *Ant.* 9.37 vs. 2 Kings 3:14-20; *Ant.* 9.48 vs. 2 Kings 4:3; *Ant.* 9.49 vs. 2 Kings 4:7 ("man of G-d"); *Ant.* 9.55 vs. 2 Kings 6:17; *Ant.* 9.56 vs. 2 Kings 6:18; *Ant.* 9.57 vs. 2 Kings 6:19; *Ant.* 9.58 vs. 2 Kings 6:21; *Ant.* 9.59 vs. 2 Kings 6:23; *Ant.* 9.60 vs. 2 Kings 6:24; *Ant.* 9.67 vs. 2 Kings 6:31; *Ant.* 9.68 vs. 2 Kings 6:32; *Ant.* 9.70 vs. 2 Kings 6:33; *Ant.* 9.72 vs. 2 Kings 7:2; *Ant.* 9.73 (*bis*) vs. 2 Kings 7:2; *Ant.* 9.86 vs. 2 Kings 7:20; *Ant.* 9.88 vs. 2 Kings 8:7; *Ant.* 9.90 vs. 2 Kings 8:10; *Ant.* 9.103 vs. 2 Chronicles 21:18; *Ant.* 9.120 vs. 2 Kings 9:25; *Ant.* 9.175 vs. 2 Kings 13:7-8; *Ant.* 9.178 vs. 2 Kings 13:14; *Ant.* 9.179 vs. 2 Kings 13:14; *Ant.* 9.182 vs. 2 Kings 13:20; *Ant.* 9.183 vs. 2 Kings 13:20; *Ant.* 9.185 vs. 2 Kings 13:25.

[3] *Ant.* 8.319 vs. 1 Kings 17:1; *Ant.* 8.323 vs. 1 Kings 17:15; *Ant.* 8.325 vs. 1 Kings 17:15; *Ant.* 8.325 vs. 1 Kings 17:18 ("man of G-d"); *Ant.* 8.327 vs. 1 Kings 17:22; *Ant.* 8.327 vs. 1 Kings 17:24 ("man of G-d"); *Ant.* 8.329 vs. 1 Kings 18:7; *Ant.* 8.331 vs. 1 Kings 18:7; *Ant.* 8.337 vs. 1 Kings 18:21; *Ant.* 8.346 vs. 1 Kings 18:46; *Ant.* 8.354 vs. 1 Kings 19:21; *Ant.* 8.360 vs. 1 Kings 21:17; *Ant.* 8.362 (*bis*) vs. 1 Kings 21:27-29; *Ant.* 8.417 vs. 1 Kings 22:38; *Ant.* 9.20 vs. 2 Kings 1:3; *Ant.* 9.119 vs. 2 Kings 9:25.

much-revered David (*Ant.* 7.65) and of David's chief warriors (*Ant.* 7.307). Moreover, it is with regard to Elisha alone that we find Josephus making an explicit connection between a prophet and history – so meaningful for Josephus, who was so proud of his craft as historian –, for Elisha's deeds are described as worthy of historical record (ἱστορίας) (*Ant.* 9.46).

2. *Elisha's Power as a Prophet*

Elisha's power as a prophet is nowhere demonstrated more graphically than in Josephus' addition, not found in the Bible (1 Kings 19:20), that after Elijah threw his mantle upon Elisha, the latter immediately began to prophesy and, leaving his oxen, followed Elijah (*Ant.* 8.354).

Elisha's power as a prophet is considerably aggrandized in Josephus' version. Thus, in the biblical narrative, the commander of King Jehoram's army is skeptical when Elisha prophesies that on the following day a miracle will occur that will bring the price of grain down drastically; he declares: "Behold, if the L-rd makes windows in the sky [that is, sends rain], will this thing come about?" (2 Kings 7:2). In Josephus' version the officer expresses much greater amazement and incredulity: "Incredible are the things you are saying, O prophet. And, as impossible as it is for G-d to rain down from heaven torrents of barley or fine flour, just as impossible is it for the things of which you have now spoken to happen" (*Ant.* 9.73). When, consequently, the prophecy does come to pass, it is all the more remarkable.

Significantly, Josephus omits the passage in which King Jehoram asks Gehazi, the servant of Elisha, to recount all the great deeds that Elisha had done (2 Kings 8:4 vs. *Ant.* 9.87). Such a request clearly implies that the king had not heard of Elisha's miracles, whereas Josephus wants the reader to think that Elisha was so remarkable that his fame had spread widely.

The greatest tribute to Elisha's power and effectiveness is conveyed by Josephus in an extra-biblical remark attributed to King Jehoash, who visits Elisha when the latter is ill with his final illness. The Bible has one brief comment, namely that Jehoash wept and said, "My master, my master, Israel's chariots and riders!" (2 Kings 13:14). Josephus has a much more elaborate scene. In the first place, Jehoash pays tribute to Elisha with his statement that because of the prophet the Israelites had never had to use arms against the enemy, but through his prophecies had actually overcome the enemy without a battle.[4] Jehoash then goes so far as to remark that Elisha's death would leave him unarmed before the Syrians and that consequently, since it would no longer be safe for him to live, he would do best to join Elisha in death (*Ant.* 9.179-80).

3. *Elisha's Loyalty to Elijah*

One of the qualities which Josephus emphasizes in his additions is Elisha's loyalty to his mentor Elijah. Thus, the biblical text declares that when Elijah selected Elisha as his successor, Elisha asked that he be permitted to bid his parents farewell; he then slaughters oxen, cooks the meat for his people, and feeds them (1 Kings 19:20). In Josephus' version Elisha leaves his oxen and immediately follows Elijah, asking only that he be allowed to take leave of his parents *(Ant.* 8.354). Indeed, whereas the biblical text declares that Elisha rose and followed Elijah and ministered to him (1 Kings 19:21), Josephus emphasizes Elisha's loyalty to a much greater degree by stating that so long as Elijah was alive Elisha was his disciple and attendant (*Ant.* 8.304).

The reader may, however, be disturbed by the fact that in the Bible when the disciples of the prophets ask Elisha whether he is aware that on that very day G-d will take away their master from them he replies that he does know but that they should keep quiet (2 Kings 2:5). We may, too, wonder why Elisha, who is twice able to revive people from the dead, does not do so in the case of his master. Apparently, realizing that readers might share this wonderment, Josephus resolves it by omitting the scene in which the prophets thus approach Elisha, as he does the scene in which Elisha, viewing the ascension of Elijah to heaven, weeps, apparently helplessly (2 Kings 2:11-14). Josephus was apparently likewise embarrassed by the fact that Elisha is unable to convince the disciples of the prophets that Elijah's disappearance is not due to his having been thrown off a mountain (2 Kings 2:16). Indeed, we are

---

[4] Similarly, rabbinic tradition remarks that so long as Elisha was alive no Syrian troops entered the Land of Israel and that the first invasion by the enemy occurred on the day of his burial (Tosefta, *Soṭah* 12.6, *Eliyahu Rabbah* 8.39).

told that they urge him until he is actually shamed into granting their request to start a search for their master (2 Kings 2:17). Again, Josephus, embarrassed that Elisha should be ashamed in this way, resolves the problem by totally omitting the scene (*Ant.* 9.28), just as he omits many other similarly embarrassing scenes.

One of the problems that clearly confronted Josephus was how to present Elisha as completely loyal to Elijah without making him totally subservient to him. In the Bible one of the servants of Jehoram, the king of Israel, tells Jehoshaphat, the king of Judah, when the latter seeks a prophet while his army is beset by thirst, that Elisha is nearby, "who poured water on Elijah's hands" (2 Kings 3:11). The implication of this remark is that Elisha was Elijah's personal servant, ministering to him to such a degree that he even poured water on his hands – a rather degrading picture, as most readers would agree. One would have expected a statement, rather, that Elisha was Elijah's disciple and successor. The rabbinic tradition, to be sure, extols Elisha for serving Elijah thus, noting that it is more meritorious to serve a teacher than to be his disciple (*Berakot* 7b). But again, Josephus resolves this dilemma by completely omitting the reference (*Ant.* 9.33).

4. *Elisha's Virtues*

If, as we may well assume, Josephus was acquainted with many traditions which are found recorded in later rabbinic texts (though, admittedly, we cannot prove that Josephus was acquainted with any particular tradition unless he actually refers to it), it would appear significant that Josephus chooses to stress Elisha's role as a prophet and not as a scholar; hence, Josephus omits reference to Elisha as embodying the quality of wisdom, which was associated with achievements of human intelligence. Thus, we do not find Josephus utilizing the rabbinic tradition that when the angel came down from heaven to take Elijah from earth, he found him so immersed in a learned discussion with his disciple Elisha that he could not get Elijah's attention and consequently had to return at another time in order to fulfill his mission (*Seder Eliyahu Rabbah* 5.22-23.90-91; cf. *Ta'anit* 10b, *Soṭah* 49a, *Berakot* 31a).

Elisha displays unusual courage when Ben-hadad, the Syrian king, attempts to capture him. In the biblical narrative, when Ben-hadad's army surrounds the city where Elisha is staying and Elisha's attendant despairs, crying out, "What shall we do?", Elisha responds in vague terms: "Have no fear, for those who are with us are more numerous than those who are with them" (2 Kings 6:15-16). In Josephus' version Elisha is much more explicit in naming G-d as his ally and displays bravery in being scornful (καταφρονῶν) of danger (*Ant.* 9.55).

Indeed, Josephus' Elisha shows all the qualities of an experienced and successful general when he brings the blinded forces of Ben-hadad, the Syrian king, to Samaria (*Ant.* 9.57). Whereas the Bible gives no further details about this happening (2 Kings 6:20), Josephus portrays Elisha as ordering (προσέταξε) King Jehoram of Israel to shut the gates and to place his army around the Syrians (*Ant.* 9.57). As a result, in a further detail unparalleled by the Bible, the Syrian forces are said to be in dire consternation (ἐκπλήξει) and helplessness (ἀμηχανίᾳ) at so divine and marvellous an event (*Ant.* 9.58).

It is significant that the term "renowned" (διαβόητος), which is used by Josephus in his extra-biblical encomium of Elisha (*Ant.* 9.182), is found only twice elsewhere in his writings, both times with reference to marvelous (θαυμαστήν, a term also used here of Elisha) military victories, in the one case those of Eleazar the son of Dodeios, in David's army (*Ant.* 7.309), in the other case Abijah's triumph over Jeroboam (*Ant.* 8.284).

As to the virtue of temperance, one incident in connection with Elisha which would surely raise questions about Elisha's self-control was the one in which some little boys jeer Elisha for his baldness, whereupon he curses them in the name of G-d; and, consequently, two she-bears come out of the forest and tear apart forty-two of them (2 Kings 2:23-24). The rabbis do try to defend Elisha by remarking that the boys were completely devoid of virtue. And yet, despite the rabbis' great admiration for Elisha, they are quick to remark that as a result of this lack of restraint by Elisha in failing to control his wrath he was punished by having to undergo a very serious sickness (*Pesahim* 66b, *Sotah* 47a). In this display of temper he apparently resembled his zealous master Elijah. Again, Josephus' resolution to this problem is to omit the incident altogether (*Ant.* 9.28).

Elisha likewise, in the biblical text, displays anger toward King Jehoram, when the latter's army is beset by thirst, telling him sarcastically, when he is consulted, to go to the prophets of his father

King Ahab and his mother Queen Jezebel (2 Kings 3:13). Elisha then adds, in utter contempt, that were it not for his respect for Jehoshaphat the king of Judah, whose army likewise was beset by the same thirst, "I would neither look at you nor would I see you." Here again the rabbis censure Elisha for losing his temper and state that at this point the spirit of prophecy forsook him, so that he had to resort to artificial means to reawaken it within himself (*Pesaḥim* 66b, *Sanhedrin* 39b). In Josephus' version Elisha eventually responds on a more positive note to Jehoram's request by remarking that he agreed to do so only because Jehoshaphat was a holy and righteous man (*Ant.* 9.35).

Another incident in which Elisha displays his anger is that in which he curses his disciple Gehazi for accepting gifts from Naaman (2 Kings 5:27). Indeed, the Talmud is clearly critical of Elisha for doing so and records the tradition that he was visited with illness – and subsequently, according to the rabbis, became the first person in history to survive an illness – for thrusting Gehazi away instead of maintaining some kind of relationship with him (*Soṭah* 46b-47a). In treating this episode thus the rabbis repeat the well-known saying that the right hand should push away but that the left hand should bring back (*Mekilta Yitro* 1.58b). Again, Josephus saves himself embarrasssment by omitting this incident completely (*Ant.* 9.51).[5]

Still another incident in which Elisha shows a burst of anger is that in which, when he is dying, he tells Jehoash, the king of Israel, to fetch arrows and to strike the ground with them. When Jehoash strikes the ground three times and stops, Elisha becomes incensed against him and tells him that he should have struck the ground five or six times, since now he is destined to strike the Syrians only three times whereas if he had struck the ground more he would have been privileged to annihilate them completely (2 Kings 13:15-19). The reader may well wonder why Elisha should be so angry when the king actually obeyed his instructions to strike

---

[5] R. Marcus (1937, 6:28-29, n. a on *Ant.* 9.51) states that there is a lacuna in Josephus' text corresponding to the biblical narrative extending from 2 Kings 4:8 to 6:8, including the accounts of the Shunammite woman and the resurrection of her dead child, the miraculous removal of the poison from the pottage, the miracle of the multiplication of loaves, the miraculous cure from leprosy of Naaman the Syrian, and the miraculous rescue of the iron axe-head from the water. But such omissions are common in Josephus and may, in this particular case especially, be explained by his tendency to avoid or to downgrade miracles.

the ground and Elisha himself had not specified how many times he should do so. Again, Josephus resolves the problem by completely omitting mention of Elisha's anger (*Ant.* 9.181).

Closely connected with moderation is the quality of modesty. Josephus must have been disturbed, as was Elijah himself in the Bible (2 Kings 2:9), by Elisha's seemingly bold and immodest desire to have Elijah bestow upon him twice as much prophetic power as he himself possessed, as witnessed by Elijah's reply that Elisha had made a difficult request (2 Kings 2:10). The rabbinic tradition, indeed, indicates that in point of fact Elisha, during his lifetime, did perform twice as many miracles (that is, sixteen) as did Elijah (*Baraita of 32 Middot*, no. 1). The very first of these, the crossing of the Jordan River, was, according to the rabbis, more remarkable in the case of Elisha than the similar crossing by Elijah, inasmuch as the former performed the miracle alone (2 Kings 2:14), whereas the latter was accompanied by Elisha when he did his (*Baraita of 32 Middot*, no. 1). Again, whereas Elijah restored one person to life, Elisha revived two people (*Hullin* 7b). Not surprisingly, Josephus' solution to this embarrassing problem is to omit Elisha's request to Elijah altogether (*Ant.* 9.28).

Elisha exemplifies the quality of justice when he performs his great miracle of sweetening the rancid waters of Jericho (2 Kings 2:19-22); in that case, Josephus is careful to remark that he did so by raising his righteous (δικαίαν) right hand to heaven (*War* 4.462). Moreover, in his extra-biblical prayer Elisha beseeches G-d to cure the waters and to make the land productive only so long as the citizens of Jericho remained a righteous (δίκαιοι) people (*War* 4.463). Finally, in his extra-biblical eulogy for Elisha the quality which Josephus singles out as the one for which he was renowned (διαβόητος, "noised abroad," "famous") is his justice (δικαιοσύνη) (*Ant.* 9.182).

Coupled with justice, as we have observed, is the virtue of humanity (φιλανθρωπία), as we have observed. In this connection, Josephus goes out of his way to credit Elisha with helping the poor widow for whom he performed the miracle of filling her many vessels with oil. In the Bible Elisha is not directly credited with this miracle (2 Kings 4:1-7), whereas in Josephus we are explicitly told that it was Elisha who freed the woman of her debts and delivered her from the harsh treatment of her creditors (*Ant.* 9.50). To be sure, Josephus does not characterize this help by means of the term φιλανθρωπία, but a reader of his Greek text might well identify it as an instance of that virtue.

Connected with the quality of φιλανθρωπία is the virtue of showing gratitude. We see the latter quality exemplified, in particular, by Elisha in Josephus' version of the incident in which Elisha cured the hitherto death-dealing waters of Jericho (2 Kings 2:19-22; *War* 4.459-64). In the biblical account there is no indication as to Elisha's motive in helping the people of Jericho, but Josephus in his version states that Elisha did so out of gratitude for having been treated by them with extreme hospitality (*War* 4.461); in response, as Josephus puts it, he conferred upon them and their country a boon for all time.

In accentuating the mercy which Elisha shows to the soldiers of the Syrian king Ben-hadad, Josephus goes considerably beyond the Bible. In the biblical narrative, when Jehoram, the king of Israel, asks Elisha whether he should slay the blinded Syrian soldiers, Elisha replies that he should not kill them, inasmuch as he had captured them, but rather should give them food and drink and let them return to their masters (2 Kings 6:21-22). Josephus in his version explains the reason for his advice, namely that these men had done no harm to Jehoram's country and that it was through the power of G-d and without their knowing it that they had come into Jehoram's power (*Ant.* 9.58). Elisha, in another extra-biblical addition, then exhibits the quality of hospitality, so prized among the ancients, when he counsels Jehoram to offer the soldiers hospitality (ξενίων) (*Ant.* 9.59).

Another indication of Elisha's sincere sympathy for his fellow man may be seen in Josephus' version of the prophet's reaction to his own prediction of the death of the Syrian king Ben-hadad. According to the biblical text, when Elisha tells the king's emissary, Hazael, that the king will not recover from his illness, Hazael makes his face expressionless and holds it thus for a long time, while Elisha himself weeps (2 Kings 8:11). In Josephus' version there is much more sympathy shown by both parties, inasmuch Hazael grieves at what he hears, even as Elisha begins to cry and sheds many tears (*Ant.* 9.90).

Another instance where Elisha shows sympathy and sensitivity to the feelings of fellow human beings is Josephus' version of the scene depicting Elisha's death. According to the Bible, when Jehoash the king of Israel visits Elisha upon his deathbed, Jehoash weeps for the forthcoming demise of his master. Elisha's immediate reaction is to tell Jehoash to fetch a bow and arrows and to strike the ground with them, thus showing no sympathy for the king (2 Kings 13:14-15). Josephus' Elisha, on the other hand, comforts (παρεμυθεῖτο) Jehoash and tells him to have a bow brought to him and to bend it as a prophecy of his forthcoming military success (*Ant.* 9.180).

Connected with the virtue of justice is the enormous responsibility to tell the truth. Thus, it is significant that, in an extra-biblical comment, Josephus tells us that King Jehoram and his retainers did not hesitate to believe Elisha because they were convinced of his truthfulness by earlier experiences (*Ant.* 9.72).

As for piety, when Josephus adds the unscriptural detail that Elisha was given a magnificent (μεγαλοπρεποῦς) burial, he justifies its splendor by noting that it was fitting for one so dear to G-d (θεοφιλῆ) (*Ant.* 9.182).

The closeness of Elisha to G-d is further to be seen in the extra-biblical remark that it was with G-d as his ally that Elisha was scornful of danger (*Ant.* 9.55; cf. 2 Kings 6:23). Elisha's intimate connection with G-d is emphasized, with particular effectiveness, by the fact that the very enemy of the Israelites, Ben-hadad, the Syrian king, instead of ascribing his defeat to the superiority of the Israelite king Jehoram and his troops, expresses amazement at the achievement of Elisha, "with whom the Deity was so evidently present," in arranging to blind his troops (*Ant.* 9.60). Indeed, so impressed is Ben-hadad with the power of Elisha's holiness that he determines to make no further secret attempts on the life of the Israelite king but rather to fight openly and to seek to overcome him through the numbers and strength of his army (*Ant.* 9.60; cf. 2 Kings 6:23-24).

One biblical title for Elisha which Josephus does not utilize is that of man of G-d (2 Kings 4:7, 4:9, 7:2), consistently calling him, rather, a prophet. Indeed, Josephus is careful to avoid extreme claims about Elisha, such as are found in the rabbinic tradition, that he was so awe-inspiring that no woman could look upon his face and live (*Pirqe de-Rabbi Eliezer* 33) and that not even a fly would approach him because so pleasant a fragrance surrounded him (*Berakot* 10b).

5. *A Gentler Elisha*

The picture of Elisha that emerges from the Bible is of a fiery prophet who is, in this respect, a worthy successor to his mentor Elijah. As such, he has all the characteristics of a zealot revolutionary; but whereas Elijah is identified in the rabbinic tradition with Phinehas, Elisha is not; and hence Josephus, like the rabbis, felt free to mould the latter into a gentler figure (see Hengel 1976, 172-75). Thus, in the Bible G-d tells Elijah that Jehu will kill those who escape the sword of King Hazael while Elisha will kill those who escape the sword of Jehu (1 Kings 19:17). This prophecy is missing in Josephus' paraphrase (*Ant.* 8.352) not only because we find no later reference to such slayings by Elisha but also because Josephus seeks to portray Elisha in a gentler light. Josephus also omits the gory scene, at the time of Elisha's call by Elijah, where Elisha takes the yoke of oxen, slaughters them, and boils their flesh (1 Kings 19:21 vs. *Ant.* 8.352).

Indeed, it is significant that in his extra-biblical eulogy for Elisha Josephus remarks that he was held in honor by G-d (*Ant.* 9.182). The verb that is here used for "held in honor," σπουδασθείς, means "to pursue with zeal." Far from showing himself zealous, as the revolutionaries did in Josephus' own day, Elisha is thus depicted as being the recipient of it from G-d.

6. *Miracles*

It is significant that when Josephus does mention the miracle performed by Elisha in curing the waters of Jericho (2 Kings 2:19-23), he does so by invoking natural causality (*War* 4.462-64). Thus, whereas in the Bible we read only that Elisha cured the waters by throwing salt into them, Josephus emphasizes that the miracle resulted from Elisha's prayer to G-d to mollify the stream and to open sweeter channels so long as the people of Jericho remained righteous. We are then told that in addition to these prayers Elisha "worked many things besides with his hands from [professional] skill" (*War* 4.464). Even so, we must note that Josephus omits this miracle from his extensive paraphrase of Elisha's deeds in the *Antiquities*; he apparently felt more comfortable inserting it in his narrative of the Jewish war against the Romans, where the intended readership, at least originally (*War* 1.3), consisted of Jews, who, in the context of the many strange and remarkable events of the war, would have been more readily disposed to give it credence. Moreover, in the *War* the passage appears in a geographical excursus and is presented as a story for which the author does not necessarily accept responsibility and which the reader is free either to accept or not (λόγος, *War* 4.460).

In the case of Elisha, Josephus likewise tones down the miracles performed at his behest. Thus, according to the biblical narrative, Elisha prophesies to King Jehoram of Israel, when the latter's army is beset by thirst, that the valley will be made, presumably miraculously, full of pools (2 Kings 3:16). In Josephus' version the miracle is much reduced in that Elisha orders the kings Jehoshaphat and Jehoram to dig many pits in the bed of the stream (*Ant.* 9.35). Again, though Elisha predicts that there would be neither cloud nor wind nor downpour of rain and yet that the stream bed would be full of water, apparently miraculously (*Ant.* 9.36), Josephus, rationalizing, explains the flow of water in the stream by remarking that G-d sent a heavy rain in the region of Idumaea, three days' journey away (*Ant.* 9.37); in contrast, the Bible says that the water came from the road of Edom without explaining how it got there in the first place (2 Kings 3:20).[6]

The miracle of the poor widow whose empty vessels are miraculously filled with oil becomes more credible by deft touches in Josephus' version (2 Kings 4:1-7; *Ant.* 9.47-50). In the first place, in contrast to the biblical narrative, which presents the incident as one which actually occurred and for which, consequently, the author takes responsibility, Josephus starts his version with the word φασι, that is, "they say," thus disclaiming responsibility for its historicity. In the second place, the miracle appears more plausible in that, whereas in the Bible the unending supply of oil is left unexplained (2 Kings 4:5-6), Josephus explicitly declares that it was G-d who kept on filling the vessels (*Ant.* 9.48).

Surely one of the most amazing miracles performed by Elisha is his revival of the dead child of the Shunammite woman (2 Kings 4:34). In addition to the difficulty of getting readers to believe such an unusual event, Josephus, at this point, may well have asked

---

[6] Rappaport (1930, 60-61, no. 251) notes that the commentator Rashi on 2 Kings 3:20 likewise derives the water from a rainstorm which fell upon Edom. Presumably here, as normally elsewhere, Rashi is relying upon an aggadic source, but that source is apparently lost.

himself why Elisha should have performed this for a mere stranger, who, to be sure, had shown him hospitality, whereas he did not do this for his own master Elijah himself (*Ant.* 9.51). The midrashic tradition, to be sure, explains that the prophet's deed serves to inculcate the duty of gratitude in return for the hospitality which the woman had shown him (*Exodus Rabbah* 4.2). But readers might still have wondered why Elisha could not also have performed the additional miracle of resuscitating his master. Again, Josephus resolves the problem by omitting the entire incident (*Ant.* 9.51).

Indeed, Josephus (*Ant.* 9.51) omits a number of other miracles which, according to the Bible, were performed by Elisha: his counteracting the poison in some pottage (2 Kings 4:38-41), his feeding one hundred men with a mere twenty loaves of bread (2 Kings 4:42-44), his curing Naaman of leprosy (2 Kings 5:1-19), his inflicting leprosy upon Gehazi (2 Kings 5:20-27), and his rescue of the iron axe-head from the water (2 Kings 6:1-7).

Likewise, when Elisha prays to G-d to open the eyes of his servant so that he may see the horses and chariots surrounding Elisha, we are told that the mountain was then filled with fiery horses and chariots (2 Kings 6:17). In Josephus' version, however, the miracle is made more credible in that there is no mention of the horses and chariots being fiery (*Ant.* 9.55). Moreover, the mountain is not full of them; rather, there is simply a large number (πλῆθος). Furthermore, whereas the Bible states that G-d, in response to Elisha's prayer, struck the enemy's army with blindness (2 Kings 6:18), Josephus rationalizes by explaining that Elisha besought G-d to blind the enemy's eyes through throwing a mist around them (*Ant.* 9.56). Furthermore, whereas in the biblical version Elisha leads the blinded army (2 Kings 6:19), Josephus explains that not only their eyes but also their understanding (διάνοιαν) was beclouded (ἐπεσκοτημένοι, "darkened") by G-d (*Ant.* 9.57). Moreover, the miracle is rendered more credible because the Syrian king, Benhadad, himself, in an extra-biblical addition expresses amazement at the unexpected (παράδοξον) deed (*Ant.* 9.60).[7]

If, as we have indicated, Josephus was well acquainted with rabbinic traditions, we should perhaps attach significance to the fact that he does not mention the tradition that Elisha was the first

---

[7] For other Josephan uses of the term παράδοξον see Attridge (1976, 95, n. 2).

person in history to survive serious illness (*Baba Mezia* 87a). Josephus, realizing that his readers would have raised their eyebrows at such a claim, omits it, despite the fact that he accentuates the wondrous achievements of Elisha in other areas.

It is this unexpected (παράδοξα)[8] and marvellous (θαυμαστά)[9] quality of his achievements which Josephus emphasizes in his extra-biblical eulogy of Elisha, and it is these deeds which, he says, are held as a glorious memory by the Hebrews (*Ant.* 9.182).

In view of what we have noted is Josephus' tendency to omit or rationalize or downgrade miracles, the reader may wonder that Josephus does include the extraordinary incident whereby a corpse that had been cast into the grave of Elisha was revived (2 Kings 13:20-21). A closer examination of this incident, however, may cast some light on Josephus' reason for including it. In the Bible we read that as the man was being buried a marauding band of Moabites appeared, and the burial party in their haste, apparently out of fear of the Moabites, threw him into Elisha's grave. When the corpse touched Elisha's bones he stood up on his feet. Josephus might well have chosen to omit this incident, inasmuch as it has no particular political or military significance for his narrative. However, we may note that in Josephus' version in place of the Moabites we have a reference to robbers (λῃστῶν), and the man who is dead is not one who has died naturally but rather one whom they have murdered (*Ant.* 9.183). The word λῃσταί in Josephus regularly refers to the revolutionaries who fought against the Romans; it is they who are the brigands at Masada, whither Simon bar Giora fled (*War* 2.653, 4.504, 4.555), and it is they who are referred to as the revolutionaries whom Titus besieged in Jerusalem (*War* 5.524). Hence, Josephus, who so bitterly opposed these brigands, uses this occasion to indicate that Elisha, far from being a Zealot, actively countered the activities of such brigands, even after his death.[10]

---

[8] Vermes (1987, 1-10) concludes that the phrase in the *Testimonium Flavianum* describing Jesus as having performed surprising (παραδόξων) feats (*Ant.* 18.63) is consonant with Josephus' style, noting that this same phrase is used of Elisha here. We may add that the fact that this phrase is here an extra-biblical Josephan addition strengthens the likelihood that it is also a Josephan expression in the *Testimonium*.

[9] Ben Sira (48.14) likewise remarks on the marvelous (θαυμάσια) works of Elisha even at his death.

[10] Begg (1994a, 39), while admitting that elsewhere Josephus does seem to

7. "Improvements" in the Story: Increased Drama, Elimination of Anthropomorphisms

In connection with Elisha, Josephus greatly elaborates and dramatizes the incident in which Elisha makes salubrious the hitherto poisonous waters of Jericho (2 Kings 2:19-22) (*War* 4.459-64). In the biblical version the waters are described as bad, while the land causes people to die (2 Kings 2:19). Josephus dramatizes by adding that the waters not only blighted the fruits of the earth and of trees but also caused women to miscarry and brought disease and destruction to everything alike (*War* 4.460). Again, whereas the Bible states merely that Elisha went out to the source of the water and threw salt therein and promptly declares that G-d cured the waters (2 Kings 2:21), Josephus, as we have mentioned, greatly elaborating the picture of a Palestinian example of a Graeco-Roman "divine man" in action, describes Elisha, in extra-biblical details, as "raising his righteous right hand to heaven and pouring propitiatory libations upon the ground," while beseeching "the earth to mollify the stream and to open sweeter channels, and heaven to temper its waters with more genial airs and to grant to the inhabitants alike an abundance of fruits, a succession of children, and an unfailing supply of water conducive to their production, so long as they remained a righteous people."[11] Josephus then adds that Elisha supplemented these prayers with various ritual ceremonies. One is reminded of the man who sacrificed to earth for treasure and of Apollonius of Tyana (*ap.* Philostratus, *Life of Apollonius of Tyana* 6.39), who assured him that he and Earth would help him.[12]

A good example of heightened dramatic interest may be seen as

---

downplay or eliminate biblical miracles, concludes, however, in view of his inclusion of this incident, that one cannot speak of a clear and consistent trend in Josephus' handling of miracles.

[11] M. Smith (1987, 254) suggests that Josephus may have found his extra-biblical details in some source and that he perceived the source to be congenial to his taste and useful for his purpose, namely "to re-do Judaism in Roman imperial style, of which an important decorative element was the occult." S. Schwartz (1990, 33) asks where else in the *War* or in the *Antiquities* Josephus so hellenizes his biblical material.

[12] S. Schwartz (1990, 33) remarks that Josephus has turned this story into a display of ἀρετή by a Hellenistic magician; but we may remark that he takes care to make it credible by explaining the miracle, at least to some degree, in naturalistic terms.

well in Josephus' elaboration of the scene in which Elisha leads to Samaria the army of Ben-hadad that had been sent to capture him and which G-d, in response to Elisha's prayer, inflicts with blindness. In the biblical version we read very simply: "And he led them to Samaria" (2 Kings 6:19). Josephus, however, has them eagerly (σπουδάζοντες, "attending to with zeal," "hastening," "being eager") following the prophet (*Ant.* 9.57).

Another instance of heightened drama may be seen in Josephus' version of the incident in which even after his death Elisha was able to resurrect a man who was thrown into his grave (2 Kings 13:21; *Ant.* 9.183). Josephus' account is more dramatic in that those who throw the man's body are identified as robbers who had murdered him.

Inasmuch as anthropomorphisms presented a considerable problem theologically to Josephus, he often avoids such language. One striking example may be found in the Elisha pericope. Where the Bible states that a musician played, and "the hand of the L-rd" came upon Elisha (2 Kings 3:15), Josephus says that Elisha became divinely inspired (ἔνθεος) (*Ant.* 9.35). In this way, as Begg (1993a, 100-1) has remarked, not only does Josephus avoid the anthropomorphic reference to G-d's hand, but he has also portrayed Elijah in a way that his non-Jewish readers might more readily understand, inasmuch as the term ἔνθεος is applied to those who are divinely possessed, as we see, for example, in poets who are inspired (Plato, *Ion* 534B). We may add that the Pythian priestess at Delphi, into whom the god Apollo supposedly entered and used her vocal chords as if they were his own, is likewise described as ἔνθεος (see Dodds 1951, 70-71 and 87-88, n. 41).[13] Likewise, Josephus avoids the anthropomorphic reference in Elisha's prophecy that the valley will be filled with water, which will be a slight achievement "in the eyes of the L-rd" (2 Kings 3:18). In Josephus we read merely Elisha's prophecy that the stream will be full of water, and that this will not be the only thing which the kings will receive from G-d, but that they will also conquer their enemies (Ant. 9.36).

---

[13] Significantly, the word ἔνθεος is not found in the Septuagint, which generally avoids Greek terms that are associated with pagan practices (see Feldman 1993a, 53).

8. Summary

In depicting the prophet Elisha Josephus was in a quandary. On the one hand, Elisha is clearly inferior to his master Elijah, who was the great popular hero and even the forerunner of the Messiah himself. But, on the other hand, Elijah was the prototype of the zealot, whom Josephus, in view of his bitter experiences with the revolutionaries in the Jewish War against the Romans, greatly despised.

That Josephus identified less closely with Elijah than with Elisha may be seen from the fact that he has a eulogy for the latter when he dies but not for the former. Moreover, he refers to Elisha as a prophet, when the Bible does not, considerably more often than he does in the case of Elijah. Furthermore, it is only in connection with Elisha that Josephus establishes links between the prophet and his own craft of history. Indeed, Elisha is a gentler prophet, and Josephus omits gory scenes from his account of Elisha's activities that would make him redolent of a revolutionary figure.

Elisha's power as a prophet is considerably aggrandized. His most remarkable achievement is his enabling the forces of the Israelite king to prevail without a battle.

Josephus succeeds in emphasizing Elisha's loyalty to Elijah without making him utterly subservient to him. In general, Josephus resolves such problems by omitting the scenes which would make Elisha appear helpless, for example, when his master disappears.

Elisha is depicted as possessing three of the four cardinal virtues – courage, temperance, and justice – as well as the virtue of piety. However, Josephus does not depict him, as do the rabbis, as a learned scholar. As for courage, Elisha not only displays this quality to an outstanding degree when the Syrian king Ben-hadad attempts to capture him, but he also causes consternation in the Syrian army because of his forceful and ingenious leadership.

As for temperance, Josephus omits, almost surely deliberately, the scene in which Elisha curses the small boys who jeered him for his baldness. Furthermore, he omits Elisha's outbursts of anger. Likewise, because modesty was considered such an essential part of moderation, Josephus is careful to pass over the scene in which Elisha asks Elijah for twice as much prophetic power as Elijah himself possessed.

The importance of Elisha's justice for Josephus may be seen

from the prophet's prayer that the rancid waters of Jericho be sweetened and remain thus only so long as the people behave justly. Again, inasmuch as humanity was so important a part of justice, Josephus stresses Elisha's manifestation of this quality in his dealings with the poor widow for whom he performed the miracle of the oil. Likewise, because gratitude was so crucial an element of justice, Josephus emphasizes that Elisha performed the miracle of sweetening the waters of Jericho out of gratitude to the people of Jericho for the hospitality that they had shown him. He also displays mercy toward the innocent enemy army and sympathy for their king. Similarly, because truthfulness is such an important element of justice, Josephus takes pains to emphasize Elisha's possession of this quality.

In connection with piety, Josephus stresses Elisha's closeness with G-d but carefully avoids calling him a "man of G-d," whether as part of an anti-Christian polemic or, more likely, because he wished to keep him from appearing the equal of the wonder-worker, G-d Himself.

Regarding the numerous miracles which Elisha is said to have performed, Josephus omits many and rationalizes others or disclaims responsibility for them, in effect leaving to the reader the decision as to whether to give credence to them. In any case, he avoids gross exaggeration, such as is frequently found in the rabbinic tradition concerning Elisha, with which Josephus seems to be well acquainted.

Finally, Josephus dramatizes several scenes far beyond the biblical original, here too seeking to win the approval of his pagan Greek audience.

CHAPTER TWENTY-THREE

JEHU

1. *Introduction*

Josephus' portrait of Jehu is of particular interest because in the Bible he has the characteristics of both a hero and a villain.

One indication of the attraction of a given biblical personality to Josephus is the sheer amount of space that he allocates to him. For Jehu (2 Kings 9:1-10:36; *Ant.* 9.105-39, 159-60) the ratio of Josephus to the Hebrew text is 2.01 (1.22 to the Septuagint), thus indicating that he was of considerable interest to the historian.[1]

2. *The Portrait of Jehu in Rabbinic Literature*

Because the Talmudic corpus is dialectical in its nature, it should not be surprising if we find that there are disagreements among the rabbis or even within the views expressed by a given rabbi in the evaluation of biblical personalities. In the case of Jehu, the rabbis were apparently in a quandary, inasmuch as, on the one hand, he is praised for annihilating the entire house of the wicked Ahab and Jezebel (2 Kings 10:30); and yet, both in the preceding verse and in the very next verse (2 Kings 10:31) we read that he did not observe the law of G-d wholeheartedly and, in particular, that he did not turn away from the sins of the despised Jeroboam in that he allowed the golden calves that had been set up by Jeroboam to remain in Bethel and in Dan.

Thus, we find the statement, ascribed to the second-century Rabbi Judah bar Ilai that Jehu was a very righteous man (*Sanhedrin* 102a); and as evidence he cites the verse noted above that Jehu did

---

[1] Evidence that Josephus used a Hebrew text for the account of Jehu may be seen in his statement, like that of the Masoretic Text (2 Kings 10:1), that Jehu sent letters to the rulers of Jezreel (*Ant.* 9.125), whereas the Greek text speaks of a letter (βιβλίον). On the other hand, that Josephus also used a Greek text may be seen from the fact that we are told, in accordance with the Greek version (2 Kings 10:2), that the rulers of Samaria had strong cities, whereas the Masoretic Text reads "city" (*Ant.* 9.125).

well in G-d's eyes (2 Kings 10:30). Immediately thereafter, however, Rabbi Judah cites the next verse, that Jehu took no heed to walk in the law of G-d.

The rabbis have several pejorative traditions about Jehu. Thus, the *Mekilta de-Rabbi Shimon ben Yoḥai*, dating perhaps from the fifth century, berates Jonadab the Rechabite for his friendship with Jehu (2 Kings 10:15-16). We may also cite the tradition, to be sure not recorded until the Geonic period in the Middle Ages, that Jehu was actually foolish by nature, inasmuch as the text states that he drove his chariot madly (*beshiga'on*) (2 Kings 9:20). In particular, we may note the criticism, in the *Midrash Hagadol* (129-30), to be sure not recorded until the thirteenth century, that although Jehu abolished idolatry, brought about the downfall of Ahab's dynasty, and was responsible for the death of the hated Jezebel, yet all his good deeds came to nought because he did not promote peace. Finally, we may remark that one way the rabbis reconciled the divergent views about Jehu was to declare, as does the tenth-century midrash, *Seder Eliyahu Zuta* (184), that at first Jehu was very pious and did not worship the golden calves set up by Jeroboam, but that when he became king he degenerated and followed in the footsteps of his predecessors. We may well postulate that Josephus was acquainted with such rabbinic traditions in general, though admittedly we may ask whether his interpretations show lack of acquaintance with a particular rabbinic tradition. Given such knowledge of rabbinic traditions, we may now ask whether and to what degree Josephus, too, had a conflicted view of Jehu.

3. *The Cardinal Virtues of Jehu*

It is true that Josephus does not specifically introduce any details to enhance Jehu's reputation for wisdom; but there may well be significance in the fact that Josephus lacks reference to the tradition, recorded in the later (probably geonic period) *Alphabet of Ben Sira*, based on the biblical statement that Jehu drove his chariot "madly" (*beshiga'on*) (2 Kings 9:20), that he was somewhat foolish by nature.

Military ability and courage are clearly prime attributes of Jehu. Indeed, when he is first introduced to the reader, Josephus, in a remark that has no parallel in the biblical source (2 Kings 8:29), records that Joram (Jehoram), the king of Israel, entrusted the command of his entire army to Jehu, and that Jehu had already succeeded in capturing the city of Aramatha by storm (*Ant.* 9.105).

In particular, we see Jehu's military ability in his clever strategy and tactics in overcoming King Jehoram. The biblical text gives none of the details as to how Jehu managed to overcome Jehoram; we hear only that Jehoram turned his hands around and fled, saying to King Ahaziah of Judah, who was then visiting him, that he was the victim of treachery (2 Kings 9:23). In Josephus' version Jehu's success is due not to treachery, which would surely have diminished his stature, but to Jehu's ability, whereby Jehoram is outmanoeuvred (κατεστρατηγῆσθαι, "outwitted," "taken by surprise," "overcome by generalship," "overcome by strategem," "out-generalled") into a trap (ἐνέδρᾳ, "ambush," "plot") and tricked (δόλῳ) (*Ant.* 9.118). We also see Jehu's initiative and fearlessness in Josephus' version of the death of Ahaziah, the king of Judah. According to the Bible, Jehu, after pursuing Ahaziah, tells his men to smite him (2 Kings 9:27). In Josephus' version Jehu pursues Ahaziah closely (ἐπιδιώξας) and himself shoots and wounds him (*Ant.* 9.121).

A key characteristic of a general is decisiveness. In the biblical account Jehu writes to the magistrates of Samaria saying that if they are on his side they should take the heads of Ahab's sons and come to him at Jezreel (2 Kings 10:6). Josephus' Jehu is much more sure of himself. He actually commands them to obey him and to cut off the heads of Ahab's sons and to send them to him (*Ant.* 9.127).

To judge from the biblical version, Jehu was hardly the paragon of moderation, the third of the cardinal virtues. In particular, we read that he was so well known for the reckless way in which he drove a chariot that a lookout of King Joram was able to recognize him by the furiousness (*beshiga'on*) of his driving (2 Kings 9:20). The Septuagint also, which Josephus generally follows in his biblical paraphrase for the period of the kings, agrees at this point with the Hebrew text in reading that Jehu drove madly (ἐν παραλλαγῇ, "in frenzy"). It is, therefore, especially significant that Josephus here follows the reading of the Targum, with which he agrees relatively infrequently when the Targum diverges in its renderings from the Masoretic Text and the Septuagint, which gives the very opposite impression of Jehu, namely that he was going along rather slowly (σχολαίτερον) (Targum Jonathan, "with gentleness") and in good order (μετ' εὐταξίας, "with good discipline") (*Ant.* 9.117).

As to the virtue of justice, to a considerable degree Josephus' version of the Jehu narrative becomes a discourse on the lawful and the unlawful. But whereas in the Bible (2 Kings 9:7) it is G-d who wreaks vengeance upon the house of Ahab for the blood of the prophets and of the servants of the L-rd generally, in Josephus it is Jehu who has been chosen by G-d to inflict vengeance upon Ahab and his descendants because the prophets have been unlawfully (παρανόμως) put to death by Ahab's wife Jezebel (*Ant.* 9.108).

Telling the truth, as we have remarked, is an integral part of justice. In the case of Jehu, when Jehu comes out to the servants of his master after he has been anointed by the young prophet, they ask him, in the biblical version, why "this mad fellow" came to him. His reply to them is "You know the fellow and his talk," whereupon they accuse him of lying: "That is false (*sheqer*); tell us now" (2 Kings 9:11-12). Such an outright accusation of lying on Jehu's part would be very embarrassing, and so Josephus simply omits it (*Ant.* 9.110).

One might likewise accuse Jehu of being less than honest in the scene where he appears before the people after the heads of Ahab's sons have been displayed and admits that he had conspired against his master, King Jehoram, but then, most disingenuously (since, after all, he had ordered the sons to be slain), asks, "Who struck down all these?" (2 Kings 10:9). Josephus' Jehu is more honest in stating that he himself had not slain the youths (*Ant.* 9.129).

Coupled with justice is the virtue of humanity (φιλανθρωπία). In the case of Jehu, Josephus was confronted with a dilemma, in that, according to the Bible, Jehu's men were obviously less than tolerant of other religions, inasmuch as they broke down the pillars of Baal and tore down the house of Baal and made it a latrine "unto this day" (2 Kings 10:27).[2] Clearly, making a shrine of another nation's gods into a latrine would be regarded as insulting by pagan readers, especially the remark that it remains a latrine

---

[2] The word for "latrine" as it appears in the written text is *limeḥora'ot* and signifies a place for a privy. It comes from the stem *ḥor*, "a hole," and alludes to the orifice from which the solid wastes are excreted. As it is read, the word is *lemoẓa'ot* and signifies a place for excretion, a version which is less explicit.

until the present day. Josephus has, therefore, very deliberately omitted these details and instead retains only the comment that they burnt down the temple of Baal, thus purging Samaria of strange rites (*Ant.* 9.138). A Roman, familiar with the banning of the Bacchanalian revels in 186 B.C.E., would have understood such a suppression.

Jehu shows his piety, the fifth of the cardinal virtues, in particular, by avenging the blood of the prophets, who had been put to death by Jezebel. For Josephus this is especially important because the prophets are, in his view, the recorders of Jewish history of the biblical period and guarantors of the validity of this account and, indeed, are the predecessors of later historians such as Josephus himself (*Ag. Ap.* 1.37).

In connection with the account of the vengeance which Jehu inflicted upon Jezebel, there are two major differences between the biblical account and that of Josephus. In the first place, in the Bible the young nameless prophet, in anointing Jehu, tells him that while he is to strike the house of Ahab G-d will avenge the blood of His servants (2 Kings 9:7), whereas in Josephus' version it is Jehu himself who is to wreak this vengeance (*Ant.* 9.108). Secondly, in the biblical version the vengeance is to be for both the prophets and all of the L-rd's servants, whereas in Josephus, who, as we have indicated, so closely identified himself with the prophets, there is no mention of anyone other than the prophets. This emphasis on Jehu as the instrument of the prophets, who, in turn, are the agents of G-d Himself, serves to justify the revolt of Jehu against the established authority of the king, whereas Josephus is normally strongly opposed to such challenges to the existing government.

Josephus' stress on Jehu as the agent of the prophets may also be seen in Josephus' version of the scene in which King Jehoram's corpse is thrown into the field of Naboth. According to the Bible, Jehu told Bidkar his aide to cast the corpse onto the plot of ground belonging to Naboth, "for remember, when you and I rode side by side beside Ahab his father, how the L-rd uttered this oracle against him" (2 Kings 9:25). Josephus' version has Jehu remind Bidkar specifically of Elijah's prophecy that both Ahab and his descendants should perish in Naboth's field (*Ant.* 9.119). To emphasize the role of the prophet Jehu then adds that while seated behind Ahab's chariot he had heard the prophet say these things;

he then, once again, mentions the role of the prophet Elijah, in an extra-biblical addition, when he declares that these things turned out in accordance with Elijah's prophecy (*Ant.* 9.120).

Furthermore, in the Bible it is G-d who promises Jehu, as a reward for his executing the members of the house of Ahab, that his descendants until the fourth generation will occupy the throne of Israel (2 Kings 10:30). In Josephus, however, it is again a prophet who plays this key role (*Ant.* 9.139).[3]

Jehu's piety is further emphasized by the fact that Jonadab (Jehonadab), the son of Rechab, the founder of the ultra-ascetic Rechabites, who are so highly praised by the prophet Jeremiah (35:18-19) for obeying the commands of Jonadab, is denominated, in an addition to the Bible, as one who had long been a friend of Jehu (2 Kings 10:15; *Ant.* 9.132). Moreover, Jonadab's endorsement of Jehu's action in extirpating the house of Ahab is much stronger in Josephus than in the Bible. In the latter we read that Jehu greeted Jonadab and asked him whether he was in agreement with him, whereupon Jonadab answered that he was and gave his hand in confirmation (2 Kings 10:15). In Josephus it is Jonadab who takes the initiative to greet Jehu and does not wait to be asked whether he is in agreement with Jehu's actions (*Ant.* 9.132). Instead, Jonadab himself, we are told in an extra-biblical comment, began to commend Jehu for having done everything in accordance with the will of G-d in eliminating the house of Ahab. Thereafter, whereas in the Bible Jehu invites Jonadab to join him and see his zeal for the L-rd (2 Kings 10:16), Josephus emphasizes Jehu's piety by having him offer to show Jonadab how he would spare no wicked man but would punish the false prophets and false priests and those who had seduced the people into abandoning the worship of G-d and bowing down to strange gods (*Ant.* 9.133). Here again, in this extra-biblical remark, we see Jehu's concern with the prophets; his additional concern for the priests may well reflect Josephus' status and pride as a priest belonging to the first of the twenty-four courses of the priests (*Life* 2). Finally, whereas in the Bible we read simply that Jehu had Jonadab ride in his chariot (2 Kings 10:16), in Josephus' version we are told that Jonadab was persuaded by Jehu's arguments and consequently got up into Jehu's chariot (*Ant.* 9.134).

---

[3] In rabbinic tradition also G-d speaks to Jehu through a prophet, who is identified as Jonah (*Seder Olam* 19).

Some of Josephus' non-Jewish readers – and it was primarily for them that he wrote – might well ask how Jehu was justified in putting to death all the false prophets. In the Bible no justification is given or, for that matter, needed (2 Kings 10:24). Josephus, however, justifies this as vengeance because the false prophets had set at naught their fathers' customs (*Ant.* 9.137). To Romans, who had been brought up on Ennius' famous line, *Moribus antiquis res stat Romana viresque*, allegiance to the ancient ways was the bulwark of Roman strength through the ages; and hence violating those customs was a sin of the greatest magnitude.

Josephus, however, apparently felt that he could not ignore the clear statement in the biblical text that Jehu continued the worship of the golden calves which were in Bethel and Dan (2 Kings 10:29). Nevertheless, even here he has toned down Jehu's failing in three respects: in the first place, unlike the biblical text, which ascribes the initiative in this worship to Jehu himself, Josephus implies that it was the Israelites who insisted on this worship, since he says that Jehu permitted them to bow down before the heifers (*Ant.* 9.139). Secondly, the Bible both here and two verses later specifically refers to Jehu as sinning in this matter (2 Kings 10:31), whereas Josephus does not mention the word "sins." And finally, and most significantly, the Bible both here and again two verses later parallels Jehu with Jeroboam, in stating that Jehu did not turn aside from the sins of Jeroboam (2 Kings 10:31), whereas Josephus, who castigates Jeroboam even more than does the Bible, does not mention the name of Jeroboam at all in connection with Jehu. Indeed, in justifying the sufferings of Israel under Jehu, who had, after all, shown such piety in wiping out Ahab's family and his adherents, Josephus, to be sure, does mention the Bible's statement that he had been careless in fulfilling his duties toward G-d (2 Kings 10:31, *Ant.* 9.160); but, most significantly, this takes second place to Josephus' own extra-biblical addition, namely that Jehu had not been prompt to oppose Hazael the king of Syria when the latter began to devastate the land of Israel.

4. *Jehu and Civil Strife*

Jehu, it would seem, was guilty of lawlessness in rebelling against the king of his nation, Israel; and Josephus was clearly in a quandary as to how to differentiate beween this rebellion and the civil strife which he so strongly condemns. It is significant, therefore, that the biblical account states that Jehu conspired (*vayiteqasher*, "joined together") against Jehoram (2 Kings 9:14). In Josephus' version, however, there is no mention of conspiracy; we hear only that Jehu collected his army and prepared to set out against Jehoram (*Ant.* 9.112). Again, whereas, after Ahab's sons had been slain, in accordance with Jehu's orders, Jehu admits to the people that it was he who had conspired (*qoshareti*, the same root as *vayiteqasher*) against King Jehoram (2 Kings 10:9), Josephus omits the element of conspiracy and has Jehu state merely that he had marched στρατεύσαιτο ("made war," "undertaken a campaign," "taken the field") against his master (*Ant.* 9.129).

Josephus, moreover, in a comment that has no parallel in the biblical source (2 Kings 9:15), stresses the loyalty (εὐνοίας), which he clearly implies was well deserved, of Jehu's followers to him, in that they declared him king because of their friendly feeling toward him (*Ant.* 9.113). As evidence of this good will, in another passage which is unparalleled in the Bible (2 Kings 9:15-16), Josephus notes that Jehu's soldiers, approving (ἡσθέντες, "delighting in," "being pleased with," "taking pleasure in") what Jehu had said, guarded the roads so that no one might escape to Jezreel, where King Jehoram was recuperating from a wound, and betray him to those who were there (*Ant.* 9.114).

Josephus, however, is careful not to give the impression, as does the Hebrew text (2 Kings 10:16), that Jehu was a zealot, inasmuch as this might associate him with the Zealots, whom Josephus excoriates as having "copied every deed of ill, nor was there any previous villainy recorded in history that they failed zealously to emulate" (*War* 7.268-74). We may note that just as Josephus avoids labeling as a zealot Phineas, the slayer of Zimri whom the Bible so denominates (Numbers 25:11 vs. *Ant.* 4.150-55), likewise here Josephus carefully avoids applying the term to Jehu (*Ant.* 9.133). Instead, Josephus puts a pious truism into the mouth of Jehu, who tells Jonadab that it is the most desirable and pleasant of sights for a good and upright man to see the wicked punished, in keeping, we may add, with the moral lesson which Josephus preaches in the proem to his *Antiquities*, namely that people are rewarded and punished by G-d in accordance with the degree to which they conform or violate the laws revealed by G-d (*Ant.* 1.14).

5. *"Improvements" in the Story: Clarifications, Better Motivation and Drama*

One of Josephus' "improvements" comes through explaining what is difficult to understand in the action of his biblical personalities. Thus, the biblical reading declares that King Jehoram of Israel's watchman reports that he sees someone coming in a chariot, and that that person's driving is like that of Jehu, "for he drives madly" (*beshiga'on*) (2 Kings 9:20). The reader at this point might well ask why, having heard such a report, Jehoram would venture out of his secure position to meet a madman. Josephus makes Jehoram's action in going forth to meet Jehu more plausible by reading "rather slowly" (σχολαίτερον), which would certainly not arouse suspicion, rather than "madly" (so Begg 1993b, 460-61).

One means by which Josephus seeks to "improve" upon the biblical narrative is through providing better motivation. We see an example of this in connection with Jehu. Whereas in the Bible we are not told why Jehu sent letters to the rulers of Samaria, and we must conjecture as to his motive from the result (2 Kings 10:1-3), Josephus spells out the motive, telling us that Jehu sent these letters because he wished to test the feelings of the Samarians toward himself (*Ant.* 9.126) – a wise move, indeed, inasmuch as if they had not been well disposed toward him he would have had to plan a military campaign against them.

Josephus' version of the anointing of Jehu illustrates his success in increasing the drama of an event. Thus, according to the biblical account, the prophet Elisha tells the nameless young prophet that after anointing Jehu he is to open the door and flee (2 Kings 9:3). Josephus elaborates, having his Elisha tell the young prophet that after anointing Jehu he is to make the journey as if he were a fugitive, in order that he may get away without being seen by anyone (*Ant.* 9.106). There is likewise increased drama in the details of the anointing ceremony itself. In the biblical version, we read that Jehu arose and went into the house, where the young prophet pours oil upon his head (2 Kings 9:6). In Josephus' version the secretiveness of the proceedings is increased, in that we find that Jehu follows the young prophet into an inner chamber (ταμεῖον, "storeroom," "warehouse," "archive-chamber," "closet") (*Ant.* 9.108).[4]

---

[4] Cf. the usage of this word in the Septuagint (Genesis 43:30), where it is

There is likewise increased drama in Josephus' description of the scene which follows. According to the biblical narrative, the young prophet opened the door and fled (*vayanos*) (2 Kings 9:10). In Josephus the prophet actually darts (ἐξεπήδησεν, "rushed out," "ran out," "departed hurriedly") out of the inner chamber, and Josephus adds that he takes care not to be seen by any of those in the army of which Jehu is the commander (*Ant.* 9.109).

Increased drama is likewise to be found in Jehu's reply to his fellow-officers when they ask why the young prophet came to him. In the Bible Jehu does not comment on the madness which the officers attribute to the prophet (2 Kings 9:11), while in Josephus Jehu tells them that they have guessed correctly, for his words were, indeed, those of a madman (*Ant.* 9.110). Thereby, he increases the anticipation of the reader, who wonders whether, indeed, the prophet's words are those of a crazy person or whether Jehu is simply trying to put off his questioners. The suspense is further increased with Josephus' addition that Jehu's fellow-officers were eager (σπουδαζόντων, "be serious," "be earnest," "be zealous") to hear the words of the prophet and begged (δεομένων) Jehu to speak (*Ant.* 9.111).

There is likewise increased drama in the scene in which Jehu is informed that the heads of Ahab's sons have been brought to him. According to the biblical narrative, a messenger came and told Jehu that the heads have been brought (2 Kings 10:8). In Josephus' version the dramatic announcement that the heads have been brought is made to Jehu as he is dining with his friends (*Ant.* 9.128).

6. *Summary*

Josephus' portrait of Jehu is of particular interest because in the Bible he has the characteristics of both a hero and a villain; and Josephus does, indeed, devote a great deal of space to him.

Josephus stresses Jehu's clever strategy and tactics, initiative, fearlessness and decisiveness. Inasmuch as moderation was so much

---

employed in connection with the inner chamber to which Joseph retires to weep privately after he sees his younger brother Benjamin in Egypt. This is also the word which is used in the Gospel according to Matthew (6:6), where Jesus counsels that one should pray in secret in one's inner chamber.

prized as a virtue by the ancients, it is most significant that Josephus speaks of Jehu as driving his chariot rather slowly and in good order rather than madly, as the Hebrew and Septuagint texts have it. Moreover, it is Jehu rather than G-d Himself, as in the Bible, who is the agent for wreaking vengeance upon the house of Ahab. Inasmuch as truth is so crucial an aspect of justice, it is significant that Josephus omits the accusation that Jehu was guilty of lying to his colleagues.

Because the Jews had been accused so often of being intolerant of other religions, Josephus, in accord with the apologetic stance of the *Antiquities*, omits the biblical statement that Jehu turned the temple of Baal into a latrine. Jehu's apparent intolerance in putting to death the false prophets is made more acceptable to the Romans in the version of Josephus, who explains that these prophets had attempted to undermine the traditions of their ancestors. As for the virtue of piety, Josephus stresses Jehu's role in avenging the deaths of the prophets and in meriting the endorsement of Jonadab the son of Rechab, the founder of the ultra-ascetic Rechabites. Finally, Josephus glosses over the most damning accusation against Jehu, namely that he had permitted the golden calves at Dan and at Bethel to be worshipped. In Josephus' version it is the people, not Jehu, who take the initiative in perpetuating this worship; moreover, he avoids the use of the word "sins"; and finally, and most important, he refrains from the biblical comparison of Jehu's misdeed with that of the much despised King Jeroboam. Again, though Jehu, like Jeroboam, is guilty of lawlessness in rebelling against a legitimate sovereign, Josephus avoids the biblical reference to his activity as a conspiracy. Furthermore, he carefully refrains from labeling him as a zealot, since this would have the unfortunate consequence of reminding the reader of the role of the Zealots, whom Josephus so despised, in the recent revolt of the Jews against the Romans.

Finally, Josephus "improves" the narrative by having Jehu drive slowly rather than madly and thus not incur suspicion on the part of King Jehoram, by providing better motivation for Jehu's sending of letters to the rulers of Samaria, and by increasing the drama in his account of the anointing of Jehu and of his conversation with his fellow-officers when they ask why the young prophet has come to him, as well as in the scene where the heads of Ahab's sons are brought to him.

CHAPTER TWENTY-FOUR

HEZEKIAH

1. *Introduction: The Problem*

Aside from the three great kings of Israel – Saul, David, and Solomon – there is no king whom the rabbinic tradition views more highly than Hezekiah, especially since, in the eyes of the rabbis, no achievement was more praiseworthy than the spread of Torah learning with which he is credited. If, indeed, as there is good reason to believe, Josephus was well acquainted with this sentiment, he may well have known the tradition, as later recorded in the Talmud, that because of Hezekiah's zeal in disseminating the study of the Torah, there was no boy or girl, man or woman, in his entire realm who was not thoroughly versed in the most intricate laws of religious cleanliness and uncleanliness (*Sanhedrin* 94b). Indeed, there was a story that a scroll of the Torah was actually placed upon his coffin and a proclamation was made: "This man fulfilled all that which is written therein" (*Baba Qamma* 16b). Another tradition declared that a college of students to study the law was set up near his sepulchre, presumably as a tribute to his devotion to the cause of Torah learning (*ibid.*).

What is even more remarkable is the tradition expounded by the third-century Bar Kappara, the student of the great patriarch (*nasi*) Judah the Prince, that G-d Himself wished to appoint Hezekiah as the Messiah and the Assyrian monarch Sennacherib as Gog and Magog, whereupon the Attribute of Justice complained that if G-d did not make King David, who uttered so many hymns and psalms, the Messiah, it was not fair to appoint Hezekiah, who, despite all the miracles performed in his behalf, did not compose any hymns or psalms (*Sanhedrin* 94a). A similar statement is recorded by the third-century Hillel II, who, as the grandson of the famous patriarch *(nasi)* Judah the Prince, was in a position of great importance in the Palestinian Jewish community, that there will be no Messiah for Israel because they have already enjoyed him in the days of Hezekiah (*Sanhedrin* 99a). Indeed, the eight names that are ascribed to Hezekiah are those ascribed by the prophet Isaiah to the Messiah (Isaiah 9:5; *Sanhedrin* 94a). To be sure, to this clear implication that King Hezekiah was the long-awaited Messiah, his contemporary Rabbi Joseph responded, "May G-d forgive him" (*Sanhedrin* 99a).[1]

And yet, there is reason to think that Josephus did not completely share this lofty view of Hezekiah. One measure of the amount of interest that a given personality has for Josephus may be seen in the sheer amount of space that he devotes to him. As for Hezekiah, the ratio is complicated by the fact that Josephus (*Ant.* 9.260-76 and 10.1-36) clearly used two sources – 2 Kings 18-20 and 2 Chronicles 29-32, and even selected portions from Isaiah – for his presentation of this king.[2] The text in Josephus comprises 353 lines, the corresponding Hebrew text of 2 Kings 162 lines, the corresponding Hebrew text of 2 Chronicles 202 lines, the Greek Septuagint text of 2 Kings 234 lines, the Greek Septuagint text of 2 Chronicles 308 lines. The ratio of Josephus to the Hebrew of the corresponding passage in Kings (which is Josephus' major source) is 2.18 (1.51 to the Septuagint); the ratio of Josephus to the Hebrew of the corresponding passage in Chronicles is 1.75 (1.15 to the Septuagint).[3] This would indicate that the Hezekiah pericope is of considerable interest to Josephus.

Another test indicating the importance to Josephus of a given biblical personality is the length and nature of the eulogy which

---

[1] To be sure, the Rabbis, to some degree at least, express reservations about King Hezekiah. They note three things which he did of which they approve: he did away with the Book of Cures, he broke into pieces the brazen serpent which had become an object of idol-worship, and he dragged the bones of his wicked father Ahaz on a bed of ropes (*Pesaḥim* 56a). They also, however, list three deeds of Hezekiah, of which they did not approve: he stopped up the waters of Gihon, he cut off the gold from the doors of the Temple and sent them to the King of Assyria, and he intercalated the month of Nisan during Nisan itself. He is also criticized (*Berakot* 10a) by the prophet Isaiah, according to the rabbinic version, for not trying to have children; and when he offers the rejoinder that he had decided not to do so because he had foreseen by the holy spirit that his children would not be virtuous, he is told that he should have done what he was commanded and let G-d do what pleases Him.

[2] As Begg (1995c, 383) notes, Josephus is indebted to a number of peculiar readings in Isaiah relevant to Hezekiah; for example, whereas neither the Hebrew nor the Septuagint of 2 Kings 20:10 mentions the sun in connection with Isaiah's miracle, Josephus, in accordance with Isaiah (38:8), does do so (*Ant.* 10.29)

[3] The ratio of Josephus to the Hebrew of the combined texts of Kings and Chronicles is .97 and of Josephus to the Greek combined texts in the Septuagint is .65.

he typically gives upon that person's death. By this criterion, however, Hezekiah seems very unimportant, inasmuch as he rates a mere five words, i.e., that he lived all his time in peace (*Ant.* 10.36). Moreover, Josephus totally omits Hezekiah's building achievements, notably the construction of a pool and conduit to bring water into the city (2 Kings 20:20; *Ant.* 10.36).

A third test of the importance of a personality is the extent to which he is referred to elsewhere in Josephus' works also; from this point of view, Hezekiah cannot have been of overriding importance to him, inasmuch as Josephus nowhere else refers to him by name, though he certainly had ample opportunity to do so, especially in the speech which he himself delivered in Jerusalem urging his fellow-Jews to surrender to the Romans, where he mentions the siege of the city of Jerusalem by Sennacherib at some length (*War* 5.387-88, 404-8).

How can we explain this mixed picture as to the importance of Hezekiah for Josephus? The answer would appear to be that Josephus had ambivalent feelings about him. On the one hand, he was proud of him as a Jewish king who was noted for his virtues, especially that of piety. On the other hand, Josephus, as a Hasmonean, a member of a dynasty which was not of Davidic descent, would not readily identify with the line of David. Secondly, Josephus must have been wary of any claims that Hezekiah was the Messiah, inasmuch as his Roman patrons, to the extent that they were aware of the beliefs of Jewish messianism, would have objected to such a political figure who would seek to re-establish an independent Jewish state, precisely the goal of the revolutionaries against Rome in Josephus' own day whom he attacks so bitterly. Similarly, we may note, Josephus omits all reference to David as ancestor of the Messiah, despite the fact that such a tradition must have been widespread in his era, because he wished to make clear to his Hellenistic Jewish readers his own repugnance for the idea of an independent Jewish state. If, indeed, Josephus was aware of the tradition, as noted above, that Hezekiah was actually viewed by some as the Messiah, this would further dampen his enthusiasm for him. We may also suggest that Josephus perhaps saw a parallel between the situation in which Hezekiah found himself opposing the military power of his day, namely Assyria, instead of realistically accommodating himself to it, and that of his own day, in which the various Jewish revolutionary groups chose the suicidal path of war against the mighty Roman Empire instead of seeking a *modus vivendi* with it. As one who chose the latter route Josephus himself may have been arguing *pro domo* in the distinct lack of enthusiasm for Hezekiah, the political figure which his presentation evidences.

That Josephus, despite his great indebtedness to the Roman imperial family, in fact still felt ambivalent toward the Roman empire may be seen in his evasiveness with regard to the meaning of the stone which, in Nebuchadnezzar's dream, destroys the kingdom of iron (Daniel 2:44-45; *Ant.* 10.210). The fact that he does not omit this reference is an indication of his deliberate ambiguity in the attempt to reach both of his audiences, the non-Jews and the Jews, for the latter of whom the reference was apparently taken to be to a Messianic kingdom which would make an end of the Roman Empire.[4] Perhaps he felt that to omit the allusion altogether would have been seen by his fellow Jews as a clear indication that he had sold out to the Romans.

Moreover, that personal considerations, notably the fact that Josephus himself was a priest, played a role in Josephus' revamping of the Hezekiah narrative may be seen in the omission of the statement that the Levites were more upright in heart than were the priests in sanctifying themselves (2 Chronicles 29:34; *Ant.* 9.263). Likewise, whereas in the Bible the Levites and the priests cleanse the Temple (2 Chronicles 29:12-17), in Josephus it is the priests alone who open the Temple and prepare the vessels of G-d (*Ant.* 9.263). Again, whereas we are told that Hezekiah spoke encouragingly to all the Levites, who had shown good skill in the service of the L-rd (2 Chronicles 30:22), Josephus shifts the credit to the priests, remarking that the priests performed everything in accordance with the law (*Ant.* 9.270). Likewise, whereas the biblical text states that the king and the people were forced to postpone their celebration of the Passover until the following month because the priests had not sanctified themselves in sufficient numbers (2 Chronicles 30:2-3), Josephus, reluctant to criticize the priests, omits this detail. Clearly, Josephus, as a priest who proudly mentions his priestly ancestry as the very first point in his *Life* (1), was embarrassed by the secondary role played by the priests during Hezekiah's reign.

---

[4] That the rabbis understood the stone (Daniel 2:44-45) to refer to the Messiah is clear from *Tanḥuma* B 2.91-92 and *Tanḥuma Terumah* 7.

2. Hezekiah's Qualities of Character

Wisdom is a quality which, as we have indicated, Josephus stresses in a number of extra-biblical comments about many of his biblical personalities. But in his portrait of Hezekiah there is nothing about his wisdom or his skill in persuasion.

Again, the second of the cardinal virtues, courage and skill in battle, is stressed by Josephus in a number of additions to the biblical narrative. However, not only does Josephus not enhance Hezekiah's courage, he even goes to the extreme of asserting that it was out of cowardice (δειλίας) that Hezekiah did not come out himself to meet the Assyrians when they encamped before the walls of Jerusalem and asked him to parley with them but sent three of his friends instead (*Ant.* 10.5). We may note that the biblical text at this point reports merely that the Assyrian generals called to Hezekiah to come out to them and that he sent three members of his staff, with no editorial indication that Hezekiah's refusal to come in person was motivated by cowardice (2 Kings 18:18). If this cowardice seems to contradict Hezekiah's apparent courage in refusing to submit to the threats of the Assyrians (2 Kings 18:14), the latter action is due not to Hezekiah's courage but rather, as Josephus indicates, his confidence in his piety toward G-d and in the prophet Isaiah, by whom, according to Josephus, he had been accurately informed of future events (*Ant.* 9.276).

Likewise, when the Assyrian general, Rab-shakeh spoke in Hebrew to Hezekiah's emissaries warning them to surrender Jerusalem, the emissaries, according to the biblical account (2 Kings 18:26), begged Rab-shakeh to speak in Aramaic rather than in Hebrew in the ears of the people on the wall. In Josephus' version, the envoys, clearly reflecting Hezekiah's own lack of courage, spell out their fear that the people may overhear them and be thrown into consternation (*Ant.* 10.8).

Indeed, to downplay Hezekiah's qualities as commander of his nation's armed forces and inspirer of his troops, and to place even further stress upon this reliance upon Divine aid, Josephus totally omits mention of the measures which the biblical Hezekiah takes to defend Jerusalem, namely stopping the water of the springs that were outside the city, building up the wall that was broken down, raising towers upon it, erecting still another wall, making shields and weapons in abundance, organizing the defense of the city by setting up combat commanders, and speaking to the people to arouse their courage (2 Chronicles 32:3-8; *Ant.* 10.16).

The third of the cardinal virtues, temperance, is likewise a recurring theme in extra-biblical additions to the portraits of his biblical heroes in Josephus, who identifies it with modesty (*Ant.* 6.63). Again, we are struck with Josephus' silence regarding Hezekiah's modesty.

But for Josephus to have presented a negative portrait of Hezekiah would surely have run counter to the description in the Bible itself and, moreover, would have violated Josephus' promise that he would, throughout his work, set forth the precise details of the Scriptures, neither adding nor omitting anything (*Ant.* 1.17). His Jewish readers would likewise certainly have expected a sympathetic portrait of the king; and hence, when Hezekiah is first introduced, Josephus describes him, in general terms, as having a character that was good (χρηστή), just (δικαία), and pious (εὐσεβής) (*Ant.* 9.260). In particular, he calls attention to Hezekiah's qualities of justice and piety, as he does with so many others of his biblical personalities. Moreover, Josephus himself apparently felt some sense of identification with Hezekiah as a fellow-townsman, since he adds the detail, not found in the Bible, that Hezekiah was a native of Jerusalem (2 Kings 18:2 vs. *Ant.* 9.260).

Piety is, indeed, the one quality which Josephus does emphasize in his recasting of the Hezekiah pericope. Thus, in paraphrasing Hezekiah's invitation to the Israelites to come to Jerusalem to celebrate the Passover (2 Chronicles 30:1), Josephus explains that Hezekiah's motive was not the political aggrandizement that one might suspect, namely that he was seeking to make them subject to him against their will, but rather true piety, in that he was striving for their own good and happiness (*Ant.* 9.264). Hezekiah's sincere piety is all the greater because the opposition which his envoys encounter is even more vicious than that described in the Bible, reaching the point where the Israelites actually killed their prophets (2 Chronicles 30:10; *Ant.* 9.265-66). Josephus also exaggerates Hezekiah's success in convincing members of the tribes of Israel to come to Jerusalem. Thus, whereas the biblical text states that only a few men of the tribes of Asher, Manasseh, and Zebulun came to Jerusalem as a result of Hezekiah's invitation and his prophets' exhortations (2 Chronicles 30:11), Josephus says both that many came and that they flocked (συνέδραμον, "ran together") to Jerusalem to worship G-d (*Ant.* 9.267).

Moreover, Josephus aggrandizes Hezekiah's personal piety. Whereas in the Bible Hezekiah presents the congregation a thousand bullocks for offerings and the princes give a thousand bullocks and ten thousand sheep (2 Chronicles 30:24), Josephus doubles the number of bullocks offered by the king and greatly decreases the number of sheep provided by the princes from ten thousand to one thousand and forty (*Ant.* 9.271). He also increases even further the splendor (λαμπρῶς) and magnificence (φιλοτίμως) with which the Passover, under the inspired leadership of Hezekiah, is celebrated (2 Chronicles 30:26; *Ant.* 9.272).

Even when Hezekiah submits to the Assyrian Sennacherib's threats and gives him a vast quantity of valuables, Josephus, clearly concerned to protect Hezekiah's reputation for piety, omits the biblical statement that he stripped the gold from the doors of the Temple (2 Kings 18:16) – an act which bordered on sacrilege and which was criticized in rabbinic tradition (*Pesaḥim* 56a); instead, we have merely the statement that he emptied his treasuries, with no indication that he despoiled the Temple (*Ant.* 10.3). Similarly, Josephus has omitted the Assyrian Rab-shakeh's reminder to Hezekiah's representatives that it would, in effect, be hypocritical for Hezekiah to say that he was relying upon G-d when it was he who had removed the high places and altars (2 Kings 18:22; *Ant.* 10.7); such a remark would again cast a bad light upon Hezekiah's reputation for piety. Likewise, when Hezekiah receives Sennacherib's ultimatum, the Bible states very simply that he read it (2 Kings 19:14); Josephus, again emphasizing Hezekiah's reliance upon G-d, adds that he made light of (καταφρονεῖ, "despise," "be indifferent," "ignore") the ultimatum because of his confidence inspired by G-d (*Ant.* 10.16).

Hezekiah exhibits his piety further, in an extra-biblical addition, by offering sacrifices of thanksgiving to G-d in gratitude for the destruction of some of the Assyrians and for the removal of the rest from Jerusalem (*Ant.* 10.24). All this he ascribes, in his piety, to the aid given by G-d as his ally.[5] Indeed, Josephus declares that

---

[5] Similarly, as Attridge (1976, 79, n. 1) remarks, Josephus frequently emphasizes the help and protection which Israel received from from G-d. Significantly, the rabbinic tradition asserts that G-d was so disappointed with Hezekiah's failure to thank Him for his rescue that He revoked His earlier decision to designate Hezekiah as the Messiah (*Midrash Song of Songs Rabbah* 4.8).

Hezekiah showed all zeal (σπουδῇ) and devotion (φιλοτιμίᾳ) in the worship of G-d (*Ant.* 10.25).

That it is Hezekiah's piety which Josephus wishes to stress may be deduced from the fact that he omits completely the biblical statement that when Hezekiah became sick he did not show the proper gratitude to G-d, "for his heart was proud," whereupon wrath came upon him and upon his people (2 Chronicles 32:25 vs. *Ant.* 10.25). Nor, for that matter, does Josephus mention Hezekiah's later humbling himself for his pride of heart (2 Chronicles 32:26). Indeed, in Josephus' version, not only is there no mention of Hezekiah's pride of heart, but, on the contrary, we read that despite the fact that he showed all zeal (σπουδῇ) and devotion (φιλοτιμίᾳ) in his worship of G-d he was smitten with a severe illness (*Ant.* 10.25).

Josephus (*Ant.* 10.25) also does not refer to the rabbinic tradition that Hezekiah was condemned to an early death because he had not tried to have children, since, according to the rabbis, the excuse alleged by Hezekiah, i.e., he had seen by the holy spirit that his children would not be virtuous, was not acceptable (*Berakot* 10a).[6] Instead, we are told, in an addition to the biblical text, that his illness was aggravated by his despair when he considered that he was about to die without leaving a legitimate successor (2 Kings 20:1 vs. *Ant.* 10.25-26).

Again, to give further emphasis to the theme of Hezekiah's piety, Josephus heightens the role of G-d in his cure by dramatizing, in a passage which has no biblical counterpart, the fact that all hope for his recovery had been given up by his physicians, and that even his friends did not expect any improvement in his condition (2 Kings 20:1 vs. *Ant.* 10.25). Hezekiah's piety is also highlighted in that his prayer for extension of his life was granted by G-d not, as the Bible implies, out of regard for his ancestor King David (2 Kings 20:5), but rather because he had sought this not for his own sake but so that a son might be born to succeed him (*Ant.* 10.27). Moreover, the cure is effected apparently by G-d's direct intervention (*Ant.* 10.28) and not by the cake of figs which the prophet Isaiah directs to be placed upon his boil (2 Kings 20:7) and which is not mentioned by Josephus. Again, when his cure is effected, the

---

[6] Cf. Jerusalem *Sanhedrin* 10.2 and other citations in Rappaport (1930, 134, n. 263). Josephus, however, does appear to be acquainted with the rabbinic tradition that he was childless at the time when he became ill (*Berakot* 10a, *Ant.* 10.25).

pious Hezekiah shows his gratitude to G-d, in an addition to the Bible (2 Kings 20:11), by going to the Temple and doing obeisance to G-d and offering prayers to Him (*Ant.* 10.29). Still further emphasis is placed upon Hezekiah's piety by his uncomplaining statement, in a Josephan addition to the Bible (2 Kings 20:19), after the prophet Isaiah has predicted the Babylonian exile, that it is not possible to alter G-d's decrees and by his subsequent extra-biblical prayer that there should be peace during his own lifetime (*Ant.* 10.34).

Josephus, moreover, felt the need to present a balanced picture of Hezekiah as a leader. Therefore, since, as both Thucydides (2.65.7) and Plato (*Republic* 7.519C-20E) had emphasized, the first concern of a leader should be for his people, it is a distinct compliment that Hezekiah's first concern, upon coming to power, was, according to Josephus' extra-biblical addition, to consider what was necessary and profitable not merely for himself but also for his subjects (*Ant.* 9.260); and hence he called together not merely the priests and the Levites, as we find in the Bible (2 Chronicles 29:3), but also the people generally. Here it is again his piety, not merely in cultic worship but in the broadest sense, which is stressed (see Attridge 1976, 89). Again, whereas the Bible says that the people brought sacrifices (2 Chronicles 29:32-33), Josephus emphasizes Hezekiah's piety in declaring that it was he who sacrificed the animals (*Ant.* 9.270).

3. *Apologetics*

Because, in effect, the *Antiquities* is an extended apology for the Jews, Josephus felt the need to defend his people against the charge that they had forfeited the protection of G-d through their heinous sins. Hence, whereas in the Bible Hezekiah paints a lurid picture of the Jews as an object of horror, astonishment, and hissing because of the sins of their fathers (2 Chronicles 29:8), Josephus tones this down considerably into the mere remark that the Jews have experienced many great misfortunes (*Ant.* 9.261). Again, whereas the Bible reports that Hezekiah broke in pieces the bronze serpent that Moses had made and which had apparently been worshipped (2 Kings 18:4) and whereas the rabbis specifically praise him for this achievement (*Pesahim* 56a), Josephus, apparently aware that this would call attention to the fickleness of the

Jews in worshipping idols despite all the miracles which G-d had brought to pass in their behalf, omits all mention of this tremendous lapse and says, in the most general way, that Hezekiah urged the priests and Levites to purify the Temple with the accustomed sacrifices (*Ant.* 9.262).

Josephus makes use of the respect which the ancients had for the general principle that the older things are the more divine and the more credible they were, so that human beings were said to be closest to the gods in the earliest times.[7] Specifically, readers would appreciate the effectiveness of Hezekiah's exhortation, not found in the biblical source (2 Chronicles 29:5-11), to the priests and Levites to restore the Temple to its ancient (ἀρχαίαν) and ancestral (πάτριον) honor (*Ant.* 9.262).

In his treatment of Hezekiah, Josephus was clearly in a quandary in that, on the one hand, as we have noted, he did not want to build up Hezekiah as a messianic figure, since that would offend the Romans; secondly, he wished, without unduly emphasizing the miracle involved, to demonstrate that the deliverance of the Jews was due to G-d's intervention; and finally, he had to avoid criticizing the Assyrians more than necessary, as he did not want to offend non-Jews unduly. Hence, in line with this last concern, he omits the biblical statement that Sennacherib wrote letters to cast contempt on the G-d of Israel (2 Chronicles 32:17); and, in particular, he omits the degrading remark of the Rab-shakeh warning that the Jews are doomed to eat their own dung and to drink their own urine (2 Kings 18:27). Indeed, he considerably abbreviates the threats uttered by the Rab-shakeh (*Ant.* 10.10).

Josephus likewise omits, in an obvious show of tolerance, the statement, in Hezekiah's prayer before G-d, that the kings of Assyria had cast the gods of other nations into the fire (2 Kings 19:17-18 vs. *Ant.* 10.16). He furthermore omits, as apparently too strong, the prophet Isaiah's blistering promise from G-d that He would put His hook in Assyria's nose and His bit in its mouth (2 Kings 19:28 vs. *Ant.* 10.16). If Sennacherib is ultimately defeated, it is not a matter of his returning to his own land because of a

---

[7] See Georgi (1986, 160 and the literature cited on 223, notes 492-94). One recalls the famous conversation of Solon, in the sixth century B.C.E., with an aged Egyptian priest (*ap.* Plato, *Timaeus* 22b) who spoke of the Greeks as children, since they had no immemorial past: "You ever remain children; in Greece there is no old man."

mere rumor, as the Bible would have it (2 Kings 19:7), since that presumably, from Josephus' point of view and from that of much of his audience, would have trivialized the whole incident, but rather because he is a victim, in a manner reminiscent of a Greek tragedy, of over-confidence (θράσους) similar to the overweening pride (ὕβρις) characteristic of the generation of the Tower of Babel and of Haman (*Ant.* 10.13). And yet, just as in the Daniel pericope Josephus shows respect for Nebuchadnezzar, Belshazzar, and Darius, so here he shows regard for Sennacherib, despite the latter's attack upon Jerusalem, as we see from his addition to the biblical statement (2 Kings 19:37), in which he points out that it was by treachery that Sennacherib was slain by his son (*Ant.* 10.23). Finally, the Bible (2 Kings 20:12-13, Isaiah 39:1-2), relates how the king of Babylon sent envoys to Hezekiah bearing letters and a gift (Septuagint, gifts) and inviting him to become his ally and how Hezekiah welcomed them and showed them his treasure house; Josephus, however, eager to demonstrate the high regard that Jews have for non-Jews and, in particular, the importance of hospitality in Hezekiah's scheme of values, adds that Hezekiah feasted the envoys and sent them back with gifts for the Babylonian king.

4. *Josephus' Theology*

Despite the fact that in his preface Josephus tells readers that the main lesson to be derived from his history is that G-d rewards those who obey His laws and punishes those who do not (*Ant.* 1.14), Josephus, apparently aware that his readers would be skeptical of such theologizing in a work that claimed to be a critical history, frequently omits or downgrades the role of the Divine in human events. That he does not do so in the case of Hezekiah may be due, as we have suggested above, to his eagerness not to aggrandize unduly the personality of Hezekiah himself.

In dealing with the miraculous rescue of the Jews from the assault of Sennacherib, however, Josephus was clearly in a dilemma. On the one hand, as a believing Jew, he could hardly deny the centrality of such miracles as the plagues in Egypt, the crossing of the Sea of Reeds, and the revelation at Sinai. On the other hand, he hardly wished to expose himself to ridicule for being so credulous and, indeed, insists that Moses wrote nothing that was unreasonable, and that everything in Scripture was in keeping with the nature of the universe (*Ant.* 1.24).

Josephus' concern for his own credibility may be seen from the fact that in the *Antiquities* he says nothing about the angel which, according to Scripture, miraculously went forth and smote 185,000 of the Assyrians (2 Kings 19:35, 2 Chronicles 32:21), but rather rationalizes, explaining that Sennacherib withdrew his forces because they were in danger from a plague which G-d had visited upon them (*Ant.* 10.21). It was this pestilence, according to Josephus, which threw Sennacherib into a state of alarm and terrible anxiety for his entire army (*Ant.* 10.22). In the *War*, however, which is addressed primarily to Jews (*War* 1.3), when he speaks to his fellow-Jews urging them to surrender to the Romans (*War* 5.362-419), Josephus adheres closely to the biblical account and unhesitatingly mentions the role of the angel in destroying the Assyrian army (*War* 5.388).

That Josephus is aware of the difficulty that his readers would have in believing in miracles may be seen in his discussion of the miracle which was performed to convince Hezekiah that he would be healed from his severe illness (2 Kings 20:8-11; *Ant.* 10.28). According to Josephus, Hezekiah himself would not believe the prophet Isaiah when he was told that he would be cured, and so he asked the prophet to perform some sign or miracle that he might believe that this announcement had come from G-d. Josephus here frankly adds that such miracles are beyond belief and surpass our hopes.

5. *Summary*

In presenting the narrative of King Hezekiah Josephus was clearly aware of the parallel between the Assyrians and the Romans in their assaults on Jerusalem. Indeed, when Josephus (*War* 5.362-419) urges the Jews to surrender to the Romans, his argument, supported by precedent after precedent from previous Jewish history, is that the Jews have been successful against their attackers only when they have committed their cause to G-d, but that now G-d has fled to the Roman side because of the enormities committed by the Jews. One of these precedents cited by Josephus is the overthrow of Sennacherib's army (*War* 5.387-88), his point being that it was not by human hands that the Jews had thus been victorious but rather because G-d, through his angel, had destroyed the Assyrian host. He repeats this reference at some length later in his speech, noting again that it was only because of G-d's aid that the Assyrians were laid low (*War* 5.404-8); and he pointedly contrasts the Assyrians, who had violated their promise not to attack the city, with the Romans, who are just and mild in their treatment of their enemies.

Here, in the Hezekiah pericope, Josephus, though he does build up Hezekiah in some respects, deliberately chooses not to build up Hezekiah as a person with the complete gamut of virtues which he emphasizes in so many other biblical personalities, but rather to portray him as the pious servant of G-d who triumphs because G-d rewards his piety. This will explain why Josephus makes the amazing and utterly extra-biblical remark about Hezekiah's actual cowardice (*Ant.* 10.5), which serves all the more to highlight his dependence upon G-d alone. Indeed, it is surely indicative of Josephus' concern not to exalt the personality of Hezekiah unduly that he omits completely the biblical statement that after the withdrawal of Sennacherib from the siege of Jerusalem many brought gifts to the Temple and precious objects to Hezekiah so that he was exalted in the sight of all nations from that time onward (2 Chronicles 32:23; *Ant.* 10.23).

CHAPTER TWENTY-FIVE

ISAIAH

1. *Issues*

Granted that Josephus is writing a history rather than a book of theology, to which he intended to devote a separate treatise, we may well ask why he gives so much more attention to Jonah and to Jeremiah than to Isaiah.[1] In the cases of Jonah and Jeremiah it would seem to be that Josephus has focused upon historical episodes centering upon their roles as historical figures and upon their political missions. But Isaiah was also very much involved with the political events of his day. Why so much less attention in his case?

As for Jeremiah, there are two major reasons why Josephus was attracted to him. In the first place, he saw a strong parallel between the advice which Jeremiah gave to King Zedekiah of Judah to submit to the Babylonians and that which he himself gave to his countrymen when they revolted against the Romans. Indeed, in the speech which he delivers to the revolutionaries in Jerusalem he makes a point of noting this parallel just as he underscores the disastrous result of Zedekiah's failure to listen to the prophetic warnings of Jeremiah (*War* 5.391). In the second place, Josephus saw a strong parallel between Jeremiah and himself personally (see Gray 1993, 72-74). Both were priests who had predicted victory for

---

[1] There has been no extended study of Josephus' portrait of Isaiah. Meyer (1964, 6:812-28) almost totally ignores Josephus' treatment of the biblical prophets. Blenkinsopp (1974, 239-62) concentrates on Josephus' self-understanding as a prophet and on the relationship of prophecy and priesthood. Delling (1974, 109-21) devotes a mere page (115) to Josephus' treatment of Isaiah. The study by van Unnik (1978, 41-54) is largely a summary of Josephus' references to prophecy but is hardly analytical. Begg (1988b, 341-57) has a brief account (348-51) of Josephus' treatment of Isaiah. I (1990, 386-422) deal with more general questions, notably the importance of the biblical prophets to Josephus, the nature of prophecy according to him, the relationship between prophecy and history, Josephus' view on the cessation of prophecy, the prophet as predicter, Josephus in comparison to pagan and Talmudic views of prophecy, and the relationship of the prophet and the priest; but I mention Isaiah only in passing. The most recent treatment of prophecy in Josephus, Gray (1993), does not deal with Isaiah at all.

the enemy and had urged the course of surrender. Both had to deal with rival prophets who had promised deliverance for their nation. Both had been accused of being traitors, and both had suffered at the hands of their countrymen. In particular, Josephus represents Jeremiah as predicting the capture of Jerusalem not only by the Babylonians but also by the Romans (*Ant.* 10.79), since he apparently interpreted the Book of Lamentations as a prophecy of both events. Finally, in extra-biblical additions, Josephus has Jeremiah predicting the destruction not only of Jerusalem but of the Temple in particular,[2] with which Josephus, as a proud priest belonging to the first of the twenty-four courses of the priests (*Life* 2), was especially concerned.

Indeed, one would have expected Josephus to devote more attention to Isaiah than to any other of the prophets. The fact is that, according to tradition, the book of Isaiah was said to have been written by none other than the school of King Hezekiah (*Baba Batra* 15a), who was regarded as the very paradigm of justice and who spread the study of Torah to such an extent that no man or woman, boy or girl, was found in the whole land who was not thoroughly versed in the laws of cleanliness and uncleanliness (*Sanhedrin* 94b). The oral tradition, with which, as we have noted, Josephus seems to have been well acquainted,[3] actually equates Isaiah with Moses as the greatest of the prophets (*Deuteronomy Rabbah* 2.4, *Pesiqta Rabbati* 4.14a).[4] What undoubtedly enhanced

---

[2] Compare Jeremiah 36:2 and *Ant.* 10.93; Jeremiah 38:17-18 and *Ant.* 10.126; Jeremiah 38:20-23 and *Ant.* 10.128; and Jeremiah 29:10, 14 and *Ant.* 10.113.

[3] In the case of Isaiah we may point, in particular, to the statement, unparalleled in the Bible, that King Hezekiah's illness was aggravated by his despair because he was childless (*Ant.*10.25). This statement has a clear parallel in the rabbinic tradition according to which Isaiah rebuked Hezekiah because he had decided not to have children, with the result that Hezekiah fell ill (*Berakot* 10a). We may also note that Josephus, interpreting Isaiah's prophecy that there shall be an altar in the midst of the land of Egypt as referring to the temple built by Onias IV (Isaiah 19:19), is paralleled in the rabbinic tradition ((*War* 7.432; *Ant.* 13.64, 68, 71; *Menahot* 109b).

[4] *Aggadat Bereshit* 14.32 speaks of Isaiah as the greatest of the prophets and of Obadiah as the most insignificant of them. Isaiah is said to be more distinguished than the other prophets in two respects. In the first place, whereas the other prophets received their spirit of prophecy from their masters, Isaiah prophesied directly from the mouth of G-d. Secondly, he repeats the introductory words of his prophecies, thus indicating that their fulfillment was certain. See Ginzberg (1928, 6:358-59, n. 32), who cites *Pesiqta de-Rav Kahana* 16.125a and *Leviticus Rabbah* 10.2.

the reputation of Isaiah was the tradition of his martyrdom at the hands of King Manasseh.[5]

That Josephus knew the entire book of Isaiah is implied from the fact that he states that Isaiah "wrote down in books all that he had prophesied and left them to be recognized as true from the event by men of future ages" (*Ant.* 10.35). In view of the fact that Josephus was so sharply criticized by his rivals and himself engaged in apologetics and polemics, he could hardly have made such a statement if he himself had not read the entire book of Isaiah. Indeed, that Josephus had a high regard for Isaiah may be inferred from the very first reference to Isaiah in Josephus, which attributes Hezekiah's disregard of Assyria's threats to his confidence in the prophet Isaiah, "by whom he was accurately informed of future events" (*Ant.* 9.276). This is a compliment of the highest value, coming not only from one who claimed predictive powers for himself in his prophecy that Vespasian would become emperor (*War* 3.399-408) but also from a historian who regarded as his supreme model Thucydides, who, it will be recalled, looked upon history as of supreme value as a guide for the future (1.22).

One indication of the popularity of the Book of Isaiah in Josephus' lifetime may be seen in that no fewer than nineteen copies of the book, most of them, to be sure, in fragmentary form, have been found among the biblical manuscripts from the Dead Sea caves. Another indication of the book's popularity is the fact that of the *haftarot* selected from the prophetic books and read in the synagogue after the weekly Pentateuch portions as well as after the holiday selections (though, to be sure, we cannot be sure when the selections were made), there are more from Isaiah than from any other source: fifteen after Pentateuch portions plus five after the holiday portions, making a total of twenty, as compared with seven after Pentateuch portions plus two after holiday portions from Jeremiah, and five after Pentateuch portions plus five after holiday portions from Ezekiel.

---

[5] See *Yevamot* 49b and *Sanhedrin* 103b, as well as the first part of the *Martyrdom and Ascension of Isaiah*, (5:1 ff., known as the *Martyrdom of Isaiah*; cf. Hebrews 11:37, which speaks of prophets who were sawn in two, presumably alluding to the tradition that Isaiah was thus sawn by King Manasseh). The Talmud (*Yevamot* 49b) cites a nameless Tanna who reports the statement of Simeon ben Azzai, who lived in Palestine in the early part of the second century, that he had found a roll of genealogical records in Jerusalem with the statement that Manasseh slew Isaiah. The *Martyrdom of Isaiah* was apparently composed by a Jew in Palestine no later than the first century C.E., the very time in which Josephus lived.

2. *Josephus' Concern with Priestly Matters*

One major reason for Josephus' great interest in Isaiah is that Isaiah prophesies the rebuilding of the Temple in Jerusalem. Indeed, Josephus specifically says that it was through reading the prophecy of Isaiah (the reference here is to Isaiah's prophecy in Chapters 44:28-45:1),[6] which Josephus notes was made some 140 years before the Temple was demolished, that Cyrus, the king of Persia, came to the realization that he had been divinely appointed to allow the Jews to return to their own land and to rebuild the Temple (*Ant.* 11.5-6). The statement that Cyrus had read the book of Isaiah, which, significantly, is not in Josephus' source at this point (whether Ezra 1:3 or 1 Esdras 2:5) enhances the importance not only of Isaiah but also of Cyrus, who, though a non-Jew, is presented as being divinely inspired – a point not lost upon Josephus in his apologetic quest to prove that Jews do not look down upon non-Jews but rather especially appreciate their efforts on behalf of Jews. Specifically, Josephus includes the passage because it refers to the rebuilding of the Temple, so dear to him, while it carefully omits all reference to the establishment of an independent nation, so abhorrent to Josephus.

We would have expected Josephus to include Isaiah's prophecy to King Ahaz of Judah (Isaiah 7:1-25), inasmuch as the context clearly refers to the historic incident of Ahaz's alliance with Assyria, the superpower of that day, against the coalition of the Kingdom of Israel and Syria. Significantly, however, Josephus omits all mention of this, presumably, at least in part, because Isaiah had prophesied the defeat of Ahaz's enemies, whereas Ahaz showed disdain for the Temple, which he shut up completely, discontinuing the customary sacrifices (2 Kings 16:14-18, 2 Chronicles 28:24, *Ant.* 9.257).[7]

Furthermore, the one prophecy of Isaiah that is mentioned in both the *War* (7.432) and the *Antiquities* (13.64, 68, 71) is that a

---

[6] From this reference we may deduce that Josephus looked upon the entire book of Isaiah as we have it as a single book and did not look upon chapters 40 and following as being by a different author, the so-called Second Isaiah.

[7] Another reason for Josephus' omission of this episode is that it culminates in the messianic prediction of the birth of a wonderful child from a young woman (Isaiah 7:14-25). Such a messianic prophecy was anathema to the Romans, since a primary function of a Messiah, as traditionally portrayed, is to establish an independent state, hence requiring a revolt against the Romans.

temple would be erected by a Jew in Egypt, representing Josephus' interpretation of Isaiah 19:19: "In that day there will be an altar to the L-rd in the midst of the land of Egypt, and a pillar to the L-rd at its border."[8] Josephus is particularly impressed, and presumably expects his readers to be similarly impressed, that Isaiah made this prediction some six hundred years before the temple of Onias was actually erected in Leontopolis (*War* 7.432).[9] Moreover, Josephus is here emphasizing that Isaiah's predictions have their effect not only across the centuries but also outside the land of Israel (so Begg 1988b, 350). Furthermore, Josephus stresses that in granting the request of Onias the non-Jews Ptolemy Philometor and Cleopatra were impressed by his statement that the prophet Isaiah had long before foretold the building of this temple, since, as they declared, they did not want to seem to have sinned against G-d in any way (*Ant.* 13.71). Furthermore, the fact that we find, in both Josephus and in rabbinic literature in a statement ascribed to the second-century Judah bar Ilai (*Menahot* 109b), the same interpretation of the passage in Isaiah as referring to the temple of Onias would seem to indicate that both reflect the same tradition.

We may conjecture, however, that one reason why Josephus the priest gives less attention to Isaiah is that Isaiah had decried the view that the sacrifices offered in the Temple were all that was needed to appease G-d: "What to me is the multitude of your sacrifices? says the L-rd; I have had enough of burnt offerings of rams and the fat of fed beasts; I do not delight in the blood of bulls, or of lambs, or of he-goats" (Isaiah 1:11). Or again: "You have not satisfied me with the fat of your sacrifices" (Isaiah 43:34). It is hard

---

[8] Presumably, in the verse before Isaiah 19:19 Josephus found a reference to Heliopolis, where the temple was to be erected, on the basis of the reading *ha-heres*, city of the sun, as found in Symmachus and the Vulgate, rather than *ha-heres*, city of destruction. See Marcus, 7:257, n. e; and Michel and Bauernfeind 1969, 2.2:284, n. 206. We may add that the reading *heres* is clearly implied in the tradition mentioned by the third-century Rabbi Joseph bar Ḥiyya (*Menahot* 110a) that the place in Egypt referred to by Isaiah is Bet Shemesh, that is, the House of the Sun, presumably Heliopolis.

[9] Thackeray (1928, 3:626, n. a) says that the period of Isaiah's prophecies was actually 800 years before Josephus' own time. However, Josephus does not say that the prediction was made 600 years before the time of Josephus; rather, he indicates that the prediction of Isaiah was made 600 years before the time that Onias set up his temple. Inasmuch as Isaiah prophesied approximately 740–700 B.C. and the temple was erected about the year 170 B.C.E., Isaiah's prophecy was made between 530 and 570 years earlier.

to imagine a priest, especially one as proud of his priesthood as was Josephus, admitting a lesser role for the sacrifices in the service of G-d. A further clue to Josephus' attitude may be seen in the fact that whereas in the Bible when Jerusalem is besieged by King Sennacherib of Assyria, King Hezekiah sends a delegation to Isaiah asking him to pray to G-d (2 Kings 19:4), in Josephus' version, very significantly, the delegation asks Isaiah not merely to pray but also to offer sacrifices (*Ant.* 10.12). Such an assimilation of the prophetic and priestly roles is likewise to be seen in Josephus' treatment of the high priest Phineas (*Ant.* 5.120), the high priest Abimelech (*Ant.* 6.254, 257), and the anonymous high priest who prophesies for David (*Ant.* 7.72) (cited by Begg 1988b, 349, n. 19).

As to Josephus' omission of Isaiah's call (Isaiah 6), as Begg correctly explains, this is in line with his general tendency to shy away from biblical accounts of intimate exchanges between G-d and prophets, since for him the crucial point is not the revelation, which, being miraculous, presented problems of credibility to Josephus and to many of his readers (see Begg 1988b, 351; Feldman 1988b, 506-7). Likewise, Josephus' omission of Isaiah's castigation of the social and ethical sins of the people of Judah is paralleled by his similar omission of such data from other prophets and may be explained by the fact that Josephus is writing a history, which, in his conception, was focused upon political and military affairs.

3. *Submissiveness to the Superpower*

Inasmuch as it was Isaiah's prophecy that the Assyrian king Sennacherib would be defeated without a battle that encouraged Hezekiah to defy the Assyrians (2 Kings 19:20-34; *Ant.* 10.13), Isaiah and Hezekiah would seem to be associated in a refusal to submit to the superpower; and hence one can understand why Josephus would seek to minimize and downgrade both of them. After all, if we compare the message of the Assyrian king Sennacherib to Hezekiah, in which he recalls to Hezekiah what has happened to all the nations that have resisted the Assyrians (Isaiah 37:11-13, 2 Kings 19:33-35), we see striking parallels with the speech of the Jewish king Agrippa II in which he lists the various nations that have been overcome by the Romans (*War* 2.358-87). Indeed, we may note that the rabbinic tradition, with which, as we have indicated, there is good reason to believe Josephus was acquainted, asserts that Hezekiah had opponents to his policy vis-à-vis the Assyrians, notably the high priest Shebnah (*Leviticus Rabbah* 5.5), who, indeed, we are told, had a greater following than the king himself (*Sanhedrin* 26a),[10] and that Shebnah even went to the extent of fastening a letter to a dart which he shot into the Assyrian camp declaring, "We and the people of Israel wish to conclude peace with thee, but Hezekiah and Isaiah will not permit it" (*Sanhedrin* 26a-b, *Leviticus Rabbah* 5.5 and 17.3, *Midrash Psalms* 11.98-99). According to this tradition, Shebnah's influence was so great that Hezekiah showed signs of yielding, but the prophet Isaiah stiffened his resistance to Sennacherib's demands. Josephus, we may surmise, would have joined the peace movement if he had lived at that time, and thus he would have countered Isaiah's militant opposition to submission.

We may also note that one of the few prophecies of Isaiah that Josephus does include is his prediction that Cyrus would cause Jerusalem and the Temple to be rebuilt (Isaiah 44:28). Josephus felt secure in reproducing this prophecy because its focus is on the Temple, to which he, the priest, was so devoted, whereas there is no mention of establishing an independent Jewish state.

4. *References to David and to the Messiah*

It is surely striking that Josephus omits all reference to David as the ancestor of the Messiah, despite the fact that such a tradition must have been widespread in his era (see Feldman 1989d, 173), because he apparently wished to stress for his Jewish readers his own repugnance to an independent state, this being generally regarded as the goal which a Messiah as a political leader would accomplish.

While it is true, as de Jonge has remarked, that an investigation of Jewish writings dating from the beginning of the Common Era reveals that the term "Messiah" is not generally used as a desigation for G-d's representative or intermediary who will effect

---

[10] Ginzberg (1928, 6:364, n. 63) remarks that, according to Jerome on Isaiah 22:15, Shebnah delivered the entire city of Jerusalem, with the exception of Mount Zion, into the hands of Sennacherib.

a new age of peace for Israel and for the world, the fact is that messianic movements do seem to have gained impetus precisely during the first century, aided and abetted by the treatment of the Jews by the Roman procurators (de Jonge 1992, 787). Thus, there were several movements in Judaea during the first century, particularly at the time of the revolt against Rome, headed by people who claimed the kingship or were proclaimed king by their followers (so Horsley 1992, 793). In view of the fact that these movements were clearly informed by traditional biblical prototypes, "the conclusion seems obvious that the groups led by the popularly proclaimed kings were 'messianic' movements based upon the prototypical messianic movements of biblical history" (so Horsley 1992, 793). To be sure, Josephus avoids using the word "Messiah," except (supposing the passages are authentic) in connection with Jesus (*Ant.* 18.63, 20.200); but the movements led by Judas in Galilee, Simon in Peraea, Athronges in Judaea, Menahem the leader of the Sicarii, and Simon bar Giora are highly reminiscent of messianic movements, even if the name "Messiah" is never used with reference to them by Josephus.

Moreover, by approximately the time that Josephus completed his *Antiquities* in 93/94, we find definite references to the expectation of a Messiah in 4 Ezra (7:30-44, 12:32) and 2 Baruch (29:3, 30:1-2, 39:7, 40:1, 40:3, 70:9, 72:2) as a royal figure who, after a period of wars, will bring about an age of complete bliss and incorruptibility that will last forever, in which only those who have not subjugated Israel will be spared, after which, when his personal reign will have come to an end, he will return in glory, and a general resurrection of the dead will follow (2 Baruch 72:2-6). There can be little doubt, then, that by the time of Josephus, there was vigorous expectation of a Davidic Messiah, at least in certain circles, as we can see in a number of documents – the Qumran scrolls, the Testaments of the Twelve Patriarchs, and the Psalms of Solomon (see Collins 1987, 104-5).

The use of the term "Messiah" in the Gospels (Mark 12:35, 15:32; Luke 2:11, 26; John 1:41; Acts 2:36, 4:26, etc.) in connection with this expectation would seem to confirm that by the end of the first century such an expectation was sufficiently widespread as to be readily understood. The fact that in the Gospel accounts of the interrogation of Jesus by the high priest, he is asked whether he is the Messiah, without further explanation of what the term

"Messiah" meant (Matthew 26:60-64, Mark 14:61-64, Luke 22:66-71), would indicate that the authors of the Gospels, toward the end of the first century, felt that its significance would be clear to their reading audience. The debates mentioned particularly in the Book of Acts (9:22, 18:5, 18:28) between the followers of Jesus and their opponents as to whether Jesus was the Messiah clearly assume that both sides expect a Messiah and that the only difference between them is that some do not regard Jesus as having fulfilled their expectations.

When de Jonge remarks that there are no messianic sayings recorded of Tannaitic scholars who died before 70, this does not imply that Jews of that period did not expect a Messiah (de Jonge 1992, 786).[11] In the first place, the Talmud records views in the names of scholars who may have lived in the third, fourth, or fifth centuries but who recall traditions that go back to an indefinite earlier period. In the second place, the Mishnah, which is where the views of rabbis who lived before its redaction about the year 200 are recorded, is a legal compendium which, as such, has relatively few references to theological matters. Nevertheless, the Mishnah, in the name of the "sages," without specifying the names or dates of those sages, says that the term "all the days of your life" (Deuteronomy 16:3) includes the messianic age (*Berakot* 1:5). Likewise, the Mishnah, in the name of Rabbi Eliezer the Great, who lived at the end of the first century and at the beginning of the second century and hence was a contemporary of Josephus, describes conditions "in the footsteps of the Messiah," that is, in the time just before the advent of the Messiah, namely that "insolence will increase and honor dwindle, the vine will yield its fruit but wine will be dear, the government will turn to heresy and there

---

[11] Neusner (1984) argues that the Messiah concept is insignificant in most early rabbinic works; this may, however, be due to the general eagerness of the rabbis not to provoke the Romans into abrogating the special privileges enjoyed by the Jews. This may be seen, for example, in the fable told by Josephus' younger contemporary, Joshua ben Ḥananiah, about the crane that extracted a thorn from the throat of a lion and upon demanding a reward was told, "Be satisfied that I allowed you to live" (*Genesis Rabbah* 64.10). If so, Josephus would be in accord with this rabbinic trend, as might be expected, given his desire not to offend his Roman beneficiaries, since a Messiah, *ipso facto*, implied revolt against Rome in order to establish an independent state. As to whether messianic expectations were avoided or, more likely, suppressed in the composition of the Mishnah, we may also note that the Mishnah is primarily a codification of law, and hence for it to discuss the Messiah would really be a digression.

will be no reproof," etc. (*Soṭah* 9:15). Moreover, a generation after the death of Josephus, we hear that Rabbi Akiva (Jerusalem *Ta'anit* 4.68d) interpreted the phrase that "a star shall come forth out of Jacob" (Numbers 24:17) messianically and recognized Bar Kochba as the Messiah. The fact that his colleague, Rabbi Joḥanan ben Torta, disagreed and declared that "grass will grow out of your cheeks and the Son of David will still not have come" would appear to indicate that he also accepted the concept of a Messiah and that his only disagreement with Akiva was whether Bar Kochba was that Messiah.

Likewise, the third-century Rabbi Tanḥum presents the tradition that six sons were destined to come forth from Ruth–David, Messiah, Daniel, Hananiah, Mishael, and Azariah (*Sanhedrin* 93b and parallels cited by Ginzberg 1928, 6:193, n.61). Clearly, the Messiah is a distinct figure here, different from David. He then quotes Isaiah 11:2-3: "And the spirit of the L-rd shall rest upon him [the shoot from the stump of Jesse], the spirit of wisdom and understanding, the spirit of counsel and might, the spirit of knowledge and the fear of the L-rd." The fact that immediately thereafter the Talmud mentions Bar Kochba's claim to be the Messiah would seem to indicate that Bar Kochba regarded himself as fulfilling the messianic characteristics cited in the passage in Isaiah. Another indication that the rabbis understood this passage in Isaiah messianically may be seen in the statement that Jesus had a disciple named Neẓer, who when brought before the court for judgment said: "Shall Neẓer be executed? Is it not written [Isaiah 11:1]: 'And Neẓer [a twig] shall grow forth out of his roots?'" (*Sanhedrin* 43a, in the uncensored text). The fact that this verse is mentioned in connection with a disciple of Jesus is again an indication of its messianic connection.

The assumption that the Messiah is descended from David is to be found not only in the rabbinic tradition, as noted above, but also in the Gospels. In Matthew 22:42 Jesus asks the Pharisees, "What do you think of the Messiah? Whose son is he?" Their reply is "The son of David." Jesus, to be sure, counters by quoting Psalm 110:1, but the Pharisees do seem to represent the usual view. Likewise, in the Dead Sea Scrolls (4 Q Flor 11-12) we find that "the Branch of David" will arise with the interpreter of the Law at the end of time. We can thus see that the Gospels, the Dead Sea sect, and the rabbinic tradition all assume that the Messiah would be descended from King David.

We should note at this point that there was a clear conflict between the Hasmonean kings, who were not descended from David, and their supporters, on the one hand, and those who looked forward to the return of the Davidic dynasty, on the other hand. This conflict is reflected in the *Psalms of Solomon*, which were probably written about 50-40 B.C.E. (so de Jonge 1992, 783), and whose authors attack the Hasmoneans because they had not discharged their priestly duties properly and had usurped both the high priesthood (8:11) and royal authority (17:5-6). Divine deliverance, these Psalms assert, is to come from a Davidic king (17:21). Because Josephus was himself descended from the Hasmonean kings rather than from the line of David and because, according to the prophecy of Isaiah (9:7), the looked-for Messiah will re-establish the kingdom of David, clearly anathema to the Romans, who realized that any attempt to re-establish the Davidic kingdom would mean revolt against Rome, Josephus could hardly be expected to endorse such a position; and, not surprisingly, he totally omits these messianic prophecies. Moreover, because of David's association with the Messiah, Josephus omits Isaiah's reporting of G-d's statement that the king of Assyria would not enter Jerusalem "for my own sake and for the sake of my servant David" (2 Kings 19:34; *Ant.* 10.16).

Isaiah 9:6 reads: "For to us a child is born, to us a son is given; and the government will be upon his shoulder, and his name will be called 'Wonderful Counselor, Mighty G-d, Everlasting Father, Prince of Peace.' Of the increase of his government and of peace there shall be no end, upon the throne of David, and over his kingdom, to establish it, and to uphold it with justice and with righteousness from this time forth and for evermore." Isaiah 11:1-2 reads: "There shall come forth a shoot from the stump of Jesse, and a branch shall grow out of his roots. And the spirit of the L-rd shall rest upon him, the spirit of wisdom and understanding, the spirit of counsel and might, the spirit of knowledge and the fear of the L-rd." Because these passages were interpreted messianically and because for Isaiah the central figure in these prophecies is a descendant of David we should not be surprised to find that Josephus omits them altogether.[12] Indeed, Josephus never men-

---

[12] Similarly, we may note that Josephus omits reference to the messianic pas-

tions David in connection with the Messiah and is content to say merely that David's house will be glorious and renowned (*Ant.* 7.94). In fact, partly at least because David was so closely associated with the Messiah, Josephus has considerably downgraded his importance, especially as compared with David's great rival, Saul, whom he aggrandizes.[13]

Another reason why Josephus may have sought to diminish the importance of Isaiah was because of the messianic associations of King Hezekiah, with whom Isaiah was so closely associated. That the rabbinic tradition understood the passage in Isaiah 9:6-7 messianically is evident from the Talmud, where the third-century Rabbi Tanḥum, in the name of Bar Kappara (the student of the great patriarch Judah the Prince), who lived at the beginning of the third century, commenting on the fact that the letter *mem* in the middle of the word *lemarbeh* ("increase") is written not as a medial but as a final *mem*,[14] explains that G-d wished to appoint Hezekiah as the Messiah and the Assyrian king Sennacherib as Gog and Magog, i.e., the tribes that will lead all nations in a tremendous attack upon Israel, whereupon an angel, the hypostasized Attribute of Justice, argued with G-d saying that if G-d did not make David, who had written so many hymns and psalms, the Messiah, how could he appoint Hezekiah, who had written no such hymns despite the miracles that G-d had wrought for him? Remarkable also is the statement recorded in the name of the third century Hillel II, who, as the grandson of the famous patriarch Judah the Prince, was in a position of great importance in the Palestinian Jewish community, that there will actually be no Messiah for Israel in the future because they have already enjoyed him in the days of Hezekiah (*Sanhedrin* 99a). Indeed, the eight names

---

sages in Jeremiah (23:3-5, 33:14-17), Ezekiel (34:23-24, 37:24-25), Haggai (2:21-23), and Zechariah (3:9-10, 4:6-10, 6:9-15).

[13] See Feldman 1982, 45-99; and 1989d, 129-74, especially 172-74. In contrast to this downgrading of David's importance, we may note that Philo, who generally has very little to say about the books of the Bible beyond the Pentateuch, elevates him, referring to him not merely as one of the disciples of Moses (*De Confusione Linguarum* 11.39) but as a member of the inner circle of Moses (*De Plantatione* 9.39). In even greater contrast to Josephus, the rabbis elevated David to the point where Rabbi Akiva declares that on the Day of Judgment David will sit on a throne adjacent to that of G-d (*Sanhedrin* 38b). See especially Feldman 1989d, 131-32, n. 6.

[14] The closing of the *mem* would appear to signify that G-d's original intention to make Hezekiah the Messiah was closed, that is, revoked.

that are ascribed to Hezekiah are the very ones used by the prophet Isaiah (9:6) of the Messiah (*Sanhedrin* 94a). To be sure, to this clear implication that King Hezekiah was the long-awaited Messiah, Hillel II's contemporary, Rabbi Joseph, responded, "May G-d forgive him" (*Sanhedrin* 99a).

Josephus may also have de-emphasized David, Hezekiah, and Isaiah, not only because of their close association with the messianic ideal but also because David and Isaiah had assumed special importance for Christianity. While it is true, as we have noted, that Jesus himself appears to have asserted that the Messiah is not descended from David (cf. Matthew 22:41-45, Mark 13:35-51, Luke 20:41-44), just as some of his contemporaries are said to be unaware of a connection between Jesus and the House of David (John 7:41-42), nevertheless, by the time of Paul, Christians already believed that Jesus was descended from the family of David (Romans 1:3), so that two of the Gospels have genealogies, differing to be sure in details, but agreeing in deriving Jesus' descent from David (Matthew 1:1-7 and Luke 3:23-38). Moreover, the Christian tradition identified the *almah* of Isaiah 7:14 with the virgin mother Mary and Immanuel with Jesus (Matthew 1:20). Indeed, the Church Fathers looked upon Isaiah as not merely the greatest of the prophets but also as an apostle and an evangelist. Hence, to counteract the importance of David and Isaiah among the Christians, Josephus may have diminished their significance, just as, we may guess, he may be reacting against the claims of Christianity in the original version of the *Testimonium Flavianum* (*Ant.* 18.63-64) (see Feldman 1982a, 179-99, 288-93), and even possibly in his version of the Flood story, in which because the reference to a covenant (διαθήκη) between G-d and man is so important for Christianity, he deliberately omits all reference to it (so Paul 1985, 473-80). The diminished emphasis on miracles in Josephus (see Feldman 1984, 477-80) may likewise perhaps be seen, in part, as a reply to the Christians, who emphasized Jesus' miracles, and as such in line with the point of view expressed in the story of Rabbi Eliezer, who appealed to miracles but yet was overruled and even excommunicated when he insisted on his Halakhic point of view after it had been backed by divine miracles (*Baba Mezia* 59b).

Still another reason for Josephus' omission of the messianic passages in Isaiah is that such a vision as that depicted in Isaiah 27:9 of the destruction of Asherim and alien incense-altars was not congruent with Josephus' view, as seen in his interpretation, in accordance with the Septuagint of Exodus 22:27, that one is not permitted to speak in a derogatory fashion about other religions (*Ant.* 4.207, *Ag. Ap.* 2.237).[15]

5. *Isaiah as Prophet*

As a historian, Josephus is critical of his predecessors for misrepresenting the facts and for not seeking accuracy (τὸ...ἀκριβὲς τῆς ἱστορίας) as their goal (*War* 1.2).

That Josephus actually had the highest regard for Isaiah may be seen in the fact that he refers to him as an unmistakably (ὁμολογουμένως) "divine" (θεῖος) prophet, just as he refers to Moses as a "divine man" (θεῖον ἄνδρα) (*Ant.* 3.180) and just as he indicates that Daniel gained credit among the multitude for his divine power (θειότητος) (*Ant.* 10.268). Indeed, in the *Testimonium Flavianum*, the authenticity of which has been so fiercely debated, Josephus refers to the prophets generally as divine (θεῖοι), presumably in the sense of being divinely inspired (*Ant.* 18.64).

The quality of Isaiah which Josephus singles out, in a kind of editorial about him, is that he was marvelously possessed of truth and was confident of never having spoken what was false (*Ant.* 10.35). Indeed, we may note that, significantly, Josephus on seven occasions[16] refers to Isaiah as a prophet where his identification as a prophet is missing in the Bible. And yet, Josephus was confronted with a major problem here, inasmuch as according to both the Book of 2 Kings (20:1) and the Book of Isaiah (38:1) Isaiah had prophesied to Hezekiah that he would not recover from his illness but would die. According to the biblical account, however, Hezekiah prayed (2 Kings 20:2-3, Isaiah 38:2-3), whereupon G-d instructed Isaiah to tell Hezekiah that He had heard his prayer and had added fifteen years to his life (2 Kings 20:4-6, Isaiah 38:4-6). In his version of this incident Josephus has made five major

---

[15] We may note that, in the interest of tolerance, Josephus has omitted the biblical passage that King Jehu's men broke down the house of the pagan god Baal and made it a latrine "unto this day" (2 Kings 10:27; *Ant.* 9.138).

[16] *Ant.* 9. 276 (vs. 2 Kings 19:5), 10.13 (vs. 2 Kings 19:5), 10:16 (vs. 2 Kings 19:20), 10.28 (vs. 2 Kings 20:4), 10.29 (vs. 2 Kings 20:9), 10.32 (vs. 2 Kings 20:16), 10.35 (vs. no particular passage).

changes (*Ant.* 10.24-25).[17] In the first place, apparently aware of the fact that Isaiah's original prophecy that Hezekiah's illness would be fatal was not fulfilled, he omits that prophecy altogether. Rather, we hear that when Hezekiah took ill, he prayed, and G-d took pity on him and granted his request to live a little longer. It is only after the request has been granted that Josephus reports that G-d sent Isaiah to inform Hezekiah that within three days he would be rid of his illness and would live an additional fifteen years and that sons would be born to him (*Ant.* 10.27). The second major change concerns G-d's instructions to Isaiah, which in the Bible read: "Go and say to Hezekiah, Thus says the L-rd, the G-d of David your father" (Isaiah 38:5). In Josephus' version there is no mention of David (*Ant.* 10.27), presumably for the reason that we have already indicated, namely that Josephus seeks to avoid the association of David, Hezekiah, and the Messiah. Thirdly, in the biblical version, after Isaiah reports to Hezekiah G-d's decision to lengthen the king's life, Isaiah, on his own initiative orders a cake of figs to be brought which he then places on Hezekiah's boil so as to cure him (2 Kings 20:7). This is completely omitted by Josephus (*Ant.*10.28), presumably because he suspected that his readers might regard this as superstition rather than as a scientific cure, and he was well aware of the charge made against the Jews that they were superstitious.[18] Fourthly, whereas in the Bible Hezekiah simply asks Isaiah for a sign to prove that G-d would fulfill his promise to heal him, without indicating why he seeks this evidence (2 Kings 20:8), Josephus, aware that his readers would be skeptical, explains that things that are beyond belief and surpass our hopes are made credible by acts of a like nature (*Ant.* 10.28). Moreover, in the Bible it is Hezekiah who asks Isaiah what sign G-d will give to verify his promised cure and Isaiah replies by telling him that the sign will be that the shadow of the sun will, in accordance with Hezekiah's request, either go forward or go backward ten steps (2 Kings 20:8). In Josephus' version the spotlight is to a greater degree on Isaiah in that it is he who takes the initiative in the first place to ask Hezekiah what sign he wishes to have to confirm G-d's prediction (*Ant.* 10.29). Fifthly, whereas in the biblical

---

[17] We may note that in the version in 2 Chronicles 32:24) there is no mention of the role of Isaiah in predicting Hezekiah's death.

[18] See, for example, Agatharchides (*ap. Ag. Ap.* 1.205-11) and Plutarch (*De Superstitione* 8.169C).

narrative there is no statement that Hezekiah was actually cured and it is merely implied that Hezekiah was cured, in Josephus' version not only is there an explicit statement that he was cured but Josephus adds that he was at once freed from his illness (*Ant.* 10.29).

6. *Summary*

Though Josephus shows a great respect for and identification with the prophets, and though Isaiah was so highly regarded by the rabbinic tradition, with which he seems to have been well acquainted, he appears to diminish the importance of Isaiah, especially as compared with Jeremiah and Jonah. There are seven major reasons for his modifications of the biblical account of Isaiah and for this de-emphasis on this prophet: (1) Josephus, the proud priest for whom the Temple and the sacrifices were so central, was disturbed by Isaiah's view that if one wishes to win the favor of G-d it is not enough to conduct the traditional sacrifices; (2) As indicated by his positive attitude toward Jehoiachin and Gedaliah, Josephus identified himself, as seen in his own submission to the Romans, with those who realistically agreed to be subservient to the superpower, whereas Isaiah had successfully counselled King Hezekiah (whom Josephus likewise downgraded, despite the extraordinary reputation that he enjoyed both in the Bible and in rabbinic tradition) to defy the Assyrians, the superpower of that day. If Josephus does include Isaiah's prophecy that King Cyrus of Persia would allow the Jews to rebuild Jerusalem and the Temple, it is because the focus there is on the Temple, which was of great importance to Josephus the priest, and does not speak of establishing an independent state. Likewise, his interpretation of Isaiah's prophecy as referring to the building of the temple at Leontopolis in Egypt is to be explained as due to Josephus' interest in priestly matters and to his opportunity here to have a non-Jew, King Ptolemy Philometor of Egypt, express admiration for the prescience of a Jewish prophet; (3) Inasmuch as the Book of Isaiah contains passages that were understood messianically, Josephus, realizing that a major function of a Messiah was to establish an independent state and being eager not to offend his Roman hosts, who would presumably be overthrown by such a Messiah, omits such passages; (4) Since, according to both the Gospels and the rabbinic tradition, the Messiah was to be descended from David, Josephus, who himself was descended from the Hasmonean kings, the rivals of the Davidic line, downgrades the prophet of such a Messiah; (5) Inasmuch as Hezekiah, with whom Isaiah is so closely identified, was himself regarded as the Messiah, at least according to one tradition, Josephus downgrades his chief supporter, Isaiah, as well; (6) Josephus may have diminished the importance of Isaiah both because of the latter's own importance and the significance of David (of whom Isaiah has so much to say) for nascent Christianity; (7) Josephus, for whom the key factor in prophecy is its truth, may have been disturbed by the fact that Isaiah had prophesied that King Hezekiah would die of the illness that had afflicted him, only to be, so to speak, overruled by G-d, who allowed Hezekiah to live for an additional fifteen years.

CHAPTER TWENTY-SIX

JONAH

1. *Introduction: Issues*

That Josephus has relatively little to say about the individual biblical prophets should not be surprising in view of the fact that he is writing a history rather than a treatise on theology or ethics. Nevertheless, it is striking that certain prophets do claim his attention, including two of the minor prophets, Jonah and Nahum. While there have been several studies dealing with Josephus' views on prophecy and prophets generally,[1] there have been only two attempts[2] – and those very brief and insufficiently analytical – to study Josephus' treatment of Jonah in particular. It is not merely that Josephus has drastically compressed the biblical account (so Begg 1988b, 345); we must also try to explain why he utilizes those aspects which he does and why he omits others. Moreover, though he attempts to note all places where Josephus parallels the rabbinic tradition, Rappaport cites no examples from the Jonah pericope (Rappaport 1930).

The present study will address the following questions in particular:

1. Why is Josephus particularly interested in Jonah when he neglects many of the other prophets? Why does he repeatedly refer to Jonah as a prophet, whereas in the Book of Jonah he is never referred to thus?

2. Why does Josephus reduce the role of G-d in the Jonah story?

3. Why does he avoid indicating that G-d repented after the city of Nineveh had repented?

4. How does Josephus handle the miracles in the biblical Jonah narrative?

5. How does he resolve the dilemma of the universalism of the biblical book as against the implied particularism of Jonah and the

---

[1] Dienstfertig 1892, 24-33; Fascher 1927, 161-64; Meyer 1964, 6.812-28; Blenkinsopp 1974, 239-62; Delling, 1974, 109-21; van Unnik 1978, 41-54; and Begg 1988b, 341-57.

[2] Begg 1988b, 345-47; and Duval 1973, 1.82-86.

Israelites? Why does he avoid indicating that the city of Nineveh repented or that Jonah was displeased with G-d's repentance?

6. How does he cope with the implication of the Book of Jonah that the sailors became proselytes or "G-d-fearers"?

7. Are there indications that he has "Hellenized" the story?

2. *The Importance of Jonah to Josephus, the Historian*

Although the Book of Jonah is reckoned among the twelve Minor Prophets, it is certainly the best known of them for Jews.[3] Indeed, according to one rabbinic view, the Book of Jonah is a book by itself and is not to be viewed as part of the book of the twelve minor prophets (*Numbers Rabbah* 18.21). This special status of the book is largely due to the fact that it is read in its entirety as the *haftarah* on the afternoon of the most sacred day in the Jewish calendar, the Day of Atonement.[4] Its uniqueness, moreover, derives from the fact that it alone of the prophetic books deals primarily not with Jews but with a heathen city and with its repentance.

There are indications in the way in which Josephus introduces the prophecy of Jonah that he is deliberately inserting a digression. He starts with an apology, that since he had promised to give an exact account of Jewish history, he deems it necessary to report what is found in the Scriptures concerning Jonah (*Ant.* 9.208). But when we consider how much of the biblical narrative Josephus has omitted in his entire paraphrase of the Bible, this seems like a mere pretext for introducing material that he thought important on other grounds. Moreover, though he promises to recount what he has found written in the Hebrew books (ἐν ταῖς Ἑβραικαῖς βίβλοις) concerning this prophet, he actually is highly selective and, indeed, omits most of what is written in the Book of Jonah, including the main point of the story. The reason, then, for this

---

[3] At least the story of the big fish that swallowed Jonah was apparently well known even to pagan intellectuals, as we can see from Celsus (*ap.* Origen, *Against Celsus* 7.53).

[4] It is so designated as the *haftarah* in the Talmud (*Megillah* 31a). That the institution of reading selections from the prophets was known in Josephus' time and goes back to at least the middle of the first century is clear from the reference in Luke 4:16-17, where we are told that Jesus on the Sabbath day in the synagogue was given the book of the prophet Isaiah from which to read. Furthermore, we read in Acts 13:15 that "after the reading of the law and the prophets" Paul was invited to speak in the synagogue. See Büchler 1907, 6:135-36.

digression would appear to be that Jonah's prophecy concerning Nineveh is important for him as an historian.

As an historian, Josephus is eager to give the impression of being precise. Thus, the Bible reports that Jonah found a ship going to Tarshish, a site whose location is left unspecified (Jonah 1:3); and one might well wonder whether the city is fictitious and whether the whole story is a mere parable. Not so in Josephus, who unambiguously identifies the city as Tarsus in Cilicia (*Ant.* 9.208).[5] Similarly, whereas the Bible states that the fish vomited out Jonah upon the dry land without indicating where this was (Jonah 2:11), Josephus is precise in identifying the place as the shore of the Euxine (Black) Sea (*Ant.* 9.213), though such an identification is nowhere to be found in the rabbinic or in any other tradition.[6] Such precision gives the historian's narrative an air of reliability, just as when Josephus identifies the spot, namely Armenia, where Noah's ark landed (*Ant.* 1.90) and even displays further precision in noting that the Armenians call that spot "Landing-Place" and show the relics there even in Josephus' own day (*Ant.* 1.92).

That, for Josephus, Jonah the prophet is to be viewed against his historical background is clear from the fact that he introduces him by citing his political role, as noted in 2 Kings 14:25, in prophesying to King Jeroboam II of Israel that he would make war on the Syrians and thus extend the borders of his kingdom, whereas most scholars agree that the protagonist of the Book of Jonah has only the loosest connection with the Jonah of the Book of Kings. It is a similar political role which is underscored by Josephus when he declares that Jonah was instructed by G-d to preach in Nineveh that it would lose its power (ἀρχήν) (*Ant.* 9.208).

Moreover, it is significant that whereas in the Book of Jonah there is not a single explicit reference to Jonah as a prophet, in

---

[5] Cf. Josephus, *Ant.* 1.127, who, paraphrasing the Table of Nations found in Genesis, chapter 10, comments on the verse that gives the name of one of Japheth's sons as Tarshish (Genesis 10:4). Josephus there declares that Tarshish was the ancient name of Cilicia, as is proven by the fact that its principal and capital city was called Tarsus. It is perhaps tempting to see a connection between this identification of Tarshish as Tarsus and the fact that a contemporary of Josephus, the apostle Paul, was, like Jonah, involved in a shipwreck; but Josephus nowhere mentions Paul or his mission; and if the passage were interpolated by a Christian one would have expected a more precise reference to Paul as well as to the gospel which he preached.

[6] This identification apparently results from Josephus' assumption that the Euxine (Black) Sea is the nearest sea to Nineveh. So Marcus 1937, 6:113, n. c.

Josephus, within a mere nine short paragraphs (*Ant.* 9.206-14), Jonah is on four occasions referred to as a prophet or as prophesying, even though in the biblical book Jonah delivers only a single prophecy (3:4) and in only five words, the rest of the book being a story *about* Jonah.[7] To be sure, Josephus does have a biblical warrant for his designation, that is, the use of the term "prophet" for Jonah in 2 Kings 14:25. But Josephus has converted the narrative of the Book of Jonah into an account dealing with the profession of the prophet, whom he regards as the twin brother, so to speak, of the historian. To him the narrative is not a midrashic legend[8] but a page of history.

Josephus is careful, however, to avoid any hint of nationalism in his portrayal of Jonah. Hence, whereas in the biblical passage Jonah tells the sailors on board the ship "I am a Hebrew" (Jonah 1:9), in Josephus Jonah says that he is a Hebrew by race (τὸ... γένος) (*Ant.* 9.211), the same expression that Josephus uses about himself (*War* 1.3), where the word γένος refers not necessarily to nation but to origin or group or family in the etymological and broadest sense.[9]

---

[7] It is true that the Book of Jonah begins in a manner similar to that of several others of the minor prophets – Hosea, Joel, Micah, Zephaniah, Malachi – namely, "The word of the L-rd [that] came to...," without mention of the word "prophet." It is clear in his case, as in that of the other prophets, that he is a prophet; his mission, which he tries to flee, is nothing if not prophetic, and the whole paradox of Jonah is that he is a prophet whose act of prophesying leads to a falsification of the prophecy. In view of all these features, readers of the Book of Jonah in Hebrew would not have been particularly sensitive about the absence of the word "prophet" in the narrative. Yet, the significant point is that Josephus keeps emphasizing that Jonah is a prophet, for the reason which we have suggested, namely that he regards the prophet as the twin brother of the historian.

[8] This is the classification given of the biblical narrative proposed by Trible (1967).

[9] Cf. *War* 1.78: Judas was of Essene extraction (Ἐσσαῖος ἦν γένος), where the reference cannot be to a nation, since the Essenes did not constitute a nation. Cf. Josephus' other references to the Essenes (*War* 2.113, 2.119; *Ant.* 13.311, 17.346). That the word γένος does not necessarily denote a nation is clear from the passage in which we are told that the procurator Florus scourged and nailed to the cross men of equestrian rank who were Jews by birth (τὸ γένος Ἰουδαῖον) (*War* 2.308), where clearly neither Josephus nor Florus would regard these equestrians as members of a Jewish nation. That the word γένος does not necessarily mean a "nation" in a political sense is also clear from Josephus' statement that the Jewish people (τὸ γὰρ Ἰουδαίων γένος) are densely interspersed among the native populations of every portion of the world (*War* 7.43). Other instances where the word γένος cannot refer to a political entity are *Antiquities* 2.78, alluding to Joseph's rank by birth (γένους); 2.179, referring to Leah's progeny (γένος); and

We may also suggest that it was similarly his desire to avoid any semblance of nationalism that may have led Josephus to avoid mention of the widespread tradition[10] that Jonah was the Zarephath widow's son resuscitated by the prophet Elijah (1 Kings 17:17-24) who is said to be the Messiah of the tribe of Joseph (cf. *Midrash Psalms* 26.220). Similarly, we may note, Josephus avoids any allusion to David as the ancestor of the Messiah, since such a reference might well have been considered by the Romans as encouraging revolt, inasmuch as the Messiah was generally regarded as a political leader who would reestablish an independent Jewish state.

Ironically, perhaps, Josephus, though dealing with a prophet, ignores the religious side of Jonah's conduct and mission and restricts himself to Jonah's political role.[11] We may here suggest that Josephus perhaps introduced his digression about Jonah in order to give him an opportunity to predict the overthrow of Assyria, which is located in precisely the area where the kingdom of Parthia, the great enemy of the Romans, was situated. Josephus, who depicts himself as a veritable prophet (*War* 3.351-53) and as a faithful lackey of the Romans, would have taken pleasure at such a prospect.

3. *The Role of G-d in Josephus' Treatment of Jonah*[12]

One might say that G-d Himself is the real hero of the biblical Book of Jonah and that the heart of the story is that, as Jonah admits in his prayer, G-d is gracious and merciful, slow to anger, and abounding in steadfast love (Jonah 4:2). This divine love, we

---

2.216, mentioning the people (γένος) who will be delivered by Moses, in all of which cases the Jewish nation has obviously not yet been constituted; likewise, in *Antiquities* 7.117 and 296 the term refers not to the nation but to the family (γένους) of Saul, just as in 8.232 and 270 it refers to the family (γένους) of David.

[10] Cf. *Seder Eliyahu Rabbah* 18.97-98; Jerome, introduction to *Commentary on Jonah*, who connects the name of Jonah's father, Amittai, with the word *'emet* ("truth") in the statement of the widow of Zarephath to Elijah, "Now I know that you are a man of G-d and that the word of the L-rd in your mouth is truth" (1 Kings 17:24).

[11] The point is made but not developed by Duval (1973, 82-86).

[12] Begg (1988b, 347) correctly notes that Josephus' version of the Jonah story lacks much of the theological depth and satiric bite of the original, but he does not develop the point further.

may remark, extends both to non-Jews, that is, the people of Nineveh, and to the recalcitrant prophet Jonah. But Josephus is writing a history of men, not of G-d, and this detheologizing is evident in his paraphrase of the Book of Jonah. Thus, for example, at almost the very beginning of the narrative, the biblical account states that the L-rd hurled a great wind upon the sea (Jonah 1:4); and the question naturally arises whether, if the storm was due solely to the presence of Jonah, other ships were able to avoid the storm (see Bickerman 1967, 10-11). The rabbinic tradition has preserved an answer to this problem, namely that the storm affected only Jonah's ship (*Pirqe de-Rabbi Eliezer* 10, to be sure not reduced to writing until perhaps the eighth century). But Josephus avoids the difficulty altogether by omitting G-d from the equation and simply stating that "a very severe storm came up" (*Ant.* 9.209).

Again, in the biblical narrative, when the storm has overwhelmed the ship carrying Jonah and when the sailors cry to their respective deities, the captain urges Jonah to call upon his G-d, in the desperate hope that perhaps his G-d will have pity on them (Jonah 1:6). In Josephus' version, however, there is no such scene (*Ant.* 9.209); and hence, again, G-d is omitted from the picture. It is only after the lots have been drawn that we hear that the sailors ask Jonah who he is (*Ant.* 9.211); and he replies by declaring that he is a Hebrew by race and that he is a prophet of G-d. Even here, whereas the Hebrew has Jonah identify himself as one who fears the L-rd, the G-d of heaven, creator of sea and land, in Josephus Jonah states merely that he is a prophet of the Most High G-d (*Ant.* 9.211), with no explicit indication, implied though that may be, that he is a G-d-fearing person or that G-d is the creator of land and sea.

Likewise, in the biblical narrative we read that the sailors accuse Jonah: "What is this that you have done?" (Jonah 1:10). A theological issue arises here, since we are informed that there has been a previous conversation between them in which Jonah had told them that he was fleeing from the presence of G-d. In Josephus, on the other hand, there is no such previous conversation, no indication that the sailors have any knowledge of why Jonah is on board the ship, and no mention at all of G-d's role (*Ant.* 9.211).

Moreover, the role of G-d is again reduced, inasmuch as Josephus totally omits the biblical statement that the L-rd came to Jonah a second time, ordering him to go to Nineveh and to proclaim the message that He will tell them (Jonah 3:1-2 vs. *Ant.* 9.214). Instead, we read that Jonah, having prayed to G-d to grant him forgiveness for his sins, went to Nineveh, without any explicit indication that G-d ordered him to go there (*Ant.* 9.214). Furthermore, there is no indication at this point that the message that he proclaims, that Nineveh will soon lose its dominance over Asia, has been dictated by G-d.

In addition, Josephus resolves the problem of how and why G-d repented of punishing Nineveh by the simple device of omitting G-d's repentance (Jonah 3:10). In addition, the biblical book ends with G-d teaching Jonah an object lesson about compassion for the inhabitants of Nineveh (Jonah 4:6-11), and nothing is said as to what happened to Jonah thereafter, whereas G-d plays no role in the ending of Josephus' version. Instead, we are told simply that after delivering his message to the people of Nineveh, Jonah departed, presumably to his native city (*Ant.* 9.214).

The climax of the Hebrew book is the lesson of the *qiqayon* (Jonah 4:6-11). Here, it is G-d who brings forth the *qiqayon* (Jonah 4:6) and causes a worm to attack the *qiqayon* and destroy it (Jonah 4:7); and it is G-d who raises a sultry east wind to beat upon Jonah to the point that he becomes so faint that he seeks to die (Jonah 4:8). There is clearly a theological lesson in all this which, in effect, is based on *a fortiori* reasoning: if Jonah found a mere plant, which was only a day old, too important to be destroyed, how could G-d not have pity on a huge city, which had existed for so long?

Still another factor is instrumental in Nineveh's survival according to the Bible, namely the degree of its repentance. One might say that G-d is trying to teach Jonah a cosmic lesson, namely that the existence of a city such as Nineveh is as important in the scheme of creation as is that of a single *qiqayon*. Josephus, however, omits the incident of the *qiqayon* altogether; and there is consequently no place for divine reasoning or for a moral to be drawn in his version.

4. *The Problem of G-d's Repentance and the Truth of Jonah's Prophecy*

If we compare the Book of Jonah with Josephus' version[13] we note that Josephus has omitted the passage which indicates that Jonah was exceedingly displeased that G-d had repented of the punishment which he had promised to inflict upon the people of Nineveh (Jonah 4:1). More particularly, in the biblical version we are told that Jonah was actually angry, presumably because G-d's action was completely contrary to what Jonah had been told to prophesy. Now, a key feature of prophecy in the sense of prediction is that it comes true. Thus, in an extra-biblical editorial, Josephus stresses that inasmuch as the prophecies spoken by Elijah and Micaiah both came true, we ought to acknowledge the greatness of G-d and should not think that statements that flatter us are more worthy of belief than the truth, "but should acknowledge that nothing is more beneficial than prophecy and the foreknowledge which it gives" (*Ant.* 8.418). Similarly, though he does not mention the majority of the twelve minor prophets at all, Josephus goes out of his way to present at length the prophecies of Nahum (*Ant.* 9.239-42) in order to give point to his conclusion that everything that Nahum foretold concerning Nineveh actually came to pass after 115 years (*Ant.* 9.242). Furthermore, the quality of Isaiah which Josephus singles out, in a kind of editorial about him, is that he was marvelously possessed of truth and was confident of never having spoken falsely (*Ant.* 10.35). Indeed, the significance of this aspect of prophecy for Josephus is to be found in his editorializing about Daniel, namely that he (Daniel) made plain the accuracy and faithfulness to truth of his prophecies (*Ant.* 10.269). This attribute of truthful prophecy, adds Josephus, is evident not only in Isaiah but also in the twelve[14] other prophets as well (*Ant.* 10.35), including, of course, Jonah.

Hence, we can understand why Josephus omits G-d's repentance, since this could be interpreted as an indication that Jonah's initial prophecy about Nineveh turned out to be actually false.

---

[13] That Josephus knew the Hebrew text of Jonah is evident from the fact that he renders it literally in the passage where Jonah says that he is a Hebrew (1:9), whereas the Septuagint reads δοῦλος κυρίου, presumably based upon a Hebrew text that read '*eved y* rather than '*ivri*, where the letter *resh* was replaced by a *daled*.

[14] Presumably the reference is to the twelve prophetic books mentioned in *Against Apion* 1.40.

Indeed, according to the rabbinic tradition, Jonah had earlier gained a reputation among the Israelites as a false prophet, inasmuch as, because the inhabitants of Jerusalem had repented and because G-d had had mercy upon them, his prophecy that Jerusalem would be destroyed had not come to pass (*Pirqe de-Rabbi Eliezer* 10, *Tanḥuma Vayiqra* 8, *Midrash Jonah* 96). Therefore, when he was sent to Nineveh to prophesy the downfall of the city, Jonah reflected that he would only confirm his reputation of being a false prophet by doing as directed, inasmuch as he knew that the Ninevites would repent and that therefore the threatened punishment would not be executed. Consequently, Josephus protects himself against the possible charge that he has misrepresented the Book of Jonah with its prediction that Nineveh would be overthrown within forty days (Jonah 3:4) (the Septuagint makes matters all the more implausible by reading three in place of forty here). In Josephus we have instead the carefully worded statement that Nineveh would be overthrown within "a very short time" (μετ' ὀλίγον πάνυ χρόνον) (*Ant.* 9.214). Such vagueness protects Jonah against the charge of being a false prophet. This concern will also help to explain why Josephus repeatedly, as we have noted, calls Jonah a prophet, namely to counteract any doubts readers might have had – given the problem of Jonah's unfulfilled prediction – concerning Jonah's status. In this connection, we may note, too, that Josephus' juxtaposition of the notice of Jonah's prediction of Jeroboam's successes and its fulfillment (*Ant.* 9.206-7) with his version of the Book of Jonah is likewise intended to promote a view of Jonah as a true prophet, since the fulfillment of his Syrian prophecy evokes the expectation that his prophecy concerning Nineveh will likewise be realized. To be sure, we may note that at the conclusion of his retelling of the Book of Jonah Josephus does not state that his word against Nineveh was, in fact, realized. That it will be, however, is effectively intimated by the "fulfillment notice" attached to Jonah's earlier prediction to Jeroboam.

In the case of Jonah, Josephus was aware that the entire Book of Nahum consists of a prophecy of the overthrow of Nineveh (*Ant.* 9.239-42). This would seem to contradict the fact that in the Book of Jonah the city of Nineveh is spared by G-d because of the repentance of its people, though, of course, one might reconcile the two books by postulating that the people of Nineveh had repented at the time of Jonah's prophecy but later reverted to their evil ways and therefore were doomed once more. To the unwary reader, however, the two books would seem to be in contradiction to one another; and hence we can understand why Josephus omits G-d's repentance and leaves us with Jonah's renewed prophecy that Nineveh would lose its dominion over Asia (*Ant.* 9.214). Indeed, Josephus' presumed contemporary, Pseudo-Philo, in his *Homily on Jonah* (6, 41, 48), obviously disturbed that Jonah should have fled from his mission, attempts (6) to justify his action by arguing that, being a prophet, he knew beforehand that his threats against Nineveh would not be fulfilled and that he would consequently be discredited as a false prophet. Likewise, in the scenario as presented by the rabbis, Jonah explains his anger by noting that now that his prophetic message had failed to materialize the nations of the world will claim that he was a false prophet and, indeed, would dismiss the whole institution of prophecy, thus bringing about the profanation of the name of G-d (*Pirqe de-Rabbi Eliezer* 10, *Tanḥuma Vayiqra* 9, *Midrash Jonah* 96). Josephus might easily, then, have resolved the problem of the apparent contradiction between Jonah and Nahum or the embarrassment which would be occasioned by the non-fulfillment of Jonah's prophecy by simply omitting the prophecies of Jonah and of Nahum, as he did so many other prophecies in the Bible.[15] For other reasons, however, he declines to take this option.

5. *Josephus' Handling of the Miracles in the Book*

If, indeed, as we have indicated, Josephus was addressing a non-Jewish literate audience in the first place, perhaps the most difficult task confronting him was what to do with the various miracles in the book – the swallowing of Jonah by the fish, Jonah's prayer from within the fish, the episode of Jonah emerging from the big fish, the conversion of the whole city of Nineveh, the plant that grew within one night, the destruction of the plant on the next day by a single worm, and the huge dimensions of Nineveh. In gen-

---

[15] Begg (1988b, 348) says that Josephus' inclusion of Nahum's prophecy gave him an opportunity to confirm and reinforce the announcement about Nineveh's overthrow. But the question still remains why Josephus should have wanted to emphasize Nineveh's overthrow instead of the point made by the Book of Jonah itself, namely the power of repentance.

eral, Josephus tends to downgrade miracles, as we have observed; and this holds true also for the book of Jonah.

In the case of the miracle of Jonah remaining alive for three days in the belly of the big fish and then emerging from it, this was apparently regarded as a major miracle, so that Celsus, in the second century, as we have noted, sarcastically declares that Christians should worship not Jesus but Jonah or Daniel, whose miracles outdo the resurrection (*ap.* Origen, *against Celsus* 7.53). Even two centuries after Celsus, to judge from Augustine (*Epistulae* 102.30), who quotes Porphyry's lost work *Adversus Christianos*, this incident was a source of ridicule among the pagans in general. Josephus might have omitted the story as being incredible (as he did the other miraculous events enumerated above), or he might have left it to the reader to decide, or he might have modified the story to conform with the somewhat similar stories told about Heracles and Hermione and Perseus and Andromache, where the fish is maimed by the hero; but Josephus chose not to depart from the biblical version, perhaps because it was so well known, even while dissociating himself from its veracity. He does so by the device of stating that the story (λόγος) has it that Jonah was swallowed by a huge fish, just as in a somewhat similar story, that of Arion who was rescued by a dolphin, Herodotus (1.24) declares, without taking responsibility for the tale, that "they say" (λέγουσι) that the dolphin took him on his back. Moreover, whereas the biblical narrative has Jonah miraculously address G-d while he is still in the big fish (Jonah 2:1-9), Josephus eliminates the miraculous element by having him do so only after he has emerged from the fish (*Ant.* 9.214). Furthermore, in the Hebrew Bible Jonah, praying from the belly of the fish (Jonah 2:1-2), declares that G-d has answered him (Jonah 2:7), whereas it is clear that the deliverance has not yet taken place. The Septuagint version resolves this difficulty by reading the optative, "May my prayer come to Thee." The Targum speaks of a future: "and it is revealed before you to raise my life from destruction." Josephus, for his part, neatly disposes of this problem by having Jonah pray after emerging from the belly of the fish (*Ant.* 9.214), as just mentioned.[16] Further-

---

[16] So also Pseudo-Philo (*Homily on Jonah* 19-25) replaces the biblical Jonah's prayer with a more appropriate supplication. It is interesting that the great twelfth-century Ibn Ezra, in his commentary on Jonah 2:2, notes that there are commentators who stress the fact that Jonah prayed not in the fish but from the

more, in the Hebrew version we read that the L-rd spoke to the fish that had swallowed Jonah and that it vomited Jonah upon the dry land (Jonah 2:10). Josephus, obviously sensitive to the charge of his credulity here, says nothing about G-d's action in speaking to the fish and instead resorts to the passive voice with the statement that after three days and as many nights Jonah was cast up on the shore of the Black Sea (*Ant.* 9.213).

6. *The Issue of Jew and Non-Jew: The Universalism of the Book of Jonah vs. the Particularism of Jonah and the Israelites*

Josephus found himself in a dilemma with the Jonah pericope. On the one hand, the biblical account highlights the universalistic attitude of Judaism in that G-d's mercy encompasses not only Israel but also the Gentiles[17] and thereby seems to provide an effective answer to the charges of misanthropy noted above. Indeed, the fact that G-d shows mercy toward the people of Nineveh, the very Assyrians who were the bitterest enemies of the Israelites and were responsible for the destruction of the Kingdom of Israel and the loss of ten of the twelve tribes of Israel, is a quite telling answer to such charges. This is reinforced by the fact that on three occasions in the biblical Book of Jonah Nineveh is termed a great city. And yet, the biblical narrative seems at the same time to reinforce the charge of misanthropy in that Jonah is portrayed as angry with G-d for showing mercy toward the people of Nineveh, and also in that it casts the Jews as a whole in a relatively bad light as compared with the people of Nineveh, who repent so sincerely. If Josephus were then to praise the people of Nineveh this would show his broadmindedness; conversely, however, if he did do so, it might reflect badly, by comparison, on his fellow-Jews, who had not heeded the admonitions of the prophets.[18] Indeed, such an

---

fish and hence deduced that he prayed after he had emerged from the fish.

[17] Duval (1973, 77) is astonished that Philo, whose universalism is not in doubt, never refers to the story of Jonah; but we may remark that it is only relatively rarely that Philo refers to books of the Bible other than the Pentateuch. In particular, he mentions only two of the twelve minor prophets and these in only three places (Hosea: *De Plantatione* 33.138; *De Mutatione Nominum* 24.139; and Zechariah: *De Confusione Linguarum* 14.62).

[18] This is actually the view expressed in the *Midrash Lamentations Rabbah*, introduction no. 31: "I sent one prophet to Nineveh, and he brought it to penitence and conversion. And these Israelites in Jerusalem – how many prophets have I sent to them!"

unfavorable comparison is already to be found in the Gospels according to Matthew (12:41) and Luke (11:32); and it is just possible that Josephus was aware of this use made by the Christians of the story of Jonah and may have attempted to respond to it by, in effect, not praising the Ninevites.[19] In this respect we may suggest that Josephus parallels the Targum of Jonah (3:5), which counters the Christian claims about Nineveh's religious conversion and faith by stressing that the Ninevites believed in the message brought by Jonah rather than in G-d.[20] We may also note that the rabbis, clearly seeking to protect the reputation of the Jews, have a tradition that the reason why Jonah boarded the ship was that he hoped that he would lose his life on the voyage and thus be spared the pain of seeing the heathen repent while the Jews failed to do so (*Pirqe de-Rabbi Eliezer* 10, *Tanhuma Vayiqra* 8, *Midrash Jonah* 96)[21].

The rabbinic tradition is well aware that a prophet who holds back his prophecy (as Jonah apparently did, according to the biblical version) is subject to the death penalty at the hands of Heaven (Mishnah, *Sanhedrin* 11:5). The rabbis, too, were confronted with the dilemma of the book's universalism as against the implied particularism of Jonah and the Israelites; and they note that G-d conferred special honor upon the inhabitants of Nineveh by sending the prophet to them – a distinction never before granted to the nations of the world.(*Pirqe de-Rabbi Eliezer* 10, *Tanhuma Vayiqra* 8, *Midrash Jonah* 96) (cited by Ginzberg 1928, 6:349, n. 27). They

---

[19] Levine (1975, 14) remarks that several early Church Fathers (e.g., Justin Martyr, *Dialogue with Trypho* 107; Jerome, *on Jonah* 1.3 and 4.1) used the motif of the Ninevites' sincere repentance in their anti-Jewish polemics to contrast this with the stubbornness of the Jews. We may also suggest that Josephus' omission of Jonah's statement that "It is better for me to die than to live" (Jonah 4:8) may be a response to Christian exegesis, which cited this verse in support of the Christian view that death was better for Jesus than life, since while alive he could save only one nation but that with his death he saved the whole world. See Bowers (1971, 58-59) and Levine (1975, 14), who note that the Targum has, by its subtle paraphrase, altered this Christian "proof-text" by rendering it "It is better that I die than that I live."

[20] See Levine 1975, 13. On the other hand, whereas in the Hebrew text (1:9) and Josephus (*Ant.* 9.211) Jonah identifies himself as a Hebrew, as do the Christian Church Fathers, the Targum identifies him as a Jew, the difference being important in polemics between Jews and Christians.

[21] Cf. Levine 1975, 10: "The spectacular discovery of the Dead Sea Scrolls and Targum Neophyti I have provided increasing indications that even targum texts of a late date may incorporate a significant amount of ancient material." See Bamberger (1949, 115-23); Bikerman (Bickerman) (1952, 44-54); R. Bloch (1955, 194-227); Macho (1960, 222-45).

further explain the forgiveness granted by G-d to the Ninevites by indicating that this was G-d's reward to them because Ashur, their ancestor, had left his native country, since he did not wish to remain among the sinful followers of Nimrod, and had founded the city of Nineveh in honor of G-d. Furthermore, there was a rabbinic tradition that the sons of Sennacherib, the famous king of Assyria who unsuccessfully besieged Jerusalem (2 Kings 19:35), marched to Jerusalem, where they became proselytes and ultimately the ancestors of the famous scholars, Shemaiah and Avtalyon, of the first century B.C.E. (*Gittin* 57b, *Sanhedrin* 96b, Targum 2 Kings 19:35, 37).

As to Nineveh, the rabbinic tradition paints in lurid colors the wickedness of the inhabitants, so that it emerges as a second Sodom (see the discussion by Bickerman 1967, 32-33). Indeed, Cyril of Alexandria (*PG* 71.601), after asking why Jonah had been sent to faraway Nineveh rather than to Tyre or to some other closer heathen city, explains that this was because Nineveh was a veritable Sodom. Hence, it is most striking that the rabbis have traditions – though, admittedly, we do not know how ancient – indicating the tremendous degree of sincerity of the Ninevites in their repentance.[22]

But the rabbis were also concerned to protect the reputation of Jonah, whose book, after all, is part of the canon of the prophets; and they therefore explain his refusal to go to Nineveh as due to his love of Israel, since he knew that the Ninevites would repent of their evil deeds and that their repentance, in turn, would lead G-d to compare the Israelites, who had not heeded the warnings

---

[22] We are told that the angel Gabriel installed Pharaoh as king of the great city of Nineveh, and that it was Pharaoh who, seized by fear and terror, covered himself with sackcloth and published the decree that men and beasts should fast. The inhabitants of Nineveh are said to have become "G-d-fearers," and some are reported to have gone so far as to destroy their palaces in order to return a single brick to the rightful owner. Some of their own accord appeared before courts of justice in order to confess their secret crimes, even though these crimes were subject to a death penalty. One tradition mentions a man who, in a building lot which he had acquired from his neighbor, found a treasure which now both buyer and seller refused to accept (*Midrash Jonah* 100-102, *Pirqe de-Rabbi Eliezer* 43, *Exodus Rabbah* 45.1). Furthermore, we are told that the sailors promised to make sacrifices to G-d upon their return to land (Targum on Jonah 1:16). Indeed, the *Midrash Jonah* states that they went up to Jerusalem, were circumcised, and after the completion of their conversion to Judaism brought sacrifices. See Ginzberg 1911, 3:29-30; and 1928, 6:10-11, n. 54).

of the prophets, unfavorably with them.[23] Similarly, Pseudo-Philo (*Homily on Jonah* 6) states that Jonah knew by prophetic clairvoyance that the city of Nineveh would be saved. Inasmuch as the Shekinah does not reveal itself outside of the Land of Israel, he hoped, by fleeing, that he would cease receiving communications from G-d to go to Nineveh (*Mekilta Bo* 1b-2a, Jerusalem *Sanhedrin* 11.30b) (cited by Ginzberg 1928, 6:349, n. 27). In this connection it is significant that in the Book of Jonah the name of Israel is not mentioned even once; and except for the fact that Jonah is a Hebrew (Jonah 1:9), the reader would see no connection between him and the Jews. In fact, in the Septuagint version even this ethnic self-identification is missing, and Jonah declares, "I am a servant of the L-rd." In Josephus, however, the Jewish associations of Jonah are clear both because he prophesies to King Jeroboam of Israel (*Ant.* 9.206) and because Josephus himself remarks that he thought it necessary to recount what he had found written in the Hebrew books concerning Jonah (*Ant.* 9.208). Moreover, that Josephus' narrative is focused on Jonah rather than on the Ninevites may be seen in the fact that Josephus adds the extra-biblical detail that after giving his prediction about Nineveh Jonah returned to his country (ὑπέστρεψε, "turned back") (*Ant.* 9.214). Here we see that the focus at the end of the pericope is on Jonah and on the land of Israel to which he returned, rather than on Nineveh.

Josephus was clearly confronted with a dilemma as to how to handle Jonah's behavior in hiding on the ship, since this would seem to indicate an attempt to shirk his duty and an indifference toward the Gentiles whom he was to warn. The Bible declares that Jonah had gone down into the inner part of the ship and had lain down and was fast asleep (Jonah 1:5). The Septuagint presents an even more degrading picture since it reads that Jonah was asleep and was snoring (ἔρεγχε). Josephus' Jonah has covered himself up (συγκαλύψας) and prostrated himself (ἐβέβλητο); there is no indication that he is asleep, let alone that he is snoring (*Ant.* 9.209) Moreover, most importantly, Josephus gives a good reason why Jonah absented himself, namely, that he did not wish to imitate any of the things (presumably an allusion to their pagan prayers) that he saw the sailors doing.

---

[23] See *Mekilta Bo* (Pisḥa) 2a. See also Jerome on Jonah 1:6.

Likewise, in passing over the exchange between Jonah and the captain of the ship (Jonah 1:6) Josephus shows his concern with upholding the status of Jonah, who should not appear to stand in need of lessons on his religious obligations, as the biblical story has it, by a pagan. Indeed, Jonah's standing is further accentuated subsequently by Josephus when he has him volunteer the advice that he be thrown overboard by the crew (*Ant.* 9.211) rather than give this counsel only in response to a question by the crew, as in Jonah 1:11-12.

Furthermore, in his version of Jonah's prayer from the belly of the fish, Josephus, instead of emphasizing Jonah's distress, has him appeal to G-d to grant him "pardon for his sins" (συγγνώμην...τῶν ἡμαρτημένων) (*Ant.* 9.214), whereas this element of self-confession is absent in the much more extended prayer in the Bible (Jonah 2:1-9). This stress on Jonah's contrite repentance would doubtless raise his stature in the eyes of readers.

Moreover, the biblical statement concerning Jonah's extreme anger with G-d because He had forgiven the Ninevites after they had repented (Jonah 4:1) might well have been interpreted as chauvinism on the part of Jonah and, through him, on the Jewish people whom he represents. The Septuagint on this verse, we may note, softens Jonah's anger by reading that Jonah was very deeply grieved (ἐλυπήθη...λύπην μεγάλην) and confounded (συνεχύθη) rather than that he was displeased and angry. Josephus avoids the problem by omitting the passage completely.

Remarkably, in contrast to the Bible (Jonah 1:2), there is no indication in Josephus that the people of Nineveh had sinned or that the city would be destroyed because of this, just as there is no indication that the prediction of Jonah remained unfulfilled. Moreover, in ignoring the repentance of the Ninevites Josephus was risking antagonizing those pagan readers who, like pseudo-Longinus (9.9), might have been acquainted with the Bible, in that his version seems to be conveying the message that there is no possibility of repentance by pagans. On the other hand, Josephus shared the concern of the rabbis that the Israelites not be viewed less favorably than the Gentiles. Moreover, as a historian rather than as a theologian, he knew that the city of Nineveh did eventually fall; and so there is no discrepancy between what he reports of Jonah's message and the historical facts.[24]

---

[24] In the apocryphal Book of Tobit (14:4) there is a reference to the proph-

7. Proselytes and "G-d-Fearers" in the Book of Jonah

Perhaps the most sensitive implication suggested by the Book of Jonah is that the sailors became proselytes or "sympathizers" with Judaism, since we read that they feared the L-rd with great fear and offered sacrifices to the L-rd and made vows" (Jonah 1:16). The Bible likewise expands on the Ninevites' piety by remarking that the people of Nineveh believed in G-d and, in their sincere repentance, proclaimed a fast and, from the greatest to the least, put on sackcloth (Jonah 3:5). Both of these statements are, significantly, missing in Josephus. In contrast, a late Midrash indicates that, like the sons of Sennacherib, the Ninevites went to Jerusalem, were circumcised, and brought sacrifices, thus completing their conversion (*Tanḥuma Vayiqra* 8 end; *Pirqe de-Rabbi Eliezer* 10.72-73; *Midrash Jonah* 97).

Josephus had to be extremely careful not to offend his Roman hosts by referring to the inroads that the Jews had made through proselytism into the Roman populace. It is surely significant that in the *Antiquities*, aside from the passage about the conversion of the royal family of Adiabene (*Ant.* 20.17-96) (which was, after all, under Parthian domination, and hence of no immediate concern to the Romans), Josephus nowhere propagandizes for proselytism.

The picture of the non-Jewish sailors in the biblical book is that of pious men who turn from the worship of their own pagan gods to the worship of the Hebrew G-d (Jonah 1:5). When the lot falls upon Jonah as the guilty one and when he asks to be thrown overboard, the sailors shudder to do so, since they shrink from shedding innocent blood and, indeed, invoke the name of the L-rd twice within a single sentence (Jonah 1:14). In fact, we are told that they feared the L-rd exceedingly and that they offered sacrifices to the L-rd and made vows (Jonah 1:16). One is reminded of the Mishnaic statement of the second-century Rabbi Judah in the name of his older contemporary Abba Gurion of Zadian, that most sailors are saintly (*Qiddushin* 4:14). The picture is very different in Josephus, where there is no indication whether the sailors were Jews or that they prayed to their own individual gods; instead we

---

ecy of Jonah according to which Assyria and Nineveh would be destroyed. This is the reading of the major manuscripts; but Zimmermann (1958, 40-41) prefers to read Nahum in place of Jonah, though it would seem more likely that both Tobit and Josephus reflect a common tradition.

are told very simply that the sailors began to pray, without being told to whom they were praying (*Ant.* 9.209). While it is true that Josephus' sailors regard it as an impious act to cast Jonah into the sea (*Ant.* 9.212), their morality is based not upon the prohibition of shedding innocent blood but rather upon the ancient Greek sanction concerning hospitality for strangers who have entrusted their lives to their hosts, a feature that a reader acquainted with Homer's *Odyssey*, with its emphasis on proper (the Phaeacians) and improper (Polyphemus the Cyclops) hospitality would have especially appreciated.[25]

The rabbinic tradition stresses the non-Jewish origin of the sailors by noting that representatives of the seventy nations of the world were on board the vessel, each with his individual idols, and that they all resolved to entreat their gods for help, with the understanding that the god from whom help would come would be recognized and worshipped as the only one true G-d (*Pirqe de-Rabbi Eliezer* 10, *Tanhuma Vayiqra* 8, *Midrash Jonah* 97) (see Ginzberg 1913, 4:247-48).[26] When help came from none of the pagan gods, the captain shows his admiration for Judaism by stating that he had heard that the G-d of the Hebrews was most powerful and that if they would cry to Him perhaps He would perform miracles. Indeed, Pseudo-Philo (*Homily on Jonah*), on the basis of the biblical statement that Nineveh was saved, conjectures that proselytism had already reached a high point where Jonah delivered his homily.

The biblical statement that the sailors feared the L-rd with great fear is surely reminiscent of the "G-d-fearers," well known from the eleven passages in Acts (10:2, 22, 35; 13:16, 26, 43, 50; 16:14, 17:4, 17; 18.7) referring to φοβούμενοι τὸν θεόν ("fearers of G-d") and σεβόμενοι τὸν θεόν ("reverencers of G-d") and from the passage in Juvenal (14.96) referring to one who fears (*metuentem*) the Sabbath and who has a son who eventually becomes a full-fledged Jew. It is true that these terms, in and of themselves, do not necessarily refer to "sympathizers" and may, indeed, designate pious Jews, as I

---

[25] Of course, the behavior of the sailors is not necessarily an indication of a Greek concept of hospitality, since such an attitude was prevalent in the Near East generally, as we see, for example, in the Bible's portrait of Abraham; but Josephus' Greek readers would most probably think of the Homeric reference.

[26] Cf. *Ant.* 1.161, where, in Josephus' addition to the biblical text, Abraham shows a similar openmindedness in declaring, upon his descent to Egypt, that if he found the doctrines of the Egyptians superior to his own he would adopt them, but that if his own doctrines appeared superior to theirs he would convert them.

have noted (see Feldman 1950, 200-8). But the new inscriptions from Aphrodisias make it more likely that these are, indeed, terms referring to "sympathizers," at least in the third century, the apparent date of the inscriptions (see Feldman 1986c, 58-69; and 1989b, 265-305).

By the third century there can be no doubt that there was such a class, as is clear from a passage in the Jerusalem Talmud which quotes Rabbi Eleazar, a third-century Palestinian rabbi, as saying that only the Gentiles who had nothing to do with the Jews during their bitter past will not be permitted to convert to Judaism in the time of the Messiah, whereas those "Heaven-fearers" (*yirei shamayim*) who had shared the tribulations of Israel would be accepted as full proselytes, with the Emperor Antoninus[27] at their head (Jerusalem *Megillah* 3.2.74a) (see Lieberman 1942, 78-80).

Finally, Josephus, we may suggest, is careful not to compliment the Ninevites, since they were, geographically at any rate, as we have noted, the ancestors of the Parthians, the great national enemy of the Romans.[28] Indeed, in Josephus Jonah is depicted as covering himself up on board the ship and not imitating any of the things, presumably referring to the sailors' idol-worship, which he saw the others on the ship doing (*Ant.* 9.209). Moreover, in the biblical narrative there is no intimation, in the rebuke of the captain of the ship to Jonah, that he might be the *cause* of the storm; rather, he berates him merely for not praying to his G-d (Jonah 1:9). In Josephus, on the other hand, there is no such scene involving the captain and Jonah; rather, we read that the sailors began to suspect, "as is natural," that one of their passengers was the cause of the storm (*Ant.* 9.210).

---

[27] Attempts to identify "Antoninus" with any of the Antonine or Severan emperors at the end of the second and at the beginning of the third century have proven unsuccessful. See Gutmann 1971, 3:165-66.

[28] On Josephus' anti-Parthian bias see Colpe (1974, 97-108). Begg (1995a, 18-19) similarly suggests that Josephus' decision to include a summary of Nahum's prophecy concerning Assyria was inspired by his desire to please his Roman patrons, who would have been pleased that a Jewish prophet had predicted the overthrow of the ancestor of their national rival, Parthia. On the other hand, Jewish readers, equating Assyria with Rome, would have been pleased with a prediction of the overthrow of the Roman Empire.

8. Hellenizations in Josephus' Account

That Josephus in his Jonah pericope is making an appeal to his Hellenized audience may be seen from the fact that he refers to Nineveh not by its usual name, as found in the Hebrew (*Nineveh*) or in the Septuagint (Νινευή) and elsewhere in Josephus himself (e.g., in the prophecy of Nahum, *Ant.* 9.239-42)[29] but rather as the kingdom of Ninos (*Ant.* 9.209).[30] By referring to the kingdom thus Josephus is reminding the reader of the husband of the legendary great Assyrian queen Semiramis, the daughter of the fish-goddess Atargatis[31] of Ascalon in Palestine, who created for her husband a tomb nine stadia high and ten in width at Nineveh and who succeeded him in the rule. By referring to Nineveh as Ninus Josephus is, furthermore, reminding the reader that Ninus, after completing great conquests, decided to found a city so great that it would not only be the largest city of all cities of the inhabited world but so large that no later king would ever establish a larger one (Ctesias, *ap.* Diodorus 2.3). To be sure, Josephus avoids expatiating on the size of the city, as does the Hebrew version (Jonah 4:11); but that may be because he seeks to avoid the charge of exaggeration.

The fact that it is to Joppa (modern Jaffa) that Jonah goes to find a ship (Jonah 1:3) supplies a further connection with Greek mythology, since it is there that Andromeda was chained to a rock (Strabo 16.2.28.758), as Josephus mentions elsewhere (*War* 3.420), whence she was rescued by the great hero Perseus, who, like Jonah, is connected with a fish, which, however, he, unlike Jonah, fought against and wounded.

---

[29] To be sure, in *Ant.* 9.239 Josephus refers to the city by both names, Ninos and Nineveh; but elsewhere, in his version of the prophecy of Nahum, the name is spelled "Ninos." The rule seems to be that when he refers to Nineveh by itself he calls it Nineveh.

[30] While it is true that Josephus does sometimes vary the spelling of proper names, the variation is seldom of the order that we find here; and, in any case, it would seem to be more than a coincidence that the variant involves a name that has such special significance as that of Ninos.

[31] We may conjecture that the fact that Ninus was the son-in-law of the fish-goddess Atargatis may have occasioned Josephus' use of this name in place of Nineveh in the story of Jonah, whose most famous incident connects him with a fish. The very name Nineveh, according to a popular etymology, means "place of the fish," and the cuneiform pictogram for the city shows Nina, representing an enclosure with a fish inside (see Speiser 1962, 552). In Hellenistic times a parallel was drawn with the Greek god Ninus, who was a fish-god.

As we have noted above, another touch which would surely have appealed to Josephus' Greek audience was his treatment of the scene in which the sailors cast Jonah into the sea. In the Hebrew the sailors try desperately to avoid throwing him into the sea because they do not want to have innocent blood on their hands through the impious act of murder (Jonah 1:13-14). In Josephus the crime which they seek to avoid is not the religious one of murder but rather the crime of inhospitality (*Ant.* 9.212), so much a concern to the Greeks, as we see particularly in Homer's *Odyssey*, since, in an extra-biblical addition, Jonah is called a stranger (ξένον) who had entrusted his life to them. This Hellenizing touch is particularly effective because Josephus, in describing the storm which brought the sailors to such desperate straits, uses a phrase (ὑπερβιαζομένου τοῦ κακοῦ) taken directly from Thucydides' description of the plague (2.52.3) which beset Athens near the beginning of the Peloponnesian War and which caused the Athenians to give up the semblance of morality and respect for law (2.52-53) – the very opposite of the attitude of the sailors under duress here.

Finally, we may note the fact that Jonah identifies himself as a prophet of "the most high G-d" (τοῦ μεγίστου θεοῦ) (*Ant.* 9.211), rather than, as in the Bible, as one who fears "the L-rd, the G-d of heaven, who made the sea and the dry land" (Jonah 1:9). Thereby Josephus appeals to his pagan audience, since such a G-d would be acknowledged by pagans as well as by Jews, as we see, for example, in the fact that when Cyrus, the king of Persia, sends his decree throughout his realm (Ezra 1:1-4) he declares, in Josephus' version that it is the most high G-d (ὁ θεὸς ὁ μέγιστος) who has appointed him king of the habitable world and that He is the god whom the Israelites also worship (*Ant.* 11.3).[32] It is this identification of the G-d of the Jews with the supreme G-d of the pagans that we find occurring in another apologetic setting, namely in the *Letter of Aristeas* (16), where the chief of the translators, at the symposium sponsored by King Ptolemy Philadelphus in their honor, explains to the king that the Jewish G-d is simply another name for Zeus, thereby seeking to diminish the theological differences between the Greeks and the Jews.

---

[32] In the Hebrew and Septuagint versions G-d is called " the L-rd, the G-d of heaven" (Ezra 1:2).

Another way in which Josephus appeals to his Greek audience is through introducing dramatic motifs and language. We may see this in his dramatization of the storm which beset the ship in which Jonah found himself. In the Bible we are told that the mariners were afraid (Jonah 1:5), whereas Josephus is more dramatic in declaring that as the vessel was in danger of sinking, not only the sailors, as in the Hebrew text, but also the pilots and even the shipmaster began to pray (*Ant.* 9.209). Josephus' detailed recapitulation of this episode is all the more remarkable, inasmuch as he so drastically compresses the whole rest of the story. All the more does the question of the reason for Josephus' procedure arise here, since the storm episode does not appear to have any crucial bearing on Josephus' underlying concern with introducing the figure of Jonah in the first place, that is, to present him as one in a long line of true prophets whose predictions do come about just as announced.

Moreover, in order not to subject himself to ridicule by his Greek audience, Josephus shuns the grotesque, as we see, for example, in his avoidance of such exaggerations in connection with Samson's strength. In the case of Jonah, the Bible states that Nineveh was an exceedingly great city, three days' journey in width (Jonah 3:3), while the rabbinic tradition goes even further in asserting that the city covered forty square parasangs and contained a million and a half human beings (*Midrash Jonah* 99-100) (cited by Ginzberg 1928, 6:350, n. 34), whereas the Bible gives the population as one hundred and twenty thousand (Jonah 4:11). Josephus simply omits such data altogether.

Similarly, the Bible declares that the king of Nineveh decreed a public fast and ordered that beasts as well as men be clad in the sackcloth of mourning (Jonah 3:6-8).[33] A scene describing beasts clad in sackcloth would surely have seemed grotesque to Josephus' Greek audience, and so he simply omits the king's orders altogether.

---

[33] Cf. Gaster 1969, 655-56. A possible parallel to beasts mourning may be found in Herodotus (9.24), where the Persians, in their mourning for Masistius, who, after Mardonius, was held in the greatest esteem by the Persians, cut the manes from their war-horses and their beasts of burden; but this is hardly as grotesque as putting sackcloth of mourning upon their beasts, as we find in the case of Nineveh.

9. Summary

Josephus has transformed what Bickerman (1967, 28) has called a morality play, which, in the Bible, focuses upon the sinful people of Nineveh, their genuine repentance, and their forgiveness by G-d, into an historical episode centering upon the figure of Jonah, who, as a prophet, is closely akin to the historian, and upon his political mission. All the reasons why the book was chosen for the *haftarah* of the afternoon service of the most sacred day of the Jewish calendar, the Day of Atonement, namely to emphasize that G-d is the G-d of all mankind, that it is impossible to flee from His presence, and that He pities His creatures and forgives those who turn to Him in truth (see Levine 1975, 9) – all these are conspicuously absent from Josephus' version. The biblical version is more an unfulfilled prophecy than a book about a prophet, whereas Josephus' is about a prophet and, via Nahum, a fulfilled prophecy. In an effort to appeal to his non-Jewish audience, Josephus emphasizes Jonah's qualities of character and mutes the role of G-d. He avoids taking responsibility for the central miracle of the book, the episode of Jonah in the big fish. Above all, in order not to offend his Roman hosts, who were very sensitive about proselytizing by Jews, he avoids reproducing the biblical indications that the inhabitants of Nineveh had repented and had turned to Judaism, in whole or, at any rate, in part.[34]

---

[34] I should like to express my sincere gratitude to Professor Christopher T. Begg for many helpful comments in connection with this essay.

CHAPTER TWENTY-SEVEN

MANASSEH

1. *Introduction*

The Talmudic tradition, with which, there is reason to believe, Josephus was well acquainted, singles out (Mishnah, *Sanhedrin* 10:2), as we have noted, three kings – Jeroboam, Ahab, and Manasseh – as so wicked that even though (Mishnah, *Sanhedrin* 10:1) all Israelites have a share in the world to come, these kings have forfeited their share. And yet, Josephus, in his paraphrase of the Bible in the *Antiquities*, deals with the three of them very differently. Jeroboam is castigated without mercy as a forerunner of the revolutionaries of Josephus' own day. On the other hand, his portrayal of Manasseh, as of Ahab, is balanced between criticism and praise.

One indication of the amount of interest that a given personality has for Josephus may be seen in the sheer amount of space that he devotes to him.

Both Jeroboam and Ahab were clearly of great interest to Josephus, as we can see from the fact that for Jeroboam (Josephus, *Ant.* 8.205-45, 265-87 [463 lines] vs. 1 Kings 11:26-40, 12:1-14:20, 2 Chronicles 13:1-20 [214 lines]) the ratio is 2.16 (1.29 as compared with the Septuagint text [360 lines]), and for Ahab it is 1.98. On the other hand, for Manasseh (Josephus, *Ant.* 10.37-46 [63 lines] vs. 2 Kings 20:21-21:18 [32 lines]and 2 Chronicles 32:33-33:20 [37 lines]) the ratio is only .91 (or, discounting the duplicate material in 2 Chronicles [32:33-33:9], 1.26).[1]

2. *The Portrait of Manasseh in Rabbinic Literature*

The rabbis give a mixed picture of Manasseh. On the one hand, they have a tradition, presented anonymously, that Manasseh ex-

---

[1] The ratio of Josephus to the Septuagint version of the passages in Kings and Chronicles (106 lines) is .59; it is .81 if the biblical version is restricted to the passage in 2 Kings, as supplemented by the material in 2 Chronicles not found in Kings.

amined the biblical narratives in order to prove them worthless and that he is consequently the arch-example of the one who acts impudently against the Torah (*Sanhedrin* 99b). In fact, the rabbis derive his very name from *nasha*, "he forgot," and interpret this to allude to the fact that he forgot his G-d and his pious father (*Sanhedrin* 102b) (so also *Ascension of Isaiah* 2:1). Indeed, he is said to have removed the divine name from the Torah. Moreover, he is the arch-idolater, as we see from the rabbinic tradition that he destroyed the altar in the Temple in Jerusalem and set up an idol with four faces, copied from the four figures on the divine throne as depicted by the prophet Ezekiel, so that regardless of the direction from which someone entered the Temple he saw the face of an idol (*Sanhedrin* 103b). Furthermore, he is said to have made an image as heavy as a thousand men, all of whom it killed every day, presumably through its enormous weight.[2] Even in his youth, when he was brought to the synagogue (or to the house of learning), he is said (*Berakot* 10a, according to the Munich Manuscript) to have poked fun at his pious father, King Hezekiah. So wicked was he that he sat in judgment on his own grandfather, the prophet Isaiah, and condemned him to death (*Yevamot* 49b). After declining to defend himself against the charge that he had contradicted the teachings of Moses, preferring that Manasseh act out of ignorance rather than out of deliberate wickedness, Isaiah fled for his life. When Isaiah pronounced the Ineffable Name of G-d a cedar tree swallowed him up (Jerusalem, *Sanhedrin* 10.1.28c), whereupon Manasseh ordered that the tree be sawed in two and thus brought about Isaiah's death (*Sanhedrin* 103b, Tosefta-Targum on 2 Kings 21:16 and Isaiah 66:1, *Pesiqta de-Rav Kahana* 4.14). Finally, he is reported, in an anonymous rabbinic comment to have violated his own sister (*Sanhedrin* 103b).[3] A similar negative picture is found in the Pseudepigrapha, according to which Satan strengthened him in causing Israel to apostasize and in fostering the lawlessness which was spread abroad in Jerusalem (*Ascension of Isaiah* 2:4-5). According to this account, he promoted the practices of witchcraft, magic, and divination, fornication and adultery, and the persecution of the righteous.

And yet, the rabbis also see redeeming features in Manasseh.

---

[2] Or, alternatively, Manasseh put them to death every day at the end of the day's work.

[3] So also, according to the *Apocalypse of Baruch* 64:2-3, he violated wedded women.

Thus, according to an anonymous comment, the same Manasseh who ridiculed the Torah was a great scholar who, in his brilliance, interpreted the book of Leviticus, with its complex laws pertaining to the priesthood, in fifty-five different ways, corresponding to the number of years of his reign (*Sanhedrin* 103b). As the rabbis remark, the greater the scholar the stronger his evil inclination (*Sukkah* 52a). The tradition of Manasseh's learning is well exemplified in the anecdote, where we hear that he appeared to Rav Ashi (335-427 C.E.) in a dream and taught him the answers to such learned and technical questions as to the part of the bread from which the blessing at the start of the meal is to be taken (*Sanhedrin* 102b). In fact, in the colloquy that ensues, Manasseh attempts to explain his worship of idols with the assertion that he was influenced by the pervasive evil environment of that time. "If you were there," he remarks, "you would have ...sped after me."

Indeed, much is said in rabbinic literatue of Manasseh's repentance. Thus, a nameless tanna asserts that Manasseh was penitent for thirty-three years (*Sanhedrin* 103a). In response to the tradition that he is one of the three kings who have no share in the world to come (Mishnah, *Sanhedrin* 10:2), the second-century Rabbi Judah bar Ilai, who was known for his outstanding piety, objects that Manasseh does indeed have a share since he repented, according to Scripture (2 Chronicles 33:13) (Mishnah, *Sanhedrin* 11:2). Likewise, the third-century Rabbi Johanan states that he who asserts that Manasseh has no portion in the world to come weakens the power of repentance (*Sanhedrin* 103a). Finally, there is a tradition that when the angels pleaded with G-d not to accept Manasseh's repentance, G-d Himself insisted that if He did not do so He would be closing the door of repentance for all repentant sinners, whereupon a wind arose and carried Manasseh back to Jerusalem from his Babylonian captivity (Jerusalem *Sanhedrin* 10.2.28c).

3. *The Impiety of Manasseh*

For Josephus, who is so proud of his priestly ancestry, as we see from the very opening of his autobiography (*Life* 1-6), piety was connected particularly with the Temple in Jerusalem. Hence, one would expect him to be particularly incensed by Manasseh's gross impiety in polluting the Temple (2 Kings 21:4=2 Chronicles 33:4), about which Josephus remarks that he even dared to pollute not only the Temple but also the city of Jerusalem and the entire country (*Ant.* 10.37).

However, Josephus' sensitivity to the charge that the Jews are illiberal toward other religions may also be seen in his treatment of Manasseh. Thus we find, in both of the biblical accounts of Manasseh's reign (2 Kings 21:5-7, 2 Chronicles 33:5-7), a description of the altars and of the graven images that he built for alien gods in the very Temple of G-d in Jerusalem. We are told further of his practices, in imitation of the idol-worshippers, of burning his son(s) as an offering, and of soothsaying, augury, and dealing with mediums and wizards. We are specifically informed that he rebuilt the high places for foreign worship which his father, the good king Hezekiah, had destroyed and of his erection of altars for the pagan Baal(s), of his making an Asherah as a cult object in imitation of the pagans, and of his worshipping all the host of heaven (2 Kings 21:3, 2 Chronicles 33:3). In the words of the Bible, found in both 2 Kings 21:2 and in 2 Chronicles 33:2, in identical language, "he did what was evil in the sight of the L-rd, according to the abominable practices of the nations whom the L-rd drove out before the people of Israel." What is most remarkable is that despite Josephus' tendency to embellish the biblical narrative, all of this material is omitted. Again, whereas the Bible compares Manasseh's abominations with those of the Amorites (2 Kings 22:11), Josephus says nothing about the Amorites but rather portrays his misdeeds as an internal matter, i.e., his seduction of the Jews (*Ant.* 10.38). Rather than attack non-Jewish religions Josephus thus shifts the blame to the Jews themselves, who, he says, "did more evil than the nations whom the L-rd destroyed before the people of Israel." Indeed, Josephus very deliberately shifts from an attack on the beliefs and practices of his pagan readers to a mere general statement that Manasseh exhibited every form of wickedness (πονηρίας) in his conduct and left no impious act (ἀσεβές) undone (*Ant.* 10.37); but Josephus is careful not to define this wickedness and impiety further. We are told not that he imitated the pagans – a charge which pagan readers might well have resented – but rather that he imitated the lawless deeds (παρανομίας, "transgressions of law") of the Israelites wherein they sinned against G-d and so perished.

4. *Manasseh's Attack on the Prophets*

In emphasizing Manasseh's failure to observe Jewish law and tradition, Josephus significantly changes the vague biblical statement that Manasseh shed very much innocent blood (2 Kings 21:16) into a statement that he killed all the righteous men among the Hebrews and, in particular, that he did not spare even the prophets, some of whom he slaughtered daily, so that Jerusalem ran with blood (*Ant.* 10.38).[4]

Whereas the Bible declares that Manasseh did not listen to the words of G-d (2 Kings 21:9, 2 Chronicles 33:10), Josephus highlights the role of the prophets, noting that it was to them that Manasseh and the people did not listen (*Ant.* 10.39); if they had listened, he says, they might have so profited as not to experience any misfortune. Here again one sees the equation of the prophet and the historian and is reminded of the famous statement by Thucydides (1.22.4), one of Josephus' favorite authors, that "whoever wishes to have a clear view of the events which have happened and of those which will some day, in all human probability, happen again in the same or a similar way" will find his history useful.

5. *Manasseh's Repentance*

The basic difference between the accounts of Manasseh in the Book of Kings and in the Book of Chronicles is that the former says nothing about Manasseh's repentance. Not only, however, does Josephus follow Chronicles in citing Manasseh's repentance but actually highlights it (*Ant.* 10.41). Thus, the biblical statement

---

[4] As we have noted, there is a rabbinic tradition (*Yevamot* 49b) that Manasseh was responsible for the death of Isaiah in particular. Cf. also the pseudepigraphical *Martyrdom of Isaiah* and the New Testament (Hebrews 11:37). Schubert (1952, 1-62) suggests that Josephus derived from the Essenes his notice that Manasseh put Isaiah to death. But Zeitlin (1958-59, 1-34) correctly points out that Josephus does not here mention Isaiah by name. Moreover, in view of the many other places where Josephus parallels rabbinic and pseudepigraphic tradition, it is more likely that Josephus derived this tradition rather from the rabbis. Cf. also Schoeps (1943, 7-8; and 1950, 130), who asserts that this Josephan paraphrase of the Bible, with its large element of fantasy, shows the role that the theme of the murder of the prophets played in the folk consciousness. We may suggest, however, that Josephus mentions the point not because it is so prominent in the folk consciousness as because it fits his goal of emphasizing the dreadfulness of Jewish sins against fellow-Jews rather than attacking non-Jewish beliefs and practices.

reads that when Manasseh was in distress, he entreated the favor of G-d and humbled himself greatly before G-d (2 Chronicles 33:12). Josephus goes further in stating that Manasseh realized in what a bad plight he was (*Ant.* 10.41). Moreover, he explicitly performs what the rabbis regard as the first step in repentance, namely confession of his sins (*Yoma* 86b). In place of the Bible's generalized statement that he humbled himself greatly, Josephus' Manasseh is said to believe himself the cause of all that came upon him. Instead of the general entreaty for the favor of G-d that we find in the biblical narrative we are told specifically that he prayed to G-d to make the enemy humane (φιλάνθρωπον) and merciful to him. Moreover, in an extra-biblical addition, Manasseh goes so far in his display of repentance as to strive (ἐσπούδαζεν) to cast from his mind the very memory of his former sins (*Ant.* 10.42). The use of the imperfect tense of the verb for "striving" here indicates a continuous effort on his part. Moreover, this verb has implications of eagerness and zeal. Manasseh then goes on to state that he was anxious (ὥρμησε, "hurried," "rushed headlong") to repent and to show G-d the utmost reverence. In addition, whereas the Bible asserts that Manasseh commanded Judah to serve the L-rd (2 Chronicles 33:16), Josephus' Manasseh is not content merely to command the people, but he teaches them to reverence G-d, based upon his personal experience, "having learned how close he had been to disaster because of following the opposite way of life" (*Ant.* 10.43). Again, there is significance in Josephus' use of the imperfect tense for "taught" (ἐδίδασκε), which indicates repeated and continuous effort to teach the people. The Bible states that the people, however, still sacrificed at the high places and did not restrict themselves to the Temple in Jerusalem (2 Chronicles 33:17); this notice, however, implies that the effectiveness of Manasseh's new policy was limited, and so Josephus simply omits it (*Ant.* 10.45). Moreover, in a passage which has no counterpart in the Bible (2 Chronicles 33:13), Josephus remarks that Manasseh underwent such a change of heart and lived the rest of his life in such a way as to be accounted a blessed (μακαριστός) and enviable (ζηλωτός) man (*Ant.* 10.45). With this use of the word ζηλωτός, so reminiscent as it is of the term ζηλωτής, with its ironic connection with the Zealots, of infamous repute from Josephus' point of view during the revolution against the Romans, Manasseh comes full circle in his enthusiastic repentance. Again, when recording the act of Manasseh's repentance, the Bible specifies that he took away the foreign gods and the idols from the Temple, as well as the altars which he had built for pagan worship (2 Chronicles 33:15). Josephus says nothing at all about this uprooting of pagan cults; instead the accent is totally on the positive, i.e., Manasseh's sanctification of the Temple and the purification of the city of Jerusalem and the consequent restoration of the Jewish worship (*Ant.* 10.42). Likewise, at the end of the biblical account we are referred to the Chronicle of the Seers for a further account of the pagan Asherim which Manasseh set up (2 Chronicles 33:19); but Josephus, presumably aware of the rabbinic maxim (Mishnah, *Baba Mezia* 4:10) that it is forbidden to say to a penitent, "Remember your former deed," and seeking not to detract from Manasseh's repentance, omits all mention of this (*Ant.* 10.45).

Josephus did not wish to denigrate the power of authority, as vested in the kingship, except in the case of a ruler such as Jeroboam, who was guilty of the grievous sin of promoting civil discord. Hence, like the Book of Chronicles and like part of the rabbinic tradition, he sought to rehabilitate the king Manasseh. One indication of this effort may be seen in his version of the biblical narrative of the capture of Manasseh by the commanders of the army of the king of Assyria (2 Chronicles 33:11). The Bible says that he was taken with hooks and bound with fetters without indicating how he was captured; and the reader may well wonder about his ignominious behavior in allowing himself thus to be taken. Josephus, however, upholds Manasseh's reputation by stating that he was captured by cunning (δόλῳ, "deceit," "treachery," "guile") (*Ant.* 10.40), and so, by implication, Manasseh should not be blamed for what happened to him.

Finally, aware that it is not enough for the penitent merely to state his remorse, Josephus' Manasseh continues with an account, not found in his biblical source (2 Chronicles 33:14), of Manasseh's deeds in improving Jerusalem, namely his providing for the security of the city by repairing the old walls with great care (σπουδῆς, "speed," "haste," "zeal," "eagerness," "assiduity," "energy," "industry," "diligence") and by adding a new one, by erecting very high towers, and by strengthening the fortresses before the city in various ways, particularly through bringing in provisions and diverse necessities (*Ant.* 10.44). As a native of Jerusalem, Josephus was especially appreciative of such improvements.

It is the quality of humanity (φιλανθρωπία, Latin *humanitas*), with which, as we have noted, Manasseh prays the enemy will be imbued (*Ant.* 10.41).

Again, whereas the Bible, in connection with Manasseh's repentance, states simply that he knew that the L-rd was G-d (2 Chronicles 33:13) and commanded Judah to serve G-d (2 Chronicles 33:16), Josephus goes much further in affirming that Manasseh's sole concern was to show his gratitude to G-d for having been saved (*Ant.* 10.42). The fact that showing gratitude to G-d was Manasseh's sole concern when he repented places him, in this respect, in a line with such revered personalities as Moses, Joshua, and David.

6. *Summary*

The rabbinic tradition, with which Josephus seems to be well acquainted, offers an ambivalent picture of Manasseh. On the one hand, he is the arch-opponent of the Torah, the arch-idolater, and he is responsible for the cruel death of the prophet Isaiah. And yet, he is also a most learned scholar and is depicted as the archetype of the repentant sinner. Josephus is likewise ambivalent, but because he is writing for a predominantly non-Jewish audience he avoids mentioning Manasseh's promotion of pagan idolatry and instead focuses upon the sins of the Jews themselves. It is the lawless deeds not of the pagans but of the Israelites which Manasseh imitates. Josephus' addition that Manasseh did not spare the prophets should be seen against the backdrop of his view of the close connection between history and prophecy, both of which crafts he himself practiced. It is in highlighting Manasseh's repentance that Josephus departs most radically from the portrait in Kings and goes considerably beyond that in Chronicles. In his sincere concern to show gratitude to G-d for saving him Manasseh is coupled with such great biblical heroes as Moses, Joshua, and David.

CHAPTER TWENTY-EIGHT

JOSIAH

1. *Introduction*

From a quantitative point of view, Josiah is of considerable interest to Josephus,[1] though less than we might have expected in view of the tremendous reverence in which he is held both in the Bible and in the rabbinic tradition. In Josephus (*Ant.* 10.48-78) the account covers 181 lines in the Loeb Classical Library edition. There are two biblical accounts: 2 Kings 22:1-23:30 covers 106 lines (157 lines in the Septuagint), whereas 2 Chronicles 34:1-35:27 contains 113 lines (184 lines in the Septuagint). This gives a ratio of 1.71 of Josephus to the account in 2 Kings (1.15 to the Septuagint) and 1.60 of Josephus to the version in 2 Chronicles (.98 to the Septuagint).

2. *The Rabbinic Account of Josiah*

The rabbis are much impressed with Josiah's greatness and note that he was the only king after Solomon who ruled over both Judah and Israel (*Megillah* 14b). In particular, they cannot say enough about Josiah's piety. We are told that when Josiah saw the Scriptural passage predicting the destruction of the Temple (Deuteronomy 28:36) he hid the ark and all its vessels in order to guard them from destruction at the hands of the enemy (*Yoma* 52b). His piety is particularly great when compared with the wickedness of his father Amon, who, according to the tradition transmitted by the third-century Rabbi Johanan ben Nappaḥa, burnt the Torah and, according to the latter's contemporary Rabbi Eleazar ben Pedat, actually had relations with his own mother simply in order

---

[1] A perusal of the various bibliographies of Josephus – Schreckenberg (1968 and 1979); Feldman (1984; 1986a; 1989c, 330-448); and Bilde (1988) – indicates that there has been no study of Josephus' portrait of Josiah even approaching comprehensiveness. Rappaport (1930) has nothing on Josephus' treatment of Josiah. There has been only one essay dealing with even a portion of the subject, namely Begg (1988a, 157-63).

to provoke G-d (*Sanhedrin* 103b). And yet, so great was the virtue of Josiah that his father was not included in the category of those who have no portion in the world to come because of it (*Sanhedrin* 104a). The rabbis even go so far as to credit Josiah with the destruction of all the idols in the Land of Israel despite the fact that he had been preceded in this enterprise by Kings Asa and Jehoshaphat. Finally, even when Josiah is dying and the prophet Jeremiah fears that perhaps he might say something improper because of the pain which he is experiencing we hear that he died humbly confessing that "the L-rd is righteous, for I have rebelled against His word" (*Ta'anit* 22b). Indeed, so great was the mourning for Josiah that when the rabbis speak of the most extensive mourning, it is the laments for him and for Ahab that they invoke (*Mo'ed Qatan* 28b).

Josiah is held in such high regard in the rabbinic tradition that there is even a debate as to whether he even sinned at all (*Shabbat* 56b). Rabbi Samuel bar Naḥmani, who lived in the Land of Israel during the late third and early fourth centuries, goes so far as to say that Josiah never sinned. This would presumably put him in the same category as the four (Benjamin, the son of Jacob; Amram, the father of Moses; Jesse, the father of David; and Kilab, the son of David) (*Shabbat* 55b) who, according to tradition, never sinned and who died only because it had been ordained that mortals must die. As to the statement that he returned (*shav*) to the L-rd with all his heart (2 Kings 23:25), while this certainly implies that he first sinned and then returned to the right path, Samuel interprets this to mean that when Josiah discovered the hidden Torah scroll, he revised every judgment which he had previously issued, since he had handed down those judgments between the ages of eight and eighteen, without the benefit of guidance from the Torah. Even Rav, the third-century Babylonian, uses the assertion that Josiah did sin in order to praise him all the more for his repentance, stating that there was no greater penitent than Josiah in his generation. Indeed, the rabbis cannot imagine that Josiah died because of his own sins, and so they ascribe his death to his godless generation and to their deception in worshipping idols without his knowledge (*Ta'anit* 22b, *Lamentations Rabbah* 1.53).

3. *Josiah as the Embodiment of the Cardinal Virtues*

In his very first words about Josiah (*Ant.* 10.49), Josephus considerably expands the biblical portrait (2 Kings 22:2). In the Bible we are told in very bland terms that he did what was right in the eyes of the L-rd, that he walked in all the ways of King David, and that he turned away neither to the right nor to the left. Josephus is much more explicit and even more laudatory. Josiah, he says, using the two words which are key terms in describing the height of excellence of character, was of an excellent (ἄριστος) character and well-disposed to virtue (ἀρετήν). Whereas the biblical text describes him as walking in the ways of David, Josephus goes further in declaring that he was an emulator (ζηλωτής, "zealous admirer," "zealous follower")[2] of the practices of David, whom he made the pattern (σκοπῷ, "aim," "target," "objective") and rule (κανόνι) of his whole manner of life (*Ant.* 10.49).

Josephus develops considerably the theme of the precociousness of Josiah. In the Bible (2 Chronicles 34:3) we read that in his twelfth year (the Septuagint adds "of his reign", which would make him twenty years old) he began to purge Judaea and Jerusalem from the high places and the groves and the carved molten images. Though Josephus generally follows the Greek he here adopts the reading of the Hebrew text, which, of course, does stress Josiah's procociousness, just as in the New Testament Jesus' precociousness is emphasized by the fact that when he similarly was only twelve years old he was already amazing scholars with his questions and answers (Luke 2:42-51). Thus, we are told that when Josiah was only twelve years old he gave proof (ἐπεδείξατο, "exhibited," "showed off," "displayed for oneself," "demonstrated," "substantiated") of his piety (εὐσέβειαν) and righteousness (δικαιοσύνην) (*Ant.* 10.50).

In an important extra-biblical remark, Josephus declares that Josiah carefully differentiated between what was sound and what was unsound in the ideas and practices of his predecessors, and wisely (συνετῶς, "intelligently," "sagaciously") corrected (διώρθου, "amended," "rectified") those errors that his forefathers had made, while keeping and imitating those practices that he found to be

---

[2] To be sure, this word is added by Dindorf; but a word is definitely missing in the text, and it is clear that that word is either a noun or an adjective.

good. In doing so, Josephus significantly remarks, he acted as if he were a very old man. Indeed, we may here call attention to the fact that in the Talmud the term "old man" (*zaqen*) is a synonym for a wise man (*Qiddushin* 32b).³ Moreover, Josephus stresses that Josiah's wisdom (σοφίᾳ) pertained to his very nature (φύσεως) and that it was not merely knowledge but discernment (ἐπινοίᾳ, "understanding," "sagacity," "craftiness") (*Ant.* 10.51). Indeed, the fact that Josephus here uses two words (σοφίᾳ and ἐπινοίᾳ) to characterize Josiah's wisdom is a clear indication that in Josephus' mind Josiah was not merely wise but also, as we can see from the various meanings of the word ἐπίνοια, perceptive, insightful, and inventive. Indeed, Josiah's reforms, as described by Josephus (*Ant.* 10.50-51) are the result of rational considerations and hence would appeal to the intelligentsia in Josephus' audience, whereas in the Bible, whether 2 Kings 23:4-24 or 2 Chronicles 34:29-33, Josiah's reforms are the result of royal ukase, with the word "wise" or "rational" significantly absent in the description of Josiah's initiative.

In fact, Josephus makes of Josiah a prototype of the Pharisees, inasmuch as, in an extra-biblical remark, he states that Josiah was guided by the counsel (συμβουλίᾳ) and tradition (παραδόσει) of the elders (τῶν πρεσβυτέρων) (*Ant.* 10.51).⁴ That Josephus has the Pharisees in mind here is indicated by the fact that we find precisely the same phraseology in the Gospels' references (Mark 7:3, 4; Matthew 15:2) to the Pharisaic teaching as ἡ παράδοσις τῶν πρεσβυτέρων, as well as a very similar phrase, παραδόσεως τῶν πατέρων in Josephus himself (*Ant.* 13.297),⁵ where he contrasts the Pharisees' regard for such traditions with the Sadducees' view that considered valid only those regulations that are written down in Scripture. Similarly, Josephus speaks of the Pharisees as intro-

---

³ Wiesenberg (1956, 213-33), though, to be sure, with some diffidence, identifies Josephus himself as the old man who was learned in Greek wisdom and who gave the advice to dispatch a swine instead of cattle for the sacrifices in the Temple during the civil war between Hyrcanus and Aristobulus (*Baba Qamma* 82b, *Soṭah* 49b, *Menaḥot* 64b); but this incident occurred in 63 B.C.E., a full century before the birth of Josephus (unless we follow the Jerusalem Talmud in placing it in the time of Titus).

⁴ To be sure, the words καὶ τῇ τῶν πρεσβυτέρων πειθόμενος ("obeying [the counsel and tradition] of the elders") are omitted in several of the manuscripts; but without some such phrase the Greek is unidiomatic.

⁵ On the significance of this phrase see Hoffmann (1883, 45-63); and Baumgarten (1987, 73-76).

ducing regulations in accordance with the tradition of their fathers (κατὰ τὴν πατρῴαν παράδοσιν) (*Ant.* 13.408). Mason[6] argues that the context in the above Josiah passage disallows the idea of Pharisaic tradition, inasmuch as Josephus combines Josiah's innate wisdom and understanding with the counsel (συμβουλίᾳ) and advice (παραδόσει) of his elders (Mason 1991, 233-34). He further claims that the parallel with συμβουλίᾳ indicates that the παράδοσις is here a present influence and not a tradition. But the most common meaning of παράδοσις is a "handing down, "bequeathing," or "transmission," whether of a legend or a doctrine, and surely does not have the meaning of "advice," which Mason assigns to it here. Mason furthermore states that Josiah predates the Pharisaic elders by several centuries and hence cannot be regarded as one of them; but, in response, we should stress that Josephus, at any rate, did not regard this as an anachronism, inasmuch as he declares that the philosophies of the Jews, including specifically that of the Pharisees, existed from the most ancient (ἐκ τοῦ πάνυ ἀρχαίου) times (*Ant.* 18.11).

In Josephus' portrayal Josiah is the great leader. We see this even – or especially – when he is wounded and in great pain (*Ant.* 10.77). At this point in the biblical narrative he tells his servants to take him away, whereupon the servants take him to Jerusalem (2 Chronicles 35:23-24). In Josephus' version, however, even though he is wounded and in great pain he is still in command and orders the call to be sounded for his army's retreat and takes an active lead in the return to Jerusalem.

The great leader must be able to inspire his people to contribute to the cause which he represents. Thus, whereas the Bible says nothing about the efforts which he made to collect money for the refurbishing of the Temple (2 Chronicles 34:8), Josephus remarks that Josiah sent emissaries through the country telling those who wished to bring gold and silver for the repair of the Temple that they were welcome to do so, each according to his inclination and ability (*Ant.* 10.54).

Likewise, Josephus adds to the biblical portrait of Josiah the fact that he was not only a king but also a teacher of his people in that

---

[6] S. Schwartz (1990, 181, n. 34) admits that the phrase τῶν πρεσβυτέρων ... παραδόσει has a Pharisaic ring to it but says that the condition of the text is so poor as to render speculation about this feature unwise.

he sought to bring them to their senses (ἐσωφρόνιζε) and urged (παρῄνει, "urged," "advised," "recommended," "exhorted") them to give up their belief in idols (*Ant.* 10.50). The fact that Josephus uses the imperfect tense for both of these verbs is evidence that he sees this effort of Josiah's as continuous.

A major incident which seems to detract from Josiah's reputation for wisdom is his refusal to listen to King Neco of Egypt when the latter requested permission to pass through Josiah's territory in order to fight against the Medes and Babylonians. According to the biblical account Neco warned Josiah that he (Neco) was inspired by G-d in making his request (2 Chronicles 35:21-22, 1 Esdras 1:27); and, indeed, in refusing him, Josephus' Josiah disregards the advice of the prophet Jeremiah, "spoken by the word of the L-rd" (1 Esdras 1:28) (*Ant.* 10.76). Such stubbornness and insubordination in the face of the word of G-d and of His prophet would constitute a tremendous flaw in Josiah's character, but Josephus justifies Josiah's action by remarking, in an extra-biblical addition clearly critical of Neco, that Neco had the desire to rule Asia (*Ant.* 10.74) and by omitting the biblical statement that Neco had divine or prophetic backing (so noted by Begg 1988a, 163). Indeed, in a significant and remarkable addition, Josephus, in a blatant attempt to excuse Josiah's action, adds to the biblical narrative (2 Chronicles 35:22) that it was Destiny (τῆς πεπρωμένης), "I believe, that urged him on to this course, in order to have a pretext for destroying him" (*Ant.* 10.76) As Begg has noted, if Josephus had followed the biblical text here he would, in effect, have led the reader to conclude that Neco obeyed the will of G-d whereas Josiah did not (Begg 1988a, 161).

Moreover, in the proem to the *Antiquities* (1.14) Josephus plainly preaches that the main lesson to be learned from his work is that those who obey the will of G-d prosper in all things beyond belief, whereas it would seem to be plain that Josiah, who most certainly did obey the word of G-d, did not prosper for long. Hence, in order not to put the finger of blame on Josiah Josephus transfers responsibility for Josiah's premature death to Destiny.

The fact that in some other contexts, as Begg has remarked, Josephus does follow the Bible in attributing disaster not to Fate but to G-d, as in the case of King Amaziah of Judaea (*Ant.* 9.199, 2 Chronicles 25:20), in foolishly attacking King Jehoash of Israel, indicates that Josephus' motive in ascribing Josiah's doom to Destiny is to save the reputation of Josiah (so Begg 1988a, 161). Undoubtedly, moreover, Josephus was troubled by the apparent inconsistency between Josiah's tragic end despite his great piety and Josephus' own insistence in the proem to the *Antiquities* (1.14) that those who conform to the will of G-d are rewarded with unlimited prosperity and happiness.

Of course, in ascribing his doom to Destiny,[7] Josephus ran the risk of leading readers to associate the good king Josiah with the evil king Ahab, whose death is similarly due to Destiny, according to him. And yet, significantly, as we have tried to show in our study of Ahab, Josephus, like the rabbis, sees positive virtues in Ahab himself.

As to the second of the cardinal virtues, courage, Josephus is careful to protect Josiah's reputation for bravery by avoiding the degrading picture of Josiah disguising himself as he went forth to battle with Neco (2 Chronicles 35:22 vs. *Ant.* 10.76). Moreover, in this battle, he displays his zeal (σπουδῆς) for battle and his inspiring leadership in riding in his chariot from one wing of his army to another – a detail which is missing in the biblical account (2 Chronicles 35:23). Furthermore, he displays extraordinary bravery and presence of mind when mortally wounded in that, despite his great pain from the wound, he manages to order the call to be sounded for his army's retreat.

Already at the tender age of twelve, as we have noted, Josiah sought to imbue his people with the quality of temperance, the third of the cardinal virtues, as we see in Josephus' extra-biblical remark that Josiah then kept on trying to make the people moderate (ἐσωφρόνιζε) (*Ant.* 10.50).

That the quality of justice is one of the major characteristics of the Josephan Josiah is evident from the fact that Josephus declares that when he was only twelve years old Josiah already gave proof of his commitment to justice (δικαιοσύνην) (*Ant.* 10.50). Furthermore, the young Josiah displays his devotion to justice particularly in following the laws, with the result, we are told, that he suc-

---

[7] Schwartz (1990, 181) concludes that Josephus used the story of Josiah to illustrate his theme that G-d rewards the just and punishes the unjust without, however, trying to reconcile Josiah's piety with his ignominious end. We may, nevertheless, remark that it is precisely because he was concerned with this apparent inconsistency that Josephus ascribed Josiah's death to Destiny rather than to G-d.

ceeded in bringing order into his government (*Ant.* 10.51). Indeed, Josephus ascribes Josiah's success in so doing to his readiness to follow the laws and to the disappearance of lawlessness (παρανομίαν) in his realm (*Ant.* 10.51). This emphasis on respect for the laws may also be seen in Josephus' version of the oath which the people take to abide by the covenant which Josiah has made with G-d (2 Chronicles 34:32 vs. *Ant.* 10.63). As Josephus has it, it is specifically to obey the laws of Moses that the people pledge themselves. Needless to say, this would have a special appeal to the Romans, who, as we have noted, traditionally and historically placed such a premium upon law and justice.

Josephus, in an important statement that has no parallel in the Bible (2 Chronicles 34:3-7) and which emphasizes the importance of justice for Josiah, remarks that Josiah appointed certain judges and overseers who, in administering the affairs of individuals, put justice (τὸ δίκαιον) above all else and treated it no less carefully than their own lives (*Ant.* 10.53). Marcus remarks that nothing is said in Scripture about Josiah's appointment of judges and wonders whether Josephus may not have confused Josiah with Jehoshaphat here (R. Marcus 1937, 6:186, n. c). More likely, however, as Schwartz has indicated, Josephus felt that Josiah's thorough re-evaluation of the Judahite constitution would have involved a reform of the judicial system as well (so S. Schwartz 1990, 181, n. 34) – especially, we may add, inasmuch as the administration of justice was so important to a significant class of Josephus' readers, namely the Romans. Indeed, so great is Josephus' admiration for Josiah's justice that, in an extra-biblical remark, he has the prophetess Huldah remark that the destined exile of the entire Jewish nation would be postponed because Josiah was a righteous (δίκαιον) man (*Ant.* 10.61); in contrast, in the Bible, it is merely Josiah himself who will be spared seeing Jerusalem's fall (2 Kings 22:19-20, 2 Chronicles 34:27-28).

That piety is the chief quality of Josiah is clear from Josephus' extra-biblical remark that when he was only twelve Josiah urged his people to give up their belief in idols and to worship the G-d of their fathers (*Ant.* 10.50). Indeed, Josephus tells us that Josiah succeeded in bringing order into his government through following the laws and through his piety (εὐσεβείας) (Ant. 10.51). Such criticism of idol worship would have found a sympathetic audience among at least some pagan intellectuals if we may judge from the case of the first century B.C.E. Varro, the most learned of the Romans, as Quintilian (10.1.95) calls him in the first century C.E., and from that of the encyclopedic historian and geographer Strabo, who lived in the latter part of the first century B.C.E. and in the early years of the first century C.E. Indeed, Varro (*ap.* Augustine, *De Civitate D-i* 4.31) says that the ancient Romans worshipped gods without an image, comparing them in this respect to the Jews, and then adds, most significantly, that if this ancient usage of the Romans had continued, their worship of the gods would have been more devout, since, he says, those who introduced images diminish reverence for the gods, inasmuch as gods in the shape of images might easily inspire contempt. In effect, we may say, in Josephus' formulation, Josiah is asserting almost the same thing as Varro, i.e., that one should revert to the theology of the ancients. That Strabo is sympathetic to Judaism when he states that Moses was critical of the Egyptians and of the Greeks for representing the Divine Being by the images of animals and of human beings respectively is clear from his remark that in arguing thus Moses persuaded not a few thoughtful (εὐγνώμονας, "reasonable," "rational," "sensible," "prudent") men (16.2.36.761) Such views had a long history in Greek philosophical, especially Stoic, thought (so Stern 1974, 1:207). In particular, Josephus' older contemporary, the Stoic philosopher and statesman Seneca the Younger (*ap.* Augustine, *De Civitate D-i* 6.10) ridicules the worship of images: "They dedicate images of the sacred and inviolable immortals in most worthless and motionless matter. ... They call them deities, when they are such that if they should get breath and should suddenly meet them, they would be held to be monsters."

Furthermore, whereas the Bible simply mentions that Josiah knocked down the statues and other appurtenances belonging to alien religions (2 Chronicles 34:3-7), Josephus places the emphasis upon Josiah's positive achievements in turning the people to the service of G-d and states that he offered upon His altar the customary sacrifices and the whole burnt-offerings (*Ant.* 10.53). Indeed, in the interest of minimizing Josiah's assault upon pagan worship, which would appear to indicate a lack of tolerance of the religious views of others, Josephus completely omits the long account of Josiah's demolition of pagan temples and monuments (2 Kings 23:7-19), as well as his elimination of the necromancers and diviners (2 Kings 23:24 vs. *Ant.* 10.53).

Again, Josephus stresses the piety of Josiah by noting that

Josiah's emissaries not only, as in the Bible (2 Chronicles 34:8), undertook the work of repairing the Temple but that they did so without allowing any postponement or delay (μηδὲν ὑπερθέσει μηδὲ ἀναβολῇ) (*Ant.* 10.56). Moreover, Josephus adds that they provided master-builders (ἀρχιτέκτονας) for the repairs. Indeed, Josephus concludes his account of this activity by adding the remark that the repair of the Temple in this fashion made clear the piety (εὐσέβειαν) of the king.

Josiah's piety is further stressed by Josephus' additions to the biblical statement regarding the money that was found in the Temple by those repairing it. In the biblical version it is Shaphan, Josiah's scribe, who reports to the king that his workmen have removed the money which they found in the Temple while they were repairing it (2 Kings 22:9). There is no indication of what they do with this money after they have found it. In Josephus' account it is Josiah himself who, in his piety, takes the initiative to send for the high priest Eliakias (Hilkiah), telling him to melt what is left over of the money and with it to make mixing-bowls and libation-cups and bowls for the Temple service, as well as to bring out whatever gold and silver he might find in the treasuries of the Temple and to spend it similarly for mixing-bowls and such vessels (*Ant.* 10.57).[8] Moreover, in an extra-biblical detail, Josephus notes that Josiah, in his reforming zeal, searched the houses and villages and cities for idolatrous objects (*Ant.* 10.69).[9]

Furthermore, Josephus spells out the fears of the pious king that G-d would punish the Jews because of the transgressions of their forefathers against the laws of Moses. In the Bible we are told merely that G-d is angry because the Jews' fathers have not hearkened to the words of the book that had been found (2 Kings

---

[8] The Bible at this point states that Hilkiah the high priest found the book of the law in the Temple (2 Kings 22:8 and 2 Chronicles 34:14); and most scholars have assumed that the Book of Deuteronomy is referred to here. They have further concluded that that book, in its present form, was written not long before Josiah became king and that his reforms are based upon the prescriptions in that book. Josephus, apparently troubled by the biblical passage and its implications, is careful to state that Hilkiah came upon the sacred books of Moses, that is, the entire Pentateuch (*Ant.* 10.58). Likewise, whereas the Bible states that Josiah read the words of the scroll of the covenant (2 Kings 23:2), Josephus specifies that he read the sacred books (*Ant.* 10.63).

[9] Josiah is similarly depicted in rabbinic literature; but there it is not Josiah himself, as in Josephus, but his emissaries who conduct the search. See Ginzberg 1913, 4:282; and 1928, 6:378, n. 119.

22:13); in Josephus the specific fear is mentioned that they may be driven into exile into a foreign land where they will be destitute (*Ant.* 10.59). One is here reminded of Socrates' description of the pain of exile, wandering from city to city and continually being expelled, when he declines to propose exile as the penalty for his conviction (Plato, *Apology* 37C-E).

Josephus was quite clearly in a quandary when he came to the biblical passage that Josiah put to death all the priests of the high places who had been guilty of idol worship (2 Kings 23:20). This was truly embarrassing, inasmuch as Josephus himself was a priest. Hence, Josephus adds the extra-biblical detail that these priests were not, as he himself was, of the family of Aaron (*Ant.* 10.65).

Moreover, it is not, for Josephus, sufficient that Josiah himself was pious. Thus, we read in the Bible that Josiah broke down the idols of his predecessors (2 Chronicles 34:6-7); the Josephan Josiah, however, is not content merely to do this: he is a teacher who goes to the people of his kingdom and persuades them also to give up their impious practices and to abandon their worship of foreign gods and to show piety (εὐσεβεῖν) and fidelity to G-d (*Ant.* 10.68).

Josephus significantly embellishes the account of the celebration of Passover by Josiah. The biblical narrative simply declares that such a Passover sacrifice had not been performed since the time of the judges (2 Kings 23:22 and 2 Chronicles 35:18). Josephus, in a distinct compliment to Josiah's piety, adds that everything was carried out in accordance with the laws (νόμους) and with the observance of their fathers' ancient customs (*Ant.* 10.72).

It is not surprising that Josiah emerges, in an extra-biblical addition, as one who lived in peace and enjoyed wealth and the good opinion of all men (*Ant.* 10.73). In these latter qualities he is thus reminiscent of such a heroic figure as Cimon in the portrayal by Cornelius Nepos (*Cimon* 4). Finally, Josephus adds the extra-biblical detail that Josiah's burial was magnificent (μεγαλοπρεπῶς) (*Ant.* 10.77).

And yet, Josephus, realizing, presumably, that his credibility would be impugned by exaggeration, is careful to avoid extravagant praise of Josiah (*Ant.* 10.73). Thus, Josephus omits the biblical statement that there was no king like him before him, "who returned to the L-rd with all his heart and with all his soul and with all his possessions," that is, in fulfillment of the central requirements of the key prayer of Judaism, the "Shema" (Deuteronomy 6:5), "according to the entire Torah of Moses" (and hence not merely in accordance with the Book of Deuteronomy), and that no one of equal piety arose after him (2 Kings 23:25).

4. Summary

For Josephus Josiah is the embodiment of the cardinal virtues – wisdom, courage, temperance, justice, and the fifth virtue of piety. Like the typical Hellenistic hero, he is depicted, in extra-biblical additions, as precocious. At the tender age of twelve he is said to possess the wisdom and discernment of an old man. His reforms, being inspired by reason, would appeal to the intelligentsia in his audience. In depicting him as guided by the traditions of the elders Josephus makes Josiah the prototype of the later Pharisees. He is able to inspire the masses of the people to contribute to his cause. Like Moses and like Plato's philosopher-king he is able to teach and persuade the people and to bring them to their senses.

Whereas the Bible is clearly critical of Josiah for not listening to the Egyptian King Neco, who had divine backing in asking permission from Josiah to pass through his territory, Josephus significantly protects Josiah's reputation by omitting the fact that Neco spoke to him in the name of G-d.

Inasmuch as, according to Josephus' own statement in the proem to the *Antiquities*, the chief lesson to the learned from his history is that G-d rewards the just and punishes the unjust, Josephus, clearly in a quandary as to how to explain Josiah's untimely death, resolves the matter by placing the blame on "Destiny." In this respect, Josiah is similar to Ahab; but the latter, in Josephus' portrayal, as noted above, is much more sympathetically presented than he is in the Bible.

As to bravery, Josiah exhibits this quality particularly during his last battle when he inspires his men riding from one wing to another and when finally, though mortally wounded, he maintains his presence of mind in giving the order for the army's retreat. He shows the quality of temperance at the tender age of twelve in constantly seeking to influence his people toward the goal of moderation. In his devotion to law and justice and in bringing order into his government Josephus' Josiah undoubtedly would appeal to his Roman readers, who were so proud of their legal achievement and who placed such a premium upon orderly administration. Piety, the salient quality of the great Roman hero Aeneas, is likewise the most prominent quality of Josiah. He is not content merely to be pious himself: he teaches and inspires his people to follow his lead. His criticism of idol worship would have found a particularly sympathetic audience among the Stoics. Yet, in the interest of religious tolerance, Josephus omits the long account of Josiah's demolition of pagan temples and monuments. Finally, he significantly embellishes the biblical account of Josiah's celebration of Passover.

CHAPTER TWENTY-NINE

JEHOIACHIN

1. *Introduction: The Problem*

We have made frequent reference to the fact that whereas Josephus promises that he will neither add to nor omit anything from the Scriptures in his history (*Ant.* 1.17), in actuality he makes numerous changes. But these are matters of mere addition or subtraction. And yet, how can we explain so notable a change as the one here, namely, the case of Jehoiachin (Jeconiah), where Josephus seems to change the biblical text completely, so that instead of characterizing Jehoiachin, as does the Bible, as one who did what was evil in the sight of the L-rd (2 Kings 24:9, 2 Chronicles 36:9), he is described as being kind (χρηστός) and just (δίκαιος) (*Ant.* 10.100)?

As to Josephus' modification of the biblical text with regard to Jehoiachin, we might perhaps explain that in omitting the phrase that Jehoiachin "did what was evil in the sight of the L-rd" Josephus is simply omitting a formula frequently found in the Bible in connection with the various kings of Judah and Israel. Alternatively, we may say that the reference in this stock phrase may be to idolatry and that it does not mean that the king to whom it is applied mistreated his subjects. However, an examination of how Josephus deals with this phrase, which in the Bible occurs in connection with 25 kings,[1] indicates that he never reproduces it as such, whereas

---

[1] Rehoboam (1 Kings 14:22, 2 Chronicles 12:14; *Ant.* 8.251), Nadab (1 Kings 15:26; *Ant.* 8.287), Baasha (1 Kings 15:34, 16:7; *Ant.* 8.299), Zimri (1 Kings 16:19; *Ant.* 8.309), Omri (1 Kings 16:25; *Ant.* 8.313), Ahab (1 Kings 16:30; *Ant.* 8.316), Ahaziah of Israel (1 Kings 22:52; *Ant.* 9.18), Jehoram of Israel (2 Kings 3:2, *Ant.* 9.27), Jehoram of Judah (2 Kings 8:18, 2 Chronicles 21:6, *Ant.* 9.95), Ahaziah of Judah (2 Kings 8:27, 2 Chronicles 22:4, *Ant.* 9.121), Jehoahaz of Israel (2 Kings 13:2, *Ant.* 9.173), Jehoash of Israel (2 Kings 13:11, *Ant.* 9.178), Jeroboam II (2 Kings 14:24, *Ant.* 9.205), Zechariah (2 Kings 15:9, *Ant.* 9.215), Menahem (2 Kings 15:18, *Ant.* 9.232), Pekahiah (2 Kings 15:24, *Ant.* 9.233), Pekah (2 Kings 15:28, *Ant.* 9.234), Ahaz (2 Kings 16:2, 2 Chronicles 28:1, *Ant.* 9.243), Hoshea (2 Kings 17:2, *Ant.* 9.258), Manasseh (2 Kings 21:2, 2 Chronicles 33:2, *Ant.* 10.37), Amon (2 Kings 21:20, 2 Chronicles 33:22, *Ant.* 10.47), Jehoahaz of Judah (2 Kings 23:32, *Ant.* 10.81), Jehoiakim (2 Kings 23:37, 2 Chronicles 36:5, *Ant.* 10.83), Jehoiachin (2 Kings 24:9, 2 Chronicles 36:9, *Ant.* 10.100), Zedekiah (2 Kings 24:19, 2 Chronicles 36:12, *Ant.* 10.103).

he specifies in various ways the nature of a given king's evildoing. In some cases Josephus explains that the evil consisted of impiety (Zimri, Omri, Jehoahaz of Israel, Ahaz); in others he says it consisted of both impiety and wickedness (Nadab, Baasha, Jehoram of Israel, Jehoram of Judah, Jeroboam II, Hoshea, Manasseh, Amon); in still others it is a matter of impiety and lawlessness or corruptness (Pekah, Jehoahaz of Judah). Again, in some cases it is left unspecified whether the king's wickedness was against G-d or toward man (Ahaziah of Israel, Ahaziah of Judah); in others it is wickedness toward G-d (Ahab); in still others one hears of wickedness and injustice, presumably toward man (Jehoiakim); and finally, there are instances involving perverseness and cruelty toward man (Menahem, Pekahiah).

Similarly, we may note that in the eight cases where the Bible states that a king did what was right in the eyes of the L-rd, Josephus never reproduces this phrase as such but spells out in various ways what the goodness involved. Thus in some cases he indicates that it consisted of piety (Jehoash), in others he identifies it with justice (presumably toward his subjects) (Amaziah), in other cases it is a matter of piety and justice (Asa, Jehoshaphat, Jotham, Hezekiah, Josiah), while finally Uzziah's righteousness lay in his goodness and justice.

We may perhaps find a parallel in Josephus' portrait of Zedekiah. According to the Bible, Zedekiah, like Jehoiachin, did what was evil in the sight of the L-rd (2 Kings 24:19); moreover, we are told that he did not humble himself before the prophet Jeremiah (2 Chronicles 36:12) and that he hardened his heart against turning to the L-rd (2 Chronicles 36:13). Josephus, to be sure, does not avoid the biblical statement that Zedekiah did what was evil in the eyes of G-d (2 Kings 24:19), and, indeed, declares that Zedekiah was contemptuous of justice (δικαίων) and duty (δέοντος) (*Ant.* 10.103); but he implicitly places the blame for this upon Zedekiah's impious (ἀσεβεῖς) contemporaries and upon the masses who had license to act as outrageously as they pleased. Again, whereas in the Bible, we hear only that Zedekiah did not humble himself before the prophet Jeremiah (2 Chronicles 36:12), Josephus blames Zedekiah's advisers, inasmuch as, in an extra-biblical addition, he states that Jeremiah specifically urged him not to pay heed to these leaders, "because there were wicked men among them," and not to put faith in the false prophets who were predicting that the Babylonian king would never again make war on Jerusalem and that the Egyptians would take the field against him and would defeat him in battle (*Ant.* 10.104). Hence, it is clear that Zedekiah's impieties (ἀσεβείας) and lawless acts (παρανομίας) were, according to Josephus, the result of listening to this poor advice (*Ant.* 10.104). The whole scene reminds one of Plato's famous allegory of the ship in which the captain of the ship (representing the naive people) listens to the sailors (representing the demagogues) rather than to the navigator (representing the philosopher) (*Republic* 6.488).

But a comparison between Josephus' Zedekiah and Jehoiachin is not really *ad rem*, inasmuch as even in the Bible Zedekiah shows pity for Jeremiah in instructing Ebed-melech the Ethiopian to rescue him from the cistern into which he had been lowered (Jeremiah 38:10); again, he secretly sends for Jeremiah in order to ask him what message he had received from G-d pertaining to him (Jeremiah 38:14); likewise, he admits to Jeremiah his fear of the Jews who have deserted to the Babylonians lest he be handed over to them and they abuse him (Jeremiah 38:19); furthermore, he makes a covenant, of which Jeremiah quite clearly approves, with all the people in Jerusalem that everyone should set free his Hebrew slaves (Jeremiah 34:8-11).

A closer parallel is to be found in Josephus' comments about Jehoash (Joash), the king of Israel. The Bible uses the familiar formula that "he did what was evil in the sight of the L-rd," and, as if this is not enough, it adds that "he did not depart from all the sins of Jeroboam the son of Nebat, which he made Israel to sin, but he walked in them" (2 Kings 13:11). The fact that he seized all the gold and silver and all the vessels of the Temple in Jerusalem would, we might expect, have led Josephus, who was so proud of his status as a priest, to condemn him utterly. Yet, Josephus has the very opposite view of Jehoash, remarking that he was a good (ἀγαθός) man and in no way like his father Jehoahaz in character (*Ant.* 9.178). It is possible that Josephus has confused the Israelite Jehoash with the king of Judah of the same name, who, indeed, is described as having done what was right in the eyes of the L-rd (2 Kings 12:2). But that this is unlikely is seen from the fact that Josephus praises Jehoash the king of Judah for his zealousness in the worship of the L-rd (*Ant.* 9.157). Another possibility is that Jehoash the king of Israel may have repented, as did his father

Jehoahaz, who is labeled as impious (*Ant.* 9.173) but then is described as repentant (*Ant.* 9.175), but against this is the fact that there is nothing in the Bible to indicate that Jehoash was repentant. The most likely explanation would seem to be that Josephus had an independent tradition indicating that Jehoash was actually a good king. In this he is similar to, if not dependent upon, the rabbinic tradition that speaks of Jehoash as being rewarded with victory over the Arameans because he had refused to listen to the accusations brought against the prophet Amos by Amaziah and had replied that even if Amos had uttered a prophecy of doom upon him he was merely obeying the command of G-d (*Seder Eliyahu Rabbah* 16.88). Here we would seem to have a clue as to Josephus' "revisionism" in his view of biblical characters, namely his awareness of oral tradition as later embodied in the rabbinic literature.

We may perhaps find another close parallel in the way in which the Talmudic rabbis treat the incident of David and Bathsheba. Although the prophet Nathan in the Bible seems to say very clearly that David, in smiting Uriah the Hittite and taking Uriah's wife to be his wife had "despised the word of the L-rd, to do what is evil in His sight" (2 Samuel 12:9), and although David himself admits, "I have sinned against the L-rd" (2 Samuel 12:13), Rabbi Samuel bar Nahmani, in the name of the third-century Rabbi Jonathan, directly contradicts the Bible by stating that whoever says that David sinned himself errs (*Shabbat* 56a).[2]

2. *The Qualities of Jehoiachin*

That the Jehoiachin pericope is of considerable interest to Josephus, although he was king for only three months (2 Kings 24:8, 2 Chronicles 36:9),[3] may be seen from the sheer amount of

---

[2] Interestingly, however, Josephus himself does not cover up David's sin but candidly declares that although David was by nature righteous and G-d-fearing, nevertheless he fell into this grave error. For a suggested explanation of Josephus' attitude see Feldman 1989d, especially 171-74.

[3] Excavations at Beth-Shemesh, Tel Beth-Mirsim, and Ramat Rahel have revealed three broken jar-handles stamped with a seal, dating from the period when Jerusalem was under siege by the Babylonians and referring to a certain Eliakim,

space that he devotes to it as compared with the attention which he gives to other episodes. For the Jehoiachin pericope (2 Kings 24:6-17, 25:27-30 [27 lines]; 2 Chronicles 36:8-10 [7 lines]; Josephus, *Ant.* 10.97-102, 229-230 [49 lines]) the ratio of Josephus as compared with the Hebrew text of 2 Kings, which is the more substantial biblical account, is 1.81, and as compared with the combined Hebrew texts of 2 Kings and 2 Chronicles is 1.44. The ratio of Josephus to the Septuagint version of 2 Kings is 1.14 and as compared with the combined Septuagint texts of 2 Kings and 2 Chronicles is .91. Hence, we see that the episode is of considerable interest to Josephus.

In describing Jehoiachin as kind (χρηστός) and just (δίκαιος) (*Ant.* 10.100), Josephus is using the same pair of adjectives that he uses of the character of the prophet Samuel (*Ant.* 6.194), the good King Hezekiah (*Ant.* 9.260), the heroic high priest Jehoiada (*Ant.* 9.166) who rescued Joash and proclaimed him king, and Nehemiah (*Ant.* 11.183). The ascription of these qualities to Jehoiachin is especially important because Josephus, throughout his version of the Bible, stresses the wisdom of seeking accommodation, as Jehoiachin did, with the superpower of his day. It is, moreover, surely significant that the corresponding nouns, χρηστότης and δικαιοσύνη, are used with regard to King Zedekiah (*Ant.* 10.120), who, as we have noted, is similarly rehabilitated by Josephus in contrast to his biblical portrayal. It is likewise notable that the quality

---

a servant of Jehoiachin. It is hard to believe that this seal was used only during the three months of the latter's rule as reported in the Bible. Apparently, then, even while his successor Zedekiah was ruling, Jehoiachin still held on to estates in Judah and enjoyed the status of king.

In addition, tablets have been found in Babylon listing payment of rations in oil, barley, and other provisions to captives and skilled workmen from many nations, including Yaukin (i.e. Jehoiachin), king of Judah. Albright (1932, 77-106; and 1942, 49-55) concludes, from these discoveries, that Jehoiachin was free to move about Babylon and that he was not only the legitimate king from the point of view of the Jewish exiles in Babylon but that he was also regarded by the Babylonians themselves as a legitimate king of Judah whom they held in reserve if circumstances should appear to require it. The Babylonians apparently alternated between favoring Zedekiah and favoring Jehoiachin from year to year. In particular, the large quantity of oil allocated to Jehoiachin personally (twelve times the amount received by each of his sons) indicates that Jehoiachin was responsible for supporting his entire household.

In addition, Berridge (1992, 662) suggests that the fact that the book of Ezekiel (e.g. Ezekiel 1:2) employs a dating system based on the year of Jehoiachin's deportation indicates that Jehoiachin was regarded as the legitimate ruler of Judah, with Zedekiah merely his regent, even after Jehoiachin's deportation.

of χρηστότης is ascribed to Gedaliah (*Ant.* 10.164), who, like Jeremiah, Zedekiah, and Jehoiachin, adopted a submissive attitude toward the Babylonians. Finally, the quality of kindness is particularly meaningful to Josephus, inasmuch as it is precisely that virtue (χρηστότητος) which, according to Josephus himself, the Emperor Vespasian displayed toward him until the very end of his (Vespasian's) life (*Life* 423).

3. *The Political Implications of Josephus' Treatment of Jehoiachin*

At first thought one might suggest that Josephus' attitude to Jehoiachin may have been influenced by a desire to present the penultimate king of Judah in a positive light in view, perhaps, of Josephus' hope of the renewal of the monarchy at some future time. But this is unlikely, inasmuch as Josephus himself traced his ancestry back, on his mother's side, to the Hasmoneans (*Life* 2), who were not of the Davidic line. Moreover, the concept of the renewal of the Davidic line was intimately connected with the expectation of a Messiah, who, traditionally, was regarded as a descendant of David; and the idea of a Messiah was surely anathema to the Romans, Josephus' patrons, inasmuch as a major achievement of the Messiah was to be the establishment of a truly independent state; and this could, of course, occur only with the end of Roman occupation of Judaea.

A more fruitful approach will be to consider the possibility that because Josephus saw a striking parallel between the events leading to the destruction of both the First and Second Temples, and because he himself acted in a fashion similar to that of Jehoiachin in surrendering to the enemy, he felt a greater necessity to defend Jehoiachin's decision.[4] It is surely striking that in his address to his

---

[4] The *Babylonian Chronicle* (British Museum 21946, verso, line 12), as published by Wiseman (1956, 73) corroborates the biblical account of the capture of Jerusalem and the exile of Jehoiachin in the seventh year of Nebuchadnezzar's reign. However, Josephus' account of the events leading to the fall of Jerusalem and to the capture of Jehoiachin differs from the *Babylonian Chronicle* in some respects, particularly inasmuch as it implies that Nebuchadnezzar himself came to Jerusalem, slew Jehoiakim, and placed Jehoiachin on the throne. Malamat (1950, 223-24) correctly remarks that the true significance of the exile of Jehoiachin is to be measured not by a quantitative but rather by a qualitative standard, since it was precisely the most important elements of the population who were exiled with him, namely the royal family, the wealthy and the aristocrats, and, above all,

rival John of Gischala and to his fellow-Jews, Josephus appeals to the same motives that led Jehoiachin to surrender, namely, to spare his country and to save the Temple from destruction. As a sole precedent, he cites the instance of Jehoiachin, whose action he refers to as a noble example, in that he voluntarily endured captivity together with his family rather than see the Temple go up in flames (*War* 6.103-4). He then, in a veritable peroration and clearly disregarding the biblical statement that he did evil, remarks that because of this action Jehoiachin is celebrated in sacred story by all Jews and will be remembered forever. It is significant, too, that aside from David and Solomon, Jehoiachin is the only king mentioned by name in the *Jewish War*.

How to justify such subservience to a foreign occupier, whether in the case of Jehoiachin or in Josephus' own case, must have presented a real problem to Josephus. His solution is that it was a matter of military necessity in both instances. Similarly, that there was no military possibility of continuing the war against Nebuchadnezzar is clear from Josephus' statement (*Ant.* 10.155) that those who were left in Judaea and over whom Gedaliah was made governor were the poor (so also Jeremiah 40:7) and the deserters (Josephus' addition).

Gedaliah's position, vis-à-vis the Babylonians at the time of the destruction of the First Temple, was more or less replicated by Josephus at the time of the destruction of the Second Temple, namely, to accept subservience to the superpower in return for religious autonomy. In this he agreed with the rabbinic leadership, at least as exemplified by Johanan ben Zakkai (*Giṭṭin* 56a-b).

Josephus was certainly aware of the criticism that must have been leveled against Jehoiachin for surrendering the city of Jerusalem, as he was of the bitter criticism which he himself suffered for surrendering Jotapata to the Romans. Thus, whereas the Bible simply states the fact that he gave himself up, together with his mother and his servants and his princes and his palace officials to the king of Babylon (2 Kings 24:12), Josephus explains the reason, namely that, being kind and just, he did not think it right to allow

---

the soldiers, craftsmen, and artisans (2 Kings 24:14-16, Jeremiah 24:1, 27:20, 29:1-2). Hence, it is the exile of Jehoiachin, rather than the exile ten years later, that the Bible regards as the decisive event (cf. Ezekiel 1:2, 2 Kings 25:27). This is particularly evident from the fact that the Bible counts the number of exiles beginning from the deportation of Jehoiachin (Jeremiah 52:28-30).

the city to be endangered on his account (*Ant.* 10.100). That this action did not turn out to the advantage of Jehoiachin and his family is then blamed not on Jehoiachin but on Nebuchadnezzar, who, we are told, failed to keep his pledge to Jehoiachin (*Ant.* 10.101).[5]

4. *The Rehabilitation of Jehoiachin in Rabbinic Literature and in Josephus*

Margaliyot remarks that the Bible says not a word that is positive about Jehoiachin (Margaliyot 1949, 86),[6] whereas the rabbinic tra-

---

[5] One would have thought that Josephus would be strongly critical of Nebuchadnezzar as the one responsible for the destruction of the First Temple, but apparently he saw an analogy between Nebuchadnezzar, the destroyer of the First Temple, and Titus, the destroyer of the Second Temple; and inasmuch as he felt that he could hardly be critical of the latter, presumably in view of all the gifts and favors which Vespasian and Titus had bestowed upon him, he often does his best to exonerate Nebuchadnezzar. Furthermore, realizing that, even so, he had not painted Nebuchadnezzar in the best light, Josephus apologizes by reminding the reader that at the very beginning of his history he had indicated that he was merely translating the Bible and had promised that he would record the narrative as he had found it there without adding or subtracting anything (*Ant.* 10.218). He then seeks to confirm his own credibility by citing four extra-biblical non-Jewish sources – Berossus, Megasthenes, Diocles, and Philostratus (*Ant.* 10.219-27) – whom he had consulted with regard to Nebuchadnezzar's deeds. That the data that he cites from these authorities only incidentally mention the Jews is an indication that his two major purposes in citing them were to build up the figure of Nebuchadnezzar himself by noting his victories in battle and his magnificent achievements in building temples and a palace and in adorning the city of Babylon and to accentuate Nebuchadnezzar's kindness in giving orders to allot to the Jewish captives, upon their arrival, settlements in the most suitable places in Babylonia. In fact, in an addition which is totally irrelevant in the history of the Jews which he is writing, Josephus cites Megasthenes as attempting to show that Nebuchadnezzar surpassed the greatest Greek mythical hero, Heracles himself, in bravery and in the greatness of his deeds and that he subdued the greater part of Africa and Spain (*Ant.* 10.227). So important were these citations from Berossus, Philostratus, and Megasthenes to Josephus that he quotes them twice, once in the *Antiquities* (10.220-26) and once in the essay *Against Apion* (1.134-41). Indeed, whereas Josephus normally provides encomia only for his Jewish personalities, he most remarkably praises Nebuchadnezzar as a man of bold action (δραστήριος, "active," "enterprising," "energetic," "determined," "spirited") and one who was more fortunate (εὐτυχέστερος) (*Ant.* 10.219). Moreover, realizing that Nebuchadnezzar might be criticized for his treatment of Jehoiachin, Josephus, in an extrabiblical addition, presents a reason for his action, namely that he feared that Jehoiachin might bear him a grudge for killing his father and might consequently lead his country in revolt (*Ant.* 10.99).

[6] Margaliyot, however, makes no attempt to explain this complete change of

dition has only complimentary statements and not a single negative remark about him. It would seem that Josephus was aware of a tradition, found among the rabbis and presumably based upon the statement in 2 Kings (25:27-30) and Jeremiah (52:31-33), that King Evil-merodach, Nebuchadnezzar's successor, rehabilitated and indeed honored Jehoiachin, and that sorrow and suffering changed the latter, as it apparently did Zedekiah, into a saint. Indeed, so great is the regard that the tradition had for Jehoiachin that one of the gates of the Temple, when it was rebuilt was named for Jeconiah (another name for Jehoiachin) (Mishnah, *Middot* 2:6). In this 180-degree shift in attitude one is reminded of the change of attitude toward Heracles and Odysseus (both of whom were regarded by the Greeks as historical personages), such as we find when we compare Homer and the Greek tragedies.

In particular, we may note the tradition that when Nebuchadnezzar threatened to destroy the Temple if the Sanhedrin refused to agree to his demand that Jehoiachin surrender, Jehoiachin, in his piety, mounted the roof of the Temple and, holding all the keys to its chambers in his hand, offered to return the keys to G-d inasmuch as G-d no longer regarded the Jews as trustworthy (*Midrash Leviticus Rabbah* 19.6). Thereupon, miraculously, a hand was stretched forth from heaven and took the keys. He then, in his piety and in his devotion to his people, because he did not wish the city of Jerusalem to be exposed to peril for his sake, surrendered himself to the Babylonians after they had sworn that neither the city nor the people should suffer harm – an oath which, as it turned out, the Babylonians did not keep.[7] Another tradition depicts Jehoiachin as responsible for the continuation of Jewish practice in Babylonia. It was he who brought the holy ark from the Temple in Jerusalem to Babylon. Furthermore, he is said to have

---

attitude toward Jehoiachin on the part of the rabbinic tradition as compared with the biblical account. Nor does he note that Josephus parallels the rabbis in this change of attitude. We may, however, point out that the closing passage in 2 Kings (25:27-30) recounting the gracious treatment of Jehoiachin and the honor accorded to him during his captivity by King Evil-merodach of Babylonia would appear to imply that the author of the biblical narrative seemed to view this easing of Jehoiachin's lot favorably.

[7] *Seder Olam* 25, *Sifre Deuteronomy* 321, *Tanḥuma Noah* 3, *Giṭṭin* 88a, *Sanhedrin* 38a, Jerusalem *Sanhedrin* 1.19a, Jerusalem *Nedarim* 7.40a, *Midrash Leviticus Rabbah* 11.7, *Midrash Numbers Rabbah* 11.3, *Midrash Esther Rabbah* introduction, cited by Ginzberg (1928, 6:379, n. 132).

erected a synagogue in the Babylonian city of Nehardea using as building materials the stones and bricks that he had brought from Jerusalem. The Shekinah – G-d's Presence – was said to have dwelt in this synagogue from time to time.[8]

The greatest compliment that the rabbinic tradition could pay to anyone is to associate him with scholarship and teaching. That is precisely the picture that emerges from the statement that illustrates G-d's righteousness by noting that He anticipated the exile of Zedekiah already during that of Jehoiachin; hence the great scholars who were exiled with Jehoiachin were still alive and were able to transmit their teachings to their posterity. So high was the level of learning among them, we are told, that when the scholars opened a learned discussion all the others became as deaf, and when they closed a discussion the result was so definitive that it was not reopened (*Sanhedrin* 38a, *Giṭṭin* 88a).

The ultimate indication of Jehoiachin's piety is to be found in the tradition that while he was a prisoner the Sanhedrin, who had been deported together with the king, feared that the royal dynasty of David would die out, and hence they besought Nebuchadnezzar for permission to allow Jehoiachin's wife to join him. Through the queen's hairdresser they succeeded in getting the Queen Semiramis to prevail upon Nebuchadnezzar. And yet, despite his great joy in being united with his wife, when she informed him that she had seen a menstrual discharge, he withdrew from her, and observed the ritual laws of family purity as specified in the Pentateuch (*Midrash Leviticus Rabbah* 19.6).[9] The Midrash comments that while he was living in Jerusalem he did not observe these precepts, but that because he was doing so now, he was pardoned for his sins, and the Sanhedrin absolved G-d from His oath that the rule should be taken from Johoiachin's descendants. In fact, the first governor of the Land of Israel after the destruction of the Temple was Jehoiachin's grandson, Zerubbabel,[10] and the Messiah is destined to be one of his descendants.[11]

---

[8] *Seder Olam* 25, Tosefta *Sheqalim* 2.18, *Yoma* 53b, cited by Ginzberg (1928, 6:380, n. 134).

[9] Africanus, *Letter to Origen* 2, identifies the wife of Jehoiachin as Susanna of the Apocryphal book. So also Hippolytus, *Commentary on Daniel* 1.

[10] *Pesiqta de-Rav Kahana* 25.163b, *Midrash Leviticus Rabbah* 10.56, *Midrash Song of Songs Rabbah* 8.6, *Sanhedrin* 37b-38a, cited by Ginzberg (1928, 6:381, n. 135).

[11] *Tanḥuma B* 1.140, *Tanḥuma Toledot* 14, *Aggadat Bereshit* 44.89, Targum on 2 Chronicles 3:24, cited by Ginzberg (1928, 6:381, n. 136).

The rabbis draw a lesson from the life history of Jehoiachin, namely that one should never despair, inasmuch as he languished in prison for thirty-seven years, but eventually not only gained his freedom but also received royal garments and an allowance and other great honors from Nebuchadnezzar's successor, Evil-merodach.[12] Indeed, according to one version, when the magnates of Babylonia objected to Evil-merodach's desire to free Jehoiachin on the grounds that a king is not permitted to revoke the edict of his dead predecessor unless he drags the corpse of the dead king from his grave, Evil-merodach actually dishonored the dead body of Nebuchadnezzar ('Avot de-Rabbi Nathan 17.37).

As to Josephus, he builds further upon the passage in 2 Kings (25:27-30) and Jeremiah (52:31-33) which tells how Evil-merodach, Nebuchadnezzar's son and successor, not only freed Jehoiachin from captivity, permitting him to put off his prison garments, but also spoke kindly to him[13] and honored him above the other kings who were with him in Babylon, even to the point of dining with him regularly at the king's table and giving him a regular allowance. In Josephus' version we are told that Evil-merodach kept Jehoiachin as one of his closest friends and gave him many gifts (*Ant.* 10.229). Josephus explains that the reason why he did so is that Nebuchadnezzar had not kept his pledge to Jehoiachin when the latter voluntarily surrendered himself together with his wives and children and all his relatives in order to save Jerusalem from a siege.[14]

In view of the change of attitude of Josephus toward Jehoiachin as compared with the view of him that we find in the Bible, one would have expected that Josephus, like the rabbis, would note that his suffering led him to repent. This presumably, as with

---

[12] *Tanḥuma B* 3.38, *Tanḥuma Tazria* 8, *Midrash Leviticus Rabbah* 18.2, 2 *'Avot de-Rabbi Nathan* 17.38.

[13] Levenson (1984, 353-61) suggests that Jehoiachin's change of clothes may signify a change of status beyond that which any inmate undergoes upon his release. He notes as well that recent Assyriological studies indicate that the phrase, which literally means "he spoke good things with him," connotes the establishment of a treaty of friendship; thus, his rehabilitation may have awakened hopes of a return among Jehoiachin's people both in exile and in Judah.

[14] On the inviolability of an oath see *War* 1.224, 260, 532; *Ant.* 1.212, 18.332. In particular, we may note the sacredness of an oath in the eyes of the Essenes (*War* 2.139, 142, 143), who were so greatly admired by Josephus. This point is particularly stressed by Josephus' statement that among the Essenes any word of theirs had greater force than an oath (*War* 2.135).

Zedekiah, would have justified the change of attitude toward Jehoiachin. And yet, one finds no such comment in Josephus' paraphrase any more than one finds it in the Bible itself.[15] We may suggest that if Josephus had referred to Jehoiachin's repentance this might have reminded the reader of the divine promise to David that he would establish David's dynasty forever (2 Samuel 7:11-16) and presumably of the traditional corollary that the Messiah would be descended from him. On the other hand, as we have noted, Josephus, being a descendant of the Hasmoneans (*Life* 2), would have regarded the Davidic dynasty as a rival to the claims of his own ancestors; and being a protégé of the Roman imperial family he could hardly highlight the expectation of the Messiah, who, according to tradition, would establish a truly independent state and hence would have to overthrow the Romans.[16]

5. *Summary*

Josephus' treatment of Jehoiachin is remarkable in that whereas the Bible states that he did evil in the sight of the L-rd, in Josephus he is described in completely opposite terms, namely as kind (χρηστός) and just (δίκαιος). That these two epithets are indeed extremely complimentary may be seen in that they are used of the prophet Samuel, King Hezekiah, the high priest Jehoiada, King Zedekiah, and Nehemiah. The ascription of the quality of kindness is particularly significant for apologetic purposes because the Jews had been accused by several intellectuals of hating mankind. It is

---

[15] Begg (1986, 49-56) notes that the biblical narrative says nothing about Jehoiachin's repentance (2 Kings 25:27-30). He also remarks on the significance of the fact that the Bible says nothing about any role of G-d in Jehoiachin's release from captivity. Granowski (1992, 173-88) concludes that the narrative, as read in the light of the story of G-d calling Abraham out of the land of the Chaldaeans (Genesis 11), as well as the account of the imprisonment and later exaltation of Joseph (Genesis 40-41) and of David's beneficent gesture toward Mephibosheth (2 Samuel 9), is deliberately ambiguous, rather than merely negative.

[16] In his portrait of Joram of Judah, as Begg (1993-94, 327-28) has indicated, Josephus likewise is careful not to ruffle Roman sensitivities with regard to Jewish messianism. Thus in both 2 Kings 8:19 and 2 Chronicles 21:7 we read of G-d's promise to "give a lamp to him [David] and to his sons forever," whereas Josephus (*Ant.* 9.96) says merely that G-d, because of His convenant with David, did not wish utterly to destroy his line, with no mention of the "everlasting lamp," which would clearly imply a resurrection of a Jewish state.

likewise significant that it is this quality that the Emperor Vespasian is said to have shown toward Josephus himself.

Josephus clearly had a vested interest in his presentation of the events leading to the destruction of the First Temple, inasmuch as he saw there a striking parallel to the events preceding the destruction of the Second Temple in his own day. He consequently felt a special need to defend Jehoiachin's decision to surrender to the enemy and devotes a considerable amount of space to this as compared with the biblical text; and, very significantly, in the one place in the *Jewish War* where he refers to this period he recalls the example of Jehoiachin as a noble precedent in seeking to spare his country and to save the Temple from destruction.

As he does in his treatment of Gedaliah and, of course, in his own surrender to the Romans, Josephus regards Jehoiachin's surrender as a matter of military necessity. In this Josephus may well have been aware of the rabbinic tradition, which likewise rehabilitates Jehoiachin completely. However, whereas the rabbis stress that it was his suffering that led Jehoiachin to repent, thus justifying their reversal of the biblical judgment upon him, Josephus mentions no such action by Jehoiachin, perhaps because to have done so might have led the reader to recall G-d's promise to David that his dynasty would last forever, as well as the prophecy that the Messiah would be descended from David, whereas Josephus himself was descended from the rival dynasty of the Hasmoneans and, as a protégé of the Romans, avoids mention of the concept of the Messiah, since, according to tradition, a major achievement of the Messiah was to establish a completely independent Jewish state and hence, in the context of Josephus' own day, was to overthrow the Roman empire.

CHAPTER THIRTY

ZEDEKIAH

1. *Introduction: The Problem in Josephus' Portrait of Zedekiah*

Normally, in his portraits of biblical figures, Josephus either enhances or diminishes their virtues or conversely exaggerates or diminishes their vices. Thus he enhances the virtues of Abraham, Isaac, Jacob, Joseph, Moses, Joshua, Gideon, Samson, Samuel, Saul, David, Solomon, Elisha, Jehoshaphat, Jonah, Josiah, Gedaliah, Daniel, Nehemiah, and Esther. On the other hand, he diminishes those of Deborah, Hezekiah, and Ezra. Again, he exaggerates the vices of Joab, Absalom, and Jeroboam, while he diminishes the vices of the Egyptian Pharaohs, Balaam, Ahab, Jehoram king of Israel, and Manasseh.

For his portrait of Zedekiah, Josephus (*Ant.* 10-102-54) appears to have consulted a number of passages in the Bible (2 Kings 24:17-25:12, 2 Chronicles 36:10-14, Jeremiah 34:1-22, 37:1-39:10, 52:1-16).[1] Here, however, he was confronted with a stark dilemma. On the one hand, the Bible asserts that Zedekiah did what was evil in the sight of the L-rd, like all that Jehoiakim had done (2 Kings 24:19), that he did not humble himself before the prophet Jeremiah (2 Chronicles 36:12), and that he hardened his heart against turning to the L-rd (2 Chronicles 36:13).

On the other hand, Zedekiah shows pity for Jeremiah in instructing Ebed-melech the Ethiopian to rescue him from the cistern into which he had been lowered (Jeremiah 38:10). Furthermore, he makes a covenant, quite clearly approved of by Jeremiah, with all the people in Jerusalem that everyone should set free his Hebrew slaves (Jeremiah 34:8-11).

The rabbinic tradition likewise contains contradictory traditions about Zedekiah. Thus, on the one hand, he is criticized for the egregious crime of swearing falsely, inasmuch as we are told that

---

[1] I have approached this study of Zedekiah independently of Begg (1989b, 96-104), who presents a fine, systematic comparison of Josephus' version with the actual texts of the various biblical passages which he is paraphrasing but who is less concerned with the rationale of Josephus' modifications.

despite the fact that he had sworn fealty to Nebuchadnezzar on a Torah scroll, as demanded by him, he nevertheless rebelled against him (*Pesiqta Rabbati* 26.3). He is likewise condemned for his faithlessness in not abiding by an oath by the name of Heaven which Nebuchadnezzar had made him take not to reveal that he had seen the latter eating flesh from a living hare (*Nedarim* 65a, *Tanḥuma B*, Exodus 33).[2] Thus Nebuchadnezzar could justify his punishment of Zedekiah because, as he put it, Zedekiah had sinned against the laws of both G-d and the state (*Pesiqta Rabbati* 26.6). There is a tradition of unknown origin reported by the eleventh-century commentator Rashi (on 2 Kings 25:4) that because of his unfaithfulness to his oath Zedekiah was punished in a most unusual way: while he was attempting to escape through a cave which extended from his house in Jerusalem to Jericho, G-d sent a deer into the Babylonian camp; and while pursuing that animal the Babylonian soldiers came to the opening of the cave precisely when Zedekiah was leaving it.[3]

On the other hand, the rabbinic tradition also recalls Zedekiah's virtues. Thus, Rabbi Eleazar ben Azariah is quoted as saying that because he had arranged to have the prophet Jeremiah lifted from the mire (Jeremiah 38:10), he was deemed worthy to be rewarded by dying in peace (Jeremiah 34:5) and to outlive Nebuchadnezzar himself (*Mo'ed Qatan* 28b). Much more positive is the statement, in connection with the discussion as to whether a given generation follows its leader or vice versa, that Zedekiah is an example of the leader who was virtuous, whereas his generation was not (*'Arakin* 17a). The third-century Rabbi Joḥanan declares, on the authority of the second-century Rabbi Simeon bar Yoḥai, that so wicked was the generation of Zedekiah that G-d was determined to reduce the world to formlessness and emptiness, but that when he considered Zedekiah his anger subsided (*Sanhedrin* 103a). To be sure, the

---

[2] According to the version in *Nedarim* 65a, Zedekiah had arranged to have himself absolved of his oath before disclosing that Nebuchadnezzar had eaten flesh from the living hare. The Talmud then presents a scenario in which Nebuchadnezzar, after learning that he was being derided, had the Sanhedrin and Zedekiah brought before him. When the Sanhedrin declared that Zedekiah had been absolved of his oath, Nebuchadnezzar asked whether one may be absolved of an oath when the object of the oath is not present. Thereupon the Sanhedrin, its legal incompetence thus revealed, was deposed.

[3] Zedekiah is likewise presented in a negative light in a Jeremiah apocryphon. See Mingana and Harris (1927, 329-42, 352-95); and Kuhn (1970, 93-135, 291-350).

Talmud notes an apparent contradiction by citing the passage that Zedekiah did what was evil in the sight of G-d (2 Kings 24:19); but Rabbi Joḥanan explains this by remarking that he could have stemmed the evil of others but did not (*Sanhedrin* 103a).[4] Indeed, the Talmud refers to him as the righteous Zedekiah and asks what he could have done on behalf of the wicked Nebuchadnezzar (*Shabbat* 149b). Likewise, he is listed as one of the eight princes among men, together with Jesse, Saul, Samuel, Amos, Zephaniah, the Messiah, and Elijah (*Sukkah* 52b). To be placed in such company is surely a high compliment. Great was the mourning when he died, and the elegy over him was: "Alas, that King Zedekiah has died, he who quaffed the lees which all the generations before him had accumulated" (*Seder Olam Rabbah* 28).

This same positive portrayal of Zedekiah appears to be reflected in several fragments discovered at Qumran near the Dead Sea and soon to be published jointly by John Strugnell and Erik Larson (4Q470).[5] One of these fragments describes the making of a covenant, through the agency of the angel Michael, between G-d and a certain Zedekiah, whom the editors identify, most persuasively, with the last king of Judah. The fact that the covenant involves both observing the Torah and causing others to observe it is an indication that the fragment looks most favorably upon the figure of Zedekiah.

2. *Josephus' Portrait of Nebuchadnezzar*

A clue to Josephus' attitude toward Zedekiah in not abiding by his oath to Nebuchadnezzar and in rebelling against him may be seen in Josephus' remarks about Nebuchadnezzar himself. One would have thought that Josephus would be strongly critical of Nebuchadnezzar as the person responsible for the destruction of the First Temple, but apparently he saw an analogy between Nebuchadnezzar, the destroyer of the First Temple, and Titus, the destroyer of the Second Temple, to whom he was so much indebted.

The rabbis frequently refer to Nebuchadnezzar as "the wicked

---

[4] Indeed, there is a tradition that the reason why the Jews went into captivity was that they had no excuse for their sinfulness, inasmuch as their king was so pious (2 Baruch 1:3).

[5] For a summary see Larson (1994, 210-28).

one" (e.g., *Berakot* 57b, *Shabbat* 149b). To show their feeling of utter disgust for him they mention that he ate the flesh of a hare while it was still alive (*Nedarim* 65a) and that he forced subject kings to have homosexual relations with him (*Shabbat* 149b). He is said to have killed numerous Jewish exiles in Babylonia (*Sanhedrin* 92b). Furthermore, he is reputed to have punished the Sanhedrin by having their hair tied to the tails of horses and by forcing them to run from Jerusalem to Lydda (*Midrash Lamentations Rabbah* 2.10.4).

Josephus, on the other hand, presents us a Nebuchadnezzar who is less chauvinistic in that, whereas the Bible states that the Jewish youth whom he captured were taught the learning and language of the Chaldeans (i.e. of the Babylonians) (Daniel 1:4), Josephus states that he had the youths taught the learning not only of the Chaldeans but also of the natives (*Ant.* 10.187). Moreover, from the biblical narrative we would deduce that Nebuchadnezzar was utterly arbitrary in insisting that his wise men not only interpret his dream but also recount the details of the dream itself to him (Daniel 2:5). Josephus' Nebuchadnezzar, however, is not so capricious in that he explains that he had forgotten his dream and therefore wished to have his wise men reconstruct it (*Ant.* 10.195).

Josephus also, to some degree, protects Nebuchadnezzar's reputation by omitting the cruel decree which the latter issued in which he declares that anyone who spoke a word against the Jewish G-d should be torn limb from limb (Daniel 3:29). To be sure, Josephus does include the story of the casting of Daniel's companions into the fiery furnace; but he does not specify, as does the Bible, that it was Nebuchadnezzar who ordered them to be immolated (Daniel 3:20); rather he uses the passive voice, "And so they were convicted and straightway thrown into the fire," without indicating who was actually responsible for convicting them (*Ant.* 10.214).

Undoubtedly the most gruesome scene in the Bible involving Nebuchadnezzar (well known through William Blake's painting) is the one in which, in fulfillment of his dream (Daniel 4:4-18), he takes to behaving like an animal, driven from men, with his hair like eagles' feathers and nails like a bird's claws, eating grass like an ox (Daniel 4:30). Such a depiction was hardly becoming a king; and Josephus, who greatly condenses the dream (*Ant.* 10.216), omits the statement that the dream had made Nebuchadnezzar afraid (Daniel 4:5). Moreover, he says merely that the king dreamt that he would make his home among the beasts rather than that he would actually take the form of a beast. Most significantly, he asserts that Nebuchadnezzar spent seven years in the wilderness without indicating his physical state during this time (*Ant.* 10.217). To be sure, Josephus' chief concern here was for his own credibility as an historian, but the net result is also that Nebuchadnezzar's reputation is protected.

In addition, Nebuchadnezzar appears in a better light in that he prays to G-d that he may recover his kingdom and does not wait to do so, as the Bible would have it (Daniel 4:31-34), until after his reason was restored to him (*Ant.* 10.217). Again, when the Bible recalls this episode, it once again paints a grotesque picture of an insane Nebuchadnezzar with the mind of a beast and dwelling among asses, eating grass like an ox (Daniel 5:21); Josephus, on the other hand, asserts merely that his way of life (δίαιταν) had been changed to that of beasts, but with no indication of his actual insanity (*Ant.* 10.242).

Moreover, realizing that even with the above changes he had not painted Nebuchadnezzar in the best light, Josephus apologizes by reminding the reader that at the very beginning of his history he had indicated that he was merely translating the Bible and had promised the reader that he would record the narrative as he had found it there without adding or subtracting anything (*Ant.* 10.218). He then seeks to confirm his own credibility by citing four extra-biblical non-Jewish sources – Berossus, Megasthenes, Diocles, and Philostratus (*Ant.* 10.219-27) – whom he claims to have consulted with regard to Nebuchadnezzar's deeds.

On the other hand, as with Zedekiah, the rabbis, to some degree, rehabilitate Nebuchadnezzar in remarking that he took pity on King Jehoiachin and on the Jewish exiles (*Midrash Leviticus Rabbah* 19.6, *Pesiqta Rabbati* 26.129). Likewise, he is represented as one of five persons who, because of their fear of G-d, were saved from the army of the Assyrians (*Sanhedrin* 95b). He showed his piety by rebuking Merodach Baladan for writing the name of King Hezekiah before that of G-d; and consequently he was rewarded by being given the rule of the entire world (*Song of Songs Rabbah* 3.4).

Finally, the reader might well wonder how Josephus could present sympathetically a king, Nebuchadnezzar, who, after putting out Zedekiah's eyes, kept him in prison. Josephus, at least to some degree, mitigates criticism of Nebuchadnezzar in this regard by remarking, in an extra-biblical addition that Nebuchadnezzar showed Zedekiah the honor of giving him a royal burial (*Ant.* 10.154).

3. *Josephus' Defense of Zedekiah*

Josephus does not avoid the biblical statement that Zedekiah did what was evil in the eyes of G-d (2 Kings 24:19), and, indeed, he declares that Zedekiah was contemptuous of justice (δικαίων) and duty (δέοντος) (*Ant.* 10.103); but he places the blame for this implicitly upon his impious (ἀσεβεῖς) contemporaries and upon the masses who had license to act as outrageously as they pleased (*ibid.*). Again, whereas in the Bible we hear at one point that Zedekiah did not humble himself before the prophet Jeremiah (2 Chronicles 36:12), Josephus shifts the blame to Zedekiah's advisers, inasmuch as, in an extra-biblical addition, he states that Jeremiah specifically urged him not to pay heed to these leaders, "because there were wicked men among them," and not to put faith in the false prophets who were predicting that the Babylonian king would never again make war on Jerusalem and that the Egyptians would take the field against him and would defeat him in battle (*Ant.* 10.104). Hence, it is clear that Zedekiah's impieties (ἀσεβείας) and lawless acts (παρανομίας), according to Josephus (*Ant.* 10.104), were the result of listening to this poor advice.

That it is Zedekiah's advisers who are really culpable, according to Josephus, is clear from the fact that whereas in the Bible Zedekiah tells his leaders that they may do to Jeremiah whatever they wish, without any indication of Zedekiah's own personal preference (Jeremiah 38:5), Josephus, in an extra-biblical addition, makes it clear that Zedekiah was personally opposed to the imprisonment of Jeremiah (*Ant.* 10.120); in fact, he goes out of his way to mention Zedekiah's goodness (χρηστότητος) and sense of justice (δικαιοσύνης), in apparent contradiction to his own earlier statement that Zedekiah was contemptuous of justice and duty (*Ant.* 10.103).[6] Likewise, when Zedekiah hands the prophet Jer-

---

[6] Begg (1989b, 100), citing this apparent contradiction, suggests that the discrepancy may perhaps be resolved by postulating that for Josephus Zedekiah is one whose instincts are right in seeking to avoid conflict but who is also derelict in justice and duty in failing to stand up to pressures from those intent on mis-

emiah over to his advisers (Jeremiah 38:5), Josephus, in a remarkable addition, states that, despite Jeremiah's dire predictions, Zedekiah, because of his goodness (χρηστότητος, "honesty," "kindness," "friendliness," "generosity") and sense of justice (δικαιοσύνης), was in no way personally (ἰδίᾳ) resentful (παρωξύνθη, "got angry," "became indignant")[7] and that it was only because he did not wish to incur the hostility of the leaders of the state at this critical moment that he gave them permission to do as they saw fit with the prophet (*Ant.* 10.120). Jeremiah, clearly echoing Josephus' own position, bids Zedekiah to take courage and to be assured that his fears are groundless, that neither he nor his family will suffer, and that he personally, as well as the Temple, will remain unharmed (*Ant.* 10.128). Josephus reiterates the same point, putting the finger of blame upon Zedekiah's friends, when he declares, in a remark not paralleled in his biblical source (2 Kings 24:19-20 or Jeremiah 37:1-2), that Zedekiah actually believed Jeremiah and agreed that everything that he said was true because he realized that it was to his interest to have faith in him, but that it was his friends who corrupted him and, winning him away from the prophet, led him wherever they pleased (*Ant.* 10.105).

Again, whereas in the Bible we hear only of "these men" (Jer-

---

leading him. Perhaps, we may add, a solution to this discrepancy may be found in the biblical statement, frequently used of the kings of Judah and Israel (e.g., with regard to Jehoiakim [2 Kings 24:5, 2 Chronicles 36:8]), referring the reader to the Book of the Kings of Israel and Judah for further information. Such additional information, whether in written or oral form, may have been available to the rabbis and Josephus. A striking parallel, this time between the Bible itself and Josephus, may be seen in Josephus' evaluation of King Jehoiachin, as we have remarked. Whereas the Bible (both 2 Kings 24:9 and 2 Chronicles 36:9, in both the Hebrew and Septuagint versions) states that Jehoiachin "did what was evil in the sight of the L-rd," Josephus describes him, as we have noted above, as kind (χρηστός) and just (δίκαιος). The fact that Josephus in this instance does not even attempt to present an explanation of his departure from the biblical text is an indication that he felt no qualms about such divergences, any more than did the rabbis in portraying Jehoiachin in a very positive light, as we see in the *Midrash Leviticus Rabbah* 19.6, where we are told that Jehoiachin was rewarded by having his sins forgiven because he kept the laws of marital purity while he was in exile. Above all, inasmuch as the rabbis valued study so highly, we may note the tremendous compliment accorded Jehoiachin in the tradition that Zedekiah's being exiled while Jehoiachin was alive was merciful because Jehoiachin was thus able to teach Torah to Zedekiah (*Gittin* 88a).

[7] Begg (1989b, 100) appositely notes that in this respect Zedekiah is differentiated by Josephus from those kings who show themselves resentful toward prophets, namely Jeroboam I (*Ant.* 8.233, vs. Jadon), Ahab (*Ant.* 8.392, vs. Micaiah), and Ahaziah (*Ant.* 9.24 vs. Elijah).

emiah 38:9), who are mentioned by name (Jeremiah 38:1) and are referred to as "princes" (Jeremiah 38:4, *ha-sarim*), in Josephus' extra-biblical addition the Ethiopian Ebed-melech blames "the friends and the leaders" (τοὺς φίλους καὶ τοὺς ἡγεμόνας) for doing wrong in sinking Jeremiah into mud and for dooming him to a death more painful than one by imprisonment in chains (*Ant.* 10.122). Significantly, whereas in the Bible when Ebed-melech takes the initiative in going to King Zedekiah to report that Jeremiah had been lowered into a cistern (Jeremiah 38:7-9), Zedekiah (Jeremiah 38:10) tells him merely to take three men with him and to lift him out of the cistern without giving specific details on how to do so, in Josephus we are told that as soon as he heard what had been done to Jeremiah, Zedekiah repented (μετανοήσας) of having delivered the prophet to the leaders (*Ant.* 10.123). He then specifically orders the Ethiopian to take thirty of the king's men with ropes, as well as whatever else he might think of use in rescuing the prophet, and to draw up Jeremiah with all haste. That Zedekiah was sincere in his repentance is clear from the statement that follows, namely that after Jeremiah had been rescued, Zedekiah sent for him secretly and asked him what message he could give him from G-d (*Ant.* 10.124), whereas in the Bible we read merely that King Zedekiah sent for Jeremiah the prophet (Jeremiah 38:14). And once again, at that meeting, in an extra-biblical addition, it is Zedekiah's friends who are blamed, this time by Jeremiah himself, for determining to destroy the prophet (*Ant.* 10.124), just as the false prophets are castigated by Jeremiah for deceiving Zedekiah into believing that Nebuchadnezzar would not march against him.[8]

At this point the reader might well ask why Zedekiah followed the advice of his friends when not only Jeremiah but also Ezekiel had prophesied that the city of Jerusalem would be captured and that Zedekiah himself would be taken captive. Josephus, clearly aware of this possible objection, adds the extra-biblical explanation, unparalleled in his biblical source (Jeremiah 34:2-7 and

---

[8] Quite clearly Josephus, as a proud priest and as a member of the first of the twenty-four courses of priests (*Life* 1-2), was particularly concerned with the destruction of the Temple. Hence, whereas in the Bible Jeremiah, in the name of G-d, tells Zedekiah that if he will surrender to the Babylonians his life will be spared and the city will not be burned with fire (Jeremiah 38:17), Josephus adds also that the Temple will remain unharmed (*Ant.* 10.128).

Ezekiel 12:13), that although the prophecies of Jeremiah and
Ezekiel agreed with each other in all other respects, they differed
in that Ezekiel prophesied that Zedekiah would not see Babylon,
whereas Jeremiah had prophesied that Nebuchadnezzar would
take him there in chains (*Ant.* 10.106). Hence, Zedekiah was convinced that since they apparently contradicted each other they
could not both be right. As things turned out, of course, as
Josephus carefully notes, both were right, inasmuch as Zedekiah,
upon being captured, was blinded, on orders of Nebuchadnezzar,
and thus did not see Babylon, where he was taken, precisely as
Ezekiel had predicted (*Ant.* 10.141).

Again, upon Nebuchadnezzar's withdrawal from Jerusalem when
the Egyptian army comes to Zedekiah's aid, the blame is placed
upon Zedekiah's advisers, in this case the false prophets, who are
said, in an addition, not found in the parallel biblical passages (2
Kings 25:1, 2 Chronicles 36:17), to deceive Zedekiah by assuring
him that Nebuchadnezzar would not make war upon him again
and that his fellow Jews whom the latter had exiled to Babylonia
would return and would even bring back all the vessels which
Nebuchadnezzar had taken from the Temple (*Ant.* 10.111). Significantly, whereas in the Bible the word of G-d comes to Jeremiah and
no mention is made of his castigating Zedekiah's advisers (Jeremiah 37:6-8), in Josephus Jeremiah clearly exonerates the king
himself in insisting that the false prophets were doing the king a
wrong by deceiving him, since no good would come to them from
the Egyptians (*Ant.* 10.112). Josephus then adds the editorial comment, unparalleled in his biblical source (Jeremiah 37:11), that in
saying these things Jeremiah was believed by most of the people
but that these leaders and their impious associates ridiculed him
as though he were out of his mind (ὡς ἐξεστηκότα τῶν φρενῶν)
(*Ant.* 10.114).

The fact, moreover, that Josephus does not compare Zedekiah
with Jehoiakim, as does the Bible (2 Kings 24:19), is another indication that he sought to absolve him of blame. Similarly, Josephus,
in exonerating the otherwise wicked Ahab, puts more blame upon
Ahab's wife, Jezebel, since she is described as being the active and
bold partner in the marriage (*Ant.* 8.318). Thus, whereas the Bible declares that it was Ahab who erected an altar to Baal and who
made an Asherah grove of trees for idol-worship (1 Kings 16:32-
33), Josephus ascribes to her the building of the temple to Baal

and the planting of the Asherah grove, and adds that she appointed priests and false prophets to Baal (*Ant.* 8.318). Ahab's wickedness is then ascribed to the bad influences upon him of these priests and false prophets rather than to any innate wickedness on his part (*Ant.* 8.318).

One possible criticism of Zedekiah is that he allowed himself to become a mere subservient vassal of Nebuchadnezzar. That he did so is emphasized in the Bible in that when he is appointed king Nebuchadnezzar actually changes his name from Mattaniah to Zedekiah (2 Kings 24:17), such a change being a symbolic expression of Zedekiah's status as a vassal of Nebuchadnezzar. Josephus, eager to rehabilitate Zedekiah as a ruler of some independence, significantly omits this change of name.

One clear flaw in Zedekiah's character is that he violated the oath which he had given to Nebuchadnezzar to attempt no uprising and to show no friendliness to the Egyptians (2 Chronicles 36:13; *Ant.* 10.102, 10.138). We need not emphasize that for the Jews in general the inviolability of an oath was absolutely crucial (see Greenberg and Cohn 1971, 1295-1301). Zedekiah is likewise reproached, after his capture, by Nebuchadnezzar for his ingratitude (ἀχαριστίαν) in having first received the kingdom from Nebuchadnezzar, who had taken it away from Jehoiachin, and then having used his power against the one who had bestowed it upon him (*Ant.* 10.139).

But though an oath is normally inviolable, in this case Josephus is apparently reluctant to condemn Zedekiah, since, in a passage which occurs just before the above text and which is unparalleled in the biblical text (2 Kings 24:10), he notes that Nebuchadnezzar, after pledging not to inflict harm upon the city of Jerusalem and the family of King Jehoiakim if he would surrender them to the Babylonians, did not keep his pledge but proceeded to take captive all the young men and craftsmen in the city, as well as Jehoiakim and his family (*Ant.* 10.99-100). Thus Zedekiah's oath-breaking has a precedent in Nebuchadnezzar's own.

Even with regard to his flight from Jerusalem, Josephus rehabilitates Zedekiah. In the Bible we are told that the king, together with all his soldiers, fled when a breach was made in the city (2 Kings 25:4, Jeremiah 39:4). Josephus, on the other hand, notes, in the first place, that Zedekiah's primary concern was for the Temple, since it is only when he learns that the Temple had been entered by the enemy that he flees (*Ant.* 10.136); and, in the second place, it is Zedekiah who assumes the initiative to take his wives and children with him in his flight, as well as his officers and friends. Moreover, in order not to attack Zedekiah as a coward, whereas the Bible indicates that it was the Babylonian army that was responsible for the pursuit and capture of the king (2 Kings 25:8), Josephus puts the blame on the Jews who had earlier deserted to the Babylonians and who inform the Babylonians of Zedekiah's attempt to escape (*Ant.* 10.137). Again, when he is finally overtaken by the Babylonians, Josephus once again blames Zedekiah's friends in declaring that they actually abandoned him, "each one determined to save himself" (*Ant.* 10.137-38), whereas the Bible says that his army was scattered from him (Jeremiah 52:8), As a result, we are told, Zedekiah was left with only a few men, and the enemy consequently captured him. Significantly, whereas in the Bible the Babylonians slay the sons of Zedekiah (2 Kings 25:7), in Josephus' version Nebuchadnezzar orders not only his sons but also his friends to be put to death on the spot (*Ant.* 10.140).

It now appears clear from the Lachish Letters, dating from the period just before Nebuchadnezzar's conquest of Jerusalem, that Judah had close ties with Egypt (see Di Vito 1992, 126-28); moreover, the fact that Nebuchadnezzar besieged Tyre for thirteen years (*Ag. Ap.* 1.156) may indicate that Tyre had joined in the anti-Babylonian coalition. Though obviously Josephus, like Jeremiah, to whom he clearly likens himself,[9] viewed Zedekiah's uprising against Nebuchadnezzar as hopelessly foolish, nonetheless, especially in view of the fact that the Jews had been reproached with cowardice by such Jew-baiters as Apollonius Molon (*Ag. Ap.* 2.148) and that Josephus himself had been subjected to such a charge (*War* 3.358), he goes out of his way, in an extra-biblical remark, to note the tremendous energy (μετὰ πάσης...φιλοτιμίας)[10] which Nebuchadnezzar put into the siege (*Ant.* 10.116) and, by implication, the great courage exhibited by the Jews and their leader in resisting him. Likewise, in a passage not paralleled in his biblical source (2 Kings 25:3), Josephus remarks that those within the city

---

[9] See Daube 1980, 18-36; S. J. D. Cohen 1982, 366-81; Gray 1993, 72-74.

[10] Josephus uses similar language (πάσῃ φιλοτιμίᾳ) in describing the tremendous energy that King Solomon employed in adorning the Temple (*Ant.* 8.85) and (πάσης φιλοτιμίας) in referring to the great zeal with which Herod helped his subjects to recover from the famine which had afflicted them (*Ant.* 15.312).

bore the siege by Nebuchadnezzar with courage and spirit, and that they did not weaken despite famine and disease (*Ant.* 10.132). On the contrary, he adds, in a further unparalleled passage, that the defenders were not dismayed by the devices and engines of war of the Babylonians but, on the contrary, devised engines of their own to counter the enemy, so that the contest came down to be one of cleverness and skill (*Ant.* 10.132-34).

4. *Summary*

In Josephus, as in the New Testament, in Pseudepigraphic literature, and in the rabbinic corpus, we find parallels being drawn between the events leading up to the destruction of the First and Second Temples.

Josephus, like the Talmudic rabbis, was confronted with a real problem in that the Bible itself seems to report both positive and negative acts of Zedekiah, the last king of Judah. We may see something of Josephus' purpose when we examine his portrait of Nebuchadnezzar, the destroyer of the First Temple; here Josephus, influenced by the Babylonian's parallel with Titus, the destroyer of the Second Temple, attempts, to some degree, to rehabilitate him.

In his defense of Zedekiah, Josephus insists on blaming not Zedekiah, whom he actually describes as good and just, but his wicked advisers, just as he blames the advisers of other biblical personalities, notably Ahab and Darius, whom he seeks to redeem. He further stresses that Zedekiah was opposed to incarcerating the prophet Jeremiah. Indeed, in Josephus' version Zedekiah repents of having turned Jeremiah over to his advisers and takes the lead in giving specific instructions concerning the rescue of the prophet. Josephus, moreover, apologizes for Zedekiah's failure to heed Jeremiah's counsel by explaining that he was misled by the fact that Jeremiah and the prophet Ezekiel gave apparently contradictory prophecies.

Josephus is careful, however, to avoid portraying Zedekiah as too subservient to Nebuchadnezzar, and so he omits the fact that Nebuchadnezzar actually changed Zedekiah's name. As for Zedekiah's failure to keep the oath of fealty that he had pledged to Nebuchadnezzar – a very serious charge, especially in Jewish eyes – Josephus, to some degree at least, exonerates him by noting that Nebuchadnezzar, after pledging not to inflict harm upon the city of Jerusalem and the family of King Jehoiakim if he would surrender them to him, did not keep his pledge but proceeded to take captive all the young men and craftsmen in the city, as well as Jehoiakim and his family.

Moreover, Josephus stresses the bravery of Zedekiah in adding that he fled Jerusalem only when he learned that the Babylonians had entered the Temple itself and then only with his wives and children, together with his officers and friends. In a further effort to uphold Zedekiah's bravery, Josephus blames those who had deserted to the enemy and who had informed the Babylonians of Zedekiah's attempt to escape. Finally, in still another extra-biblical detail, he has Zedekiah captured only when his friends abandon him.

CHAPTER THIRTY-ONE

GEDALIAH

1. Introduction

When one examines the six fast days in the present-day Jewish calendar one notes that three of them (the Tenth of Tevet, the Seventeenth of Tammuz, and the Ninth of Av) are connected with the destruction of the Temple in Jerusalem. The Day of Atonement is based on Leviticus 16:29, 23:27, and Numbers 29:7, while the Fast of Esther is based on Esther 4:16. The most unusual of these fast days is the Fast of Gedaliah, which is nowhere mentioned as such in the Bible, though it is said to be alluded to by Zechariah's reference to the fast of the seventh month (8:19) (*Rosh Hashanah* 18b). It is significant that when the rabbis comment on this fast day they compare it with the three fast days connected with the destruction of the Temple, since, they say, "the death of the righteous is put on a level with the burning of the House of our G-d." One is naturally led to wonder why the assassination of a minor Jewish official, serving as the apparent puppet governor, a collaborator no less, of a foreign conqueror king – indeed, the very king, Nebuchadnezzar, responsible for the destruction of the Temple itself –, should occasion such outpouring of mourning that it ended up becoming part of the religious calendar forever.

That Josephus should evince great interest in Gedaliah should occasion no surprise since he apparently recognized in him a predecessor of himself, just as he did with Joseph, Jeremiah, Daniel, Esther, and Mordecai, all of whom had prophetic powers (such as he claimed for himself) and all of whom suffered for their people (see Daube 1980, 18-36). The analogy with Gedaliah is perhaps the closest of all, however, inasmuch as both he and Josephus advocated subservience to the foreign power and an end to the desire for an independent state.

How to justify such subservience, whether in the case of Gedaliah or in his own, must have presented a real problem to Josephus. His solution is that it was a matter of military necessity. Thus, whereas the Bible indicates that Gedaliah was appointed by King

Nebuchadnezzar of Babylon (2 Kings 25:22, Jeremiah 40:7), in Josephus' version the appointment is made by Nebuchadnezzar's general Nabuzardanes (*Ant.* 10.155). Moreover, that there was no military possibility of continuing the war against Nebuchadnezzar is clear from Josephus' statement that those who were left in Judaea and over whom Gedaliah was made governor were the poor (so also Jeremiah 40:7)[1] and the deserters (Josephus' addition) (*ibid.*).

2. *Gedaliah's Virtues*

When Josephus first introduces us to Moses' father Amram, his initial remark is that he was a Hebrew "of noble birth" (εὖ γεγονότων) (*Ant.* 2.210). Josephus likewise, in a detail not found in the Bible (1 Samuel 9:1), speaks of the good birth (εὖ γεγονώς) of Kish, the father of Saul (*Ant.* 6.45). Precisely the same phrase (εὖ γεγονότων) is found, in an extra-biblical addition, with reference to Gedaliah's noble family (*Ant.* 10.155).

It is significant that when Gedaliah is first introduced to the reader he is described, in extra-biblical additions, as kind (ἐπιεικῆ, "moderate," "suitable," "considerate," "understanding," "generous," "magnanimous," "genial," "friendly," "gentle," "peaceable") and just (δίκαιον) (*Ant.* 10.155). Elsewhere Gedaliah is characterized as acting φιλανθρώπως ("humanely," "kindly," "friendly," "magnanimously," "high-mindedly," "graciously," "affably," "hospitably") (*Ant.* 10.163), as possessing φιλανθρωπία ("humanity," "kindliness," "friendliness," *Ant.* 10.164), as being friendly (φιλοφρονούμενος (*Ant.* 10.168), and as exhibiting the quality of kindness (χρηστότης, "honesty," "friendliness," "generosity," *Ant.* 10.164).

Of his biblical figures Josephus applies the terms φιλανθρωπία and φιλάνθρωπος most frequently to David (*Ant.* 6.299, 6.304, 7.118, 7.184, 7.391); hence we may infer that this application of these terms to Gedaliah is a tremendous compliment. These terms are likewise employed by Josephus in calling attention to the hu-

---

[1] Generally speaking, Josephus in his *Antiquities* follows the Greek biblical text. Here, however, he quite clearly is following the Hebrew text, inasmuch as the Greek version of this passage does not mention the poor and says only that the Babylonians committed to Gedaliah the men and their wives.

manity of the Jewish law (*Ag. Ap.* 2.146, 2.213, 2.261). Likewise, the term χρηστότης is used to characterize the laws of the Torah (*Ant.* 4.237, 266).

In view of the extraordinary brevity of the passage in Josephus about Gedaliah the repetition concerning his quality of kindness or friendliness is striking. It is surely significant that the two qualities, ἐπιεικής and δίκαιος, ascribed to Gedaliah when he is first mentioned by Josephus, are singled out in Josephus' encomium of David (*Ant.* 7.391). Indeed, we may note that two of Gedaliah's qualities, being ἐπιεικής and χρηστός, are found in juxtaposition in connection with two of the personalities most admired by Josephus, namely Samuel (*Ant.* 6.92) and David (*Ant.* 7.391). Likewise, the qualities of being χρηστός and δίκαιος are found, we recall, in juxtaposition in connection with several personalities highly esteemed by Josephus, namely Jehonadab (*Ant.* 9.133), Jehoiada (*Ant.* 9.166), Hezekiah (9.260), Jehoiachin (*Ant.* 10.100), Nehemiah (*Ant.* 11.183), and Ptolemy Philometor (*Ant.* 13.114). Similarly, the qualities of being ἐπιεικής and φιλάνθρωπος are found in juxtaposition as the virtues which the Roman Emperor Claudius, in his edict addressed to the rest of the world, sought to have the Jews continue to exemplify (*Ant.* 19.290).

The chief quality of a ruler is to be concerned for the care of his subjects, and it is this trait which is singled out by Josephus in connection with Gedaliah. Thus, whereas the Bible is content merely to state that the captain of the Babylonian guard gave the prophet Jeremiah an allowance of food and a present and then let him go (Jeremiah 40:5), in Josephus the Babylonian general contacts Gedaliah and asks him, presumably confident that his instructions would be obeyed, to take all possible care (πρόνοιαν, "carefulness," "careful attention," "concern," "forethought," "consideration") of Jeremiah and to provide him with everything that he might possibly need (*Ant.* 10.157). If the Babylonian commander felt that Gedaliah could be trusted to take care of Jeremiah, he probably also felt confident that Gedaliah could similarly be trusted to take care of the Judaeans as a whole.

3. *Contemporary Associations*

It is significant to note in what context Josephus elsewhere uses the same epithets that he applies to Gedaliah. Thus we find that the epithet φιλάνθρωπος and its adverb φιλανθρώπως are employed four times in connection with Titus (*War* 4.96, 5.335, 6.324, and 7.107) and twice of Vespasian (*War* 6.340, 341). Moreover, the corresponding noun, φιλανθρωπία, is used with reference to the friendliness of the Romans to the Jews (*Ant.* 14.267), as seen in the many decrees which the Romans issued on behalf of the Jews, in Augustus' treatment of Herod's sons (*Ant.* 15.343) and in Tiberius' courteous reply to Agrippa (*Ant.* 18.162). The particular import of this term may be discerned in Titus' address to the revolutionaries in calling attention to the humanity displayed by the Romans toward the Jews (*War* 6.333), as well as in Agrippa's speech to them emphasizing the same point (*War* 2.399). Indeed, it is almost as if Gedaliah is a "stand-in" for Josephus, and as if Ishmael, who is responsible for the plot to assassinate Gedaliah, is a "stand-in" for Josephus' great enemy, John of Gischala; in fact, we find that John of Gischala hypocritically affects Gedaliah's very quality of humanity (ὑποκριτὴς φιλανθρωπίας) (*War* 2.587). Furthermore, we find the terms φιλοφρονούμενος (*War* 3.408) and χρηστότης (*Life* 423) used of Vespasian's treatment of Josephus himself.

Likewise, we note that Josephus (*Ant.* 10.160), in his description of Ishmael the son of Nethaniah, who was responsible for the assassination of Gedaliah, refers to him as wicked (πονηρός) and very crafty (δολιώτατος). It is no coincidence that these epithets are used by him on a number of occasions of John of Gischala, Josephus' bitter rival. Thus Josephus remarks that John, aspiring to despotic power, began to disdain the position of mere equality in honors with his peers and gathered around himself a group of the more depraved (πονηροτέρων) (*War* 4.389). Again, speaking of the rivalry between John and another revolutionary, Simon bar Giora, Josephus says, quite cynically, that the one who gave his comrades no share in the proceeds from the miseries of others was ranked a scurvy villain (πονηρός) (*War* 5.441). Indeed, Josephus remarks that the people of Galilee, knowing that John was a perjured villain (πονηρός), pressured Josephus to lead them against him (*Life* 102). In point of fact, however, it was no easy matter to shake off one who had gained such influence through his villainy (πονηρίας, *War* 4.213).

As to Ishmael's trickery, we may note that Josephus' source (Jeremiah 40.8), when first mentioning Ishmael, says nothing about this quality of his. Josephus, however, as we have noted, describes him as wicked and very crafty (*Ant.* 10.161), almost the exact terms which he uses of John of Gischala, whom he calls the most unscrupulous (πανουργότατος) and most crafty (δολιώτατος) of all who have ever gained notoriety by such infamous (πονηρεύμασιν) means (*War* 2.585). Likewise, he describes John as a man of extreme cunning (δολιώτατος) who carried in his breast an insatiate passion for despotic power and who had long been plotting against the state (*War* 4.208).[2]

Josephus assigns the same quality of villainy to his great literary rival, Justus of Tiberias. Thus, using the well-known rhetorical device of praeteritio, Josephus remarks that while veracity is incumbent upon a historian, he is nonetheless at liberty to refrain from harsh scrutiny of the misdeeds (πονηρίας) of individuals such as Justus, not from any partiality for the offenders but because of his own moderation (*Life* 339).

Josephus also paints the other revolutionary groups of his own time with the same brush of villainy. Indeed, he remarks, that period had somehow become so prolific of crime (πονηρίας) of every description among the Jews that no deed of iniquity was left unperpetrated (*War* 7.259). In particular, he notes that the Sicarii only oppressed the more those who in righteous self-defense reproached them with their villainy (πονηρίαν) (*War* 7.258). As for the followers of Simon bar Giora, they considered it an act of petty malice (πονηρίας) to do injury to a foreigner (*War* 7.266).

Likewise, in his description of the plot to assassinate Gedaliah, Josephus clearly has John of Gischala in mind. In the biblical version, when Johanan the son of Kareah warns him of the plot and suggests a preemptive strike against Ishmael, Gedaliah's reply is to forbid such a strike, "for you are speaking falsely of Ishmael" (Jeremiah 40:16). Josephus develops the scene considerably. In the first place, he adds a motive for the plot (*Ant.* 10.164), namely Ishmael's ambition to rule over the Israelites, inasmuch as he was of royal descent. In his reply to Johanan Gedaliah notes that Ishmael had been well treated by him and that he could not therefore believe that a person who had not wanted for anything in the midst of such scarcity should be so base (πονηρόν) and ungrate-

---

[2] Thackeray (1929, 119-20) aptly suggests that this passage recalls Sallust's portrait of Catiline (*De Catilinae Coniuratione* 5), where *subdolus* is the equivalent of δολιώτατος.

ful (ἀνόσιον, "unholy," "wicked") toward his benefactor; rather, he says, in his trusting naiveté, it would be a wicked thing in itself for such a person not to seek to save him if he were plotted against. Finally, even if it were true that a plot was being hatched to assassinate him, it would be better to die thus than to put to death a man who had take refuge with him and had indeed entrusted his very life to him (*Ant.* 10.166-67).

The episode is clearly reminiscent of John of Gischala's plot against Josephus. There, too, envy is said to be the motive (*Life* 85), though we may suspect that an additional, and perhaps primary, motive on Ishmael's part was to overthrow Babylonian rule. Likewise, Josephus has no suspicion of any malign (πονηρόν) intention; indeed, he does not prevent John's coming but even goes so far as to write separate letters to those to whom he had entrusted the administration of Tiberias, directing them to show him proper hospitality (*Life* 86).

Josephus likewise elaborates and renders much more dramatic the scene in which Gedaliah entertains Ishmael. In the biblical version we read that Ishmael came with ten men to Gedaliah and that they ate bread together (Jeremiah 41:1), whereupon Ishmael and his cohorts struck down Gedaliah and killed him. As Josephus tells it, Gedaliah entertained Ishmael and his friends with a splendid banquet and presents, and in his cordial reception (φιλοφρονούμενος) of Ishamel and those with him actually went so far as to become drunk (*Ant.* 10.168). Thereupon, seeing that Gedaliah had sunk into unconsciousness and a drunken sleep, Ishmael sprang up with his ten friends and slaughtered Gedaliah, together with those who were reclining with him at the banquet table (*Ant.* 10.168). The fact that the slaughter takes place at night makes it all the more dramatic.

4. *Why the Whitewash of Gedaliah?*

We may wonder why Gedaliah was appointed as governor in the first place. Neither the Bible nor Josephus gives us any clue. We may suggest, however, as does Ginzberg, that a hint may be found at the beginning of the *Apocalypse of Daniel*, where we read that it was Gedaliah who told Nebuchadnezzar's general Nebuzaraden the cause of the seething blood in the Temple, namely that this was the blood of the prophet Zechariah, who had been murdered by the Judaeans because he had prophesied the destruction of the Temple; consequently, Gedaliah won the favor of Nebuzaraden and was later appointed governor of Judaea (Ginzberg 1928, 6:396, n. 30). Josephus, as we have indicated, was acquainted with much rabbinic tradition; his omission of such a tradition may well have been deliberate since it would cast a cloud over Gedaliah as an active collaborator with the enemy.

Gedaliah's position, vis-à-vis the Babylonians at the time of the destruction of the First Temple, was more or less replicated by Josephus at the time of the destruction of the Second Temple, namely, to accept subservience to the superpower in return for religious autonomy. In this he agreed with the stance adopted by the rabbinic leadership, at least as exemplified by Johanan ben Zakkai (*Gittin* 56a-b); Josephus' aggrandizing the role of Gedaliah likewise finds a parallel in the rabbis' declaring the day of his assassination a day of national mourning comparable to the fast days commemorating the events leading to and including the destruction of the Temple.

In the biblical version (Jeremiah 40:9) Gedaliah tells the Judaean delegation that they should not be afraid to serve the Babylonians and that if they do they will prosper. Josephus has Gedaliah spell out his assurance that if anyone molested them they would find him ready to help (*Ant.* 10.161). Moreover, he takes the initiative, not noted in the Bible, of advising his people to settle down in whatever cities they chose and to send others along with their own men to rebuild the foundations there. Furthermore, like a latter-day Joseph he warns the people, while there is still time, to prepare stores of food in the summer in order to have food throughout the winter (*Ant.* 10.162).

But Gedaliah is not merely a governor, as in the Bible (Jeremiah 40:11), obeying the commands of the king who appointed him. In Josephus' version he receives the fugitives with friendliness (φιλανθρώπως) (*Ant.* 10.163). Indeed, the returnees are so impressed[3] with his kindness (χρηστότητα) and friendliness (φιλανθρωπίαν) that they develop a very great affection (ὑπερηγάπησαν) for him, which prompts Johanan and others to warn him of the plot of Ishmael (*Ant.* 10.164). Moreover, we see Gedaliah's popularity in

---

[3] The received text reads "When they observed (the nature of) the land;" but Naber suggests reading χάριν ("graciousness") for χώραν, "land."

that whereas, according to the account in Jeremiah (41:5), after the murder of Gedaliah eighty men appear in mourning for the destroyed Temple, Josephus depicts them as coming with gifts for Gedaliah (*Ant.* 10.170).

Josephus' identification with Gedaliah's policy of subservience to the superpower should be understood in the light of his sensitivity to the charge that the Jews constituted a nation within a nation whose allegiance, wherever they were scattered, was to an independent state in the Land of Israel and hence that they would forever be subversive until their return from captivity. In effect, Josephus, unlike the Fourth Philosophy, whose adherents fought the Romans during the Great War of 66-74, did not regard nationhood as the *sine qua non* of Judaism; a policy such as that advocated by Gedaliah would, he believed, bring peace and prosperity to the Jews.

5. *"Improvements" in the Story: Elimination of Improbabilities*

True, Gedaliah shows his magnanimity in refusing to listen to the advice of Johanan and, by a preemptive strike, to murder Ishmael in order to abort the latter's plan to murder Gedaliah (Jeremiah 40:15-16; *Ant.* 10.164-67). But, after all, Gedaliah had a duty not only to protect himself but also those who had taken refuge with him (*Ant.* 10.161). Moreover, how could Ishmael with ten men assassinate, without any apparent resistance, Gedaliah and all those who were with him? The Bible (Jeremiah 41:2-3) offers no explanation. Josephus, however, in an extra-biblical addition, offers an explanation, namely that the reception which Gedaliah gave to Ishmael and his men at Mizpah was not merely one at which they ate bread together (Jeremiah 41:1) but rather was a lavish banquet at which Gedaliah went so far as to become drunk (*Ant.* 10.168). "Seeing him in this condition, sunken into unconsciousness and a drunken sleep" (*Ant.* 10.169), Ishmael and his ten friends had no problem in dispatching Gedaliah and those reclining with him at the banquet table (so Begg 1994, 33).

Another problem arises in connection with the biblical account of what happened on the day after the murder of Gedaliah. According to the Bible, before anyone had learned of the murder of Gedaliah, eighty men arrived at Mizpah from Shechem, Shiloh, and Samaria, with beards shaved, clothes torn, and bodies gashed, bringing cereal offerings and incense for the Temple in Jerusalem.

Ishmael, weeping, invited them to see Gedaliah, whereupon he and the men with him slew the visitors, except for ten who offered stores of food (Jeremiah 41:4-8). Several problems immediately present themselves. In the first place, why should Samaritans be arriving to present offerings in the Temple in Jerusalem, which had been destroyed by the Babylonians and when, in any case, their sacred temple was on Mount Gerizim?[4] Secondly, why should they be coming to Mizpah when their destination is Jerusalem? Thirdly, why are they in mourning if they do not yet know of the murder of Gedaliah? Fourthly, why does Ishmael weep, as if in mourning, when his plan is to deceive them? Josephus resolves these problems by not specifying that the visitors were from Samaria but rather, vaguely, from the country (ἀπὸ τῆς χώρας). He gives no indication that their purpose in coming is to present offerings to the Temple; rather, they have come with gifts for Gedaliah, since they did not know what had happened to him. There is no indication that they are in mourning, nor does Ishmael greet them with weeping (*Ant.* 10.170) (see Begg 1994, 33-35).

6. *Summary*

In his portrayal of Gedaliah Josephus paints a self-portrait of one who, like himself, advocated subservience to a foreign power out of military necessity.

He aggrandizes Gedaliah's noble ancestry and, above all, describes him as kind and just, qualities that he ascribes to Samuel and David among others. Moreover, he singles out his concern for his subjects.

Josephus' Gedaliah has considerable contemporary associations. In particular, the epithet φιλάνθρωπος, which he applies to Gedaliah, is employed several times by him in connection with his own

---

[4] Begg (1994, 34 n.33) notes several attempts by scholars to understand "the house of the L-rd" (Jeremiah 41:5) as referring not to the Temple in Jerusalem but rather to a place in Mizpah. But it is hard to believe that the author of the Book of Jeremiah would have used the phrase "house of the L-rd" to refer to any temple other than the one in Jerusalem. Moreover, the very fact that Josephus makes no mention of the "house of the L-rd" would appear to indicate that he understood the phrase to refer to the Temple in Jerusalem and, realizing the problem involved, resolved it by omitting all reference to it (*Ant.* 10.170).

patrons, Titus and Vespasian. Just as Gedaliah emerges as a "stand-in" for Josephus, so his assassin, Ishmael, is described as wicked and very crafty, almost the exact terms used by Josephus to delineate his great enemy, John of Gischala. In particular, in his description of the plot to assassinate Gedaliah, Josephus has in mind John's plot against himself. In both cases the victim has no suspicion of malign intent, and in both cases envy is the motive.

Finally, Josephus tidies the account. Thus, whereas the biblical narrative raises questions as to how Gedaliah and his followers could have been dispatched so easily, Josephus explains that at the lavish banquet which they gave for Ishmael, Gedaliah became drunk. As to the aftermath of the assassination, the visitors from Samaria, dressed in clothes of mourning, who have come with offerings for the Temple in Jerusalem have become visitors from the country who have come with gifts for Gedaliah, with no mention of their mourning garb.

CHAPTER THIRTY-TWO

EZRA

1. *Introduction: The Problem*

We might expect that Josephus would magnify the figure of Ezra,[1] inasmuch as the rabbis do elaborate on his tremendous achieve-

---

[1] There has been no substantial study of Josephus' treatment of Ezra hitherto. Rappaport (1930), who attempts to cite all midrashic parallels to Josephus, has nothing at all on Ezra. Likewise, Attridge (1976) has not a single reference to Ezra. The only works that even attempt to evaluate Josephus' treatment of Ezra are Treuenfels (1850, 693-98); Pohlmann (1970, 74-114; and Williamson (1977, 21-29). Treuenfels and especially Pohlmann are concerned with the relationship between Josephus and 1 Esdras and amply demonstrate, through a comparison of vocabulary and phraseology, especially in the documents which Josephus cites, that Josephus followed this source very closely, presumably because he was attracted to its more elegant Greek style, as suggested by Thackeray (1899, 759). Where there are differences these are due to Josephus' attempt to remove chronological discrepancies or repetitious material. Thackeray concludes that there is no evidence of embellishment on the basis of our Hebrew text of Ezra. Both he and Williamson are concerned with vocabulary and style rather than with content, and particularly with the question of the nature of the text of Ezra which was available to Josephus. Pohlmann, Williamson, and Thackeray, however, seem to be going too far when they insist that Josephus has used only the Greek text of 1 Esdras. That Josephus also knew the Hebrew text would seem evident from the fact that he knows the entire canon of the Bible, including Ezra-Nehemiah (*Ag. Ap.* 1.40). Moreover, 1 Esdras 8:66 (63) mentions twelve goats for a peace-offering among the sacrifices offered by Ezra, whereas Josephus clearly follows the Hebrew text here (Ezra 8:35) in mentioning twelve goats as a sin-offering (*Ant.* 11.137). Another instance where Josephus seems to be dependent upon the Hebrew text is in *Antiquities* 11.144, where he states that Ezra besought G-d, "who had preserved a seed and remnant out of their recent misfortune." Here 1 Esdras 1:78 remarks that "we still have a root and a name in the place of thy sanctuary" but says nothing of a remnant, whereas the Hebrew Ezra 9:8 specifically does mention a remnant. Hölscher (1916, 1953) argues that Josephus did not use the Bible as a direct source but rather a Hellenistic targum-like version with large-scale midrashic elements; but it seems unlikely that one who was born in Jerusalem and achieved, at least according to his own report, such a high degree of proficiency in the traditional texts, should not have used them directly for his paraphrase. In any case, as Pohlmann (91) has shown, Josephus' dependence upon 1 Esdras for his choice of words is striking, and there is almost nothing in his account that cannot be traced back directly to 1 Esdras. Hampel (1969) concludes that Josephus did not know Ezra-Nehemiah in either the Hebrew or Aramaic or even in Greek but rather used an unknown Jewish source, as well as an anti-Samaritan document; but Pohlmann's comparison of Josephus' version with 1 Esdras, phrase by phrase,

ments as chief priest, scholar, teacher, legislator, prophet, and holy man. Indeed, Ezra's work was probably as all-encompassing as that of Moses himself, since his ambitious aim was to rebuild Israel as the nation of twelve tribes, including even the Samaritans (see Koch 1974, 196).[2] We would also expect Josephus to give much more attention to Ezra in view of the latter's great knowledge of and general antagonism toward the Samaritans (see Feldman 1992a),[3] who, in turn, according to the Second Samaritan Chronicle, looked upon Ezra as their arch-enemy because he altered the script and contents of the Torah.

That, on the contrary, Ezra held much less interest for Josephus than several other biblical figures may be seen in the sheer amount of space which he devotes to him. Thus, in the portion of 1 Esdras 8-9 (Hebrew Ezra 7-10) which Josephus paraphrases (*Ant.* 11.121-58) there are 304 lines in Rahlfs' text (183 lines in the Hebrew version, chapters 7-10, corresponding to this). This gives a ratio of only .72 of Josephus to 1 Esdras and of 1.20 to the Hebrew text. Moreover, whereas such major biblical figures as Abraham, Isaac, Jacob, Joseph, Moses, Joshua, Saul, David, and Solomon are mentioned by Josephus on numerous occasions outside the pericope

---

convincingly shows that he has followed this as his main source. Ararat (1971) concludes that Ezra, 1 Esdras, Josephus' account of Ezra, and the legends of the rabbinic sages pertaining to the Persian era are all based upon a lost source which he calls the "Comprehensive Chronicle"; if so, it seems remarkable that no trace of this lost source has come down to us. Tuland (1966, 176-92) is concerned with the technical question of the names of the several Persian kings mentioned by Josephus and is critical of Josephus' corrections of the biblical sequences for the Persian kings. Also concerned with this question, though with a more positive view of it, is Emery (1987, 33-44). In any event, if, as Grabbe (1987, 231-46) claims, Josephus does not offer a consistent, clear account of the period and has confused his data, this applies to the chronology of the Persian kings but not to his narrative data concerning Ezra.

[2] To be sure, as M. Smith (1971, 122) has noted, beyond the traditions which are preserved in the Books of Chronicles and in 1 Esdras, Ezra cuts no great figure in early Jewish legend. Thus, for example, Ben Sira (49:11-13), in his list of heroes, does not mention him but rather praises Nehemiah; similarly, he is ignored by 2 Maccabees. However, by the time of Josephus, if we may judge from rabbinic literature, Ezra had come to be regarded as a key figure in Jewish history.

[3] A late rabbinic tradition recalls the total excommunication of the Samaritans, allegedly proclaimed by Ezra with great solemnity in the presence of three hundred priests, three hundred children, and three hundred scrolls of the Torah and to the accompaniment of three hundred trumpets (*Tanḥuma Vayeshev* 2 end, *Pirqe de-Rabbi Eliezer* 37 [38]).

devoted specifically to them, once Josephus completes his narrative of Ezra with mention of his death, he nowhere refers to him again.

2. *Ezra as Priest and Scribe in Rabbinic Tradition*

Ezra is said by the rabbis to have been of such stature that he would have been high priest even if Aaron himself were alive in his time (*Ecclesiastes Rabbah* 1.4).[4] Furthermore, we hear that he reached such a level of holiness that he was able to pronounce the Divine name "as it is written" (*Yoma* 69b).[5] Indeed, he is one of five men (Abraham, Moses, Aaron, Hezekiah, and Ezra) whose piety is especially extolled by the rabbis (*Midrash Psalms* on 105.2). In fact, the *Apocalypse of Ezra* (4 Ezra), written somewhere between 95 and 100 C.E. in Palestine, describes Ezra as communicating with angels and as receiving seven prophetic visions which summarize the whole course of human history up to his own day. There is a clear parallel here between Ezra and Moses, the receiver of biblical revelation, since in the last vision of this work Ezra, prior to his assumption into heaven, receives the twenty-four books of the Bible, together with seventy books of esoteric, apocalyptic lore. In particular, there is a parallel with Moses in that in the seventh vision he, like Moses, hears a voice from a thorn-bush warning him to guard the secrets that have just been revealed to him. Here, too, the process of revelation is said to take forty days; but whereas in the Bible it is G-d who reveals the Torah to Moses, in the *Apocalypse of Ezra* G-d's role is to bid Ezra to dictate to his scribes the history of the world since creation. Indeed, this work depicts Ezra as beseeching G-d that the holy spirit may descend upon him be-

---

[4] In fact, the Midrash is so convinced of Ezra's superior attainments as a priest that it feels compelled to explain why he remained in Babylon after Daniel's departure for Palestine (*Song of Songs Rabbah* 5.5). The reason given is that he was considerate of the feelings of Joshua the son of Jehozadak, who was of the high-priestly family of Zadok. Joshua, according to the Midrash, would have been embarrassed by Ezra's presence in the Land of Israel in view of the latter's obviously superior qualifications. Hence, G-d, who dislikes taking honors away from one family and giving them to another, commanded Ezra to remain in Babylon so long as Joshua was alive. It was only after the death of Joshua that Ezra went to the Land of Israel, where he served as high priest.

[5] Cf. Tosefta *Berakot* 7.23; Jerusalem *Berakot*, 4.11c, 9.14a; *Midrash Psalms* 36.251.

fore he dies, in order that he may record all that has occurred since the creation of the world as set down in the Torah. Thereupon, in still another parallel with Moses, who was on Mount Sinai for forty days, G-d bids Ezra to take five experienced scribes[6] and to dictate to them for forty days. But whereas in the case of Moses in the Pentateuch it is G-d who dictates and Moses who writes, in this instance Ezra transcends the role of Moses, since he dictates and the five scribes write. Moreover, apparently, there was widespread agreement among the rabbis that Ezra was actually identical with the prophet Malachi, since both spoke of the necessity of putting away non-Jewish wives (*Megillah* 15a)[7]. In short, it is not surprising that this glorification of Ezra reached such proportions that in the Koran Mohammed accuses the Jews of regarding Ezra as the veritable son of G-d (Sura 9:30).

3. *Ezra's Genealogy in Josephus*

If, indeed, as we have suggested, Josephus was acquainted with many or even most of the above traditions, what does he make of them? In the first place, as a priest, Josephus is so proud of his priestly ancestry that this is the very first point that he makes in his autobiography (*Life* 1). Hence, we should expect that Josephus would pay particular attention to Ezra, who, when he is first introduced in the biblical account (Ezra 7:1-5, 1 Esdras 8:1-2), has his pedigree carefully traced back no fewer than sixteen generations to the first high priest, Aaron. Furthermore, it is Josephus' wont elsewhere to embellish the genealogies of his biblical heroes. Tracing Ezra's genealogy should, it seems, have been a matter of importance to Josephus, inasmuch as, according to rabbinic tradition, Ezra himself had carefully worked out his own pedigree before consenting to leave Babylonia (*Baba Batra* 15a) and inasmuch as one of his chief achievements was checking the genealogies of those who went with him from Babylonia to Palestine (Ezra 8:1-20, 1 Esdras 8:28-49). Josephus knows of Ezra's status as a leading priest, since he refers to him as a foremost priest (πρῶτος ἱερεύς) (*Ant.* 11.121), while, unlike 1 Esdras (9:40), which refers to him as

---

[6] The fact that there are five scribes would appear to represent a deliberate parallel with the five books of Moses.

[7] Cf. Targum *Malachi* 1:1; Jerome, introduction to his commentary on Malachi.

high priest, he is apparently aware that he did not serve as high priest while Joiakim the son of Joshua was still alive, inasmuch as he mentions Joiakim as high priest in the sentence before he introduces Ezra to the reader (*Ant.* 11.121). To our amazement, however, not only is there no aggrandizement, but there is even no mention of Ezra's genealogy in Josephus. On the other hand, Josephus was apparently embarrassed by the lack of observance by the priests, according to the biblical text; hence, whereas 1 Esdras 9:40 states that he brought the law to all the multitude, as well as to the priests, Josephus says merely that Ezra stood up in the midst of the multitude to read the Law and omits mention of the priests altogether (*Ant.* 11.155). Again, inasmuch as the rabbis, as we have noted, looked upon Ezra as a second Moses, it is instructive to note that Josephus has several extra-biblical details adding to Moses' pedigree. Thus, when Josephus first introduces us to Moses' father Amram, his initial remark is that he was a Hebrew of noble birth (εὖ γεγονότων) (*Ant.* 2.210).[8] Like Demetrius (*ap.* Eusebius, *Pr. Ev.* 9.29.2), Philo (*De Vita Mosis* 1.2.7), and the rabbis (*Genesis Rabbah* 19.7, *Song of Songs Rabbah* 5.1, *Pesiqta de-Rav Kahana* 2.343-44), Josephus also presents the extra-biblical addition[9] that Moses was the seventh generation after Abraham; and, like the rabbis, he actually mentions Moses' ancestors by name (*Ant.* 2.229). All this stands in marked contrast with Josephus' total omission of Ezra's extensive and glorious genealogy.

4. *The Virtues of Ezra: Wisdom*

In the rabbinic tradition Ezra is depicted as a great scholar who was still studying in Babylonia under Baruch ben Neriah, the scribe of the prophet Jeremiah, when Daniel and his companions left for Palestine (*Song of Songs Rabbah* 5.5). So serious was he in his study of the Torah that he regarded it as of even greater importance than the task of rebuilding the Temple, so that he waited until

---

[8] So also in rabbinic tradition (*Sifre Numbers* 67, *Exodus Rabbah* 1.8).

[9] Thackeray (1930, 4:264, n. a), in his note on this passage, remarks that the sentence stating that Moses was the seventh generation after Abraham and enumerating these seven generations has been viewed by some editors as an interruption of the narrative and that it may be a postscript of the author; but in view of Josephus' emphasis elsewhere on genealogy, as we have noted, the greater likelihood is that it is authentic.

after his teacher's death before he decided to go to Jerusalem with his fellow exiles in order to rebuild the Temple. Moreover, he is depicted as so zealous in disseminating the Torah that the famous second-century Rabbi Yose ben Ḥalafta spoke of him as if he were a second Moses, inasmuch as he said of him that if Moses had not preceded him, Ezra would have been worthy of receiving the Torah for Israel (*Sanhedrin* 21b).[10] Indeed, the third-century Resh Laqish is quoted as saying that when, in ancient times, the Torah was forgotten in Israel, Ezra came up from Babylon and established it (*Sukkah* 20a; cf. *Sifre Deuteronomy* 48, *Midrash Tannaim* 43). The comparison of Ezra with Moses is clear likewise from the remark of the second-century Simeon ben Eleazar ascribing to Ezra the division of the Torah into portions to be read on Sabbaths, as well as on Mondays and Thursdays, during the course of the year (*Megillah* 31b, Jerusalem *Megillah* 4.1.75a). That Ezra was viewed as a lawgiver comparable to Moses may also be inferred from the fact that it was at his instigation that the very letters of the Bible were rewritten in "Assyrian" characters (*Sanhedrin* 21b), with the old Hebrew characters being left to the Samaritans. Ezra is, moreover, said to be the author of not only the book of the Bible which bears his name but also of the genealogies of the Book of Chronicles up to his own time (*Baba Batra* 15a), as well as of a portion of the Psalms (*Song of Songs Rabbah* 4.19). There is even a tradition that the Mishnah itself was written by Ezra and five of his companions (*Masseket Kelim* 88).[11] The rabbinic tradition speaks of him as a great educator who, on the ground that competition among educational institutions would result in better schools, ordered additional schools to be established everywhere, even though the old ones were sufficient to meet the demands of the day (*Baba Batra* 21b). His importance as a legislator is seen in the tradition that the Great Assembly, which laid the foundation of rabbinic Judaism, carried on its beneficent activities under his direction. As legislator Ezra is noted for the ten ordinances which he issued on religious, economic, and social matters, including such intimate matters as the requirement that women wear certain garments for the sake of modesty, that garlic be eaten on Fridays as an aphrodisiac,

---

[10] Cf. Tosefta, *Sanhedrin* 4.7; Jerusalem *Megillah* 1.21b; Tertullian, *De Cultu Feminarum* 3; Jerome, *Adversus Helvidium* 7.

[11] See Adolf Jellinek, *Beit Hamidrash* 2 (1853) 88, and the discussion by Ginzberg (1919, 37).

and that pedlars be allowed to travel about in towns to provide toilet articles to be used by women to beautify themselves (*Baba Qamma* 82a-b, Jerusalem *Megillah* 4.1.75a).

Though Josephus adds extra-biblical remarks about the wisdom of so many of his biblical heroes, in the case of Ezra, however, we are told nothing about his wisdom but only that he was very learned in the laws of Moses (*Ant.* 11.121), another clear indication that Josephus wishes to stress Ezra's subordination to Moses. Furthermore, whereas the biblical text describes Ezra as a teacher who is to see to the instruction of those who lack theological knowledge (1 Esdras 8:23), Josephus does not depict Ezra as a teacher but rather declares that he will give those ignorant of the law an opportunity to learn it (*Ant.* 11.129). The emphasis in Josephus is on Ezra as a teacher of obedience to law, again a point which would clearly have appealed to the Romans, with their strong tradition of abiding by the law at all costs. Thus, whereas the biblical text states that the whole Jewish people listened intently while Ezra read the Law (1 Esdras 9:41 and Nehemiah 8:3), Josephus elaborates by declaring that the people were moved to tears as they reflected that they would not have suffered any of the evils which they had experienced if they had observed the law (*Ant.* 11.155). In the biblical text Ezra teaches the people to be pious (1 Esdras 9:52); in Josephus they are taught to be just (δίκαιοι), that is, to obey the law (*Ant.* 11.155). Again, in an extra-biblical addition, it is obedience to the law of the community (πολίτευμα) that Ezra teaches; and consequently the people are grateful to him for rectifying offenses against these laws (*Ant.* 11.157). Furthermore, whereas, in the biblical text, Ezra is termed a scribe on ten occasions (Ezra 7:6, 11, 12, 21; Nehemiah 8:1, 4, 9, 13; 12:26, 36), and whereas, as we have noted, in rabbinic tradition Ezra is termed a scribe comparable in Moses in transcribing the laws, Josephus never calls him a scribe but is content to describe him as sufficiently skilled (ἱκανῶς ἔμπειρος) in the laws of Moses (*Ant.* 11.121). Again, although it is Josephus' practice to present an extra-biblical eulogy upon the death of his biblical heroes, it is particularly striking to find that his encomium of Ezra consists of a single sentence of two and a half lines (*Ant.* 11.158), which actually contains only a single element of eulogy, namely that he was honored by the people.

5. *Ezra as Political Leader*

Josephus' chief aim, in his reworking of the biblical Ezra narrative, is to stress Ezra's loyalty to his ruler and, by implication, to underscore the similar loyalty of Jews to the government of the state in which they reside. It is particularly important, therefore, that when Ezra is first introduced by Josephus he is termed, in an addition not to be found in 1 Esdras 8:4, "friendly" (φίλος, *Ant.* 11.121) to King Xerxes (biblical Artaxerxes). A precedent for Ezra's status here may be seen in Josephus' references to Hezekiah, who was invited by the king of Babylon, Berodachbalaban, to become his ally and "friend" (*Ant.* 10.30), as well as to Daniel, who was given the extraordinarily high honor of being designated by King Darius of Media as the first of his "friends" (*Ant.* 10.263), and to Zerubbabel, who had an "old friendship" with King Darius of Persia and who was on that account "judged worthy of a place in the king's bodyguard" (*Ant.* 11.32).

Ezra's usefulness to the Persian king, as portrayed by Josephus, is chiefly political. Thucydides, whom Josephus admired and imitated so much, cites (2.65.4) the truism that the way of the multitude is fickle. It is, therefore, indeed, significant that when Ezra is first introduced, Josephus, in an extra-biblical addition, notes that he enjoyed the good opinion (δόξης) of the masses (*Ant.* 11.121). With the huge Persian kingdom, consisting, as it did, of so many nationalities and with the Persians themselves being a distinct minority within it, a person such as Ezra, who had the ear of the Jewish masses, would prove extremely useful to his overlord. However, this quality would not necessarily raise Ezra in the esteem of Josephus' reading audience, since Josephus, particularly in his portrayal of Moses, stresses that the true leader is not swayed by the multitude. It is only a rabble-rousing demagogue such as Korah who caters to the multitude and who is consequently the candidate of the people (*Ant.* 4.15, 4.20), whereas the multitude itself is actually bent on stoning Moses (*Ant.* 4.22). Again, Josephus stresses that the natural state of the multitude is anarchy, noting that once their great leader Joshua had died, the people continued in a state of anarchy for a full eighteen years (*Ant.* 6.84).

Hence, Josephus is concerned to balance his picture of Ezra's popularity with the masses with one of Ezra as a leader, inasmuch as, on the one hand, it would have made no sense for the Persian king to entrust such an important position to Ezra if he lacked qualities of leadership; while, on the other hand, it would also have been degrading for the Jews to have as their leader someone who lacked such qualities. Consequently, whereas the biblical text employs the passive voice in stating that Ezra was accompanied to Jerusalem by some Israelites (1 Esdras 8:4), Josephus represents Ezra as assuming the lead in deciding to go to Jerusalem and in taking with himself some of the Jews (*Ant.* 11.122). Again, whereas 1 Esdras 8:8 claims to be quoting a copy of the mandate which King Artaxerxes gave to Ezra, in Josephus Ezra takes the initiative in requesting the king to give him a letter to take to the satraps of Syria (*Ant.* 11.122). Furthermore, the biblical text says merely that Ezra took courage from the help of the L-rd and gathered Jews to accompany him on his trip to Palestine (1 Esdras 8:27), whereas Josephus' Ezra shows much more leadership in not only reading the letter of King Xerxes to the Jews in Babylon but also in taking charge of the whole undertaking by sending a copy of the letter to the Jews in Media (*Ant.* 11.131). Ezra's qualities in organizing the trip to Jerusalem would likewise be called into question by the biblical scene at the river with the returnees (1 Esdras 8:41-59), since Ezra himself admits that he was ashamed to ask the king to supply footmen and horsemen so necessary to safeguard the trip, inasmuch as he had told the king that G-d would protect them; but Josephus avoids such embarrassment by greatly condensing the account (*Ant.* 11.133). Moreover, the king had already spoken about the return of the Levites (*Ant.* 11.123); hence Ezra would appear a poor organizer and leader if he first thought of the matter only at the Euphrates. Ezra's ability as a leader would likewise seem to be impugned by his three-day delay, with no reason being given for it, once he had gathered the returnees on the way to Palestine (1 Esdras 8:41); Josephus removes this blot on Ezra's leadership by explaining that the three days were devoted to a fast to enlist divine aid (*Ant.* 11.134).

Again, Ezra emerges as a more effective leader in that whereas the biblical text declares that Ezra sat down perplexed and miserable when he heard of the intermarriages that had taken place among the Jews (1 Esdras 8:71), Josephus' Ezra is much stronger in his reaction by actually throwing himself upon the ground (*Ant.* 11.141). Likewise, 1 Esdras 9:48-49 indicates that it was the thirteen Levites, whose names it cites, who taught the people the Law, whereas Josephus omits the names of the Levites (*Ant.* 11.155), thus keeping the focus more directly upon Ezra's activity; again, in the biblical text it is the Levites who command the people how to celebrate the holiday (1 Esdras 9:53), whereas in Josephus it is Ezra who, excellent leader that he is, does not command but rather successfully exhorts (προετρέπετο, "urged," "encouraged") the people to repentance, assuring them that they would thus gain security (*Ant.* 11.156).

Ezra's loyalty to his monarch may be seen in Josephus' reduction of the gifts which he receives from the Persian king. Thus, according to 1 Esdras 8:19-20, Artaxerxes directs his treasurers to give Ezra whatever he might request up to a hundred talents of silver, a hundred sacks of wheat, a hundred casks of wine, and salt without limit. The Hebrew version adds a hundred baths of oil. Josephus, though it is his wont to give precise figures, here on the contrary, apparently realizing the extravagance of such amounts, particularly since it might provoke the charge that the Jews are greedy, omits these figures altogether and states merely that the king gave orders that his treasurers should grant Ezra's request (*Ant.* 11.127).

That Josephus presents Ezra's mission as chiefly political is clear also from his addition to the Persian king Xerxes' instructions. Whereas, according to the biblical text, Xerxes wrote to his satraps that whoever does not obey the law of G-d and of the king shall be punished by death or degradation or fine or exile (1 Esdras 8:24, Ezra 7:26), in Josephus' version, there is a further phrase, namely that ignorance of the law will not be accepted as an excuse (*Ant.* 11.130). Josephus also highlights the patriotic loyalty of the Jews to the king when he adds to the biblical text (1 Esdras 8:25) that when the Jews of Media learned of Xerxes' orders and of his piety toward G-d, as well as of his goodwill toward Ezra, they were all greatly pleased (*Ant.* 11.132-33). Indeed, even when given permission to leave for Palestine, we are told, in an extra-biblical addition to 1 Esdras 8:27 (Ezra 7:28), that the Israelite nation as a whole (ὁ δὲ πᾶς λαός) opted to remain in the Median country (*Ant.* 11.133).

In connection with Ezra himself Josephus' stress is on his loyal service to the king and his concern for upholding the law. Thus, whereas in 1 Esdras 8:36 it is the Jewish exiles who deliver the orders of the Persian king to the governors of the province Across the River, in Josephus it is Ezra himself who does so (*Ant.* 11.138); and this results, in an extra-biblical apologetic addition, in the governors' being compelled to honor the Jewish nation and to assist them in all necessary ways. Again, whereas in the biblical text we are told that the leaders and principal men of the Jews share in the violation of the law (1 Esdras 8:70), and whereas in Josephus we are informed that they violated the constitution and broke their ancestral laws (*Ant.* 11.140), Ezra is urged by some of the leaders to come to the aid of the laws (*Ant.* 11.141). It is this quality of Ezra's obedience to the law that is also stressed by Josephus in an addition to the Bible (1 Esdras 8:68), when he declares that Ezra took the leadership in planning (ἐβουλεύσατο), but that it was due to G-d that all turned out well for him, since G-d saw fit to reward him for his goodness (χρηστότητα) and for his righteousness (δικαιοσύνην) (*Ant.* 11.139). This latter term, "righteousness," is clearly related to observance of the law (δίκη).

Thus, Ezra's role, as highlighted by Josephus, is that of upholding the law, surely a role that would have appealed to the Romans, who placed such a premium upon obedience to the law.

6. *Josephus' Aims: Moralizing about Intermarriage*

Josephus, as we have pointed out, was confronted with a dilemma with regard to the intermarriage issue, in that, on the one hand, the Bible clearly forbids it (Deuteronomy 7:3), while, on the other hand, too strenuous an opposition to the practice would be construed as confirmation of the charge of Jewish misanthropy. In the case of Ezra, though his breaking up of intermarriages is central to his biblical role, in Josephus Ezra does not take the lead in this matter. Indeed, in an extra-biblical addition (1 Esdras 8:68-70), Josephus stresses that the initiative to enforce the law regarding intermarriage came from others who, in turn, besought Ezra to take action (*Ant.* 11.141). Specifically, in the Bible it is a Jew named Shecaniah (Jechonias, 1 Esdras 8:92-95) who boldly calls out and asks Ezra to take strong action to dissolve the intermarriages; but in Josephus this is watered down, so that Achonios (=Shecaniah) tried to persuade (ἔπειθε) Ezra to adjure the Jews to put away their foreign wives and the children born of them (*Ant.* 11.145); the use of the imperfect tense of the verb "to persuade" indicates that he had to attempt repeatedly to convince Ezra. When the biblical Ezra is told about the intermarriages (1 Esdras 8:72), he sits appalled, full of heaviness, unable to act, but we are not told why. Josephus is not ashamed to be explicit in telling his readers that the reason why Ezra was immobilized is his realization that the intermarried Jews will not listen to him in any case if he commands them to put away their wives and children (*Ant.* 11.142). In the biblical text when Ezra is approached by Jechonias he does take action and does assume responsibility, forcing all the Jews to swear that they will do as he dictates to them (1 Esdras 8:96). Josephus' Ezra stresses that he is acting thus because he has been persuaded (πεισθείς) by the counsel of Achonios (κατὰ τὴν 'Αχονίου συμβουλίαν) (*Ant.* 11.146). In fact, Ezra's particular concern, in another addition to the Bible (1 Esdras 8:70) is not with intermarriage generally but rather the danger of mixture in the line of priestly families such as his own (*Ant.* 11.140). Moreover, a careful comparison of the language of the Bible (1 Esdras 9:8-9) with Josephus' shows that whereas in the former Ezra orders the Jews to send away their foreign wives, in the latter he diplomatically suggests merely that they will do what is pleasing to G-d and beneficial to themselves if they send away their wives (*Ant.* 11.149). Again, when the Jews finally do separate themselves from their foreign wives it is not, as in the biblical text (1 Esdras 9:16-17), Ezra who takes the initiative, but rather the other leaders (*Ant.* 11.151).

Moreover, Josephus omits the long list of names of sixteen priests, six Levites, four temple-singers and door-keepers, and seventy-five Israelites who had taken foreign wives, offering no rationale for this other than that he thought it unnecessary to give their names (*Ant.* 11.152). But aside from the embarrassment that mention of them would cause their descendants, the omission also serves to further diminish the biblical emphasis on the vast number of such intermarriages. Finally, as in the case of the Midianite women and Samson, Josephus' opposition to the intermarriages is based on his concern about yielding to passion – grounds that would appeal especially to the Stoics in his audience – and on his conviction that intermarriage violated the constitution (πολιτείαν) and broke the laws of the country; consequently, when the Jews do dismiss their foreign wives, he, in an extra-biblical comment (1 Esdras 9:20), remarks that in doing so they had more regard for the observance of the laws than for the objects of their affection (φίλτρων, "love potions") (*Ant.* 11.152). Here again we see Josephus' emphasis on obedience to law that was so important to the Persian government and would be so impressive to his Roman readers. Finally, Ezra, in an addition to the biblical text (1 Esdras 9:36) is credited not merely with resolving the immediate matter of the mixed marriages but also with setting a standard of obedience to the law "so that it remained fixed for the future" (*Ant.* 11.153). Indeed, once the matter of mixed marriages is viewed, as it is by Josephus, in political terms, Greek readers might well have thought of the parallel to the citizenship law of 451/450 attributed to the much-admired Pericles, which restricted citizenship to those who could prove that both their parents were citizens of Athens.[12]

7. *Apologetics for the Jews in Josephus' Account of Ezra*

One of Josephus' major goals in writing his *Antiquities*, no less than in his essay *Against Apion*, was to defend the Jews against the charges of pagan intellectuals. One of the basic reasons for hatred of the Jews was their wealth, as we may discern from the tone of Cicero's remarks (*Pro Flacco* 28.66-69), especially since their wealth was constantly being sent off to the Temple in Jerusalem. Tacitus also alludes to this charge when he speaks bitterly about proselytes to Judaism who keep sending tribute to Jerusalem, "thereby increasing the wealth of the Jews" (*Histories* 5.5.1), and shortly thereafter refers to the Temple possessing enormous riches (*immensae opulentiae templum*) (*Histories* 5.8.1). In his address to the revolutionaries, Josephus likewise bitterly reminds them that the Romans allowed the Jews to collect the tribute for the Temple "only that you might grow richer at our expense and make preparations with our money to attack us!" (*War* 6.335).

Hence, it is a sensitive matter when the biblical book lists the silver, gold, and sacred vessels which had been presented to those returning to Palestine by the king, his counsellors, and all the Jews (1 Esdras 8:55-57). According to the biblical account, these included a hundred talents of gold, twenty pieces of gold plate, and twelve vessels of brass so fine that it gleamed like gold. Such tre-

---

[12] See Ostwald (1986, 182-83), and the literature cited there. Ostwald, 507-8, notes that following the restoration of the democracy after the end of the Peloponnesian War this restrictive provision of the citizenship law was revived.

mendous wealth seems to confirm contemporary critics' claims about the Jews sending vast sums to the Temple in Jerusalem. In Josephus' version the list has been considerably trimmed to gold vessels weighing twenty talents and vessels of bronze weighing twelve talents (*Ant.* 11.136).

Again, Josephus' treatise *Against Apion*, in large part, is intended to refute the charge that the Jews are an insignificant people who have, for good reason, been ignored by the Greeks (*Ag. Ap.* 1.60-68). Hence, it is important that the biblical text notes that when the returnees to Palestine deliver the king's orders to the royal treasurers and governors of Coele-Syria and Phoenicia, the latter added luster to (ἐδόξασαν, "extolled," "magnified") the Jewish nation and the Temple (1 Esdras 8:67). In Josephus' magnified version the governors are spoken of as actually compelled to carry out the king's commands; and, moreover, they not only honor the Jewish nation but they also assist it in all necessary ways (*Ant.* 11.138).

If charges are to be brought against the Jews the best source, it would seem, is the Bible itself. It is not surprising, therefore, that Josephus, the apologist for the Jewish people, has omitted, as we have noted, a number of apparently embarrassing passages. Likewise, in the biblical narrative of Ezra the Jews themselves admit that their sins are so great as to tower above their heads (1 Esdras 8:74-90). Josephus, however, in his desire to withhold giving ammunition to the enemies of the Jews, seeks to avoid indicting the Jewish people so strongly and prefers to tone down their humiliation. Hence, this extended confession of sins is very much abbreviated by Josephus (*Ant.* 11.143). Likewise, whereas the biblical text declares that Ezra neither ate food nor drank water while he mourned over the serious violations of the law by the community (1 Esdras 9:2), Josephus at this point avoids mentioning the embarrassing fact of the sins of the Jews and says merely that Ezra fasted because of his grief (*Ant.* 11.147). Similarly, whereas in 1 Esdras 9:13 Ezra persuades the Jews who have taken foreign wives to assemble at a fixed time so that the fierce wrath of G-d may be averted from them for this matter, in Josephus there is no mention of such divine wrath (*Ant.* 11.150). In like fashion, whereas in the Bible Ezra has a long prayer to G-d in which he rehearses Israelite history, including such unflattering episodes as the building of the Golden Calf (Nehemiah 9:6-38), and states that the Israelites had rebelled against G-d, killed His prophets, and committed great blasphemies (Nehemiah 9:26), Josephus again avoids such embarrassments by omitting the prayer altogether (*Ant.* 11.158).

One of the most embarrassing passages in the biblical narrative is the statement that when Ezra read the Law to the Jews in Jerusalem on the festival of Tabernacles, the people made *sukkot*, inasmuch as they had not observed the commandment to dwell in *sukkot* since the days of Joshua (Nehemiah 8:14, 17). That the Jews for so long a period of time had not observed a festival so explicitly enjoined in the Pentateuch raises the question whether they had the Pentateuch at all during this period or whether perhaps it was not given by G-d at Sinai but rather was written much later, possibly even by Ezra himself, as critics such as Spinoza were later to suggest.[13] Hence, Josephus discreetly avoids stirring up this hornet's nest by omitting the passage altogether (*Ant.* 11.157).

8. *Summary*

It is more by what Josephus omits than by what he says about Ezra that we can gauge how he appraised him. Unlike the rabbis, who compare Ezra's achievements as legislator and teacher to those of Moses, Josephus has diminished his role considerably. Though Josephus, in his portraits of other biblical personalities, gives much attention to genealogy and though the Bible itself traces Ezra's pedigree back sixteen generations, Josephus omits such data in his case. Again, though Josephus routinely adds to the Bible remarks about the wisdom of biblical characters, he says nothing about Ezra's wisdom as such other than that he was learned in the laws of Moses. Rather, Josephus emphasizes Ezra's role as teaching obedience to law – a point which would endear him to his Roman imperial sponsors. Furthermore, though it is Josephus' practice to present an encomium, often at length, upon the death of his biblical heroes, he summarizes Ezra's achievements in a mere two and a half lines, with only one phrase of eulogy, namely that he was honored by the people.

Josephus' portrait of Ezra is influenced primarily by his desire to defend the Jewish people against charges by their intellectual opponents. In particular, in response to the accusation that the

---

[13] Benedict Spinoza, *Theologico-Political Tractate*, chapter 8.

Jews are not loyal to the Empire, especially as seen in their massive revolt during the years 66-70, Josephus stresses Ezra's loyalty to his ruler. He is depicted as an effective leader who took the initiative in organizing the return to Palestine, thus strengthening the Persian Empire on its fragile borders. His righteousness is clearly related to his strict observance of the law – a note calculated to appeal to the Romans.

Ezra's most important achievement, according to the biblical narrative, was in breaking up the numerous intermarriages of Jews with foreigners. Yet, Josephus was here, as in his treatment of Samson, confronted with a dilemma, inasmuch as, though the Bible emphatically forbids intermarriage, too strenuous an objection to the practice would appear to confirm the frequent charge of misanthropy made by intellectual opponents of the Jews. Josephus resolves the difficulty by stressing that the initiative in enforcing the prohibition of intermarriage came from others, who besought Ezra to take action. Josephus' Ezra bases his opposition to such mixed marriages on his aversion to yielding to passion – grounds that would certainly appeal to Stoics in his audience. His concern, in an extra-biblical addition, is not with intermarriage in general but rather with the mixture in the strain of priestly families such as his own. In the end, Ezra does not, as in the Bible, actually order the Jews to send away their wives but rather merely suggests that they will please G-d if they do so.

Josephus also uses the opportunity in his portrait of Ezra to respond to the charge that the Jews drain the wealth of the Empire by reducing considerably the amount of wealth sent to Palestine by the king and by the Jews. To the charge that the Jews are an insignificant people justly ignored by others, he replies, in an extra-biblical addition, that the Persian governors were ordered by their king both to honor the Jewish nation and to assist it in every way. Finally, Josephus discreetly omits the embarrassing statement that it was not until Ezra read the Pentateuch to them that the Jews realized that they had been negligent in building *sukkot* since the days of Joshua.

CHAPTER THIRTY-THREE

NEHEMIAH

1. *Introduction: The Problem*

It is Josephus' wont, as we have seen, in his paraphrase of the Bible in the *Jewish Antiquities*, to expand considerably the treatment of the great biblical personalities. In particular, because to a writer of a history of the Jews like himself Nehemiah's memoir would be of immense importance and because, indeed, a whole biblical book is devoted to Nehemiah,[1] and, finally, because of his crucial importance in the rebuilding of Jerusalem and of the Temple, which were so important to Josephus, who was born in Jerusalem and who, as a priest, had a special attachment to the Temple, one would expect Josephus to aggrandize his portrait.[2]

An indication, however, of Josephus' relative lack of interest in Nehemiah may be seen in the sheer amount of space that he devotes to him. Thus, in the portion of 2 Esdras 11-23 (Hebrew Nehemiah 1-13) which Josephus paraphrases (*Ant.* 11.159-83: 144 lines in the Loeb Classical Library text) there are 792 lines in Rahlfs' text (589 lines in the Hebrew version corresponding to this). This gives a ratio of only .18 of Josephus to the Greek of 2

---

[1] Marcus (1937, 6:400-1, n. b, on *Ant.* 11.179) remarks that according to the Bible it took only fifty-two days to complete the building of the wall of Jerusalem (Nehemiah 6:15), whereas according to Josephus it took two years and four months or three years and four months (*Ant.* 11.179). He suggests that this would indicate that Josephus had before him a text of Nehemiah, whether Hebrew or Greek, that was different from ours, unless we assume, with Bewer (1924, 224-26), that Josephus' text is corrupt. We may, however, note that it is precisely in such numbers that corruptions are most likely to occur in texts.

[2] No substantial study of Josephus' treatment of Nehemiah has been made. Rappaport (1930), who attempts to cite midrashic parallels for all of Josephus, has nothing at all on Nehemiah. Likewise, Attridge (1976) has not a single reference to Nehemiah. Blenkinsopp (1974, 58) mentions, in passing, that Josephus is at pains to present Nehemiah in as favorable a light as possible and notes that he passes over in silence allusions to internal difficulties and opposition during his administration but does not supply details. The only work that even attempts to consider at all systematically Josephus' treatment of Nehemiah is Pohlmann (1970, 114-26); but Pohlmann makes no attempt to evaluate the significance of the differences between the biblical text and Josephus.

Esdras and of .24 to the Hebrew text. This is by far the lowest ratio for all the biblical figures that we have examined. We may attribute this brevity in part to Nehemiah's unpopularity in his own lifetime[3] or to the fact that he was supposedly excessively self-complacent (*Sanhedrin* 93b) or to the relative paucity of aggadic material about Nehemiah or to Josephus' desire to give greater attention to the priest Ezra, the other great figure involved in the resettlement of Jerusalem with whom Josephus would have identified more closely, inasmuch as he, too, was a priest.[4] Nevertheless, the fact that Nehemiah was identified with the famed Zerubbabel (*Sanhedrin* 38a), the leader of the original caravan of repatriates who is spoken of as the builder of the Temple which frequently bears his name (Ezra 3:2), should, it would seem, have induced Josephus, who was so proud of his priesthood, to give him much more attention. In any case, it is very hard to explain his omission of vast portions of the biblical Nehemiah narrative.

2. *Nehemiah as a Political Figure*

The very beginning of Josephus' account of Nehemiah calls attention to his relationship to the king. Whereas in the biblical account it is not until after eleven verses of the first chapter that Nehemiah is identified as the cupbearer of the king (Nehemiah 2:1), a position of crucial importance requiring the complete confidence of the monarch, Josephus' very first sentence so describes him (*Ant.* 11.159).

In Josephus' reworking of the biblical narrative, Nehemiah emerges, in an extra-biblical detail, as the Persian king's loyal servant who gave stability to the land of Palestine at a time when it was being overrun by marauders who plundered it by day, did mischief to it at night, and carried off many captives from the country and even from Jerusalem itself (*Ant.* 11.161). The biblical text simply states that the inhabitants of Palestine were in great affliction and reproach (Nehemiah 1:3). Josephus adds that highwaymen had made the roads unsafe, so that they were full of corpses (*Ant.*

---

[3] Cf. *Sanhedrin* 103b, which points out that Nehemiah, like David, had many enemies, yet both were truly righteous men.

[4] For Ezra, as we have noted, the ratio of Josephus to 1 Esdras is .72; the ratio to the Hebrew text is 1.20. This too, as we have noted, is much lower than the ratio for a number of other biblical personalities.

11.161). Inasmuch as roads were the great pride of both the Persians (cf. Herodotus 8.98) and the Romans, the fact that Nehemiah secured the safety of these roads, according to Josephus' extra-biblical addition, must have made an extremely strong impression upon his readers.

Again, Josephus dramatically illustrates the loyalty of Nehemiah to the Persian king by adding to the biblical passage (Nehemiah 2:1) that Nehemiah, in his fidelity to the king, hastened just as he was and without even bathing to perform the service of bringing the king his drink (*Ant.* 11.163).

The king's confidence in Nehemiah is also illustrated by the omission of a biblical passage. In Nehemiah 2:6 the king is represented as asking him how long he will be gone and when he will return, whereupon Nehemiah, of course, answers him by setting a time. Apparently, Josephus regarded such an inquiry as itself a sign of lack of confidence in Nehemiah, and so he simply omits it (*Ant.* 11.166). An indication of Nehemiah's persuasiveness and of the king's confidence in him may likewise be seen in Josephus' addition to the biblical text (Nehemiah 2:8) that it took the king only one day to fulfill his promise to Nehemiah and to give him a letter to the governor of Syria (*Ant.* 11.167).

Nehemiah, as representative of the Persian king, could hardly afford to show hesitation or fear, and yet the biblical text indicates that whereas he heard in Kislev about the difficulties in Jerusalem (Nehemiah 1:1), it was not until four months later in Nisan that he went to the king with a request to remedy the situation (Nehemiah 2:1). Such a delay is obviously not consonant with dynamic leadership, and so Josephus has Nehemiah go immediately to the king after hearing of the troubles of the Jews in Jerusalem (*Ant.* 11.163). Moreover, according to the Bible, when the king asked him why he was sad, he became very much afraid (Nehemiah 2:2). Josephus, however, obviously found such a detail unseemly in a leader and simply omits it (*Ant.* 11.164).

A major ingredient of Nehemiah's character, as highlighted by Josephus and crucial in his capacity as the right-hand man of the Persian king, is respect for law (*Ant.* 11.183). Indeed, it is significant that in his brief encomium for Nehemiah, consisting of a single sentence, Josephus calls attention to his being just (δίκαιος), that is, observant of the proper way (δίκη) (*Ant.* 11.183). We have noted that the same two adjectives used here of Nehemiah, χρηστός and δίκαιος, are employed also for the prophet Samuel (*Ant.* 6.294) and for the model king Hezekiah (*Ant.* 9.260), as well as for Jehonadab (*Ant.* 9.133), Jehoiada (*Ant.* 9.166), and Jehoiachin (*Ant.* 10.100).

A crucial quality of a leader, as we may see in the portrait of Pericles by Thucydides, is the ability to persuade. In the case of Nehemiah, in a supplement to the biblical narrative, Josephus says that Nehemiah, before approaching the king for permission to go to Jerusalem, prays to G-d to give his words some measure of grace and persuasion (πειθώ) (*Ant.* 11.165).

That Nehemiah was indeed gifted in the art of persuasion is clear from the fact that he gains his request. Moreover, whereas the Bible remarks that the king granted it, "for the good hand of my G-d was upon me" (Nehemiah 2:8), Josephus omits the role of G-d altogether and attributes Nehemiah's success solely to his own efforts (*Ant.* 11.166).

As for Nehemiah's mission itself in going to Palestine, it is significant that the Bible speaks only of its religious dimension, emphasizing the importance of the tombs of the ancestors, in that Nehemiah asks the king to send him to Judaea, "to the city of my fathers' sepulchres, that I may rebuild it" (Nehemiah 2:5). In Josephus' version the mission is both religious and, more especially, political, inasmuch as Nehemiah puts the emphasis on the need to repair the walls and the gates of the city of Jerusalem when he declares that the occasion for his mission is the report that he has heard that the walls of his native city of Jerusalem, where the graves and the monuments of his forefathers are located, have been thrown to the ground and its gates burnt (*Ant.* 11.165).

Nehemiah's qualities of leadership may be discerned also in the fact that whereas the biblical text asserts that only a few men accompanied him (Nehemiah 2:12), Josephus states that many of his countrymen went with him and, what is more, did so voluntarily – a clear indication of his ability to inspire confidence in his followers (*Ant.* 11.168). Again, although the biblical text is generally much longer than Josephus' version of the Nehemiah narrative, Josephus considerably amplifies Nehemiah's speech (Nehemiah 2:17-18), encouraging the Jews in their work of rebuilding Jerusalem, and thereby underscores his qualities of inspiring leadership (*Ant.* 11.169-71). In particular, by his extra-biblical remarks, Nehemiah instills confidence in his hearers that they will, with G-d's help, be able to withstand the hostility of their neighbors.

To the reader of the biblical narrative Nehemiah emerges as a kind of "tyrant," very similar to those of the Greek cities along the coast of the Aegean Sea.[5] Whereas it was typical of tyrants to have the backing of only one segment of the people, through whose aid they came to power, and whereas the biblical Nehemiah (2:16) at first works secretly with a small group of followers, in Josephus he summons the people of Jerusalem and is viewed as a leader by all of them (*Ant.* 11.168). Again, whereas one of the common characteristics of the Greek tyrants was utter secrecy and the general distrust thus evoked, Josephus leaves out the biblical report (Nehemiah 2:12-16) that Nehemiah made a secret inspection of Jerusalem's walls at night (*Ant.* 11.168).

An important change from the biblical portrait of Nehemiah may be seen in Josephus' paraphrase of the description of his repairs of the various gates of the city of Jerusalem (Nehemiah 3:1-32). In particular, he leaves aside all of these biblical details and instead focuses upon the picture of Nehemiah as leader and organizer, stressing that Nehemiah himself promised to assist in building together with his servants (*Ant.* 11.172). In extra-biblical additions we are given a portrait of an excellent administrator who assigns the work on the wall of Jerusalem by villages and cities, bearing in mind the abilities of each person (*ibid.*). One is reminded of the scene in Virgil in which Dido, queen of Carthage, is similarly depicted as directing the building of the walls of Carthage, apportioning by just division or by lot the tasks to be done (*Aeneid* 1.507-8). Likewise, to emphasize Nehemiah's ability in organizing the builders, whereas the Bible states merely that he stationed a trumpeter near him (Nehemiah 4:12), Josephus is much more elaborate and precise in saying that he stationed trumpeters at intervals of five hundred feet with the command to give the signal to the people if the enemy appeared (*Ant.* 11.177).

Nehemiah's achievement as a leader is all the greater because of Josephus' exaggeration of the difficulties that he faced. Thus in the biblical text the adversaries of the Jews threaten to slay them (Nehemiah 4:5), whereas in Josephus they actually kill many (*Ant.*

---

[5] See Andrewes (1956); Picket (1969, 19-61); M. Smith (1971, 136-47); Drews (1972, 129-44); and Sealey (1976, 38-65). Smith, 141-44, notes that the similarity of Nehemiah to the Greek tyrants is no mere matter of general outline; it extends to every detail.

11.174). Moreover, in an addition having no parallel in the Bible (Nehemiah 4:8), Josephus adds to the obstacles which confronted Nehemiah by noting that the enemies of the Jews instilled fear and alarm in them and spread rumors, undoubtedly more frightening than the attacks themselves, that many nations were about to attack them, so that as a result the Jews very nearly gave up their building work (*Ant.* 11.175).

The fact that, like the Greek tyrants, Nehemiah, according to Josephus, surrounded himself with a bodyguard would raise the obvious suspicion in the mind of Josephus' readers that Nehemiah was more concerned with his own safety than he was with the well-being of the Jews (*Ant.* 11.176). Josephus, clearly well aware of this problem, in an addition to the Bible (Nehemiah 4:8), goes out of his way to stress Nehemiah's unwearying zeal and insensibility to hardship. He carefully and apologetically explains that the reason why he took forethought for his own safety was not that he feared death but rather that he was convinced that should he be slain the Jews would be leaderless and unable to continue rebuilding the walls of the city (*Ant,* 11.176).

Though, as we have noted, Josephus has greatly condensed the biblical narrative, yet, in order to emphasize Nehemiah's energy, indeed, Josephus asserts that he ate and slept not for pleasure but only out of necessity (*Ant.* 11.178). Most significantly, in the very brief summary which Josephus gives of Nehemiah's achievements he singles out his extraordinary eagerness to serve his countrymen (περὶ τοὺς ὁμοεθνεῖς φιλοτιμότατος) (*Ant.* 11.183).

Again, whereas the biblical text calls attention to the sufferings of the people and paints a dark picture of their heavy burdens of taxation and their general degradation (Nehemiah 5:2-5, 14-15), Josephus shifts the emphasis to Nehemiah himself and speaks of the hardships that he endured for two years and four months (*Ant.* 11.179).

Furthermore, in an addition to the Bible, Josephus proudly reports that Nehemiah built houses for the priests and the Levites at his own expense in order to increase the population of the city of Jerusalem, which had apparently declined in numbers (*Ant.* 11.181). Here, as we would expect from one so proud of his priestly status, Josephus shows his pro-priestly bias, inasmuch as the corresponding biblical passage speaks not of priests and Levites but of nobles, officials, and the people generally (Nehemiah 7:4-5).[6] In addition, the Bible co-ordinates the efforts of Ezra the priest-scribe and Nehemiah the governor (Nehemiah 8:1, 9), but since the net result of this coupling would be to detract from the achievements of both figures, Josephus never brings them into juxtaposition.

In order to focus greater attention on his biblical heroes Josephus, as we have remarked, frequently reduces the role of G-d. Thus, in order to accentuate the achievements of Nehemiah, Josephus omits Nehemiah's prayer to G-d (Nehemiah 4:9), as well as his statement to his workers (Nehemiah 4:20) that G-d will fight for them (*Ant.* 11.177). Instead he mentions only Nehemiah's organizing achievements and his orders to his men. It is only when the walls are finally completed that Nehemiah sacrifices to G-d (*Ant.* 11.180).

Likewise, the Bible declares that it was G-d who frustrated the plans of the enemies of Jews who had sought to stop the rebuilding of the city (Nehemiah 4:15). Again, when the enemies hear that the wall of the city has been completed, all the neighboring nations, according to the Bible, were afraid because they concluded that the work had been accomplished with divine help (Nehemiah 6:16). To Josephus, however, the credit belongs to Nehemiah and his leadership, and so he omits such statements (*Ant.* 11.179).

3. *Apologetics for the Jews*

Similarly, whereas in the biblical text Nehemiah weeps, confessing the sins of the Israelites and recalling G-d's promise that He would scatter the Israelites if they proved unfaithful to Him (Nehemiah 1:5-11), Josephus' Nehemiah also bursts into tears but says nothing about the people's sins, which would, indeed, have given ammunition to the Jew-baiters, but rather expresses his pity for the misfortunes of his countrymen (*Ant.* 11.162).

---

[6] Blenkinsopp (1974, 58) conjectures that the detail that Nehemiah built houses in Jerusalem is perhaps taken from Ecclesiasticus 49:13; but that passage most probably alludes to Nehemiah's rebuilding of the outer walls and gates of the city, inasmuch as it refers to his erecting walls, gates, and bars and his raising up of ruins, presumably of the walls of the city. In any case, it does not speak of Nehemiah doing so at his own expense. For other examples of Josephus' pro-priestly revisions of the biblical narrative see S. Schwartz (1990, 89-90).

In particular, the biblical text records that Nehemiah saw people violating the Sabbath by treading winepresses and bringing in heaps of grapes and loading them on asses on that day (Nehemiah 13:15-22), whereupon Nehemiah took action to enforce Sabbath observance (Nehemiah 13:19-22). That the Jews were so remiss in observing so central a commandment as the Sabbath obviously reflects badly on them. Josephus consequently passes over this notice (*Ant.* 11.179).

In view of the fact that the Jews were known for their loyalty and compassion toward one another (cf. Tacitus, *Histories* 5.5.1), it would, needless to say, have been very awkward for Josephus to reproduce the biblical narrative of their discord in the days of Nehemiah. In particular, the Bible records Nehemiah's charges, obviously embarrassing to the reputation of the Jews, that Jewish nobles and officials were exacting interest from their fellows and were selling them into slavery (Nehemiah 5:6-7). Likewise, Nehemiah 5:12 alludes to Nehemiah's quarrel with the priests and to his insistence that they swear an oath to do as they had promised. We hear also of his quarrel with Eliashib the priest, who, during Nehemiah's absence, assigned one of the chambers of the Temple to his opponent, Tobiah, whereupon Nehemiah in a fit of anger threw Tobiah's furniture out of the chamber (Nehemiah 13:4-9). Again, according to the biblical text, Nehemiah discovered that the Levites had not been given their portions and that they had fled, being forced to seek a livelihood elsewhere, whereupon he remonstrated with the officials (Nehemiah 13:10-11). Josephus discreetly omits all these data (*Ant.* 11.179) and states merely that Nehemiah urged the priests and Levites to leave the countryside and to move to the city of Jerusalem without indicating why they were no longer living in the city at the moment (*Ant.* 11.181).

One of the recurring accusations made against the Jews, as we see from the remarks of Lysimachus, for example, is that they are an ignoble people, afflicted with leprosy and various other diseases, leading a mendicant existence and therefore hardly worthy of respect (*ap.* Josephus, *Ag. Ap.* 1.305). In connection with Nehemiah, whereas the Bible is silent concerning the king's order that the satraps should pay Nehemiah honor (Nehemiah 2:7-8), Josephus adds that the king specifically instructed the satraps to do so, giving Nehemiah a letter to this effect to carry to the governor of Syria (*Ant.* 11.166). Such honor quite clearly redounded not only to Nehemiah but to the Jewish people at large as well.

Another charge frequently made against the Jews is hatred of mankind. In reply, Josephus stresses the Jewish quality of φιλανθρωπία, closely connected with which is the virtue of gratitude. Thus, in an addition to the biblical text (Nehemiah 2:8), Josephus' Nehemiah gives thanks (εὐχαριστήσας) to the king for his promise to help in the rebuilding of Jerusalem (*Ant.* 11.167).

In the Nehemiah pericope, Josephus is concerned to underscore the allegiance of the Jews to the state, as we may see in his omission (*Ant.* 11.170) of the biblical charge, made by Sanballat the Horonite, Tobiah the servant, the Ammonite, and Geshem the Arab, that the Jews were rebelling against the Persian king (Nehemiah 2:19-20, 6:6). These neighbors likewise tried to reduce to absurdity the action of the Jews in rebuilding the wall; indeed, the biblical text observes that they derided and despised them. Josephus omits such disparaging remarks. Again, whereas the Bible stresses that Sanballat and Tobiah the Ammonite had ridiculed the Jews by remarking that if a fox were to climb the wall he would break it down (Nehemiah 4:1, 4), Josephus sigificantly omits the mention of ridicule and instead limits the reaction of the various neighboring tribes to anger and plots to hinder the Jews (*Ant.* 11.174).

In the Bible, Sanballat, the chief enemy of the Jews, is said to have sent a letter to Nehemiah for the fifth time repeating the accusation, as "reported among the nations," that the Jews intended to rebel against the Persians, that Nehemiah himself was seeking to become their king, and that all this would be reported to the Persian monarch (Nehemiah 6:5-7). The biblical narrative, of course, vehemently denies all this; the very thought, however, that such charges could be made against him was apparently embarrassing to Josephus, who, not surprisingly, omits them altogether.

4. *The Problem of Intermarriage*

Intermarriage, as we have repeatedly noted, presented Josephus with a dilemma, since an attack upon it might well be construed as proof of Jewish misanthropy. As for Nehemiah, it is he as governor who heads the list in the Bible of those who solemnly promise not to allow their children to marry non-Jews (Nehemiah 10:1-30).

Moreover, he adopts the strongest measures against Jews who intermarried with neighboring nations and no longer spoke Hebrew (Nehemiah 13:23-29). In fact, in an unseemly and intemperate outburst, Nehemiah curses and beats them, and even pulls out their hair (Nehemiah 13:25). All this is passed over by Josephus.

Indeed, when one considers how important genealogy was to Josephus, it is striking that he omits all mention of Nehemiah's role in assembling, on G-d's initiative, the nobles and the officials and the people generally to examine the crucial matter of their pedigrees (Nehemiah 7:5). This omission is particularly striking in view of the fact, as we have noted, that his own genealogy is the very first point that Josephus presents in his autobiography (*Life* 1), just as he stresses, again with obvious pride, almost immediately thereafter, that his mother sprang from the rulers of the Hasmonean dynasty, who were not only kings but also high priests (*Life* 2). If Josephus (*Ant.* 11.179) omits the extensive biblical lists of those who returned to Palestine (Nehemiah 7:6-65), we can understand this in view of his general disinclination to list such names (*Ant.* 1.176) (presumably because such directories would be boring to the reader); but the Bible clearly views Nehemiah's concern with establishing the genealogy of the people as a crucial achievement, inasmuch as it is said to have been prompted by G-d Himself (Nehemiah 7:5). Hence, Josephus' total disregard of Nehemiah's concern with verifying genealogies seems surprising. The explanation would appear to be the same as with regard to Josephus' treatment of intermarriage; to highlight this issue would be to play into the hands of those who accused the Jews of misanthropy. Josephus, the theological and literary, no less than political, coward, simply sidesteps the issue by not mentioning it.

5. *Summary*

Josephus' portrait of Nehemiah is very condensed compared with that of the Bible, perhaps because he sought to give more prominence to the other key figure in the return of the Jews from Babylonian captivity, Ezra, who like Josephus was a priest, whereas Nehemiah was a mere layman.

To the extent that he adds to the biblical account, Josephus emphasizes Nehemiah's service to the Persian king and his respect for law, features which would answer the accusation that the Jews cannot be trusted, as witnessed by their recent revolt against the Romans.

Nehemiah, in his role as right-hand man of the king, emerges, to judge from Josephus' additions to the narrative, as another Joseph, with all the qualities of an effective leader, including, especially, the ability to persuade his people and his magnanimity in building houses for the priests and Levites at his own expense. The obstacles facing him are even greater than those mentioned in the biblical narrative. In order to call greater attention to his achievements, Josephus diminishes the role of G-d. He is careful, however, to divest him of the qualities of a typical Greek "tyrant," whom he otherwise resembles in many respects.

Josephus omits a number of details which in the Bible cast the Jews in a bad light, in particular the dissension among them in which Nehemiah became involved.

As in his paraphrase of the Ezra pericope so in that of Nehemiah, Josephus was confronted with a dilemma regarding the intermarriage problem of that era. His solution, in order to avoid the charge of misanthropy which had been made frequently by intellectuals against the Jews, is to omit all mention of Nehemiah's role in examining the crucial matter of the pedigrees of the Jews.

CHAPTER THIRTY-FOUR

AHASUERUS

1. *The Rabbinic Portrayal of Ahasuerus*

The story of Esther and Ahasuerus was clearly one of the most popular narratives among the Jews, as we can see from the fact that a holiday, Purim, was established to commemorate the deliverance of the Jews. Every year on this holiday the Book of Esther was read twice, once in the evening and once in the morning of the day of Purim. Moreover, an entire tractate of the Talmud, *Megillah*, is devoted to the story and to the laws pertaining to the observance of Purim. Its popularity may be seen in the fact that in the synagogue of Dura Europus in Babylonia one of the wall panels depicts Haman leading Mordecai through the streets of Susa while Ahasuerus and Esther are enthroned.

One would suppose that the rabbis, at least those living in Babylonia under the Parthians (and after 226 the Sassanians), who regarded themselves as the direct successors of the Persians, would be careful not to offend their hosts by making derogatory comments about the Persian kings. Nevertheless, the rabbinic tradition, while acknowledging the might of King Ahasuerus in depicting him as one of only three kings who ruled over the entire earth (the other two being Ahab and Nebuchadnezzar) (*Megillah* 11a, 2 Targum on Esther 1:2), and while presenting one view that Ahasuerus at the banquet that he arranged for his subjects actually had regard for the Jews' dietary laws and their rule forbidding wine to be drunk that had been touched by a non-Jew (*Pirqe de-Rabbi Eliezer* 49, *Abba Gorion* 13, *Midrash Esther Rabbah* 1.8), gives, on the whole, a very negative picture of him. In the first place, the view is expressed by some of the rabbis that Ahasuerus was actually unfit to be king but that he raised himself to that position by virtue of his mere wealth (*Megillah* 11a). Secondly, and most unforgivably, he is said, when he saw that seventy years had been completed and that the Jews had not yet been redeemed, to have desecrated the Temple vessels (*Abba Gorion* 9, *Panim Aherim* 58, 2 Targum *Esther* 1.4, cited by Ginzberg 1928, 6:452, n. 11) and to have arrayed himself in the robes belonging to the high priest (*Abba Gorion* 2-8, 1 *Targum Esther* 1.2, cited by Ginzberg 1928, 6:452, n.13) at the feast which he made for all the princes of his kingdom even though he was well aware of what had happened to Belshazzar for such conduct (*Megillah* 11b, *Seder Olam* 28).[1] Indeed, he is said, in a play on his name, to be the brother of the head (*'aḥiv shel rosh*), and is thus compared by the third-century Rav with Nebuchadnezzar, the king who was responsible for the destruction of the First Temple, and is referred to as his brother in the sense of his counterpart in that "the one slew, the other sought to slay; the one laid waste, the other sought to lay waste" (*Megillah* 11a). Though Rav's contemporary, Samuel, is often represented as disputing with him, in this disparaging portrayal of Ahasuerus he is in agreement, since he says, with another play on the name of Ahasuerus, that in the latter's days the face of Israel was blackened (*hushḥaru*) like the sides of a pot. His contemporary Rabbi Joḥanan ben Nappaḥa, in still another derogatory play on Ahasuerus' name, remarks that everyone who thought of him said, "Alas for my head (*'aḥ le-rosho*). Still another pun on his name comes from his contemporary, Rabbi Ḥanina, basing himself on the verse in Esther 10:1 ("And the king Ahasuerus laid a tribute"), that all became poor (*rashin*) in his days (*Megillah* 11a).

In view of the great respect that the rabbis generally had for rulers, the fact that Ahasuerus is referred to over and over again as wicked (e.g., *Megillah* 12a-b) is surely significant. Thus, in an anonymous comment on the very first verse in the Book of Esther, we are told that the word *hu* ("he") indicates that Ahasuerus persisted in his wickedness from beginning to end; and the analogy is made with the occurrence of this same word in connection with a series of rogues – Esau (Genesis 36:43), the arch-rebels against Moses, Dathan and Abiram (Numbers 26:9), and King Ahaz (2 Chronicles 28:22), who likewise persisted in their wickedness from beginning to end (*Megillah* 11a). In fact, in a remarkable parable, the point of which is that Ahasuerus was as eager as Haman to get rid of the Jews, the third-century Rabbi Abba compares Ahasuerus and Haman to two men one of whom had a mound and the other of whom had a ditch in the midst of their respective fields and

---

[1] According to *1 Targum Esther* 1.10, Mordecai spent a whole week in fasting and prayer to G-d to punish Ahasuerus for desecrating the Temple vessels.

each of whom was eager to have what was to the other an obstacle, whereupon they made the exchange without cost and to their great satisfaction (*Megillah* 13b-14a). Indeed, in a striking comment on the scene in which Esther at her banquet identifies Haman as her enemy, the third-century Rabbi Eleazar ben Pedat remarks that Esther was actually pointing at Ahasuerus himself when she said these words, but that an angel pushed her hand so as to point to Haman (*Megillah* 16a). Moreover, whereas in the biblical statement Ahasuerus reports to Esther the number of their enemies slain by the Jews in Susa (Esther 9:12), the rabbinic tradition reports that an angel came and slapped him on the mouth, presumably because he was angry that the Jews had taken revenge (*Megillah* 16b).

Moreover, in his greed Ahasuerus is compared to a bear; and the phrase from Proverbs (28:15), "a ravenous bear," is said to apply to him (*Megillah* 11a). Additionally, he is depicted as a drunkard. Thus, his wife Vashti taunts him, reminding him that her father, who is said to have been King Belshazzar, drank in the presence of a thousand and still did not get drunk, whereas Ahasuerus became senseless with wine (*Megillah* 12b).

Furthermore, the rabbis stress Ahasuerus' immorality, noting that he ordered that force be used in taking maidens away from their parents and wives from their husbands in acquiring them for his harem (*Panim Aḥerim* 65). Likewise, they remark that Vashti was a fit queen for him, since she had an immoral purpose in making a feast for the eminent people in the royal family (Esther 1:9; *Megillah* 12a).

There is an apparent difference of opinion as to whether Ahasuerus was clever or foolish, with Rav saying that he was clever because he entertained his distant subjects first, since he realized that he could win over his nearer subjects at will, while Samuel says that he should have entertained his nearer subjects first, so that if the more distant subjects rebelled he would have had a solid base of support among his nearer subjects (*Megillah* 12a). Moreover, in contrast to the Jews, who begin their meals with discourses on the Torah, Ahasuerus, says Rav, began his feast with words of silliness (*tifelut*, "frivolity, "trivialness," "obscenity"). In fact, in a comment on Ahasuerus' decision to appoint commissioners to gather all beautiful young maidens throughout his kingdom (Esther 2:3), he is regarded as the epitome of foolishness (since all who had young daughters hid them, knowing that he would try them all but choose only one), for whom the verse in Proverbs (13:16) is particularly applicable, "In everything a prudent man acts with knowledge, but a fool flaunts his folly" (*Megillah* 12b). Indeed, the fourth-century Raba explains the delay of the Jews in taking measures to avoid their destruction when they were given almost a year of advance warning (Esther 3:12-13) by remarking that the people had seen how foolish the king was from the letter which he sent out stating what was so clearly obvious, namely that every man should rule in his own home (Esther 1:22; *Megillah* 12b). In short, Ahasuerus is presented as the archetypal fool (*Midrash Esther Rabbah* 1.22).

Furthermore, in explaining why Esther invited Haman to her banquet, Rabban Gamaliel conjectures that she did so because Ahasuerus was so changeable (*Megillah* 15b), presumably her hope being that she would be able to persuade him to alter his decision to destroy the Jews while Haman was present so that he would not have time to change his mind again. His instability is illustrated by the fact that he sacrificed his wife Vashti in listening to his friend Memucan (who is identified with Haman) and later in sacrificing his friend Haman to his wife Esther (*Abba Gorion* 1, *Esther Rabbah* introduction 9). His chameleon character is likewise seen in the fact that after deposing Vashti, when he became sober, he turned furiously against those who had counselled him to depose her and ordered them to be put to death (*Abba Gorion* 17-18).

There is good reason to think that Josephus was acquainted with the oral tradition, as later codified by the rabbis, with regard to the story of Esther in particular, as we have noted.

2. *Josephus' Portrait of Ahasuerus*[2]

Because of his reverence for the concepts of law and order and for the institution of kingship it should not be surprising, as we have

---

[2] There are a number of indications that it is the Greek text that is Josephus' primary source for his version, most notably in his close paraphrase of a number of extensive additions which are found only in the Greek. Moreover, like the Greek, he repeatedly introduces the role of G-d into the narrative, whereas the very name of G-d is totally absent from the Hebrew text. We may cite as an example Esther 6:1, where, in the Hebrew text, we read that "On that night the king could not sleep." The Greek text, introducing the role of G-d, reads, "The L-rd

seen, that Josephus, likewise in extra-biblical comments, presents non-Jewish kings, such as the Egyptian Pharaohs, Nebuchadnezzar, Belshazzar, and Darius, in a better light.

What is most striking about Josephus' version of Ahasuerus is that there is not even a single hint in it that is negative. Indeed, almost at the very beginning of the narrative, whereas, as we have seen, the rabbis portray him as a drunkard, based, presumably, on the biblical passage that on the seventh day of his feast, the heart of Ahasuerus was merry with wine (*ketov lev hamelekh bayayin*) (Esther 1:10), Josephus totally omits his drunkenness as the background of his order to his queen Vashti to appear at the banquet (*Ant.* 11.190).

Moreover, most significantly, the pericope in Josephus' hands becomes an instrument for preaching the importance of obeying the law, a feature which, as we have noted, he stresses so often elsewhere. Indeed, the word νόμος, "law," appears no fewer than fourteen times in Josephus' paraphrase of the Esther story (*Ant.* 11.191, 192, 193, 195, 205, 210, 212, 217, 228, 230, 231, 238, 239, and 281); and what is particularly impressive is that in eight of these instances (*Ant.* 11.191, 195, 205, 210, 230, 231, 238, 239) neither the word νόμος nor any corresponding word is to be found in the corresponding passages (Esther 1:12, 2:1, 2:14, 3:2, Addition C [*bis*], 7:2 [*bis*]) in the Septuagint, the prime source of his account. We may note, in particular, that Josephus makes a point of adding the extra-biblical statement that the reason why Queen Vashti did not appear at the banquet when summoned by Ahasuerus was that she was observing the laws of the Persians which forbade women to be seen by strangers (*Ant.* 11.191). Again, as Josephus depicts it, so great is Ahasuerus' regard for law that, in an extra-biblical statement, though he had a deep love for Vashti and clearly had a change of heart after dismissing her (the scene is reminiscent of Herod's attitude toward Mariamne after he had ordered her to be put to death), he declines to recall her because the law forbade such a reconciliation (*Ant.* 11.195).

The biblical account stresses Ahasuerus' rage at Vashti's refusal to appear at the banquet when summoned by him and gives the reader the distinct impression that Ahasuerus' dismissal of Vashti was capricious (Esther 1:12); but Josephus, as in the Lucianic ver-

---

removed sleep from the king"; and Josephus (*Ant.* 11.248) clearly follows this text when he writes, "That night He [i.e. G-d] deprived the king of sleep."

sion, protects the king's reputation by making it clear that he had sent for her not merely once but repeatedly (*Ant.* 11.191). This point is reiterated by Josephus' addition that Ahasuerus said that he had been insulted (ὑβρισθείη) by her, "for though she had repeatedly been called by him to the banquet, she had not once obeyed" (*Ant.* 11.192). This arrogance is all the greater since Ahasuerus is said to have power over all men (*Ant.* 11.194). The key word here is ὑβρισθείη – a word that his audience, brought up as they undoubtedly were, on the Greek tragedies, would have appreciated, since such insolence (ὕβρις) merited the most severe penalty. Indeed, it is this word which is repeated by Muchaios (Memucan), one of the Seven Persians who were the king's closest advisers, who stresses that such an insult affected not only Ahasuerus but all the Persians (*Ant.* 11.193).

One of the embarrassing aspects of the story is that it would appear that Esther, the heroine, was actually only the favored woman in Ahasuerus' harem (Esther 2:17). Hence, it is significant that Josephus makes it very clear that he made her his lawful (νομίμως) wife (*Ant.* 11.202). Here, once again, we see the emphasis on Ahasuerus as concerned with obeying the law. Indeed, whereas the biblical text, in the Septuagint version, asserts that Esther was taken to Ahasuerus in the twelfth month, that is Adar (Esther 2:16), Josephus makes this the date that he actually married her (*Ant.* 11.202).

Moreover, Josephus expands greatly in his depiction of the gentleness of Ahasuerus and of his tender concern for Esther's well-being (*Ant.* 11.236). Thus, whereas Addition D in the Greek text indicates that when Esther fearfully, without being summoned, approached the king to invite him to her banquet, he changed his initial reaction of anger to gentleness, Josephus adds that he feared that his wife might have suffered some very serious injury through her fear, whereupon he embraced her and spoke to her endearingly and urged her to take heart and not to be afraid of a gloomy fate (*Ant.* 11.238). Indeed, he reminds her, in another addition, that she ruled equally with himself and thus had complete security. Again, in Addition D, where the king is described as troubled when Esther faints, it is his servants who comfort her; in Josephus' version, on the other hand, it is Ahasuerus who sympathetically is seized by anguish (ἀγωνία) and alarm (ταραχή) and who then takes the initiative to encourage her to be of good cheer and to hope for the best (*Ant.* 11.241). We also see and admire Ahasuerus' deep love for Esther when Esther tells him that Haman plans to kill her people. At this point, in the biblical version we are told that Ahasuerus rose up from the banquet to go into the garden (Esther 7:7); Josephus' Ahasuerus reacts much more strongly: in his perturbation (ταραχθέντος) he actually leaps up (ἀναπηδήσαντος) from the banquet hall into the garden (*Ant.* 11.265). He then shows his intense anger with Haman by calling him, in a further addition to the biblical text, "O basest of all men." Likewise, after Haman has been punished, in the biblical text Ahasuerus tells Esther to write, in his name, as seems best to her on behalf of the Jews (Esther 8:8), whereas Josephus' Ahasuerus shows even more concern for her when he adds his promise that nothing should be done to distress her nor any opposition be made to what she strives after (*Ant.* 11.271).

In addition, Ahasuerus is, in a supplement to Addition E, represented as noted for his loyalty to his benevolent (εὐνοούντων, "well-disposed") friends (*Ant.* 11.278). Furthermore, the statement, after all the benefactions that he had performed on behalf of the Jews, that Ahasuerus then proceeded to levy a tax upon his kingdom both by land and sea (Esther 10:1), an act that was hardly likely to endear him to his subjects, or for that matter to his readers, is significantly omitted altogether by Josephus (*Ant.* 11.296), though he otherwise follows the biblical text closely.

We have already noted the ridicule poured upon Ahasuerus by the rabbinic tradition for his foolishness in sending out an order stating what was so obvious, namely that every man should rule in his own home (Esther 1:22; *Megillah* 12b). Josephus omits this statement completely and instead has Ahasuerus announce to the nations merely what had been decreed against Vashti (*Ant.* 11.194). Furthermore, that Ahasuerus is identified in Josephus with good sense and reason is manifest from the fact that whereas, in his edict in favor of the Jews, Ahasuerus asserts that Haman was overcome by the pride of his station (Addition E), Josephus' Ahasuerus castigates Haman for not bearing his prosperity with prudent reasonableness (σώφρονι λογισμῷ) (*Ant.* 11.277), a quality which Josephus clearly feels is identified with Ahasuerus.

That Ahasuerus' concern is with his subjects is clear from the appeal which Haman, in an extra-biblical remark, makes to him. "If you wish to lay up a store of good deeds (εὐεργεσίαν καταθέσθαι) with your subjects, you will give orders to destroy this nation root and branch" (*Ant.* 11.213), he says, with the obvious indication that his appeal will strike a responsive chord. Indeed, Ahasuerus is represented as the ideal ruler whose goal, in an extra-biblical addition, is peace and good government (εὐνομίας) with the aim that his subjects may enjoy these forever (*Ant.* 11.216). Εὐνομία, we recall, is personified as the daughter of Themis in Hesiod (*Theogony* 902), is the very title of a famous poem by Tyrtaeus (cited by Aristotle, *Politics* 1307A), and is the goal of Plato's ideal system of education (*Republic* 4.425A).

Furthermore, to enhance the picture of Ahasuerus as a serious and effective ruler, whereas the biblical text states merely that when the king could not sleep he had his servant read from his chronicles (Esther 6:1), Josephus adds a motive for these instructions, namely, that he did not wish to waste his wakeful hours in idleness but to use them for something of importance to his kingdom by hearing the record of deeds of those kings who were before him as well as of his own deeds (*Ant.* 11.248), thus showing concern for the welfare of his subjects and, in particular, his eagerness to learn from history.

Moreover, Josephus enhances the gratitude which Ahasuerus feels towards those who have done good to him. Thus, whereas in the biblical text, when the chronicle is read to him telling how Mordecai had saved him from the conspiracy of Bigthan and Teresh, Ahasuerus asks what honor had been bestowed upon Mordecai (Esther 6:3), Josephus adds that the reader was already passing on to another incident when Ahasuerus took the initiative to stop him in order to inquire how Mordecai had been rewarded (*Ant.* 11.250). That, indeed, magnanimity is the quality most closely associated with Ahasuerus may be seen from the fact that whereas in the Bible the king asks Haman what should be done to the man whom the king delights to honor (Esther 6:6), in Josephus' version Ahasuerus asks Haman to advise him, in a manner worthy of his magnanimity (μεγαλοφροσύνης), how to honor one whom he greatly cherished (*Ant*, 11.252). Moreover, in a supplement to Addition E, Josephus remarks that Haman enjoyed the hospitality and kindness which he shows to all people (*Ant.* 11.277).

One major obstacle to the rehabilitation of the reputation of Ahasuerus is that, after all, Ahasuerus did send out the edict condemning all the Jews to death (Esther 3:12); but Josephus diminishes the blame accorded to Ahasuerus by remarking that it was Haman who sent out the edict in the king's name (*Ant.* 11.215). Moreover, in a supplement to Addition E, Josephus has Ahasuerus defend himself by remarking that those who had been entrusted with the administration of the government had misled their masters by false charges and slanders and had thus persuaded them (including Ahasuerus himself) to vent their anger on people who had done no wrong (*Ant.* 11.275). In a further addition Ahasuerus then promises that in the future he will take care not to pay attention to such slanders and accusations but rather to rely upon his own knowledge (*Ant.* 11.276). Indeed, Ahasuerus more than makes up for his past errors by declaring, in a supplement to Addition E, that it is his will that the Jews be shown every honor (*Ant.* 11.280).

3. *Novelistic, Romantic, and Dramatic Elements*

The Hellenistic novels tend to elaborate the descriptions of palaces and royal banquets. Here, too, Josephus adds a number of details not found in the Hebrew original or in the Septuagint. Thus we are given a detail not found in the Bible (Esther 1:6), that the pavilion where Ahasuerus' banquet was held was so large that many tens of thousands could recline there at the tables (*Ant.* 11.187). Again, though Josephus does omit a few details concerning the banquet-couches and the pavement upon which they were set (Esther 1:6 vs. *Ant.* 11.187), he adds, following the Septuagint, as against the Hebrew text, that the bowls from which the guests were served were made not only of gold (Esther 1:7) but also of precious stones (*Ant.* 11.188). The gala nature of the king's celebration is magnified by Josephus' addition, for which there are no rabbinic parallels, that the king sent messengers throughout his realm to proclaim that his subjects might rest from their work and celebrate for many days in honor of his reign (*Ant.* 11.189). Later, when Ahasuerus makes a feast to celebrate his wedding with Esther (Esther 2:18), Josephus magnifies its dimensions by stating that the king dispatched messengers called *angaroi* to every nation, inviting them to join in the celebration (*Ant.* 11.203).

The novels tend not to cite too many difficult and exotic names, since these would be difficult for the reader to pronounce. Josephus also omits lists of names because of their difficulty; thus he deliberately omits for this reason the names of Jacob's seventy descendants that entered Egypt (*Ant.* 2.176), as well as the names of the families that returned to Jerusalem (*Ant.* 11.68) from the Babylonian captivity or the names of the Jews who put away their foreign wives at the behest of Ezra (*Ant.* 11.152) or those of the seventy elders sent by Eleazar to translate the Torah (*Ant.* 12.57). He likewise omits, presumably for the same reason, the names of King Ahasuerus' seven chamberlains (Esther 1:10 vs. *Ant.* 11.190) and of his seven counsellors (Esther 1:14 vs. *Ant.* 11.192), as well as those of Haman's ten sons (Esther 9:7-9 vs. *Ant.* 11.289).

Josephus adds a number of details to enhance the romance and the drama of his narrative. To build up the erotic aspect, Josephus adds to Scripture (Esther 1:12) by giving a reason for Vashti's refusal, namely, that the Persians' laws forbade wives from being viewed by strangers (*Ant.* 11.191). Both Herodotus (5.18 and 9.110) and the Bible itself (Esther 5:4 ff. and Nehemiah 2:6) make it clear that the queen could be present at banquets (so Paton 1908, 149-50); hence Josephus' addition here seems calculated solely to increase the erotic interest, a motif prominent in the Greek romances.[3] Again, the dramatic interest of the narrative is increased by Josephus' description of the king's reaction when Vashti refuses to come to the banquet. The Bible says merely that "the king was very wroth, and his anger burned in him" (Esther 1:12). Josephus' Ahasuerus is more dramatic in his reaction; he breaks up (λῦσαι) the banquet (*Ant.* 11.192).

The reader may be critical of Ahasuerus for turning so quickly against his loyal prime minister, Haman. But Haman's punishment is justified by Josephus in terms that his Greek audience would especially appreciate, for Josephus (*Ant.* 11.273-83), in a paraphrase of Apocryphal Addition E 2-4, notes that Haman has allowed, in a sequence familiar to those who know Greek tragedy, the κόρος, the abundance of his good fortune, to lead him, with utter disregard for prudence and reason, to ὕβρις against his very benefactors. To Ahasuerus, as he notes in an edict issued to his empire, it

---

[3] See Goethals 1959, 89. Moehring (1957) has noted the novelistic-erotic elements in several passages from Josephus' account of the Hellenistic period, namely, the life of Herod the Great, the relations between Herod and Mariamme, the death of Herod, the four sects of the Jews, and the account of the persecution of the Jews in Rome in 19 C.E.

is intolerable that Haman, himself an alien, who had received hospitality from Ahasueres, should manifest such ingratitude as to plot against the kingdom and Ahasueres' very life in demanding the destruction of Mordecai, the king's benefactor and savior, and Esther, who shared the king's life and throne.

There is likewise a greater build-up of suspense toward the climax of Esther's selection as successor in Josephus' further elaboration of the feeling of remorse that Ahasuerus feels after he has deposed Vashti (*Ant.* 11.195). The Bible reports that Ahasuerus "remembered Vashti, and what she had done and what was decreed against her" (Esther 2:1). Josephus adds that the king was in love with her and could not bear the separation, yet, because of the law, could not be reconciled to her (*Ant.* 11.195). A similar motif is to be found in the Greek romances (cf., e.g., Parthenius 8). Indeed, there is in Josephus a shift of emphasis from Ahasuerus the ruler of a great empire to Ahasuerus the lover, so characteristic of the Greek romances (see Perry 1967, 149-53). Josephus further adds the element of grief to the king's emotional state, noting that Ahasuerus continued (διετέλει, the imperfect tense indicating repeated action) to grieve (λυπούμενος) at not being able to obtain his desire (*Ant.* 11.195). In the Bible, the advice to seek a beautiful young replacement for the deposed queen is presented as a political decision, coming from the king's servants who minister to him (Esther 2:2). In Josephus, as in the Greek plays and novels, the love-tormented hero who has lost his sweetheart is advised by confidants or friends (φίλοι), who, seeing him in so unhappy a station (οὕτως ἔχοντα χαλεπῶς), command him to cast out his memory of his wife and his love (ἔρωτα) for her, since this was doing him no good (μηδὲν ὠφελούμενον), and to seek a beautiful virgin to replace her (*Ant.* 11.195). They give the standard advice of confidants to lovers, not paralleled in the Bible (Esther 2:4), namely, that the fire of his tender love (φιλόστοργον, "passion," "affection") for Vashti would be quenched (σβέννυσθαι) by replacing her with another, and that thereby his affection (εὔνουν) for her would be gradually (κατὰ μικρόν) diverted to her successor (*Ant.* 11.196).[4]

---

[4] The erotic motif is perhaps found even in Josephus' portrayal of Mordecai, for he remarks, in an extra-biblical detail that Mordecai shared the royal power with the king, "at the same time also enjoying the companionship of the queen" (ἀπολαύων ἅμα καὶ τῆς κοινωνίας τοῦ βίου τῇ βασιλίσσῃ) (*Ant.* 11.295).

Ahasuerus' anger at Haman is exaggerated in his exclamation upon his return, "O basest of all men" (*Ant.* 11.265). Whereas the Hebrew Esther is silent as to Haman's reaction when the king thus accuses him of trying to violate his wife (Esther 7:8), Josephus generates a greater sense of drama by noting Haman's inability to utter any further sound (*Ant.* 11.266).[5]

4. *Summary*

In his *Antiquities* Josephus is largely concerned with answering the anti-Jewish canard that Jews hate Gentiles. In reply and because of his reverence for the concepts of law and order and for the institution of kingship Josephus also presents non-Jewish kings – notably the pharaohs of Abraham's and Joseph's times and even of the Exodus – in a more favorable light. Even Nebuchadnezzar, who was responsible for the destruction of the First Temple, is presented in a less derogatory tone than he is in the Bible; and the same is true for Belshazzar and Darius.

As to Ahasuerus, the rabbinic tradition generally portrays him in tones distinctly less favorable than would be apparent from the biblical text. Thus he is said to have attained power only because of his wealth. Moreover, he is said to have desecrated the Temple vessels. He is repeatedly described as wicked, no less so than Haman himself. They stress his greed, drunkenness, immorality, stupidity, and fickleness.

Though there is good reason to believe that Josephus was acquainted with much of this rabbinic tradition, he portrays Ahasuerus in much more favorable terms. In the first place, there is no mention of Ahasuerus' drunkenness. Josephus, above all, stresses Ahasuerus' respect for law. His apparently capricious treatment of Queen Vashti is explained as due to her insolence after she had been summoned repeatedly by her husband. And even then, Josephus expands on his deep love for her and on his remorse.

As to Ahasuerus' relationship with Esther, though there is good reason to question its nature, Josephus insists that it was lawful. He expands on his gentle and tender concern for Esther. The actions

---

[5] The Septuagint likewise notes Haman's reaction ("his face changed"; διετράπη τῷ προσώπῳ) (Esther 7:8), but this is hardly as effective as Josephus' description of Haman's speechlessness.

that the rabbis found foolish are carefully omitted, and the quality of prudent reasonableness is ascribed to him. Indeed, he is glorified as the ideal ruler whose goal is peace and good government for his subjects. He is particularly magnanimous toward those who do favors for him. If he did send out the edict condemning all the Jews in his realm to be put to death the blame is placed upon his advisers.

In his account of Ahasuerus Josephus includes a number of novelistic elements, which tend to enhance the stature of Ahasuerus. In particular, he elaborates the details of Ahasuerus' banquet at the beginning of the narrative, as well as of the feast with which he celebrates the wedding with Esther. He builds up the erotic aspect by giving a reason for Vashti's refusal to appear at Ahasuerus' banquet. The dramatic interest is heightened by Josephus' description of Ahasuerus' reaction at Vashti's refusal. Moreover, Josephus enhances the picture of Ahasuerus as the love-tormented king who is unable to cast out from his memory his love for Vashti.

CHAPTER THIRTY-FIVE

ESTHER

1. *Introduction*

One indication of the importance of a given episode for Josephus is the sheer amount of space that he devotes to it. For the Esther pericope Josephus (*Ant.* 11.184-296, 643 lines in the Loeb text) uses 1.04 times the space of the biblical Greek text (621 lines). This would appear to make the Esther story of only moderate importance to Josephus, but when we subtract the 226 lines in the additions to the Greek text which have no parallel in the Hebrew and which Josephus uses only very selectively, the ratio becomes 1.63, which indicates that, in fact, the episode is of major interest to Josephus. Its importance is due to three major factors: first, the narrative offers an idealized version of the figures of Esther and Mordecai, whom he may thus present as role models for his Jewish readers; second, for apologetic reasons, so crucial to Josephus' purposes in writing the *Antiquities*, Josephus' version serves to defend the Jews against the charges of their opponents; and third, the account engages the interest of the reader more than almost any other in the *Antiquities* because of its novelistic, romantic, and erotic elements.

2. *The Qualities of Esther and of Mordecai*

The heroine in Greek novels is usually portrayed as being of lofty, often royal, ancestry, though this ancestry is not revealed in many cases until late in the story. Similarly, Josephus starts his narrative of Esther by describing her as being of royal family (τοῦ γένους... τοῦ βασιλικοῦ) (*Ant.* 11.185). To be sure, in the Bible itself, Mordecai, her cousin, is described as being a descendant of Shimei, the son of Kish (Esther 2:5); and rabbinic tradition[1] identified this Kish as the father of King Saul. But if Mordecai's royal ancestry is,

---

[1] Cf. *Megillah* 13b, Targum 1 on Esther 2:5. See Ginzberg (1913, 4:381-83 and 1928, 6:458); and Rappaport (1930, 68, no. 282, and 134, n. 277).

in fact, being referred to here, it would seem more reasonable to refer to King Saul rather than to Saul's father. The fact that Josephus follows the rabbinic tradition[2] in ascribing royal ancestry to Mordecai (and consequently to Esther) seems deliberate and gives his heroine a characteristic feature of Hellenistic novels (see Goethals 1959, 1 ff.). Josephus further stresses Mordecai's prominence by noting that not only was he, as the Bible says, of the tribe of Benjamin (Esther 2:5), but that he was one of the chief men among the Jews (τῶν δὲ πρώτων παρὰ τοῖς Ἰουδαίοις) (*Ant.* 11.198).

It is characteristic of the Hellenistic novel to build up the stature of the hero and of the heroine. This is true of Josephus' Esther narrative also, for he exalts the character of both Esther and Mordecai. In reading the biblical narrative, one might conclude that Hegai, the eunuch in charge of the king's harem, showed special favoritism to Esther, since we read that "he advanced her and her maidens to the best place in the house of the women" (Esther 2:9). Josephus is careful to avoid this charge of special treatment by omitting this statement and by saying merely that she received every attention (*Ant.* 11.200). He likewise avoids the possible charge of undue favoritism shown by Hegai to Esther by omitting mention of Esther's refusal to take anything, when she goes to see Ahasuerus, except what Hegai recommends. A possible implication in the biblical narrative is that Esther thus relied upon Hegai because of the favoritism that he had shown her; Josephus avoids such a suggestion completely. Moreover, the question of Esther's relationship with Ahasuerus before their marriage (Esther 2:16) is avoided by Josephus by having him lawfully (νομίμως) make her his wife immediately after falling in love with her (*Ant.* 11.202).

In the biblical narrative Esther is completely subordinated, at least at the beginning of the tale, to Mordecai. But Josephus, though in general he tends to downgrade his biblical heroines (see Amaru 1988, 143-70; and Brown 1992), wants to focus attention on Esther, and so he omits the statement "Esther did the command

---

[2] Mordecai is cited by the rabbis as being as prominent among his contemporaries as Moses was among his. See Rappaport (1930, 68, no 283, and 135, n. 278), who cites *Midrash Esther Rabbah* 6.2 and *Menaḥoth* 65a.

of Mordecai, just as when she was brought up by him" (Esther 2:20 vs. *Ant.* 11.203).³

Esther's stature would likewise be decreased if Josephus had mentioned the second gathering of the virgins that is cited in the Bible (Esther 2:19), with the implication that Ahasuerus, even after making Esther his queen, was not content with her but sought new concubines. Josephus, like the Septuagint, avoids such an implication by omitting the episode completely (*Ant.* 11.204).

Esther's courage is exalted by Josephus' added remark that around King Ahasuerus' throne stood men with axes to punish those who approached without being summoned (*Ant.* 11.205). Hence, when Esther later decides to approach Ahasuerus on behalf of her people, even though she has not been summoned for a month, her great courage is manifest. In contrast to the simple biblical statement that she should petition the king on behalf of her people (Esther 4:8), Josephus builds up the drama with Mordecai's stern injunction to Esther that she should not consider it beneath her dignity (ἀδοξῆσαι) to put on humble dress and to intercede for the Jews (*Ant.* 11.225).

As co-hero of the narrative, Mordecai must not have anything unbecoming associated with him. In the biblical account we read: "And when the virgins were gathered together the second time, and Mordecai sat in the king's gate" (Esther 2:19). The connection between Mordecai's sitting in the king's gate with the gathering of the virgins is not clear (so Paton 1908, 188). To suppose, as do the older versions and many commentators, that Mordecai was a royal official who had charge of the reception of the virgins would be to ascribe something unseemly to him; Josephus avoids doing so by omitting mention of the gathering of the virgins (*Ant.* 11.204).⁴

---

³ That Josephus does not always denigrate biblical women may be seen in his portrait of Abigail, who, as Begg (1996, 32-33) has shown, emerges even more positively than she does in the Bible, notably as an effective speaker. In this case, however, Josephus may have chosen to present Abigail in a better light in order to make an even sharper contrast than does the Bible with her first husband, the churlish Nabal, and perhaps also to detract somewhat from David, whom she impresses with her sagacity and who later marries her. On Josephus' downgrading of David see Feldman (1989d, 172-74).

⁴ On the questions connected with Mordecai's lingering before the palace each day see Hoschander (1923, 20-21), who finds no difficulty in accepting the biblical account.

Mordecai's relationship with the king, even in the early days of Esther's reign, becomes closer in Josephus. Thus, after Mordecai saves Ahasuerus' life by revealing the conspiracy of Bigthan and Teresh, whereas the Bible merely records that the deed was noted in the royal book of chronicles (Esther 2:23), Josephus adds that the king ordered that he remain in the palace as a very close (ἀναγκαιότατον) friend (φίλον) of the king (*Ant.* 11.208).

One might well question why Mordecai does not prostrate himself before Haman. The Bible gives no explanation but merely states the fact (Esther 3:2). Josephus, in contrast, explains that Mordecai did so because of his wisdom (σοφίαν)[5] and his native law (τὸν οἴκοθεν αὐτοῦ νόμον), which forbade such prostration before any man (*Ant.* 11.210). There is no such Jewish law (so Bickerman 1967, 179); but this explanation would make a particular appeal to a Greek audience, which might well recall, for example, the refusal of the Spartan ambassadors to prostrate themselves before Xerxes as violating their sense of freedom (Herodotus 7.136). Mordecai's refusal to bow down is made all the more dramatic by Josephus' omission of the initial attempt of the king's servants to get Mordecai to agree to prostrate himself (Esther 3:3-4); in Josephus Haman himself observes Mordecai's refusal directly and inquires from what people he comes (*Ant.* 11.210).

3. *Novelistic, Romantic, and Dramatic Elements*

Martin Braun, in his detailed analysis of Josephus' rehandling of the episode of Joseph and Potiphar's wife, shows how he transforms a biblical narrative into a Hellenistic romance (Braun 1934). The relationship between historiography and romance had already been stressed by Schwartz,[6] who argued that the Greek romances

---

[5] Mordecai's knowledge is also stressed by the rabbis, who remark that as a member of the Sanhedrin, he knew seventy languages, which knowledge enabled him to understand the conversation of Bigthan and Teresh when they were plotting against the king, and that he maintained an academy. See *Menaḥoth* 65a, *Midrash Panim Aḥerim* 62; but the compliment about Mordecai's wisdom in not bowing down before Haman is unique to Josephus.

[6] On the emotional qualities, so characteristic of the novels, that mark Hellenistic historiography, see Scheller (1911, 79 ff.) Some of the motifs in the romances, such as travel and adventure, though not love, are also found in Egyptian narratives, and may have their origin there. See Giangrande (1962, 143, n. 1). To judge from the story of Gyges in Herodotus and Plato and from Xenophon's *Cyropaedia*, some of these motifs may well have arisen in the Near East.

originated in the fusion of Alexandrian love elegies and Hellenistic historiography (Schwartz 1896, 154). In view of the parallels between the stories of Joseph and Esther,[7] notably their common portrayals of Israelites who through their beauty and high position in a foreign royal court rescue their people from misfortune; and in view of similar parallels with the story of Judith in the Apocrypha (see Stiehl 1956, 4-22; and Bardtke 1958, 703-8), which Wilamowitz calls a typical Hellenistic novel, with its heroine-savior and its erotic aspect (Wilamowitz-Moellendorff 1912, 189), one should not be surprised to discover that Josephus has added a number of Hellenizations to his version of the Esther narrative,[8] including several touches characteristic of Hellenistic novels.[9] While it is true, despite Hoschander, that several of Josephus' additions are also paralleled in rabbinic midrashim (Hoschander 1923, 39), most of them are not to be found, despite Paton, in the Talmudic literature (Paton 1908, 39); and even those that do appear there seem deliberately to have been selected by Josephus because they serve his purpose.

One characteristic of Josephus' novelistic treatment is his concern with the beauty of biblical women. Josephus exaggerates the beauty of a number of women in his *Antiquities* – Rachel (*Ant.* 1.288), Samson's mother (*Ant.* 5.276), Bath-sheba (*Ant.* 7.130), and David's daughter Tamar (*Ant.* 7.162). Similarly, Vashti, who in the Bible is described merely as "fair to look on" (Esther 1:11), is

---

[7] See L. A. Rosenthal 1895, 278-84; and 1897, 125-28; Riessler 1896, 182; and Gan 1961-62, 144-49. Gan notes several more precise parallels: in both stories there are two attendants who sin against the king, and in both the heroes remain forgotten despite a confirmation of their revelations. Moreover, Gan points to a number of parallel expressions and figures of speech unique to the stories of Joseph and Esther. Talmon (1963, 454-55) describes both stories as "historicized wisdom tales."

[8] The Book of Esther is classified as a historical novel by Gunkel (1916, 75-76); Eissfeldt (1956, 628-29); Bentzen (1958, 2:192-95); and Kaufmann (1963, 4.1:439-48). But Cazelles (1961, 20) has rightly challenged this classification, since the marriage of Esther is not the center of interest in the work, and since the description has little of the sentimental in it, this incident being merely the preamble to the deliverance of the Jews. It is Josephus who by his changes gives the narrative much more of the appearance of an historical novel.

[9] Despite the fact that the earliest complete extant Greek novel probably dates from the second century C.E., a period somewhat later than Josephus, the discovery of the fragmentary Ninus romance, dating from no later than the first century C.E. and perhaps a hundred years earlier, shows that the typical motifs of these novels must go back to an earlier period. See Perry (1967, 153-54).

spoken of by Josephus as one who "surpassed all women in beauty" (κάλλει τὰς γυναῖκας ἁπάσας ὑπερβάλλουσαν) (*Ant.* 11.190). Again, Ahasuerus' search for fair young virgins to be gathered together by his officers from all the provinces of his kingdom (Esther 2:3) becomes a world-wide beauty contest, one encompassing the entire habitable (οἰκουμένην) world (*Ant.* 11.196). Furthermore, whereas the rabbis remark that Esther was not a real beauty but rather a seventy-five-year-old woman who captivated those whom she met by her grace and charm,[10] Josephus aligns himself on this point rather with the tradition of the Hellenistic novels (see Goethals 1959, 134 ff.) by depicting her as another Vashti, surpassing all women in beauty (πασῶν...τῷ κάλλει) (*Ant.* 11.199), though he does follow the rabbis in noting that the grace of her countenance (τὴν χάριν τοῦ προσώπου) greatly attracted (μᾶλλον ἐπάγεσθαι) the eyes of those who beheld her (τὰς ὄψεις τῶν θεωμένων).

It is significant, too, that Josephus, who, when he follows the Septuagint's additions to Esther, does so rather closely, departs from these in his highlighting of novelistic elements. Thus in his version of Addition C, which contains Esther's prayer to G-d before she goes to King Ahasuerus to plead for her people, Josephus says that Esther prayed for two things, for eloquence and for greater beauty than she had ever had before, so that she might by both these means turn aside the king's anger (*Ant.* 11.232); the Septuagint, by contrast, lacks the request for additional beauty and mentions merely her desire for eloquence. Finally, whereas the Apocryphal Addition (D 5) describes Esther as radiant in the perfection of her beauty and as endowed with a happy and lovely countenance, Josephus' Esther is warmer and more picturesque, her face covered with blushes, adorned with a sweet (προσηνές, "soft," "gentle," "soothing") and dignified (σεμνόν, "solemn," "august," "stately," "majestic") beauty (κάλλος) (*Ant.* 11.234).

The Hellenistic novels are much interested in the cosmetics and unguents with which women adorn themselves. The Bible says that Hegai, the keeper of Ahasuerus' harem, speedily supplied Esther with ointments and food (Esther 2:9); Josephus elaborates, remarking that Esther was anointed with an abundance of spices and

---

[10] See *Midrash Genesis Rabbah* 39.13 and *Esther Rabbah* 2.7, cited by Ginzberg (1913, 4:384; and 1928, 6:459, n. 68).

costly unguents such as women's bodies need (*Ant.* 11.200). The novels likewise are addicted to giving exact details about erotic matters; here too Josephus adds to the biblical account (Esther 2:9) by giving the exact number of maidens in Ahasuerus' harem, namely 400 (*Ant.* 11.200), an addition the source of which Benno Jacob finds it difficult to explain (Jacob 1890, 296). Again, Josephus, unlike the Hebrew text (Esther 2:18), gives the exact length of time during which Ahasuerus entertained his guests in honor of his marriage; the Septuagint says that he did so for seven days, but Josephus increases this to a full month.

In addition, as in the Hellenistic novels, Josephus is more explicit in his references to sexual intercourse. The Bible speaks of every maiden in the king's harem having her turn to go in to the king (Esther 2:12) and says that in the evening a maiden went and returned the following day to the second house for the women (Esther 2:14). Josephus remarks that when the virgins had received sufficient care and were now deemed fit for the king's bed by the eunuch in charge, the eunuch would send one every day to lie with the king, who, after having intercourse with her, sent her back at once to the eunuch. The picture thus presented is similar to that in Herodotus (3.69), where the wives of the false Smerdis visit him in turn.[11]

The soul of the narrative art of the Hellenistic romance is love. The romantic element in Josephus is often emphasized, as we see in Josephus' expanded treatment of the Egyptians' frenzy for women in connection with the story of Sarah and Abraham in Egypt (*Ant.* 1.162), Dinah's seduction (*Ant.* 1.327), the story of Joseph and Potiphar's wife (*Ant.* 2.53), Moses' marriage to the Ethiopian princess Tharbis (*Ant.* 2.252-53), the seduction of the Israelite youths by the Midianite women (*Ant.* 4.134), the affair of the Levite concubine (*Ant.* 5.136-37), the seizure of the women of Shiloh by the Benjaminites (*Ant.* 5.172-73), Manoah's mad love for his wife (*Ant.* 5.277), the love affair of David and Michal (*Ant.* 6.196 and 215), etc. Romance is similarly heightened by Josephus' version of the Bible's statement that "the king loved Esther above all the women" (Esther 2:17), according to which he actually fell

---

[11] Talmon (1963, 450) has noted that the stories of Esther and of Judith and Herodotus' account of the Magi (1.68-70) are all set in the Persian era and that all have the common theme of a courageous woman who rids or helps to rid her people of a tyrant.

in love with the maiden (πεσὼν τῆς κόρης εἰς ἔρωτα) (*Ant.* 11.202). One is reminded of Josephus' portrayal, with its extra-biblical color, of Jacob's falling in love with Rachel at first sight (*Ant.* 1.288).[12] Suspense is the hallmark of the Greek romances. The extent of Mordecai's devotion to Esther is increased by Josephus' shifting the statement that Mordecai took Esther for his own daughter from the beginning of the narrative about Esther (Esther 2:7) to the point where Esther is separated from him and enters the king's palace as his queen (Esther 2:11); at that point there is further suspense, for Mordecai lingers about the palace inquiring about Esther, "for he loved her as his own daughter" (*Ant.* 11.204).

In Apocryphal Addition D 8 we read that Esther fainted in the presence of Ahasuerus when she came to invite him and Haman to her feast. There is increased drama in Josephus' supplement (*Ant.* 11.237), according to which Ahasuerus feared that she had suffered serious injury.[13] There is greater warmth and added romance as well in Josephus' supplement to Addition D 8, noting that after Ahasuerus had brought Esther back to consciousness, he embraced (κατασπαζόμενος) her and spoke to her endearingly (προσομιλῶν ἡδέως) (*Ant.* 11.238). There is greater drama, too, in Josephus' version of the scene found in Apocryphal Addition D 15, which states that while Esther was speaking she fell swooning and that the king was troubled. In Josephus' account Esther speaks with difficulty (μόλις) and weakly (μετὰ ἀσθενείας), while anguish (ἀγωνία) and alarm (ταραχή) seize Ahasuerus (*Ant.* 11.241).

The intensity of Ahasuerus' reaction is likewise increased in Josephus' version of what happens after Esther has told him that Haman plans to kill her people. In the Bible the king arises in his wrath from the banquet and goes into the palace garden (Esther 7:7). In Josephus the king in his perturbation (ταραχθέντος) actually leaps up (ἀναπηδήσαντος) from the banquet-hall into the garden (*Ant.* 11.265).[14]

---

[12] The theme of love at first sight is common in the Greek romances: see Parthenius 1.1, Chariton 1.1-6-7, Xenophon of Ephesus 1.3.12, Achilles Tatius 1.4.2-5, and Heliodorus 3.5.4-5.

[13] For swooning as an expression of awe, cf., e.g., Chariton 3.6.4 and 4.9.1, as noted by Bickerman (1951, 117).

[14] Similarly, Josephus emphasizes Solomon's eagerness to do obeisance to G-d by having him leap up (ἀνεπήδησεν) from his bed when he hears G-d's promise to preserve his kingdom (*Ant.* 8.25). Again, Josephus adds excitement to his narrative of Ahab by having him leap up (ἀναπηδήσας) from his bed when in-

One of the most characteristic features of the Hellenistic novel, undoubtedly due to the influence of Greek tragedy, is its high degree of irony.[15] This is also one of the characteristics of Josephus' version of the Esther story. Thus in the Hebrew version (Esther 5:9), after Haman receives his invitation to Esther's second banquet, he is described as going forth in joy and in gladness of heart, but the reason for his joy is only implied in terms of the events that have preceded. It is characteristic of Greek tragedy that just before the περιπέτεια there is a moment of ironically increased rejoicing, which in effect heightens the reversal that is to follow. This is particularly true in Josephus' version of the Esther story. Josephus is explicit in giving as the reason for Haman's joy the fact that he alone had been deemed worthy to dine with the king at Esther's palace; and the irony of Haman's imminent fall is increased by the further statement that no one had previously obtained a similar honor from any of the kings before Ahasuerus (*Ant*. 11.244). The irony of Haman's fall through the efforts of Esther is accented by Josephus' omission of Haman's boasting of his riches and of the multitude of his children (Esther 5:11 vs. *Ant*. 11.245); instead and more effectively, in Josephus' version, he concentrates on the honor shown him by the queen, who on the following day is to point him out to the king as the villain who seeks to destroy her people.

At the highest moment in Haman's fortunes, when he has received the exclusive invitation to join Esther and Ahasuerus a second time at her banquet and when he has built the gallows to hang his arch-enemy Mordecai, Josephus typically, just before the περιπέτεια, introduces G-d's ironic laughter at these events: "But G-d mocked (κατεγέλα) Haman's wicked hopes, and, knowing what was to happen, rejoiced (ἐτέρπετο) at the event" (*Ant*. 11.247).

The reversal of fortunes of Mordecai, and consequently of Haman, is heightened by Josephus' version of Ahasuerus' sleepless night (*Ant*. 11.249). According to the Bible and Septuagint (Esther 6:1-2), Ahasuerus asks to have the chronicles read, and it was found written that Mordecai had saved the king's life. More dramatic is Josephus' account, according to which the readers first tell

---

formed by Jezebel that Naboth has been killed and that he can take possession of his vineyard without paying for it (*Ant*. 8.360).

[15] Cf., e.g. Achilles Tatius 5.11, 6.11-12; Heliodorus 1.18, 1.28-31, 6.15, 8.17, and 9.2. See Wolff 1912, 213-17.

of the land, the name of which was also written, awarded a certain man for his bravery. Then, after mentioning the gift awarded to another for his loyalty, they come to the story of how Mordecai had saved the king from the plot of Bigthan and Teresh. There is increased drama because the scribe merely states the fact, ever so briefly, of Mordecai's rescue of the king and is already passing on to another incident when the king stops him and asks what reward had been given Mordecai (*Ant.* 11.250).[16]

That the reading had gone on for some time is clear from the additional remark in Josephus that the king told the scribes to stop and inquired of his attendants what hour of the night it was (*Ant.* 11.250-51). When told that it is already morning, he asks to have admitted to him any of his friends who might be waiting before the court. Josephus, following the Lucianic version, adds to the irony by noting that Haman had come that day before the usual hour (*Ant.* 11.251); and it is against this background that the scene between Ahasuerus and Haman takes place. Haman's anticipation that it is he whom the king wishes to honor is heightened because, whereas in the Bible Ahasuerus asks Haman what should be done for the man whom the king wishes to honor (Esther 6:6), Josephus' Ahasuerus seeks advice as to how to honor, in a manner worthy of his magnanimity (μεγαλοφροσύνης), a man who was greatly cherished (στεργόμενον: frequently used with reference to the mutual love of parents and children) by him (*Ant.* 11.252). Moreover, Ahasuerus introduces his question by adding the remark, particularly ironic in the context, that he knows that Haman is the only friend loyal (εὔνουν, "well-disposed," "kindly," "friendly") to him (*Ant.* 11.252).

It is natural, in such circumstances, for Haman to deduce that he is the person intended by the king; and here, too, Josephus adds to the irony by stating that Haman thought that he was the only one loved (φιλεῖσθαι, implying affection) by the king (*Ant.* 11.253). Haman's thinking of himself as the one loved by the king is further underscored with a third additional reference in Josephus (and with a third different word for love). "If you wish to

---

[16] Josephus' statement that the reader was ready to pass on to another incident may well have a parallel with rabbinic tradition, according to which the office of reader was being filled by one of Haman's sons (*Ant.* 11.250). See Ginzberg (1913, 4:434; and 1928, 6:476, n. 168), who cites *Midrash 2 Panim Aḥerim* 75 and *Yalquṭ* 2.1057.

cover with glory the man whom you say you love (ἀγαπᾶν, implying regard), let him ride on horseback," says Haman (*Ant.* 11.254); the Hebrew speaks merely of "the man whom the king delighteth to honor" (Esther 6:7). There is further irony in that whereas in the biblical text Haman recommends that the person whom the king wishes to honor should be paraded on horseback through the city square (Esther 6:9), in Josephus' version Haman suggests that one "of your close friends" (τῶν ἀναγκαίων φίλων) – obviously, in Haman's mind, himself – should precede him (*Ant.* 11.254). The word "love" is again introduced with ironic effect in Josephus' version of the words later spoken by Haman in leading Mordecai about. In the Bible these words are: "Thus shall it be done unto the man whom the king delighteth to honor" (Esther 6:11). Josephus' Haman proclaims that this is the reward given by the king "to him whom he loved (στέρξῃ, "cherished") and held worthy of honor" (*Ant.* 11.258).

The irony of Josephus' account is emphasized by Josephus' repetition, not found in the Hebrew text (Esther 6:10), of the statement that Haman gave his advice in the belief that the king would reward him (*Ant.* 11.255). There is added irony in the implied equation of Mordecai and Joseph,[17] for whereas Scripture speaks of the royal crown being placed upon the horse that Mordecai rides (Esther 6:8), Josephus, perhaps because this seemed awkward or incongruous, substitutes a necklace of gold to be placed on Mordecai himself (*Ant.* 11.254). In the account of Pharaoh's elevation of Joseph, we likewise read that Pharaoh put a gold chain about his neck (Genesis 41:42) (to be sure, omitted in Josephus' paraphrase of the passage, *Ant.* 2.90).[18] There is further irony in Josephus' remark that Ahasuerus was pleased (ἡσθείς) with Haman's counsel (*Ant.* 11.255); the biblical text does not record the king's reaction to Haman's advice (Esther 6:10). The irony is all the greater when Ahasuerus tells Haman to do to Mordecai

---

[17] The Midrash likewise compares the story of Esther with that of Joseph in several respects: thus we are told that not even Joseph could vie with Esther in grace (Ginzberg 1913, 4:385). Hegai (Ginzberg 1913, 4:386) loads Esther with jewels just as Joseph loaded Benjamin her ancestor. The agreement between Ahasuerus and Haman to destroy the Jews is a punishment for the sale of Joseph (Ginzberg 1913, 4:413, who cites 2 Targum 3.14-15).

[18] Later in the narrative Josephus adds to the biblical account (Esther 8:15) by noting that Mordecai donned the royal necklace when he assumed the position of the king's prime minister (*Ant.* 11.284).

what he has advised. In the Hebrew text Ahasuerus says merely, "Let nothing fail of all that thou hast spoken" (Esther 6:10). In Josephus the ironical effect is all the sharper, for Ahasuerus adds the reason why he has chosen Haman to carry out what he calls Haman's "good counsel," "since you are my close friend." The word which Ahasuerus uses here for "close friend" (ἀναγκαῖος) (*Ant.* 11.253) is the same as that used by Haman in his advice that one of the king's close friends should precede the man whom he proposes to honor (*Ant.* 11.254); and the irony is consequently heightened.

Again, whereas the Bible does not give any description of Haman's state of mind after he has been told to lead Mordecai about, and merely records that he took the apparel and the horse (Esther 6:11), Josephus notes first of all that the king's words were – the very essence of irony – contrary to all of Haman's expectations, and that Haman was consequently oppressed (συνεσχέθη) in spirit and stricken (πληγείς) with helplessness (ἀμηχανίας) (*Ant.* 11.256).[19] The irony of having the great and powerful Haman lead Mordecai is increased in Josephus' version; for whereas the Bible reports merely that Haman took the apparel and the horse and arrayed Mordecai (Esther 6:11), Josephus dwells on the contrast between Mordecai in his sackcloth, in which state Haman finds him, and the new garments which he is now told by Haman to put on instead (*Ant.* 11.256).

Dramatic suspense is increased by Josephus' additional detail, found in the Lucianic version but not in the Hebrew or in the standard Septuagint, that Mordecai at first was suspicious of Haman's intentions and, thinking that he was being mocked (χλευάζεσθαι), bitterly remarked: "O basest of all men, is this the way you make sport (ἐπεγγελᾷς) of our misfortunes?" (*Ant.* 11.257). It is only after he is convinced that Haman is sincere that he puts on the robes offered him by Haman.[20] The περιπέτεια in Haman's fortunes is magnified in that Haman leads Mordecai not merely through the streets of the city (Esther 6:11) but completely around the city (ἐκπεριῆλθον, *Ant.* 11.259).

There is likewise a heightening of dramatic suspense in Jose-

---

[19] So also the Lucianic version. The rabbis likewise (Ginzberg, 4.436-37) elaborate on Haman's feeling of disappointment.

[20] For rabbinic parallels see *Megillah* 16a and other passages cited by Ginzberg (1928, 6:476, n. 170).

phus' introduction of Harbonah at an earlier point than he appears in the biblical narrative. In the Bible it is not until Haman has been pointed out by Esther as the one who sought to destroy her people that Harbonah remarks that Haman had also built gallows for Mordecai, and the king thereupon orders Haman to be hanged thereon (Esther 7:9). In Josephus Harbonah, as one of Esther's eunuchs sent to hasten Haman's coming to the banquet, notices the gallows, learns that they ironically have been prepared for the queen's uncle Mordecai, and for the time being holds his peace (*Ant.* 11.261). As a storytelling device, such a detail builds up suspense, and Harbonah's later revelation is therefore all the more effective.

Josephus makes a special point of commenting on the supreme irony that Haman himself should have been hanged on the gallows that he had prepared for his enemy Mordecai and marvels at G-d's wisdom and justice in bringing this about (*Ant.* 11.268). Esther heightens this drama in Josephus' account by actually showing King Ahasuerus the letter that Haman had sent throughout the country enjoining the destruction of the Jews (*Ant.* 11.270).

Josephus adds a dramatic dimension to the hatred of Haman for the Jews by remarking that he was of Amalekite descent[21] (Esther 3:1 says only that he was an "Agagite"), and hence an ancestral enemy of the Jews (*Ant.* 11.209).[22] Ironically, he, like the Jews

---

[21] The Septuagint (Apocryphal Addition E 10 and Esther 9:24) speaks of Haman as a Macedonian, that is, in terms of Hellenistic history, an enemy of both the Persians and the Jews. Likewise, in the Latin Josephus (*Ant.* 11.277) Haman is termed *Macedo*, though this is, as Niese (1892), *praefatio*, vol. 3, p. xxxix, notes, an obvious correction on the basis of the Septuagint.

[22] Presumably, Josephus derives the notion of Haman's Amalekite descent from the fact that Agag was king of the Amalekites (1 Samuel 15:8). The rabbis (see *Megillah* 13a, *Pesiqta Rabbati* 12 [ed. Friedmann 51b], and *Midrash Esther Rabbah* 3.1, 7.4 [see Rappaport-1980, notes 281 and 282]) likewise speak of Haman as an Amalekite. The Septuagint, on the contrary, knows of no tradition of Haman as an Amalekite. See Jacob 1890, 291. Jacob, 262, is mistaken in his contention that Josephus used the Septuagint to the exclusion of the Hebrew, although there are places where this is the case: e.g., in *Ant.* 11.219, Josephus follows the LXX in stating that the Jews were to be massacred on the fourteenth day of the twelfth month, whereas the Hebrew text gives the date as the thirteenth day of the twelfth month (Esther 3:13); similarly, in *Ant.* 11.221, Josephus follows the Septuagint (Esther 4:1) in having Mordecai cry out that the Jewish nation had done no wrong; furthermore, he agrees with the Septuagint (Esther 4:5) in stating that Esther summoned Hasach, who happened to be nearby (*Ant.* 11.223). Likewise, Torrey (1944, 38) is not justified in postulating that Josephus used only the Aramaic version in a Greek translation but gives no evidence of

themselves, is described as "an alien among those of Persian blood" (*Ant.* 11.277). Josephus specifically remarks, in a detail not found in Scripture (Esther 3:6), that Haman decided to exterminate Mordecai's whole nation, "for he naturally hated the Jews because the race of Amalekites, from whom he was descended, had been destroyed by them" (*Ant.* 11.211). Josephus, moreover, takes pains to explain Haman's enmity for Mordecai personally by being more explicit than the biblical narrative, which says that all the king's *servants* who were in the king's gate used to bow down and prostrate themselves before Haman (Esther 3:2); Josephus says

---

acquaintance with the Hebrew. Hoschander (1923, 6-7) cites evidence that Josephus also used the Hebrew version. Furthermore, while there is a resemblance between the Lucianic text and Josephus, there are too many differences between them (so Jacob, 259 and 262) to posit that he used this text to the exclusion of all others.

The question as to which Greek text Josephus had before him for the narrative of Esther is extremely complex. H. Bloch (1879, 78-79) concludes that Josephus was following the Septuagint; but while it is true that at times, e.g., in stating that Ahasuerus married Esther in the twelfth month, Josephus does agree with the Septuagint (Esther 2:16; *Ant.* 11.202), at other times he rather follows the Old Latin, and at still other times the Lucianic version, as noted by Motzo (1928, 84-105). At still other times he agrees with the Hebrew text as against the Greek; for example, he states that the celebration of the wedding of Ahasuerus and Esther lasted a whole month (*Ant.* 11.203), whereas the Septuagint indicates that it lasted only seven days. Hölscher (1904, 52), in his search for a single source to explain the many deviations of Josephus from all known sources, declares it very probable that for the Book of Esther Josephus' sole source was the work of Alexander Polyhistor, *On the Jews*; but inasmuch as among the fragments of his work that have survived in the writings of Clement of Alexandria and Eusebius not a single one deals with any aspect of the Esther story, this suggestion is difficult to accept. Bickerman (1951, 104) concludes that Josephus was following a particular recension of the Greek Esther, namely the one popular among the Jews in Rome, where Josephus wrote his *Antiquities*, but which is now lost. Lévy (1949, 114) goes so far as to postulate that the Book of Esther was originally composed in Greek in substantially the form that it appears in Josephus, and that our Hebrew text is an extract from this. Seyberlich (1964, 363-66), remarking that the second edict of King Ahasuerus is found only in Josephus (*Ant.* 11.273-83) and in the Aramaic *Targum Sheni* 8.12, broaches the possibility that Josephus' source may have been an Aramaic, Targum-like paraphrase, but she ultimately dismisses this hypothesis on the ground that since Josephus, at the time of the completion of the *Antiquities*, had spent twenty years in Rome, it is improbable that he would have used an Aramaic Targum there. More likely, such parallels are due instead to his recalling some details of Pharisaic midrashim that he had heard in his earlier years. However, the text of the edict in Josephus is actually a close paraphrase of Addition E of the Septuagint version; and in view of the continuing contacts between the Jewish communities of Palestine and Rome throughout this period, it seems likely that Josephus would also, in fact, have had access to an Aramaic Targum.

specifically that both the foreigners and Persians prostrated themselves before him (*Ant.* 11.209).²³ This helps in the dramatic build-up of Haman's anger and of his hatred of Jews, for he contrasts this subservience with Mordecai's refusal, amplifying Scripture (Esther 3:9), urging Ahasuerus to order the Jews to be destroyed "root and branch" (πρόρριζον) and leave not a remnant of them to be kept either in slavery or in captivity" (*Ant.* 11.213).²⁴ Haman's hatred of the Jews is further exaggerated by Josephus' increase, from 10,000 to 40,000 talents of silver, not found in the Hebrew (Esther 3:9) or Septuagint versions, in the amount of the bribe offered by Haman to those who carry out the destruction of the Jews (*Ant.* 11.214).²⁵ Josephus adds the plausible explanation that Haman offered this amount to offset the loss in revenue that the king would suffer as a result of the elimination of the Jews (*Ant.* 11.214). Subsequently, too, there is a higher pitch of drama in Josephus, for whereas the Bible says that Ahasuerus' edict was to be published so that all people would be ready to attack the Jews on the given day (Esther 3:14), Josephus reports that when the decree was brought to the various cities and country districts, the people all actually readied themselves to annihilate the Jews on the appointed day (*Ant.* 11.220).

It is Josephus' contention that Haman deserved his fate because, like a classical Greek tragic figure, he did not know how to use his prosperity appropriately. Josephus elsewhere generalizes that men are apt to lose control of reason (λογισμοῦ) when blessed by good fortune (εὐτυχήσαντας) (*Ant.* 6.116), and he likewise notes, commenting on Rehoboam's degeneracy, that it is the very greatness in a man's affairs (τὸ τῶν πραγμάτων μέγεθος) and the improvement in his position that leads to evil and lawlessness (παρανομίας) (*Ant.* 8.251). Again, commenting on King Uzziah's degeneracy, he remarks that it was because of his successes (εὐπραξίας), his brilliant good fortune (ἡ τῶν ἀγαθῶν λαμπρότης), and his great power (τὸ μέγεθος τῶν πραγμάτων) that he fell into sin

---

²³ For rabbinic parallels see *Sanhedrin* 61b, *Pirqe de-Rabbi Eliezer* 50, *Midrash Esther Rabbah* 2.5 and 3.1-2, Targum Esther 3.2, *Abba Gorion* 22, 2 *Panim Aherim* 46, cited by Ginzberg (1928, 6:463, n. 100).
²⁴ The Midrash also amplifies Haman's hatred of the Jews. See Ginzberg (1913, 4:369, 393, 402, 410, 412, and notes thereon).
²⁵ The rabbis also amplify Haman's wealth. See *Pirqe de-Rabbi Eliezer* 50, *Panim Aherim* 46, *Midrash Esther Rabbah* 3.1, cited by Ginzberg (1928, 6:462, n. 93).

(*Ant.* 9.122). Likewise, he notes that G-d punishes the insolence of those who are ungrateful to Him (*Ant.* 5.200). Here, too, he cites as an example of the tragic process how Haman's great wealth led to κόρος ("satiety"), which, in turn, led to ὕβρις, which, in turn, brought about his νέμεσις. Josephus stresses Haman's lack of restraint as well: whereas the biblical narrative notes that when Haman saw that Mordecai did not stand up before him when he returned from Esther's first banquet, he was filled with wrath but nevertheless restrained himself (Esther 5:9-10), in Josephus' version Haman is highly indignant, and there is no mention of any restraint (*Ant.* 11.244). Again, whereas the Apocryphal Addition (E 12) remarks that Haman, made overbearing by his proud position (ὑπερηφανίαν, "arrogance"), took counsel to deprive Ahasuerus of his kingdom, Josephus castigates him, in terms of classical Greek tragedy, for not showing moderation in his time of prosperity: he did not bear his good fortune (εὐτυχίαν) wisely, and did not husband (ἐταμίευσεν)[26] the abundance (μέγεθος) of his prosperity (ἀγαθῶν) with prudence (σώφρονι, "moderation") and reason (λογισμῷ) (*Ant.* 11.277).[27] Josephus likewise stresses Nimrod's insolence (*Ant.* 1.113) and that of Hagar (*Ant.* 1.188-89) in order to justify the latter's expulsion by Abraham.

Josephus justifies Haman's punishment in terms familiar from Greek tragedy, for he adds to the biblical narrative (Esther 7:10) the remark that Haman was destroyed through his having used his position of honor immoderately (ἀμετρήτως, "indiscreetly," "excessively") (*Ant.* 11.269). In a paraphrase of an Apocryphal Addition (E 2-4), Josephus stresses Haman's ὕβρις toward those who had benefited and honored him and his lack of appreciation of his blessings (*Ant.* 11.273-74). He is further censured, again in terms of Greek tragedy, for turning his κόρος ("satiety," i.e., the consequences of satiety) against those who had benefited him (*Ant.* 11.274). Josephus attacks Haman particularly because, in a supplement to an Apocryphal Addition (E 6), he had acted on the prompting of a private grudge (μῖσος ἴδιον) (*Ant.* 11.275).

---

[26] R. Marcus (1937, 6:448) notes that a similar phrase, "husbanded ... good fortune" (ταμιεύεσθαι τὴν τύχην) is likewise found in Dionysius of Halicarnassus (*Ant. Rom.* 1.65).

[27] We may also note that Josephus, so as to concentrate attention on Haman and his family, omits the mention of Haman's friends joining Haman's wife Zeresh in advising him to build a gallows for Mordecai; instead the advice comes solely from Zeresh (*Ant.* 11.246).

Josephus takes care to paint Haman in still darker colors than he appears in the Apocryphal Addition (E 12-14). There mention is made only of Haman's plot against Ahasuerus' kingdom and against the lives of Mordecai and Esther. Josephus adds to the gravity of the charge by asserting that Haman also plotted against Ahasuerus' very life (*Ant.* 11.278). By the use of stronger language, i.e., that Haman "treacherously and deceitfully" demanded the destruction of Mordecai and of Esther, thus seeking to deprive him of "my (Ahasuerus') loyal friends," Josephus makes it easier to comprehend the king's speedy and drastic action in condemning Haman.

4. *Apologetic Elements*

A major purpose of Josephus' *Antiquities*, as of the essay *Against Apion*, is to answer the charges of the vilifiers of the Jews. Haman, in the biblical narrative, attacks the Jews as a people whose laws are different from those of every other people (Esther 3:8). Josephus amplifies this charge in terms similar to those used by the Alexandrians whom he answers in his *Against Apion*. The Jews, says Haman, refuse to mingle with others (ἄμικτον – a term used of Centaurs and Cyclopes)[28] and are unsocial (ἀσύμφυλον, "not akin," "incompatible," "unsuitable"). They do not have the same religion (θρησκείαν), nor do they practice the same laws as other peoples, but in both their customs (ἔθεσι) and in practices (ἐπιτηδεύμασιν) they are the enemy of the Persians and indeed of all mankind (ἅπασιν ἀνθρώποις) (*Ant.* 11.212). If, then, suggests Haman, Ahasuerus wishes to seek the welfare of his subjects, he will order the destruction of this people (*Ant.* 11.213). The Jews' purported hatred of monarchy in particular is singled out in Josephus' version of Ahasuerus' edict (*Ant.* 11.217); the Septuagint's Addition B 4 is more mild in stating that the Jews habitually neglect "the ordinances of the kings, so that the consolidation of the kingdom honorably intended by us cannot be brought about."

Haman's charges against the Jews are a concise summary of the most frequently recurring indictments against them from the time of Hecataeus of Abdera, one of the first Greeks, if not the first Greek, to describe the Jews, and who terms their way of life as ἀπ-

---

[28] Sophocles, *Trachiniae* 1093; Euripides, *Cyclops* 429.

ἄνθρωπον ("misanthropic," "unsocial") and μισόξενον ("hostile to strangers") (*ap.* Diodorus 40.3.5). Thus, it is significant that though he generally follows the Apocryphal Addition C, containing Esther's prayer to G-d, rather closely, Josephus omits the abhorrence of foreigners expressed there by Esther: "I detest the bed of the uncircumcised and of any alien" (C 26-27). Josephus even omits the separatism implicit in Esther's claim that she has not eaten or drunk forbidden food at the king's or Haman's table (C 28).

It is likewise significant that though Josephus introduces a certain number of adaptations of the Apocryphal additions, he omits completely Mordecai's dream (Addition A) and its interpretation (Addition F). In the dream, the conflict between Haman and Mordecai is presented not in terms of Haman's personal antagonism against the Jews but rather in terms of the eternal struggle of Gentile against Jew. Both additions were available to Josephus (so Motzo 1928, 86-87; and Bickerman 1951, 107, n. 17), since the statement that the king commanded Mordecai to wait upon him in the palace (*Ant.* 11.208), as well as the names of the eunuchs in *Antiquities* 11.207, for example, come from Addition A; but Josephus, for apologetic reasons, seeks to avoid the notion that there are two lots, one for the Jews, the other for the remaining nations, and that the Jews and Gentiles are by nature at odds with each other (see Bickerman 1944, 360-61). On the contrary, Josephus presents the unscriptural detail attributing Haman's hatred of the Jews not, as Haman later tells Ahasuerus, to the Jews' misanthropy (*Ant.* 11.212) but rather as a natural (φύσει) consequence of his being descended from the Amalekites, who had been destroyed by the Jews (*Ant.* 11.211). Here hatred of the Jews is depicted not as an eternal Jewish-Gentile conflict but rather as the result of a particular, even a personal, grudge.

Moreover, whereas Esther justifies the suffering of the Jews by admitting that they have sinned before G-d in that they have given glory to the gods of the Gentiles (Addition C 17-18), Mordecai, in Josephus' version specifically declares that it was not for any sin that they were in peril of being ingloriously put to death (*Ant.* 11.230).

Additionally, whereas in Addition E 20, Ahasuerus, in his edict, orders that the Jews be reinforced so that on the thirteenth day of the month of Adar they may defend themselves (ἀμύνωνται) against those who attacked them in the time of their affliction, in Josephus, presumably reflecting contemporary realities, the decree permits the Jews "by all means" not merely to defend themselves but to take more active measures to prepare themselves to fall upon (μετέλθωσιν) their enemies (*Ant.* 11.283). Moreover, whereas in the biblical text, when Mordecai is honored the city of Shushan shouts in gladness (Esther 8:15), in Josephus it is not merely that Mordecai is being honored but rather that his good fortune is shared by all the Jews (Esther 8:15)(*Ant.* 11.284).

Most remarkably, when Mordecai sends a eunuch to tell Esther not to look out for her own safety as much as for the common safety of the Jewish people, he warns her that if she neglects her people she and her family will be destroyed by those who had been neglected, that is, by her fellow-Jews (*Ant.* 11.227), whereas in the Bible Esther is told that if she neglects to help her fellow-Jews at this critical moment relief and deliverance will come from another (unspecified) quarter and that she and her father's house will perish (Esther 4:14), but with no indication as to how and by what means this will come about. Hence, in stressing the theme of the importance of Jewish unity, Josephus is, in effect, commenting upon its lack during the war against the Romans and its fatal consequences for the Jewish people.

The charge that the Jews were intolerant of other religions is sharply refuted by Josephus in his version of the Book of Esther as elsewhere. Thus, though Josephus generally follows the Apocryphal Addition C, containing Esther's prayer to G-d, he omits her bitter attack on the idol-worship of the non-Jews: "And now they [i.e. the enemies of the Jews] have not been satisfied with the bitterness of our captivity, but they have laid their hands (in the hands of their idols), to remove the ordinance of Thy mouth, and to destroy Thine inheritance, and to stop the mouth of them that praise Thee, and to quench the glory of Thy house and Thy altar, and to open the mouth of the nations to give praise to vain idols, and that a king of flesh should be magnified forever. Surrender not, O L-rd, Thy sceptre unto them that be not gods" (Addition C 19-22). Similarly, Josephus lacks the midrashic tale that Haman fostered idol-worship by having an image of an idol fastened on his clothes so that whenever someone prostrated himself before him he simultaneously worshipped that idol.[29]

---

[29] *Pirqe de-Rabbi Eliezer* 50, *Abba Gorion* 22, *Panim Aḥerim* 46, *Midrash Esther*

5. *Resolution of Difficulties in the Biblical Narrative*

Among the most common charges against the Jewish Scriptures (cf. *Ag. Ap.* 1.69 ff.) was the contention that they contained details in their chronology that would tax a reader's credulity. Josephus an an apologist is consequently concerned with avoiding these whenever possible. Thus, one of the problems in the Hebrew text of Esther is the statement that Mordecai was one of the captives who had been carried away by Nebuchadnezzar with Jeconiah (Jehoiachin) the king of Judah (597 B.C.E.) (Esther 2:6).[30] Even if Mordecai was then an infant, he would still be 123 years old in the twelfth year of Xerxes' reign (with whom most scholars identify Ahasuerus).[31] Josephus avoids the problem by omitting the statement that Mordecai had been carried off to Babylon. Esther's age, particularly if she is the daughter of Mordecai's uncle (Esther 2:7), presents a problem, since it seems unlikely that the king would be captivated by so old a woman; but as Mordecai's niece (*Ant.* 11.198) Esther's age is reduced, and the problem consequently lessened.

A question of credibility arises also with regard to the long period required to prepare the maidens before they could go in to King Ahasuerus. The Bible puts the length of this period at twelve months (Esther 2:12); Josephus reduces it to six months (*Ant.* 11.200) and thereby makes the matter more credible.

Another problem that arises is how Mordecai could gain daily access to the royal harem after Esther had been taken there (Esther 2:11) (see Paton 1908, 176). Josephus avoids the problem by omitting any mention here of Mordecai's visits (*Ant.* 11.201).

The Bible tells us merely that the conspiracy of two eunuchs Bigthan and Teresh "became known to Mordecai," but it does not tell us how this came about (Esther 2:22). The rabbis were much concerned to explain how Mordecai obtained his knowledge (*Megillah* 13b); and Josephus, likewise concerned with the problem, presents a plausible explanation, namely, that a certain

---

Rabbah 2.5 and 3.1-2, Targum Esther 3.2, *Sanhedrin* 61b (cited by Ginzberg 1928, 6:463, n. 100).

[30] Hebrew usage demands that the relative pronoun in Esther 2:6 refer to Mordecai.

[31] See, however, Hoschander (1923, 18-19).

Barnabazos[32] the servant of one of the eunuchs, who was a Jew by birth, discovered the plot and revealed it to his fellow-Jew Mordecai (Ant. 11.207). This explanation is found in no other source; in the Septuagint Mordecai himself overhears the plot (Addition A).

Another difficulty that faced Josephus is the apparent discrepancy as to the date set for the massacre of the Jews by Haman. The Hebrew and Lucianic texts say that after lots (Hebrew *purim*) had been cast, the date was set for the thirteenth day of Adar (Esther 3:10), whereas the Septuagint omits the date. Elsewhere the Septuagint gives the date as the fourteenth day of Adar (Esther 3:7 and Addition B), and it is this latter date which is adopted by Josephus (*Ant.* 11.219), who omits mention of the casting of lots altogether, presumably because he regarded such an etymology for the name of the festival, Purim, as unseemly and preferred the Septuagint's etymology from φρουραί, "guards" (*Ant.* 11.295).[33]

Another apparent difficulty which Josephus removes is the delay of almost a year in the carrying out of Ahasuerus' edict to destroy the Jews. According to the biblical version, the edict was promulgated on the thirteenth day of the first month (Esther 3:12) but was not carried out until the thirteenth day of the twelfth month (Esther 3:13). If the Jews had been warned almost a year in advance, they would probably have found a means of escape (so Paton 1908, 209). Josephus avoids the difficulty by omitting the date of the edict's promulgation.

That Esther abstained from eating and drinking forbidden food at Ahasuerus' and Haman's table even while keeping her origin secret seems difficult to credit (so Bickerman 1951, 125). Hence it is not surprising that Josephus omits mention of this fact (*Ant.* 11.233), though it is found in the Apocryphal Addition (C 28) which he otherwise follows rather closely.

A good storyteller avoids a *deus ex machina* to resolve loose ends. For example, in the biblical narrative, the question naturally arises as to how Harbonah knew about the gallows that Haman had built for Mordecai (Esther 7:9). Josephus answers this question by noting that he had seen the gallows when he went to summon Haman

---

[32] Jacob (1890, 295) suggests that the name points to its Hellenistic origin.
[33] This etymology is favored by Motzo (1924, 107 ff.).

to Esther's second banquet and had asked one of the servants of Haman's household for whom it was intended (*Ant.* 11.261 and 266).

One of the difficulties in the Hebrew text is that, after the Jews slay Haman's ten sons (Esther 9:7-10), Esther pursues her vengeance to the point of asking to have them hanged also (Esther 9:13). Josephus avoids this display of extreme vengeance by omitting the initial account of the slaying of the sons (*Ant.* 11.288). Here an apparently needless repetition is avoided, as it is when Josephus omits Esther's and Mordecai's second letter concerning Purim (Esther 9:29-32 vs. *Ant.* 11.295).

Another difficulty, which would probably perplex the average reader, is why Jews who live in unwalled towns are to celebrate the festival of Purim on the fourteenth day of the month of Adar, whereas those who live in walled cities are to celebrate it on the following day (Esther 9:19). Again, Josephus resolves the problem by omitting this detail altogether (*Ant.* 11.292).

6. *The Role of G-d*

Perhaps the greatest difficulty posed by the Hebrew Book of Esther, as many commentators have noted, is that it lacks a single mention of G-d;[34] and this is probably the chief reason why there was a debate as to whether the book should be canonized.[35] The

---

[34] The reason usually given for this omission is that since the celebration of Purim is often rather boisterous, the rabbis sought to eliminate the possibility of a descration of G-d's name by omitting the name from the Hebrew book. Torrey (1944, 11-12) objects that those who translated the book into Greek presumably knew the nature of the celebration and yet included the name of G-d in many places. Alternatively, the Greek book may have been intended to be read privately for propagandistic purposes, whereas the Hebrew version was intended to be read in the synagogue on Purim itself, when the celebration often does get out of hand, though there is a real question whether this was true in antiquity. In any case, there is a Talmudic dispute (*Megillah* 18a) as to whether it is permissible for the Purim Megillah (the Book of Esther) to be read in Greek, which is resolved by the statement that the two greatest rabbis of the third century, Rav and Samuel, agreed that those who read the Book of Esther in Greek have fulfilled the rabbinic obligation to read the Book on Purim.

[35] Cf. *Megillah* 7a: "Rab Judah said in the name of Samuel [third century C.E.]: [The scroll of] Esther does not make the hands unclean [i.e. is not canonical]. Are we to infer from this that Samuel was of the opinion that Esther was not composed under the inspiration of the holy spirit? How can this be, seeing that Samuel has said that Esther was composed under the inspiration of the holy

fact that not a single fragment of the book has been found among the Dead Sea Scrolls would seem also to reflect misgivings about its status.³⁶ As Torrey has remarked, the Jews were always a religious people, no people more so (Torrey 1944, 1). Surely the story of Esther signified the regard which G-d had for Israel. The Septuagint, for apologetic reasons, attempts to remedy this state of affairs by introducing the name of G-d on sixteen occasions and the word "L-rd" on seventeen occasions. Josephus, likewise, for apologetic reasons, attempts to remedy the original's deficiency by introducing references to G-d on thirteen occasions, far fewer, to be sure, than does the Septuagint.³⁷ Thus, in an obvious suppression of G-d's name in the Hebrew text, Mordecai tells Esther that if she does not speak to the king, "then will relief and deliverance arise to the Jews *from another place*" (Esther 4:14).³⁸ The Lucianic version and Josephus specify here that this help will come from G-d (*Ant.* 11.227). Again, Josephus follows the Apocryphal additions in inserting Mordecai's and Esther's prayers to G-d (*Ant.* 11.229-33).

But in line with his general tendency to diminish the role of G-d, Josephus tones down the intervention of G-d; for where the Apocryphal Addition (D 8) says that G-d changed the spirit of Ahasuerus into mildness, Josephus states: "But the king, by the will of G-d, I believe (οἶμαι), changed his feeling" (*Ant.* 11.237).

Josephus likewise, tends to omit references to the supernatural, particularly to angels, presumably because his rationalistic readers would have found such details difficult to believe. Thus, whereas the Apocryphal Addition (D 13) reports that Esther, explaining why she had fainted, said that she had seen Ahasuerus as an angel

---

spirit? It was composed to be recited [by heart], but not to be written." Another possible reason why there was some rabbinic opposition to canonization of the book is the fact that Esther was apparently married to a non-Jew and lived in a non-Jewish environment and ate non-Kosher food.

³⁶ Milik (1992) 321-405, however, has now published fragments of an Aramaic text from Cave IV of Qumran, which he calls "Proto-Esther."

³⁷ Most commentators assert that the purpose of the Additions to Esther, as contained in the Apocrypha, is to supply the religious atmosphere lacking in the Hebrew. But, as Torrey (1944, 1-2) has noted, only Addition C contributes appreciably toward this end; moreover, as the colophon at the end of the Greek version attests, this version was composed in Palestine; and finally, several of the expansions seem plainly to have been translated from the Semitic.

³⁸ It is possible, as Talmon (1963, 428-29) suggests, that the term "from another place" is here actually a substitute for the divine name.

of G-d,[39] in Josephus she says that she fainted as soon as she saw him "looking so great and handsome and terrible" (*Ant.* 11.240).

G-d, however, is depicted by Josephus as ironically laughing at Haman's apparent prosperity after he has reached the high point in his fortunes, with his second invitation to Esther's banquet and with the building of a gallows for Mordecai (*Ant.* 11.240). Again, whereas the Hebrew text says that on that night the king could not sleep (Esther 6:1), it is G-d in Josephus, as in the Septuagint, Who is said to be responsible for depriving the king of sleep, thus causing the king to ask that the chronicles be read and ultimately leading to the ironic honoring of Mordecai by Haman (*Ant.* 11.247).

A divine dimension is likewise introduced by Josephus in his version of the statement made to Haman by his friends and wife after he has suffered the disgrace of leading Mordecai about the city. In the Bible they predict that Haman will not prevail against Mordecai but will surely fall before him (Esther 6:13). Josephus follows the Septuagint in giving a reason why Haman will be unable to avenge himself upon Mordecai, namely, that G-d is with Mordecai (*Ant.* 11.259).

In a striking addition to the biblical narrative, Josephus moralizes, following Haman's condemnation to death on the gallows that he had prepared for Mordecai and marveling at G-d's wisdom and justice in contriving that Haman should fall by the very instrument that he had devised against his enemy (*Ant.* 11.268). That G-d directs the universe, rewarding those who obey Him and punishing those who do not, is stated by Josephus himself to be the chief lesson to be learned from his history (*Ant.* 1.14).

Finally, the festival of Purim itself is presented not merely as a time for feasting and gladness (Esther 9:22) but also as an occasion for giving thanks to G-d for delivering the Jews from their enemies (*Ant.* 11.294).

---

[39] Cf. Gregg (1913, 1:679): "The expression ['angel of G-d'] does not accord well with the scrupulosity shown by Esther in Addition C: it comes strangely from a Jew to a heathen. Perhaps this is why it does not appear either in Josephus or the Midrash or in Bin-Gorion."

7. Summary

In terms of the sheer amount of space that Josephus devotes to the Esther pericope, it is clearly one of the greatest importance for him. Esther and Mordecai are presented as role models, with emphasis on their good birth. In particular, Josephus praises Esther's courage. Likewise, he takes pains not to have Mordecai associated with anything unbecoming.

Sophie Trenker defines the *novella* as "an imaginary story of limited length, intended to entertain, and describing an event in which the interest arises from the changes in the fortunes of the leading characters or from behaviour characteristic of them; an event concerned with real-life people in a real-life setting" (Trenker 1958, xiii). Josephus, of course, did not regard the story of Esther as imaginary, but his narrative comes close to qualifying as a *novella* on Trenker's definition. In stressing the royal origins of Esther, in building up her stature, in emphasizing her beauty (which he makes warmer and more picturesque), in adding to the Bible's mention of cosmetics and unguents, in elaborating the descriptions of the palace and the royal banquets, in eliminating the enumeration of difficult and exotic names, in amplifying the erotic aspect particularly with regard to the harem and in evoking a romantic mood, in being explicit in referring to sexual relations, in building up suspense, in highlighting the irony in the reversal of fortunes, and in making use of the classical Greek tragic sequence of ὕβρις and νέμεσις, Josephus incorporates novelistic motifs and methods into his version of the Esther story.

Still more important for Josephus here, as in his treatment of other biblical episodes, is the concern to answer the charge that Jews are misanthropic and to counter the accusation that the Jews are intolerant of other religions

Furthermore, Josephus, in his version, attempts to resolve apparent contradictions and discrepancies in the biblical text of chronology and other matters, especially details that would tax the reader's credulity.

Though Josephus elsewhere tends to downgrade the divine role in human affairs, here, confronted by the fact that the Hebrew biblical text totally avoids mention of G-d, he follows the Septuagint's additions by including a limited number of references to

G-d and by noting G-d's ironic laughter at Haman's prosperity and by moralizing about his downfall.

By thus dressing up his narrative Josephus hoped to make his whole work more attractive to his Greek readers, who would find in it many apologetic motifs and replies, explicit and implicit, to anti-Jewish propaganda.

CONCLUSION

1. Introduction

Two basic conclusions emerge from our study. In the first place, Josephus is not a mere copyist or compiler. He has his own views – historiographical, political, religious, and cultural –, and these are consistently seen throughout the *Antiquities*, particularly in the changes which he has made in his paraphrase of the biblical text. Secondly, there is a consistent point of view in all of his works, so that the *Antiquities* is to be seen side by side with his other treatises. In effect, he is saying that the various themes and personalities in the *War* had their precursors in the themes and personalities in biblical history, as he describes it in his *Antiquities*.

Josephus is eclectic in the texts which he uses, generally preferring the Septuagint, but not infrequently using the Hebrew, the Aramaic Targumim, and the proto-Lucianic text; his preference for any given one of these texts varies from book to book, though, of course, it is possible that he had a text different from any of those that are extant. On the other hand, Hölscher's theory that he used an eclectic Greek sourcebook seems unlikely, since we have found not a single fragment of such a work. He is, however, eclectic in the authors which he has read and whose style he imitates. His favorite is Thucydides, both in his conception of historiography and in his style and vocabulary. Others who particularly influenced him are Plato and Sophocles.

2. Josephus' Violation of His Promise Not to Add to or Subtract from the Biblical Narrative

One question that constantly keeps arising is how to explain the fact that, on the one hand, Josephus solemnly assures his readers that he has set forth the precise details of the Scriptures, neither adding nor omitting anything (*Ant.* 1.17), when, in point of fact, he adds, subtracts, and modifies, usually in minor respects, but sometimes, as we have seen, in major shifts as well. One such case is that of Jehoash, who, in the Bible (2 Kings 13:11), is said to have done evil in the sight of the L-rd, yet in Josephus (*Ant.* 9.178) is described as a good man. Again, Josephus goes so far as to transform Jehoiachin, who, in the Bible (2 Kings 24:9, 2 Chronicles 36:9), is said to have done evil in the sight of the L-rd, into a king who is described (*Ant.* 10.100) as kind and just. It seems hardly convincing to say that Josephus is simply not telling the truth or that he is careless or that he depends upon the ignorance of his readers, knowing how difficult it would be for them to check up on him, with manuscripts being relatively scarce and with their being no indices. After all, since the *Antiquities* was written in Greek, it would appear likely that his readers, some of whom were presumably Hellenized Jews (see Feldman 1988b, 471), would have access to the Septuagint; moreover, if we may judge from Pseudo-Longinus' paraphrase of Genesis 1:3 and 1:9-10 (*On the Sublime* 9.9), the Septuagint was sufficiently well known, at least to some intellectuals, so that Pseudo-Longinus, presumably a non-Jew, does not have to bother to identify the "lawgiver of the Jews" (see Feldman 1993, 312). It is clear, moreover, from the high praise that Pseudo-Longinus gives to the Bible that he was acquainted with much more from the Bible than this passage alone.

Furthermore, the craft of historian was a highly competitive one if we may judge from the fact that the Jewish war, for example, did not lack its historians (*War* 1.1-2, *Ag. Ap.* 1.46); hence, Josephus, who, especially in his essay *Against Apion* (1.23-27), is so critical of the Greek historians because of their regard for style rather than for truth, had to be careful lest he himself be criticized as a hypocrite. Moreover, Josephus himself, because of the murky circumstances surrounding his surrender to the Romans and the many gifts and privileges granted to him by Vespasian and Titus (*Life* 423), was subjected to numerous accusations (*Life* 425); such a person had to be particularly careful in his behavior, public and private. Finally, Josephus spent at least a dozen years (79/81-93/94) writing the *Antiquities*, living on an imperial pension and without, it would seem, having any additional duties or responsibilities. This would come to writing an average of about ten lines of Greek per day (see Feldman 1982, 97 n.94).

Apparently, this kind of programmatic statement, as we see in other historians of the era (e.g. Dionysius of Halicarnassus, *Thucydides* 5 and 8), is intended merely to assure the reader that the historian has done his research honestly. The historian, as the successor to the prophets, is one who views matters in the large and consequently, to the ordinary reader, may appear at times to distort details.

Moreover, in taking such liberties, Josephus had the precedent of the Bible itself, namely the Book of Chronicles, which often differs in attitude and in specific details with the corresponding treatments in the books of Samuel and Kings. Another precedent was supplied by the translators of the Septuagint, which, though supposedly done under divine inspiration (*Letter of Aristeas* 306; Philo, *De Vita Mosis* 2.7.37; *Megillah* 9a), contains numerous changes, major and minor, from the original. And yet we are told that the Greek translation corresponded literally with the original, that the translation was one and the same as the original both in matter and words (Philo, *De Vita Mosis* 2.7.38-39), and that the translators were veritable prophets and priests of the mysteries (Philo, *De Vita Mosis* 2.7.40). Significantly, in his lengthy paraphrase of the *Letter of Aristeas*, while stating that the translators "set to work as ambitiously and painstakingly as possible to make the translation accurate" (*Ant.* 12.104), Josephus does not say that the translators made no changes in their version as compared with the original or that the translation was actually perfect; but he does say that since the work of translation was accomplished "well" (καλῶς) (he does not say perfectly or without alterations), and that it should remain as it was and should not be altered (*Ant.* 12.108); and, repeating this thought, he concludes with the statement that the leaders of the Alexandrian community decided that what had been judged to have been done well should remain forever (*Ant.* 12.109). Apparently the curse pronounced upon anyone who dared to make any changes in the translation (*Letter of Aristeas* 311) was not taken very seriously, since we find three major recensions (Aquila, Symmachus, and Theodotion) by the end of the second century.

A statement which has somehow escaped notice of the commentators on Josephus is the one which he makes immediately after the promise not to add to or subtract from the Scriptural details, namely that *almost* (σχεδόν, "nearly," "approximately") everything related in his version of the Pentateuch is dependent (ἀνήρτηται) on the wisdom (σοφίας) of the lawgiver Moses (*Ant.* 1.18). Why *almost*? If Moses simply transcribed what G-d had dictated, what "wisdom" was required of him? Apparently, then, according to Josephus, Moses himself did play a role in the transmission of the

Scriptures.[1] We may wonder, in view of the biblical statement itself that one is not permitted to add to or subtract from the Law (Deuteronomy 4:2, 12:32), that the rabbis (*Megillah* 9a), no less than Philo and Josephus, gave their enthusiastic approval to various changes made by the translators; but the prohibition of change may apply only to the actual commandments in the Law rather than to the narrative portion, which is, for the most part, where Josephus makes his changes; and even in those respects where Josephus differs with the legal portions of the Torah (Goldenberg 1978; Feldman 1988b, 507-18), he understands the Law to include the Oral Law (*Ant.* 13.297), of which he has an interpretation.

As to the changes which Josephus has made in the narrative portions of the Bible, perhaps what he means when he says that has set forth the precise details of the Scriptures is that he has not modified the Jewish tradition generally, which included the oral tradition as later embodied in the midrashim. If the objection is offered that aggadic material had not been reduced to writing by the end of the first century, the fact is that we do have midrashic and midrashic-like traditions in the Septuagint and in such writers as Demetrius, Artapanus, Eupolemus, Pseudo-Eupolemus, Cleodemus Malchus, Aristeas, Pseudo-Hecataeus, Theophilus, Thallus, Theodotus, Ezekiel the tragedian, Philo the epic poet, Philo, Jubilees, the *Genesis Apocryphon*, and Pseudo-Philo's *Biblical Antiquities*. The practice of "rewriting" the Bible was apparently well established among the Dead Sea sect, so that it is frequently impossible to tell whether a given fragment represents an alternate reading of a text or an interpretation of it (see Bernstein 1994).

In addition, as we see in Cicero's famous letter to his friend Lucceius (*Ad Familiares* 5.12), there is precedent, even in the much admired historian Polybius (7.7.6), for exaggerating and for disregarding the canons of history when writing a monograph. Apparently, Josephus has extended this to writing the history of a whole people, the Jews. Finally, in his rewriting of the sacred text,

---

[1] A possible clue that a similar view may have been held by some of the rabbis is found in a Midrash (*Exodus Rabbah* 47), which relates that the angels, in their jealousy that Moses and not they had been chosen as G-d's agency to bring the Torah to the Israelites, warned G-d that Moses might write his own ideas into the Torah. One would have expected G-d to answer that he was sure that Moses would not alter one syllable of what He would dictate. Instead, G-d's answer is that if Moses were to do so (the implication being that he might choose to interpret the Torah), he could be relied upon not to misrepresent the will of G-d.

Josephus has the precedent of the Greek tragedians, with whom he was well acquainted, who, even at the religious festivals of the god Dionysus, did not hesitate, unabashedly, to remold the familiar myths as they saw fit. Even Plato (*Republic* 2.377) and the Stoics, who object to the degrading portrayal of the gods, do not object to the fact that the myths are interpreted with such latitude and, in fact, seek to have them interpreted even more liberally.

3. *Factors That Influenced Josephus in His Rewriting of the Bible*

We may now enumerate some of the factors and goals that influenced Josephus most in his rewriting of the Bible:

1. *Josephus' Non-Jewish Audience*

That Josephus' primary audience consisted of non-Jews is clear from his statement that his work was undertaken in the belief that the whole Greek-speaking world would find it worthy of attention (*Ant.* 1.5). The fact that he asks whether, on the one hand, Jews in the past have been willing to communicate information about their earlier history and whether, on the other hand, non-Jews have been interested in learning about this history is a clear sign that there is a precedent for his work and that Gentiles are interested in the subject (*Ant.* 1.9). Josephus states as the precedent for his work the translation of the Pentateuch undertaken at the behest of a non-Jewish king, Ptolemy Philadelphus (*Ant.* 1.10). The person who urged him to write it is his patron, Epaphroditus, a non-Jew. The fact that, according to his own statement (*Ant.* 20.263), he worked hard to master the Greek language and literature would indicate that he sought an audience that would appreciate this knowledge. Finally, the fact that at the close of his work Josephus boasts that no one else would have been equal to the task of composing such a work for the Greek world indicates that his primary audience consisted of non-Jews (*Ant.* 20.262).

2. *Josephus' Jewish Audience*

Secondarily, Josephus' audience consisted of Jews. In his day, in all probability, Greek was the chief language for a high percentage, perhaps even the majority, of the Jews in the world. As one who had himself become a Diaspora Jew, he might very well hope to reach them and especially to defend himself against the accusations that were constantly being brought against him. The fact that he apologizes for rearranging the order of the biblical narrative with the statement that perhaps "any of my countrymen who read this work should reproach me" (*Ant.* 4.197) is an indication that he did expect some Jews to read the work. Moreover, only Jews would appreciate the cryptic references to the fall of the Roman empire in Balaam's prophecy (*Ant.* 4.125) and in Nebuchadnezzar's dream (*Ant.* 10.210) and, in particular, in the latter passage the invitation to read the Book of Daniel.

3. *Concern with Assimilation and Intermarriage*

In addressing Jews in his audience, notably in his account of the Israelites' sin with the Midianite women (*Ant.* 4.131-55, increased in length from nine verses [Numbers 25:1-9] to twenty-five paragraphs [*Ant.* 4.131-55]), Samson's affairs with non-Jewish women (*Ant.* 5.286-313), and Solomon's excesses of passion (*Ant.* 8.191-98), Josephus stresses the dangers of assimilation and intermarriage. And yet, aware that excessive objection to intermarriage would play into the hands of those who had charged the Jews with misanthropy, Josephus modulates Samson's parents' objection to his proposed intermarriage (*Ant.* 5.286), and he omits marriage with Moabites from his list of prohibited marriages (*Ant.* 3.274-75, 4.244-45), in view of Boaz's marriage with Ruth a Moabite. Even Ezra, whose break-up of intermarriages is so central to his mission, is not portrayed as taking the lead in doing so (*Ant.* 11.141 vs. 1 Esdras 8.68-70). Furthermore, his concern is not with intermarriage generally but rather with the danger of compromising the purity of the priestly line (*Ant.* 1.140). Moreover, Josephus' opposition to intermarriage is based on opposition to yielding to passion, a point of view that would have especially appealed to Stoics, and on the principle that such marriages broke the law of the country, a view that would have especially appealed to the Romans.

4. *Respect for the Prophets*

One would think that as an historian Josephus would not be especially interested in the Hebrew prophets. The fact, however, is that the prophets played a crucial role in the political events of their day. Moreover, he regarded the prophets as the immediate predecessors of historians, their common denominator being an utter regard for truth; indeed, the reason why, according to Josephus, there are no discrepancies in what is written in the Bible is that it is the prophets alone who had the privilege of recording events (*Ag. Ap.* 1.37). Undoubtedly, one major factor that influenced Josephus' high regard for the prophets was that he regarded himself as having a special gift for prediction, as shown by his foretelling that Vespasian would become emperor (*War* 3.400-2). Because the chief quality of a prophet, according to Josephus, is his truthfulness, Josephus, aware that Isaiah's original prophecy (Isaiah 38:1) that Hezekiah's illness would prove to be fatal was actually not fulfilled, omits that prophecy.

5. *Regard for the Priesthood and Especially for the Temple in Jerusalem*

The very first statement that Josephus makes in his autobiography is that he traces his descent back to priestly ancestors and that, among Jews, the connection with the priesthood is the hallmark of an illustrious line (*Life* 1). He then goes on to assert, with great pride, that not only were his ancestors priests but that they belonged to the very first of the twenty-four courses of priests. In fact, he states this even before he informs his readers that he is of royal blood (*Life* 2). As a priest, it is not surprising that Josephus takes pains to defend the choice of Aaron as the first high priest, asserting that he was even more just than Moses himself (*Ant.* 3.190). As for the blots on Aaron's record, notably his participation in the creation of the golden calf (Exodus 32) and his criticism of Moses for marrying an Ethiopian woman (Numbers 12:1), Josephus conveniently omits them. If, to be sure, Aaron is relatively downgraded this would seem to be due to Josephus' aim to preserve the primacy of Moses. Because Josephus was sensitive to the attempt of the Levites to raise their status vis-à-vis the priests (*Ant.* 20.218), he condemns the Levite Korah's attempt to become high priest in even stronger terms. In negative terms, Josephus is particularly upset by the fact that Jeroboam set up his own alternative to the Temple and, above all, that he selected priests and Levites from the people themselves (*Ant.* 8.227-28, 265). Another indication of the importance of the priesthood for Josephus may be seen in the fact that he gives much more attention to Ezra, who happened to be a priest, than to Nehemiah, who was not. The fact that Josephus gives less attention to Isaiah than to other prophets may well be due, in part, to that prophet's attack (e.g., Isaiah 1:11) on those who deemed that sacrifices alone in the Temple were sufficient to appease G-d.

6. *Concern to Show That His Biblical Heroes Are Fully Comparable to Pagan Heroes*

Because eminent intellectuals, such as Apollonius Molon and Apion, had accused the Jews of not having produced any outstanding inventors in the arts or eminent sages and, indeed, of not having added anything useful to human civilization (*Ag. Ap.* 2.135, 148), Josephus felt a need to prove, through his delineation of biblical personalities, that the Jews had indeed produced such virtuous and outstanding leaders. He stresses the high regard of Jewish leaders for the virtue of command of one's passions, so intimately associated with the Stoics, for whom he had such high regard. Not coincidentally, it is these qualities (especially wisdom and courage) that Josephus himself claims to possess (see Neyrey 1994, 192-96).

a. *Good Birth*

The importance for the Greeks and Romans of genealogy may be seen especially in Herodotus' history and in Cornelius Nepos' and Plutarch's biographies of famous heroes. The importance of good birth for Josephus is manifest from the very beginning of his autobiography where he traces his ancestry to the Hasmonean kings and to the very first of the orders of the priests (*Life* 1-6). At the very beginning of the Korah episode Josephus stresses his eminence by reason of his good birth (*Ant.* 4.14). Others whose genealogy is elevated are Abraham (*Ant.* 1.148), Rebekah (*Ant.* 1.247), Jacob (*Ant.* 1.288-90), Joseph (*Ant.* 2.9), Amram (*Ant.* 2.210), Moses (*Ant.* 2.229), Aaron (*Ant.* 4.26), Korah (*Ant.* 4.14), Gideon (*Ant.* 5.213), Jephthah (*Ant.* 5.257), Samson (*Ant.* 5.276), Saul (*Ant.* 6.45), Shallum (*Ant.* 10.59), Gedaliah (*Ant.* 10.155), and Esther (*Ant.* 11.185).

b. *Precociousness*

Great heroes, such as Romulus or Alexander, were expected to show their precocity at an early age. Josephus himself (*Life* 9) depicts himself as so learned that at the age of fourteen the leading men of Jerusalem would come to him constantly for information about the laws. Among biblical figures whose precocity he emphasizes are Moses (*Ant.* 2.233), who, though only an infant, throws down the crown placed upon his head by Pharaoh, and Josiah (*Ant.* 10.50), who, though only twelve years old, showed his piety by endeavoring to get his people to give up their idolatry.

c. *Handsome Stature*

The importance for the Greeks of beautiful appearance may be discerned from Plato's remark (*Republic* 7.535A) that the rulers in his ideal state should, if at all possible, be the most handsome persons. To Josephus it is Joseph's handsomeness that made him especially beloved to his father (*Ant.* 2.9) as well as to Potiphar's wife (*Ant.* 2.41). Pharaoh's daughter is enchanted with the beauty of the infant Moses (*Ant.* 2.224). Likewise, Josephus calls attention to Saul's and David's handsomeness (*Ant.* 6.45, 6.164). Absalom's beauty, we are told, surpassed even those who lived in great luxury (*Ant.* 7.189).

d. *Wealth*

One of the charges frequently made against the Jews in antiquity is that they are a nation of beggars (Lysimachus, *ap.* Josephus, *Ag. Ap.* 1.305; Martial, 12.57.1-14; Juvenal, 3.10-16, 296; 6.542-47). Josephus stresses Abraham's wealth (*Ant.* 1.243). When he first introduces Korah Josephus asserts as part of his claim to leadership the fact that he is wealthier than Moses (*Ant.* 4.14). Furthermore, he calls attention to the great wealth of Solomon (*Ant.* 8.185) and Josiah (*Ant.* 10.73).

e. *Wisdom*

The chief virtue of the philosopher-king, as Plato emphasizes, is wisdom. Because the Jews had been accused by Apion (*ap. Ag. Ap.* 2.135) and others of not having produced wise men comparable to Socrates, Josephus constantly stresses the presence of this virtue in his biblical figures. Abraham is a veritable philosopher (*Ant.* 1.154) who presents an original proof of the existence of G-d (*Ant.* 1.156). Jacob shows wisdom in understanding the significance of Joseph's dreams (*Ant.* 2.15). Joseph's wisdom is likewise manifest in his interpretation of the dreams of the butler, the baker, and Pharaoh (*Ant.* 2.63-65, 84-87). Moses is said to have surpassed all others in understanding (*Ant.* 4.328). Among others whose wisdom is noted are Saul (*Ant.* 6.45), Abner (*Ant.* 7.31), David (*Ant.*7.158), and especially Solomon (*Ant.* 8.34).

Among those most highly endowed with the ability to persuade, which is an important aspect of wisdom, are Abraham (*Ant.* 1.154), Moses (*Ant.* 3.13, 4.328), Joshua (*Ant.* 3.49, 5.118), and Nehemiah (*Ant.* 11.165). The most important example of the importance of the latter quality is the advice given to but disregarded by Rehoboam by his older advisers to speak to the people in a friendly spirit and to show flexibility when they ask him to lighten their yoke (*Ant.* 8.215).

f. *Courage*

Josephus felt a particular need to stress the courage of his biblical heroes because Jews had been reproached with cowardice by such influential intellectuals as Apollonius Molon (*Ag. Ap.* 2.148). Furthermore, Josephus himself had been similarly accused (*War* 3.358). Hence he expatiates the description of the courage of Abraham in his fight against the Assyrians (*Ant.* 1.172), of Abraham's sons (*Ant.* 1.120-41) in their joint effort with the renowned Heracles, and of Moses in his conquest of Ethiopia (*Ant.* 2.238-53) and in his conduct of war after the exodus from Egypt. Moreover, he is careful to protect the reputation for courage of even a relatively minor figure, Jehoshaphat, so that whereas the Bible (1 Kings 22:32, 2 Chronicles 18:31) depicts him as crying out when he is discovered by the Syrians and as being rescued by G-d, in Josephus he does not cry out, nor does he need G-d to rescue him (*Ant.* 8.414)

g. *Temperance*

The stress that the Greeks placed upon temperance may be seen in the motto inscribed in Delphi, μηδὲν ἄγαν. Moses is praised for his command of his passions (*Ant.* 4.318-29). The direct opposite of temperance is to be seen in Jeroboam, who is described as hotheaded by nature (*Ant.* 8.209) and, in Josephus' own day, in the Zealots (*War* 4.292). The Bible has an embarrassing scene in which Elisha loses his self-control and curses some little boys who jeered for his baldness (*Ant.* 8.414); Josephus, who clearly admires Elisha, omits the incident altogether. In the case of Jehu, whom Josephus seeks to rehabilitate, both the Hebrew and Septuagint texts (2 Kings 9:20) indicate that he drove his chariot madly; Josephus says that he drove slowly and in good order (*Ant.* 9.117). Likewise, Josephus, seeking to praise Elisha and realizing that the virtue of modesty is allied to that of temperance, omits Elisha's request to have his mentor bestow twice as much prophetic power as he himself possessed (2 Kings 2:9; *Ant.* 9.28). The virtue of modesty is particularly to be seen in Moses (*Ant.* 4.328-29), Gideon (*Ant.* 5.230), Saul (*Ant.* 6.63), David (*Ant.* 7.391), and Solomon (*Ant.* 8.146-49), the last most remarkably in recognizing that he had proven inferior to a Tyrian lad Abdemon in proposing and in solving riddles.

h. *Justice (including especially respect for truth, humanity (φιλανθρωπία), mercy, hospitality, gratefulness, and generosity)*
The fact that justice is the subject of the most famous and most influential of Plato's dialogues, *The Republic*, is an indication of the importance of this virtue. Plutarch, Josephus' contemporary and the most influential of biographers of great men, concludes that it is justice which is the most appropriate attribute of a king (*Demetrius* 42.5-9). Likewise, the Torah underlines its importance in the commandment: "Justice, only justice shalt thou pursue" (Deuteronomy 16:20). This virtue is central in Josephus' depiction of most of the major personalities of the Bible, such as Abraham (*Ant.* 1.158), Moses (*Ant.* 3.66-67), Samuel (*Ant.* 6.36, 294), Saul (*Ant.* 6.212), David (*Ant.* 6.290, 7.110), Solomon (*Ant.* 8.21), Josiah (*Ant.* 10.50), Gedaliah (*Ant.* 10.155), Daniel (*Ant.* 10.246), Ezra (*Ant.* 11.121), and Nehemiah (*Ant.* 11.183). Typically, Josephus, sensitive to the importance of this virtue, omits the killing of two captured kings of the Midianites by Gideon (Judges 8:18-21).

Since truthfulness is so intimately connected with justice, as we see, for example, in Cephalus' definition of justice in Plato's *Republic* (1.331C), Josephus emphasizes the presence of this quality in such key personalities as Moses (*Ant.* 4.303) and David (*Ant.* 7.110, 269).

The presence of φιλανθρωπία ("humanity,"), which is so closely connected with justice, is particularly important to Josephus in his answer to the charge that Jews hate other peoples (Apion, *ap. Ag. Ap.* 2.121, 148). Hence, this virtue is ascribed to Rebecca (*Ant.* 1.250), Joseph (*Ant.* 2.101, 136, 145), David (*Ant.* 6.299, 304; 7.118, 184, 391), Solomon (*Ant.* 8.116-17), Gedaliah (*Ant.* 10.163, 164), and Zerubbabel (*Ant* 11.87). In the case of Gedaliah, for example, the returnees to Judaea are so impressed with his kindness (χρηστότης) and friendliness (φιλανθρωπία) that they develop a very great affection for him. Indeed, generosity is a prime quality of Samuel (*Ant.* 6.194), Jehonadab (*Ant.* 9.133), Jehoiada (*Ant.* 9.166), and Hezekiah (*Ant.* 9.260).

One aspect of φιλανθρωπία which was of special significance for the ancients was hospitality, as we see, for example, in the concept of guest-friendship as enunciated in the meeting of Glaucus and Diomedes in Book 6 of Homer's *Iliad* and in the reception accorded Odysseus by the Phaeacians in Books 6-8 of the *Odyssey*. Josephus is particularly eager to answer the charge of inhospitality, as found in such writers as Juvenal (*Satires* 14.103-4), that the Jews show the way or a fountain to none except fellow Jews. Hence, he stresses the presence of this quality in such key figures as Moses (*Ant.* 3.63), Boaz (*Ant.* 5.330), and David (*Ant.* 7.54). It is particularly prominent in Gedaliah, who, when warned of the plot against his life by Ishmael, responds that he prefers to die by Ishmael's hands rather than to put to death a man, namely Ishmael, who had taken refuge with him and had entrusted his very life to him. Likewise, we see the importance of regard for a suppliant in Josephus' expansion (*Ant.* 8.386) of the reception which Ahab gave to Ben-hadad. Jehoram's subjects have reasons to be fully confident that Jehoram will judge them fairly and will empathize with them, as seen in the case of the woman who had made a pact with her neighbor to cook their sons (*Ant.* 9.64).

Another important aspect of justice is gratefulness. This is displayed, in extra-biblical additions, by Joseph (*Ant.* 2.152), Jethro's daughters (*Ant.* 2.262), Moses (*Ant.* 2.262), Joshua (*Ant.* 5.30, 95), Saul (*Ant.* 6.145), David (*Ant.* 7.69, 111, 160, 272-74), Jehoshaphat (*Ant.* 9.2), and Mordecai (*Ant.* 11.294).

i. *Piety*

That piety is to be regarded as the fifth of the cardinal virtues is clear from Plato (*Protagoras* 330B, 349B). Moreover, that *pietas* is the great Roman virtue is clear from the fact that it is the key quality of Aeneas in the great national epic of the Romans, Virgil's *Aeneid*. It was particular important for Josephus to stress this virtue in his biblical heroes inasmuch as the Jews had been accused of teaching impiety (*ap. Ag. Ap.* 2.291). Thus Josephus makes a point of stressing that it is especially in piety that Moses trained the Israelites (*Ant.* 1.6). Again, Jehoshaphat shows his piety in that he tells his people that they must show their faith in the prophet Jahaziel by not even drawing themselves up for battle (*Ant.* 9.12). Conversely, because it clearly implies impiety, Josephus is careful to omit the account of Gideon's making of an ephod out of the earrings formed from spoils of war which led all Israel astray (*Ant.* 5.232). However, Josephus does not hesitate to condemn Jephthah for carrying out his vow in sacrificing his daughter, when, says Josephus, that sacrifice was not sanctioned by law nor was pleasing to G-d (*Ant.* 5.266). As for filial piety, the importance of which is so greatly emphasized in Virgil's portrayal of Aeneas' devotion to his father Anchises, Josephus calls attention to its opposite in his characterization of Absalom (*Ant.* 7.198).

7. Qualities of Leadership

Certainly the chief lesson of both Thucydides in his history and Plato in the *Republic* is that a nation can succeed only if it has the proper leadership, inasmuch as the masses cannot be trusted. A leader must devote his full attention to the needs of his people. That, too, is how the Roman Republic was able to become the great nation that it ultimately became. And that is also how the Jewish people became a great nation, having as its leader the great Moses. Indeed, Josephus downgrades the role of Aaron, so that he, rather than Aaron, performs miracles (*Ant.* 2.280, 284, 287). He is the incomparable patron and protector of the people, as the people realized while he was gone for forty days (*Ant.* 3.98). Despite the occasional ugly mood of the people toward him, he, the psychologist, was able to analyze the cause of their depression (*Ant.* 3.310) and to inspire faith in his teachings (*Ant.* 3.317). He could have chosen to live a life of ease but chose instead to share his people's perils (*Ant.* 4.42).

8. Importance of Repentance

Realizing that many of his biblical heroes had considerable flaws in their character and achievements, Josephus stresses their repentance in a number of instances beyond what we find in the biblical text. Thus Josephus emphasizes the contriteness of Saul (*Ant.* 6.329) and of Rehoboam (2 Chronicles 12:6 vs. *Ant.* 8.256-57). Ahab, one of the most wicked of all the kings, is considerably rehabilitated because of his repentance (*Ant.* 8.362): we read that he did not make a new departure in his wickedness and that he merely imitated his predecessors, notably Jeroboam, in his behavior (*Ant.* 8.316); furthermore, Josephus puts more blame on Ahab's wife, Jezebel (*Ant.* 8.318). Manasseh, the most wicked of all the kings of Judah, goes so far, in Josephus' extra-biblical addition, in his repentance as to attempt to cast from his mind even the memory of his previous sins (*Ant.* 10.42). Josephus likewise emphasizes the sincerity of Zedekiah's repentance in that after the prophet Jeremiah has been rescued Zedekiah sends for him secretly and asks what message he can give him from G-d (*Ant.* 10.124).

9. *Respect for Law and Order*

This goal would especially appeal to the Romans, with their pride in their legal tradition going back to the Twelve Tables. Thus Josephus emphasizes that Absalom's greatest sin is lawlessness and rebellion against established authority. It is Jeroboam's lawlessness that Josephus particularly denounces (*Ant.* 9.282). His chief criticism of Ahab is that he violated his country's laws (*Ant.* 8.361). On the other hand, in his portrait of Ezra Josephus stresses his role as teacher of obedience to law (*Ant.* 11.155). Furthermore, crucial to Nehemiah's position as most trusted assistant to the Persian king is his respect for law (*Ant.* 11.183).

10. *Respect for the Concept of a Just War*

The Romans felt strongly about the concept of a "just war," that is, that a war is permitted to be waged only when all attempts at a peaceful solution have failed and when the enemy is guilty of having launched an unjust attack (Cicero, *De Officiis* 1.11.34-36; *De Re Publica* 3.23.34-35). Thus, for example, before going to war against the Syrians and to justify that war, Josephus (*Ant.* 8.399) carefully expands on the history of Ahab's claims against Syria. On the other hand, one might well wonder whether Saul's war against the Amalekites and especially Samuel's criticism of him for failing to fulfill the commandment to wipe them out were justified. However, Josephus' extra-biblical explanation that the war was justified as vengeance for what the Amalekites had done to the Israelites after the exodus is more convincing (*Ant.* 6.133), since the Romans had such high regard for their ancestors.

11. *Contempt for the Masses*

Here Josephus followed in the footsteps of Thucydides (2.65.4) and Plato (*Republic* 8.557-61), and here, too, there are clear overtones in his attitude toward the role of the masses in the war against Rome (*War* 3.475, 7.191). He stresses the disorderliness of the mob that supported Korah (*Ant.* 4.22). It is precisely because the masses are so fickle that responsible and inspired leadership is so important, as we see particularly in Josephus' treatment of the period of the judges. His negative attitude toward the mob is seen in his statement that it was the leaders of the rabble who were responsible for the rise of Jeroboam and consequently for the secession of the northern kingdom (*Ant.* 8.212).

12. *Disdain for Demagogues*

Here again Josephus followed in the footsteps of Thucydides (3.36, 6.19) and Plato (*Republic* 6.488-89). Korah is condemned as a demagogue who gives the impression of being concerned with the general welfare when actually he is seeking power for himself (*Ant.* 4.20). Likewise, Absalom plays the demagogue with the multitude when he rebels against his father King David, and, in particular, is condemned for making an appeal to those who lost their legal cases (*Ant.* 7.196-97).

13. *Realistic Attitude and Even High Regard for the Superpower of the Day*

In his reworking of the narrative of Gedaliah, the client governor of Judaea appointed by Nebuchadnezzar, and with clear implications for the contemporary position of Jews vis-à-vis the Romans, Josephus stresses that it is a matter of military necessity for the Jews to remain subservient to the superpower. Thus, despite the Bible's strongly positive view of Hezekiah, Josephus is clearly critical of Hezekiah for not realistically accommodating himself to the superior power of that day, Assyria; and, drawing a parallel to the situation of the Jews vis-à-vis the Romans, Josephus is less than enthusiastic about him, even going to the point of asserting that it was cowardice that influenced Hezekiah not to come out himself to meet the Assyrians (*Ant.* 10.5). The fact that Hezekiah was encouraged by the prophet Isaiah to resist the Assyrians may help to explain Josephus' relative downgrading of Isaiah's importance. On the other hand, Josephus, in contrast to the Bible (2 Kings 14:9, 2 Chronicles 36:9), presents a very positive view of Jehoiachin (*Ant.* 10.100), presumably because he saw a striking parallel between the events surrounding the destruction of the two temples, and because Jehoiachin, as Josephus himself did later, realized the power of the enemy and surrendered to him in order to save the Temple from destruction; significantly, in his address to his fellow-Jews urging the Jews to surrender, the one precedent for his recommendation that he cites is that of Jehoiachin (*War* 6.103-4). Josephus, in particular, justifies the subservience of Gedaliah to the Babylonians, where Gedaliah is a thinly-veiled version of Josephus, and Ishmael, his assassin, is a thinly-veiled version of John of Gischala (*Ant.* 10.164-66). Significantly, the same damning epithets are applied to Ishmael, the assassin of Gedaliah, as are used of John (*Ant.* 10.160 = *Life* 85, 102; *War* 2.585, 4.208, 4.389, 5.441).

14. *Opposition to Messianic and Messianic-like Movements*

Inasmuch as the concept of a messiah *ipso facto* meant revolt against Rome in order to establish an independent Jewish state, it is not surprising that Josephus avoids any overt inkling that he favored such a doctrine – hence his relative downgrading of Ruth as the ancestor of David, of David as the ancestor of the Messiah, and of Hezekiah, whose messiahship was apparently recognized by some. Thus, in the words of Balaam, the goal of the Jews is not to dominate the world but rather merely to be happy (*Ant.* 4.114). Nor is the goal to have an independent state in Palestine but rather to live eternally (δι' αἰῶνος) in the entire habitable world, that is, the Diaspora. Indeed, one reason, we have suggested, why Josephus identified himself more closely with Elisha than with the latter's mentor Elijah, who was the forerunner of the Zealots, whom Josephus, in view of his bitter experiences with the revolutionaries in the war against the Romans, greatly despised. We may see Josephus' opposition to the re-establishment of an independent Jewish state in the fact that whereas in the Bible King Jehoshaphat reminds G-d that it is He who has driven out the non-Jewish inhabitants of Judaea and has given it to the Jews as a possession which G-d has given the Jews to inherit (2 Chronicles 20:5-

12), Josephus' Jehoshaphat speaks not of the land as a possession which the Jews have inherited but rather as a place in which to live (κατοίκησιν) (*Ant.* 9.8-9). It should not surprise us that Josephus has omitted the passages in Isaiah which were interpreted messianically (9:6-7, 11:2-3). And yet, lest he be regarded as having sold out to the Romans, Josephus does not omit but rather adopts cryptic language in referring to Balaam's prophecy of the overthrow of cities of the highest celebrity (*Ant.* 4.125), just as he does not omit but deliberately avoids explaining the meaning of the stone which, in Nebuchadnezzar's dream, destroyed the kingdom of iron (*Ant.* 10.210), which the rabbinic tradition understood to refer to the triumph of the Messiah (*Tanḥuma* B 2.91-92 and *Tanḥuma Terumah* 7).

15. *Contempt for the Revolutionaries of His Own Day*

Like his beloved model, Thucydides, Josephus believed that history more or less repeated itself, inasmuch as its chief ingredients consisted of people, who have not changed very much through the centuries in the factors that drive them. Hence, he finds many parallels between biblical events and personalities and those of his own day, particularly during the war against the Romans. On the one hand, he is careful to avoid denominating Phineas, the slayer of Zimri, a zealot, as the Bible does, indeed, term him (Numbers 25:11), since Phineas was, like Josephus, a priest, and since G-d Himself gave approval, according to the Bible, to his act in ridding the Israelites of succumbing to sexual temptation. On the other hand, he has recast the figure of Joab so as to parallel John of Gischala. Jeroboam, in his "ambition for great things" (*Ant.* 8.209), is the prototype of Josephus' rivals, John of Gischala and Justus of Tiberias, of whom a similar phrase is used (*War* 2.587, *Life* 36). Josephus decries Jeroboam's lawlessness (*Ant.* 9.282), the very sin which he ascribes to the Sicarii in rebelling against legitimate authority (*War* 7.262). On the other hand, he omits mention of the zealotry of the popular prophet Elijah (1 Kings 19:9, 19:14); but even so he identifies more closely with Elisha than with Elijah, who was the popular prototype of the zealot and the forerunner of the Messiah, as may be seen from the fact that he omits the prophecy that Elisha will kill those who escape the sword of Jehu (1 Kings 19:17) and, above all, from the notable fact that he has a eulogy for Elisha but not for Elijah. Indeed, Elisha thus emerges as a gentler prophet.

16. Abhorrence of Civil Strife

Clearly, this grew out of Josephus' own experience in the war against the Romans. Almost at the very beginning of his narrative, Josephus indicates how self-defeating this is by stating that this is the penalty imposed by G-d upon the builders of the Tower of Babel (*Ant.* 1.117). Again, to indicate how terrible the rebellion of Korah was, he declares that it was a sedition (στάσις) unparalleled in the history of the world (*Ant.* 4.12). Most significantly, Josephus asserts that Gideon did a greater service in assuaging the Ephraimites and thus avoiding civil strife than he accomplished through his military successes (*Ant.* 5.231). Of course, the crucial instances of civil strife are the civil war between Saul and David, Joab's murder of Abner and Amasa, Absalom's rebellion against David, and the secession of the Kingdom of Israel from Judah. Thus, very typically, Josephus describes Jeroboam's sedition in language very similar to that which he uses to describe his great enemy, John of Gischala (*Ant.* 8.209, *War* 2.587). Significantly, in his eagerness to promote the unity of the Jewish people, Josephus omits the criticism leveled by Eliezer the son of Dodavahu against Jehoshaphat for forming an alliance with the king of Israel, Ahaziah (2 Chronicles 20:37).

17. Loyalty to Rulers

Josephus felt it particularly important, in view of the recent disastrous revolt of the Jews against the Romans, to stress that the proper policy for the Jews was to be loyal to their rulers. Thus, despite his high station, Joseph has no design to supplant Pharaoh; indeed, Josephus significantly omits Judah's remark to Joseph, "Thou art even as Pharaoh" (*Ant.* 2.140). In particular, in his rewriting of the books of Ezra (*Ant.* 11.121) and Nehemiah, he stresses their loyalty to their rulers. Nehemiah, indeed, is so loyal that he hastens even without bathing to bring drink to the king (*Ant.* 11.163).

18. Loyalty to Mentors and Friends

Here a prime example is Elisha, who in Josephus' version leaves everything at once in order to follow Elijah (*Ant.* 8.354). Because the reader might well ask why Elisha, who is able to revive the dead, does not do so for his master, Josephus omits the scene in which the prophets ask Elisha whether he is aware that Elijah will die on that day (2 Kings 2:5 vs. *Ant.* 9.20). And yet, Josephus omits the scene in which Elisha is depicted as completely subservient to Elijah (2 Kings 3:11).

19. *Tolerance and Respect toward Non-Jews and Especially Non-Jewish Leaders*

One of the recurring charges against Jews was that they had an implacable hatred of non-Jews. It is to answer this charge, as made by Apollonius Molon and Lysimachus (*Ag. Ap.* 2.145) and repeated by Tacitus (*Histories* 5.5.1), that Josephus goes out of his way to stress that Jews show compassion for non-Jews. Joseph sells grain to all people and not merely to native Egyptians (*Ant.* 2.94, 101). In particular, Jethro is seen in a most favorable light; when he wishes to criticize the way in which Moses is administering justice, he shows remarkable sensitivity in taking him aside so as not to embarrass him. Again, Solomon, in dedicating the Temple, asks that G-d grant the prayers not only of Jews but also of non-Jews (*Ant.* 8.116-17). Whereas the biblical Jonah appears to be indifferent to the Gentiles whom he is to warn, since we find him, at the beginning of the account, fast asleep and even, according to the Septuagint, snoring (Jonah 1:5), Josephus' Jonah is not asleep and, we are told, has absented himself only because he did not wish to imitate what the sailors were doing. Φιλανθρωπία ("humanity") is a quality which Josephus ascribes to Cyrus (*Ag. Ap.* 1.153) and Xerxes (*Ant.* 11.123). The other non-Jewish leaders whom Josephus presents in a more favorable light include Balaam, Eglon the king of Moab, Nebuchadnezzar, Belshazzar, Darius, Ahasuerus, and even the various pharaohs (especially the one connected with Joseph) that are mentioned in the Bible. For example, Josephus stresses Ahasuerus' undeviating respect for law (*Ant.* 11.195), portrays his relationship with Esther as a lawful marriage (*Ant.* 11.202), stresses his tender concern for her (*Ant.* 11.236), and depicts him as the ideal ruler who is totally concerned with peace, good government, and the welfare of his subjects (*Ant.* 11.216, 213). Furthermore, when Mesha, the king of the Moabites, sacrifices his own son to his god, the Bible says nothing about the reaction of Kings Jehoshaphat and Jehoram (2 Kings 3:27); Josephus, on the other hand, calls attention to their humanity and compassion (*Ant.* 9.43). Where he does criticize non-Jewish leaders he usually puts the blame on their advisers. And yet, aware that his readership included Jews as well, Josephus is careful not to refer to Balaam as a prophet (προφήτης) but rather as a craftsman or μάντις ("diviner," "seer").

20. *Tolerance toward Non-Jewish Religions*

In an interpretation of Exodus 22:27 [28], wherein he follows the Septuagint, Josephus declares that Jews are forbidden to speak ill of the religion of Gentiles out of respect for the very word "god" (*Ant.* 4.207 and *Ag. Ap.* 2.237). Thus, Josephus simply omits the passage in which Gideon, upon instructions from G-d, pulls down the altar of Baal and the Asherah tree that was worshipped beside it (Judges 6:25-32). Inasmuch as mystery cults were held in such high regard by many non-Jews, it is not surprising that Josephus altogether omits the statement, as found in the Septuagint translation, that King Asa ended the mystery cults (1 Kings 15:12). Furthermore, he omits the statement that Jehoshaphat removed the pagan high places and Asherim (2 Chronicles 17:6 vs. *Ant.* 9.1). He likewise omits King Jehu's conversion of the temple of Baal into an outhouse (2 Kings 10:27).

21. *Insistence that Gentiles Do Not Hate Jews*

In his effort to establish better relations between Jews and non-Jews Josephus emphasizes that Gentile nations are not motivated by hatred of the Jews. Thus Balak and Balaam are motivated not by Jew-hatred but rather by a desire to defeat them militarily (*Ant.* 4.112). In Josephus' view, Balaam's readiness to curse the Israelites is due not to hatred for them but rather to his friendship with Balak (*Ant.* 4.120-21). Again, Haman's hatred for the Jews is presented not as part of an eternal Jewish-Gentile conflict but rather as a personal grudge, since he is an Amalekite (*Ant.* 11.212).

22. *Compliments by Non-Jews*

It is particularly effective to have the Jews complimented by non-Jews. Indeed, Jethro is so impressed with Moses that he even adopts him as his son (*Ant.* 2.263). Again, Balaam, who has been sent to curse the Jews, declares that they have been invested by G-d with superior (περιόν) bravery (ἀνδρείας, *Ant.* 4.117). Finally, the supreme example of compliments directed toward Jews by non-

Jews is to be found in connection with Solomon. Thus, we read that the Queen of Sheba's strong desire to see Solomon arose from the daily reports which she received about his country (*Ant.* 8.165). Furthermore, we read of the compliment paid to Solomon by a certain Dios, who wrote a history of Phoenicia and who reported how honest and modest Solomon was in acknowledging that he had been bested in the solving of riddles by a Tyrian lad named Abdemon (*Ant.* 8.149, *Ag. Ap.* 1.114-15).

23. *Concern to Refute the View That the Jews Are Aggressive in Seeking Converts*

That the Romans were particularly sensitive about alleged Jewish aggressiveness in proselyting activities may be seen not only in the remarks of satirists such as Horace (*Satires* 1.4.139-43) and Juvenal (*Satires* 14.96-106) and the historian Tacitus (*Histories* 5.5.1) but also in the fact that on at least two occasions (139 B.C.E. and 19 C.E.) the Jews were expelled from Rome because of alleged missionary activities (see Feldman 1993a, 300-4). Since the Jews insisted that the convert give up the belief in the pagan gods, this meant to the Romans that proselytes had given up their belief in the gods that had been responsible for the triumphs of the Romans through the centuries. Hence, aside from his account of the conversion of the royal family of Adiabene (*Ant.* 20.17-96), Josephus nowhere propagandizes for proselytism. One can see this sensitivity in Josephus' handling of Jethro. Whereas in the Bible Jethro blesses G-d for delivering the Israelites from the Egyptians and offers a sacrifice to Him, implying that he had become a proselyte (Exodus 18:8-12), Josephus says only that he welcomed Moses and that Moses offered a sacrifice (*Ant.* 3.63). Moreover, though it would seem that a major point of the Book of Ruth, at least as the rabbinic tradition understood it, is her conversion to Judaism, Josephus says nothing about her conversion. Again, the book of Jonah states that the people of Nineveh had faith in G-d (Jonah 3:5), which seems to imply that they had become proselytes; Josephus, on the other hand, says merely that they prayed, without indicating to whom they prayed (*Ant.* 9.209). Furthermore, the biblical text declares that after the sailors had thrown Jonah into the sea and the storm ceased, they feared G-d exceedingly (Jonah 1:16), which might well imply that they had become

"G-d-fearers" (see Feldman 1993a, 342-82). In Josephus' version we read only that the storm was stilled (*Ant.* 9.213).

24. *Insistence that Jews Are Not Busybodies*

One of the charges which Josephus seeks to defuse in the *Antiquities*, presumably growing out of their tremendous increase in numbers and in influence, especially in the Ptolemaic and Roman Empires, is that the Jews seek to dominate the entire world. Thus, Josephus goes out of his way to state most emphatically that Balak, in his concern that the Israelites were growing so great, had not learned that they were actually content merely with the conquest of Canaan and that G-d Himself had forbidden them to interfere in the affairs of other countries (*Ant.* 4.102).

25. *Establishment of the Historicity of Biblical Events*

One of the most serious charges against the Jews, as we see from Josephus' reply, was that the Bible lacked historicity, particularly as to the antiquity of the Jews (*Ag. Ap.* 1.69 ff.). Thus, to refute the claim that the Flood, as described in the Bible, is a myth, Josephus very effectively cites the evidence of non-Jewish writers, namely Berossus, Hieronymus, Mnaseas of Patara, and Nicolaus of Damascus (*Ant.* 1.93-94), and asserts that the relics of the ark have been preserved in Armenia (*Ant.* 1.95). The fact that Josephus uses the same word for Noah's ark (λάρνακα, *Ant.* 1.77) which is used by Apollodorus (1.7.2), Lucian (*De Dea Syria* 12, and Plutarch, (*De Sollertia Animalium* 13.968F) for Deucalion's ark, rather than the Septuagint's word (κιβωτός, Genesis 6:14) shows that he sought to have his reader identify the two floods. Likewise, he cites Menander to confirm the historicity of a drought during the reign of Ahab, even when the non-Jewish author in part contradicts the Bible (*Ant.* 8.324).

26. *Improvements in the Narrative through Removal of Difficulties and Contradictions*

There are a number of difficulties in the biblical text which Josephus seeks to remove. The reader may wonder at the biblical statement that Noah was perfect (Genesis 6:9); Josephus omits this statement. Likewise, one may wonder how Noah's ark had managed to float so far away from its starting point and had come to rest in Armenia; Josephus explains this through his addition that Noah had left the country of his origin before the flood (*Ant.* 1.74). The Bible presents the confusing spectacle of calling Jethro by seven names; Josephus consistently calls him Raguel but explains that his surname was Ietheglaeus, that is Jethro (*Ant.* 2.264). In the Balaam episode a question arises why G-d should have been angry with Balaam when, after all, it was He who had allowed Balaam to go to curse the Israelites (Numbers 22:20); Josephus explains that Balaam failed to understand that G-d was speaking sarcastically (*Ant.* 4.107). Again, Josephus totally omits a number of obscure details in the account of Ehud's plan to assassinate Eglon (Judges 3:16-25 vs. *Ant.* 5.191-4). Furthermore, there is an apparent inconsistency between the statement that the heart of King Asa was blameless all his days and the statement in the same passage that he did not eliminate the high places where forbidden sacrifices took place (1 Kings 15:14, 2 Chronicles 15:17); Josephus resolves the problem by omitting both statements.

Likewise, Josephus removes chronological difficulties. Thus he explains the longevity of the patriarchs by citing the evidence of a number of non-Jewish historians that the ancients generally lived for a thousand years (*Ant.* 1.107-8). Again, according to the biblical narrative, Mordecai, having been taken captive when King Jehoiachin was exiled in 597 B.C.E., must have been 122 years old at the time of the Haman episode (Esther 2:6). Esther, being his cousin (Esther 2:7), must likewise have been old. Josephus resolves this problem by giving no indication as to when Mordecai was carried off to Babylonia and by asserting that Esther was Mordecai's niece (*Ant.* 11.198). The reader may also wonder why if the edict to destroy the Jews was issued almost a year before it was to be carried out (Esther 3:12), the Jews did not find some means of escape. Josephus neatly resolves this problem by simply omitting the date of the edict.

Already in the twelfth century Abraham Ibn Ezra, in his commentary on Deuteronomy 1:1, cited six passages in the Bible (Genesis 12:6, Genesis 22:14, Exodus 24:4, Deuteronomy 1:1, Deuteronomy 3:11, Deuteronomy 34:1-12) which presented serious questions as to the authorship of the Pentateuch; all of them are, significantly, omitted by Josephus. Likewise, the rabbis list five passages in the Pentateuch (Genesis 4:7, 49:6-7; Exodus 17:9, 25:33; and Deuteronomy 31:16), the grammatical construction of which is ambiguous (*Yoma* 52a-b); Josephus, significantly, omits all of them.

Josephus seeks to provide better motivation for events. Thus the reader will want to know why Noah offered a sacrifice upon emerging from the ark. Josephus says, very understandably, that he did so in order to beseech G-d not to send another flood (*Ant.* 1.96).

How was Mordecai able to discover the conspiracy of Bigthan and Teresh (Esther 2:22)? The Bible has no answer. Josephus very plausibly, and uniquely, supplies an answer: the plot was exposed by a certain Jew, Barnabazos, the servant of one of the eunuchs, who revealed it to Mordecai (*Ant.* 11.207).

Finally, there are a number of passages which seem to exaggerate unduly. For example, the Bible says that Niveveh was so great a city that it was three days' journey in width and that it had a population of 120,000 (Jonah 3:3); Josephus resolves this problem of credulity by simply omitting such data.

An embarrassing question arises in connection with the passage that when Ezra read the Torah to the Jews on Tabernacles they made *sukkot*, inasmuch as they had not observed the holiday since the days of Joshua many hundreds of years earlier (Nehemiah 8:14, 17). This raises the question whether the Jews had the Torah at all that they could have neglected a commandment spelled out there so explicitly. To avoid the problem Josephus discreetly omits it (*Ant.* 11.157).

27. *Stylistic Improvements*

To a certain degree, as we can see from the proem of the *Antiquities*, where he cites the Septuagint as the precedent (*Ant.* 1.10-12), Josephus' work is a kind of second edition of the Septuagint. Although Josephus insists that he has added nothing to the biblical text for the sake of embellishment, he also is careful to underline that he has made one innovation, namely that he has arranged the subject matter in a more orderly fashion and, indeed, almost as if he were a general in the literary sphere, uses a military term, τάξαι, which implies that he has arranged his words and sentences, like troops, in an orderly battle formation (*Ant.* 4. 196-97). Indeed, clearly aware, as he puts it, that his fellow-Jews, in reading his work, might criticize him for changing the order and wording of the Torah, he specifically adds that Moses left the Torah in a scattered condition (σποράδην) as he had received it from G-d and that he therefore deemed it desirable to rearrange its subject matter more logically (*Ant.* 4.197) (see Cohen 1979, 32-33, 39-42). Josephus, in the belief that the Bible is not always sufficiently coherent, systematically, as he puts it, seeks to preserve a methodical arrangement (*Ant.* 8.224), again using military language (εὔτακτον), as if he were marshalling troops for battle.

28. *Hellenization of the Narrative for His Greek Readers*

That Josephus is, indeed, influenced by Greek tragedy may be deduced from the fact that, in one of his typical generalizations about human nature, he declares that when men attain power they lay aside their moderate ways "as if they were stage masks" (ὥσπερ ἐπὶ σκηνῆς προσωπεῖα) (*Ant.* 6.264). Aware that his Greek readers would appreciate motifs familiar from Greek tragedy, Josephus rewrites the biblical narrative of the Flood by stressing that mankind was full of overweening pride (ὕβρις, a key word in Greek tragedy) (*Ant.* 1.73, 100). Likewise, we are told, G-d tried to tame the Israelites' insolence (ὕβρις) before Deborah's judgeship began, so that they might be more moderate (σωφρονῶσιν, another key word in Greek tragedy) in the future (*Ant.* 5.200). Over and over again Josephus' refers to Jeroboam's outrages against G-d and the laws as ὕβρις (*Ant.* 8.245, 265, 277). Again, Ahasuerus' justification for his dismissal of Vashti is her ὕβρις (*Ant.* 11.192-93). If Jephthah and Saul make rash vows they are criticized for losing control of reason (*Ant.* 5.266, 6.117); and in an explanation so often found in Greek tragedy this is said to be due to success or prosperity. Uzziah, he says in words that are almost taken out of a Greek tragedy, was led to sin "by his brilliant good fortune and the greatness of his power" (*Ant.* 9.223). Again, Josephus condemns Haman, in terms familiar from Greek tragedy, for not showing moderation in time of his prosperity (*Ant.* 11.277).

29. *Increased Suspense, Drama, and Irony*

There is increased suspense in the fact that Mordecai lingers about the palace inquiring about Esther, "for he loved her as his own daughter" (*Ant.* 11.204).

Josephus' treatment of the Korah episode is particularly dramatic, expecially the excited reaction of the multitude (*Ant.* 4.22), the description of the earthquake that destroyed Dathan's company (*Ant.* 4.51), and the details of the fire that consumed Korah's company (*Ant.* 4.54-56). Moreover, the reconciliation of David and Absalom is much more dramatic, with Absalom throwing himself down upon the ground and David raising him up (*Ant.* 7.193). There is also increased drama in that when the chronicles are read to Ahasuerus, the scribe, after briefly mentioning how Mordecai had saved the king from a plot, is already passing on to another incident when the king stops him. There is likewise greater drama when Esther faints in the presence of King Ahasuerus and he fears that she has suffered serious injury (*Ant.* 11.237).

The fact that Absalom urges his sister to show moderation, a quality which he distinctly lacks, increases the irony (*Ant.* 7.172). It is further ironic that Absalom speaks to losers in law suits to join him in a rebellion which will end in complete loss on his part (*Ant.* 7.195). Most ironic of all is the fact that it is precisely Absalom's beauty that becomes the means of his death (*Ant.* 7.238). Josephus heightens the irony by having G-d laugh at Haman's hopes just before the turn in events known as the περιπέτεια (*Ant.* 11.247). Likewise, there is additional irony in that Ahasuerus asserts that he knows that Haman is the only friend loyal to him (*Ant.* 11.252).

Josephus is clearly influenced by Sophocles in presentation of Solomon as a Jewish Oedipus. Thus the four elements that he has added in his treatment of the case of the two harlots who gave birth to children (*Ant.* 8.30) are to be found in Sophocles' *Oedipus the King*, namely: others had attempted and failed to determine who the real mother was; most strikingly, these others are spoken of as mentally blinded; to solve the question required the use of intelligence; and, most strikingly, the case is compared to a riddle. Again, the final disappearance of Elijah (*Ant.* 9.28) clearly parallels that of Oedipus in *Oedipus at Colonus*.

30. *Derogatory View of Women*

We may perceive Josephus' condescending attitude toward women from the way in which he disparages Queen Salome Alexandra for allowing the Pharisees to take advantage of her naiveté (*War* 1.111-12). Women are coupled with children as too feeble to respond to Moses' oral admonition (*Ant.* 3.5). Women are insidiously clever in their counsel from the very beginning of human history (*Ant.* 1.49). Such comments would have reminded Josephus' Greek audience of misogynistic comments in Homer (*Odyssey* 11.436-39), Plato (*Timaeus* 90E), and Aristotle (*De Generatione Ani*-

malium 775A). Especially when his account is compared with that of Pseudo-Philo and the rabbis, we see that Josephus has downgraded Deborah as poetess (totally omitting the Song of Deborah, including the factual details), military leader, and judge. Unlike Pseudo-Philo, he does not make a heroine out of Jephthah's daughter, especially when we compare his treatment of her with his treatment of Isaac, whose proposed sacrifice is clearly parallel. At least in part, the diminished importance of Ruth for Josephus is to be explained by his misogyny. If Esther is built up it is because she is a queen and, like Josephus, has made the realistic adjustment to subservience to a superpower in the Diaspora.

31. *Increased Romantic Element*

Herodotus, the father of history, had established the tradition of enhancing the interest of historical narrative by introducing romantic motifs. Josephus introduces the erotic element in a number of episodes: Sarah and Pharaoh (*Ant.* 1.162), Dinah's seduction (*Ant.* 1.327), Joseph and Potiphar's wife (*Ant.* 2.53), Moses and the Ethiopian princess Tharbis (*Ant.* 2.252-53), the seduction of the Israelite youths by the Midianite women (*Ant.* 4.134), the affair of the Levite concubine (*Ant.* 5.136-37), the seizure of the women of Shiloh by the Benjaminites (*Ant.* 5.172-73), Manoah's mad love for his wife (*Ant.* 5.277), David and Michal (*Ant.* 6.196, 215), etc. Again, Ahasuerus' search for beauties is throughout the entire habitable world (*Ant.* 11.196), Esther's beauty is described in additional detail (*Ant.* 11.199), and Ahasuerus actually falls in love with Esther (*Ant.* 11.202). The erotic aspect is enhanced by Josephus' addition of the reason why Vashti refuses to heed Ahasuerus' orders (*Ant.* 11.191), and the dramatic interest is increased by the description of Ahasuerus' reaction in breaking up the banquet when she refuses (*Ant.* 11.192), and by his later feeling of remorse (*Ant.* 11.195). Furthermore, Josephus is more explicit in his references to sexual intercourse (*Ant.* 11.202).

32. *Introduction of Wise Sayings*

Ancient historians believed that it was necessary for the historian not merely to inform but also to instruct. Josephus' great model, Thucydides (1.22), had insisted that there is a crucial purpose in the writing of history, namely that it be useful (ὠφέλιμα) for readers, inasmuch as history tends to repeat itself in the same or a similar way. Furthermore, Dionysius of Halicarnassus, whose work (*Roman Antiquities*) bears a title similar to Josephus' (*Jewish Antiquities*), which also consisted of twenty books and which in language and motifs anticipates Josephus (see Sterling 1992, 284-90), praises the historian who fills his history with philosophic reflections (*Ant. Rom.* 6.78.4). Consequently, Josephus frequently introduces wise sayings and proverb-like reflections: e.g., those who obey well will know to rule well (*Ant.* 4.186); men lose control of reason when blest by fortune (*Ant.* 6.116); the greatness of kings' power forbids them to be less than wholly good (*Ant.* 6.349); we have more faith in what we do ourselves than in what is done through others (*Ant.* 7.29); to preserve is greater than to acquire (*Ant.* 8.121); fate is not deceived by a change of garments (*Ant.* 8.413); buildings, like men, in time turn grey and lose strength and beauty (*Ant.* 10.265).

33. *Appeal to Philosophic Interests*

Because many in his audience were well versed in the philosophies of the day, notably Epicureanism and Stoicism, Josephus appeals to these interests. Thus he concludes his account of Daniel with a long statement emphasizing how mistaken the Epicureans are in claiming that the world runs automatically without Providential guidance (*Ant.* 10.27-81). Since he remarks that the Pharisees, with whom he associated in public life, resemble the Stoics (*Life* 12), and since he shared the attitude of the Stoics in accepting the *status quo* as that which must be, we should not be surprised to find a number of allusions to Stoic concepts in his rewriting of the Bible. Thus he constantly uses the Stoic term πρόνοια in alluding to G-d's providence; additionally, he says that all things spring up spontaneously through G-d's providence (*Ant.* 1.46). Again, he describes the decline from the ideal of the Golden Age in Stoic terms (*Ant.* 1.60-62). Likewise, it is G-d's providence (πρόνοια) that is preserving the Israelites, according to Balaam (*Ant.* 4.128). Josephus also uses Stoic terminology in connection with Abraham's proof for the existence of G-d (*Ant.* 1.156). Furthermore, Josephus constantly uses key Stoic terms for fate and necessity. In Josephus fate takes the place of a prophet's lying spirit in explaining the death of Ahab (*Ant.* 8.409). He blames destiny for leading Josiah to ignore Necho's request and consequently to bring about his death (*Ant.* 10.76). In commenting on the capture and exile of

King Zedekiah, he reiterates that it is impossible to escape from one's fate (*Ant.* 10.142).

34. *Interest in Military Details*

It should not be surprising that Josephus, who himself served as a general during the war against the Romans, should emphasize military details, especially since the Jews had been accused of being cowards (*Ag. Ap.* 2.148). Thus, we are given additional graphic details concerning Abraham's role as a general against the Assyrians (*Ant.* 1.177). He adds a new dimension to Moses in depicting him as a highly resourceful general in his campaign against the Ethiopians (*Ant.* 2.243-53). Moreover, he presents a much more dramatic account of the rout of the Midianite army by Gideon (*Ant.* 5.226).

35. *Analysis of the True Motives of People*

Like his model, Thucydides, Josephus believes that the historian must be a psychologist and analyze the true motives of people behind their overt appearance. Thus in response to Korah's charge that Moses, in appointing his brother Aaron as high priest, was guilty of nepotism, Moses replies that actually he should have appointed himself, since he is a nearer kinsman to himself than is his brother (*Ant.* 4.27). Likewise, G-d Himself reminds Gideon of the proneness of human nature to self-love (*Ant.* 5.215).

Again, Josephus comments, in connection with Joab's murder of Abner, on the degree to which greed and power will lead men to be reckless (*Ant.* 7.37). In particular, jealousy, to which Josephus claims he had been subjected (*Life* 80), particularly during his campaign in Galilee (*Life* 84-85, 122, 204, 230), and which he feels was a crucial factor in the loss of the war to the Romans (*War* 2.620), is a motif which he constantly stresses in his rewritten Bible. Furthermore, in emphasizing Joab's envy of Abner (*Ant.* 7.31), Josephus uses terminology very similar to that describing the envy of John of Gischala toward himself.

36. *G-d's Reward for Those Who Obey His Laws and Punishment for Those Who Do Not*

The main lesson, says Josephus to be learned from his history is that those who obey the laws of G-d prosper, while those who do not suffer irretrievable disaster (*Ant.* 1.14). One of many examples is to be found in the statement by the prophet Azariah that if King Asa and his people continued to be righteous and pious G-d would bring them military victory and happiness but that if they did not the reverse would be true (*Ant.* 8.296). If, as in the case of Josiah, G-d does not seem to reward the pious, Josephus places the blame on Destiny (*Ant.* 10.76).

37. De-emphasis on G-d's Role in History

In an effort to place greater stress on the achievements of the human characters in his history, Josephus de-emphasizes, in general, the Divine role. Thus to highlight Gideon's own role in his exploits he omits the statement that the spirit of the L-rd clothed Gideon (Judges 6:34). Most extraordinarily, though the biblical account of Ruth mentions G-d seventeen times, Josephus mentions Him only at the very end (*Ant.* 5.337). In the Jonah pericope he omits the theological lesson of the *qiqayon* (Jonah 4:6-11).

When, on the other hand, Josephus does not de-emphasize the role of G-d, as in his portrait of Moses, this would seem to be because the Greeks believed that great leaders, such as Lycurgus, had to be divinely directed. Again, if he stresses the role of G-d in the Deborah pericope this is because his misogyny leads him to avoid building up her character. Likewise, the fact that Josephus does not downgrade the role of G-d in the case of Hezekiah is apparently due to his eagerness not to unduly aggrandize the personality of Hezekiah himself because the latter did not accommodate himself to the superpower of his day, Assyria. Again, the reader may wonder why, if, as is true, the Book of Esther has not a single mention of the name of G-d, Josephus has introduced such mention into his narrative on thirteen occasions. The reason may be that Josephus in this pericope is following the Septuagint, which does mention G-d many times; and because of the apparent popularity of the book in its Greek version and for the sake of those in his audience who are Jewish he includes it.

38. De-emphasis on Miracles

Because one of the stock charges against the Jews is excessive credulity (e.g., Horace, *Satires* 1.5.97-103), Josephus tends to downgrade miracles or to present scientific-like explanations of them or to give the reader the choice as to how to interpret them. Thus, he makes the miracle of the crossing of the Sea of Reeds more credible by pointing to an actual incident in Greek history, namely the case where the Pamphylian Sea retired before the advance of the army of Alexander the Great (*Ant.* 2.348). Again, he presents the miracle of the earth opening her mouth and swallowing up Korah and his followers as an earthquake (*Ant.* 4.51). Likewise, instead of an angel appearing to Gideon we have a specter (φάντασμα) (Judges 6:11 vs. *Ant.* 5.213). Moreover, Josephus omits Gideon's challenge to the angel to produce miracles (Judges 6:13 vs. *Ant.* 5.214). The Apocryphal Addition (D 13) states that Esther fainted when she saw Ahasuerus as an angel; Josephus says not that she saw him as an angel but rather that he looked great, handsome, and terrible (*Ant.* 11.240).

Josephus tones down the miracle of the feeding of Elijah by the ravens (1 Kings 17:2-4) by omitting G-d's command to the ravens and by stating instead that the ravens brought food to him every day, presumably of their own accord (*Ant.* 8.319). He scientifically explains the miracle of the fire licking up the water at Mount Carmel by saying that the water came up as steam (*Ant.* 8.342). Instead of the miracle of Elijah's ascension in a whirlwind in a chariot of fire (2 Kings 2:11-12) he says simply that Elijah disappeared without giving any further details (*Ant.* 9.28).

To be sure, Josephus does include Balaam's speaking ass (*Ant.* 4.109), but this may not have been so incredible to students of Homer, who mentions Achilles' speaking horse (*Iliad* 19.408-17); and, in any case, at the end of the entire Balaam pericope Josephus adds his familiar disclaimer: "On this narrative readers are free to think what they please" (*Ant.* 4.158). If he does mention Elisha's miracle of curing the waters of Jericho (2 Kings 2:19-23), he explains it by natural means, and this too only in the *War* (4.462-64), where his intended audience consisted of Jews (*War* 1.3), rather than in the *Antiquities*, where his readership consisted primarily of non-Jews. As to the miracle whereby, due to Elisha, the widow's empty vessels are filled with oil, he disclaims responsibility by asserting "they say" (*Ant.* 9.47-50). Furthermore, he omits completely Elisha's greatest miracle, the revival of the dead child of the Shunammite woman (2 Kings 4:34). If he includes the miracle of Jonah's remaining alive for three days in the belly of the big fish (Jonah 1:17), he is careful to present it as a story (λόγος, *Ant.*

9.213); and, in an obvious disclaimer, he adds that he has simply recounted the story as he had found it written down (*Ant.* 9.214). Interestingly, in the *Antiquities*, addressed as it is primarily to non-Jews, Josephus ascribes Sennacherib's withdrawal to a plague (*Ant.* 10.21); in the *War* (5.388), addressed primarily to Jews, he cites the role of an angel.

39. *Resolution of Theological Problems*

That Josephus was concerned with resolving theological problems is clear from the fact that he tells us that he intended to write a work on customs and causes (*Ant.* 4.198, 20.268). Though he did not actually write such a work, he copes with a number of such problems in the *Antiquities*, perhaps because anti-Jewish intellectuals had pointed them out. Thus, the reader of the Bible might well ask why G-d, being perfect, should have changed his mind and repented that He had created man. Josephus solves this problem by omitting the passage altogether (*Ant.* 1.73). One might also have expected that G-d would give mankind some warning before destroying the world, but there is none such in the Bible. Josephus, like the Rabbis (*Sanhedrin* 108a-b), describes Adam as urging his fellow men to repent (*Ant.* 1.74).

Sometimes Josephus seeks to avoid anthropomorphisms. For example, the Bible says that G-d breathed the breath of life in man's nostrils (Genesis 2:7), a seemingly grotesque anthropomorphism. Josephus avoids this by saying that He instilled into man spirit and soul (*Ant.* 1.34). For similar reasons Josephus omits the statement that G-d smelled the savor of Noah's sacrifice (Genesis 8:21 vs. *Ant.* 1.92).

There are a number of instances in the Bible which raise the question of G-d's justice. Thus, one might well ask why G-d should have punished Pharaoh after He Himself had hardened his heart. Here Josephus, as is his wont, simply omits all mention of the hardening of Pharaoh's heart (e.g., *Ant.* 2.288).

In conclusion, the result is a "smartened up," more credible, more interesting, more philosophical, more penetrating psychologically, second edition of the Bible, so to speak, one particularly designed at once to answer critics of the Jews and to instill in Jews a sense of pride in their history and to teach them how to avoid the mistakes of the past and to learn from them.

ABBREVIATIONS

ABD	*The Anchor Bible Dictionary*, ed. David N. Freedman. 6 vols. New York: Doubleday, 1992
Ag. Ap.	Josephus, *Against Apion*
AJP	*American Journal of Philology*
Ant.	Josephus, *Jewish Antiquities*
Ant. Rom.	Dionysius of Halicarnassus, *Antiquitates Romanae*
AR	*Archiv für Religionswissenschaft*
AUSS	*Andrews University Seminary Studies*
BA	*Biblical Archaeologist*
BAGB	*Bulletin de l'Association G. Budé*
BAR	*Biblical Archaeology Review*
Bib. Ant.	Pseudo-Philo, *Biblical Antiquities*
BJRL	*Bulletin of the John Rylands Library*
BM	*Beth Mikra*
CBQ	*Catholic Biblical Quarterly*
CP	*Classical Philology*
CQ	*Classical Quarterly*
DSD	*Dead Sea Discoveries*
EB	*Estudios Biblicos*
EJ	*Encyclopaedia Judaica*. 16 vols. Jerusalem: Macmillan, 1971.
ETL	*Ephemerides Theologicae Lovanienses*
FRLANT	*Forschungen zur Religion und Literatur des Alten und Neuen Testaments*
HT	*History and Theory*
HTR	*Harvard Theological Review*
HUCA	*Hebrew Union College Annual*
JAOS	*Journal of the American Oriental Society*
JBL	*Journal of Biblical Literature*
JE	*Jewish Encyclopedia*. 12 vols. New York: Funk and Wagnalls, 1901-9
JHI	*Journal of the History of Ideas*
JJLP	*Journal of Jewish Lore and Philosophy*
JJS	*Journal of Jewish Studies*
JNES	*Journal of Near Eastern Studies*
JNSL	*Journal of Northwest Semitic Languages*
JQR	*Jewish Quarterly Review*
JSJ	*Journal for the Study of Judaism*
JSOT	*Journal for the Study of the Old Testament*
JSP	*Journal for the Study of the Pseudepigrapha*
JSQ	*Jewish Studies Quarterly*
JSS	*Journal of Semitic Studies*
JTS	*Journal of Theological Studies*
LCL	*Loeb Classical Library*
LS	*Louvain Studies*
MWJ	*Magazin für die Wissenschaft des Judentums*
NTS	*New Testament Studies*
OCD	*Oxford Classical Dictionary*, ed. Nicholas G. L. Hammond and Howard H. Scullard. 2nd ed. Oxford: Clarendon, 1970
OLZ	*Orientalistische Literatur-Zeitung*
PAAJR	*Proceedings of the American Academy for Jewish Research*

PG	*Patrologia Graeca*, ed. Jacques P. Migne. 161 vols. Paris: Seu Petit-Montrouge, 1857-66
PL	*Patrologia Latina*, ed. Jacques P. Migne. 221 vols. Paris: Migne, 1841-79
PR	*Psychoanalytic Review*
Pr. Ev.	Eusebius, *Praeparatio Evangelica*
RB	*Revue Biblique*
RE	*Realencylcopaudie der klassischen Altertumswissenschaft*, ed. August Pauly, Georg Wissowa, Wilhelm Kroll, Karl Mittelhaus, Konrat Ziegler. Erste Reihe, 47 vols.; zweite Reihe, 18 vols; 15 supplementary vols. Stuttgart: Metzler, Druckenmüller, 1893-1979
REJ	*Revue des Études juives*
RQ	*Revue de Qumran*
RSC	*Rivista di Studi Classici*
RSR	*Recherches de science religieuse*
SBLSP	*Society of Biblical Literature Seminar Papers*
SMSR	*Studi e Materiali di Storia delle Religioni*
SP	*Studia Patristica*
ST	*Studia Theologica*
TAPA	*Transactions of the American Philological Association*
TDNT	*Theological Dictionary of the New Testament*, ed. Gerhard Kittel and Gerhard Friedrich. Trans. by Geoffrey W. Bromiley. 10 vols. Grand Rapids: Eerdmans, 1964-76
TWNT	*Theologisches Wörterbuch zum Neuen Testament*, ed. Gerhard Kittel and Gerhard Friedrich. 9 vols. Stuttgart: Kohlhammer, 1933-73
VT	*Vetus Testamentum*
VTS	*Vetus Testamentum Supplements*
WB	*Warburg Bibliothek*
WZKM	*Wiener Zeitschrift für die Kunde der Morgenländer*
ZAW	*Zeitschrift für die alttestamentliche Wissenschaft*
ZDPV	*Zeitschrift des deutschen Palästina-Vereins*
ZKT	*Zeitschrift für katholische Theologie*

BIBLIOGRAPHY

Aberbach, Moses. 1971. Pharaoh and the Egyptians in the Aggadah. *EJ* 13:360-62.
Albright, William F. 1932. The Seal of Eliakim and the Latest Pre-exilic History of Judah, with Some Observations on Gebal. *JBL* 51:77-106.
———. 1942. King Joiachin in Exile. *BA* 5:49-55.
———. 1963. Jethro, Hobab and Reuel in Early Hebrew Tradition. *CBQ* 25:1-11.
Alter, Robert. 1981. "Sacred History and Prose Fiction." In *The Creation of Sacred Literature: Composition and Redaction of the Biblical Text*, ed. Richard E. Friedman. Berkeley: University of California Press. 7-24.
Amaru, Betsy H. 1980-81. Land Theology in Josephus' Jewish Antiquities. *JQR* 71:201-29.
———. 1988. Portraits of Biblical Women in Josephus' *Antiquities*. *JJS* 39:143-70.
Andrewes, Antony. 1956. *The Greek Tyrants*. London: Hutchison University Library.
Aptowitzer, Victor. 1922. *Kain und Abel in der Agada, den Apokryphen, der hellenistischen, christlichen, und Muhammedanischen Literatur*. Wien: Löwit.
Ararat, Nisan. 1971. Ezra and His Deeds in the Sources [Hebrew]. Ph.D. diss., Yeshiva University, New York. Published in part as Ezra and His Deeds in the Biblical and Post-Biblical Sources [Hebrew]. *BM* 17 (1971-72):451-92; 18 (1972-73) 85-101, 130-32.
von Arnim, Hans F. A., ed. 1903-24. *Stoicorum Veterum Fragmenta*. 3 vols. Leipzig: Teubner, 1903-5; vol. 4, ed. Maximilian Adler, 1924.
Astour, Michael. 1965. *Hellenosemitica*. Leiden: Brill.
Attridge, Harold W. 1976a. *The Interpretation of Biblical History in the Antiquitates Judaicae of Flavius Josephus*. HTR, Harvard Dissertations in Religion, vol. 7. Missoula: Scholars Press.
Balsdon, John P. V. D. 1979. *Romans and Aliens*. London: Duckworth.
Bamberger, Bernard J. 1939. *Proselytism in the Talmudic Period*. Cincinnati: Hebrew Union College.
———. 1949. The Dating of Aggadic Materials. *JBL* 68:115-23.
Bardtke, Hans. 1958. *Die Religion in Geschichte und Gegenwart*, 3rd ed. Vol. 3:703-8.
Baskin, Judith R. 1983. *Pharaoh's Counsellors: Job, Jethro, and Balaam in Rabbinic and Patristic Tradition*. Chico, California: Scholars Press.
Basser, Herbert W. 1987. Josephus as Exegete. *JAOS* 197:21-30.
Baumgarten, Albert I. 1987. The Pharisaic Paradosis. *HTR* 80:73-76.
Baumgartner, Walter. 1915. Jephtas Gelübde Jud. 11.30-40. *AR* 18:248-49.
Begg, Christopher. 1986. The Significance of Jehoiachin's Release: A New Proposal. *JSOT* 36:49-56.
———. 1988a. The Death of Josiah: Josephus and the Bible. *ETL* 64:157-63.
———. 1988b. The 'Classical Prophets' in Josephus' Antiquities. *LS* 13:341-57.
———. 1989a. The Death of King Ahab according to Josephus. *Antonianum* 64:225-45.
———. 1989b. Josephus' Zedekiah. *ETL* 65:96-104.
———. 1990. Josephus's Portrayal of the Disappearances of Enoch, Elijah, and Moses: Some Observations. *JBL* 109:691-93.
———. 1993. *Josephus' Account of the Early Divided Monarchy (AJ 8,212-420): Rewriting the Bible*. Leuven: University Press.
———. 1993a. Filling in the Blanks: Josephus' Version of the Campaign of the Three Kings, 2 Kings 3. *HUCA* 64:89-109.

———. 1993b. Josephus's Version of Jehu's Putsch (2 Kgs 8,25-10,36). *Antonianum* 68:450-84.
———. 1993-94. Joram of Judah according to Josephus. *JSQ* 1:323-39.
———. 1994. The Gedaliah Episode and Its Sequels in Josephus. *JSP* 12:21-46.
———. 1994a. Joash and Elisha in Josephus, *ANT.* 9.177-185. *Abr-Nahrain* 32:28-46.
———. 1995. Josephus' Portrait of Jehoshaphat: Compared with the Biblical and Rabbinic Portrayals. *BN* 78:39-48.
———. 1995a. Josephus and Nahum Revisited. *REJ* 154: 5-22.
———. 1995b. Jehoshaphat at Mid-Career according to *AJ* 9, 1-17. *RB* 102: 379-402.
———. 1995c. Hezekiah's Illness and Visit according to Josephus. *EB* 53:365-85.
———. 1995d. Ahaziah's Fall (2 Kings 1): The Version of Josephus. *Sefarad* 55: 25-40.
———. 1996. The Abigail Story (1 Samuel 25) according to Josephus. *EB* 54:5-34.
Bentzen, Aage. 1958. *Introduction to the Old Testament*, 4th ed. Copenhagen: Gad.
Bernstein, Moshe J. 1994. 4Q252: From Re-Written Bible to Biblical Commentary. *JJS* 45:1-27.
Berridge, John M. 1992. Jehoiachin. *ABD* 3:661-63.
Betz, Otto. 1987. Miracles in the Writings of Flavius Josephus. In *Josephus, Judaism, and Christianity*, ed. Louis H. Feldman and Gohei Hata. Detroit: Wayne State University Press.
Bewer, Julius A. 1924. Josephus' Account of Nehemiah. *JBL* 43:224-26.
Bickerman (Bikerman), Elias (Élie). 1944. The Colophon of the Greek Book of Esther. *JBL* 63:339-62.
———. 1951. Notes on the Greek Book of Esther. *PAAJR* 20:101-33.
———. 1952. La Chaine de la Tradition pharisienne. *RB* 59:44-54.
———. 1967. *Four Strange Books of the Bible: Jonah, Daniel, Koheleth, Esther*. New York: Schocken.
Bilde, Per. 1988. *Flavius Josephus between Jerusalem and Rome: His Life, His Works, and Their Importance*. Sheffield: Sheffield Academic Press.
Blenkinsopp, Joseph. 1974. Prophecy and Priesthood in Josephus. *JJS* 25:239-62.
Bloch, Heinrich. 1879. *Die Quellen des Josephus in seiner Archäologie*. Leipzig: Teubner.
Bloch, Renée. 1955. Note méthodologique pour l'étude de la littérature rabbinique. *RSR* 43:194-227.
Bode, George H., ed. 1834. *Scriptores Rerum Mythicarum Latini Tres Romae Nuper Reperti*. Calle: Schulze.
Bowers, Robert H. 1971. *The Legend of Jonah*. The Hague: Nijhoff.
Braude, William G. 1940. *Jewish Proselyting in the First Five Centuries of the Common Era: The Age of the Tannaim and Amoraim*. Providence: Brown University Press.
Braun, Martin. 1934. *Griechischer Roman und hellenistische Geschichtsschreibung (Frankfurter Studien zur Religion und Kultur der Antike, 6)*. Frankfurt-am-Main: Klostermann.
———. 1938. *History and Romance in Graeco-Oriental Literature*. Oxford: Blackwell.
Braverman, Jay. 1974. Balaam in Rabbinic and Early Christian Traditions. In *Joshua Finkel Festschrift: In Honor of Joshua Finkel*. New York: Yeshiva University Press. 41-50.
Brown, Cheryl A. 1992. *No Longer Be Silent: First Century Jewish Portraits of Biblical Women: Studies in Pseudo-Philo's Biblical Antiquities and Josephus's Jewish Antiquities*. Louisville: Westminster/John Knox Press.
Büchler, Adolph. 1907. Haftarah. *JE* 6:135-36.
Bultmann, Rudolf. 1910. Der Stil der paulinischen Predigt und die kynisch-stoische Diatribe. In *Forschungen zur Religion und Literatur des Alten und Neuen*

Testament, vol. 13. Göttingen: Vandenhoeck & Ruprecht.
Bury, John B. 1920. *The Idea of Progress: An Inquiry into Its Origin and Growth*. London: Macmillan.
Cassuto, Umberto. 1961. *A Commentary on the Book of Genesis, Part 1: From Adam to Noah*. Jerusalem: Magnes.
Cazelles, Henri. 1961. Note sur la Composition du Rouleau d'Esther. *Festschrift für H. Junker*. Trier: Paulinus.
Cohen, Chayim. 1971. "Right and Left." *EJ* 14:177-79. Jerusalem: Macmillan.
Cohen, Shaye J. D. 1979. *Josephus in Galilee and Rome: His Vita and Development as a Historian*. Leiden: Brill.
———. 1982. Josephus, Jeremiah, and Polybius. *HT* 21:366-81.
Cohn, Leopold. 1898. An Apocryphal Work Ascribed to Philo of Alexandria. *JQR* (Old Series) 10:277-332.
Collins, John J. 1987. Messianism in the Maccabean Period. In *Judaisms and Their Messiahs at the Turn of the Christian Era*, ed. Jacob Neusner et al. Cambridge: Cambridge University Press. 97-109.
Colpe, Carsten. 1974. Die Arsakiden bei Josephus. In *Josephus-Studien: Untersuchungen zu Josephus, dem antiken Judentum und dem Neuen Testament: Otto Michel zum 70. Geburtstag gewidmet*. Göttingen: Vandenhoeck & Ruprecht. 97-108.
Colson, Francis H. and Whitaker, George H., ed. and trans. 1929-62. *Philo*. 10 vols. *LCL*. London: Heinemann.
Daube, David. 1980. Typology in Josephus. *JJS* 31:18-36.
Delling, Gerhard. 1971. Von Morija zum Sinai (Pseudo-Philo Liber Antiquitatum Biblicarum 32, 1-10. *JSJ* 2:1-18.
———. 1974. Die biblische Prophetie bei Josephus. In Otto Betz, Klaus Haacker, and Martin Hengel, eds. *Josephus-Studien: Untersuchungen zu Josephus, dem antiken Judentum und dem Neuen Testament; Otto Michel zum 70. Geburtstag gewidmet*. Göttingen: Vandenhoeck & Ruprecht. 109-21.
Dienstfertig, Meyer. 1892. Die Prophetologie in der Religionsphilosophie der ersten nachchristlichen Jahrhunderts, unter besonderer Beachtung der Verschiedenheit in den Auffassungen des Philon von Alexandrien und des Flavius Josephus. Diss., Erlangen (Breslau: Schatzky). 24-33.
Di Vito, Robert A. 1992. Lachish Letters. *ABD* 4:126-28.
Dodds, Eric R. 1951. *The Greeks and the Irrational*. Berkeley: University of California Press.
Drews, Robert. 1972. The First Tyrants in Greece. *Historia* 21:129-44.
Droge, Arthur J. 1989. *Homer or Moses? Early Christian Interpretations of the History of Culture*. Tübingen: Mohr.
Duval, Yves-Marie. 1973. *Le livre de Jonas dans la littérature chrétienne grecque et latine; sources et influence du Commentaire sur Jonas de saint Jérôme*. Vol. 1. Paris: Études augustiniennes. 82-86.
Ehrenzweig, A. 1915. Kain und Lamach. *ZAW* 35:1-9.
———. 1919-20. Biblische und klassische Urgeschichte. *ZAW* 38:65-86.
Eissfeldt, Otto. 1956. *Einleitung in das Alte Testament unter einschluss der Apocryphen und Pseudepigraphen*, 2nd ed. Tübingen: Mohr.
Emery, David L. 1987. Ezra 4 – Is Josephus Right after All? *JNSL* 13:33-44.
Evans, John K. 1978. The Role of *Suffragium* in Imperial Political Decision-Making: A Flavian Example. *Historia* 27:102-28.
Fascher, Erich. 1927. Προφήτης. Giessen: Töpelmann. 161-64.
Feldman, Louis H. 1950. Jewish 'Sympathizers' in Classical Literature and Inscriptions. *TAPA* 81:200-8.
———. 1958-59. Philo-Semitism among Ancient Intellectuals. *Tradition* 1:27-39.

———. 1965. Ed. and trans. *Josephus*, vol. 9. *LCL*. London: Heinemann.
———. 1968a. Hellenizations in Josephus' Account of Man's Decline. In *Religions in Antiquity: Essays in Memory of Erwin Ramsdell Goodenough*, ed. Jacob Neusner. Leiden: Brill. 336-53.
———. 1971. Prolegomenon. In reprint of Montague R. James, *The Biblical Antiquities of Philo* (London, S.P.C.K., 1917). New York: Ktav. vii-clxix.
———. 1974. Epilegomenon to Pseudo-Philo's Liber Antiquitatum Biblicarum (*LAB*). *JJS* 25:305-12.
———. 1982. Josephus' Portrait of Saul. *HUCA* 53:45-99.
———. 1982a. The *Testimonium Flavianum*: The State of the Question. In *Christological Perspectives*, ed. Robert F. Berkey and Sarah A. Edwards. New York: Pilgrim. 179-99, 288-93.
———. 1984. *Josephus and Modern Scholarship (1937-1980)*. Berlin: de Gruyter.
———. 1984a. Abraham the General in Josephus. In *Nourished with Peace: Studies in Hellenistic Judaism in Memory of Samuel Sandmel*, ed. Frederick E. Greenspahn, Earle Hilgert, and Burton L. Mack. Chico, California: Scholars Press. 43-49.
———. 1984-85. Josephus as a Biblical Interpreter: the 'Aqedah. *JQR* 75:212-52.
———. 1986a. *Josephus: A Supplementary Bibliography*. New York: Garland.
———. 1986b. Josephus' Portrait of Deborah. In *Hellenica et Judaica: Hommage à Valentin Nikiprowetzky*, ed. André Caquot, Mireille Hadas-Lebel, and Jean Riaud. Leuven-Paris: Éditions Peeters. 115-28.
———. 1986c. The Omnipresence of the G-d-Fearers. *BAR* 12.5:58-69.
———. 1988a. Josephus' Version of Samson. *JSJ* 19:171-214.
———. 1988b. Use, Authority, and Exegesis of Mikra in the Writings of Josephus. In *Mikra: Text, Translation, Reading and Interpretation of the Hebrew Bible in Ancient Judaism and Early Christianity* (*Compendia Rerum Iudaicarum ad Novum Testamentum*, Sect. 2, vol. 1), ed. Martin J. Mulder and Harry Sysling. Assen: Van Gorcum. 455-518.
———. 1988-89. Josephus' Portrait of Jacob. *JQR* 79:101-51.
———. 1989a. Josephus' *Jewish Antiquities* and Pseudo-Philo's *Biblical Antiquities*. In *Josephus, the Bible, and History*, ed. Louis H. Feldman and Gohei Hata. Detroit: Wayne State University Press.
———. 1989b. Proselytes and 'Sympathizers' in the Light of the New Inscriptions from Aphrodisias. *REJ* 148:265-305.
———. 1989c. A Selective Critical Bibliography of Josephus. In *Josephus, the Bible, and History*, ed. Louis H. Feldman and Gohei Hata. Detroit: Wayne State University Press.
———. 1989d. Josephus' Portrait of David. *HUCA* 60:129-74.
———. 1990. Prophets and Prophecy in Josephus. *JTS* 41:386-422.
———. 1991-92. Josephus' Portrait of Moses. *JQR* 82:285-328; 83 (1992-93):7-50, 301-30.
———. 1992a. Josephus' Attitude toward the Samaritans: A Study in Ambivalence. In *Jewish Sects, Religious Movements, and Political Parties*, ed. Menachem Mor. Omaha: Creighton University Press. 23-45.
———. 1993a. *Jew and Gentile in the Ancient World: Attitudes and Interactions from Alexander to Justinian*. Princeton: Princeton University Press.
Fontenrose, Joseph E. 1970. Prophetes. *OCD*, rev. ed. Oxford: Clarendon Press. 887.
Fordyce, Christian J., ed. 1961. *Catullus*. Oxford: Clarendon.
Fornaro, Pierpaolo. 1979. Il cristianesimo oggetto di polemica indiretta in Flavio Giuseppe (Ant. Jud. IV 326). *RSC* 27:431-46.

Franxman, Thomas W. 1979. *Genesis and the "Jewish Antiquities" of Flavius Josephus.* Rome: Biblical Institute Press.
Gager, John G. 1972. *Moses in Graeco-Roman Paganism.* Nashville: Abingdon.
Gan, Moshe. 1961-62. The Book of Esther in the Light of the Story of Joseph in Egypt [Hebrew]. *Tarbiz* 31:144-49.
Gaster, Moses. 1927. *The Asatir: The Samaritan Book of the 'Secrets of Moses' together with the Pitron or Samaritan Commentary and the Samaritan Story of the Death of Moses.* London: Oriental Translation Fund, N.S. vol. 26.
Gaster, Theodor H. 1969. *Myth, Legend and Custom in the Old Testament: A Comparative Study with Chapters from Sir James G. Frazer's "Folklore in the Old Testament."* New York: Harper.
———. 1975. *Man, Legend and Custom in the Old Testament.* New York: Harper.
Georgi, Dieter. 1986. *The Opponents of Paul in Second Corinthians.* rev. ed. Philadelphia: Fortress Press.
Giangrande, Giuseppe. 1962, On the Origins of the Greek Romance: The Birth of a Literary Form. *Eranos* 60:132-59.
Gibbs, John G. and Feldman, Louis H. 1985-86. Josephus' Vocabulary of Slavery. *JQR* 76:281-310.
Ginzberg, Louis. 1909-38. *The Legends of the Jews.* 7 vols. Philadelphia: Jewish Publication Society.
———. 1919. The Mishnah Tamid: The Oldest Treatise of the Mishnah. *JJLP* 1:33-44, 197-209, 265-95.
Glaser, O. 1932. Zur Erzählung von Ehud und Eglon. *ZDPV* 55:81-82.
Goethals, T. R. 1959. The Aethiopica of Heliodorus: A Critical Study. Ph.D. diss., Columbia University, New York.
Goldenberg, David. 1978. The Halakhah in Josephus and in Tannaitic Literature: A Comparative Study. Ph.D. diss., Dropsie University, Philadelphia.
Grabbe, Lester L. 1987. Josephus and the Reconstruction of the Judean Restoration. *JBL* 106:231-46.
Graf, Heinrich E. 1884. *Ad Aureae Aetatis Fabulam Symbola.* Ph.D. diss., Leipzig.
Granowski, Jan J. 1992. Jehoiachin at the King's Tables: A Reading of the Ending of the Second Book of Kings. In *Reading between Texts: Intertexuality and the Hebrew Bible,* ed. Danna Nolan Fewell. Louisville: Westminster/John Knox Press. 173-88.
Gray, Rebecca. 1993. *Prophetic Figures in Late Second Temple Jewish Palestine: The Evidence from Josephus.* New York: Oxford University Press.
Greenberg, Moshe and Cohn, Haim Hermann. 1971. Oath. *EJ* 12:1295-1301.
Greene, John T. 1989. Balaam: Prophet, Diviner, and Priest in Selected Ancient Israelite and Hellenistic Jewish Sources. *SBLSP.* Atlanta: Scholars Press. 57-106.
Gregg, J. A. F. 1913. The Additions to Esther. In *The Apocrypha and Pseudepigrapha of the Old Testament in English,* ed. Robert H. Charles. Vol. 1. Oxford: Clarendon Press. 665-84.
Gruppe, Otto. 1920-21. Kain. *ZAW* 39:67-76.
Gunkel, Hermann. 1916. *Esther.* Tübingen: Mohr. 395-404.
Gutmann, Joshua. 1971. Antoninus Pius. *EJ* 3:165-66.
Hackett, Jo Ann. 1980. *The Balaam Text from Deir 'Alla.* Chico: Scholars Press.
Hadas, Moses. 1959. *Hellenistic Culture: Fusion and Diffusion.* New York: Columbia University Press.
Halpern, Baruch. 1988. *The First Historians: The Hebrew Bible and History.* San Francisco: Harper.
Hampel, Ido. 1969. The Historiography of Josephus Flavius for the Period 'Shivat

Zion' – The Return of Zion [Hebrew]. M.A. diss., Tel-Aviv University.
Harrington, Daniel J., ed. 1976. *Pseudo-Philon Les Antiquités Bibliques*, vol. 1. Paris: Les Éditions du Cerf.
Headlam, Walter. 1934. Prometheus and the Garden of Eden. *CQ* 28:63-71.
Hengel, Martin. 1976. *Die Zeloten: Untersuchungen zur jüdischen Freiheitsbewegung in der Zeit von Herodes I bis 70 n. Chr.* 2nd ed. Leiden: Brill.
Hoffmann, David. 1883. Über die Männer der grossen Versammlung. *MWJ* 10:45-63.
Holladay, Carl R. 1983-89. *Fragments from Hellenistic Jewish Authors*, vol. 1: *Historians*. Chico: Scholars Press; vol. 2: *Poets*. Atlanta: Scholars Press.
Hölscher, Gustav. 1904. Die Quellen des Josephus für die Zeit vom Exil bis zum jüdischen Kriege. Ph.D. diss., Marburg. Leipzig: Teubner.
———. 1916. Josephus. *RE* 18:1934-2000.
Horsley, Richard A. 1992. Messianic Movements in Judaism. *ABD* 4:791-97.
Hoschander, Jacob. 1923. *The Book of Esther in the Light of History*. Philadelphia: Dropsie College.
Jacob, Benno. 1890. Das Buch Esther bei den LXX. *ZAW* 10:241-98.
Jacobson, Howard. 1983. *The Exagoge of Ezekiel*. Cambridge: Cambridge University Press.
———. 1996. *A Commentary on Pseudo-Philo's Liber Biblicarum Antiquitatum*, 2 vols. Leiden: Brill.
Jellicoe, Sidney. 1968. *The Septuagint and Modern Study*. Oxford: Clarendon.
de Jonge, Marianus. 1974. Josephus und die Zukunftserwartungen seines Volkes. In *Josephus-Studien: Untersuchungen zu Josephus, dem antiken Judentum und dem Neuen Testament Otto Michel zum 70. Geburtstag gewidmet*, ed. Otto Betz, Klaus Haacker, and Martin Hengel. Göttingen: Vandenhoeck & Ruprecht. 205-19.
———. 1992. Messiah. *ABD* 4:777-88.
Katzoff, Ranon. 1986. Suffragium in Exodus Rabbah 37.2. *CP* 81:238-39.
Kaufmann, Yehezkel. 1963. *Toledot Ha'emunah ha-Yisrae'elit* [Hebrew], 3rd ed. Vol. 4.1. Tel-Aviv: Mosad Bialik.
Klausner, Joseph. 1925. *Jesus of Nazareth*. New York: Macmillan.
———. 1949. *History of the Second Temple* [Hebrew]. Vol. 5. Jerusalem: Ahiasaf.
Klingender, Johann Wilhelm. 1856. *De Aureae Aetatis Fabula Disputatio*. Cassel.
Koch, Klaus. 1974. Ezra and the Origins of Judaism. *JSS* 19:173-97.
Kraeling, Emil G. 1935. Difficulties in the Story of Ehud. *JBL* 54:205-10.
Krämer, Hans J. 1968. "Προφήτης." *TDNT* 6:781-96.
Kretschmer, Paul. 1909. Remus and Romulus. *Glotta* 1:301.
Kuhn, K. H. 1970. A Coptic Jeremiah Apocryphon. *Le Muséon* 83:93-135, 291-350.
Larson, Erik. 1994. 4Q470 and the Angelic Rehabilitation by King Zedekiah. *DSD* 1:210-28.
Le Déaut, Roger. 1964. φιλανθρωπία dans la littérature grecque jusqu'au Nouveau Testament (Tite III,4). In *Mélanges Eugène Tisserant*. Vatican City: Bibliotheca apostolica vaticana. 1:255-94.
Levenson, Jon D. 1984. The Last Four Verses in Kings. *JBL* 103:353-61.
Levine, Etan. 1975. *The Aramaic Version of Jonah*. Jerusalem: Jerusalem Academic Press.
Levison, John R. 1988. *Portraits of Adam in Early Judaism: from Sirach to Baruch*. Sheffield: Journal for the Study of the Pseudepigrapha.
———. 1991. Josephus's Version of Ruth. *JSP* 8:31-44.
———. 1994. The Debut of the Divine Spirit in Josephus's *Antiquities*. *HTR* 87:123-38.
Lévy, Isidore. 1949. La Repudiation de Vasti. *Actes du XXIe Congrès International des*

Orientalistes (1948). Paris: Imprimerie nationale , Société asiatique de Paris. 114-15.
Lewinsky, Abraham. 1887. *Beiträge zur Kenntnis der religionsphilosophischen Anschauungen des Flavius Josephus*. Breslau: Preuss & Jünger.
Lewis, Jack P. 1978. *A Study of the Interpretation of Noah and the Flood in Jewish and Christian Literature*. Leiden: Brill.
Lieberman, Saul. 1942. *Greek in Jewish Palestine*. New York: Jewish Theological Seminary.
Lovejoy, Arthur O. and George Boas. 1935. *Primitivism and Related Ideas in Antiquity*. Baltimore: Johns Hopkins University Press.
Macho, Alejandro Diez. 1960. The Recently Discovered Palestinian Targum: Its Antiquity and Relationship with Other Targumim. *VTS* 7:222-45.
Macurdy, Grace H. 1940. *The Quality of Mercy: The Gentler Virtues in Greek Literature*. New Haven: Yale University Press.
Malamat, Abraham. 1950. The Last Wars of the Kingdom of Judah. *JNES* 9:218-27.
Marcus, David. 1986. *Jephthah and His Vow*. Lubbock: Texas Tech Press.
Marcus, Ralph, ed. and trans. 1934-63. *Josephus*, vols. 5-8. LCL; London: Heinemann.
Margaliyot, Eliezer. 1949. *Ha-hayavim bamiqra vezakaim batalmud uvemidrashim [Positive (Depictions) in the Bible and Negative (Depictions) in the Talmud and in the Midrashim]* [Hebrew]. London: Ararat.
Mason, Steve. 1991. *Flavius Josephus on the Pharisees: A Composition-Critical Study*. Leiden: Brill.
McKenzie, John L. 1966. *The World of the Judges*. Englewood Cliffs: Prentice-Hall.
Meyer, Rudolf. 1938. Levitische Emanzipationsbestrebungen in nachexilischer Zeit. *OLZ* 41:721-28.
———. 1964. προφήτης. *TWNT* 6:812-28.
Michel, Otto and Bauernfeind, Otto. 1969. *Flavius Josephus, De Bello Judaico: Der Jüdische Krieg*. Vol.2.2. München: Kosel.
Mingana, Alfonse and Harris, James Rendell. 1927. A New Jeremiah Apocryphon. *BJRL* 11:329-42, 352-95.
Moehring, Horst R. 1957. Novelistic Elements in the Writings of Flavius Josephus. Ph.D. diss., University of Chicago.
Milik, Jósef T. 1992. Les Modèles Araméens du Livre d'Esther dans la Grotte 4 de Qumran. *RQ* 15.3:321-405.
Moore, George F. 1898. *A Critical and Exegetical Commentary on Judges*, 2nd ed. New York: Scribner's.
———. 1927. *Judaism in the First Centuries of the Christian Era: The Age of the Tannaim*. 3 vols. Cambridge, Mass.: Harvard University Press.
Moscovitz, Larry. 1979. Josephus' Treatment of the Biblical Balaam Episode. M.A. diss., Yeshiva University, New York.
Motzo, Bacchisio R. 1924. *Saggi di storia e Letteratura Giudeo-Ellenistica*. Florence: Le Monier.
———. 1928. Il testo di Ester in Giuseppe. *SMSR* 4:84-105.
Murray, Robert H. 1920. The Conception of Progress in Classical and Renaissance Writers. Appendix in his *Erasmus and Luther: Their Attitude to Toleration*. London: SPCK. 401-46.
Neusner, Jacob. 1984. *Messiah in Context: Israel's History and Destiny in Formative Judaism*. Philadelphia: Fortress.
Neyrey, Jerome H. 1994. Josephus' *Vita* and the Encomium: A Native Model of Personality. *JSJ* 25:177-206.

Niese, Benedictus, ed. 1888-95. *Flavii Josephi Opera*. 7 vols. Berlin: Weidmann.
Noy, Dov. 1971. Absalom in Folklore. *EJ*, vol. 2. Jerusalem: Macmillan. 175.
Ostwald, Martin. 1986. *From Popular Sovereignty to the Sovereignty of Law: Law, Society, and Politics in Fifth-Century Athens*. Berkeley: University of California Press.
Paton, Lewis B. 1908. *Critical and Exegetical Commentary on the Book of Esther*. New York: Scribner.
Paul, André. 1985. Flavius Josephus' "Antiquities of the Jews": An Anti-Christian Manifesto. *NTS* 31:473-80.
Pease, Arthur S. 1958. *M. Tulli Ciceronis De Natura Deorum Libri Tres*. 2 vols. Cambridge, Mass.: Harvard University Press.
Penna, Angelo. 1961. The Vow of Jephthah in the Interpretation of St. Jerome. *SP* 4:163.
Perrot, Charles and Bogaert, Pierre-Maurice, eds. 1976. *Pseudo-Philon, Les Antiquités Bibliques*. Vol. 2. Paris: Les Éditions du Cerf.
Perry, Ben E. 1967. *The Ancient Romances*. Berkeley: University of California Press.
Pfeiffer, Augustus. 1679. *Dubia Vexata Scripturae Sacrae*. Dresden: Huebner.
Picket, H. W. 1969. The Archaic Tyrannis. *Talanta* 1:19-61.
Pohlmann, Karl-Friedrich. 1970. Studien zum dritten Esra. Ein Beitrag zur Frage nach dem ursprunglichen Schluss des chronistischen Geschichtswerkes. Diss., Marburg, 1968-69. Reprinted in *FRLANT*, 104. Göttingen: Vandenhoeck & Ruprecht. 3: Das Zeugnis des Josephus. 74-126.
Rabinowitz, Louis I. 1971. Hevra Kaddisha. *EJ*. Jerusalem: Macmillan. 8:442-46.
Rappaport, Salomo. 1930. *Agada und Exegese bei Flavius Josephus*. Vienna: Alexander Kohut Memorial Foundation.
Reitzenstein, Richard. 1926. *WB* 7:38 ff.
Rendtorff, Rolf. 1968. Προφήτης: Navi in the Old Testament. *TDNT* 6:796-812.
Riessler, Paul. 1896. Zu Rosenthal's Aufsatz, Bd. XV, S. 278 ff. *ZAW* 16:182.
Rose, Herbert J. 1914. Divination (Greek). In *Encyclopaedia of Religion and Ethics*, ed. James Hastings. Edinburgh: Clark. 4:796-99.
———. 1970. Devotio. *OCD*. 333.
Rösel, Hartmut N. 1977. Zur Ehud-Erzählung. *ZAW* 89:270-72.
Rosenmeyer, Thomas G. 1957. Hesiod and Historiography. *Hermes* 85:257-85.
Rosenthal, Ludwig A. 1895. Die Josephsgeschichte mit den Büchern Ester und Daniel verglichen. *ZAW* 15:278-90.
———. 1897. Nochmals der Vergleich Ester, Joseph-Daniel. *ZAW* 17:125-28.
Rosenthal, Judah. 1947-48. Ḥiwi al-Balkhi. *JQR* 38:317-42, 419-30; 39:79-94..
Rouillard, Hedwige. 1985. *La Péricope de Balaam (Nombres 22-24): La Prose et les "Oracles."* Paris: Lecoffre.
Ryberg, Inez S. 1958. Vergil's Golden Age. *TAPA* 89:112-31.
Saller, Richard P. 1982. *Personal Patronage under the Empire*. Cambridge: Cambridge University Press.
Schäfer, Peter. 1996. The Exodus Tradition in Pagan Greco-Roman Literature. In *The Jews in the Hellenistic-Roman World: Studies in Memory of Menahem Stern*, ed. Isaiah M. Gafni, Aharon Oppenheimer, and Daniel R. Schwartz. Jerusalem: Zalman Shazar Center for Jewish History. 9*-38*.
Schalit, Abraham, trans. 1944. *Josephus, Antiquitates Judaicae* [Hebrew]. Vol. 1. Jerusalem: Bialik.
Scheller, Paul. 1911. De Hellenistica Historiae Conscribendae Arte. Ph.D. diss., Leipzig.
Schoeps, Hans-Joachim. 1943. *Die jüdischen Prophetenmorde*. Zürich and Uppsala: Niehaus.

———. 1950. *Aus frühchristlicher Zeit. Religionsgeschichtliche Untersuchungen.* Tübingen: Mohr.
Schreckenberg, Heinz. 1968. *Bibliographie zu Flavius Josephus.* Leiden: Brill.
———. 1979. *Bibliographie zu Flavius Josephus: Supplementband mit Gesamtregister.* Leiden: Brill.
Schubert, Kurt. 1952. Die jüdischen und judenchristlichen Sekten im Lichte des Handschriftenfundes von 'En Fescha. *ZKT* 74:1-62.
Schürer, Emil. 1973-86. *The History of the Jewish People in the Age of Jesus Christ (175 B.C.-A.D. 135),* ed. Geza Vermes and Fergus Millar. 3 vols. Edinburgh: Clark.
Schwartz, Eduard. 1896. *Fünf Vorträge über den griechischen Roman.* Berlin: Reimer.
Schwartz, Seth. 1990. *Josephus and Judaean Politics.* Leiden: Brill.
Sealey, Raphael. 1976. *A History of the Greek City-States 700-338 B.C.* Berkeley: University of California Press.
Séchan, Louis. 1929. Pandora, l'Eve grecque. *BAGB*:3-36.
Seidenberg, Robert. 1966. Sacrificing the First You See. *PR* 53:53.
Seyberlich, Rose-Marie. 1964. Esther in der Septuaginta und bei Flavius Josephus. *Neue Beiträge zur Geschichte der Alten Welt.* Band 1: *Alter Orient und Griechenland* (II. Internationale Tagung der Fachgruppe Alte Geschichte der Deutschen Historiker-Gesellschaft vom 4.-8. Sept. 1962 in Stralsund, ed. Charlotte Weiskopf). Berlin: Akademie-Verlag. 363-66.
Shochat, Azriel. 1953. The Views of Josephus on the Future of Israel and Its Land [Hebrew]. In *Yerushalayim* (review for *Erez-Israel Research Dedicated to Isaias Press*). Jerusalem: Mosad HaRav Kuk. 43-50.
Shutt, Robert J. H. 1961. *Studies in Josephus.* London: SPCK.
Smith, Kirby F. 1908. Ages of the World (Greek and Roman). In *Encyclopaedia of Religion and Ethics,* ed. James Hastings. Vol. 1. Edinburgh: Clark. 192-200.
Smith, Morton. 1971. *Palestinian Parties and Politics That Shaped the Old Testament.* New York: Columbia University Press.
———. 1987. The Occult in Josephus. In *Josephus, Judaism, and Christianity,* ed. Louis H. Feldman and Gohei Hata. Detroit: Wayne State University Press. 236-56.
Smits, Edmé R. 1992. A Contribution to the History of Pseudo-Philo's Liber Antiquitatum Biblicarum in the Middle Ages. *JSJ* 23:197-216.
Snowden, Frank M. 1970. *Blacks in Antiquity: Ethiopians in the Greco-Roman Experience.* Cambridge, Mass.: Belknap Press of Harvard University Press.
———. 1983. *Before Color Prejudice: The Ancient View of Blacks.* Cambridge, Mass.: Harvard University Press.
Speiser, Ephraim A. 1962. Nineveh. *Interpreter's Dictionary of the Bible.* Vol. 3. Nashville: Abingdon. 552.
Spengel, Leonardus. 1854. *Rhetores Graeci.* Vol. 2. Leipzig: Teubner.
Spicq, Ceslaus. 1958. La philanthropie hellénistique, virtu divine et royale. *ST* 12:169-91.
———. 1978. *Notes de lexicographie néo-testamentaire.* 2 vols. Göttingen: Vandenhoeck & Ruprecht.
Spiro, Abram. 1953. Manners of Rewriting Biblical History from Chronicles to Pseudo-Philo. Ph.D. diss., Columbia University, New York.
Stachowiak, L. R. 1957. *Chrestotes. Ihre biblisch-theologische Entwicklung und Eigenart.* Freiburg.
Stagg, Evelyn and Frank. 1978. *Women in the World of Jesus.* Philadelphia: Westminster Press.
Stein, Edmund. 1931. *Philo und der Midrasch: Philons Schilderung der Gestalten des Pentateuch verglichen mit der des Midrasch.* Giessen: Töpelmann.
Sterling, Gregory E. 1992. *Historiography and Self-Definition: Josephos, Luke-Acts and*

Apologetic Historiography. Leiden, Brill.
Stern, Menahem, ed. 1974-84. *Greek and Latin Authors on Jews and Judaism*. 3 vols. Jerusalem: Israel Academy of Sciences and Humanities.
Stiehl, Ruth. 1956. Das Buch Esther. *WZKM* 53:4-22.
Sypherd, William O. 1948. *Jephthah and His Daughter: A Study in Comparative Literature*. Newark: University of Delaware Press.
Tabor, James D. 1989. "Returning to the Divinity": Josephus's Portrayal of the Disappearances of Enoch, Elijah, and Moses. *JBL* 108:225-38.
Talbert, Charles H. 1980. Prophecies of Future Greatness: The Contribution of Greco-Roman Biographies to an Understanding of Luke 1:5-4:15. In *The Divine Helmsman: Studies on G-d's Control of Human Events Presented to Lou H. Silberman*, ed. James L. Crenshaw and Samuel Sandmel. New York: Ktav. 129-41.
Talmon, Shemaryahu. 1963. Wisdom in the Book of Esther. *VT* 13:419-55.
Tarn, William W. and Guy T. Griffith. 1952. *Hellenistic Civilisation*. 3d ed. London: Arnold.
Taylor, Margaret E. 1955. Primitivism in Virgil. *AJP* 76:261-78.
Teggart, F. J. 1947. The Argument of Hesiod's *Works and Days*. *JHI* 8:45-77.
Thackeray, Henry St. J. 1899. Esdras, First Book of. In *A Dictionary of the Bible*, ed. James Hastings. Vol. 1. Edinburgh: Clark. 758-63.
———. ed. and trans. 1926-34. *Josephus*, vols. 1-5. *LCL*; London: Heinemann.
———. 1929. *Josephus the Man and the Historian*. New York: Jewish Institute of Religion.
Torrey, Charles C. 1944. The Older Book of Esther. *HTR* 37:1-40.
Trenker, Sophie. 1958. *The Greek Novella in the Classical Period*. Cambridge: Cambridge University Press.
Treuenfels, Abraham. 1850. Über den Bibelkanon des Fl. Josefus: Über das apokryphische Buch Esra. *Oriens* 11:693-98.
Trible, Phyllis. 1967. Studies in the Book of Jonah. Ph.D. diss., Columbia University, New York.
———. 1984. *Texts of Terror: Literary-Feminist Readings of Biblical Narratives*. Philadelphia: Fortress.
Troiani, Lucio. 1986. I lettore delle "Antiquitates Judaicae" di Giuseppe. *Athenaeum* 64:343-53.
Tuland, C. G. 1966. Josephus, Antiquities, Book XI: Correction or Confirmation of Biblical Post-Exilic Records? *AUSS* 4:176-92.
Türck, Hermann. 1931. *Pandora und Eva: Menschwerdung und Schöpfertum im griechischen und jüdischen Mythus*. Weimar: Verus.
Ulrich, Eugene C. 1989. Josephus' Biblical Text for the Books of Samuel. In *Josephus, the Bible, and History*, ed. Louis H. Feldman and Gohei Hata. Detroit: Wayne State University. 81-96.
van Unnik, Willem C. 1974. Josephus' Account of the Story of Israel's Sin with Alien Women in the Country of Midian (Num. 25.1 ff.). In *Travels in the World of the Old Testament: Studies Presented to Professor M. A. Beek*, ed. Matthieu S. H. G. Heerma von Voss (*Studia Semitica Nerlandica*, 16). Assen: Van Gorcum. 241-61.
———. 1978. Die Prophetie bei Josephus. In his *Flavius Josephus als historischer Schriftsteller*. Heidelberg: Schneider. 41-54.
Varneda, Villalba I. 1986. *The Historical Method of Flavius Josephus*. Leiden: Brill.
Vermes, Geza. 1973. *Scripture and Tradition in Judaism: Haggadic Studies*. 2nd ed. Leiden: Brill.
———. 1987. The Jesus Notice of Josephus Re-examined. *JJS* 38:1-10.

Vogelstein, Heinemann. 1889. *Der Kampf zwischen Priestern und Leviten seit den Tagen Ezechiels.* Stettin: Nagel.
Wehrli, Fritz R. 1944. *Die Schule der Aristoteles, Texte und Kommentar.* Vol. 1. Basel: Schwabe.
Weinfeld, Moshe. 1982. The King as Servant of the People: The Source of the Idea. *JJS* 33:189-94.
Weiss, K. 1973. χρηστός. *TWNT* 9:472-88.
Wendland, Paul. 1912. *Die hellenistisch-römische Kultur, in ihren Beziehungen zu Judentum und Christentum,* 3rd ed. Tübingen: Mohr.
White, Hugh G. Evelyn, trans. 1914. *Hesiod. LCL;* Cambridge, Mass.: Harvard University Press.
Wiese, Kurt M. 1926. *Zur Literarkritik des Buches der Richter.* Ph.D. diss., Königsberg. Stuttgart.
Wiesenberg, Ernest. 1956. Related Prohibitions: Swine Breeding and the Study of Greek. *HUCA* 27:213-33.
von Wilamowitz-Moellendorff, Ulrich. 1912. *Die Griechische und Lateinische Literatur und Sprache,* 3rd ed. Leipzig: Teubner.
Williamson, Hugh G. M. 1977. *Israel in the Books of Chronicles.* Cambridge: Cambridge University Press.
Wiseman, Donald J. 1956. *Chronicles of Chaldaean Kings 626-556 B.C. in the British Museum.* London: British Museum.
Wolff, Samuel L. 1912. *The Greek Romances in Elizabethan Prose Fiction.* New York: Columbia University Press.
Wolfson, Harry A. 1947. *Philo: Foundations of Religious Philosophy in Judaism, Christianity, and Islam.* 2 vols. Cambridge, Mass.: Harvard University Press.
Zeitlin, Solomon. 1958-59. The Medieval Mind and the Theological Speculation on the Dead Sea Scrolls. *JQR* 49:1-34.
Zimmermann, Frank, trans. and ed. 1958. *The Book of Tobit.* New York: Harper.

INDEX OF PASSAGES FROM ANCIENT TEXTS

Jewish Scriptures

1 Chronicles		15:17	268 (*bis*), 561
2:10-15	67	16:2	268
19:13	208	16:7	114 n. 9 (LXX)
21:3	207	16:7-10	269
21:6	208	16:10	114 n. 9 (LXX),
26:28	114 n. 9 (LXX)		269 n. 5 (LXX)
2 Chronicles		16:12	269 (*bis*)
10:1-12:16	244, 244 (LXX)	16:14	269
10:3	246	17:1-21:1	307, 307 (LXX)
10:5	248, 255	17:3	314, 319
10:9	257	17:4	316
10:13	257	17:6	319, 558
10:15	257	17:7-8	308
10:16	257, 259	17:7-9	314
10:18	258 (*bis*)	17:10	314, 319
11:4	253, 257	17:11	318
11:13	256, 259	17:12	311 (*bis*), 311 (LXX)
12:1	260	17:15	318
12:5	260	17:16	318
12:6	260, 551	18:1-2	316
12:7	261	18:2	282, 282 n. 5 (LXX), 309, 316-317, 317
12:9	261		
12:14	256, 260, 437 n. 1		
13:1-20	233, 233 (LXX), 416, 416 (LXX)	18:3	311, 317
		18:6	314
13:4-12	236	18:7-8	314
13:17	236, 238	18:31	311, 548
14:1-16:14	263	18:33	283-284 n. 6
14:2	267	19:2	114 n. 9 (LXX), 307 n. 1 (LXX), 317
14:3	269		
14:5	269		
14:6-7	265	19:3	319
14:11	265, 267 (*bis*)	19:4	313, 315
14:12	265	19:6	309, 313
14:13	265, 265 n. 2 (LXX)	19:8	307 n. 1 (LXX)
		19:9-10	313
14:14	265 (*bis*)	19:11	308
15:2	266 (*bis*)	20:1-2	312
15:2-7	266, 271	20:5-12	315, 315 n. 7, 554
15:8	266, 270	20:7	320
15:9	270, 270 (LXX)	20:11	320
15:12-13	270	20:12	312
15:16	268, 268 n. 4 (LXX)	20:17	307 n. 1, 307 n. 1 (LXX)

20:18	313	33:13	418, 421, 423
20:20	307 n. 1 (LXX), 315	33:14	422
		33:15	422
20:21	308, 316	33:16	421, 423
20:26	316	33:17	421
20:29	316	33:19	422
20:30	315	33:22	437 n. 1
20:36	310	34:1-35:27	424, 424 (LXX)
20:37	317, 556	34:3	426, 426 (LXX)
21:5-8	328	34:3-7	431, 432
21:6	437 n. 1	34:6-7	434
21:7	448 n. 16	34:8	428, 433
21:15	304	34:14	433 n. 8
21:18	335 n. 2	34:27-28	431
22:2	332	34:29-33	427
22:4	437 n. 1	34:32	431
25:20	284, 429	35:15	114 n. 9 (LXX)
28:1	437 n. 1	35:18	434
28:22	501	35:21	283
28:24	379	35:21-22	429
29-32	364, 364 (LXX)	35:22	429, 430
29:3	371	35:23	283 n. 6, 430
29:5-11	372	35:23-24	428
29:8	371	36:5	440 n. 1
29:12-17	366	36:8	456 n. 6
29:30	114 n. 9 (LXX)	36:8-10	441, 441 (LXX)
29:32-33	371	36:9	437, 440, 440 n. 1, 456 n. 6, 456 n. 6 (LXX), 540, 554
29:34	366		
30:1	368	36:10-14	450
30:2-3	366	36:12	438 (*bis*), 440 n. 1, 450, 455
30:10	368		
30:11	368	36:13	438, 450, 459
30:22	366	36:17	458
30:24	369	Daniel	
30:26	369	1:4	453
32:3-8	368	2:5	453
32:17	372	2:44	118
32:21	374	2:44-45	366, 366 n. 4
32:23	375	3:20	453
32:24	390 n. 17	3:29	453
32:25	370	4:4-18	453
32:26	370	4:5	453
32:33-33:9	416,	4:30	453
32:33-33:20	416, 416 n. 1 (LXX)	4:31-34	454
		5:21	454
33:2	419, 437 n. 1	5:23	74
33:3	419	5:29	75
33:4	418	6:7	75
33:5-7	419	6:9	75
33:10	420	6:16	75
33:11	422	6:24	75
33:12	421	7:18	118

INDEX OF PASSAGES FROM ANCIENT TEXTS

Deuteronomy		2:6	532, 532 n. 30, 561
1:1	561 (*bis*)	2:7	520, 532, 561
2:9	121	2:9	514, 518, 519
3:11	561	2:11	520, 532
4:2	542	2:12	519, 532
4:10-5:33	292	2:14	504, 504 (LXX), 519
6:5	435		
6:8-9	219 n. 7	2:16	505, 514, 526, 525 (LXX)
6:11	219 n. 7		
6:18	219 n. 7	2:17	505, 519
6:20	219 n. 7	2:18	508, 519
7:3	130, 197, 483	2:19	515 (*bis*)
8:8	155 n. 5	2:20	515
9:20	60	2:22	532, 562
10:6	71 n. 11	2:23	516
12:32	542	3:1	525
16:3	384	3:2	504, 504 (LXX), 516, 526
16:20	549		
18:3	96	3:3-4	516
18:4	96	3:6	526
18:10-11	169	3:7	533
21:18	218	3:8	529
22:10	96	3:9	527 (*bis*)
23:3	197	3:10	533
23:5	113 n. 8	3:12	508, 533, 561
26:2	96	3:12-13	503
28:36	424	3:13	525 n. 22, 525 n. 22 (LXX), 533
30:4	293 n. 3		
31:16	561	3:14	527
33:1-29	160 n. 10	4:1	525 n. 22 (LXX)
34:1-12	561	4:5	525 n. 22 (LXX)
34:5	301	4:8	515
34:8	71	4:14	531
34:10	43, 94, 112 n. 6, 231, 310	4:16	463
		5:4 ff.	509
Esther		5:9	521
1:1	501	5:9-10	528
1:6	508 (*bis*)	5:11	521
1:7	508	6:1	503 n. 2, 503-504 n. 2 (LXX), 507
1:9	502		
1:10	504, 509	6:1-2	521
1:11	517	6:3	507
1:12	504 (*bis*), 504 (LXX), 509 (*bis*)	6:6	507, 522
		6:7	523
1:14	509	6:8	523
1:22	503, 506	6:9	523
2:1	504, 504 (LXX), 510	6:10	523 (*bis*), 524
		6:11	523, 524 (*ter*)
2:2	510	6:12	521, 521 (LXX)
2:3	502, 518	7:2	504 (*bis*), 504 (LXX) (*bis*)
2:4	510		
2:5	513, 514	7:7	506, 520

7:8	511, 511 n. 5 (LXX)	6:16-20	67
		6:18	293 n. 3
7:9	525, 533	6:23	66
7:10	528	6:25	52
8:8	506	7:1-2	66
8:15	523 n. 18, 531 (bis)	7:1-13	64 n. 8, 64 n. 8 (LXX)
9:7-9	509		
9:7-10	534	7:8-9	66
9:12	502	7:10	66
9:13	534	7:19-21	64 n. 8, 64 n. 8 (LXX)
9:19	534		
9:24	525 n. 21, 525 n. 21 (LXX)	7:20	67
		8:1-21	64 n. 8, 64 n. 8 (LXX)
9:29-32	534		
10:1	501, 506	8:2	67
Exodus		8:4	66
1:8	79, 84, 89	8:13	67
1:8-10	85	8:19	88
1:11	311	8:21	66
1:15	85	8:25	67
1:22	80	9:8	67
2:3	28	9:8-10	64 n. 8, 64 n. 8 (LXX)
2:10	85		
2.15-21	39	9:12	88
2:16	39, 40, 44	9:22	536
2:16-21	38, 38 (LXX)	9:27	66, 67
2:17	46	9:27-28	64 n. 8, 64 n. 8 (LXX)
2:18	39		
2:20	46	9:27-30	88
2:21	43, 47	10:3	67
3:1	52	10:3-8	64 n. 8, 64 n. 8 (LXX)
3:2	292		
4:1	169	10:7	88
4:10	64	10:16	67
4:14	65, 535	10:16-17	66
4:14-16	64 n. 8, 64 n. 8 (LXX)	10:16-18	64 n. 8, 64 n. 8 (LXX)
4:18	52 (bis)	11:10	64 n. 8, 64 n. 8 (LXX), 67
4:27-29	57		
4:27-31	64 n. 8, 64 n. 8 (LXX)	12:1	64 n. 8, 64 n. 8 (LXX)
4:30	65	12:28-31	64 n. 8, 64 n. 8 (LXX)
5:1	65 (bis)		
5:1-21	64 n. 8, 64 n. 8 (LXX)	12:30	88
		12:43	64 n. 8, 64 n. 8 (LXX)
5:2	79		
5:4	65	12:50	64 n. 8, 64 n. 8 (LXX)
5:19-21	66		
6:1	536	13:19	59
6:12	65	14:5	88
6:13	66, 536	14:8	88
6:14-25	66	15:1-18	58, 160

INDEX OF PASSAGES FROM ANCIENT TEXTS 589

15:20	64 n. 9, 183 n. 7		(LXX)
15:21	160	28:30	69
16:2-3	64 n. 8, 64 n. 8 (LXX), 67	28:35-39	64 n. 8, 64 n. 8 (LXX)
16:6-7	64 n. 8, 64 n. 8 (LXX)	28:38	69
		28:41	68
16:9	68	29:1-46	64
16:9-10	64 n. 8, 64 n. 8 (LXX)	29:44	64 n. 8, 64 n. 8 (LXX)
16:10	68	30:30	64 n. 8, 64 n. 8 (LXX)
16:33-34	64 n. 8, 64 n. 8 (LXX)	32	60, 545
17:8-16	47, 121	32:1-25	64 n. 8, 64 n. 8 (LXX)
17:9	561		
17:10	64 n. 8, 64 n. 8 (LXX)	32:21	60
		32:21-25	61
17:12	55 n. 1, 68	32:24	60 (*bis*)
18:1	47, 49	32:25	60
18:1-27	38, 38 (LXX)	32:26-29	60
18:5	46, 48, 49	32:35	60, 64 n. 8. 64 n. 8 (LXX)
18:7	49		
18:8-12	51, 559	Ezekiel	
18:9	49 (*bis*)	1:2	443 n. 4
18:10	45 (*bis*), 49 (*bis*), 50, 51	12:13	458
		34:23-24	387 n. 12
18:11	42, 49	37:24-25	387 n. 12
18:12	49, 51 (*ter*), 59	Ezra	
18:14	48	1:1-4	413
18:17	42	1:2	413, 413 (LXX)
18:17-23	42	1:3	379
18:19	50	3:2	490
18:21	50	7:1-5	476
18:23	50 (*bis*)	7-10	474
19-20	48	7:6	479
19:16-20:21	292	7:11	479
19:24	64 n. 8, 64 n. 8 (LXX)	7:12	479
		7:21	479
19:25	68	7:26	482
22:27 (28)	74 (LXX), 389 (LXX), 558 (LXX)	7:28	482
		8:1-20	476
24:1	64 n. 8, 64 n. 8 (LXX), 68	8:35	473 n. 1
		9:8	473 n. 1
24:1-11	68	Genesis	
24:4	561	1:3	540
24:9-10	64 n. 8, 64 n. 8 (LXX)	1:9-10	540
		2:7	2 n. 6, 570
24:10	68	2:10	1
24:14	64 n. 8, 64 n. 8 (LXX)	2:11	1
		2:13	2
25:33	561	3:1	2, 2 n. 6
28:1	57	3:14	2 n. 6
28:1-3	64 n. 8, 64 n. 8	3:16	7

590 INDEX OF PASSAGES FROM ANCIENT TEXTS

3:17	4, 8	22:2	185, 185 (LXX), 185 n. 13
4.2	9		
4:3	8	22:14	561
4:4	8	25:3	52 n. 14 (LXX)
4:4-5	8	28:13-15	120 n. 17
4:7	8 (LXX), 8 n. 18, 561	35:22	60
		36:43	501
4:16	10	40-41	448 n. 15
4:17	13	41:15	83
4:22	13	41:37	83
5:6	13	41:38-41	79
5:28-9:29	17, 17 (LXX)	41:39	83
5:29	18	41:42	523
6:2	20	41:45	83
6:3	4 n. 10	43:30	360 (LXX)
6:4	15	45:16	84
6:5	15, 24	46:34	84
6:6	21	47:1	84
6:7	21 (LXX)	49:6-7	561
6:8	27	49:27	139
6:9	24, 25, 26, 560	50:25	59
6:13	22 (*bis*), 26	Haggai	
6:14	28 (LXX), 560	2:21-23	387 n. 12
6:14 ff.	21 n. 6	Hosea	
8:4	30	7:4-7	233
8:11	29	Isaiah	
8:20	30 (*bis*)	1:11	380, 546
8:21	30, 31 (*bis*), 570	6	381
8:21-22	31	7:1-25	379
9:1	35	7:14	388
9:6	32 (LXX)	7:14-25	379 n. 7
9:9	37 n. 17, 37 n. 17 (LXX)	9:5	364
		9:6	386, 388
9:11	31	9:6-7	387, 555
9:13	33	9:7	386
9:13-17	33	11:1	385
9:16	33	11:1-2	386
9:18	34	11:2-3	385, 555
9:20-21	20 n. 5	19:19	377 n. 3, 380, 380 n. 8
9:27	35		
10	395 n. 5	22:15	382 n. 10
10:4	395 n. 5	27:9	388
10:29	1	34:8-11	439
11	448 n. 15	37:11-13	381
11:2	34	38:1	389, 545
12:6	561	38:2-3	389
12:10-20	78	38:4-6	389
12:11-12	82	38:5	390
12:15	78	38:8	364
12:16	83	39: 1-2	373, 373 (LXX)
13:18	20-21, 20-21 (LXX)	43:34	380
18:23-30	31	44:28	382

INDEX OF PASSAGES FROM ANCIENT TEXTS

44:28-45:1	379	1:6	398, 408
66:1	417	1:9	396, 400 n. 13, 400 n. 13 (LXX), 405 n. 20, 407, 407 (LXX), 413
Jeremiah			
2:18	2 n. 4 (LXX)		
23:3-5	387 n. 12		
24;1	443 n. 4	1:10	398
27:20	443 n. 4	1:11-12	408
29:1-2	443 n. 4	1:13-14	413
29:10	377 n. 2	1:14	409
29:14	377 n. 2	1:16	406 n. 22, 409 (*bis*), 559
34:1-22	450		
34:2-7	457	1:17	569
34:5	451	2:1-2	403
34:8-11	450	2:1-9	403, 408
35:18-19	357	2:2	403 n. 16
36:2	377 n. 2	2:7	403, 403 (LXX)
37:1-2	456	2:10	404
37:1-39:10	450	2:11	395
37:6-8	458	3:1-2	399
37:11	458	3:3	414, 562
38:4	457	3:4	396, 401, 401 (LXX)
38:5	455, 456		
38:7-9	457	3:5	409, 559
38:9	456-457	3:6-8	414
38:10	439, 450, 451, 457	3:10	399
38:14	439, 457	4:1	400, 408, 408 (LXX)
38:17	457 n. 8		
38:17-18	377 n. 2	4:2	397
38:19	439	4:6	399
38:20-23	377 n. 2	4:6-11	399 (*bis*), 568
39:4	459	4:7	399
40:5	465	4:8	399, 405 n. 19
40:7	443, 464 (*bis*)	4:11	412, 414
40:8	466	Joshua	
40:9	469	2:1	179
40:11	469	13:27	172
40:15-16	470	24:10	113 n. 8
40:16	467	Judges	
41:1	468, 470	1:16	52
41:2-3	470	3:9	138 n. 2, 163 (*bis*)
41:4-8	471	3:11	138 n. 2
41:5	470, 471 n. 4	3:12	144, 145, 239 n. 5
52:1-16	450	3:12-30	137, 137 (LXX)
52:8	460	3:13	145
52:28-30	443 n. 4	3:14	145
52:31-33	445, 447	3:15	138 n. 2, 139 (*bis*), 140 (LXX), 142, 142 (LXX), 142 n. 8, 142 n. 8 (LXX) (*bis*), 143, 163
Jonah			
1:2	408		
1:3	395, 412		
1:4	398		
1:5	407, 407 (LXX), 409, 414, 557	3:16	140, 146, 148, 148 (LXX)

592 INDEX OF PASSAGES FROM ANCIENT TEXTS

3:16-25	561	7:4-8	174
3:17	146, 146 n. 13 (LXX)	7:5-7	172
		7:10	166
3:19	147 (*bis*), 148	7:12	173
3:20	139, 147, 149	7:13-14	173
3:21	140, 149	7:16	173
3:22	146, 146 n. 13	7:18	170
3:24	146, 146 n. 14 (LXX), 148, 149	7:21-22	174
		7:22	173, 174
3:25	148, 150	7:23	175
3:27	141	8:1-3	171
3:28	141	8:4-17	172
3:29	150	8:18-21	168, 549
3:30	138 n. 2, 141 (*bis*), 141 (LXX)	8:24-27	169
		8:28	167
3:31	163	8:31	178 (*bis*)
4:1	239 n. 5	9:4	178, 178 (LXX)
4:1-5:31	153, 153-154 (LXX)	9:28-41	138 n. 2
		10:1	163
4:2	155	10:6	239 n. 5
4:3	154, 155, 156	10:17-18	178
4:4	155 n. 5, 157	11:1	178, 179, 180, 180 n. 3
4:6	155, 156		
4:8-9	156	11:2	180, 180 n. 3 (*bis*), 180 n. 3 (LXX), 188 n. 21
4:11	39, 52		
4:12-16	157		
4:18	160	11:3	178
4:23	159	11:6-8	179
5	160	11:7	188 n. 21
5:14-18	161	11:8	179
5:19	161	11:9	187, 189 n. 22
5:20	157	11:24	188
5:20-21	157	11:27	188, 189 n. 22
5:23	158, 161	11:29	187, 189 n. 22
5:28	161	11:30	187
5:31	161	11:31	182 (*bis*), 182 (LXX), 184, 187
6:11	165, 569		
6:11-8:35	164, 164 (LXX)	11:32	178, 187
6:12	168, 171	11:33	181
6:13	171, 569	11:34	185, 185 n. 13, 186 (*bis*)
6:14	163		
6:15	163, 165, 166, 167	11:36	190, 191
6:17	169	11:37	184, 184 n. 11
6:17-18	171	11:38	184 (*bis*)
6:25-32	168, 558	11:39	184 (*bis*), 186 n. 15
6:32	164, 168	11:39-40	184
6:34	170, 170 (LXX), 568	12:3	181
		12:20	179
6:36-40	171	14:1-16:31	131, 294
7:2	167	19:25	43
7:3	174	1 Kings	
7:4	170	2:5	209

INDEX OF PASSAGES FROM ANCIENT TEXTS 593

2:28	206	16:25	437 n. 1
6:29-22:40	273, 273 (LXX)	16:30	239, 277, 437 n. 1
11:1	197 n. 1	16:31	277
11:26	238, 240	16:32-33	277, 458
11:26-40	233, 233 (LXX), 416, 416 (LXX)	16:33	230, 274
		17-19	295, 295 (LXX), 334-335, 334-335 (LXX)
11:29	231		
12:1-24	244		
12:1-14:20	233, 233 (LXX), 416, 416 (LXX)	17:1	300 n. 7, 335 n. 3
		17:2-4	298, 569
12:5	255	17:10	303
12:7	247	17:13	296
12:9	257	17:15	300 n. 7, 335 n. 3 (*bis*)
12:12	257 n. 20		
12:13	257	17:17-24	397
12:14	257 n. 20	17:18	300 n. 7, 301, 301 n. 8, 304, 335 n. 3
12:15	257		
12:16	257, 259	17:19	296, 303
12:18	258 (*bis*)	17:21	303
12:24	253 (*bis*), 254, 257	17:22	300 n. 7, 303, 335 n. 3
12:24b	238 (LXX)		
12:26-27	232, 234	17:24	300 n. 7, 301, 301 n. 8, 335 n. 3, 397 n. 10
12:28	235, 240		
12:30	233		
12:31	237	18:6	278
12:32	234, 235, 255	18:7	286, 300 n. 7 (*bis*), 335 n. 3 (*bis*)
13:1	235		
13:3	241	18:8	285
13:4	241 (*bis*)	18:10	286
13:5	241	18:15	296
13:7	241	18:18	297
13:11	233 n. 1 (LXX), 235	18:21	300 n. 7, 335 n. 3
		18:25	303
13:24	235	18:30	303
13:33	236, 239 n. 5	18:38	298
13:34	235	18:40	302
14:1 ff.	256	18:41	298
14:21-31	244	18:43	299
14:22	239 n. 5, 437 n. 1	18:46	300 n. 7, 335 n. 3
15:6	253	19:4	296
15:9-24	263	19:5	300
15:11	267	19:8	299
15:12	267, 269, 558	19:9	299, 304, 555
15:13	268 (*bis*)	19:10	302
15:14	268 (*bis*), 561	19:11	303
15:23	269	19:11-12	292, 299
15:24	239	19:14	302, 555
15:26	437 n. 1	19:17	344, 555
15:29	236	19:19	335 n. 2
15:34	236, 437 n. 1	19:20	296, 336, 337
16:7	327 n. 1	19:21	300 n. 7, 335 n. 3, 337, 344
16:19	437 n. 1		

INDEX OF PASSAGES FROM ANCIENT TEXTS

20:4	279	1:6	297
20:6	279	1:9	297, 301
20:7	279	1:10	301
20:10	280 (*bis*)	1:11-12	301
20:12	280	1:15	300 (*bis*)
20:13	280	1:17	295 n. 5 (LXX), 335 n. 1
20:14	280		
20:15	282	2:1-25	335, 335 (LXX)
20:19	281	2:5	337, 557
20:20	281	2:8	299
20:21	281 (*bis*)	2:9	341, 549
20:22	279	2:10	341
20:27	274 n. 2 (LXX)	2:11	302 n. 9 (LXX)
20:29	281 (*bis*)	2:11-12	569
20:31	284	2:11-14	337
20:32	285	2:12	310
20:33	285	2:14	341
21:2	286	2:16	317
21:6	278	2:17	338
21:9	286	2:19	348
21:16	286	2:19-22	341, 342, 348
21:17	300 n. 7, 335 n. 3	2:19-23	344, 569
21:17-29	295, 295 (LXX)	2:21	348
21:19	284	2:23-24	339
21:27	261, 274 n. 2, 278 (*bis*)	3:1-27	322, 322 (LXX)
		3:2	437 n. 1
21:27-29	300 n. 7, 335 n. 3	3:3	328
21:29	278	3:6	328
22:3	283, 319	3:7-27	307, 307 (LXX)
22:4	282, 311	3:8	310, 318, 323
22:5	311	3:9	318, 323 (*bis*)
22:7	314	3:10	329
22:8-9	314	3:11	338, 557
22:19-23	287	3:11-20	335, 335 (LXX)
22:24	283	3:12	329
22:24-25	283	3:13	329, 340
22:30	273 n. 2, 273 n. 2 (LXX), 282, 287, 307 n. 1, 307 n. 1 (LXX), 312	3:14	330 (*bis*)
		3:14-20	335 n. 2
		3:15	349
		3:16	345
22:32	312, 548	3:18	349
22:34	280, 283 n. 6	3:20	345, 345 n. 6
22:35	280	3:27	557
22:38	300 n. 7, 335 n. 3	4:1-7	341, 345
22:41-51	307, 307 (LXX)	4:1-44	335, 335 (LXX)
22:43	319 n. 10	4:3	335 n. 2
22:43-44	308	4:5-6	345
22:52	437 n. 1	4:7	335 n. 2, 343
2 Kings		4:8-6:8	340 n. 5
1:3	300 n. 7, 335 n. 3	4:9	343
1:3-2:12	295, 295 (LXX), 335, 335 (LXX)	4:34	345, 569
		4:38-41	346

INDEX OF PASSAGES FROM ANCIENT TEXTS 595

4:42-44	346	9:10	361
5:1-19	346	9:11	361
5:8-7:2	335, 335 (LXX)	9:11-12	355
5:20-27	346	9:14	359
5:27	340	9:15-16	359
6:1-7	346	9:15-26	322, 322 (LXX)
6:8-23	322, 322 (LXX)	9:17	325
6:10	330	9:20	325 n. 1, 325 n. 1
6:15-16	339		(LXX), 353 (bis),
6:17	335 n. 2, 346		354, 360, 548
6:18	335 n. 2, 346	9:21	325
6:19	335 n. 2, 346, 349	9:23	354
6:20	330, 339	9:25	300 n. 7, 335 n. 2,
6:21	330, 335 n. 2		335 n. 3, 356
6:21-22	342	9:27	354
6:23	330, 335 n. 2, 343	9:29	332
6:23-24	343	9:43	326 n. 2
6:24	323, 335 n. 2	10:1	352 n. 1
6:25	324	10:1-3	360
6:26	324	10:2	352 n. 1
6:26-31	326	10:6	354
6:27	324, 326, 327	10:8	361
6:30	327	10:9	355, 359
6:31	327, 335 n. 2	10:15	357 (bis)
6:32	329 (bis), 335 n. 2	10:15-16	353
6:33	326, 331, 335 n. 2	10:16	357 (bis), 359
7:1-2	331 (bis)	10:24	358
7:2	335 n. 2, 336, 343	10:27	355, 389 n. 16, 558
7:10-20	322, 322 (LXX)	10:29	358
7:11-12	324	10:30	352, 353, 357
7:12	324	10:31	352, 358 (bis)
7:16	322	12:2	439
7:16-8:15	335, 335 (LXX)	13:2	437 n. 1
7:20	335 n. 2	13:7-8	335 n. 2
8:4	336	13:11	437 n. 1, 439, 539
8:7	335 n. 2	13:14	335 n. 2 (bis), 336
8:10	335 n. 2	13:14-15	343
8:11	342	13:14-21	335, 335 (LXX)
8:15	325	13:15-19	340
8:18	437 n. 1	13:20	335 n. 2 (bis)
8:19	448 n. 16	13:20-21	347
8:25	331	13:21	349
8:26	331-332	13:25	335 n. 2 (bis)
8:27	437 n. 1	14:9	554
8:28	325	14:24	437 n. 1
8:28-29	322, 322 (LXX)	14:25	395, 396
8:29	325, 353	15:9	437 n. 1
9:1-3	335, 335 (LXX)	15:18	437 n. 1
9:1-10:36	352, 352 (LXX)	15:24	437 n. 1
9:3	360	15:28	437 n. 1
9:6	360	16:2	437 n. 1
9:7	355, 356	16:14-18	379

17:2	437 n. 1	22:19-20	431
18-20	364, 364 (LXX)	23:2	433 n. 8
18:2	368	23:4-24	427
18:4	309, 371	23:7-19	432
18:7	372	23:20	434
18:14	367	23:22	434
18:16	369	23:24	432
18:18	367	23:25	425, 435
18:22	369	23:32	437 n. 1
18:26	367	23:37	440 n. 1
19:4	381	24:5	456 n. 6
19:5	389 n. 16 (bis)	24:6-17	441, 441 (LXX)
19:7	373	24:8	440
19:14	369	24:9	437, 440 n. 1, 456 n. 6, 456 n. 6 (LXX), 540
19:17-18	372		
19:20	389 n. 16		
19:20-34	381	24:10	459
19:28	372	24:12	443
19:33-35	381	24:14-16	443 n. 4
19:34	386	24:17	459
19:35	374, 406 (bis)	24:17-25:12	450
19:37	373, 406	24:19	438 (bis), 440 n. 1, 450, 452, 455, 458
20:1	370 (bis), 389		
20:2-3	389	24:19-20	456
20:4	389 n. 16	25:1	458
20:4-6	389	25:3	460
20:5	370	25:4	451, 459
20:7	370, 390	25:7	460
20:8	390 (bis)	25:8	460
20:8-11	374	25:22	464
20:9	389 n. 16	25:27	443 n. 4
20:10	364, 364 (LXX)	25:27-30	441, 441 (LXX), 445, 445 n. 6, 447, 448 n. 15
20:11	371		
20:12-13	373		
20:16	389 n. 16	Leviticus	
20:19	371	8:1-36	64 n. 8, 64 n. 8 (LXX)
20:20	365		
20:21-21:18	416, 416 n. 1 (LXX)	9:15	62
		10:3	56, 58, 64 n. 8, 64 n. 8 (LXX), 69
21:2	418, 437 n. 1		
21:3	418		
21:4	418	10:16-20	62
21:5-7	419	10:19	62
21:9	420	16:29	463
21:16	230, 417, 420	19:19	96
21:20	437 n. 1	21:1-4	59
22:1-23:30	424, 424 (LXX)	22:7	309
22:2	426	23:22	96
22:8	433 n. 8	23:27	463
22:9	433	Malachi	
22:11	419	3:23-24	291
22:13	433-434	Nehemiah	
		1-13	489

INDEX OF PASSAGES FROM ANCIENT TEXTS 597

1:1	491	Numbers	
1:3	490	1:17	69
1:5-11	495	1:44	69
2:1	490, 491 (bis)	2:3	66
2:2	491	2:3-4	66
2:5	492	2:18	52
2:6	491, 509	6:22-27	64 n. 8, 64 n. 8
2:7-8	496		(LXX)
2:8	491, 492, 497	7:12-17	67
2:12	492	10:14	66
2:12-16	493	10:29	52, 52 n. 14
2:16	493	12:1	43, 545
2:17-18	492	12:1-12	64 n. 8, 64 n. 8
2:19-20	497		(LXX)
3:1-32	493	12:3	231, 309
4:1	497	14:5	64 n. 8, 64 n. 8
4:4	497		(LXX)
4:8	494 (bis)	14:10	63
4:9	495	14:19	63
4:12	493	14:26-35	64 n. 8, 64 n. 8
4:15	495		(LXX)
4:20	495	15.37-39	93
5:2-5	494	16:1	94
5:6-7	496	16:1-35	91, 91 (LXX)
5:12	496	16:2	105, 106
5:14-15	494	16:3	64 n. 8, 64 n. 8
6:5-7	497		(LXX), 69-70, 103
6:6	497		(bis), 106 (LXX)
6:15	489 n. 1	16:5	103
6:16	495	16:5-11	107, 107 (LXX)
7:4-5	495	16:10	100
7:5	498 (bis)	16:10-11	64 n. 8, 64 n. 8
7:6-65	498		(LXX)
8:1	479, 495	16:15	107, 107 (LXX)
8:3	479	16:16-22	64 n. 8, 64 n. 8
8:4	479		(LXX)
8:9	479, 495	16:18	107
8:13	479	16:31	107
8:14	487, 562	16:31-32	105
8:17	487, 562	16:31-34	108
9:6-38	486	16:32	105, 108 (bis)
9:26	487	16:35	105 (bis), 108 (ter)
10:1-30	497		
12:26	479	17:5	70
12:36	479	17:6-25	64 n. 8, 64 n. 8
13:2	113 n. 8		(LXX)
13:4-9	496	17:17	71
13:10-11	496	18:1-7	64 n. 8, 64 n. 8
13:15-22	496		(LXX)
13:19-22	496	18:8	96
13:23-29	498	18:14	96
13:25	498	18:15	96

18:21	96	24:7	119 (LXX)
20:2	64 n. 8, 64 n. 8 (LXX)	24:8	119
		24:14	119
20:6	64 n. 8, 64 n. 8 (LXX)	24:16	110 n. 2, 110 n. 2 (LXX)
20:8	63	24:17	385
20:10	63, 64 n. 8, 64 n. 8 (LXX)	24:17-18	119
		24:24	119
20:12	64 n. 8, 64 n. 8 (LXX)	24:25	133 (*bis*)
		25:1	125
20:22-28	71	25:1-5	133 (*bis*)
20:23	71	25:1-9	130, 294, 544
20:23-29	64 n. 8, 64 n. 8 (LXX)	25:6	134
		25:6-13	133
20:24	64	25:6-18	125 (*bis*)
20:28	71	25:7-8	334
20:29	71	25:11	359, 555
22-24	113 n. 8	25:12	293 n. 3
22:2-24:25	111 n. 3	26:2	328
22:2-25:9	110, 110 (LXX)	26:9	501
22:8	116	26:51	328
22:12	122	26:62	328
22:13	122 (*bis*), 126	29:7	463
22:15	124	31:8	126
22:17-18	124	31:16	133
22:20	131, 561	31:27-30	100
22:21-35	128	Proverbs	
22:22	131	11:10	275
22:27	129	13:16	503
22:28	129 (*bis*)	28:15	302
22:29	129 (*bis*)	Psalms	
22:30	130	55:24	113 n. 6
22:32	129	69:16	140 n. 4
22:34	125, 129	99:6	95
22:37	123	106:16	97
22:41	117, 123, 124, 127	110:1	385
23:2	110 n. 2, 110 n. 2 (LXX), 116, 116 (LXX)	Ruth	
		1:4	197
		1:6	196
23:4	126	1:8	193, 196
23:5	131	1:8-18	199
23:9	117	1:10	197
23:10	120	1:13	196
23:16	127	1:16	196 (*bis*), 197, 199
23:21	117, 120	1:17	196
23:24	120	1:20	196
23:25	116	1:21	196 (*ter*)
23:26	132	1:22	197
23:27	125	2:2	197
24:2	110 n. 2	2:4	196 (*bis*)
24:4	110 n. 2, 110 n. 2 (LXX)	2:6	197
		2:8-14	200

2:10	198	13:12	216
2:12	196 (*ter*)	13:20	226
2:18	195	13:20-19:8	215, 215 (LXX)
2:19	199	13:21	217
2:20	196	13:22	226
2:21	197	13:23	227
3:2-4	200	13:27	215 n. 1 (LXX)
3:7	193	14:1	207
3:13	196	14:13	217
3:14	200	14:13-17	225
4:5	197	14:21	218
4:10	197	14:25	220
4:11	196	14:26	221
4:12	196	14:27	225
4:13	196	14:29	222
4:14	196	14:30	222-223
4:20-22	67	14:32	223 (*bis*)
1 Samuel		14:33	223 (*bis*), 227
2	293 n. 3	15:1	221
2:1-10	160 n. 10	15:2	221
9:1	464	15:2-3	222, 227
10:7	216 n. 2	15:2-6	224
12:11	163, 166, 181	15:5-6	226
15:8	525 n. 22	15:6	224
18:6	183 n. 7	15:7	215, 215 n. 1(LXX), 221 n. 11
2 Samuel			
1:19-27	160 n. 10	15:11	224
2:22	206	15:12-13	224
2:24	204, 205	16:21	219
2:26	208	18:5	220
2:32	205	18:9	228
3:1	208	18:14	206
3:25	207, 209	18:15	206
3:26	211	18:18	225
3:27	211	19:1	220
3:29	264	19:2	220
3:34	211	19:6-7	207
7:11-16	448	20:8	207
8:15-16	203	20:19	208
9	448 n. 15	23:8	203 n. 1
9:1	219	24:1	69
10:12	208	24:3	207
10:13	205	24:9-11	328
11:1	205	Zechariah	
11:2-17	60-61	3:9-10	387 n. 12
12:9	440	4:6-10	387 n. 12
12:13	440	6:9-15	387 n. 12
12:27	205	8:19	463
13:1-14	61		

APOCRYPHA

Ben Sira: see Ecclesiasticus
Ecclesiasticus
   24:27   2 n. 4
   48:14   347 n. 9
   49:11-13   474 n. 2
   49:13   495 n. 6
1 Esdras
   1:27   429
   1:28   429
   1:78   473 n. 1
   2:5   379
   8:1-2   476
   8:4   481
   8:8   481
   8:19-20   482
   8:23   479
   8:24   482
   8:25   482
   8:27   481, 482
   8:28-49   476
   8:36   482
   8:41   481
   8:41-59   481
   8:55-57   485
   8:66 (63)   473 n. 1
   8:67   486
   8:68   483
   8:68-70   483, 544
   8:70   483, 484
   8:71   481
   8:72   484
   8:74-90   486
   8:92-95   483
   8:96   484
   9:2   486
   9:8-9   484
   9:13   486
   9:16-17   484
   9:20   484
   9:36   485
   9:40   476
   9:41   479
   9:48-49   481
   9:52   479
   9:53   482
2 Esdras
   11-23   489
Esther (Additions)
   A   530 (*bis*), 533
   B   533
   B 4   529
   C   504 (*bis*), 518, 531, 536
   C 17-18   530
   C 19-22   531
   C 26-27   530
   C 28   530, 533
   D   505 (*bis*)
   D 5   518
   D 8   520 (*bis*), 535
   D 13   535, 569
   D 15   520
   E   506 (*bis*), 526 n. 22
   E 2-4   509, 528
   E 6   528
   E 10   525 n. 21
   E 12   528
   E 12-14   529
   E 20   530
   F   530
Tobit
   14:4   408 n. 24

PSEUDEPIGRAPHA

Apocalypse of Baruch: see *2 Baruch*
Apocalypse of Daniel   468
Apocalypse of Ezra: see *4 Ezra*
Ascension of Isaiah: see *Martyrdom and Ascension of Isaiah*
2 Baruch
   1:3   452 n. 4
   29:3   383
   30:1-2   383
   39:7   383
   40:1   383
   40:3   383
   64:2-3   417
   70:9   383
   72:2   383
   72:2-6   383
4 Ezra   475 (*bis*)
   7:30-44   383
   12:32   383

INDEX OF PASSAGES FROM ANCIENT TEXTS 601

Jubilees		*Paralipomena Jeremiae*	153
3:28	2	*Psalms of Solomon*	
Letter of Aristeas		8:11	386
16	29, 413	17:5-6	386
306	541	17:21	386
311	541	*Sibylline Oracles*	
Martyrdom and Ascension of Isaiah		Book 1	25 n. 10
420 n. 4		3.689-690	23 n. 9
2:1	417	*Vita Adae et Evae*	
2:4-5	417	49-50	14 n. 34
5:1 ff.	378 n. 5	49.3	23 n. 9

Dead Sea Scrolls

4Q470	452	4QSam$_a$	215 n. 1
4QFlor			
11-12	385		

Philo

De Abrahamo		6.19	77
5.27	26	9.35-10.36	42
6.34	26	10.36	42 (*bis*)
7.36	26	10.37	42 (*bis*)
21.103	76, 77	11.41-45	42
De Agricultura		19.77	76
10.43	41, 41 n. 8	24.95-96	60
		29.111	77
De Cherubim		32.124-126	60
10.32	112	50.208	76
14.49	268	50.209	76
23.74	76	51.210	76
De Confusione Linguarum		*De Fuga et Inventione*	
2.2-5	20 n. 4, 29	23.124	76
		23.126	76
3.6	2	26.145	92, 93 (*bis*)
9.29-30	77		
11.39	387 n. 13	26.146	93
		De Gigantibus	
11.41	55 n. 1	11.50	41 n. 8
14.62	404 n. 17	*De Josepho*	
		26.151	76 (*ter*)
19.88	75, 76	26.153	76
31.159	112 n. 5 (*bis*)	*De Migratione Abrahami*	
		14.78	55
De Congressu Quaerendae Eruditionis Gratia		18.103	55 n. 1
		20.113	112 n. 5
21.115	30	29.160	76
De Decalogo		32.179	240 n. 6
30.164	251	*De Mutatione Nominum*	
De Ebrietate		3.19	77
5.18	77	17.103	41 n. 8

17.104	41, 42	2.42.277	76
17.105	42, 43	De Specialibus Legibus	
19.110	42	1.9.53	74
22.128	77	4.8.49	186 n.
24.139	404 n.		16
	17	4.33.173-174	41 n. 7, 43
31.171	76		
32.173	76 (bis)	De Virtutibus	
33.175	77	7.34-35	133 n.
37.202	112 n. 5		28
37.208	55	7.34-42	134
39.223	186 n.	De Vita Mosis	
	16	1.1.1-2	177
44.255	251 n.	1.2.7	477
	16	1.11.58-59	43
De Plantatione		1.48.263-300	112 n. 5
9.39	387 n.	1.48.264	115 n.
	13		12
11.43	28	1.48.266	122
33.138	404 n.	1.48.267-268	124
	17	1.48.268	124
De Posteritate Caini		1.49.274	125
12.42-43	12 n. 29	1.50.275	123
18.63	55 n. 1	1.50.277	110 n. 2, 116
33.115	76 (bis)		
34.117	13 n. 32	1.53.294-55.304	133
De Praemiis et Poenis		1.54.295-304	131
5.28	186 n.	2.2.9	251
	16	2.7.37	541
13.74	93	2.7.38-39	541
13.75	93	2.7.40	541
13.78	93	2.15.71	268
De Sacrificiis Abelis et Caini		2.28.142	56
1.2	9	2.31.161-162	60
11.48	77	2.37-38.203-208	74
12.50	41 n. 8	2.48.263	23
19.69	76, 77 (bis)	2.50.277-278	92
		2.50.279	92
27.88-89	8	2.50.280	93
De Sobrietate		2.50.284	93
7.32	35	2.50.285	93
10.44-48	35	2.50.286-287	93
De Somniis		In Flaccum	78
2.27.182	77	Legatio ad Gaium	
2.27.183	77	18-19.120-131	78
2.27.184	77	Legum Allegoria	
2.30.200-201	76	3.4.12	77
2.31.211	77	3.4.13	76, 77
2.32.215	76	3.15.45	56 n. 1, 71-72 n.
2.32.219	76 (bis)		11
2.35.234	56	3.33.103	56, 63
2.36.237	77	3.44.128	56

INDEX OF PASSAGES FROM ANCIENT TEXTS

3.45.132	56	3.9	132 n.
3.46.135	56		27
3.75.212	76 (*bis*), 77 (*bis*)	*Quis Rerum Divinarum Heres*	
		12.60	77 (*bis*)
3.81.228	186	53.265	186 n.
3.84.236	77		16
3.87.243	75-76, 77	*Quod Deterius Potiori Insidiari Solet*	
		20.71	112 n. 5
Quaestiones et Solutiones in Exodum		25.95	77
2.5	74	44.161-162	77
Quaestiones et Solutiones in Genesin		*Quod D-us Immutabilis Sit*	
1.74	10 n. 23	5.21-22	21
1.100	22	25.117	26
2.50 (on Genesis 8:20)	30	37.181	112 n. 5
2.54 (on Genesis 8:21)	31	*Quod Omnis Probus Liber Sit*	
2.64 (on Genesis 9:13-17)	33	2.13	76
2.77 (on Genesis 9:27)	35		

Pseudo-Philo

Biblical Antiquities	162	31.2	155, 158
2.3	13 n. 30	31.3	160
3.3	21	32	160
3.4	26	32.1-4	161
3.4-5.8	19	32.16	158
3.8	30 (*bis*)	33.1-5	161
3.9	14 n. 34, 23, 31, 31 n. 16	33.6	161
		34.1	138 n. 2
4.2-5.8	19	35.1	163
9.5	43	35.6	169
9.10	43	35.7	169
10.2	88	36.2	170
10.6	88	36.3	169
12.2	60	36.3-4	163
12.3	60	36.4	169
16.1	93	39.1	178 n. 2
16.3	94	39.2	180 n. 4
18.2	115 n. 12	39.4	187 n. 19
18.3	112 n. 4	39.5	187 n. 19 (*bis*)
18.9	128 n. 24	39.6	187 n. 19 (*bis*)
18.10	101 n. 7, 115	39.7	187 n. 19
18.13-14	43, 131	39.8	187 n. 19 (*bis*)
19.11	33	39.9	187 n. 19, 188
25-28	163	39.10	187 n. 19
29	137	39.11	187 n. 19
29.1	138 n. 2 (*ter*)	40.1	187-188 n. 19, 190
29.3	138 n. 2	40.2	190 n. 24
29.4	138 n. 2	40.3	190
30-33	154	40.4	188 n. 19
30.5	138 n. 2, 157	44.2	138 n. 2
30.7	157	45.3	43
31.1	156, 158	47.1	137

604 INDEX OF PASSAGES FROM ANCIENT TEXTS

48.1	291	*Homily on Jonah*	410
48.1-2	293, 334	6	402, 407
61.6	195	19-25	403 n. 16
		41	402
		48	402

Josephus

Against Apion		2.290	177
1.23-27	540	2.291	550
1.37	111, 291, 356, 545	*Antiquities*	
1.40	400 n. 14, 473 n. 1	1.5	102, 543
1.41	114	1.6	551
1.46	540	1.9	543
1.60-68	486	1.10	543
1.69 ff.	560	1.10-12	562
1.112-125	245	1.13	206
1.113	528	1.14	212, 266, 273, 288,
1.114-115	559		359, 373, 430, 536,
1.130	29		568
1.134-141	444 n. 5	1.15	20
1.153	251, 557	1.17	19 n. 3, 244, 273,
1.156	460		291, 368, 437, 539
1.186	251	1.18	541
1.188-189	528	1.20	196
1.203	115	1.24	252, 374
1.204	115	1.25	196
1.236	115	1.34	570
1.256	115	1.38	1 (*bis*)
1.257	115	1.39	2
1.258	115, 123 n. 20	1.41	2
1.267	115	1.45	3
1.306	115	1.46	3, 4 (*bis*), 566
1.312	115 n. 12	1.49	4 (*bis*), 7 (*bis*), 564
2.40	251	1.50	2 n. 6 (*bis*)
2.202	33	1.52	9
2.135	546	1.53	9
2.145	177	1.53-59	216
2.146	465	1.54	4, 7, 8, 9
2.148	127, 460, 546, 548,	1.59	9
	567	1.60	10
2.154	69	1.60-62	10, 11, 566
2.162	115, 115 n. 11	1.61	12
2.199-203	198	1.64	13
2.206	218	1.66	12
2.210	248	1.69	13
2.213	465	1.70	14
2.225	69	1.70-71	23
2.237	74, 389, 558	1.72	13
2.257	198	1.73	15, 20, 22 (*bis*),
2.261	198, 465		563, 570

INDEX OF PASSAGES FROM ANCIENT TEXTS

1.74	18, 25 (*bis*), 561, 570	1.172	548
1.74-108	17	1.177	174, 281, 567
1.75	18, 26, 27	1.180	9
1.76	27	1.186	21
1.76-78	18	1.192	196
1.77	28, 560	1.200	249
1.80-88	18, 19	1.205	154
1.89-92	18	1.212	447 n. 14
1.90	395	1.222	185
1.92	29, 31, 32, 395, 570	1.225	185
1.93-94	29, 560	1.232	189
1.93-95	18, 19, 245	1.240	115 n. 12
1.94	29	1.240-241	39
1.94-95	28	1.243	547
1.95	29, 560	1.247	249, 546
1.96	30, 31, 562	1.250	549
1.97	31	1.256	288 n. 11
1.99	27, 31 (*bis*)	1.264	249
1.99-103	18-19	1.280-283	120 n. 17
1.100	22, 23, 563	1.282	120 n. 17
1.102	32	1.288	517
1.103	33 (*bis*), 34, 37	1.288-290	546
1.104-108	19 (*bis*)	1.327	519, 565
1.107-108	561	1.346	288 n. 11
1.108	10 n. 26	2.9	546, 547
1.109	34	2.10	85
1.109-112	19	2.15	123 n. 20, 547
1.110	34	2.22	216 n. 3
1.110-112	34	2.41	547
1.113	22 n. 8 (*bis*)	2.51-52	201
1.113-119	22 n. 8	2.53	519, 565
1.113-121	19	2.63-65	547
1.117	22 n. 8, 556	2.65	123 n. 20
1.120-141	548	2.72	123 n. 20
1.122-129	2	2.78	396 n. 9
1.122-139	19 (*bis*)	2.80	83
1.127	310, 395 n. 5	2.84-87	547
1.140-142	19	2.89	83
1.141	35	2.91	83
1.142	35	2.94	557
1.148	546	2.101	549, 557
1.154	47, 547, 548	2.136	549
1.155	143	2.140	249, 556
1.156	240, 547, 566	2.145	549
1.157	240	2.149	249
1.158	549	2.152	550
1.161	410 n. 26	2.157	249
1.162	82, 519, 565	2.159	258
1.163-164	82	2.176	509
1.165	38, 82, 83	2.179	396 n. 9
1.169	34	2.185	38, 84 (*bis*)

INDEX OF PASSAGES FROM ANCIENT TEXTS

2.194-195	132	2.347-349	104 n. 8
2.195	249	2.348	104 n. 8, 245, 569
2.196	288 n. 11	3.5	564
2.198	288 n. 11	3.11-12	67
2.201	84	3.13	98, 548
2.201-202	84	3.23	141, 177
2.202	84	3.24	68
2.205	85	3.40	121
2.206	85 (*bis*)	3.49	143, 548
2.207	85	3.54	64, 68
2.210	464, 477, 546	3.62	48
2.217	123 n. 20	3.63	46, 48, 49 (*bis*), 51, 550, 559
2.224	28, 547		
2.229	477, 546	3.63-74	38
2.232-233	85	3.64	49, 51, 58, 59, 64
2.233	86, 547	3.65	47, 49, 68
2.238-253	38, 86, 548	3.66-67	549
2.241	86 n. 9, 115	3.67	48
2.242	86	3.68	50
2.243-253	567	3.70	50 (*bis*)
2.252-253	519, 565	3.72	50 (*bis*)
2.257-264	38	3.75	68
2.258	46	3.84	68
2.261	47	3.98	551
2.262	47, 550 (*bis*)	3.136	100
2.263	47, 558	3.143	196
2.264	52, 561	3.159	69
2.277	52	3.171	69
2.279	57, 64	3.178	69
2.280	65, 551	3.180	389
2.281	65 (*bis*), 86	3.188	57, 57 n. 3
2.284	66 (*ter*), 87, 551	3.188-192	64
2.287	66, 551	3.189-190	58
2.288	87, 570	3.190	58, 59, 545
2.290	66, 87	3.191	58
2.291	66	3.192	58
2.294	67	3.205-207	64
2.295	87	3.205-211	64
2.296	67, 87, 154 n. 4	3.208	58, 59
2.300	67	3.211	69
2.301	87 (*bis*)	3.274-275	198, 544
2.302	67, 88	3.277	59
2.304	67	3.287	69
2.305	67	3.307	63, 64
2.306	67	3.310	64, 258, 551
2.307	88	3.312	218
2.313	88	3.317	551
2.314	67	4.11	101, 102
2.319	59, 64	4.11-56	101
2.320	88 (*bis*)	4.12	101 (*bis*), 102, 556
2.343	158	4.13	101 (*bis*)
2.346	58, 132, 161	4.14	94 (*bis*), 98 (*ter*), 546 (*bis*), 547

INDEX OF PASSAGES FROM ANCIENT TEXTS 607

4.15	64, 70, 103, 480	4.102	121 (*bis*), 122, 560
4.15-19	106, 237	4.102-158	110
4.16	103, 106	4.103	122
4.17	103	4.104	115
4.18	64	4.105	116, 122, 123, 247
4.18-19	70	4.106	122, 126, 127 (*bis*)
4.19	98 (*bis*), 101	4.107	38, 124 (*quater*),
4.20	101, 102, 106, 480,		131, 561
	553	4.108	129 (*bis*)
4.21	64, 101	4.108-109	129
4.22	70, 102, 103 (*bis*),	4.108-111	128
	107, 480. 553, 563	4.109	129 (*ter*), 130, 569
4.23	103, 237	4.110	129
4.23-24	64	4.111	125, 129
4.24	70	4.112	115, 117, 123 (*ter*),
4.25	98, 99		124, 127 (*bis*), 558
4.25-34	107	4.113	110 n. 2 (*bis*), 116
4.26	70, 98, 546		(*bis*), 126, 131, 132
4.26-34	64	4.114	117, 120 (*bis*), 126,
4.27	567		127, 554
4.29	107	4.114-117	132
4.29-30	70	4.115	118, 120
4.30	101, 102	4.115-116	120
4.32	101, 102, 103, 107	4.116	120, 127 (*bis*)
4.33	104	4.117	126, 127, 128, 558
4.34	104	4.118	116, 117, 132
4.35	103, 107	4.119	133
4.36	101, 103 (*bis*)	4.120-121	125, 558
4.37	102, 103 (*bis*), 107	4.120-122	128
4.40-50	107	4.121	124, 133
4.42	551	4.122	127
4.46	64	4.123	124, 125 (*bis*)
4.47-48	104	4.125	110 n. 2, 118, 119
4.48	105		(*quater*), 119 n. 14,
4.49	99		544, 555
4.51	105, 108 (*bis*), 563,	4.126	126, 133
	569	4.126-130	126, 133 (*bis*)
4.51-53	105, 108	4.126-151	133
4.52	108	4.127	124
4.53	108	4.127-128	118
4.54	104, 106	4.128	118, 126, 566
4.54-56	105, 108 (*bis*), 564	4.130	134
4.54-58	64	4.131	134
4.55	105, 108, 109	4.131-155	130, 294, 544 (*bis*)
4.56	70	4.131-158	111
4.59	103	4.131-164	126
4.64	71	4.132	130
4.64-66	64	4.133	134
4.66	71, 104	4.134	519, 565
4.83	64, 71 (*bis*)	4.134-138	134
4.83-85	64	4.135	130, 131
4.84	71	4.137	117

INDEX OF PASSAGES FROM ANCIENT TEXTS

4.140	127, 130	5.185-197	137
4.145-149	131	5.186	138 n. 2, 144 n. 11, 145
4.146	131 (bis)		
4.148	131	5.188	140, 142 n. 8, 143, 149, 149 n. 17
4.149	131		
4.150-151	294	5.189	142, 149, 150
4.150-155	359	5.190	149 (bis), 150
4.152	294	5.191	142, 143, 149
4.152-155	133	5.191-194	561
4.157	115, 127	5.192	144, 144 n. 10, 150
4.158	111, 128, 569	5.193	140, 146 (bis), 149 (bis), 150
4.161	126		
4.165	296	5.194	141 (bis), 147
4.167	11 n. 28	5.195	141, 150 (bis), 151
4.186	566	5.196	150 (bis)
4.188-189	219 n. 8	5.197	138 n. 2, 141 (bis)
4.196-197	562	5.198	144
4.197	544, 563	5.198-200	239
4.198	196, 570	5.199	156
4.207	74, 389, 558	5.200	154 (bis), 528, 563
4.212	219 n. 7	5.200-210	153
4.213	219 n. 7	5.201	156
4.216	167	5.202	156
4.224	100	5.203	156 (bis)
4.237	465	5.204	159 (bis)
4.244-245	198, 544	5.205	158
4.261-262	219	5.205-209	132
4.266	465	5.207	160
4.303	132, 549	5.209	159, 160, 161
4.304	100	5.213	165 (bis), 166, 168, 171, 546, 569
4.318-329	548		
4.320	132	5.213-233	164
4.326	301	5.214	166, 167 (bis), 171, 569
4.328	65, 98, 547, 548		
4.328-329	549	5.215	165, 167, 170 (bis), 171, 174, 567
4.328-331	288 n. 11		
4.329	160 n. 10	5.216	172, 174
5.30	550	5.217	166
5.95	550	5.218	166
5.98	248	5.220	173
5.118	288 n. 11, 548	5.223	173
5.120	381	5.224	173
5.132	11 n. 28, 141	5.225	170
5.136-137	519, 565	5.226	173, 174 (bis), 567
5.150-165	254	5.227	174-175
5.151	254	5.230	165 (bis), 167, 549
5.159	180	5.231	171, 172, 556
5.162	175 n. 6	5.232	167, 170, 551
5.172-173	519, 565	5.233	178
5.179	141, 144	5.234	216
5.179-180	11 n. 28	5.253	115 n. 12
5.184	138 n. 2	5.255	145, 239
5.185	144, 239		

INDEX OF PASSAGES FROM ANCIENT TEXTS 609

5.257	144, 165, 178, 180, 546	6.117	186, 563
5.258	144, 179 (*ter*), 180, 188 n. 21	6.126	186, 189
		6.127	189, 190
5.259	178, 180	6.133	553
5.260	144, 178, 179 (*ter*), 187	6.137	285
		6.144	285
5.261	144, 178, 181	6.145	550
5.261-262	181	6.164	547
5.262	181, 188	6.177	143
5.263	181, 183, 187 (*bis*)	6.194	249, 441, 550
5.264	185, 185 n. 13, 187, 189	6.196	265, 519, 565
		6.208	249
5.265	184, 189, 190, 191	6.210	143
5.265-266	191	6.212	249, 549
5.266	184, 185 (*ter*), 187 (*bis*), 189, 190, 551, 563	6.215	519, 565
		6.254	381
		6.257	381
		6.264	212, 563
5.267-268	181 (*bis*)	6.264-268	260
5.268	181	6.266	168
5.276	165, 517, 546	6.290	549
5.277	519, 565	6.292-294	288 n. 11
5.286	544	6.294	169, 492, 549
5.286-313	131, 294, 544	6.299	464, 549
5.298	143	6.304	464, 549
5.317	191, 288 n. 11	6.327	115, 115 n. 12
5.321-322	199	6.329	261, 551
5.322	195, 199 (*bis*)	6.330	115
5.323	200	6.331	115 (*bis*)
5.324	193, 195, 200 (*bis*)	6.335	265
5.325	195 (*bis*)	6.338	115
5.326	195	6.341	247
5.328	193, 200	6.343-350	288 n. 11
5.329	193, 195, 200	6.349	250, 566
5.330	200, 201, 550	6.363	281 n. 4
5.335	200 n. 3	7.4	160 n. 10
5.336	125	7.6	132
5.337	196 (*bis*), 202, 568	7.13	205
5.347	160 n. 10	7.15	206
6.34	11 n.28	7.16	205
6.36	549	7.17	208
6.43	258	7.18	205
6.45	464, 546, 547, 548	7.29	566
6.57	216 n. 2	7.30	116, 247
6.63	368, 549	7.31	209, 548, 567
6.81	264	7.31-32	211
6.84	145, 480	7.33	211
6.90	166, 181 (*bis*)	7.34	211, 212 (*bis*)
6.92	249, 465	7.36	212 (*bis*)
6.102	258	7.37	213, 567
6.111	143	7.37-38	212
6.116	186, 527, 566	7.38	212

INDEX OF PASSAGES FROM ANCIENT TEXTS

7.41	248	7.241	206
7.42	132	7.243	225
7.43	249	7.252	220 (*bis*)
7.54	550	7.254-257	207
7.65	336	7.269	549
7.69	550	7.270	249
7.72	381	7.272-274	550
7.94	387	7.284	207 (*bis*), 213
7.109	265	7.285	213
7.110	549 (*bis*)	7.289	208
7.111	219, 550	7.296	397 n. 9
7.117	397 n. 9	7.301	143
7.118	464, 549	7.302	143
7.125	206, 208 (*bis*)	7.305	132
7.126	205	7.307	336
7.129	205	7.309	339
7.130	239, 517	7.319	208
7.130-158	201	7.319-321	328
7.137	212	7.320	208
7.142	143	7.337	35
7.158	548	7.372	34
7.159	205	7.383	287
7.160	205, 550	7.386	209
7.162	517	7.390-391	288 n. 11
7.168	216	7.391	248, 249, 464, 465 (*bis*), 544 (*bis*)
7.172	226 (*bis*), 227, 564		
7.172-257	215	8.1	265
7.173	217, 226	8.13	206
7.174	215 n. 1, 227	8.15	207
7.177	217	8.21	549
7.181	207, 218	8.25	520 n. 14
7.184	249, 464, 549	8.30	564
7.184-185	225	8.34	548
7.185	217	8.85	460 n. 10
7.186	207, 218	8.108	240
7.189	217, 221 (*bis*), 547	8.116-117	549, 557
7.191	222, 258	8.121	566
7.192	223 (*ter*), 225	8.144-149	245
7.193	207, 223 (*ter*), 227, 564	8.146-149	549
		8.149	559
7.194	221, 227	8.165	559
7.195	222 (*bis*), 226, 227, 564	8.185	547
		8.191	197 n. 2
7.196	215 n. 1, 224 (*bis*), 228	8.191-198	544
		8.205	238, 241
7.196-197	553	8.205-245	233, 416
7.197	224	8.209	234 (*bis*), 238 (*bis*), 255, 548, 555, 556
7.198	218 (*bis*), 219, 551		
7.213	219	8.211	288 n. 11
7.214	219	8.212	237, 246, 553
7.235	220	8.212-224	244
7.238	228, 564	8.213	247 (*bis*), 248, 249

INDEX OF PASSAGES FROM ANCIENT TEXTS 611

8.214	248, 249, 251, 255, 256 (*bis*)	8.286	263
		8.287	437 n. 1
8.215	237, 246, 247, 248, 548	8.289	236, 256
		8.290	264, 267 (*bis*), 270
8.216	247, 256, 257	8.290-297	263
8.217	257	8.293	265, 267 (*bis*)
8.218	251, 257	8.294	265 (*quater*)
8.219	257, 259 (*bis*)	8.295	265, 266
8.220	258 (*bis*)	8.296	266, 568
8.221	259	8.296-297	271
8.223	253 (*bis*), 254, 257 (*bis*)	8.297	266 (*bis*), 267
		8.299	236, 437 n. 1
8.224	256, 563	8.300	237 (*bis*)
8.225	234	8.304	269, 337
8.227	240	8.304-306	263
8.227-228	235, 545	8.307	287
8.228	237	8.309	437 n. 1
8.229	233	8.313	437 n. 1
8.230	235, 255	8.314	239, 266
8.231	235 (*bis*)	8.314-315	263
8.232	241, 397 n. 9	8.315	263
8.233	241 (*ter*), 456 n. 7	8.316	239, 277, 437 n. 1, 552
8.234	241		
8.235	234	8.316-317	283
8.236	233 n. 1, 234, 241	8.316-392	273
8.238	235	8.317	255, 277
8.241	235	8.318	255, 277 (*bis*), 278 (*bis*), 458, 459 (*bis*), 552
8.245	235, 236 (*bis*), 239, 254, 563		
8.246	247	8.319	298, 300 n.7, 335 n. 3, 569
8.246 ff.	256		
8:246-265	244	8.319-354	295, 335
8.248	256, 259	8.321	303
8.251	245, 254, 260, 437 n. 1. 527	8.322	273 n. 2, 296
		8.323	300 n. 7, 335 n. 3
8.251-253	239, 260	8.324	560
8.252	246	8.325	300 n. 7 (*bis*), 303, 304, 335 n. 3 (*bis*)
8.255	246, 260		
8.256	260	8.325-327	298
8.256-257	551	8.326	296, 303
8.257	261	8.327	300 n. 7 (*bis*), 301, 303 (*bis*), 335 n. 3 (*bis*)
8.258	261		
8.260-262	245		
8.261	246	8.329	300 n. 7, 335 n. 3
8.263	245, 253, 256, 261	8.329-330	278
8.264	254 (*bis*)	8.331	286, 300 n. 7, 335 n. 3
8.265	236, 545, 563		
8.265-287	233, 416	8.332	286
8.270	397 n. 9	8.334	296
8.277	236, 563	8.336-342	298
8.278	258	8.337	300 n. 7, 335 n. 3
8.284	236, 239, 339	8.339	115 n. 12

612 INDEX OF PASSAGES FROM ANCIENT TEXTS

8.340	303	8.398-420	273
8.342	298, 569	8.399	282, 283, 311, 317, 319, 552
8.343	299, 302		
8.344	299	8.401	283, 319
8.346	300 n. 7, 335 n. 3	8.402	314
8.348	296	8.403	314
8.349	299, 300	8.405	283
8.350	299, 302	8.406	283
8.351	299, 304	8.408-409	283
8.352	303, 344 (*bis*)	8.409	283, 286, 287 (*bis*), 566
8.353	304		
8.354	296, 300 n. 7, 335 n. 2, 335 n. 3, 336, 337, 556	8.412	273 n. 2, 282, 287 (*bis*), 307 n. 1, 312
		8.413	566
8.356	278, 286	8.414	312, 315 n. 7, 548 (*bis*)
8.358	286		
8.360	286, 300 n. 7, 335 n. 3, 521 n. 14	8.415	280 (*bis*)
		8.417	300 n. 7, 335 n. 3
8.360-362	295, 335	8.418	99, 274, 400
8.361	278, 284, 552	8.418-420	286
8.362	261, 274 n. 2, 278 (*bis*), 300 n. 7 (*bis*), 335 n. 3 (*bis*), 552	8.419	287, 288
		8.420	289
		9.1	307 n. 1, 317, 319, 558
8.364	279	9.2	313 (*bis*), 315, 550
8.367	279	9.3	313
8.368	279	9.4	307 n. 1, 313
8.369	279 (*bis*)	9.5	313 (*ter*)
8.370	279	9.6	308
8.371	280	9.7	312
8.372	280	9.8-9	555
8.373	280 (*bis*)	9.9	312, 315, 315 n. 7, 320
8.374	280		
8.376	281	9.11	307 n. 1, 313
8.377	281	9.12	308, 316 (*bis*), 551
8.378	279 (*bis*), 281 (*bis*)	9.14	316
8.382	281	9.16	313 (*bis*), 315 (bis), 316
8.383	282 (*bis*)		
8.385	284	9.17	310, 317
8.386	285 (*bis*), 550	9.18	242, 277, 437 n. 1
8.387	285	9.19-44	307
8.388	285	9.20	300, 300 n. 7, 335 n. 3, 557
8.391	285		
8.392	456 n. 7	9.20-28	295, 335
8.393-9.17	307	9.21	297
8.394	313 (*bis*), 315, 316, 319 (*bis*)	9.23	297, 301 (*bis*)
		9.24	297, 456 n. 7
8.395	308, 314 (*bis*)	9.26	300 (*bis*)
8.396	311, 318, 319	9.27	295 n. 5, 322, 327, 328, 335 n. 1, 437 n. 1
8.397	318		
8.398	247, 282, 282 n. 5, 316, 317 (*bis*)	9.28	299, 301, 302, 335,

INDEX OF PASSAGES FROM ANCIENT TEXTS 613

	338, 339, 341, 549, 564, 569	9.84	322, 323
		9.85-92	335
9.29-41	322	9.86	335 n. 2
9.31	318 (*bis*), 322, 323	9.87	336
9.32	323, 329 (*bis*)	9.88	335 n. 2
9.33	313, 318, 338	9.90	335 n. 2, 342
9.34	329 (*bis*)	9.94	325
9.34-37	335	9.95	437 n. 1
9.35	313 (*bis*), 315, 340, 345, 349	9.96	448 n. 16
		9.101	304
9.36	345, 349	9.102-154	450
9.37	335 n. 2, 345	9.103	335 n. 2
9.43	326, 326 n. 2, 557	9.105	325, 354
9.44	311	9.105-106	322, 325
9.46	330, 335	9.105-139	352
9.46-60	335	9.106	360
9.47-50	345, 569	9.106-107	335
9.48	335 n. 2, 345	9.108	355, 356, 360
9.49	335 n. 2	9.109	361
9.50	341	9.110	355, 361
9.51	330, 340, 340 n. 5, 346 (*ter*)	9.111	361
		9.112	359
9.51-52	322	9.112-119	322
9.55	335 n. 2, 339, 343, 346	9.113	359
		9.114	359
9.56	335 n. 2, 346	9.115	325
9.57	330, 335 n. 2, 339 (*bis*), 346, 349	9.117	325, 355
		9.118	354
9.58	330, 335 n. 2, 339, 342	9.119	300 n. 7, 335 n. 3, 356
9.59	327, 330, 331, 335 n. 2, 342	9.120	335 n. 2, 357
		9.121	354, 437 n. 1
9.60	335 n. 2, 343 (*bis*), 346	9.122	528
		9.125	352 n. 1 (*bis*)
9.60-73	322	9.126	360
9.61	323	9.127	354
9.62	324	9.128	361
9.63	324	9.129	355, 359
9.64	324, 327, 550	9.132	357 (*bis*)
9.65	326	9.133	249, 357, 359, 465, 492, 550
9.67	327 (*bis*), 335 n. 2		
9.67-74	335	9.134	357
9.68	329, 335 n. 2	9.137	358
9.69	329	9.138	356
9.70	326, 327, 331, 335 n. 2	9.139	357, 358
		9.157	439
9.72	331, 335 n. 2, 343	9.159-160	352
9.73	335 n. 2 (*bis*), 336	9.160	358
9.81	324	9.166	249, 441, 465, 492, 550
9.81-86	322		
9.82	325	9.173	437 n. 1, 440
9.83	323	9.175	335, 335 n. 2, 440

9.178	335 n. 2, 437 n. 1, 539	9.276	367, 378, 389 n. 16
9.178-183	335	9.282	220, 239 (*bis*), 253, 328, 552, 555
9.179	335 n. 2	10.3	369
9.179-180	337	10.5	295 n. 4, 367, 375, 554
9.180	343		
9.181	341	10.7	369
9.182	288 n. 11, 295, 335, 335 n. 2, 339, 341, 343, 344, 347	10.8	367
		10.10	372
		10.12	381
		10.13	373, 381, 389 n. 16
9.183	335 n. 2, 347, 349	10.16	368, 369, 372 (*bis*), 386, 389 n. 16
9.185	335 n. 2		
9.199	284, 429	10.21	374, 570
9.205	437, n. 1	10.22	374
9.206	407	10.23	375
9.206-207	401	10.24	369
9.206-214	396	10.24-25	390
9.208	394, 395 (*bis*), 407	10.25	370 (*quater*), 370 n. 6, 377 n. 3
9.209	398 (*bis*), 407, 410, 411, 412, 414, 559	10.25-26	370
9.210	411	10.27	370, 390 (*bis*)
9.211	396, 398 (*ter*), 405 n. 20, 408, 413	10.27-81	566
		10.28	370, 389 n. 16, 390 (*bis*)
9.212	410, 413		
9.213	395, 404, 560, 569-570	10.29	364 n. 2, 371, 389 n. 16, 390, 391
9.214	399 (*ter*), 401, 402, 403 (*bis*), 407, 408, 570	10.30	480
		10.31	323
		10.32	389 n. 16
9.215	437 n. 1	10.34	371
9.223	254, 260, 563	10.35	378, 389, 389 n. 16, 400 (*bis*)
9.232	437 n, 1		
9.233	437 n. 1	10.36	365 (*bis*)
9.234	437 n. 1	10.37	419 (*bis*), 437 n. 1
9.239	412 n. 29	10.37-46	416
9.239-242	400, 401, 412	10.38	419, 420
9.242	400	10.39	420
9.243	437 n. 1	10.40	422
9.257	379	10.41	420, 421, 423
9.258	437 n. 1	10.42	421, 422, 423, 552
9.260	249, 368 (*bis*), 371, 441, 465, 492, 550	10.43	421
		10.44	255, 423
		10.45	255, 421 (*bis*), 422
9.260-276	364	10.47	437 n. 1
9.261	371	10.48-78	424
9.262	372 (*bis*)	10.49	426 (*bis*)
9.263	366	10.50	426, 429, 430 (*bis*), 431, 547, 549
9.264	368		
9.265-266	368		
9.270	366, 371	10.50-51	427
9.271	369	10.51	427 (*bis*), 431 (*ter*)
9.272	369	10.53	431, 432 (*bis*)

INDEX OF PASSAGES FROM ANCIENT TEXTS 615

10.54	428	10.139	459
10.56	433	10.140	460
10.57	433	10.141	458
10.58	433 n. 8	10.142	288 n. 9, 567
10.59	434, 546	10.154	455
10.61	431	10.155	443, 464 (*quater*), 546, 549
10.63	431, 433 n. 8		
10.65	434	10.157	465
10.68	434	10.160	466, 554
10.69	433	10.161	467, 469, 470
10.72	434	10.162	469
10.73	434 (*bis*), 547	10.163	464, 469, 549
10.74	429	10.164	249, 442, 464 (*bis*), 467, 469, 549
10.76	283, 429 (*bis*), 430, 566, 568		
		10.164-166	554
10.77	428, 434	10.164-167	470
10.78	132	10.166-167	468
10.79	377	10.168	464, 468 (*bis*), 470
10.81	440 n. 1	10.169	470
10.83	440 n. 1	10.170	470, 471, 471 n. 4
10.93	258	10.187	453
10.97-102	441	10.195	115, 453
10.99	444 n. 5	10.210	118, 119, 366, 544, 555
10.99-100	459		
10.100	249, 437, 440 n. 1, 441, 444, 465, 492, 540, 554	10.214	453
		10.216	453
		10.217	38, 454 (*bis*)
10.101	444	10.218	444 n. 5, 454
10.102	459	10.219	444 n. 5
10.103	438, 440 n. 1, 455 (*bis*)	10.219-227	444 n. 5, 454
		10.220-226	444 n. 5
10.104	439 (*bis*), 455 (*bis*)	10.227	444 n. 5
10.105	456	10.229	447
10.106	458	10.229-230	441
10.111	458	10.233	74
10.112	458	10.242	74, 454
10.113	377 n. 2	10.246	38, 75, 288 n. 9, 549
10.114	458		
10.116	460	10.247	74
10.120	249, 441, 455, 456	10.254	38, 75
10.122	457	10.256	143
10.123	457	10.258	75
10.124	457 (*bis*), 552	10.262	75
10.126	377 n. 2	10.263	480
10.128	377 n. 2, 456, 457 n. 8	10.265	566
		10.268	389
10.132	461	10.269	400
10.132-134	461	10.277-281	104
10.136	460	11.5-6	379
10.137	460	11.32	480
10.137-138	460	11.68	509
10.138	459	11.87	549

11.121	476, 477, 479 (*bis*), 480 (*bis*), 549, 556	11.179	489 n. 1 (*bis*), 494, 495, 496 (*bis*), 498
11.121-158	474	11.180	495
11.122	481 (*bis*)	11.181	494, 496
11.123	251, 481, 557	11.183	249, 441, 465, 491 (*bis*), 494, 549, 552
11.127	482		
11.129	479, 481	11.185	513, 546
11.130	482	11.187	508 (*bis*)
11.131	481	11.188	508
11.132-133	482	11.189	508
11.133	481, 482	11.190	504, 509, 518
11.134	481	11.191	504 (*ter*), 505, 509, 565
11.136	486		
11.137	473 n. 1	11.192	504, 505, 509 (*bis*), 565
11.138	483, 486		
11.139	249, 483	11.192-193	563
11.140	483, 484, 544	11.193	504, 505
11.141	481, 483 (*bis*), 544	11.194	505, 506
11.142	484	11.195	504 (*ter*), 510 (*quater*), 557, 565
11.143	486		
11.144	473 n. 1	11.196	510, 518, 565
11.145	483	11.198	514, 532, 561
11.146	484	11.199	518, 565
11.147	486	11.200	514, 519 (*bis*), 532
11.149	484	11.201	532
11.150	486	11.202	505 (*bis*), 514, 520, 526 n. 22, 557, 565 (*bis*)
11.151	484		
11.152	484 (*bis*), 509		
11.153	485	11.203	508, 515, 526 n. 22
11.155	477, 479 (*bis*), 482, 552	11.204	515 (*bis*), 520, 563
		11.205	504 (*bis*), 515
11.156	482	11.207	530, 533, 562
11.157	479, 487, 562	11.208	516, 530
11.158	479, 487	11.209	525, 527
11.159	490	11.210	504 (*bis*), 516 (*bis*)
11.159-183	489	11.211	526, 530
11.161	490, 490-491	11.212	504, 529, 530, 558
11.162	495	11.213	507, 527, 529, 557
11.163	491 (*bis*), 556	11.214	527
11.164	491	11.215	508
11.165	492 (*bis*), 548	11.216	38, 507, 557
11.166	491, 492, 496	11.217	504, 529
11.167	491, 497	11.219	525, 533
11.168	492, 493 (*bis*)	11.220	527
11.169-171	492	11.221	525 n. 22
11.170	497	11.223	525 n. 22
11.172	493 (*bis*)	11.225	515
11.174	493-494, 497	11.227	531, 535
11.175	494	11.228	504
11.176	494 (*bis*), 498	11:229-233	535
11.177	493, 495	11.230	504 (*bis*), 530
11.178	494	11.231	504 (*bis*)

INDEX OF PASSAGES FROM ANCIENT TEXTS 617

11.232	518	11.299	239
11.233	533	12.32	251
11.234	518	12.46	251
11.236	505, 557	12.57	509
11.237	520, 535, 564	12.104	541
11.238	504 (bis), 505, 520	12.108	541
11.239	504 (bis)	12.109	541
11.240	536 (bis), 569	12.122	252 (bis)
11.241	506, 520	13.64	377 n. 3, 379
11.244	521, 528	13.68	377 n. 3, 379
11.245	521	13.71	377 n. 3, 379, 380
11.246	528 n. 27	13.74	250
11.247	521, 536, 564	13.76	250
11.248	504 n. 2, 507	13.114	249-250, 465
11.249	521	13.297	427, 542
11.250	507, 522, 522 n. 16	13.311	396 n. 9
11.250-251	522	13.312	115 n. 11, 115 n. 12
11.251	522		
11.252	507, 522 (bis), 564	13.313	115 n. 11
11.253	522, 524	13.316	216 n. 3
11.254	523 (ter), 524	13.330	224 n. 15
11.255	523 (bis)	14.68	10 n. 26, 140 n. 7
11.256	524	14.174-175	111
11.257	524	14.195	251
11.258	523	14.208	251
11.259	524, 536	14.267	466
11.261	525, 534	14.313	251
11.265	506, 511, 520	15.312	460
11.266	511	15.343	466
11.268	525, 536	16.93	216 n. 3
11.269	528	16.177	248
11.270	525	16.396-404	288
11.271	506	17.4	111
11.273-274	528	17.43	111
11.273-283	509, 526 n. 22	17.121	115 n. 12
11.274	528	17.204	259
11.275	508, 528	17.209	259
11.276	508	17.215-218	259
11.277	186, 506, 507, 525 n. 21, 526, 528, 563	17.248	247
		17.345	115, 115 n. 12
		17.346	396 n. 9
11.278	506, 529	18.11	428
11.280	508	18.15	99 n. 4
11.281	504	18.63	347 n. 8, 383
11.283	531	18.63-64	388
11.284	523 n. 18	18.64	389
11.288	520, 534	18.81-84	198
11.289	509	18.116-119	37 n. 17
11.292	534	18.162	466
11.294	536, 550	18.167	143
11.295	510 n. 4, 533, 534	18.217	115
11.296	506	18.223	115

18.332	447 n. 14	204	210, 567
18.340-352	199	230	567
19.208	99	325	248
19.290	249, 465	339	467
19.330	250, 251	356	210 n. 2
19.334	249	423	210, 250, 442, 466, 540
19.340-342	121		
19.347	288	425	211, 540
20.17-96	198, 409, 559	*War*	
20.24	248	1:1-2	540
20.24-25	29-30	1.2	291, 389
20.25	28 n. 12	1.3	344, 374, 396, 569
20.90	250	1.10	171, 253
20.109	238	1.18	300
20.144	109	1.79	115 n. 11
20.168	196	1.80	115 n. 12
20.178	249	1.111-112	564
20.198-200	37 n. 17	1.126	143
20.200	383	1.224	447 n. 14
20.201	249	1.233	288 n. 9
20.216-218	100	1.260	447 n. 14
20.218	100, 545	1.275	288 n. 9
20.262	543	1.532	447 n. 14
20.263	543	2.4	259
20.268	570	2.8	259
Life		2.11-13	259
1	62, 100, 308, 366, 476, 498, 545	2.37	247
		2.112	115
1-2	91, 457 n. 8	2.113	396 n. 9
1-6	418, 546	2.119	396 n. 9
2	169, 235, 357, 377, 442, 448. 498, 545	2.135	447 n. 14
		2.139	447 n. 14
9	546	2.142	447 n. 14
10	111	2.143	447 n. 143
12	111, 566	2.159	111
18	254	2.308	396 n. 9
36	212, 238, 555	2.358-387	381
40	224	2.399	251, 466
70	209	2.464	213 n. 5
74-76	213	2.585	210, 467, 554
76	210	2.586	210
80	209, 567	2.587	238, 252, 466, 555, 556
84-85	567		
85	209, 468, 554	2.591-592	213
86	210, 468	2.614	209
87	238	2.620	210, 567
102	210, 466, 554	2.627	210
113	198	2.653	347
122	209, 567	3.347	250
132-144	259	3.351-353	397
176	249	3.353	132 n. 27
183	248	3.358	460, 548

INDEX OF PASSAGES FROM ANCIENT TEXTS

3.399-408	378	5.387-388	365, 374
3.400-402	111, 274, 291, 545	5.388	374, 570
3.408	466	5.391	376
3.420	412	5.393	239 n. 5
3.475	246, 553	5.404-408	365, 375
4.33	132 n. 27	5.441	466, 554
4.96	251, 466	5.442	239 n. 5
4.107	246	5.514	288 n. 9
4.134	239 n. 5	5.558	213
4.144	239 n.5	5.572	288 n. 9
4.155	239 n. 5	6.49	288 n. 9
4.208	467, 554	6.103-104	443, 554
4.212	99	6.115	248
4.213	466	6.122	239 n. 5
4.225	99	6.124	216 n. 3
4.292	548	6.314	119 n. 14, 288 n. 9
4.339	239 n. 5	6.324	252, 466
4.351	239 n.5	6.333	251, 466
4.357	210	6.335	485
4.389	466, 554	6.340	251, 466
4.393	210	6.341	251, 466
4.459-464	348	6.347	216 n. 3
4.460	345, 348	6.395	254
4.461	342	6.420	156
4.462	341	7.43	396 n. 9
4:462-464	344, 569	7.107	466
4.463	341	7.191	553
4.464	344	7.196	143
4.504	347	7.256	213
4.524	347	7.258	467
4.555	347	7.259	467
4.566	210	7.262	239, 328, 555
4.625	115 n. 11, 115 n. 12	7.266	467
		7.267	216 n. 3
5.335	251, 466	7.268-274	359
5.343	239 n. 5	7.332	238
5.362-419	374 (*bis*)	7.423	247
5.367	119 n. 16	7.432	377 n. 3, 379, 380

OTHER (ALLEGED) GRAECO-JEWISH WRITERS

Artapanus
ap. Eusebius, *Praeparatio Evangelica*
9.27.7   86 n. 10
9.27.11-13   86 n. 10
9.27.19   40
9.27.20   80

Cleodemus-Malchus
ap. Josephus, *Ant.* 1.240   115 n. 12
ap. Josephus, *Ant.* 1.240-241   39

Demetrius
ap. Eusebius, *Praeparatio Evangelica*
9.29.1   39-40
9.29.2   477

Ezekiel
The Exodus
ap. Eusebius, *Praeparatio Evangelica*
9.28.4b   40
ap. Eusebius, *Praeparatio Evangelica*
9.29.4   40-41

Rabbinic and Allied Literature

Mishnah

'Avot
1:12	57, 61
3:2	139 n. 3
5:6	33
5:18	232
5:19	113 n. 6, 124
6:8	94, 310 (*bis*)

Baba Meẓia
4:10	422

Berakot
1:5	384

'Eduyyot
8:7	294

Megillah
4:10	61 (*bis*)

Middot
2:6	445

Qiddushin
4:14	409

Sanhedrin
10:1	97, 218, 275 (*bis*), 416
10:2	113 n. 6, 230 (*bis*), 232, 275, 416, 418
10:3	97, 97 n. 3
11:2	418
11:5	405

Soṭah
1:8	228 n. 17
9:15	385
9:15 end	291

Tosefta

Berakot
7.23	475

'Eduyyot
3.4	294

Sanhedrin
4.7	478 n. 10
13.89	97 n. 3

Sheqalim
2:18	446 n. 8

Soṭah
3.14	158 n. 9
12.1-2	264
12.6	337 n. 4
12.13	264

Ta'anit
4.7	232

Jerusalem Talmud

'Avodah Zarah
1.1.39b	232, 233

Berakot
4.11c	475 n. 5
9.13b	309, 314 n. 5
9.14a	475 n. 5

Makkot
2.31a	204 n. 3
2.31d	203

Megillah
1.14.72c	163
1.21b	478 n. 10
3.2.74a	411
4.1.75a	478, 479

Nedarim
7.40a	445 n. 7

Qiddushin
1.16a	204 n. 3

Sanhedrin
1.19a	445 n. 7
10.1.27d-28a	96
10.1.28a	96
10.1.28b	276
10.1.28c	417
10.1.29c	97 n. 3
10.1.50a	94 n. 2
10.2	370 n. 6
10.2.28c	418

Soṭah
1	204 n. 2

Ta'anit
4.2.68a	276
4.68d	385
69d	119

Terumah
8.10.46b	293

Babylonian Talmud

'Arakin
17a	451

'Avodah Zarah
2b	119 n. 15
18b	292
44a	268 n. 3

INDEX OF PASSAGES FROM ANCIENT TEXTS

Baba Batra		13a	525 n. 22
14b	112 n. 6	13b	513 n. 1, 532
15a	377, 476, 478	13b-14a	502
21b	478	14a	157 (*bis*)
74a	97	14b	155, 156, 424
121b	293	15a	159, 476
Baba Mezia		15b	503
59b	388	16a	502, 524 n. 20
83b-84a	292	16b	502
85b	294	18a	534 n. 34
87a	347	25a	61
Baba Qamma		25a-b	177
10a	364 n. 1	31a	394
16b	363 (*bis*)	31b	478
82a-b	479	*Menaḥot*	
82b	427 n. 3	64b	427 n. 3
92b	178	65a	514 n. 2, 516 n. 5
Berakot		109b	377 n. 3, 380
7b	338	110a	380 n. 8
10a	314 n. 5, 370, 370 n. 6, 377 n. 3, 417	*Moʿed Qatan*	
		16a	158
10b	343	28b	232, 276, 425, 451
31a	338	*Nazir*	
57b	453	4b-5a	221 n. 11
ʿEruvin		23b	139, 159
13b	22 n. 7	*Nedarim*	
Giṭṭin		38a	94, 310
56a-b	293, 443, 469	65a	451, 451 n. 2, 453
57b	406	*Niddah*	
88a	445 n. 7, 446, 456 n. 6	13b	46
		24b	225
Horayot		55b	159
10a-b	245 n. 6	*Pesaḥim*	
Ḥullin		56a	364 n. 1, 369, 371
4b-5a	309	66b	331, 339, 340
6b	309	118b	157
7b	341	119a	94, 264, 310
60b	330	*Qiddushin*	
Ketubot		32b	427
103b	310	70b	46
Makkot		*Rosh Hashanah*	
24a	310	18b	463
Megillah		25a-b	163
3b	276	25b	164 (*bis*), 165, 180
7a	534 n. 35	*Sanhedrin*	
9a	541, 542	6b	309
10b	81	7a	61
11a	500 (*bis*), 501 (*ter*)	10a	95
11b	501	21a	216 n. 4
12a	502 (*bis*)	21b	478 (*bis*)
12a-b	501	26a-b	382
12b	503 (*bis*), 506	37b-38a	446 n. 10

38a	445 n. 7, 446, 490	*Shevuot*	
38b	387 n. 13	6b	119 n. 15
39b	81, 340	*Soṭah*	
43a	385	9b	221 n. 12
48b	245 n. 6, 264	10a	263 (*bis*), 264
48b-49a	204 n. 3	10b	220 n. 9
49a	203 (*ter*), 204 (*ter*)	11a	79 (*bis*), 80, 225 n. 16
56a-60a	19		
57b	32 (*bis*)	11b	80
60a	139 (*bis*)	34a	244
61b	527 n. 23, 532 n. 29	36b	79
		37a	67
91b	32	42b	195
92b	453	46b-47a	340
93b	385, 490	47a	339
94a	45, 363 (*bis*), 364	49a	338
94b	363, 377	49b	427 n. 3
95b	454	*Sukkah*	
96b	406	5a	302 n. 9
98a	292	20a	478
99a	363, 364, 387, 388 (*bis*)	52a	418
		52b	452
99b	417	*Ta'anit*	
101b	231 (*bis*), 232 (*bis*)	4a	185
102a	231, 352	10b	338
102b	230 (*bis*), 233, 242, 275 (*quinquiens*), 276 (*bis*), 417, 418	22b	425 (*bis*)
		23a	292
		Yevamot	
103a	418 (*bis*), 451, 452	7b	308 n. 2, 309
103b	218, 230 (*bis*), 231, 378 n. 5, 417 (*ter*), 418, 425, 490 n. 3	47b	46
		49b	378 n. 5 (*bis*), 417, 420
104a	425	103a	146 n. 14, 159
105a	112 n. 6, 122	*Yoma*	
105b	112 n. 6, 113 n. 6	52a-b	8 n. 18, 562
106a	44, 113 n. 6, 131, 133 n. 28	52b	424
		53b	446 n. 8
106b	112 n. 6 (*bis*), 113 n. 6	69b	475
		86b	421
108a	21, 27 (*bis*)	*Zevaḥim*	
108a-b	24 (*bis*), 570	116a	14, 24, 48
108b	25 n. 11		
109b	97	**Minor Tractates**	
110a	94, 97 (*bis*), 105 n. 9	*'Avot de-Rabbi Nathan*	
		A 4.22-24	293
110a-b	97	A 9.4	310, 317 n. 8
Shabbat		A 12	61
33b	292	A 17.37	447
56a	440	A 23	123 n. 21
56b	263, 425	A 29	124
113b	201	B 6.19	293
149b	452, 453 (*bis*)		

B 17.38	447 n. 12	on Exodus	
B 49	124	6:18	293 n. 3

TARGUMIM

on 1 Chronicles
  2:54   204
on 2 Chronicles
  3:24   446 n. 11
on Genesis
  2:7   2 n. 6
on Isaiah
  66:1   417
on Jonah
  1:16   406 n. 22
on Jonah
  3:5   405
on 2 Kings
  19:35   406
on 2 Kings
  19:37   406
on 2 Kings
  21:16   417
on Malachi
  1:1   476 n. 7
on Ruth
  1:1   194

Jonathan
on Judges
  3:24   146 n. 14
on 2 Kings
  9:20   354

Onkelos on Genesis
  8:4   30
  on Numbers
  23:2   116 n. 13

1 Yerushalmi (Pseudo-Jonathan)
  1.1   81 n. 6
on Deuteronomy
  30:4   293 n. 3
on Esther
  1:2   501
on Esther
  1:10   501 n. 1
on Esther
  2:5   513 n. 1
on Esther
  3:2   527 n. 23, 532 n. 29
on Exodus
  3:23   80

on Exodus
  6:18   293 n. 3
on Genesis
  26:1   78
on Judges
  11:39   186 n. 15
on Numbers
  16:22-34   96
on Numbers
  16:34   97 n. 3
on Numbers
  23:2   116 n. 13
on Numbers
  25:12   293 n. 3

Targum Sheni (2) (on Esther)
  1:2   500
  1:4   500
  8:12   526 n. 22

2 Targum Yerushalmi (Fragmentary Targum)
  1.1   81
  3.14-15   523 n. 17

MIDRASHIM AND OTHER RABBINIC WORKS

Abba Gorion
  1   503
  2-8   501
  9   500
  13   500
  17-18   503
  22   527 n. 23, 531 n. 29
  27   155 n. 7, 157 n. 9
  27-28   155 n. 6

Aggadat Bereshit
  14.32   377 n. 4
  44.89   446 n. 11
  65.131   122 n. 19

Aggadat Esther
  56 (ed. Buber, p. 25)   94 n. 2

Aggadat Shir Ha-Shirim
  95   231

Aggudat Aggadot
  77   155 n. 7, 157 n. 9
  77-78   155 n. 6

Alphabet of Ben Sira
  (Blau Festschrift, p. 269)   158 n. 9
  14a   317 n. 8

Baraita of 32 Middot
  no. 1   341 (*bis*)
Beit Hamidrash (ed. Jellinek)
  2.88   478 n. 11
  5.52-53   204
  6.108   96
Deuteronomy Rabbah
  2.4   377
Divre Hayamim
  1   80
Ecclesiastes Rabbah
  1.4   475
  4.7   186 n. 15
  5.12   94 n. 2
Eliyahu Rabbah (see *Tanna debei Eliyahu Rabbah*)
Esther Rabbah
  Introduction   445 n. 7
  Introduction 9 503
  1.8   500
  1.22   503
  2.5   527 n. 23, 532 n. 29
  2.7   518 n. 10
  3.1   525 n. 22, 527 n. 25
  3.1-2   527 n. 23, 532 n. 29
  6.2   514 n. 2
  7.4   94 n. 2, 525 n. 22
  7.13   292
  10.9   292
Exodus Rabbah
  1.8   79 (*bis*), 477 n. 8
  1.15   80
  1.18   80
  1.28   80
  1.32   44 (*bis*)
  1.34   80 (*bis*)
  4.2   346
  5.14   81 (*bis*)
  5.21   80
  7.3   81
  8.2   80
  10.48   159
  15.5   81
  21.5   81
  27.2   44
  27.6   44, 45
  31.3   94 n. 2
  31.9   331 n. 6
  37.2   61, 70 n. 10
  41.7   61
  45.1   406 n. 22
Genesis Rabbah
  9.7   32
  19.7   477
  21.5   293
  22.5   8 n. 19
  22.12   9 n. 23
  23.1   13 n. 30
  23.3   13 n. 32
  25.1   293
  26.5   22
  27.4   21 (*bis*)
  30.7   25
  30.9   27 (*bis*)
  31.3-5   22
  31.6   22
  32.6   27
  32.8   25 n. 11
  34.9   30
  36.7   35 (*bis*)
  39.13   518 n. 10
  41.2   78
  45.1   78
  47   542
  60.3   182 n. 6
  64.10   293-294, 384 n. 11
  71.9   292
  89.4   79
  91.7   79
  94.9   293
  97   309
  98.8   276
  99.3   139
Book of Jashar
  5.6-8   25
  5.11   25
Lamentations Rabbah
  Introduction, no. 30   264
  Introduction, no. 31   404 n. 18
  1.5.31   293
  1.53   425
  2.10.4   453
Leviticus Rabbah
  5.3   94 n. 2
  5.5   382 (*bis*)
  7 (end)   157, 157 n. 9
  10.2   377 n. 4
  10.56   446 n. 10
  11.7   445 n. 7
  17.3   382

INDEX OF PASSAGES FROM ANCIENT TEXTS 625

18.2	447 n. 12	*Midrash Psalms*	
19.6	445, 446, 454, 456 n. 6	1.15	96
		4.3	309, 314
20.4	56	5.55	231
23.10	159	11.98-99	382
28.6	173 n. 5	15.6	331
30.3	309	15.118	310, 318 n. 9
34.8	292	26.220	397
37.4	182 n. 6	36.251	475 n. 5
Likkutim		60.1	204
1.23b	96	79.1	264
Masseket Kelim		105.2	475
88	478	*Midrash Samuel*	
Mekilta, Baḥodesh		5.61-62	97 n. 3
4.65b	302 n. 9	20.106-108	195
Mekilta, Beshallaḥ		25.123-124	204 n. 3
1	44	25.124	204 n. 3
1.26b-27a	81	*Midrash Song of Songs*	
5	67	7b	81
6	82	8a	81
Mekilta, Bo		*Midrash Tannaim*	
1b-2a	407	43	478
2a	407 n. 23	*Mishnat Rabbi Eliezer*, ed. Enelow	
13	82	p. 304	44, 45
Mekilta, Yitro		*Neveh Shalom*	
1	44 (*bis*), 45 (*bis*)	47	155 n. 6, 155 n. 7, 157-158 n. 9
1.58b	340		
2	45	*Numbers Rabbah*	
Mekilta de-Rabbi Shimon ben Yoḥai		9.24	225
18b (*Beshalaḥ* 14.13)	353	11.3	445 n. 7
43-44	81	16.1	95
162	329 n. 3	18.2	95 (*bis*)
Midrash Aggadah		18.4	95
on Numbers 22:13		18.8	95
(ed. Buber 2.134)	122	18.13	94 n. 2, 97 n. 3
Midrash Al-Jithallal (ed. Jellinek)		18.19	97
6.107	94 n. 2	18.21	394
Midrash Hagadol		20.4	122
1.626	79	20.9	124 n. 22
2.7	79	20.11	124 n. 22
2.12	80	20.12	122 n. 19, 131
2.20	80	20.14-15	125 n. 23
2.43	81	20.19	122 n. 19
129-130	353	21.3	293, 293 n. 3
Midrash Jonah		22.7	94 n. 2
96	401, 402, 405 (*bis*)	23.13	203, 204 n. 3
97	409, 410	*2 Panim AhDerim*	
99-100	414	1	94 n. 2
100-102	406 n. 22	46	527 n. 23, 527 n. 25, 531 n. 29
Midrash Proverbs			
11.27	94 n. 2	58	500
26.101	81	62	516 n. 5

65	502	18.97-98	397 n. 10
74	158	26	112 n. 6
75	522 n. 16	31.117	81

Pesiqta de-Rav Kahana

Seder Eliyahu Zuta

2.343-344	477	3.177	310
4.14	417	184	353
12.11	45		

Seder Olam

16.124a	197 n. 1	16	264
16.125a	377 n. 4	17	264 (*bis*), 317
25.163b	446 n. 10	19	357 n. 3

Pesiqta Rabbati

		25	445 n. 7, 446 n. 8
4.13	292 n. 2	28	452, 501
4.14a	377		

Shibbole Ha-Leqet

11.43b	203	55-56	80
12	525 n. 22		

Shu'aib

26.3	451	Numbers 16:2	95
26.6	451		

Sifra

26.129	454	45d	71
		46a	57

Pirqe de-Rabbi Eliezer

Sifre Deuteronomy

10	398, 401, 402, 405 (bis), 410	48	478
		321	445 n. 7
10.72-73	409	338-339	57
11	34	357.2	112 n. 6 (*bis*)

Sifre Numbers

22	12 n. 29	67	477 n. 8
23	25	78	45
24	34	80	45
26	78	117	97
33	343	157	122
37 (38)	474 n. 3	end	25

Song of Songs Rabbah

43	82, 406 n. 22	1.6, no. 1	294
44	293 n. 3	2.13, no. 4	292
47	293	3.4	454
49	500	4.8	369 n. 5
50	94 n. 2, 527 n. 23, 527 n. 25, 531 n. 29	4.19	478
		5.1	477
		5.5	475 n. 4, 477

Pirqe Rabbenu ha-Qadosh, ed. Gruenhut

		8.6	446 n. 10
3.72	220 n. 10		

Tanḥuma Balak

Ruth Rabbah

1.14	195	5	122 n. 19
2.4	194	6	122
2.9	139, 194	8	122 n. 19, 131
5.6	292	11	9 n. 21, 123 n. 21
7.14	195	12	122 n. 19

Ruth Zuta

Tanḥuma Exodus

49	195	27	56
		29	275

Seder Eliyahu Rabbah

Tanḥuma Korah

3.14	309	1	95
5.22-23.90-91	338	3	95
7.44	80		
15.74	81		
16.88	440		

Tanḥuma Maseʻei		2.16	276
12	203, 204 n. 3	2.91-92	366 n. 4, 555
Tanḥuma Matot		3.38	447 n. 12
5	94 n. 2	4.85	95
Tanḥuma Mishpatim		4.86-88	95
8	94 n. 2	4.89	95
9	331 n. 6	4.93	97
Tanḥuma Noah		4.94	97 n. 3
1	31 n. 15	4.97	96
3	445 n. 7	4.134	113 n. 6, 122
5	25	4.136	122 n. 19
Tanḥuma Pequdei		4.136-137	122
1	95	4.137	122 n. 19, 131
Tanḥuma Pinehas		4.139	125 n. 23
1	293 n. 3	4.140	123 n. 21
Tanḥuma Tazria		4.142	122 n. 19
8	447 n. 12	4.160	94 n. 2
Tanḥuma Terumah		4.166	203
7	366 n. 4, 555	4.167	204 n. 3
Tanḥuma Toledot		*Tanna debei Eliyahu Rabbah*	
14	446 n. 11	8.39	337 n. 4
Tanḥuma Vaera		9.49	276
5	81 (*bis*)	13.63	61
Tanḥuma Vayaqhel		29.142	122 n. 19
4	80	31.157	61
Tanḥuma Vayeshev		*Ve-Hizhir*	
2 end	474 n. 3	on *Beshallaḥ*, ed. Freimann	
Tanḥuma Vayiqra		p.21b	105 n. 9
8	401, 405 (*bis*), 410	*Yalquṭ*	
8 (end)	409	Judges 64	170 n. 2
9	402	on 1 Kings 18:25	303 n. 11
Tanḥuma B		665	139
Exodus		2.62	172 n. 4
26	82	2.1067	522 n. 16
29	276	*Yashar Lek*	
33	451	32a	78
71	44	*Yashar Shemot*	
73	45	112b	79
75	45	125a-b	79
vol. 2, p.4	79	127b	80
vol. 2, p. 19	81	128b-130b	80
vol.2, p.122	80	133a	80
Genesis		*Yelammedenu*	
33	78	ap. ʻAruk, s.v. *Bevoah*	172 n. 4
Tanḥuma B (ed. Buber)		ap. *Yalquṭ* 2.219	276
1.140	446 n. 11	*Zohar Hadash*	
1.183	172 n. 4	Noah 29a	30 n. 14
1.208	195		

MEDIEVAL BIBLICAL COMMENTARIES AND OTHER MEDIEVAL JEWISH WORKS

Abraham Ibn Ezra
  on Deuteronomy 1:1   561
  on Jonah 2:2   403 n. 16
David Kimhi
  on Judges 11:39   184
Nachmanides
  on Genesis 4:2 9

Rashi
  on Genesis 4:22   13 n. 32
  on 2 Kings 3:20   345 n. 6
  on 2 Kings 25:44   51
Yannai
  Uvechen Vayehi Baḥazi Halailah   158

NEW TESTAMENT

Acts
2:36	383
4:26	383
9:22	384
10:2	410
10:22	410
10:35	410
13:16	410
13:26	410
13:43	410
13:50	410
16:14	410
17:4	410
17:17	410
17:22-31	25 n. 10
18:5	384
18:7	410
18:28	384

Hebrews
11:32-34	164, 182
11:37	378 n. 5, 420 n. 4

John
1:41	383
7:41-42	388

Jude
1:11	113 n. 7, 124

Luke
2:11	383
2:26	383
2:42-51	426
3:23-38	194, 388
4:16-17	394 n. 4
9:30-31	292 n. 2

16:8	26
20:41-44	388
22:66-71	384

Mark
6:15	298
7:3	427
7:4	427
9:4-5	292 n. 2
9:11-13	292
12:35	383
13:35-51	388
14:61-64	384
15:32	383

Matthew
1:1-7	194, 388
1:20	388
6:6	361
11:10-15	292
15:2	427
17:3-4	292 n. 2
17:10-13	292
22:41-45	388
22:42	385
26:60-64	384

1 Peter
3:20	25 n. 10

2 Peter
2:5	25 n. 10
2:15	113 n. 7, 124

Revelation
2:14	113 n. 7

Romans
1:3	194, 388

CHRISTIAN CHURCH FATHERS

Africanus
  Letter to Origen
    2   446 n. 9

Augustine
  Epistulae
    102.30   403

INDEX OF PASSAGES FROM ANCIENT TEXTS 629

Locutionum in Heptateuchum
82   51 n. 13

Cyril of Alexandria
PG 71.601   406

Eusebius
Praeparatio Evangelica
9.29.1   39

Helinand
Chronicon   32 n. 16

Hippolytus
Commentary on Daniel
1   446 n. 9

Jerome
Adversus Helvidium
7   478 n. 10
Adversus Jovinianum
1.23
(*PL* 23.253) 187 n. 17
on Hosea
7:4-7   233

on Jonah
introduction 397 n. 10

1.3   405 n. 19
1.6   407 n. 23
4.1   405 n. 19
Quaestiones Hebraeae in Libros Regum
on 1 Samuel 2 293 n. 3

Justin Martyr
Dialogue with Trypho
107   405 n. 19

Lactantius
De Origine Erroris (*PL* 6.326-327)
     20 n. 5

Origen
PG 12.683D 112 n. 4
Commentary on John
28.12 (*PG* 14.707) 115 n. 12

Tertullian
De Cultu Feminarum
3   478 n. 10

Theophilus
Ad Autolycum
2.19   20
3.29   20

KORAN

Sura
9:30   476

PASSAGES FROM CLASSICAL GREEK AUTHORS

Achilles Tatius
1.4.2-5   520 n. 12
5.11   520 n. 15
6.11-12   520 n. 15

Aeschylus
Agamemnon
176-178 154
Prometheus Bound
232-233 16
312   86
447-506 10 n.25

Aesop   3

Agatharchides
ap. Josephus, *Ag. Ap.* 1.205-211
     390 n. 18

Alexander Polyhistor
On the Jews 526 n. 22

Apion
ap. Josephus, *Ag. Ap.* 2.135
     547

Apollodorus
1.7.2   27, 28, 560
2.4.1   287
3.12.5   287

Apollonius Molon
ap. Josephus, *Ag. Ap.* 2.145
     557

Apollonius of Rhodes
1.622   28

Aratus
  Phaenomena
    108-109   5
    125   5
Aristophanes
  Lysistrata   134 n. 29
  Plutus
    913   121 n. 18
Aristotle
  De Generatione Animalium
    775A   564-565
  Nicomachean Ethics
    1.8.1099A31-1099B8   14
    1.9.1100A4-9   14
    1.10.1100A10-11   14
  Politics
    5.7.1307A   507
Berossus
  ap. Syncellus 53-56   28 n. 13, 29
Celsus
  ap. Origen, *Contra Celsum*
    1.19   20
    4.11   20
    4.42   20
    7.53   394 n. 3, 403
Chariton
  1.1.6-7   520 n. 12
  3.6.4   520 n. 13
  4.9.1   520 n. 13
Clearchus
  ap. Stobaeus, *Eclogae* 1, p. 171   15
Ctesias
  ap. Diodorus 2.3   412
Dicaearchus of Messene
  frag. 49 (*ap.* Porphyry, *De Abstinentia* 4.2)   3, 5
Dio Cassius
  57.18.5a   198
Diodorus Siculus
  3.2   63 n. 7
  5.62   28
Dionysius of Halicarnassus
  Roman Antiquities   566
  1.64.4   302
  1.65   528 n. 26
  1.87.4   13 n. 31
  2.21   101 n. 6
  2.56.2   302
  2.62.5   314 n. 6
  6.78.4   566
Thucydides
  5   540
  8   540
Ecphantus
  Treatise on Kingship
    277.9-11   246
    278.10-11   246
Euripides
  Bacchae
    298 ff.   132 n. 27
    300   132 n. 27
    885   154 n. 4
    1124   132 n. 27
  Cyclops
    429   529 n. 28
  Hecuba
    1182   183 n. 9
  Helen
    1301   286 n. 7
  Hippolytus
    1146   286 n. 7
    1256   286 n. 7
  Rhesus
    864   183 n. 9
Eustathius
  ad Iliad p. 771,
    55 ff.   13
Hecataeus of Abdera
  ap. Diodorus
    40.3.4   62, 101
  ap. Diodorus
    40.3.5   529-530
Heliodorus
  1.18   521 n. 15
  1.28-31   521 n. 15
  3.5.4-5   520 n. 12
  6.15   521 n. 15
  8.17   521 n. 15
  9.2   521 n. 15
Heraclitus
  ap. Diogenes Laertius 9.8
    (=frag. 66D, 26B)   15

INDEX OF PASSAGES FROM ANCIENT TEXTS

Herodotus
1.24	403
1.30	297
1.68-70	519 n. 11
1.94	34
1.95	240
2.23	1
2.59	29
2.102 ff.	245-246
2.144	29
3.15	121 n. 18
3.69	519
5.18	509
7.14-18	286-287 n. 7
7.17	287 n. 7
7.136	516
8.98	491
9.24	414 n. 33
9.110	509

Hesiod
Theogony
902	507

Works and Days
90-93	4
112-120	4
118-120	4
120	3
150-154	13
176-178	4
189	10
191	10
192	10

Homer

Homeric Hymns
Aphrodite	200
Apollo	
13.126	33

Iliad
1.14	33
1.84-91	83
1.423	63
5.688	127
6	550
6.212-236	285
9.225-605	179
9.529-605	179
17.547-550	33
19.404-417	3
19.408-417	128, 569
21.483	33
24	285

Odyssey
6-8	550
6.203	3
7.201-206	3
9.109	4
11.436-439	8, 564
17.384	114

Iambulus
  ap. Diodorus Siculus 2.57.1 5
  ap. Diodorus Siculus 2.57.4 5

Julian
  Contra Galilaeos
  346E-347C   8

Pseudo-Longinus
  On the Sublime
  9.9   408, 540

Lucian
  De Syria Dea
  12   23, 27-28, 28, 560

Lysimachus
  ap. Josephus, *Ag. Ap.* 1.305   496, 547
  ap. Josephus, *Ag. Ap.* 2.145   557

Marcus Aurelius
  Meditations
  6.4   15

Nonnos
  Dionysiaca
  3.204 ff.   20

Numenius of Apamea
  ap. Origen, *Against Celsus* 4.51   111

Panaetius
  ap. Cicero, *De Officiis* 2.15-16   5 n. 13

Parthenius
  1.1   520 n. 12
  8   510

Philemon
  frag. inc.   4

INDEX OF PASSAGES FROM ANCIENT TEXTS

Philostratus
  Life of Apollonius of Tyana
    6.39   348

Plato
  Apology
    37C-E   434
  Ion
    534B   132 n. 27, 349
  Laws
    2.672B   132
    3.677B1-3   34
    3.678E9-679A2   14
    3.679B3-C2   5
  Phaedrus
    245A   132
  Protagoras
    330B   550
    349B   550
  Republic   549
    1.331C   549
    1.332A   46
    2.377   543
    4.425A   507
    4.433A   121 n. 18
    6.488   42, 439
    6.488-489   102
    6.492   234
    7.519C-520E   371
    7.535A   547
    8.557-561   553
    9.571D-572A   170
  Statesman
    272A   5
    272C   2
  Symposium
    202E-203A   129
  Timaeus
    22B   372 n. 7
    22C   24
    22C-D   15
    90E   564

Plutarch
  De Sollertia Animalium
    13.968F   28, 560
  De Superstitione
    8.169C   390 n. 18
  Demetrius
    42.5-9   549
  Quaestiones Conviviales
    4.6.2   29
  Romulus
    10   13 n. 31

Pseudo-Plutarch
  De Fluviis
    9.1   183

Polemo
  ap. Diogenes
    Laertius 7.87   7

Polybius
  7.7.6   542

Porphyry
  Adversus Christianos   403

Posidonius
  ap. Seneca, *Epistulae*
    90.5-6   5

Simonides
  37.1   28

Solon
  frag. 1   186

Sophocles
  Oedipus at Colonus   564
    20   10 n. 24
    1655-1656   301
    1660   301
  Oedipus the King   564
  Trachiniae
    1093   529 n. 28
  Fragments
    401   33

Strabo
  14.2.7.653-654   13
  16.2.28.759   412
  16.2.36.761   432

Thucydides
  1.22   212, 378, 565
  1.22.2   297 n. 6
  1.22.4   420
  2.47   236 n. 2
  2.52-53   413
  2.52.3   413
  2.60.6   98
  2.65   102, 107, 178
  2.65.2-3   102
  2.65.4   480, 553
  2.65.7   371
  2.77   108-109
  3.36   553

INDEX OF PASSAGES FROM ANCIENT TEXTS   633

3.36.6	99	Tyrtaeus	
3.80-83	14	frag. 6-7, line 6	127
3.82.8	213	Xenophanes	
3.82-84	82, 34, 102	*Anabasis*	
4.21.3	99	5.1.15	121 n. 18
6.19	553		
6.35.2	99	Xenophon of Ephesus	
		1.3.12	520 n. 12

PASSAGES FROM CLASSICAL LATIN AUTHORS

Aetna (anonymous)		*Satires*	
16	3	1.1.69-70	244
		1.4.139-143	559
Apuleius		1.5.97-103	568
Metamorphoses	88	2.3	25 n. 10
Augustus		Hyginus	
Monumentum Ancyranum	325	*Fabulae*	
Caesar, Julius		63	287
Bellum Gallicum	11	91	287
Catullus		Juvenal	
45	140 n. 6	3.10-16	547
		3.296	547
Cicero		6.542-547	547
Ad Familiares		14.96	410
5.12	542	14.96-106	559
De Divinatione		14.103-104	550
1.1.1	114		
2.32.69	299	Lactantius Placidus	
De Natura Deorum		on Statius, *Thebaid* 5.427	63 n. 7
2.63	6	Livy	
2.64-69	9	1.7.2	13 n. 31
De Officiis		1.9	10 n. 26
1.11.34-36	181, 282, 552	1.16	13 n. 31, 302
De Re Publica		1.20.1	101 n. 6
3.23.34-35	181, 282, 552	1.26.9	217 n. 5
		1.27-28	142
Pro Flacco		2.12	140
28.66-69	485	2.12.7	311
Ennius	358	8.9	190
First and Second Mythographers		Lucretius	
	183 n. 8	*De Rerum Natura*	
Horace		2.1158	6
Odes		5.933-938	6
		5.982-987	9
1.3.27-33	4 n. 10	5.1000-1001	13
3.6.46-48	10 n. 25	5.1105-1116	11

INDEX OF PASSAGES FROM ANCIENT TEXTS

Martial
  12.57.1-14   547

Nepos, Cornelius
  Cimon
    4   434

Ovid
  Amores
    3.8.35-36   11 n. 28
    3.8.39-40   6
    3.8.41   12
  Fasti
    2.481-509   302
  Metamorphoses
    1.101-104   6
    1.109-110   6
    1.127-131   11
    1.128-162   23
    1.135-136   11
    1.139-150   11
    1.142-143   13
    1.250-252   26
    1.253-261   15, 24
    14.805-885   302
    15.99-103   5

Pliny the Younger
  6.16   109

Pompeius Trogus
  ap. Justin, *Historiae Philippicae*
    36, *Epitome* 2.16   69

Pomponius Mela
  3.85   63 n. 7

Propertius
  3.9.50   13 n. 31

Quintilian
  10.1.95   432

Sallust
  De Catilinae Coniuratione
    5   467 n. 2

Seneca the Younger
  Epistulae
    90.37   7
    90.40   7
  Hercules Furens
    38-41   63 n. 7
  Phaedra
    486   6
    527-528   6
    528-529   12
    531-532   12
  ap. Augustine, *De Civitate De-i* 6.10   432

Pseudo-Seneca
  Octavia
    401   12
    404-405   7
    420-422   12
    427-428   6

Servius
  on Virgil, *Aeneid*
    3.121-122   183 n. 8
  on Virgil, *Aeneid*
    11.264   183 n. 8

Suetonius
  Tiberius
    36   198
  Titus
    8   252 (*bis*)
  Vespasian
    12   252
    22   252

Tacitus
  Annals
    2.85   198
  Histories
    5.2.2   63
    5.5.1   485, 557, 559

Tibullus
  1.3.43-44   11
  2.5.23-24   13 n. 31

Valerius Maximus
  1.3.3   198

Varro
  ap. Aulus Gellius 16.17.2
     299
  ap. Augustine, *De Civitate D-i* 4.31
     432
  ap. Augustine, *De Civitate D-i* 21.8
     20

Virgil
  Aeneid
    1.142-143   171
    1.148-153   171
    1.202   296

INDEX OF PASSAGES FROM ANCIENT TEXTS

1.207	296	*Eclogues*	
1.507-508	493	4.18-20	6
Book 2	25 n. 11	4.32-33	12
2.634-751	216	*Georgics*	
3.121-122	183 n. 8	1.121-146	6 n. 16
6.852	325	1.125	6
9.176-502	143	1.126-127	11
11.264	183		

INDEX OF NAMES AND SUBJECTS

Aaron, brother of Moses, 55-73; details of marriage to Elisheba omitted by Josephus, 66-67; lack of encomium for by Josephus, 71; silence at death of his sons, 69; spokesman for Moses, 64-71; subordination of to Moses, 55-57, 69

Abel, Josephus' etymology of his name, 9; reason why his gift was favored by G-d, 8-9

Abimelech, Israelite ruler of Shechem in period of Judges, derogatory description of by Josephus, 178

Abiram, rebel against Moses, death of, 108

Abner, captain of King Saul's army, calumniated to King David by Joab, 211

Absalom, son of and rebel against King David, 215-229

Adam, associates freely with G-d, according to Josephus, 3; predicts destruction of universe by fire and water, 14-15, 23-24

Ahab, king of Israel, 273-289; discerns the true motives of Syrian king Ben-hadad, 279; expresses remorse, 278; not blamed for heeding the false prophet Zedekiah, 283; treatment of by rabbis, 230; wickedness of according to Josephus, 276-278

Ahasuerus, king of Persia identified by Josephus with Artaxerxes, 500-512; deep love of for Esther, 506; gentleness of, 505

Ahaz, king of Judah, omission of Isaiah's prophecy to, 379

Amalek, king who opposed Israelites in the Sinai desert, role of Moses and Aaron in fight against, 68

Amasa, military commander of Absalom's army, deceived by and slain by Joab, 213

angels, de-emphasis on in Elijah narrative, 300; de-emphasis on in Gideon narrative, 171; omission of from Hezekiah pericope of angel that smote 185,000 of the Assyrians, 374; sons of, compared with Greek giants, 15

annus magnus, end of in primal fire according to Stoics, 15

anthropomorphisms, avoided by Josephus in account of Elisha, 349; avoided by Josephus in account of Flood, 21-22, 30-31

Apollodorus, similarity in language of to Josephus' account of Flood, 27

Archilaus, successor to King Herod, paralleled with Rehoboam, 259

Aristaeus, Letter of, Pseudepigraphic work, equates G-d with Zeus, 29

ark of Noah, relics of preserved in Armenia according to Josephus, 29-30

Artapanus, (alleged) Graeco-Jewish historian, account of Jethro in, 40

Asa, king of Judah, 263-272

ass, speaking, in Balaam pericope, 128-130

assimilation, Josephus' concern with, 544; preaching by Josephus against in Balaam pericope, 130-131

audience of Josephus: Jewish, 543-544; non-Jewish, 543

Azariah, prophet, advises King Asa of Judah, 266; warns Asa, 271

Baasha, king of Israel, wickedness of, 236

Babylonian Chronicle, tablets containing data about history of seventh and sixth century BCE Babylonia, 442 n. 4

Balaam, pagan prophet, 110-136; ecstatically possessed and no longer his own master, 132-133; fame of as a soothsayer, 113-114

Balak, king of Moab, pressures Balaam to curse the Israelites, 122-126

INDEX OF NAMES AND SUBJECTS   637

Barak, leader with Deborah in struggle against Sisera, 158-159; role of enhanced by Josephus, 159, 161
beauty, of biblical heroes, 547; of Absalom, 220-221; of Esther, 518; of Vashti, 517-518
Belshazzar, Babylonian king, punished because he had blasphemed G-d, 74; viewed more favorably by Josephus, 75
Ben-hadad, Syrian king, his true motives in attacking Ahab discerned by Ahab, 279
Berossus, his account of the Flood paralleled with Josephus', 29
boundaries, marking out of, as sign of decline from Golden Age, 11-12

Cain, builds a city, 13; ending of his life of simplicity, 11-12; his fear that he will fall prey to wild beasts, 9; reason for condemnation of his gift by G-d, 8; his travels, 9-10
census, opposition of Joab to, 207-208; taken by Jehoram but omitted by Josephus, 328
Christians, claims of for Jesus as "man of G-d" avoided by Josephus, 301
chronology in Esther narrative, problems in, resolved by Josephus, 532-533
civil strife, abhorrence of, 556; avoidance of by Gideon, 171-172; avoidance of by Jehu, 358-359; consequences of in connection with Jeroboam, 237, 253-255; consequences of in connection with Joab, 208
colonies, failure of Noachides, according to Josephus, to send them out, 34-35
compassion, shown by Jehoram for Israelite woman who is ready to eat her son, 326-327; for Israelites shown by Moses and Aaron, 63; for non-Jews shown by Jehoram and Jehoshaphat, 326
contradictions and difficulties, removed by Josephus, 560-561
courage, of biblical heroes, 548; of Aaron, 58; of Ahab, 279-282; of Elisha, 338-339; of Esther, 515; of Gideon, 165-166; of Jehoram, 323-325; of Jehoshaphat, 311-312; of Jehu, 353-354; of Jephthah, 181; of Joab, 204-205; of Josiah, 430
cowardice, of Hezekiah, 367; of Joab, 206
Cushite woman, married by Moses, 62-63
Cyrus, Persian king, read book of Isaiah, according to Josephus, 379

Darius, Persian king, reputation of protected by Josephus, 75
Dathan, rebel against Moses, death of, 108
David, king, reference to as ancestor of Messiah omitted by Josephus, 382
Deborah, Israelite prophetess and judge, 153-162; meaning of her name, 154-155; song of, significance of omission of by Josephus, 160-161; song of, treatment by rabbis of, 157-158
deceit, of Joab in promise to Uriah, 212; of Joab in slaying of Amasa, 213
demagogues, disdain for, 553
Demetrius, (alleged) Graeco-Jewish historian, account of Jethro in, 39-40
demagoguery, of Absalom, 223-224
democracy, attacked by Josephus in account of choice of Absalom as king, 224; attacked by Josephus in account of choice of Jeroboam as king, 237
Deucalion, Greek eqivalent of Noah, 20
Diaspora, Josephus' attitude toward as seen in prophet Azariah's warning, 271
dramatic interest, 563-564; increase of in Josephus' account of Absalom, 227; increase of in Josephus' account of Ahab, 286; increase of in Josephus' account of Ahasuerus and Esther, 509; increase of in Josephus' account of Balaam, 131-134; increase of in Josephus' account of Ehud, 149-151; increase of in Josephus' account of Elijah, 304; increase of in Josephus' account of Elisha, 348-349;

increase of in Josephus' account of Esther, 521, 525; increase of in Josephus' account of Gedaliah, 468; increase of in Josephus' account of Gideon, 174-175; increase of in Josephus' account of Jehu, 360-361; increase of in Josephus' account of Jeroboam, 240-241; increase of in Josephus' account of Jonah, 414; increase of in Josephus' account of Korah, 106-109

Ecphantus, author of treatise on kingship, view of that subjects of a ruler imitate his conduct, 246
Eglon, king of Moab, assassinated by Ehud, 137-152; rehabilitated by Josephus, 144-146; respected by rabbis, 139
Egyptians, contempt for in Josephus, 84
Ehud, Israelite hero, courage of, 143-144; deliverer of Israelites from Eglon, king of Moab, 137-152; ingenuity of, 142-143; lefthandedness of, 140; resolution by Josephus of difficulties in biblical account of, 147-149; trickery of, 141-142;
Eleazar, son of Aaron, anger of Moses with, 62
Elijah, prophet, 291-306; death of rationalized by Josephus, 301-302; omission of Zealot features in Josephus' portrayal, 302-303; references to as "man of G-d" omitted by Josephus, 301
Elisha, prophet, 334-351; displays anger, 339-341; loyalty of to Elijah, 337-338; not called "man of G-d" by Josephus, 343
envy, disastrous effects of in connection with Joab, 209-213
ephod, priestly vestment, made by Gideon, significance of Josephus' omission of this incident, 169-170
erotic motifs, 565;in accounts of Ahasuerus and Esther, 509, 519-520; in account of Balaam, 133-134; in account of Ruth, 199-201
Esther, chosen as queen by Ahasuerus, 513-538; made Ahasuerus' lawful wife, 505
Evil-merodach, Babylonian king, successor to Nebuchadnezzar, honors Jehoiachin, 447
exaggeration, avoided by Josephus in account of Absalom, 225; avoided by Josephus in account of Gideon, 173; avoided by Josephus in account of Jehoshaphat, 312, 318; avoided by Josephus in account of Jonah, 414; avoided by Josephus in account of Josiah, 434-435
Ezekiel, Graeco-Jewish tragedian, account of Jethro in, 40-41
Ezra, Jewish leader responsible for religious reforms upon return from Babylonian captivity, 473-488; loyalty to Persian king stressed by Josephus, 480-483

Fate, blamed for hastening Ahab's end, 283-284, 286-288; blamed for Josiah's doom, 429-430
Flood, comparison of accounts of in Bible, Greek sources, and Josephus, 27-30
forgiveness, of David toward Absalom, 219-220

Gedaliah, Babylonian-appointed governor of Judaea, 463-472; submission of to the Babylonians paralleled with Josephus' to the Romans, 443, 468-470
genealogy, of biblical heroes, 546; of Esther, 513; of Ezra, 476-477; of Gedaliah, 464; of Gideon, 165; of Jephthah, 179-180; of Korah, 97-98; of Mordecai, 513-514; of Ruth, 194
Gentiles, alleged hatred by toward Jews, refuted by Josephus in Balaam pericope, 121-126
geography, biblical, according to Josephus, 1-2
Gideon, biblical judge, genealogy of enhanced by Josephus, 165; treatment of by Pseudo-Philo, rabbis, and Josephus, 163-176; virtues of enhanced by Josephus, 165-170

INDEX OF NAMES AND SUBJECTS 639

Gihon, river identified with Nile by Josephus, 2
G-d, de-emphasis on His role in history, 568; has no special place, according to Jeroboam, 240; identified with the supreme G-d of the pagans, 413; intends to replace wicked race with another, 26; persuaded by Noah to promise that He will not send another deluge, 31; rationalization of role of in Elijah narrative, 299; reduced role of in Asa narrative, 265; reduced role of in Esther narrative, 534-536; reduced role of in Jonah narrative, 397-399; reduced role of in Nehemiah narrative, 495; reduced role of in Ruth narrative, 196; repentance of omitted by Josephus in Jonah pericope, 400; rewards and punishes, 567-568; role of enhanced in Deborah narrative in Josephus, 156-159; role of in Gideon narrative, 170; role of in Jephthah narrative diminished by Josephus, 187-188; role of in Jethro narrative, 49-50
G-d-fearers, in book of Jonah and Josephus, 410-411
Golden Age, in Josephus and in classical writers, 3-8
golden calf, treatment by Philo of, 60; treatment by rabbis of, 60-1; treatment of Aaron's role in by Josephus, 59-62
gratitude, as shown by Ahasuerus, 507; as shown by Elisha, 342; as shown by Jehoshaphat, 313; as shown by Jethro, 46-47; lack of in Absalom, 218-219; lack of in Haman, 509-510

Hadoram (Adoniram), emissary sent by King Rehoboam to appease revolting people and stoned to death, 258-259
Ham, son of Noah, why not cursed by Noah, 35
Haman, prime minister of Ahasuerus, charges of against Jews parallel to those from the time of Hecataeus of Abdera, 529-530; overcome by pride of his station, 506, 527-528
Hanani, prophet, criticism by of King Asa omitted by Josephus, 269
Hasmonean kings, conflict of with those who looked for return of Davidic dynasty, 386
hatred of Jews by Gentiles alleged, 558
hatred of Jews by Haman, due to his descent from Amalek rather than as part of an eternal Jewish-Gentile conflict, 530
hatred of Romans by Jews, alleged, response of Josephus to in Balaam pericope, 118-119
Havilah, identified with India by Josephus, 1-2
Hellenizations, 563; in account of pride of generation of the Flood, 22-23
Hezekiah, king of Judah, 363-375; avoidance of buildup of as a messianic figure, 372; lofty view of not held by Josephus, 364-366; messianic associations of, 387-388
high priesthood, qualifications of Aaron for, 58; vestments of, 68-69

historicity of biblical events, 560
hospitality, shown by Balaam, 116; shown by Jehoram, 327
humanity, of biblical heroes, 549-550; held up as an ideal for rulers by advisers to Rehoboam, 251-252; of Elisha, 341-342; of Gedaliah paralleled with that of Vespasian and Titus, 464-466; of Gideon, 168; of Jehu, 355-356; of Nehemiah, 497

Iddo, prophet, predicts that Jeroboam's altar will be broken in an instant, 241
intermarriage, Josephus' concern with, 544; omission by Josephus of measures taken by Nehemiah against Jews who had intermarried, 498; omission by Josephus of names of those who had taken foreign wives, 484-485; reaction by Ezra to, 481, 483-484; treatment of by Josephus in account of Ruth, 196-198

Iron Age, described by Ovid, 11
irony, 564; in Josephus' account of Absalom, 227-228; in Josephus' account of Ahab, 286; in Josephus' account of Esther, 521-525
Isaiah, prophet, 376-392; importance of diminished in Josephus, 387-389; prophesies that Cyrus will cause Jerusalem and the Temple to be rebuilt, 379; reasons for diminished importance of in Josephus, 391-392; why and why not of special interest to Josephus, 377-378, 380-381
Ishmael son of Nethaniah, assassin of Gedaliah, paralleled in trickery with John of Gischala, 466
Ithamar, son of Aaron, anger of Moses with, 62

Jael, slayer of Sisera, role of in rabbis, Pseudo-Philo, and Josephus, 159-160
Jehoash (Joash), king of Israel, pays tribute to Elisha's effectiveness, 336-337; termed good whereas Bible says that he did evil, 439-440
Jehoiachin, king of Judah, 437-449; Josephus' defense of his decision to submit to the Babylonians paralleled with Josephus' own submission to the Romans, 442-444; omission by Josephus of biblical statement that he did what was evil in the sight of the L-rd, 437-440
Jehoram, king of Israel, 322-333; consults with Elisha, 329-331
Jehoshaphat, king of Judah, 307-321
Jehu, king of Israel, 352-362; as agent of prophets, 356-357; continued to worship golden calves, 358; not a zealot, 359; vengeance inflicted by upon Jezebel, 356
Jephthah, Israelite judge, 177-192; daughter of, 182-191; virtues of, 179-181; vow of, 182-191
Jeremiah, prophet, why Josephus was attracted to, 376-377
Jeroboam, founder of Kingdom of Israel, 230-243; precedent for Ahab's wickedness, 277
Jethro, father-in-law of Moses, 38-54; acknowledgment of greatness of Moses by, 49; criticism by of Moses' administration of justice, 48; many names of, 52; motive and setting of visit of to Moses, 47-48
Jezebel, wife of King Ahab, condemned by Josephus, 277-278
Joab, King David's general, 203-214
John of Gischala, rival of Josephus as general, craftiness of paralleled with that of Ishmael, Gedaliah's assassin, 466-468; greed of paralleled with that of Joab, 213; jealousy of toward Josephus paralleled with that of Korah, 109; his jealousy paralleled with that of Joab, 209-211; sedition of paralleled with that of Jeroboam, 238; only pretends to be humane, 252
Jonah, prophet, 393-415; importance of to Josephus the historian, 394-397; introduced by Josephus by citing his political role, 395, 397
Jonadab (Jehonadab), founder of ascetic Rechabites, long a friend of Jehu, 357
Josephus, ambivalent attitude of toward Roman Empire, 366; de-emphasizes David, Hezekiah, and Isaiah because of their importance for Christianity, 388; theology of, 373-374
Josiah, king of Judah, 424-436
"just war," concept of, 552-553; adhered to by Ahab, 282-283, 319
justice, of biblical heroes, 549-550; of Aaron, 59; of Asa, 265-266; of Elisha, 341; of Gideon, 167-168; of Jehoiachin, 441; of Jehoram, 326; of Jehoshaphat, 312-313; of Jehu, 355; of Jephthah, 181; of Josiah, 430-431
Justus of Tiberias, literary rival of Josephus, hypocrisy of paralleled with that of Joab, 212; villainy of paralleled with that of Ishmael the son of Nethaniah, 467

Korah, ability of as a speaker, according to Josephus, 98-99; ability of as a speaker, according to rabbis, 94-95; attack of upon the Torah, according to rabbis, 96-97;

INDEX OF NAMES AND SUBJECTS   641

challenge of to leadership of Moses and Aaron, 69-71, 91-109; death of, contradictory accounts of, 104-105; death of, dramatic enhancement of, 107-109; genealogy of, according to Josephus, 97-98; rebellion of as an attack on the priesthood, 100; rebellion of motivated by jealousy, 101; rebellion of, political aspects, 101-104; wealth of, according to Josephus, 98; wealth of, according to rabbis, 94

land of Israel, converted from political to religious gift in Josephus' account of Jehoshaphat, 320
language, earliest, according to Josephus, 2-3
Lappidoth, husband of Deborah, significance of name of, according to the Talmud, 157
law and order, respect for, 552
leadership of biblical heroes, 551
Leontopolis, temple of Onias at, alleged prediction by Isaiah of, 379-380
Levites, attempt of to usurp the status of priests, 100; names of omitted in Ezra pericope, 481-482; omission of in Josephus' account of Jehoshaphat, 308; omission in Hezekiah pericope of statement that they were more upright in heart than were the priests, 366
loyalty to friends, 556-557
loyalty to state, 556; of Ezra, 479-483; of Gedaliah, 469-470; of Nehemiah, 490-492
Lucian, similarity in language with Josephus' account of Flood, 27-28

magnanimity, of Gedaliah, 470
Manasseh, king of Judah, 416-423; rehabilitated by Josephus, 255; treatment of by rabbis, 230
masses, contempt for by Josephus, 480, 553
meddlesomeness of Jews, alleged, 560; refuted by Josephus in Balaam pericope, 121
Meribah, scene where Moses smites rock instead of speaking to it, 63-64
mercy, begets crime unwittingly, 285; of Elisha, 342; of Gideon, 168
Messiah, awaited by Jews of first century, 384-385; descent of from David mentioned in rabbinic tradition, in Gospels, and in Dead Sea Scrolls, 385-386; Elijah's role as forerunner of, 292; opposition to concept of, 554-555; references to in Isaiah omitted by Josephus, 386-387; references to in Pseudepigrapha, Dead Sea Scrolls, and Gospels, 383-384;
Micaiah, prophet, shown regard by Ahab, 283
Midianite women, seduce Israelite men, treatment of by Josephus, 130-131, 133-134
Midianites, rout of, described by Josephus, 174-175
midwives, identified as Egyptian by Josephus, 85
military details, 567; emphasized in Josephus' account of Balaam, 127-128
miracles, 568-570; avoided by Josephus in account of death of Korah, 105; avoided by Josephus in account of Deborah, 158; de-emphasized in Gideon narrative, 170-171; performed by Aaron, 65-67; performed by Elijah, 298-302; performed by Elisha, 344-347; performed by Moses, 66; skepticism of Hezekiah about, 374; treatment of in Balaam pericope, 128-130; treatment of in Jonah narrative, 402-404
misanthropy, charge of against Jews, refuted by Josephus in Balaam narrative, 117-118
misogyny of Josephus, 564; in Deborah narrative, 154-155, 156-157; in Ruth narrative, 202

Moabitess, reduced mention of Ruth as in Josephus, 197-198
moderation, of Absalom, 222-223
modesty, of Elisha, 341; of Gideon, 167; of Joab, 205
Mordecai, cousin of Esther, co-hero of the narrative, 513-516; omission of unbecoming details concerning, 515; reason for his not prostrating himself before Haman, 516
Moses, Israelite leader, chosen as general by Pharaoh, 86; elevated by Josephus, 55, 65-71; elevated by Philo, 56; as infant tears off pharaoh's crown, 85-86
music, role of in accounts of Moses and Aaron, 58
mythology, avoided by Josephus, 20

Naboth, owner of vineyard seized by Ahab, who later expresses regret, 278
nationalism, avoided by Josephus in portrayal of Jonah, 396-397
Nebuchadnezzar, Babylonian king, defense of by Josephus, 452-455
Nehemiah, Jewish cupbearer to Persian king Xerxes, 489-499; honored by the people upon order of Persian king, 496-497; as leader and organizer, 493-494; loyalty of to king, 490-491; respect of for law, 491-492; as "tyrant," 493-494
nepotism, alleged in Moses' appointment of Aaron as high priest, 57-58
Nicolaus of Damascus, Greek historian, account of Flood in, 28
Ninos, Josephus' name for Nineveh, 412
Noah, drunkenness of, 35; identified by Josephus with the survivor of the Babylonian flood, 28-29; perfection of omitted by Josephus, 26-27; survivor of the Flood, 17-37; treatment of by Philo, 26; treatment of by Pseudo-Philo, 26-27; treatment of by rabbis, 27; urges his fellow men to repent, 25
Noachides, descendants of Noah, all Gentiles, 19; Josephus omits tradition that more is expected of them than of Jews, 32-33
novelistic details, in account of Esther, 516-520

oath, violation of by Zedekiah justified by Nebuchadnezzar's violation, 459
obedience to law, emphasized in Josephus' treatment of Ahasuerus, 504
Ogygian Flood, known by Josephus, 20-21
Okeanos, stream flowing around the earth, 1
original sin, omitted by Josephus, 31-32

pagan cults, destruction of by Asa not mentioned by Josephus, 269-270
persuasion, gift of Nehemiah in, 492
pharaoh, etymology of according to Philo, 76-77
Pharaoh (of the Exodus), affectionate attitude of toward the infant Moses, 85-86; not identified with Pharaoh of Joseph's era, 84; omission of hardening of heart of, 87; reaction of to the plagues, 87-88
Pharaoh (of Joseph's era), admired by Josephus, 83-84
pharaohs, account of in Philo, 75-78; account of by rabbis, 78-82, Josephus' account of, 82-88
Philo, Graeco-Jewish philosopher, account of Aaron in, 55-56; account of Jethro in, 41-43; account of Korah in, 92-94; account of the pharaohs in, 75-78
philosophic interests, 566-567
Phinehas, biblical zealot, identified with Elijah, 293
piety, of biblical heroes, 550-551; lack of in Jephthah criticized by Josephus, 187-189; lack of in Jeroboam, 234-237; lack of in Joab, 207; lack of in Manasseh, 418-419; of Aaron, 59; of Asa, 267-269; of Deborah, 157; of Elisha, 343; of Gideon, 168-170; of Hezekiah, 368-371; of Jehoram, 327-331; of Jehoshaphat, 313-316; of Jehu, 356-357; of Josiah, 431-435

INDEX OF NAMES AND SUBJECTS   643

Pishon, river identified with Ganges by Josephus, 1
Plato, influence of *Timaeus* of on Josephus' account of Flood, 24; influence of on Philo, 76
Plutarch, similarity in language with Josephus' account of Flood, 28
praise of Jews by Gentiles, 558-559
precociousness, of biblical heroes, 546-547; of Josiah developed by Josephus, 426
priesthood, emphasis upon in Josephus' account of Jehoshaphat, 308; Josephus' concern with, 379, 545-546
promise of Josephus not to add to or subtract from biblical text, 539-543
prophecy, gift of Aaron for, 58
prophet(s), attack on by Manasseh, 420; role of Elijah as, emphasized, 300; use of term by Septuagint and Josephus, 114-115
proselytism, avoidance of mention of in Josephus' account of Asa, 270; in the book of Jonah, 409-410; conversion of Ruth, 198-199; denial that Jews are agressive in, 559-560; Jethro the non-proselyte, 50-51
providence, directs all, as seen in Korah episode, 104
Pseudo-Philo, failure of to mention Jethro, 43; on Jonah, 407; Ehud said to be identified with Zebul by, 137-138; treatment of Deborah by, 157; treatment of Elijah by, 293; treatment of Gideon by, 163; treatment of Korah by, 93-94

qiqayon, significance of omission of in Josephus' narrative of Jonah, 399

rabbis, heightened respect for Eglon by, 139; partial rehabilitation of Nebuchadnezzar by, 454; references by to Messiah, 385; treatment of Aaron by, 56-57; treatment of Ahab by, 274-276; treatment of Ahasuerus by, 500-503; treatment of Asa by, 263-264; treatment of Deborah by, 156-158; treatment of Ehud by, 139; treatment of Elijah by, 291-294; treatment of Ezra by, 475-479; treatment of Gideon by, 163-164; treatment of Hezekiah by, 363-364; treatment of Isaiah by, 377, 382; treatment of Jehoiachin by, 444-447; treatment of Jehoshaphat by, 309-310; treatment of Jehu by, 352-353; treatment of Jeroboam by, 230-233; treatment of Jethro by, 43-46; treatment of Joab by, 203-204; treatment of Jonah by, 405-407; treatment of Josiah by, 424-425; treatment of Korah by, 94-97; treatment of Manasseh by, 416-418; treatment of Noah by, 27; treatment of Zedekiah by, 450-452
rainbow, significance of in Josephus, 33-34
rationalizations, in Balaam narrative, 128-130; in Deborah narrative, 158; in Elijah narrative, 298-303; in Elisha narrative, 344-347; in Gideon narrative, 170; in Korah narrative, 105
Rehoboam, king of Judah, 244-262; failure of to listen to advice of advisers, 247; humbles himself, 260-261; rehabilitated by Josephus, 255-261
repentance, of biblical heroes, 551-552; of G-d omitted by Josephus in Jonah pericope, 400; of Manasseh highlighted by Josephus, 420-423; of Ninevites ignored by Josephus, 408
revelation at Sinai, role of Aaron in, according to Josephus, 68
revolutionaries, contempt for, 555
Romans, overthrow of, intimated in Balaam pericope, treatment of by Josephus, 118-119
Rome, Jewish rebellion against, parallel to Jeroboam's rebellion, 239
Ruth, biblical proselyte to Judaism, 193-202, why included in Josephus' history, 194
Sanballat, satrap of Samaria, report of that Jews intend to rebel against the Persians omitted by Josephus, 497
Sarai, wife of Abram, incident of with Pharaoh, 82-83

Saturnian Age, depicted by Virgil, 6, 11
Septuagint, translation of Pentateuch into Greek, use of προφήτης by, 114
Seth, descendants of exalted by Josephus, 13-14
Shishak, king of Egypt, fails to abide by agreement with Rehoboam, 261
sins of Jews, omitted by Josephus in narrative of Ezra, 486-487; omitted by Josephus in narrative of Nehemiah, 495-496
Sisera, Canaanite general defeated by Barak, 156; depiction of struggle against by Deborah and Barak, 158; number of troops of exaggerated by Pseudo-Philo and rabbis, 155-156
Spinoza, Benedict, author of *Theologico-Political Tractate*, 487
Stoics, Golden Age as depicted by, 5-7; influence of on Josephus' account of Balaam, 126-127; influence of on Josephus' account of Gideon, 166-167; view of that G-d has no special place, 240
stylistic improvements by Josephus, 562-563
subservience of Jews, 553; in Balaam pericope, 120-121
suppliants, regard of Ahab for, 285
suspense, 563; in Josephus' account of Absalom, 226-227; in Josephus' account of Ahab, 285-286; in Josephus' accounts of Ahasuerus and Esther, 510, 524-525; in Josephus' account of Ehud, 150-151

temperance, of biblical heroes, 548-549; lack of in Jehu, 354-355; lack of in Jeroboam, 234; of Aaron, 58-59; of Elisha, 339; of Gideon, 166-167; of Jehoram, 326; of Jephthah, 181; of Josiah, 430; omission of in Hezekiah pericope, 368
Temple in Jerusalem, alternative to set up by Jeroboam, 235; enhancement of details by Josephus of Josiah's work on repairs of, 432-433; Josephus' regard for, 545-546
theological problems resolved by Josephus, 570
tolerance of Jews for non-Jewish religions, 558; seen in Josephus' attitude of Gideon toward altar of Baal and Asherah tree, 168; seen in Josephus' account of Asa's failure to pull down pagan cult objects, 269-70; seen in Josephus' account of Jehoshaphat, 318-319; seen in omission by Josephus of Esther's attack on idol worship of non-Jews, 531; seen in omission by Josephus of Isaiah's depiction of destruction of Asherim and alien incense-altars, 388-389; seen in omission by Josephus of Josiah's actions against idol worship, 432, 434; seen in omission by Josephus of Manasseh's idol worship, 419; seen in omission from Hezekiah pericope of Isaiah's promise from G-d that He would put His hook in Assyria's nose, 372-373; seen in omission from Hezekiah's prayer of statement that Assyrian kings had cast the gods of other nations into the fire, 372; seen in omission of Jehu's making a pagan shrine into a latrine, 355-356
tolerance of Jews for non-Jews and especially non-Jewish leaders, 557-558
truthfulness, 567; lack of in Joab, 207; of Elisha, 343; of Isaiah, 389-391; of Jehu, 355; of Jonah's prophecy, 400-402
Tubal-Cain (Jubel), forging of metal by connected with art of war, 13

unity of Jewish people, stressed by Josephus in account of Jehoshaphat, 316-318
Uriah, heroic warrior in King David's army, deceived by Joab, 212
Uzziah, king of Judah, led to sin, according to Josephus, by good fortune, 260

Varro, Roman polymath, views of on theology echoed in statements ascribed to Josiah by Josephus, 432
vow, of Jephthah, 182-191
Vashti, wife of King Ahasuerus, dismissal of not capricious, 504-505

INDEX OF NAMES AND SUBJECTS   645

vengeance of Esther, omitted by Josephus, 534
virtues of biblical heroes, comparable to those of pagan heroes, 546

wealth of biblical heroes, 547; of Jews, de-emphasized by Josephus in Ezra narrative, 485-486
wisdom, of biblical heroes, 547-548; lack of in Jehu, 353; lack of in Jephthah criticized by Josephus, 185-187; lack of in Jeroboam, 233-234; of Ahab, 282; of Ezra, 477; of Gideon, 165; of Jehoram, 322-323; of Josiah, 426-429; omission of in description of Hezekiah, 367
wise sayings introduced by Josephus, 565-566
women, status of, according to Josephus, 7-8

Zambrias, Israelite, defends relationship with Midianite woman, 131
Zaphenath-paneah, name given to Joseph by Pharaoh, 83-84
Zedekiah, king of Judah, 450-462; advisers of blamed by Josephus, 438-439, 455-458, 460; change of name of to Mattaniah omitted by Josephus, 459; contradictory statements in Bible about, 450; positive portrayal of in Dead Sea fragments, 452

INDEX OF GREEK, LATIN, HEBREW, AND ARAMAIC WORDS

Greek Words

ἀγαθοὶ καὶ δίκαιοι	50, 256, 259	ἀλόγου	93
ἀγαθός	439	ἄλσει	268
ἀγαθούς	50	ἀλώμενος περιπέσῃ	9
ἀγαθῶν	528	ἀμαθίας	12
ἀγανακτήσασα	156	ἁμαρτίας ἀνθομολο-	
ἀγαπήσειν	247	γουμένους	261
ἀγαπήσομεν	130	ἀμείνων	140
ἀγαπητόν	185, 185 n. 13	ἀμετρήτως	528
		ἀμηχανήσας	87
ἄγγαροι	508	ἀμηχανίᾳ	150, 339
ἄγγελοι	20	ἀμηχανίας	524
ἀγνωμονοῦντος	154 n. 4	ἄμικτον	529
ἀγνωμοσύναν	154 n. 4	ἀμύνωνται	530
ἀγνωμοσύνη	154 (bis)	ἀμφοτεροδέξιον	140, 142 n. 8
ἀγωνία	505	ἀμφοτέρων	83
ἀδικία	5	ἀναγκαῖος	524
ἀδικίας	239	ἀναγκαιότατον	516
ἀδίκου	216	ἀνάγκη	286 n. 7
ἀδικουμένῳ	180	ἀνάγκην	223
ἀδοξῆσαι	515	ἀνάγκης	288 n. 9
ἀεὶ...ἐπιθυμήσας		ἀναισθήτους εὐεργεσιῶν	47
μεγάλων	238	ἀνακλαιομένη	304
ἀηδῶς	317	ἀναπηδήσαντος	506, 520
ἀηδῶς ἔχων	25	ἀναπηδήσας	286, 520 n. 14
ἀθέμιστα ἔργα	23		
ἀθεότητος	20 n. 4	ἀναρχία	145
αἰκιζομένη	304	ἀναρχίας	144
ἀιστώσας	26	ἀνδραγαθίας	49
ἀκέραιον	12	ἀνδρείας	128, 558
ἀκοσμίαν	145	ἀνδρειότατος	143
ἀκοσμίας	144	ἀνεπήδησεν	520 n. 14
ἀκόσμως	102, 107	ἀνηρέθιστο	107
ἀκούει	240	ἀνήρτηται	541
ἀκούειν	240	ἀνθομολογέομαι	261
ἀκρατῶς	12	ἀνθρώπινον	326
ἄκρος	165	ἀνθρώπινόν τι	326
ἀλαζόνας	254	ἀνθρωπίνων	50
ἀλαζών	254	ἀνθρωπόμορφος	30
ἀλγήσαντες	257	ἀνόητος	254
ἀληθῆ	168	ἀνοήτως	254
ἀλήτην	271	ἄνοια	277
ἀλλοτριώτατα	117	ἀνομημάτων	236

INDEX OF GREEK, LATIN, HEBREW, AND ARAMAIC WORDS 647

ἀνόσιον	468		ἀσύμφυλον	529
ἀνοσίως	207		ἀσχήμονος μυθολογίας	20
ἀντιλαμβάνεσθαι	141		ἀτόποις	212
ἄξαντος	108		ἄτοπον	107
ἀξιολογώτατοι	57		ἄτροπον	126
ἀξιόμαχον	323		αὐτοκράτορι λογισμῷ	165
ἀπάθεια	6		αὐτόματα	5
ἀπαθῆ	6		αὐτομάτη	4
ἀπάνθρωπον	529-530		αὐτομάτης	5
ἀπάνθρωπόν τινα καὶ			αὐτομάτους	5
μισόξενον βίον	62 n. 6		αὐτομάτων	4
ἅπασιν ἀνθρώποις	529		αὐτομάτως	4, 104 (ter), 207
ἀπάτην	210			
ἀπὸ τῆς χώρας	471		ἀφανισμόν	14
ἀπὸ τῶν ὑψηλῶν	34		ἀφανισμὸς...τῶν ὅλων	23
ἀποκτενοῖ τοὺς πόδας	146 n. 14		ἀφίστασθαι	238
ἀπόλαυσιν	4		ἀφορῶν	267
ἀπολαύων ἅμα καὶ			ἀχαριστίαν	459
κοινωνίας τοῦ βίου			βεβαία	168
τῇ βασιλίσσῃ	510 n. 4		βιάζεσθαι	106
ἀπόνοιαν θράσους	12		βίας	11
ἀπονοίας	219		βιβλίον	352 n. 1
ἀποσημαίνων	33		βίον εὐδαίμονα	3
ἀποχωρήσει	146 n. 14		βλασφημήσαντος	331
ἀποχωρήσει τοῦ			βουλεύσασθαι	248, 256
κοιτῶνος	146 n. 14		βούλησιν	11 n. 28
ἀπραγμοσύνην	12		γενναίως	58
ἀρετή	348 n. 12		γένοιτο δ' ἄν	28
ἀρετήν	22, 57, 165, 426		γένος	396, 396 n. 9 (quater), 397 n. 9
ἀρετῆς	47			
ἄριστα	41 n. 7, 323		γένους	397 n. 9
ἄριστα συνεβούλευσεν	43		γῆρας	4 (bis)
ἄριστος	83, 267, 426		γοητείαν	88
ἁρπαγῆς	11		γυμνοῖς τοῖς ποσὶ διῆγεν	274 n. 2
ἀρχαίαν	372		γυναικείας συμβουλίας	7
ἄρχει	40		γυναικῶν	25
ἀρχήν	395		δέησιν	124
ἀρχῆς	212		δειλίας	295 n. 4, 367
ἀρχιτέκτονας	433		δεινόν	106, 209, 327
ἄρχοντι	40			
ἄρχων	40		δείσας	85, 87
ἀσεβείᾳ	327		δελεασθέν	234
ἀσεβείας	218, 236, 439, 455		δεξιότητα	300
ἀσεβεῖς	438, 455		δεομένων	361
ἀσεβές	207, 419		δέοντος	438, 455
ἀσεβής	236		δεύτερος	56
ἀσθενείας	180		δεχόμενος	49
ἀσμένως	49		δημαγωγέω	224
ἀστεῖον	300		δημαγωγῶν	224, 224 n. 15
ἀστεῖος	146 n. 13			

δημιουργός	114	δόξης	480
δήμοις	99 n. 4	δοῦλος κυρίου	400 n. 13
δήμοις ὁμιλεῖν πιθανώα-		δραστήριον	277
τος	98	δραστήριος	328 (ter), 444
δημοτικώτερον	247		n. 5
δι' αἰῶνος	554	δυνατώτατος	143 (bis)
δι' ἐρωτικὴν ἐπιθυμίαν	180	δύσκολον	258
διὰ τὴν ἐπὶ τῇ δυνάμει		δυσκόλων	258
πεποίθησιν	22	δυσσεβεῖς	20 n. 4
διὰ τὴν πατρῴαν ἀρετήν	180	δυσχεραίνοντος	116
διαβαλεῖν	211	δυσχεραίνων	25
διαβασανίσας	185	δώροις ὑπελθών	142
διαβόητος	339, 341	ἐβέβλητο	407
διαβολαῖς	106	ἐβουλεύσατο	483
διαβολάς	209	ἐγκρατείας	234
διαθήκη	388	ἐδίδασκε	421
διαθήκην	37 n. 17 (bis)	ἐδόξασαν	486
δίαιταν	454	ἔθεσι	529
διαλλάξῃς	223	εἶδεν ἐν ὕπνῳ	110 n. 2
διάνοιαν	25, 346	εἰς γυναῖκα	160
διάταξιν τοῦ πολιτεύ-		εἰς ὁμιλίαν αὐτῷ	3
ματος	102	εἰς τὰ πεδία	34
διέλιπεν	236	εἰς φθόνον...οὔτι μέ-	
διετέλει	510	τριον	209
δικαία	368	ἐκ τοῦ πάνυ ἀρχαίου	428
δικαίαν	341	ἐκ...τῶν ὑψηλῶν	34
δίκαιοι	341, 479	ἐκαρτέρουν	197
δίκαιον	254, 315,	ἐκέλευεν	314
	431, 464	ἐκηβόλος	33
δίκαιος	313, 315,	ἐκκλησίαν	102
	437, 441,	ἐκλιπαρησάντων	179
	448, 456 n.	ἐκμιμησάμενος	277
	6, 465	ἐκπεριῆλθον	524
	(bis), 491,	ἐκπλήξει	339
	492	ἐκπύρωσις	15
δίκαιος, τέλειος ὢν ἐν		ἐκφορά	269
τῇ γενεᾷ αὐτοῦ	26	ἐλεεινόν	326
δικαιοσύνη	315, 341	ἐλευθερίας	141
δικαιοσύνην	426, 430,	ἐλευθέρων	131
	483	ἐλυμήνατο	269 n. 5
δικαιοσύνης	455, 456	ἐλυπήθη...λύπην	
δικαιότερον	59	μεγάλην	408
δικαίου	266	ἐμφύλιος	208
δικαίους	266	ἐμφυλίου...στάσεως	172
δικαίων	438	ἐν ὀλίγοις	165
δίκη	483, 491	ἐν παραλλαγῇ	325 n. 1, 354
δίκη δ' ἐν χερσί	10	ἐν ταῖς Ἑβραικαῖς	
διώρθου	426	βίβλοις	394
δοκησίσοφος	42	ἐνέδρᾳ	354
δολιώτατος	210, 466, 467	ἐνέδραν	324
	(bis)	ἐνεδρευθείς	212
δόλκῳ	354, 422	ἐνέδυσε	170

INDEX OF GREEK, LATIN, HEBREW, AND ARAMAIC WORDS 649

ἐνεθυμήθη	21	ἔργῳ	102
ἔνθεος	349 (ter), 349 n. 13	ἔρεγχε	407
		ἔριδα	208
ἔνθους	132 n. 27	ἔρωντα	510
ἐννοίᾳ	283	ἐσπούδαζεν	421
ἐξεπήδησεν	361	ἐσπουδακότος	257
ἐξετάσεις	50	Ἐσσαῖος ἦν γένος	396 n. 9
ἐξετράπη	254	ἐσωφρόνιζε	429, 430
ἐξυβρίζειν	106	ἑταίρας	180 n. 3 (bis)
ἐξυβρίζων	236	ἐταμίευσεν	528
ἐξύβρισεν	235, 236, 255	ἑτέρας	180 n. 3
		ἐτέρπετο	521
ἐπαχθεῖσαν	180	εὖ γεγονότων	464, 477
ἐπεγγελᾷς	524	εὖ γεγονώς	464
ἐπεδείξατο	426	εὐγένειαν	210
ἐπεί σφισιν ἐγγύθεν		εὐγνώμονας	432
εἰμέν	3	εὐδαίμονα	168
ἔπειθε	483	εὐδαιμονεῖν	22 n. 8
ἐπενόησεν	277	εὐδαιμονία	14
ἐπεσκοτημένοι	346	εὐδαίμων	120
ἔπηλυν	271	εὐεργεσίαν καταθέσθαι	506-507
ἐπὶ δικαιοσύνῃ ...		εὐεργεσίας	285
ἀγαπῶν	27	εὐεργετηθεῖσαι	46
ἐπὶ τὰ πεδία	34	εὐεργετηκότα	47
ἐπιγελῶν	35	εὐήθεις	5
ἐπιδιώξας	354	εὐθέως	241
ἐπιείκεια	248, 249, 252	εὐθύς	255, 260
		εὐμενείας	266
ἐπιεικείᾳ καὶ φιλανθρωπίᾳ	249	εὔνοιαν	224
		εὐνοίας	195, 205, 359
ἐπιείκειαν	247, 248, 249	εὐνομία	507
		εὐνομίαν	228
ἐπιείκειαν καὶ μεγαλοφροσύνην	252	εὐνομίας	507
		εὐνοούντων	506
ἐπιεικέσι	278	εὔνουν	510, 522
ἐπιεικέστατοι	249	εὔνους	211, 248
ἐπιεικέστεροι	249	εὐνούστεροι	248
ἐπιεικέστερον	249	εὐποιίαν	46
ἐπιεικῆ	464	εὐπραξίας	527
ἐπιεικής	249 (bis), 465 (ter)	εὐσέβεια	168
		εὐσεβείᾳ	315
ἐπιεικοῦς	249	εὐσέβειαν	22, 267, 315, 426, 433
ἐπιθυμίαν ἔχοντα	209		
ἐπιμέλειαν	178	εὐσεβείας	431
ἐπίνοια	427	εὐσεβεῖν	434
ἐπινοίᾳ	427 (bis)	εὐσεβής	315, 368
ἐπισυνέρρευσεν	224	εὔτακτον	256, 563
ἐπιτηδεύμασιν	529	εὐταξίας	31
ἐπιφανοῦς	261	εὐτυχέστερος	444 n. 5
ἐπραγματεύετο	106	εὐτυχήσαντας	527
ἔργα	143	εὐτυχίαν	528

εὐχαριστήσας	497	θαυμαστά	347
εὐχαριστία	47	θαυμαυστήν	339
εὐχαριστίας	218 n. 7	θεία προνοία	126
ἐφθόνησε	209	θεῖοι	389
ἐφορᾷ	240	θεῖον	235
ἐφορᾶν	240	θεῖον ἄνδρα	389
ἐχέτω ὑμῖν	106	θεῖος	389
Ζεὺς Ξένιος	43	θεῖος ἀνήρ	301 n. 8 (bis)
ζῆλοι	5	θειότητος	389
ζηλοτυπίαν	209	θεοφιλῆ	343
ζηλώσας	277	θεραπεύων	142
ζήλωσιν	13	θερμός	234
ζηλωτής	421, 426	θηρώμενον	106
ζηλωτός	421 (bis)	θίβις	28
ἡ δὲ σωτερίη ἥδε ἐγένετο	27	θορυβέω	103
		θόρυβος	102, 103
ἡ παράδοσις τῶν πρεσβυτέρων	427	θορύβου	102
		θορύβου καὶ ταραχῆς	107
ἡ τῶν ἀγαθῶν λαμπρότης	527	θορυβώδης	103
		θράσους	373
ἠγάπα	282	θρησκείαν	529
ἡγεμόνας	324	θρησκεύειν	327
ἡγεμονία	178	ἰδίᾳ	456
ἡγεμονία	141	ἰδιοτρόπους	117
ἡγεμών	120	ἱερουργίαν	103
ἡδόμενος τῇ πρὸς αὐτὸν ὁμιλίᾳ	3	ἱκανὸς δημαγωγεῖν	224
		ἱκανὸς...εἰπεῖν	98
ἡδονήν	4, 11, 11 n. 28	ἱκανῶς ἔμπειρος	479
		Ἰοθόρ	39
ηδονῆς	11 n. 28	Ἰοθώρ	39
ἡδύ	315	ἱστορίας	336
ἡμερῶσαι	223	Ἰωβάβ	39
ἠντιβόλει	220	καὶ τῇ τῶν πρεσβυτέρων πειθόμενος	427
ἤνυσαν μήτε αὐτοὶ φρονεῖν ὑπὸ τῆς δυστυχίας ὄντες ἀγαθοί	154	καινίσας	277
		κακία	87
ἠπείλησαν	259	κακίας	13
ἠρέμει	234	κάκιστον	237
ἠρέμησεν	236	κακοήθως	106
ἡσθείς	523	κακοῦ παντὸς ἀπαθῆ	3
ἡσθέντες	359	κακουργήματα	210 n. 4
ἡσυχάζειν	226	κακουργία	87, 210
ἡσυχίᾳ	254	κακοῦργον	211
ἡσυχίαν ἦγε	48	κακουργοῦσι	106
ἥττονα	7	κακῶν	4
ἤχθετο	217	κακῶν ῥεκτῆρα καὶ ὕβριν	10
θαρρεῖ	280		
θαρρεῖν	296	κακώσεως	145, 145 n. 12
θάρσος	166		
θαρσοῦσα	296	κάλλει τὰς γυναῖκας ἁπάσας ὑπερβάλλουσαν	518
θαυμάσαντος	83		
θαυμάσια	347 n. 9	κάλλος	518

INDEX OF GREEK, LATIN, HEBREW, AND ARAMAIC WORDS

καλῶς	541	κύριος	167
κανόνι	426	κωλυθείς	257
καρτερηθεῖσα	58	λαμπραί	335
κατ' ἰσχὺν πυρός	14, 23	λαμπρᾶς	335
κατ' οὐδὲν ὁμοίᾳ	187	λαμπρός	335
κατὰ βίαν καὶ πλῆθος		λαμπρότατος	261
ὕδατος	14, 23	λαμπρῶς	317, 322, 330, 369
κατὰ μικρόν	510		
κατὰ τὴν Ἀχονίου		λανθάνειν	106
συμβουλίαν	484	λανθάνων	226
κατὰ τὴν οἰκείαν τάξιν	19 n. 3	λάρνακα	27, 28, 560
κατὰ τὴν πατρῴαν		λάρνακος	28, 29
παράδοσιν	428	λάρναξ	28 (quater), 28 n. 12 (bis)
κατὰ φύσιν	7 (bis), 9		
καταβαίνειν	34	λέγουσι	403
κατάβασιν	34	λέγων	102
καταβήσομαι	184 n. 11	λειτουργοῦσαν	268 n. 4
καταγηράσκουσιν	4	λεληθότως	106
καταγνούς	326, 331	λησταί	347
καταδείσας	129	λῃστείαν	11, 12
καταπραΰναι	222	λῃστῶν	347
καταπραΰνῃ	258	λογισμός	165, 185 n. 14, 186 (bis), 186 n. 16
κατασπαζόμενος	520		
καταφρονεῖ	369		
καταφρονήσαντα	144	λογισμοῦ	186, 527
κατεγέλα	521	λογισμῷ	185, 528
κατεστρατηγῆσθαι	354	λόγος	55 (bis), 55 n. 1, 345, 403, 569
κατοίκησιν	320, 555		
κατῴκτειραν	326		
κατωρθωμένοις	264	λυπούμενος	510
κατωρθωμένων	264	λῦσαι	509
κελεύσαντος	314	μακαριστός	421
κελεύσειεν	330	μάλιστα	277
κενοί	178	μᾶλλον ἐπάγεσθαι	518
κενούς	178	μανία	114 n. 10
κερδαίνειν	213	μαντεία	114, 115 n. 12
κεχαρισμένην	189		
κεχειροτονημένος	104	μαντεῖον	114, 115 n. 11
κεχειροτονήσαντος	104		
κεχειροτονήσεται	104	μαντεύομαι	114
κήρυκα	25 n. 10	μάντις	114 (quater), 114 n. 10, 115, 115 n. 11, 134, 558
κιβωτός	28, 28 n. 12, 560		
κινεῖν	238		
κόρος	509, 528 (bis)	μάχαιρα	148, 148 n. 16
κόσμος	103	μεγαλοπρεποῦς	343
κόσμου	141	μεγαλοπρεπῶς	434
κρίνει	40	μεγαλοφροσύνης	507, 522
κτῆσις	9	μεγαλόψυχον	12
κύρια	168	μεγάλων ἐπιθυμητὴς	
κύριοι	167	πραγμάτων	238

652 INDEX OF GREEK, LATIN, HEBREW, AND ARAMAIC WORDS

μέγεθος	528	Νινευή	412
μέγεθος τῶν πραγμάτων	254	νόμιμον	187, 189
μέλισσα	155 n. 5	νομίμων	267 (bis)
μερίμνης	5	νομίμως	505, 514
μετ' εὐταξίας	325 n. 1, 355	νόμους	434
μετ' ὀλίγον	299	νόμων	141
μετ' ολίγον πάνυ		ξαινόμενοι	4
χρόνον	401	ξενίᾳ	116
μετὰ ἀσθενείας	520	ξενισθείς	322
μετὰ πάσης...φιλοτιμίας	460	ξενίων	327, 342
μετὰ χρόνον τινὰ	316	ξένον	180, 413
μεταβεβουλευμένος	329	ξιφίδιον	148 n. 16,
μετάμελος	278, 326 n. 2		149
μετανοήσας	457	ὁ δὲ πᾶς λαός	482
μετεώρου	257	ὁ ἐκπορευόμενος ὃς ἂν	
μέτριος	166	ἐξέλθῃ	182
μετρίως	226	ὁ θεὸς ὁ μέγιστος	413
μὴ στασιάζοιεν	34	οἱ Ἰουδαίων τύραννοι	171
μηδὲν ἄγαν	548	οἰκουμένην	285, 518
μηδὲν ὑπερθέσει μηδὲ		οἶμαι	260, 283,
ἀναβολῇ	433		535
μηδὲν ὠφελούμενον	510	οἷς ἐξύβριζον	22, 23
μηχανὴν...καὶ πόρον		ὀκνηρός	12
πρὸς σωτηρίαν	27	ὁμιλία	143
μῖσος ἴδιον	528	ὁμιλίαν	142 n. 9
μόλις	520	ὁμολογουμένως	389
μιαρᾶς	216	ὁμοφύλους	254
μιαροῖς	216 n. 3	ὁμοφύλων	238
μιαρόν	216 n. 3	ὁμοφωνούντων	2
μιαρώτερον	235, 236	ὀξεῖαν	178, 181
μιαρώτατοι	216 n. 3 (bis)	ὅσιον	200, 315
μιαρώτερον	216 n. 3	ὅσιος	103
μιμητής	311	ὁσίους	266
μισοξενία	62 n. 6	οὐ γὰρ ὄντα ὁμομήτριον	180
μονογενής	185	οὐδὲν τῆς εἰς τὸ πλῆθος	
μυθυπλαστοί	2	κακώσεως παρέλιπεν	145 n. 12
ναῦς	28 n. 13	οὐδὲν ὑποθωπεύσας	297 (bis)
νεανίσκου	171	οὐθέν	9
νεκράν	241	οὐκ ἀηδῶς	190
νέμεσις	22, 22 n. 8,	οὐκ ὢν ἐν ἑαυτῷ	132
	23, 92, 227	οὐκέτι	87
	(bis), 229,	οὕτως ἔχοντα χαλεπῶς	510
	242, 528,	ὄχλον	246
	537	ὄχλος	224
νεναρκηκυῖαν	241	ὄχλος...ἄλλως	246
νεότητα	184	ὄχλων	224, 237, 246
νεωτέρων	209	πάθει μάθος	154
νεωτέρων...ἐπεθύμει		πάθος	304
πραγμάτων	238	παῖδάς τε καὶ γυναῖκας	
νεωτέρων ἐπιθυμοῦντας		ἑαυτοῦ	28
πραγμάτων	238	παῖς	193
νεωτέρων ἐπιθυμοῦντες		πᾶν ὅ τι καὶ πρῶτον	183
αἰεὶ πραγμάτων	238		

INDEX OF GREEK, LATIN, HEBREW, AND ARAMAIC WORDS 653

πανουργία	87	περὶ τοὺς ὁμοεθνεῖς	
πανουργίαν	12	φιλοτιμότατος	494
πανουργότατος	210, 467	περιδεής	206
παντελῶς ἀνόσιον	207	περιέστη	160
παντὸς ὑπερόπτας		περιόν	558
καλοῦ	22	περιπέτεια	186, 521,
παρὰ τοῖς ἐκεῖ	33		524, 564
παράδοξα	347	περιπίπτει	186
παράδοξον	83, 346, 346 n. 7	περισσός	41
		περιφανῶς	180
παραδόξων	347 n. 8	πεσὼν τῆς κόρης εἰς	
παραδόσει	427, 428	ἔρωτα	520
παραδόσεως τῶν		πιθανώτατοι	99 n. 4
πατέρων	427	πιθανώτατος	99 (bis)
παράδοσις	428 (bis)	πιθανώτερα	99
παραιτουμένη	197	πιθανώτερος	99 (bis)
παρανομήσαντι	242	πικρῶς	331
παρανομίᾳ	327	πίστεως	205
παρανομίαν	239 (ter), 277, 328	πλέγμα	28
		πλείστην	173
παρανομίας	236, 239, 419, 439, 455, 527	πλεονεκτῶν	12
		πλεονεξία	213 (quater), 213 n. 5
		πλεονεξίας	212
παρανόμως	355	πληγείς	524
παρανομωτέροις	219	πληγέντες	257
παραυτίκα	256	πλήθει χρημάτων	11
παραχρῆμα	241, 256	πλήθεσιν ὁμιλεῖν	99
παρείθη	241	πλήθεσιν ὁμιλεῖν	
παρεκάλει	197	πιθανώτατος	98
παρεκάλεσε	282, 317	πλήθεσιν ὁμιλῆσαι	
παρεκελεύετο	296	κεχαρισμένος	98
παρεμυθεῖτο	343	πλῆθος	224, 346
παρεφύλαττεν	226	πλοῖον	28 n. 13
παρῄνει	429	πλοῦτον	11 n. 28
παροξυνθείς	241	πόλεις ὀχυράς	311 (bis)
παρρησίαν	206	πολέμου ἐμφυλίου	210
παρωξύνθη	456	πολιτείαν	484
πάσῃ φιλοτιμίᾳ	460 n. 10	πολιτείας	141
πάσης φιλοτιμίας	460 n. 10	πολίτευμα	479
πάσχοντες	154	πολλὴν δ' ἐπελθὼν γῆν	10
πασῶν...τῷ κάλλει	518	πολλῆς ἠξιωμένου τιμῆς	46
πάτριον	372	πολυανθρωπίαν	34
πατρῴαν ἀρετήν	144	πολυπραγμονεῖν	121
παῦλαν	37 n. 17	πονηρεύμασιν	467
πειθόμενος	330	πονηρία	87
πειθώ	492	πονηρίᾳ	277
πεισθείς	484	πονηρίαν	467
πεπηλωμένης	29	πονηρίας	419, 466, 467 (ter)
πεπιστευκέναι	186		
πεπρωμένην	288 n. 9	πονηρόν	211, 467, 468
πεπρωμένης	283, 288 n. 9	πονηρός	210 (bis), 466 (ter)
πεπρωμένος	287 n. 9		

πονηροτέρων	466	σκοπῷ	426
πόνοιο	4	σοφία	322
πόνου	4	σοφίᾳ	427 (bis)
πονοῦσι	4	σοφίαν	83, 516
πόνων	4, 5	σοφίας	541
πόρνη	180 n. 3	σπιθαμή	148
πόρνης	179, 180 n. 3	σποράδην	19 n. 3, 562
πράγματα	209	σπουδάζοντες	349
πρό + φημί	115 n. 11	σπουδαζόντων	361
προαίρεσιν	257	σπουδασθείς	344
προγνώσεως	274	σπουδῇ	370 (bis)
πρόγνωσιν	111	σπουδήν	122
προετρέπετο	482	σπουδῆς	47, 205, 422, 430
προθυμία	205		
προθυμίαν	122	στάντας	307 n. 1
πρόνοια	104, 136, 566 (bis)	στάσει	82
		στάσεως	102
προνοίᾳ	104	στασιάζοντας	102
πρόνοιαν	4, 88, 266, 465	στάσις	2 n. 8, 34, 82, 130, 556
		στάσις οἰκεία	171
προπετές	258	στέαρ	146 n. 13
προπετῶς	254	στέλλειν ἀποικίας	34
πρόρρησιν	123	στεργόμενον	522
πρόρρησις	123 n. 20 (bis)	στέργοντες	319
		στερρός	58
πρόρριζον	527	στέρχῃ	523
πρὸς ἡδονήν	222, 234	στῆτε	307 n. 1
προσδοκῶσα	296	στρατεύσαιτο	359
προσέταξε	339	στρατηγήσας	224
προσηλύτους	270	στρατηγήσοντος	178
προσηνές	247, 315, 518	στρατηγούντων	166, 181
		στρατηλάτης	40
προσλαβόμενος	51	στρατόπεδον	123, 127
προσομιλῶν ἡδέως	520	στρατός	127
		συγγένειαν	35
προσστερνισάμενος	85	συγγνώμην...τῶν ἡμαρτημένων	408
προφῆται	115 n. 11		
προφητείαν	58	συγκαλέσας	314
προφήτης	114 (quinquiens), 114 n. 9 (bis), 115 n. 11 (ter), 134, 558	συγκαλύψας	407
		συλλήψεσθαι	159
		συμβουλίᾳ	427, 428 (bis)
		σύμμαχον	120
		συμμονωθείς	48
πρόχειρον	248	συμπίπτοντα	58
πρῶτος ἱερεύς	476	συμφέροντα	41 n. 7
Ῥαγουήλ	39	σὺν τῇ μητρὶ τῶν παίδων καὶ τοῖς τούτων γυναιξίν	28
ῥίψαντος	223		
σβέννυσθαι	510		
σεβόμενοι τὸν θεόν	410	συνέδραμον	369
σεμνόν	518	συνέθεντο	312

INDEX OF GREEK, LATIN, HEBREW, AND ARAMAIC WORDS

συνέσεως	84		τὸ...ἀκριβὲς τῆς ἱστορίας	389
σύνεσιν ἱκανώτατος	83		τὸ γὰρ Ἰουδαίων γένος	396 n. 9
συνεσχέθη	524		τὸ...γένος	396
σύνετε	307 n. 1		τὸ γένος Ἰουδαῖον	396 n. 9
συνετῶς	426		τὸ γύναιον	277
συνετώτατα	323		τὸ δίκαιον	431
συνεχύθη	408		τὸ θεῖον	277, 301
συνιδεῖν	209		τὸ μεγεθος τῶν	
σύνοδον	268		πραγμάτων	527
συντελεῖ	4		τὸ τῶν πραγμάτων	
συντύχοι	183		μέγεθος	527
σφοδρῶς	327		τὸ χρεόν	287 n. 8
σχεδόν	541		τὸ χρεών	283 (bis),
σχολαίτερον	354, 360			286 n. 7, 287
σῶφρον	22			(bis), 287 n.
σωφρονεῖν	87 (bis)			9 (ter), 288
σώφρονι	528			n. 9
σώφρονι λογισμῷ	506			(quinquiens)
σωφρονιζομένου	88		τὸ χρηστόν	248 (bis)
σωφρονῶσιν	154, 181, 563		τοῖς ἔργοις τριβομένοις	4
σωφροσύνη	166		τοῖς κατ' ἐπίνοιαν ἀνθρώπου πλεονέκτου	
σωφροσύνης	99		[καὶ] βίᾳ πεφυκόσιν	8
ταῖς ψυχαῖς ἀνέπεσον	261		τοῖς κατωρθωμένοις	187
ταλαιπωρίας	4		τοῖς πολλοῖς	99
ταμιεῖον	360		τόλμαν	212
ταμιεύεσθαι τὴν τύχην	528 n. 26		τολμάω	143
τάξαι	19 n. 3, 562		τολμηρόν	277
τάξιν	93		τολμηροτέραν	211
ταραττομένου	129		τόλμης	218
ταραχή	102, 505, 520		τολμῆσαι	143
			τολμῶσιν	212
ταραχῆς	102 (bis)		τὸν οἴκοθεν αὐτοῦ	
ταραχθέντος	520		νόμον	516
τὰς ὄψεις τῶν			τόξον	33
θεωμένων	518		τοξοφόρος	33
τὰς πράξεις μεταφέρειν	25		τότε	48
τελευτάς	267		τοῦ γένους...τοῦ	
τελέως	222, 222 n. 13		βασιλικοῦ	513
			τοῦ κοινοῦ	102
τετολμημένων	236		τοῦ μεγίστου θεοῦ	413
τέχνη	106		τοῦ χρεών	286 n.7, 287 n. 9, 288 n. 9
τέχνην	324			
τὴν οἰκουμένην	120		τοὺς ἀρετῇ διαφέροντας	165
τὴν χάριν τοῦ			τοὺς φίλους καὶ τοὺς	
προσώπου	518		ἡγεμόνας	457
τὴν ψυχὴν ἀνέπεσε	261		τραπέντας	204
τῆς δικαιοσύνης			τρυφᾶν ἀπόνως	11 n. 28
ἠγάπησε	27		τρυφή	11 n. 28
τι	247		τρυφήν	11 n. 28
τιμῆς	57		τρυφῆς	11 n. 28
τινα	62 n. 6		τύραννος	40

τυράννων...τρόπῳ	103	φθόνον	209, 210
τύχαι	206		(quater)
τῷ δήμῳ	99	φθόνου	209
τῷ πλήθει	99	φιλανθρωπία	46, 63, 168,
τῶν ἀναγκαίων φίλων	523		249, 251
τῶν δὲ πρώτων παρὰ			(bis), 252,
τοῖς Ἰουδαίοις	514		327, 342
τῶν ἐκτὸς ἀγαθῶν	14		(bis), 355,
τῶν ὄχλων	237, 246		423, 464,
τῶν πραγμάτων			466, 497,
μέγεθος	260		549 (bis),
τῶν πρεσβυτέρων	427		550 (bis),
τῶν πρεσβυτέρων...			557
παραδόσει	428 n. 6	φιλανθρωπίᾳ	249, 251,
τῶν τότε	115		341
ὕβρεων	236	φιλανθρωπίαν	251, 469
ὑβρίζων	12	φιλανθρωπίας	252
ὕβριν	46, 145, 154,	φιλανθρώποις	251
	226, 239,	φιλάνθρωπον	248, 251,
	277		257, 421
ὕβρις	5, 22, 22 n. 8	φιλάνθρωπος	249, 251,
	(bis), 23		464, 465,
	(bis), 92,		466, 471
	154, 227	φιλανθρώπους	251, 284
	(ter), 229,	φιλανθρώπων	252
	236 (bis),	φιλανθρώπως	464, 466,
	242 (bis),		469
	373, 505,	φίλαυτον	167
	509, 528	φιλεῖσθαι	522
	(bis), 537,	φίλοι	510
	563	φίλοι μακάρεσσι θεοῖσιν	3
	(quater)	φίλον	516
ὑβρίσθαι	226	φίλον τῷ θεῷ	168
ὑβρισθείη	278, 505	φιλονικεῖν	213
	(bis)	φίλος	211, 480
ὑβρισταὶ κάρτα	23	φίλος τῷ θεῷ	169
ὑβριστάς	15, 22 (bis)	φιλόστοργον	510
ὑπεκρίνετο	212	φιλοτεχνεῖ	207
ὑπερβιαζομένου	413	φιλοτιμία	370 (bis)
ὑπερηγάπησαν	469	φιλοτιμίαν	213
ὑπερηφανίαν	528	φιλοτίμως	330, 369
ὑπερόπτας	15	φιλοφρονούμενος	464, 466,
ὑπερχόμενος	142		468
ὑπέστρεψε	407	φιλοφρόνως	116, 247,
ὑπηρετήσοντος	58		317
ὑποθεμένου	27 (bis)	φιλόφρων	247
ὑποκρίνονται	212	φιλοχρηματία	213
ὑποκριτής	252	φίλτρων	484
ὑποκριτὴς		φιτῦσαι	26
φιλανθρωπίας	466	φοβούμενοι τὸν θεόν	410
φαυλότητος	87	φρονεῖν	154
φθόνοι	5	φρόνημα	166

INDEX OF GREEK, LATIN, HEBREW, AND ARAMAIC WORDS 657

φρονήματος	93		6, 465, 491-492
φρονήσει	87		
φρόνησιν	83	χρηστότης	250, 252, 441, 442, 464, 466, 550
φροντίδι	3		
φρουραί	533		
φυλακήν	267		
φύσει	530	χρηστότητα	31, 469, 483
φύσεως	427	χρηστότητος	250 (bis), 442, 455, 456
φύσιν	319		
φῶς	55 n. 1		
χαίρων	241	χώραν	469 n. 3
χαλεπῶς	226	ψηφοφορίαν	104
χάριν	70, 469 n. 3	ὡλοκαύτωσεν	185
χάριτος	47	ὠμότητος	239
χειροδίκαι	10	ὡρμήκεσαν	12
χευάζεσθαι	524	ὥρμησαν	260
χρησμολόγοι	115 n. 11	ὥρμησε	421
χρηστή	368	ὠφέλιμα	565
χρηστοῖς	250	ὡς	302 n. 9
χρηστόν	250	ὡς ἐξεστηκότα τῶν φρενῶν	458
χρηστός	249 (bis), 250, 250 n. 13, 437, 441, 448, 456 n.	ὥσπερ ἐπὶ σκηνῆς προσωπεῖα	563
		ὥστε μὴ εἶναι ἐν αὐτοῖς περιποίησιν	265 n. 2

Latin Words

acceptum est	30	conversationem	144 n. 11
adorabat	169	devotio	190
Aetas parentum, peior avis, tulit nos nequiores, max daturos progeniem vitiosiorem	10 n. 25	eius	57 n. 3
		eius secretum	142 n. 9
		fides Punica	106, 142
		figura	31 n. 16
amor sceleratus habendi	11	fortissime	144 n. 10
annus magnus	15	fortissimus	163
benevolentissimus	252	fraude	5
caeso moenia firma Remo	13 n. 31	fraudesque dolusque insidiaeque	11
civilis	252	gratiam et misericordiam	26
clemens	252	humanitas	423
comissimus	252	hunc sacerdotem nobis credidit iustiorem	59 n. 4
credulitas	5		
de nobis fabula narratur	91, 244	immensae opulentiae templum	485
desciit	32 n. 16 (quater)		
descisco	32 n. 16	in laeva manu maximam fortitudinem habens	140 n. 5
desiit	31-32 n. 16 (ter)	induit	170
desipit	32 n. 16 (ter)	insidiis	5
despiciens inhonestam		insufferibilis	93

658 INDEX OF GREEK, LATIN, HEBREW, AND ARAMAIC WORDS

interpretem somniorum	115 n. 12		216 n. 2, 296, 305
iustus et inmaculatus in progenie tua	26	plerique Hebraeorum	187 n. 17
Macedo	525 n. 21	praesumeret	144 n. 11
metuentem	410	revocate animos	296
moribus antiquis res stat Romana viresque	358	sponte sua	6 (bis)
		suam	57 n. 3
nullo cogente	6	ultro	7
odor requietionis	30-31	vis	11
pacisque imponere morem	325	vosmet rebus servate secundis	296
penitet me	21	voti temerarii	187 n. 17
per se	6	zelaret	180 n. 4
pietas	216 (bis),		

Hebrew and Aramaic Words

ah le-rosho	501	ʿivri	400 n. 13
ʾaḥiv shel rosh	501	keniyah	325 n. 1
ʾanshei-shem	95, 106	kohen	44
ʿarei misekenot	311 (bis)	laveshah	170
aṭ	274 n. 2	lemarebeh	387
ben-hamerazeaḥ	329 n. 4	lemozaʾot	355 n. 2
berit	37 n. 17	limehoraʾot	355 n. 2
beshigaʿon	325 n. 1, 353 (bis), 354, 360	maʿalah	302 n. 9
		maʿase ʾavot siman lebanim	244
daber yedaber	65	marom	302 n. 9
ʾemet	397 n. 10	mem	387, 387 n. 14
ʿeved y	400 n. 13		
haftarah	394, 394 n. 4, 415	memalelaʾ	2 n. 6
		mesik huʾ et ragelav	146 n. 14
hagillulim	267	mezuzah	96 (bis)
ha-heres	380 n. 8	mezuzot	219 n. 7
ha-ḥeres	380 n. 8	mifelezet	268
hanevalah	216	moshiaʿ	143
haqadosh	103	navi	114 n. 9
haqedeshim	267	Nineveh	412
ha-sarim	457	nofel	110 n. 2
ḥayah	2 n. 6	pesilim	147 (ter)
ḥayat ha-sadeh	2 n. 6 (bis)	pundaqita	179
hebel	9	purim	533
hen	27	qalei ʿolam	164
ḥerev	148, 148 n. 16	qanoʾ qineʾti	302 (bis)
		qedoshim	103
ḥesed	193	qezeph	326
hu	501	qiqayon	399 (quinquiens), 568
hushḥaru	501		
ʿimedu	307 n. 1		
ʾish ʾiṭer yad-yemino	140 n. 4	qoshareti	359
ʾishah ʾaḥeret	180 n. 3	rav lakem	106
ʾiṭer	140 n. 4 (bis)	rashin	501

INDEX OF GREEK, LATIN, HEBREW, AND ARAMAIC WORDS 659

reiqim	178 (bis)	vayesitehu	282, 316
ro'eh	114 n. 9	vayiqah	94
semal	138 n. 2	vayiteqasher	359 (bis)
serefah	269	Yad Avshalom	218
shamayim	302 n. 9	yaheif	274 n. 2
shav	425	yaza' liqrat	182
Shekinah	45 (bis)	yehidah	185
sheqer	355	yehideka	185
sukkot	488, 562	yirei shamayim	411
tefillin	219 n. 7	zaddik	9 n. 21
tekelet	96 (ter)	zaddik tamim hayah	
tevah	21 n. 6	bedōrōtav	26
tifelut	502	zaqen	427
vayanos	361	zarah	180 n. 3
veyaradeti	184 n. 11	zonah	179, 180 n. 3

INDEX OF MODERN SCHOLARS

Aberbach, Moses, 80 n. 4
Albright, William F., 52 n. 14, 441 n. 3 (bis)
Alter, Robert, 146
Amaru, Betsy H., 37 n. 17, 153 n. 1, 157, 177 n. 1, 189, 514
Andrewes, Antony, 493 n. 5
Aptowitzer, Victor, 8 n. 19
Ararat, Nisan, 474 n. 1
Astour, Michael, 21 n. 6
Attridge, Harold W., 10 n. 26, 92, 120, 185 n. 14, 221 n. 12, 314 n. 6, 346 n. 7, 369 n. 5, 371, 473 n. 1, 489 n. 2
Balsdon, John P. V. D., 84 n. 8
Bamberger, Bernard J., 44 n. 9, 46 n. 11, 405 n. 21
Bardtke, Hans, 517
Baskin, Judith R., 39, 41 n. 7, 44 n. 9, 45 n. 10, 110 n. 1, 112 n. 4, 124 n.22
Basser, Herbert W., 1 n. 1, 2 n. 6
Baumgarten, Albert I., 427 n. 5
Baumgartner, Walter, 183
Begg, Christopher, 244 n. 2, 244 n. 4, 246 n. 9, 249 n. 12, 250 n. 13, 251 n. 15, 256 n. 19, 256 n. 20, 260 n. 22, 261, 261 n. 24, 273 n. 1, 282, 283, 283 n. 6 (bis), 284, 300, 302, 307 n. 1, 309 n. 3, 311 n. 4, 319, 332, 347 n. 10, 349, 360, 364 n. 2, 376 n. 1, 380, 381 (bis), 393, 393 n. 1, 393 n. 2, 397 n. 12, 402 n. 15, 411 n. 28, 415 n. 34, 424 n. 1, 429 (ter), 430, 448 n. 15, 448 n. 16, 450 n. 1, 455 n. 6, 456 n. 7, 470, 471, 471 n. 4, 515 n. 3
Bentzen, Aage, 517 n. 8
Bernstein, Moshe J., 202 n. 4, 542
Berridge, John M., 441 n. 3
Betz, Otto, 301 n. 8
Bewer, Julius A., 489 n. 1
Bickerman, Elias, 398, 405 n. 21, 406, 415, 516, 520 n. 13, 526 n. 22, 530 (bis), 533
Bilde, Per, 424 n. 1
Blenkinsopp, Joseph, 284, 286, 376 n. 1, 393 n. 1, 489 n. 2, 495 n. 6

Bloch, Heinrich, 526 n. 22
Bloch, Renée, 405 n. 21
Bode, George H., 183 n. 8
Bogaert, Pierre-Maurice, 137, 138 n. 2 (bis)
Bowers, Robert H., 405 n. 19
Braude, William G., 46 n. 11
Braun, Martin, 134 n. 29, 516
Braverman, Jay, 112 n. 4
Brown, Cheryl A., 153 n. 1, 155 n. 5 (ter), 160 n. 10, 161, 162, 177 n. 1, 514
Büchler, Adolph, 394 n. 4
Bultmann, Rudolf, 25 n. 10
Bury, John B., 7
Cassuto, Umberto, 8, 9
Cazelles, Henri, 517 n. 8
Cohen, Chayim, 140 n. 4
Cohen, Shaye J. D., 460 n. 9, 563
Collins, John J., 383
Colpe, Carsten, 411 n. 28
Colson, Francis H., 20 n. 4, 41 n. 8 (bis)
Daube, David, 37 n.17, 460 n. 9, 463
Delling, Gerhard, 153 n.2, 376 n. 1, 393 n. 1
Dienstfertig, Meyer, 393 n. 1
Dindorf, Karl W., 426 n. 2
Di Vito, Robert A., 460
Dodds, Eric R., 132 n. 27, 349
Drews, Robert, 493 n. 5
Droge, Arthur J., 1 n. 1, 1 n. 3, 9 n. 20
Duval, Yves-Marie, 393 n. 2, 397 n. 11
Ehrenzweig, A., 13 n. 31
Eissfeldt, Otto, 517 n. 8
Emery, David L., 474 n. 1
Evans, John K., 70 n. 10
Fascher, Erich, 393 n. 1
Feldman, Louis H., 1 n. 1, 49 (bis), 82 n. 7 (bis), 88 n. 11, 92 n. 1, 94, 97, 100 n. 5, 111, 115 n. 12, 131 (bis), 153 n. 1 (bis), 153 n. 2, 156 n. 8, 163 n. 1, 174, 189, 189 n. 23, 198, 215, 244 n. 1, 244 n. 5, 245 n. 7, 245 n. 8, 246 n. 10, 247 n. 11 (bis), 250 n. 14, 253 n. 17, 255 n. 18, 260 n. 21, 260 n. 22, 261 n.

INDEX OF MODERN SCHOLARS 661

23, 261 n. 25, 266, 270, 273 n. 1, 274, 288 n. 10, 291 n. 1, 300, 335, 349 n. 13, 376 n. 1, 381, 382, 387 n. 13 (*bis*), 388 (*bis*), 411 (*ter*), 424 n. 1 (*quater*), 440 n. 2, 474, 515 n. 3, 540, 542, 559, 560
Fontenrose, Joseph E., 115 n. 11
Fordyce, Christian J., 140 n. 6
Fornaro, Pierpaolo, 301
Franxman, Thomas W., 17 (*bis*)
Friedrich, Gerhard, 250 n. 13
Gager, John G., 69
Gan, Moshe, 517 n. 7
Gaster, Moses, 15 n. 35
Gaster, Theodor H., 185 n. 12, 414 n. 33
Georgi, Dieter, 372 n. 7
Giangrande, Giuseppe, 516 n. 6
Gibbs, John G., 115 n. 12
Ginzberg, Louis, 2, 22, 25 n. 11, 30, 30 n. 14, 56, 78 n. 2, 80 n. 4, 81 n. 5, 81 n. 6, 94 n. 2, 113 n. 6, 137, 137 n. 2, 155 n. 6, 155 n. 7, 158 n. 9, 172 n. 4, 186 n. 15, 195, 203 n. 1, 217 n. 4, 231 (*bis*), 232, 276 n. 3, 293 n. 3, 302 n. 9, 314 n. 5, 377 n. 4, 382 n. 10, 385, 405, 406 (*bis*), 407, 410, 414, 433 n. 9 (*bis*), 445 n. 7, 446 n. 8, 446 n. 10, 446 n. 11, 469, 478 n. 11, 500, 501, 513 n. 1 (*bis*), 518 n. 10 (*bis*), 522 n. 16 (*bis*), 523 n. 17 (*ter*), 524 n. 19, 524 n. 20, 527 n. 23, 527 n. 24 (*quinquiens*), 527 n. 25, 532 n. 29
Glaser, O., 148
Goethals, T. R., 509 n. 3, 514, 518
Goldenberg, David, 542
Grabbe, Lester L., 474 n. 1
Graf, Heinrich E., 7
Granowski, Jan J., 448 n. 15
Gray, Rebecca, 376, 376 n. 1, 460 n. 9
Greenberg, Moshe and Cohn, Haim Hermann, 459
Greene, John T., 110 n. 1
Gregg, J. A. F., 536 n. 39
Gruppe, Otto, 13 n. 31
Gunkel, Hermann, 517 n. 8
Gutmann, Joshua, 411 n. 27
Hackett, Jo Ann, 114
Hadas, Moses, 25 n. 10
Halpern, Baruch, 147, 148 (*bis*)
Hampel, Ido, 473 n. 1

Harrington, Daniel J., 154 n. 3
Headlam, Walter, 3, 4 n. 10, 7 n. 17
Hengel, Martin, 344
Hoffmann, David, 427 n. 5
Holladay, Carl R., 39 (*bis*), 40 n. 3 (*bis*), 40 n. 4, 40 n. 5, 80 n. 3
Hölscher, Gustav, 15 (*bis*), 473 n. 1, 526 n. 22, 539
Horsley, Richard A., 383 (*bis*)
Hoschander, Jacob, 515 n. 4, 517, 526 n. 22, 532 n. 31
Jacob, Benno, 519, 525 n. 22, 526 n. 22, 533 n. 32
Jacobson, Howard, 40 n. 5, 40-41, 41 n. 6, 138 n. 2
de Jonge, Marianus, 119 n. 16, 383, 384, 386
Katzoff, Ranon, 70 n. 10
Kaufmann, Yehezkel, 517 n. 8
Kittel, Gerhard, 250 n. 13
Klausner, Joseph, 113 n. 6
Klingender, Johann W., 7 n. 17
Koch, Klaus, 474
Kraeling, Emil G., 147, 147 n. 15, 148
Krämer, Hans J., 114
Kretschmer, P., 13 n. 31
Kuhn, K. H., 451 n. 3
Larson, Erik, 452, 452 n. 5
LeDéaut, Roger, 250 n. 15
Levenson, Jon D., 447 n. 13
Levine, Etan, 405 n. 19 (*bis*), 405 n. 20, 405 n. 21, 415
Levison, John R., 16, 129, 196, 202 n. 4
Lévy, Isidore, 526 n. 22
Lewinsky, Abraham, 2
Lewis, Jack P., 17, 27
Lieberman, Saul, 411
Lovejoy, Arthur O. and Boas, George, 5 n. 13, 7 n. 17, 10 n. 25
Macho, Alejandro Diez, 405 n. 21
Macurdy, Grace H., 10 n. 27
Malamat, Abraham, 442 n. 4
Malbim, Meir L., 18 n. 2, 244 n. 3
Marcus, David, 177 n. 1, 183, 184, 184 n. 10, 188 n. 22, 189
Marcus, Ralph, 222 n. 13, 236 n. 2, 340 n. 5, 380 n. 8, 395 n. 6, 431, 489 n. 1, 528 n. 26
Margaliot, Eliezer, 444
Mason, Steve, 99, 99 n. 4, 428 (*quater*)

McKenzie, John L., 188 n. 20
Meyer, Rudolf, 100 n. 5, 376 n. 1, 393 n. 1
Michel, Otto and Bauernfeind, Otto, 380 n. 8
Milik, Jósef T., 535 n. 36
Mingana, Alfonse and Harris, James Rendell, 451 n. 3
Moehring, Horst R., 509 n. 3
Moore, George F., 100, 148, 182 n. 5, 184, 185 n. 12
Moscovitz, Larry, 110 n. 1, 119 n. 14, 126, 128 n. 25, 132, 132 n. 27
Motzo, Bacchisio R., 526 n. 22, 530, 533 n. 33
Murray, Robert H., 7
Naber, Samuel A., 469 n. 3
Neusner, Jacob, 384 n. 11
Neyrey, Jerome H., 546
Niese, Benedictus, 525 n. 21
Noy, Dov, 218 n. 6
Ostwald, Martin, 485 n. 12 (*bis*)
Paton, Lewis B., 509, 515, 517, 532, 533
Paul, André, 37 n. 17, 301, 388
Pease, Arthur S., 9 n. 22
Penna, Angelo, 187 n. 17
Perrot, Charles, 137, 138 n. 2 (*bis*)
Perry, Ben E., 510, 517 n. 9
Pfeiffer, Augustus, 182
Picket, H. W., 493 n. 5
Pohlmann, Karl-Friedrich, 473 n. 1, 489 n. 2
Rabinowitz, Louis I., 59
Rahlfs, Alfred, 18 n. 2, 244 n. 3
Rappaport, Salomo, 1, 1 n. 2, 1 n. 3, 2 n. 4, 2 n. 5, 7, 9 n. 21 (*bis*), 9 n. 23, 10 n. 23, 12 n. 29, 13 n. 32, 14, 14 n. 33, 14 n. 34, 15 n. 35, 17 n. 1. 47 n.12, 94 n. 2, 105 n. 9, 133 n. 28, 158 n. 9. 345 n. 6, 370 n. 6, 393, 424 n. 1, 473 n. 1, 513 n. 1 (*bis*), 514 n. 2 (*bis*), 525 n. 22(*bis*)
Reitzenstein, Richard, 4 n. 11
Rendtorff, Rolf, 114 n. 9
Riessler, Paul, 517 n. 7
Rose, Herbert J., 114, 190
Rösel, Hartmut N., 147, 147 n. 15, 148, 148 n. 16
Rosenmeyer, Thomas G., 3 n. 7
Rosenthal, Judah, 8, 21

Rosenthal, Ludwig A., 517 n. 7 (*bis*)
Rouillard, Hedwige, 110 n. 1
Ryberg, Inez S., 5 n. 13, 6 n. 15, 6 n. 16
Saller, Richard P., 70 n. 10
Schäfer, Peter, 62 n. 6
Schalit, Abraham, 2 n. 5, 13, 14 n. 34, 120 n. 17
Scheller, Paul, 516 n. 6
Schoeps, Hans-Joachim, 420 n. 4 (*bis*)
Schreckenberg, Heinz, 82 n. 7, 153 n. 1, 273 n. 1, 424 n. 1 (*bis*)
Schubert, Kurt, 420 n. 4
Schürer, Emil, 119 n. 15
Schwartz, Daniel, 37 n. 17
Schwartz, Eduard, 516-517
Schwartz, Seth, 100, 131, 284, 348 n. 11, 348 n. 12, 428 n. 6, 430 n. 7, 431, 495 n. 6
Sealey, Raphael, 493 n. 5
Séchan, Louis, 7 n. 17
Seidenberg, Robert, 190
Seyberlich, Rose-Marie, 526 n. 22
Shochat, Azriel, 271 n. 6
Shutt, Robert J. H., 13
Smith, Kirby F., 3, 10 n. 25
Smith, Morton, 348 n. 11, 474 n. 2, 493 n. 5 (*bis*)
Snowden, Frank M., 63 n. 7 (*bis*)
Speiser, Ephraim A., 412 n. 31
Spengel, Leonardus, 165
Spicq, Ceslaus, 250 n. 13, 251 n. 15 (*bis*)
Spinoza, Benedict, 487 n. 13
Spiro, Abram, 293 n. 3
Sragow, Howard M., 151 n. 18
Stachowiak, L. R., 250 n. 13
Stagg, Evelyn, 153 n. 1 (*bis*)
Stagg, Frank, 153 n. 1 (*bis*)
Stein, Edmund, 8 n. 19
Sterling, Gregory E., 566
Stern, Menahem, 432
Stiehl, Ruth, 517
Strugnell, John, 452
Survius, Bernardin, 218 n. 6
Sypherd, William O., 184 n. 11
Tabor, James D., 301-302
Talbert, Charles H., 165
Talmon, Shemaryahu, 517 n. 7, 519 n. 11, 535 n. 38
Tarn, William W. and Griffith, Guy T., 7
Taylor, Margaret E., 5 n. 13, 6 n. 15

INDEX OF MODERN SCHOLARS 663

Teggart, F. J., 7 n. 17
Thackeray, Henry St. J., 6 n. 14, 13, 18 n. 2, 25 n. 10, 29, 57 n. 3, 59 n. 4, 145 n. 12, 175 n. 6, 380 n. 9, 467 n. 2, 473 n. 1, 477 n. 9
Torrey, Charles C., 525 n. 22, 534 n. 34, 535, 535 n. 37
Trenker, Sophie, 537
Treuenfels, Abraham, 473 n. 1
Trible, Phyllis, 187 n. 18
Troiani, Lucio, 130
Tuland, C. G., 474 n. 1
Türck, Hermann, 7 n. 17
Ulrich, Eugene C., 215 n. 1
van Unnik, Willem C., 101 n. 7, 130, 131, 133, 376 n. 1, 393 n. 1
Varneda, Villalba I., 110 n. 1

Vermes, Geza, 112 n. 4, 347 n. 8
Vogelstein, Heinemann, 100 n. 5
Weinfeld, Moshe, 237 n. 3
Weiss, K., 250 n. 13
Wendland, Paul, 25 n. 10
Wiese, Kurt M., 147
Wiesenberg, Ernest, 427 n. 3
von Wilamowitz-Moellendorff, Ulrich, 517
Williamson, Hugh G. M., 473 n. 1
Wiseman, Donald J., 442 n. 4
Wolff, Samuel L., 521 n. 15
Wolfson, Harry A., 240 n. 6, 251 n. 16, 300
Zeitlin, Solomon, 420 n. 4
Zimmermann, Frank, 409 n. 24

www.ingramcontent.com/pod-product-compliance
Lightning Source LLC
Chambersburg PA
CBHW020259010526
44108CB00037B/153